PET/CBM
Personal
Computer
Guide

PET/CBM
Personal
Computer
Guide

Adam Osborne
Carroll S. Donahue

OSBORNE/McGraw-Hill
Berkeley, California

Published by
OSBORNE/McGraw-Hill
630 Bancroft Way
Berkeley, California 94710
U. S. A.

For information on translations and book distributors outside of the U. S. A. , please
write OSBORNE/McGraw-Hill at the above address.

PET/CBM PERSONAL COMPUTER GUIDE
SECOND EDITION

567890   DODO   8987654321

ISBN 0-931988-55-1

PHOTO CREDITS

Commodore Business Machines: pp. 2, 3, 4 (top, bottom), 40 (bottom)
Joe Mauro: p. 28
Harvey Schwartz: pp. 5, 15, 18, 20, 23, 24, 25, 26, 30, 32 (top, bottom), 35, 37, 38

COVER DESIGN: Timothy Sullivan

Contents

Preface

This edition of the *PET/CBM Personal Computer Guide* is a major revision of the original book published under the same title.

This book describes all models of CBM computers: the original PET 2001 which made Commodore famous, and the more recently introduced PET 2001/N, CBM 2001/B and the 80-column CBM 8000. Peripherals described include cassette drives, two floppy disk units (the Model 2040 and the Model 8050), and two printers (the Model 2022 and the Model 2023).

Also described are recent software products introduced by Commodore: BASIC 4.0, the most recent version of Commodore's BASIC programming language, and two new versions of the disk operating system, DOS 2.1 and DOS 2.5, collectively referred to as DOS 2.0 in product literature.

The discussion of BASIC programming has been greatly expanded. Even if you have never programmed a computer before, this book will teach you how to write your own BASIC programs for any CBM computer system.

This is a large book, containing a great deal of information about CBM computer systems. Depending on your needs you may not use all of the information provided.

Perhaps you have no intention of ever becoming a programmer. Chapters 1, 2 and 3 tell you everything you need to know in order to run programs that have already been written. You can skip the rest of the book until you become more ambitious and want to do a little programming for yourself.

Chapters 4, 5 and 8 teach BASIC programming. Every CBM BASIC statement is described rigorously, but concisely, in Chapter 8. Chapter 4 describes elementary BASIC programming, while Chapter 5 covers more advanced programming techniques. Both of these chapters rely on Chapter 8 for actual statement definitions.

Chapter 6 explains programming techniques required by peripheral units including cassette drives, diskette drives and printers.

Chapter 7 is for the programming expert only. This chapter covers advanced topics such as random diskette access and assembly language programming.

Nothing teaches you programming as effectively as examples. Therefore this book is full of short programs. Whenever you encounter a programming example, key it into your computer and run it. You should also save it for future use (assuming that you have cassette or diskette drives). Every programming example presented in this book has been run on a CBM computer. That guarantees the programs are accurate as run. But only an arrogant or foolish programmer will claim that his or her programs are truly free of errors. The programs presented in this book may well have errors which you will stumble on when you try to run them in novel ways. When you enter a program and try to run it, if it does not work, do not immediately assume that the program is wrong. Carefully check your entry and execution procedure. But remember that programming errors may exist, and if you do find any, please tell us about them.

CBM computers all have two character sets: standard and alternate. Throughout this book we have used the standard character set to illustrate programs and program execution examples. If your computer is to reproduce these illustrations exactly, then you must make sure that you are using the standard character set. Using the alternate character set will make the program or illustration appear different.

The different versions of disk operating systems affect the way you program a CBM computer, but these effects are largely masked by the different versions of BASIC. Therefore we will continuously refer to different levels of CBM BASIC, but we will only occasionally identify a different version of disk operating system.

There have been three releases of CBM BASIC, designated by numbers 1.x, 3.x, and 4.x. 'x' is a number specifying a subrelease. The most significant changes in CBM BASIC were made with release 4.0. In this book we will generally divide BASIC into release 4.0 and earlier releases. These are designated as follows:

1. BASIC 4.0 for any BASIC 4.x.
2. BASIC<3.0 for all earlier releases of BASIC.

Acknowledgments

Portions of this book have been taken from the first edition which was co-authored by Janice Enger. The Blanket program was written by Janice Enger, and the manner in which this program is used to illustrate text was her idea.

Patrick L. McGuire was author of the Digital Display Clock program listed in Chapter 5.

Jim Butterfield supplied much of the memory map information included in the first edition, which has been included also in this second edition.

Commodore personnel, in general, and Chuck Peddle, in particular, were very helpful, providing newly released hardware and software products, then arranging for technical review of manuscripts.

The names PET and CBM are registered trademarks with regard to any computer product, and are owned by Commodore Business Machines, a division of Commodore International. Permission to use the trademark names PET and CBM has been granted by Commodore Business Machines, and is gratefully acknowledged.

Chapter 1

Introducing CBM Computers

This book describes the following Commodore computers:

1. The PET 2001/8K
2. The PET 2001/8N, 2001/16N and 2001/32N
3. The CBM 2001/16B and 2001/32B
4. The CBM 4000 series
5. The CBM 8000 series

In 1977, Commodore Business Machines released the first of the CBM series, the PET 2001 (Personal Electronics Transactor). The PET 2001 is a self-contained unit with a compact graphic keyboard and built-in tape cassette unit. The CBM 2001, which was released next, has an expanded, full-size graphic keyboard. Although functionally the same as the PET, the CBM 2001 and subsequent CBM models do not have a built-in cassette tape unit; instead they depend on external peripherals to store information. The CBM 2001/B business computer is a variation of the CBM 2001. The major physical difference between the CBM 2001 and the CBM 2001/B lies in the keyboard; the CBM 2001 has a full-size keyboard with graphic symbols, whereas the CBM 2001/B has a standard typewriter keyboard without graphic symbols on the keys. CBM 8016 and CBM 8032 business computers are the most recent introductions; they both have an 80-column CRT display, but are otherwise the same as the CBM 2001/B. The CBM 8032 has twice as much memory as the CBM 8016; in other respects these two models are identical.

Commodore has also released printers and disk drives. Continual updates for Commodore BASIC and disk operating system software are being released.

Figure 1-1. CBM 8000 Computer

Commodore's original computer was the PET, and this name became well known. But recently introduced computers have a CBM model designation. Therefore **this book will adopt the convention of referring to the entire computer product line as CBM computers, unless only the original PET is specifically referenced.** We will refer to both the CBM 8016 and CBM 8032 models using the general model name CBM 8000, unless one model or the other needs specific reference.

Currently CBM computers are available with 8K, 16K, or 32K bytes of memory. Only the original PETs had a 4K memory byte option. 1K means 1024 (2^{10}). One byte holds one character of data. The 8K, 16K and 32K designations refer to the amount of usable read/write memory. Every CBM computer has additional memory that is inaccessible to users. It is important to know how much usable read/write memory is available to you. A CBM computer with more memory can run longer programs and handle more data.

CBM MODELS

The CBM 8000 (CBM 8016 and 8032)

The CBM 8000 is shown in Figure 1-1. Its main distinguishing feature is the enlarged 80-column Cathode Ray Tube (CRT) display, or screen. It has a full-size typewriter keyboard, some unique screen editing keys, and a numeric keypad to the right. The CBM 8016 has 16K bytes of read/write memory. The CBM 8032 comes with 32K bytes of read/write memory. The CBM model number correlates with the amount of available read/write memory. To complete the business system, an external cassette tape unit or CBM disk drive must be attached. A printer will also probably be needed.

THE CBM 2001/B

The CBM 2001/B, like the CBM 8000, is a business computer; it is shown in Figure 1-2. The CBM 2001/B CRT display is 40 columns wide; that is half the width of the CBM 8000 display. The CBM 2001/B has a full-size typewriter keyboard, with screen editing keys and a numeric keypad to the right. The CBM 2001/B is available with 16K or 32K bytes of read/write memory. Like the CBM 8000, a CBM 2001/B will need an external cassette tape unit or disk drive, and probably a printer as well.

THE PET 2001/N

The PET 2001/N series, shown in Figure 1-3, is a modified and improved version of the original PET computer. The CRT display is identical to the 2001/B. What separates the PET 2001/N from the business computers are the graphic symbols displayed on the front of the PET 2001/N keys. The PET 2001 is available with 8K (/8N), 16K (/16N), or 32K (/32N) bytes of read/write memory. The PET 2001/N and the CBM 2001/B have the same external device requirements (for cassette tape or disk, and printer).

THE PET 2001/8K

The PET 2001/8K was the first computer released by Commodore Business Machines. All of the CBM models have evolved from the PET 2001/8K. With the same CRT display as the CBM 2001, the PET 2001/8K can easily be differentiated from the other CBM models by its compact, multi-colored keyboard and numeric keypad. There are graphic symbols displayed on the top of the PET 2001/8K keys, **shown in Figure**

Figure 1-2. CBM 2001/B Computer

Figure 1-3. PET 2001/N Computer

Figure 1-4. PET 2001/8K Computer

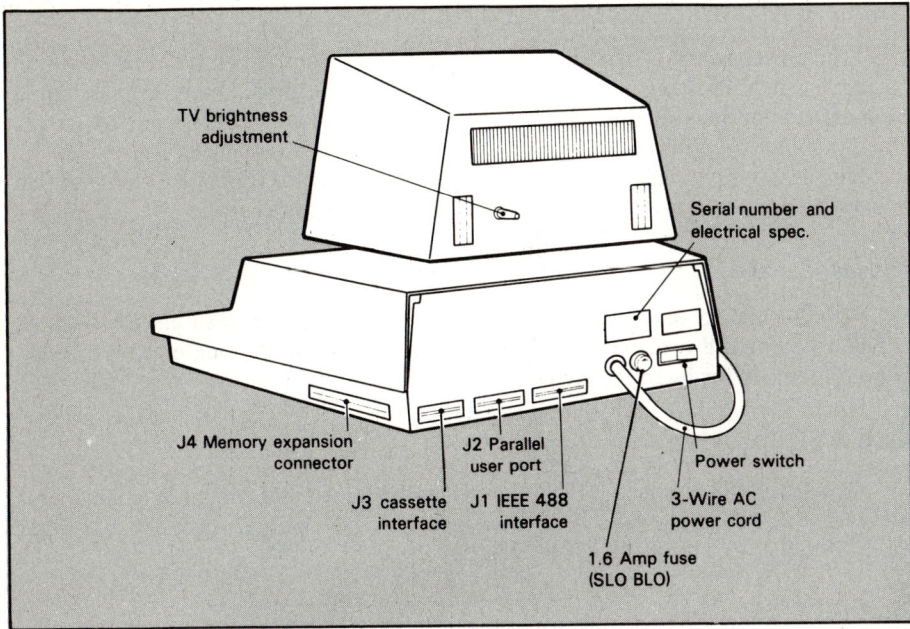

Figure 1-5. Rear View of CBM

1-4. Because of the keyboard's small size, a built-in cassette tape unit is located to the left of the keyboard. The PET 2001/8K is the only model available with a built-in cassette unit. The price you pay for having an internal tape unit is the compact keyboard. The PET 2001/8K has 8K bytes of read/write memory. 16K and 32K memory expansion options are available. A 4K version is available as a special order. The PET, like all other CBM computers, has additional read-only memory (or ROM) which is not available to users. This ROM holds permanent programs that give the computer its model personality. **Many PET computers have an "old" personality, characterized by an old set of ROMs.**

An external cassette tape unit may be connected to the PET computer. A printer and/or disk drives may be attached to a PET 2001/8K only if it has Revision level 3 ROMs.

CBM FEATURES

REAR PANEL

All switches, connectors and interfaces are located at the back of your CBM computer. Figure 1-5 shows a rear view of the CBM computer, with each component labeled, followed by a description of each part. It is important to know the location and function of each part so that you do not damage your CBM computer by using connections incorrectly.

Power Switch

The power switch is located on the left side of the back panel. It is a two-position "rocker" switch. Pressing on the outer side of the switch turns power on; pressing on the inner side of the switch turns power off.

As soon as you turn the power on, the CBM computer is ready for use. When you turn the power off, you lose anything stored in the computer's read/write memory; that includes all programs and data you entered after turning power on.

Power Cord

The 3-wire AC power cord connects the CBM computer to an electrical outlet. The power cord will connect directly to any household three-prong electrical outlet, without the need for intermediate transformer or adapter.

IEEE 488 Interface

The IEEE-488 interface (J1 in Figure 1-5) allows the CBM computer to communicate with external peripherals. IEEE cable will connect a printer, disk drive or other IEEE 488 device into the IEEE 488 interface.*

Parallel User Port

This interface (J2 in Figure 1-5) can be used instead of the IEEE-488 connector to attach peripherals to a CBM computer. You need not know anything about this port. If, by chance, you have a peripheral unit that uses this port, accompanying documentation will tell you how to connect to it.

Cassette Interface

This interface (J3 in Figure 1-5) is designed specifically for an external cassette tape unit. This interface is on the far right side, easily identifiable by its smaller size.

Memory Expansion Connector

Located on the back right side of the CBM (J4 in Figure 1-5), this is another connector that you need to know very little about. Extra read/write memory can be added to your CBM computer. Extra memory is attached to the Memory Expansion Connector.

TV Brightness Adjustment Knob

This knob controls the brightness of the CRT display. While facing the front of the computer, turn the knob to the left to darken the screen; turn to the right to brighten. Notice the change of character sharpness as you adjust the brightness.

---

*For detailed description of the IEEE 488 interface, refer to *PET and the IEEE 488 Bus (GPIB)* by E. Fisher and C.W. Jensen, Osborne/McGraw-Hill, 1980.

CRT DISPLAY

The CRT display is similar to a black and white television screen, but it has higher resolution, which means that you can see small images and characters with greater clarity. **Depending upon the model, either 1000 or 2000 character positions are displayed, in 25 rows of 40 characters, or 25 rows of 80 characters.** Characters are created by displaying appropriate dots within an 8 × 8 dot block (also called a matrix). This is illustrated in Figure 1-6.

The various CRT displays are described separately below. If you have the CBM 8000, read the following description and then skip to the keyboard section. If you have the CBM 2001/B, 2001 or PET skip the section on the CBM 8000.

CBM 8000

The CBM 8000 CRT display separates the CBM 8000 from the other CBM models. The screen is divided into 2000 equal spaces, arranged in 25 rows of 80 characters each. One character per space is displayed. Every space on the screen has a memory byte assigned to it.

Alphabetic and numeric characters, special symbols and graphic symbols can be displayed. The CBM 8000 normally displays lower and upper-case alphabetic characters using a character set that is usually referred to as the alternate character set. There is also a standard character set, which displays numerous graphic characters, but no lower case letters.

CBM 2001/B, PET 2001/N, PET 2001/8K

The CRT displays on the CBM 2001/B, PET 2001/N and the PET/8K are basically the same. The CRT is divided into 1000 spaces, arranged in 25 rows of 40 characters each. One character is displayed in each space.

All models display two types of characters: alphanumeric (alphabetic, numeric, special character symbol) and graphic symbols. The CBM 2001/B, like the CBM 8000, normally displays the alternate character set of lower- and upper-case alphanumerics; graphics are part of the standard character set. The PET normally displays the standard character set consisting of upper-case alphanumerics and graphics. Upper- and lower-case alphanumerics are in the alternate character set.

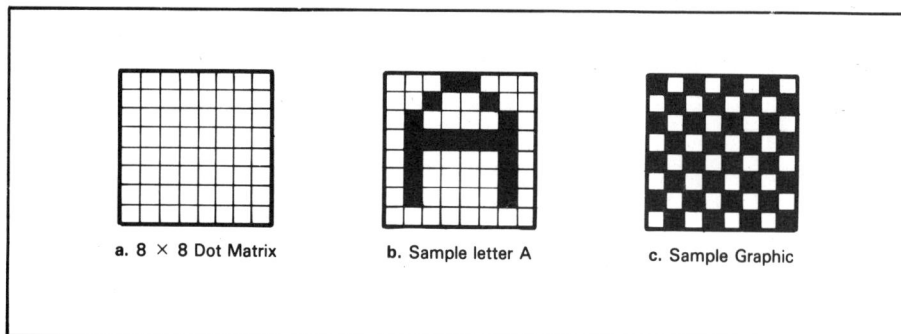

a. 8 × 8 Dot Matrix   b. Sample letter A   c. Sample Graphic

Figure 1-6. The 8 × 8 Dot Matrix

POWER UP

To "start up" your CBM computer follow these steps:

1. Plug the AC power cord, located on the console's rear panel, into a three-hole grounded electrical outlet. Notice that the power cord has a three-prong power plug. *Do not attempt to plug the cord into a two-hole (ungrounded) outlet. Do not attempt to remove the ground prong.* If the unit is not properly grounded, you may receive an electrical shock. Grounding adapters that convert a two-prong outlet into a three-prong (grounded) outlet are available from your hardware store or electrical supply house. *CAUTION: Do not use a three-prong adapter unless you ground it properly when installing it.*

2. Switch power on. The power switch is located on the left side of the console's rear panel. It is a two-position "rocker" switch. Pressing on the outer side of the switch turns power on; pressing the inner side of the switch turns power off.

3. Wait for READY display. About three seconds after switching power on, a message similar to the following one is displayed on the screen:

```
### COMMODORE BASIC ###

xxxxx BYTES FREE

READY.
▓
```

The four lines of display have the following meanings:

`### COMMODORE BASIC ###`	This line indicates that the BASIC language has been activated
`xxxxx BYTES FREE`	This line shows how much memory is available to you.
	3071 (or a similar number) will be displayed for a 4K PET system
	7167 (or a similar number) will be displayed for an 8K CBM system
	15359 (or a similar number) for a 16K CBM system
	31743 (or a similar number) for a 32K CBM system
`READY.`	The CBM computer is ready to receive input from the keyboard
`▓`	The flashing cursor is displayed at the position on the screen where the next character typed in from the keyboard will appear

If you do not get the display illustrated above after turning power on, then turn power off, wait a few seconds, and turn power back on. The display may first be filled with random characters for a second or so. This is normal; just ignore it. The random character display may appear whenever the CBM is turned off and then on again within about ten seconds.

CBM COMPUTER KEY GROUPS

The CBM computer keyboard is used to enter statements, programs and data required by programs. The type of keyboard depends on which model CBM you have. With a few exceptions, the same keys are present on both the compact and full size keyboards. Some keys have different locations on the various computer models.

Keys on the CBM computer keyboard can be grouped as follows: Alphabetic keys, numeric keys, special symbol keys, graphic keys, function keys, and cursor control keys.

Alphabetic Keys

The alphabetic keys provide the 26 letters of the alphabet, A to Z. Upper and lower-case letters are available on all CBM models.

Numeric Keys

The numeric keys provide the digits 0, 1, 2, 3, 4, 5, 6, 7, 8, and 9.

Special Symbol Keys

Special symbols and characters may represent standard punctuation marks and commonly used symbols. For example, there is a period, a comma, "+" for addition, "−" for subtraction, etc. Characters that have widely recognized interpretations include "$" for dollar sign, "%" for the percent sign, etc.

Some characters represent a specific operation, or have special meaning in a BASIC statement. For details see Chapter 4.

Graphic Keys

The CBM keyboard contains 62 graphic symbols, accessed using shifted data keys. With so many graphic characters available on the CBM computer, you can create some rather sophisticated display drawings.

Graphic characters are listed in Table 1-1; each is given a name. Similar symbols are grouped to make graphic options immediately obvious. **Note that the square enclosing the graphic symbols in Table 1-1 is not part of the symbol; the square enclosure has been added to show the symbol's location within a grid space.**

Function Keys

SHIFT. The SHIFT key is pressed simultaneously with any other key to access the key's shifted character. All keys display different characters in shifted and unshifted modes. The lower key symbol is accessed when unshifted. The upper key symbol is accessed when shifted.

There are two identical SHIFT keys located on the main keyboard, one at the lower left and one at the lower right.

SHIFT LOCK (full size keyboard only). CBM computer keyboards have a SHIFT LOCK key located directly above the left-hand SHIFT key. Pressing the SHIFT LOCK key until it "clicks" into place holds SHIFT down so that both hands are free to type in shifted mode. Press the SHIFT LOCK key again to release it; both SHIFT keys return to their unshifted position.

RETURN. The RETURN key is the equivalent of a carriage return on a typewriter; when depressed, it **causes the cursor to move to the beginning of the next line on the screen.**

A RETURN given anywhere on the last line of the screen causes all of the screen text to move, or scroll, up one line. The top line rolls up off the screen and a blank line rolls onto the bottom line of the screen, with the cursor left at the beginning of the blank line.

Table 1-1. Graphic Chararacter Keys

Line Horizontal	Thin Bar	Quarter Block Solid	T
`#` Top	`7` Top	`>` `<` Top Left, Top Right	`1` Top
`E` 3/4 Top	`/` Bottom	`;` `,` Bottom Left, Bottom Right	`2` Bottom
`D` 2/3 Top	`4` Left	`?` Diagonal	`3` Left
`C` Middle	`*` Right		`+` Right
`@` Near Middle		**Quarter Block Open (Angle)**	
`F` 2/3 Bottom	**Thick Bar**	`=` `—` Top Left, Top Right	**Symbol**
`R` 3/4 Bottom	`8` Top	`.` `Ø` Bottom Left, Bottom Right	`V` X
`S` Bottom	`9` Bottom		`[` Cross
Line Verticai	`5` Left	**Corner**	`N` Diagonal Acute
`%` Left	`6` Right	`O` `P` Top Left, Top Right	`M` Diagonal Grave
`T` 3/4 Left		`L` `:` Bottom Left, Bottom Right	
`G` 2/3 Left	**Half Block**		**Grid**
`B` Near Middle	`/` Left	**Rounded Corner**	`&` Full
`]` Middle	`//` Bottom	`U` `I` Top Left, Top Right	`\` Half Left
`H` 2/3 right		`J` `K` Bottom Left, Bottom Right	`(` Half Bottom
`Y` 3/4 right	**Triangle Solid**	**Suit**	**Circle**
`,` Right	`)` Top Left	`A` `S` Spade, Heart	`W` Solid
	`←` Top Right	`Z` `X` Diamond, Club	`Q` Outline

Before RETURN　　　　　　　　　　　**After RETURN**

```
                                          ,Top line scrolled off screen

Line
 1      10 ?"NOW IS THE TIME"              20 ?"FOR ALL GOOD PEOPLE"
 2      20 ?"FOR ALL GOOD PEOPLE"          30 READ X2
        30 READ X2

 24     90 A=B+C-D                         90 A=B+C-D
 25     100 IF A=1 GOTO 10                 100 IF A=1 GOTO 10

                    `Cursor                       `Cursor
                                      `Blank line scrolled in
```

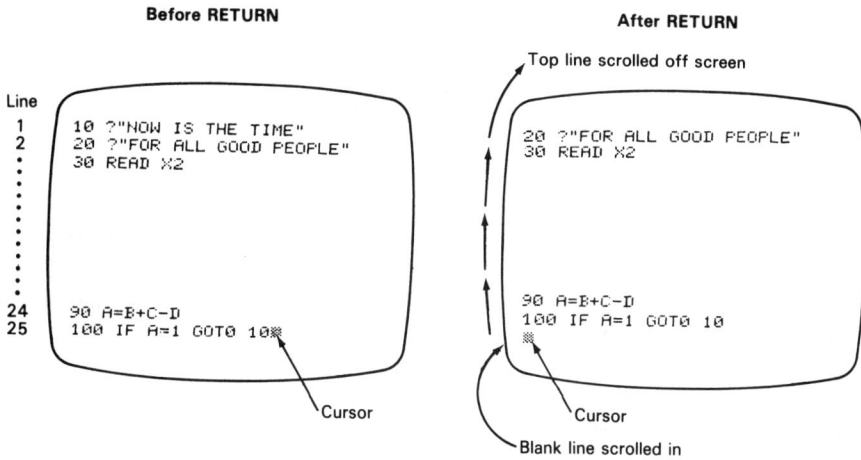

REVERSE ON/OFF. The Reverse key allows you to reverse the black and white parts of characters; REVERSE is like the negative of a photograph. The normal mode for this key is "off." To activate the REVERSE key, press it in unshifted mode. The next character keys you press will be displayed in reverse field. REVERSE ON stays in effect until you either press REVERSE OFF (the REVERSE key shifted) or until you press the RETURN key.

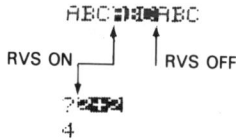

```
                ABC□□□ABC
                     ↑     ↑
        RVS ON ──────┘     │ RVS OFF

                ?□□□□
                4
```

Note: Reverse field terminated by carriage return

RUN/STOP. STOP is the unshifted half of the RUN/STOP key. **STOP stops any program that is being executed by the computer and reconnects the computer with the keyboard.** If you want to test the STOP key, try entering the following one line program, without trying to understand what it means. Key in the shaded line. When you press the RETURN key, a vertical column of numbers will be displayed, as shown. When you press the STOP key, the display will "freeze."

```
        FOR I=1 TO 100:?I:NEXT I
        1
        2
        3
        4
        5
        6
        7
        8
        9
        10 ◄─── Press STOP key

        BREAK
        READY.
```

The STOP key does nothing if there is nothing to stop, i.e., the CBM computer is not running a program.

RUN is the shifted half of the RUN/STOP key. **RUN loads and executes a program from an external peripheral (tape unit or disk drive).**

Cursor Control Keys

The remaining four keys are cursor control and edit keys. They include CLEAR SCREEN/HOME, CURSOR UP/DOWN, CURSOR LEFT/RIGHT, and INSERT/DELETE.

HOME is an unshifted cursor control key that moves the cursor to the "home" position at the upper left-hand corner of the screen.

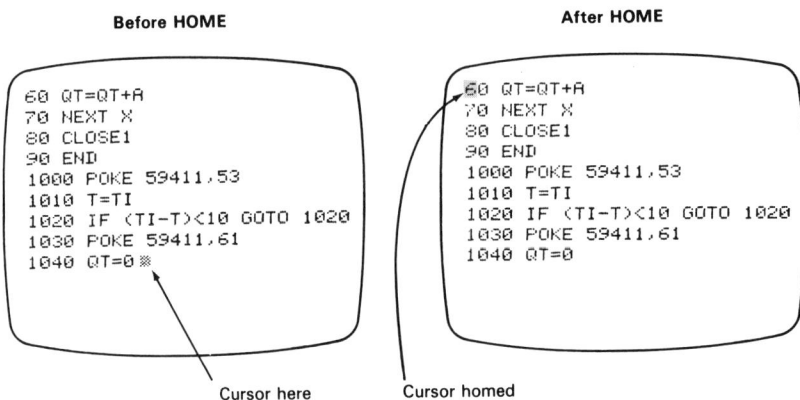

Before HOME   After HOME

```
60 QT=QT+A                          60 QT=QT+A
70 NEXT X                           70 NEXT X
80 CLOSE1                           80 CLOSE1
90 END                             90 END
1000 POKE 59411,53                 1000 POKE 59411,53
1010 T=TI                          1010 T=TI
1020 IF (TI-T)<10 GOTO 1020        1020 IF (TI-T)<10 GOTO 1020
1030 POKE 59411,61                 1030 POKE 59411,61
1040 QT=0 ※                        1040 QT=0
```

            Cursor here   Cursor homed

CLEAR SCREEN, obtained by pressing the CLEAR SCREEN/HOME key in shifted mode, **homes the cursor and blanks the entire display screen.**

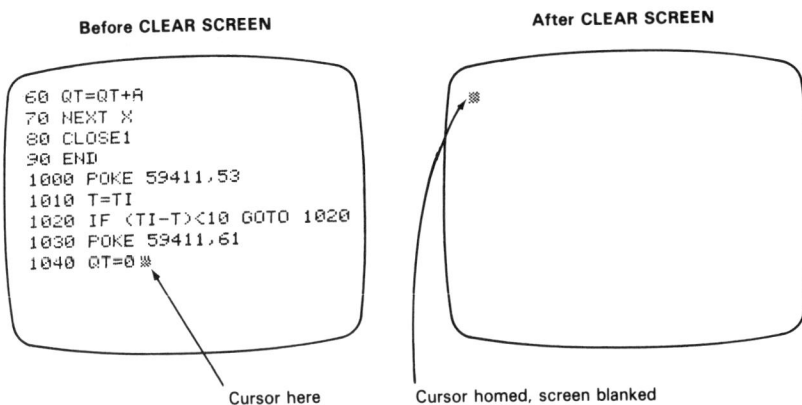

Before CLEAR SCREEN   After CLEAR SCREEN

```
60 QT=QT+A                          ※
70 NEXT X
80 CLOSE1
90 END
1000 POKE 59411,53
1010 T=TI
1020 IF (TI-T)<10 GOTO 1020
1030 POKE 59411,61
1040 QT=0 ※
```

            Cursor here   Cursor homed, screen blanked

CURSOR UP, obtained by pressing the CURSOR UP/DOWN key in shifted mode, **moves the cursor up one line within the same physical column of the screen.**

CURSOR UP

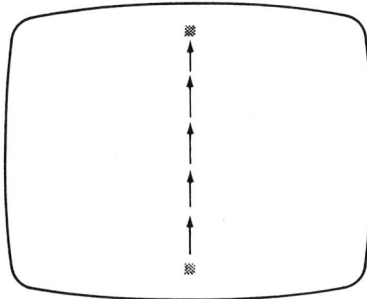

If the cursor is on the top line of the display, CURSOR UP has no effect.

The cursor moves over characters without changing them.

CURSOR DOWN, obtained by pressing the CURSOR UP/DOWN key in unshifted mode, **moves the cursor down one column.**

CURSOR DOWN

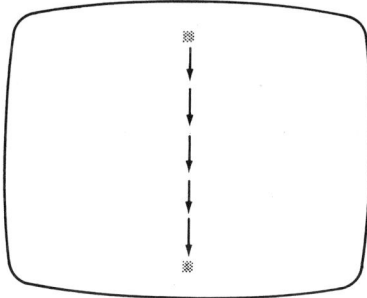

Blank lines scrolled onto screen when cursor is at bottom line

If the cursor is on the bottom line of the screen, CURSOR DOWN scrolls the display up one line.

CURSOR LEFT, obtained by pressing the CURSOR LEFT/RIGHT key in shifted mode, **moves the cursor left one position within the same horizontal row.**

CURSOR LEFT

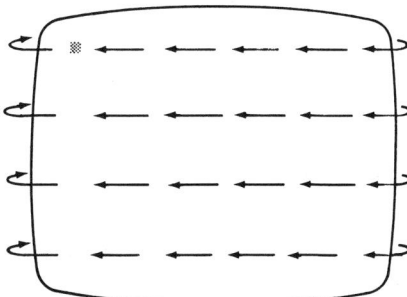

CURSOR LEFT has no effect if the cursor is in the HOME position.

CURSOR RIGHT, obtained by pressing the CURSOR LEFT/RIGHT key in unshifted mode, **moves the cursor right one character position within the same row.**

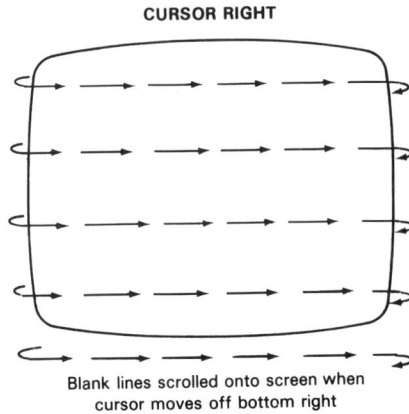

CURSOR RIGHT

Blank lines scrolled onto screen when
cursor moves off bottom right

CURSOR RIGHT and CURSOR LEFT "wrap around," moving from the end of one line to the beginning of the next, or vice versa.

If the cursor is at the end of the bottom line, CURSOR RIGHT will scroll the screen up one line and move the cursor to the start of the bottom line.

CURSOR LEFT/RIGHT are used to type over text. When editing, the cursor does not alter the display as it moves. This is equivalent to backspacing or spacing forward on a typewriter.

The INSERT/DELETE key in unshifted mode selects **DELETE. It deletes the character to the immediate left of the cursor and moves any characters to the right of the deleted character, headed by the cursor, one character position to the left.**

```
NOW IS THE TIME█
NOW IS THE TIM█
NOW IS THE TI█
```

The INSERT/DELETE key in shifted mode selects **INSERT. It opens a single character space in the line at the current position. You can then insert an additional character into the space.**

```
NOW IS█THE TIME
NOW IS█ THE TIME
NOW IS█  THE TIME
```

CBM computers treat all text as a sequence of 80-character lines. You can delete up to, but not beyond the start of an 80-character line. You can insert until current text reaches the end of the 80-character line.

THE CBM 8000 and CBM 2001/B KEYBOARDS

The CBM 8000 and CBM 2001/B keyboards are similar to a standard typewriter keyboard, with a numeric keypad to the right as shown in Figure 1-7. The keyboard may be used in two typing modes to produce two character sets.

In **Alternate Mode,** unshifted keys produce lower-case alphanumerics on the CRT, and shifted keys produce capital, or upper-case alphanumerics. The alternate character set is active on power-up.

Figure 1-7. The CBM 8000 and 2001/B Keyboard

Standard Mode (forced by typing a system command) displays upper-case alphanumerics when keys are pressed unshifted; shifted keys display graphic characters. **To activate the standard character set, type in:**

POKE 59468,12 *(RETURN)*

or on the CBM 8000 only:

?CHR$(142)

This will immediately change character sets. **To bring back the alternate set, type in:**

POKE 59468,14 *(RETURN)*

or on the CBM 8000 only:

?CHR$(14)

Unless stated otherwise, we will assume that the standard character set is being used. Also we will assume that every statement ends with a RETURN, as shown above.

In the following key descriptions, the keyboard is illustrated by key groups, with the particular key group shaded.

Alphabetic Keys

Alphabetic keys are shaded in the illustration above. In alternate mode, alphabetic keys display lower case letters unshifted, and upper case letters if shifted. In standard mode, alphabetic keys display upper case letters unshifted, and graphic characters if shifted.

Numeric Keys

The numeric keys (shaded) occur twice, on the top row of the typewriter keyboard, and on the numeric keypad to the right. The number keys on the top row are accessed in unshifted mode only. The numeric keypad may be accessed in standard and alternate mode. For touch typing, key number 5 has a small bump in the center of the key.

Special Symbol Keys

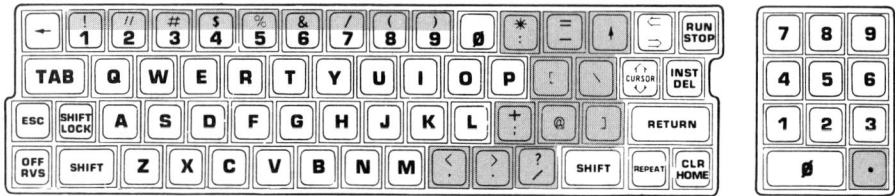

Special symbols are shaded in the illustration above. Symbols located on the top half of the numeric keys are accessed in shifted alternate mode. Other symbol keys are accessed in shifted or unshifted mode.

Graphic Keys

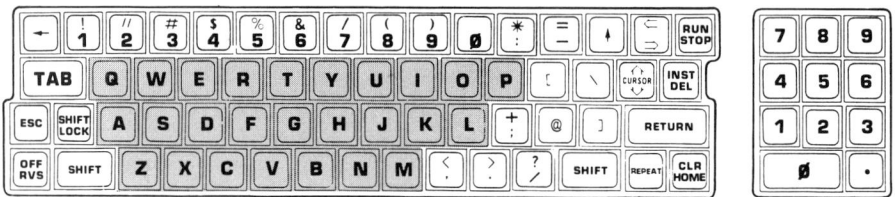

Graphic symbols are not shown on the business keyboards, but they are available. **Select the standard mode with POKE 59468,12. Keys depressed in shifted mode then access and display graphic symbols.** The illustration above shows where graphic characters available from the keyboard are located on a business keyboard.

Function Keys

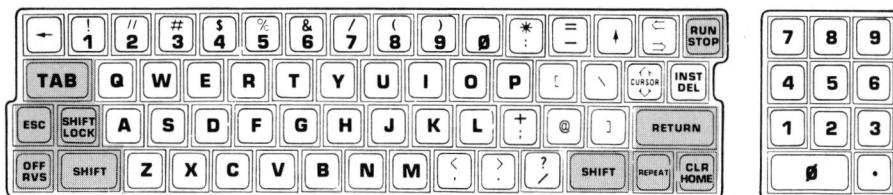

The CBM 8000 and 2001/B have three extra function keys not described in the "CBM Key Groups" section; the TAB, ESCAPE (ESC), and the REPEAT keys.

TAB. This key is used to set and clear tabs, and to jump to the next tab set column.

ESC. (CBM 8000 series only). This key has two uses: it cancels the effect of an insert, reverse character or text entry condition; it also is used in conjunction with certain other keys to create special editing functions (described in Chapter 5).

REPEAT. This key causes repeated entry of any key that is pressed simultaneously.

Cursor Control Keys

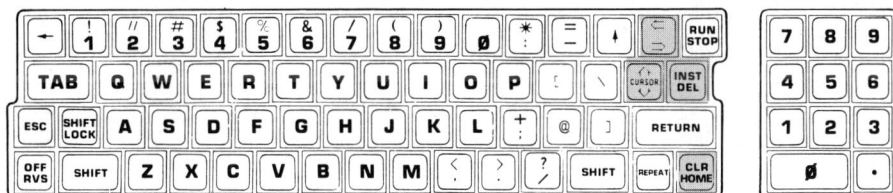

These keys are described in the "CBM Key Groups" section.

THE PET 2001/N KEYBOARD

The PET 2001/N keyboard has a full-size typewriter keyboard with graphic symbols on the front of the keys (see Figure 1-8). This keyboard also has two typing modes: standard and alternate. **Standard mode is selected when you first turn power on.** To activate alternate mode, type in:

POKE 59408,14

To change back to the standard character set, type in:

POKE 59408,12

Figure 1-8. PET 2001/N Keyboard

CBM 2001 Alphabetic Keys

The alphabetic keys shaded above access upper case alphabetics in unshifted standard mode. Lower and upper case alphabetics are accessed in alternate mode.

Numeric Keys

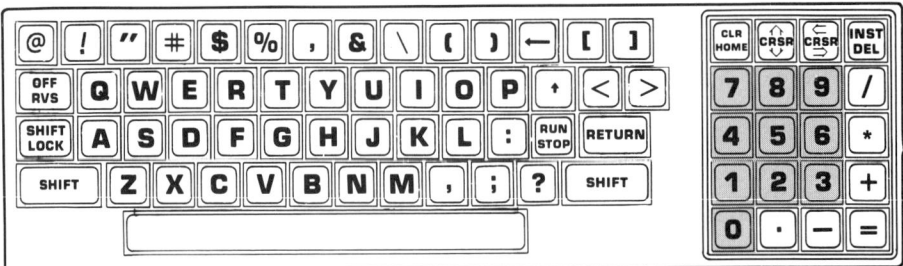

The numeric keys are on the numeric keypad to the right of the full-size keyboard. Numbers are accessed in unshifted mode only.

Special Symbol Keys

The special symbols are located on the typewriter keyboard and on the numeric keypad. These are only available as unshifted keys.

Graphic Keys

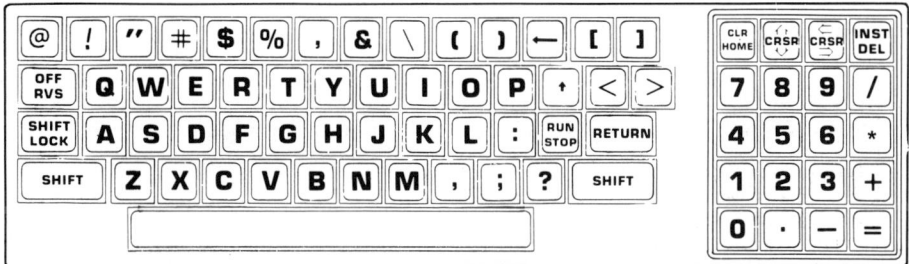

The graphic symbols are located on the front of all non-function keys and cursor keys. **Graphics are only accessed in shifted standard mode.**

Function Keys

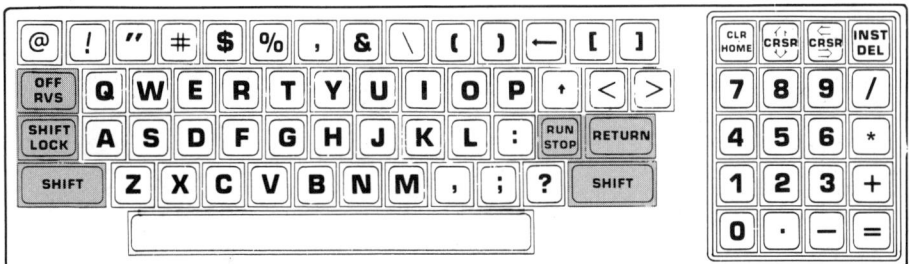

The CBM 2001 has Pi (π), a function key not on the business keyboards. It is located on the ↑ key.

Pi (π) is a circle's circumference, divided by its diameter. **When this function key is depressed, the value 3.14159265 is accessed.** To check this out, type in the shaded line; end with a RETURN and see the display:

```
?π
3.14159265

READY.
▩
```

π is not evaluated as 3.14159265 if it appears within quotation marks. Then it is treated as a graphic character. To check this out, type in the shaded line again, as follows:

```
?"π"
π

READY.
※
```

π will be displayed, as shown above, when you press the RETURN key.

Cursor Control Keys

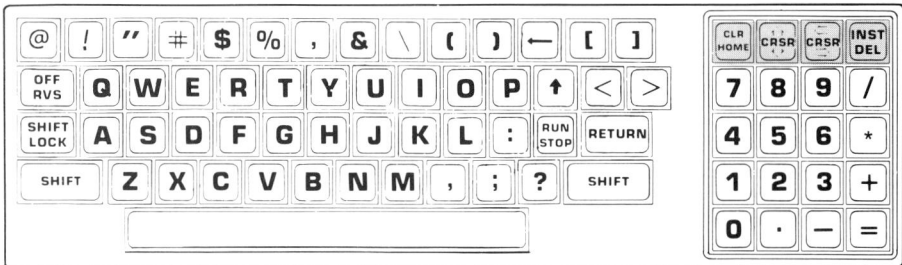

Cursor control keys operate as described earlier in this chapter.

PET 2001/8K KEYBOARD

The PET 2001 has a compact, multi-colored keyboard; like all other keyboards, this one accesses different character sets in standard and alternate modes. Like the PET 2001/N, standard mode is selected when you turn power on. To activate the alternate character set, type in:

POKE 59468, 14

To return to standard character, set type in:

POKE 59468, 12

Figure 1-9 illustrates the PET 2001 keyboard.

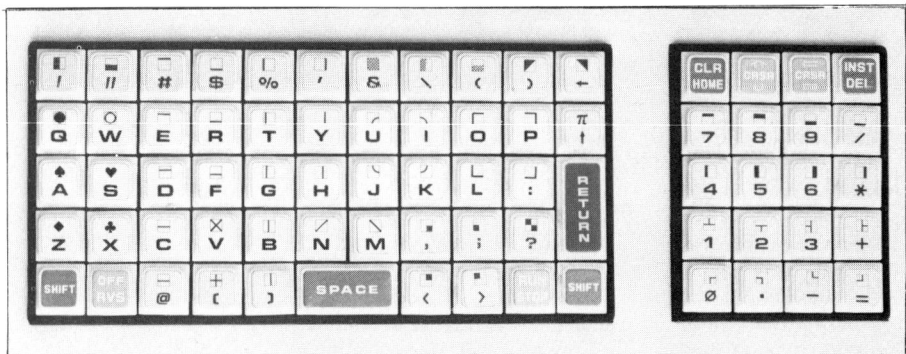

Figure 1-9. PET 2001/8K Keyboard

Alphabetic Keys

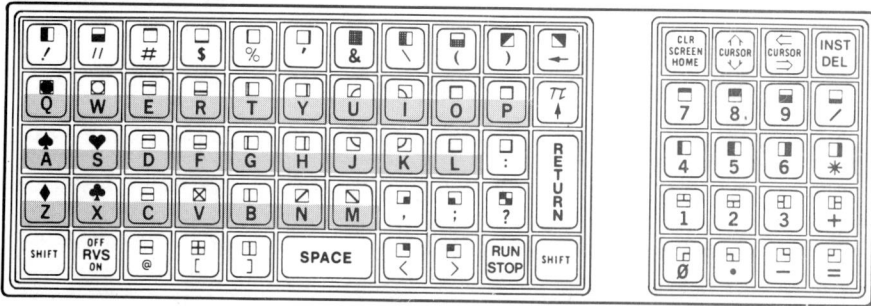

Letters of the alphabet are located on the silver-color keys; they access upper-case letters in unshifted standard mode. The alternate set accesses upper-case letters when unshifted and lower-case letters when shifted.

Numeric Keys

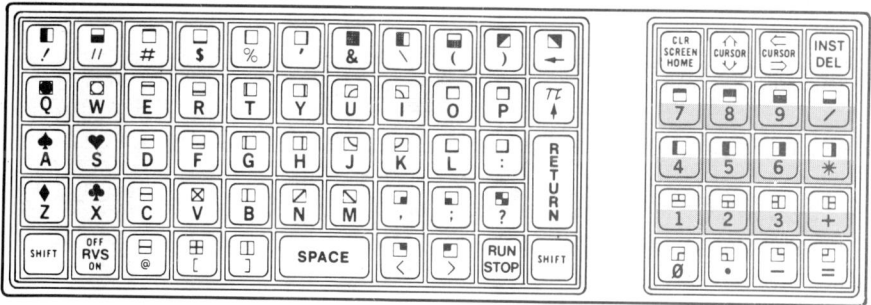

The numeric keys are silver-colored, on the keyboard to the right. Numbers are displayed in unshifted mode.

Special Symbol Keys

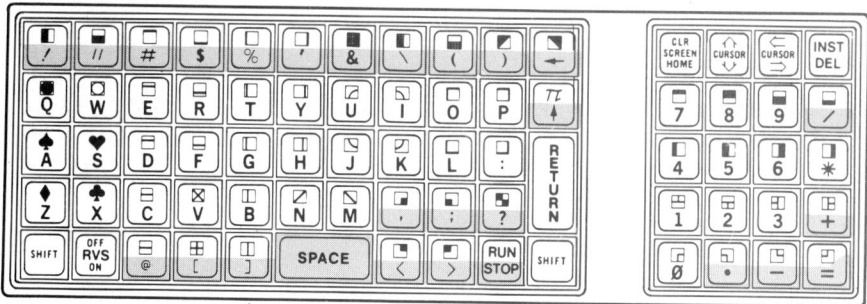

The special symbol keys, shaded above, are light blue on the keyboard and numeric keypad; special symbol keys are grouped together along the top, bottom and right side of the keyboard, and along the right side and bottom of the numeric keypad. These symbols are available only in unshifted mode.

Graphic Keys

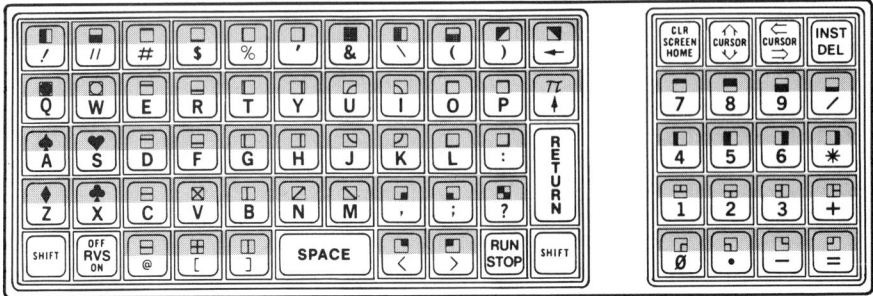

The graphic symbols are located on the front of all non-function and cursor control keys. **Graphics are displayed in shifted standard mode only.**

Function Keys

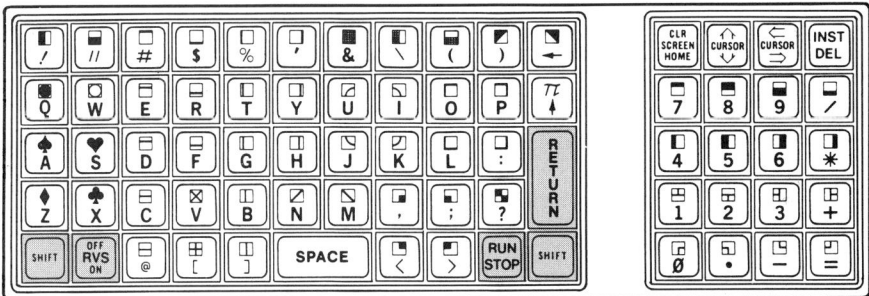

PET 2001 function keys are either red or blue. **The PET is missing the SHIFT/ LOCK key, normally located above the left shift key. However, like the PET 2001/N it has a pi (π) symbol located on the** ↑ **key.** For a description of the pi key see the PET 2001/N description.

Cursor Control Keys

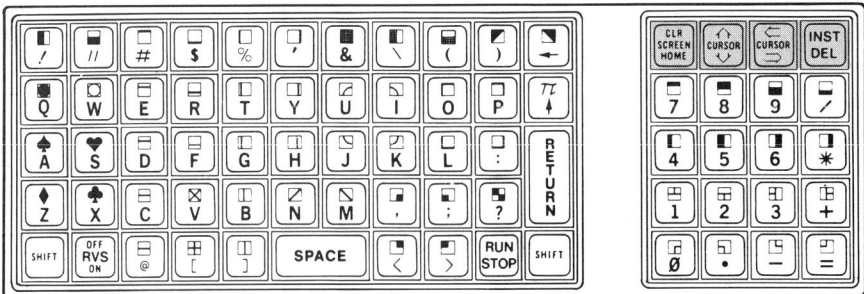

The four cursor control keys are the red and blue keys located on the top row of the numeric keyboard.

Figure 1-10. PET 2001 Internal Tape Drive

THE CASSETTE TAPE UNIT

The cassette tape unit is built into the PET console but must be connected separately to CBM models. The internal and external cassette units are basically the same. The tape drive allows you to store programs and data on cassette tape. You can also load stored programs and data from cassette tape into computer memory.

The computer can connect to more than one cassette tape drive, but only one of the tape drives is the "primary" or "console" cassette tape drive. For the PET the console tape drive is the built-in tape unit (see Figure 1-10). For CBM computers the console tape drive is the tape unit connected at the J1 interface port.

The External Tape Drive

The external tape unit is shown in Figure 1-11.

A maximum of two cassette drives may be used at one time. On the PET that has a built-in cassette drive next to the keyboard, a second cassette drive may be attached at cassette interface J3, shown in Figures 1-5 and 1-13a. On all other models, the first cassette drive is externally connected at the J3 interface. For the 2001 models, a second external cassette drive may be attached to a connector inside the computer as shown in Figure 1-13b. For the CBM 8000, see Figure 1-13c.

Other peripherals such as the printer or disk drives may be connected to the IEEE 488 interface without affecting the operation of the cassette drives.

Figure 1-11. An External Tape Drive

Cassette Tape Operation

When attaching an external cassette to any connector, you can either connect the cassette correctly, or you can break the connector. This is because the connector has an acentric slot:

The cassette drive plug has a divider that fits into the slot:

So long as the divider slides into the slot, you can be sure that a proper connection has been made.

The procedure to plug an external cassette drive into an *outside* cassette interface (such as the J3 connector) is given below.

1. Turn the power off.
2. Hold the connecting plug at the end of the cable so that the "blue" wire is on the right.
3. Gently push the plug onto the interface as in Figure 1-12. *Do not force the connection.*
4. Make sure the connection fits securely.
5. Turn on power.

To plug a cassette drive into the printed circuit board connector *inside* the CBM computer, follow these steps:

1. Turn the power off and unplug the computer.
2. Move the front of the computer out from the supporting surface so that you can see the four retaining screws on the bottom. With a screwdriver unscrew the four retaining screws.

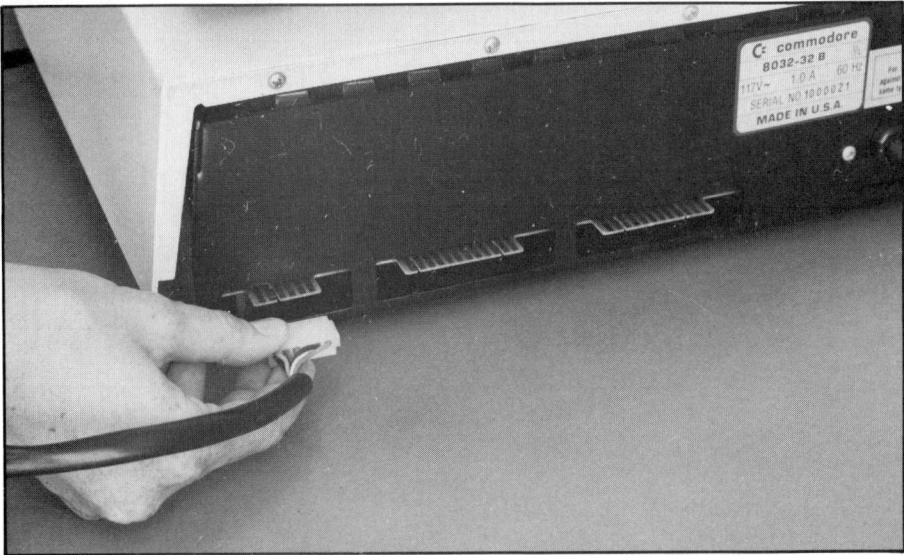

Figure 1-12. Connecting Second External Cassette Unit to CBM Computer

3. Lift the cover all the way up, being careful not to move it so far back that it pulls any of the cords.

4. Locate the supporting rod on the inner left side of the computer (if available on your model). Push the rod up to disengage it from its holder, then move it forward and secure it in the back screw hole on the left side. This holds the cover up so you have both hands free.

5. Locate the cassette interface on the left edge of the printed circuit board as shown in Figure 1-13b.

6. Hold the connecting plug at the end of the cable so that the off-center slot on the circuit board matches the off-center divider on the cassette plug.

7. Gently push the plug onto the connector as shown in Figure 1-13b. *Do not force the connection.*

8. Make sure the connection fits securely.

9. Put cover down; screw in retaining screws.

10. Plug the CBM computer in. Turn on power.

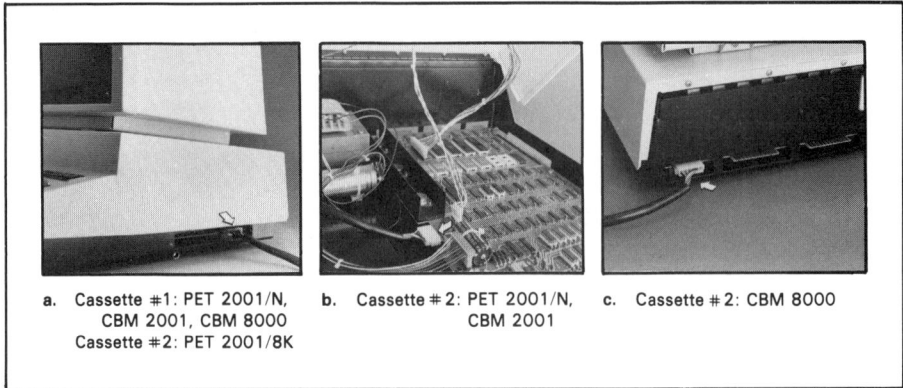

a. Cassette #1: PET 2001/N,   b. Cassette #2: PET 2001/N,   c. Cassette #2: CBM 8000
    CBM 2001, CBM 8000   CBM 2001
Cassette #2: PET 2001/8K

Figure 1-13. Plug External Cassette into Circuit Board

Operation Test

Before continuing further, you should check the mechanical operation of the cassette unit(s). Below is a simple test to make sure that all control keys and inner mechanical components are functioning correctly.

1. Turn the CBM computer on. Make sure none of the cassette keys is depressed and that the cassette drive motor is not running.

2. Open the cassette door on the top of the unit by pressing the STOP/EJECT key (or manually on the older models). While looking inside the unit, press the PLAY key. You should see the tape heads move out toward the spindles. The pinch roller should simultaneously move out, touch and rotate the capstan in a counterclockwise direction. The inside of the unit should look like Figure 1-14.

3. Press the STOP/EJECT key once. The tape heads should draw back out of view and the spindles should stop rotating.

4. Press the FFWD (Fast Forward) key. The tape heads should remain hidden and the take-up spindle on the right should move counterclockwise very fast.

5. Press the STOP/EJECT key once. The take-up spindle should stop rotating.

6. Press the REW (Rewind) key. The tape heads should remain hidden. The supply spindle on the left should move clockwise very fast.

7. Press the STOP/EJECT key once. The supply spindle should stop rotating.

8. Very gently press the REC (Record) key. The key should remain locked and not move. This key will not move unless the PLAY and REC keys are simultaneously pressed with a cassette tape inserted in place.

If all the above steps worked correctly your cassette unit is ready to begin operation. If some or all of the above steps do not work, check the following: make sure that power is on, that you did not try to press two keys simultaneously (i.e., holding down the STOP key accidentally) and that you pressed the keys down until they clicked and stayed in place. If the cassette unit is still not functioning correctly, contact your Commodore dealer.

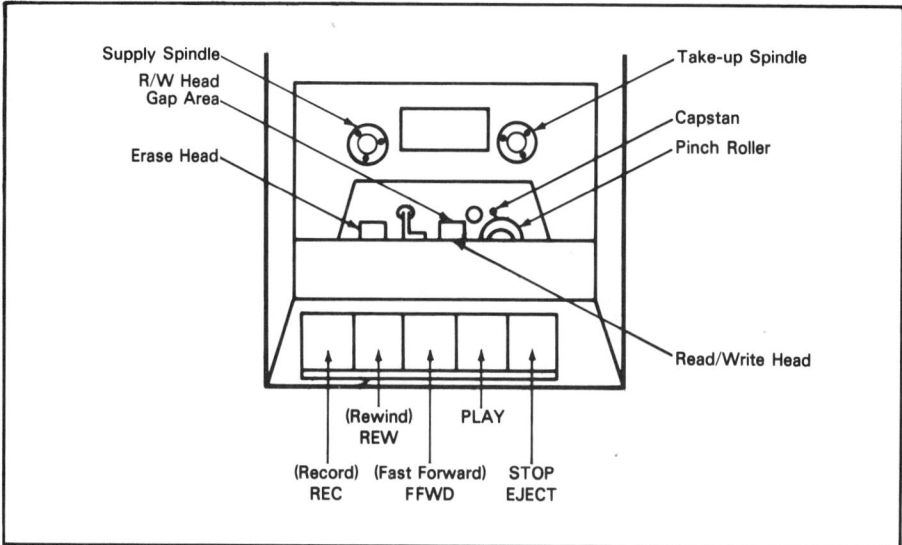

Figure 1-14. Mechanical Components on Cassette Unit

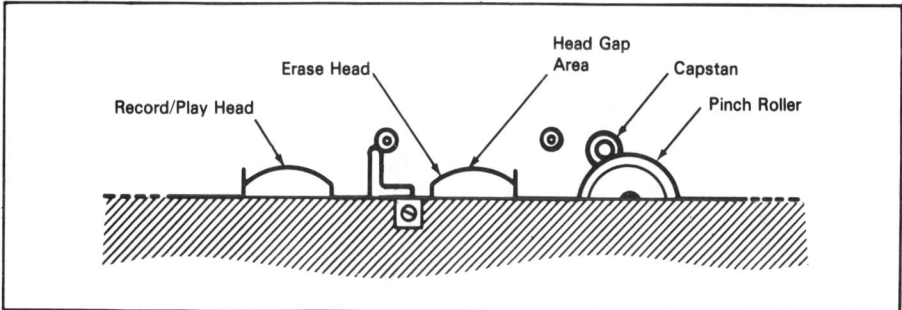

Figure 1-15. Cassette Drive Tape Head

Cleaning and Demagnetizing the Tape Head

The head area of the cassette drive can be seen by opening the cassette drive door with power *off* and depressing the PLAY key. This juts the tape head mount out where it is marginally reachable for maintenance. **The tape head is shown in Figure 1-15**

The tape head is the portion of the cassette unit that the magnetic tape contacts when you record or play back. The oxide coating on the magnetic tape gradually deposits a film on the tape head and surrounding area; this deposit must be removed periodically by cleaning the tape head to assure reliable operation of the cassette unit. **To clean the tape head, use a cotton swab soaked with a commercially formulated tape head cleaner (e.g., Nortronics brand). Do NOT use tri-cloroethylene, plastic solvent, or rubber cement. Alcohol may be used occasionally, but it is not recommended for regular use.** Clean both heads and also the capstan and pinch roller. Allow the area to dry completely before closing the cover.

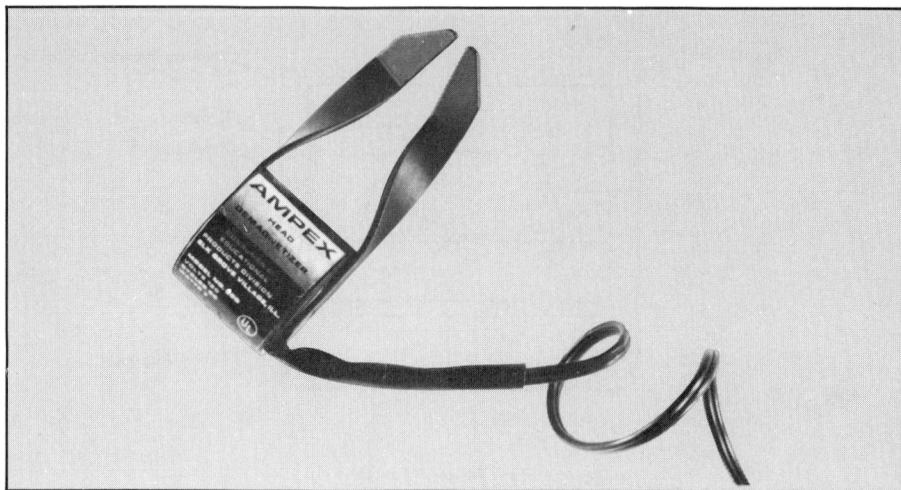

Figure 1-16. A Typical Tape Head Demagnetizer

The tape head also needs to be demagnetized periodically. The tape heads gradually become magnetized through use. This affects recording fidelity and eventually causes recording errors. To demagnetize the tape heads, you will need a tape head demagnetizer (Figure 1-16); this is an inexpensive unit that can be purchased at most audio equipment stores.

To demagnetize the tape heads, have the cassette drive door open and the PLAY key depressed. To use the demagnetizer, have it at least two feet away from the cassette drive before plugging in the demagnetizer (the cassette drive should be *off*). *Slowly* bring the demagnetizer towards the cassette drive until it contacts the head surface; carefully move it around on one head surface, then the other head surface, then all metal surfaces that are directly adjacent to the heads. *Slowly* move the demagnetizer back at least two feet before unplugging it.

Caution: Keep your pre-recorded cassette tapes away from the demagnetizer. The demagnetizer is an effective tape eraser. Keep it at least five feet away from any pre-recorded cassettes.

The more you use your cassette drives, the more often the drive will need to have the tape heads cleaned and demagnetized. Do it at least once a month — more often if you are experiencing load problems or tape degradation.

Cassette Tape Drive Controls

The cassette tape control keys are located at the forefront of the cassette drive.

RECORD (REC). The RECORD key lets you write from computer memory onto the magnetic tape cassette.

REWIND (REW). The REWIND key rewinds the magnetic tape at high speed, to its beginning. To rewind the tape, depress the REWIND key.

You will use REWIND often to rewind tape cassettes back to their beginning point before removing them from the tape drive. You will also use REWIND any time you want the computer to start searching for information beginning at an earlier point on the magnetic tape.

FAST FORWARD (FFWD). FAST FORWARD winds the magnetic tape forward at high speed.

Computers write onto magnetic tape, read from the tape, and search for information on the tape all at PLAY speed, which is slower.

PLAY. The PLAY key enables the computer to search the tape for a program, and to load the program from the tape into computer memory. You also use PLAY to write from computer memory to tape if the RECORD key is also pressed.

STOP/EJECT. The tape STOP key disengages any of the other control keys. If one of the other keys does not respond, press the tape STOP key and press the other control key again.

EJECT. The EJECT key automatically opens the tape drive door so that a cassette tape may be inserted or withdrawn. The Eject option was not available on the earliest PET tape drives.

Loading/Unloading a Cassette Tape

Use the following procedure to insert a cassette into a tape drive (refer to Figure 1-17):

1. Press EJECT. The tape drive door will lift up automatically.
2. Holding the magnetic tape cassette as shown, push the cassette along the glide paths on the underside of the tape drive window until the cassette clicks into place.
3. Push down the tape drive door. This aligns the path of the exposed magnetic tape with the tape drive head area.

To remove a cassette tape, lift up the tape drive door or push the eject key if the drive has one. Pull the cassette tape out of the tape drive, then close the tape drive door.

CASSETTE TAPES

You will probably buy cassette tapes that have prerecorded programs on them. You will probably also buy blank tape cassettes on which to record your own programs or data.

The cassette tape that fits into the cassette drive and stores your information is shown below.

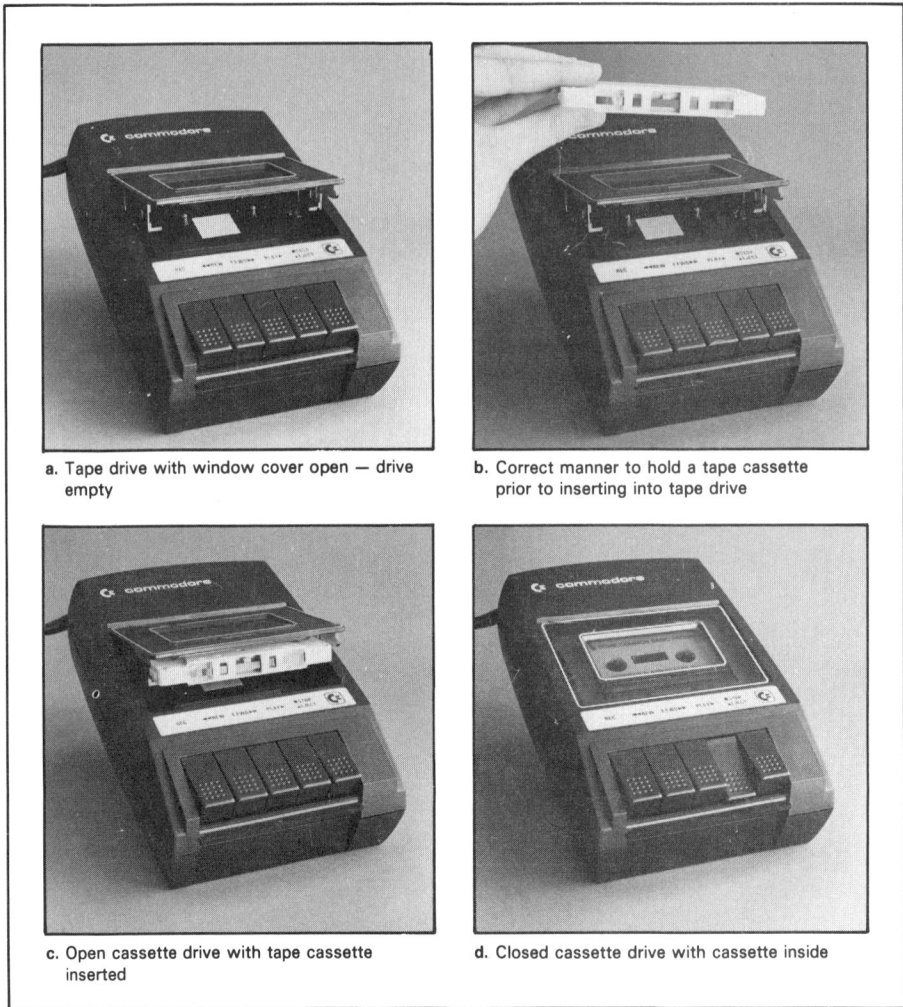

a. Tape drive with window cover open — drive empty

b. Correct manner to hold a tape cassette prior to inserting into tape drive

c. Open cassette drive with tape cassette inserted

d. Closed cassette drive with cassette inside

Figure 1-17. Inserting a Cassette Tape

Care of Cassette Tapes

Below are a few tips on taking care of your cassette tapes.

First, when you get a new cassette tape (blank or prerecorded), balance its tension by fast forwarding to the end of the tape and rewinding back to the beginning before loading the first time. This is just a precautionary measure that may prevent reading errors (also called LOAD errors).

When buying blank cassette tapes, do not buy long ones — 15 to 30 minutes are sufficient. This not only cuts down the search time, but gives you tape that is thicker and stronger than long-playing tapes. Select high quality, low noise, high output, ferric oxide tapes; bargain brands are generally less satisfactory. Store the cassettes in a cool place away from magnets and electronic equipment.

Be careful not to touch the oxide coated surface when handling tapes.

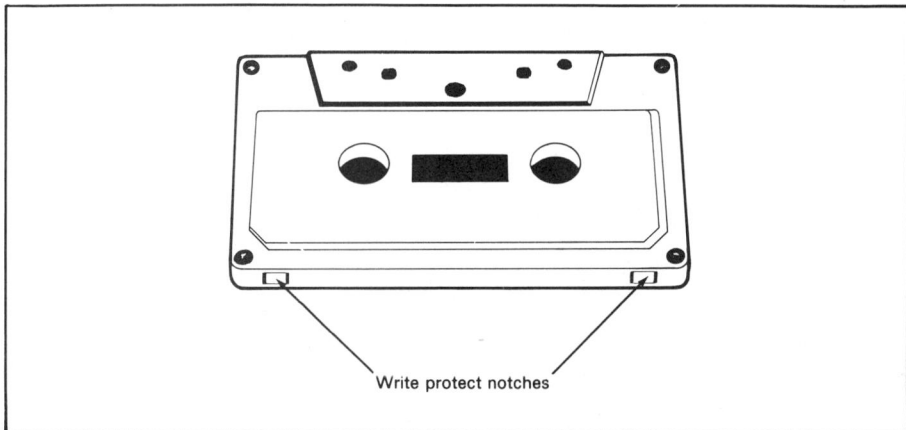

Figure 1-18. Write Protect Notches

Cassette Tape Write-Protect

You can prevent any cassette from being recorded on by "write-protecting" it. A cassette tape has two write-protect notches, one for each side to the tape, located on the side opposite the tape access opening (see Figure 1-18). When you buy pre-recorded tapes, or when your own tapes have information stored on them, you can protect these tapes from accidentally being written on by punching out the write-protect tabs. To write-protect just one side of the tape, punch out the tab that is on the left when you have the side you want to write-protect facing upward.

If you write-protect a tape and then decide you want to reuse it, just place a piece of scotch tape over the write-protect opening.

CBM DISK DRIVE

Commodore has two dual-drive floppy disk units available: the CBM 8050 and the CBM 2040. Disk drives store programs and data on diskettes. A diskette is a flexible disk, approximately the size and shape of a 45 rpm record.

The CBM 8050 and 2040 are shown in Figures 1-19 and 1-20. The CBM 2040 stores approximately 171,500 bytes of data on a diskette; it is called a "single density" drive in computer jargon. The CBM 8050 is a "double density" drive in computer jargon, and stores approximately 522,000 bytes of data per diskette. **Disk drive specifications are given in Tables 1-2 and 1-3.**

Connecting the Disk Drive to the CBM

To connect a disk drive to your CBM computer, follow these steps:

1. Disconnect the computer's AC power cord from the electrical outlet.

2. Using a CBM to IEEE cable, plug the small end into the interface slot on the upper left rear panel of the disk drive (see Figure 1-21). Secure the connector by turning the two screws clockwise until tight.

Figure 1-19. CBM 8050 Dual-Drive Floppy Disk Unit

Figure 1-20. Model 2040 Dual-Drive Floppy Disk Unit

3. Gently push the "flared" connector into the center interface slot (J1 in Figure 1-5) on the back of the CBM console. Make sure the connector side with "Commodore" stamped on it is facing up. The hookup should look like Figure 1-21.
4. Plug the disk drive's AC power cord into an electrical outlet.
5. Plug the CBM computer's AC power cord into an electrical outlet.

Having connected the disk drive to the computer, proceed to the power-on test.

Table 1-2. Model 8050 Dual-Drive Floppy Disk Specifications

Physical:			Electrical:	
Material:	18 gauge steel		Power requirements:	
Dimensions:			Voltage	100, 117, 220 or
Height	6.5''			240 VAC
Width	15''		Frequency	50 or 60 hertz
Depth	14.35''		Power	50 watts
			Drives:	
IC's:			Shugart	SA390 (2)
			Diskettes	Standard mini, 5¼''
Controller:			**Storage (each disk):**	
6502	Microprocessor			
6530	I/O, RAM, ROM		Total capacity	533,248 bytes
6522	I/O, interval timers		Sequential	521,208 bytes
Interface:			Relative	464,312 to 517,398
6502	Microprocessor			bytes, depending on
6532 (2)	I/O, RAM, interval timers			file size
6564 (2)	ROM		Sectors per track	23 to 29
			Bytes per sector	256
Shared:			Tracks	77
6114 (8)	4 × 1K RAM		Blocks	2083

Table 1-3. Model 2040 Dual-Drive Floppy Disk Specifications

Physical:			Electrical:	
Material:	18 guage steel		Power requirements:	
Dimensions:			Voltage	120 VAC
Height	6.5''		Frequency	60 Hertz
Width	15''		Power	50 watts
Depth	14.35''			
			Drives:	
IC's:			Shugart	SA390 (2)
Controller:			Diskettes	Standard mini, 5¼''
6504	Microprocessor			
6530	I/O, RAM, ROM		**Storage (each disk):**	
6522	I/O, interval timers		Total capacity	176640 bytes
Interface:			Sequential	170180 bytes
6502	Microprocessor		Random	170850 bytes
6532 (2)	I/O, RAM, interval timers		Sectors per track	17 to 21
6332 (2)	ROM		Bytes per sector	256
Shared:			Tracks	35
6114 (8)	4 × 1K RAM		Blocks	690

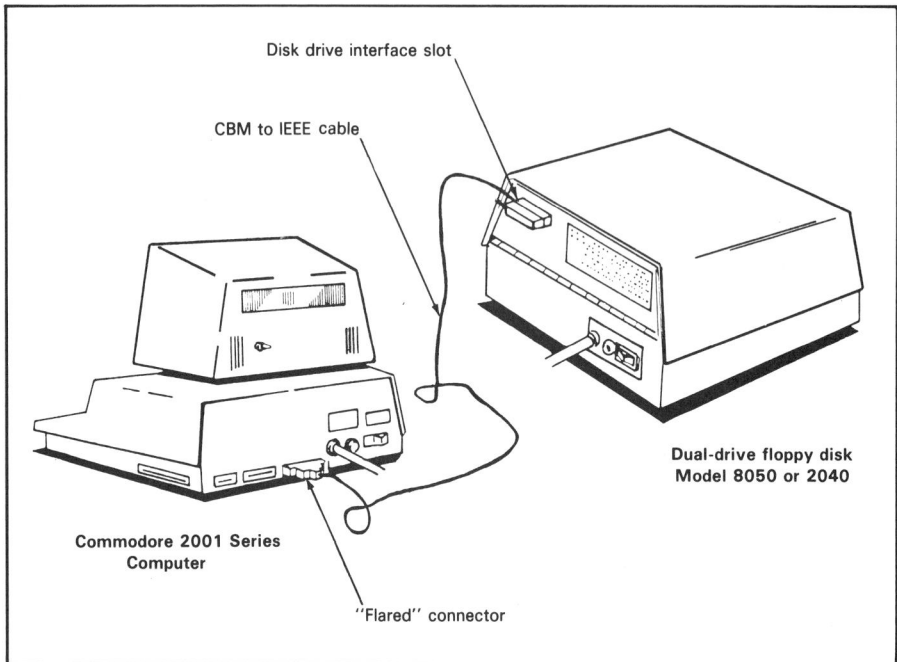

Figure 1-21. CBM-Floppy Disk Drive Connection

Power-On Test

1. Turn on power to the CBM computer. Make sure the console is working correctly.
2. If you have Model 2040 disk drives, open both drive doors by placing your forefingers under the drive doors and gently pulling your fingers forward until the doors spring open. If you have model 8050 disk drive, skip this step.
3. Make sure both disk drives are empty.
4. Turn on power to the disk drive by pressing the rocker switch on the left rear side of the disk drive.

Model 8050: All three green indicator lights on the front panel should flash twice. The left and right lights above the drives should go out. The center light should remain lit.

Model 2040: All three red indicator lights on the front panel should flash on briefly and then go out. Some disk drives may make a soft "purring" noise during initialization.

If several indicator lights remains lit, turn off the disk drive. Wait five minutes and power up the disk drive again. If the lights still remain lit, contact your Commodore dealer.

Indicator Lights

Both disk drive models have three indicator lights on the front panels (see Figure 1-22). These indicator lights are called LEDs (Light Emitting Diodes). Drive 0

Figure 1-22. Dual Drive Floppy Disk LED Indicator Lights

and drive 1 have their own LEDs that turn on when that disk drive is in operation. The center light is an error light.

The 8050 has three *green* LEDs. As previously stated, the lights above the disk drives turn on when that drive is in operation, and turn off when the operation is complete. The center LED turns on when the 8050 is receiving power; this light is also used as an error indicator. **When an error occurs the center LED changes to** *red* **and remains lit until the error is corrected.**

The 2040 has three *red* LEDs. The lights above the disk drives specify when that drive is in operation. They glow red until the operation is complete. **The LED in the center is an error indicator only. It lights up when an error occurs and remains lit until the error is corrected.**

Loading and Unloading Diskettes

Each diskette comes in a storage envelope. *Remove the diskette from the envelope before loading* it into the disk drive.

The circular diskette is held in a square protective jacket as shown in Figure 1-23. This jacket guards the diskette from foreign substances and breakage or bending. *Do not remove the jacket.* **When buying diskettes for any CBM computer, buy** *soft-sectored* 5-1/4'' diskettes. If you are unsure whether your diskette is soft-sectored, here is a simple test (see Figure 1-24):

1. Take the diskette out of its envelope (not the jacket) and hold it by the jacket.
2. Insert two fingers inside the center hole.
3. Locate the small hole next to the center hole (see Figure 1-23).
4. *Carefully* rotate the diskette with your fingers until you align a small hole in the diskette with the outer small hole in the jacket.

If you find only one hole in the diskette the diskette is soft-sectored. If you find multiple holes, it is not soft-sectored.

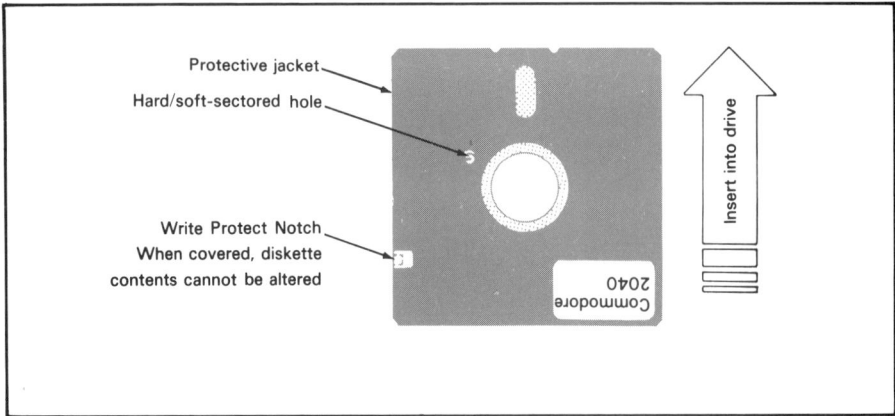

Figure 1-23. Floppy Diskette

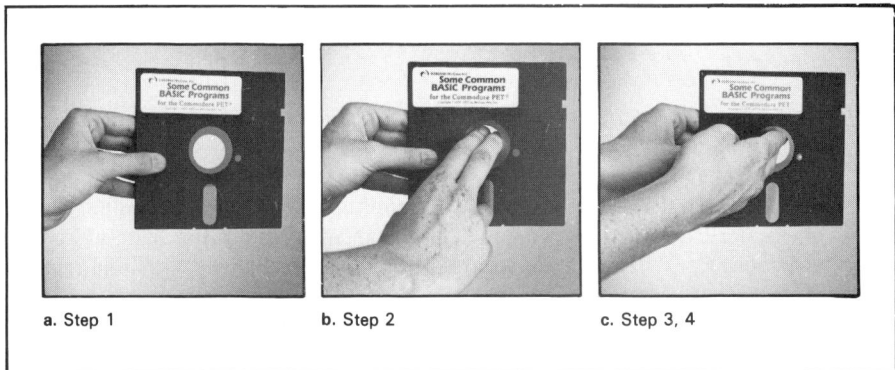

a. Step 1   b. Step 2   c. Step 3, 4

Figure 1-24. Test for Soft-Sectored Diskette

Model 8050 Load

1. Hold the diskette by the plastic jacket. *Do not touch the exposed sections of the diskette.* The diskette should be facing up with the write-protect notch on the left side.

2. Carefully guide the diskette into one of the slots (Figure 1-25) until you hear a loud click. Do not push the diskette further in. If it doesn't slide in smoothly, immediately withdraw it and try again. *Do not force the diskette* or you may damage both the diskette and the disk drive.

3. With two fingers, press down firmly on the lever in the disk drive door until the lever stays down.

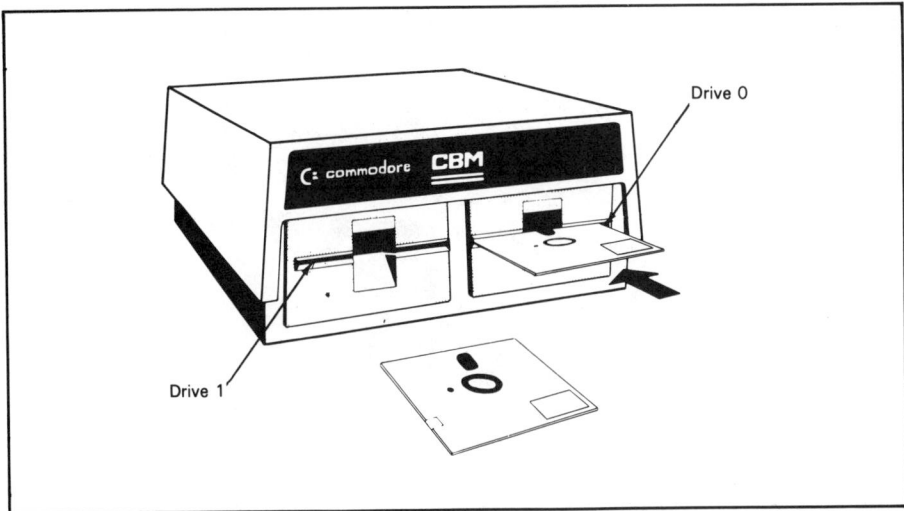

Figure 1-25. Inserting the Diskettes (Model 8050)

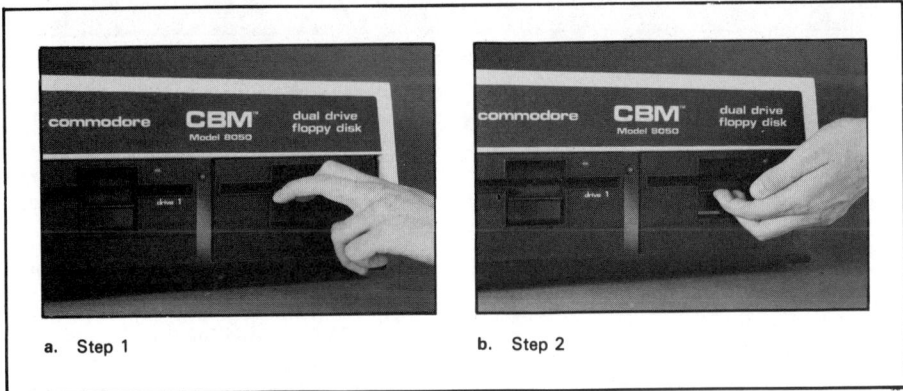

a. Step 1   b. Step 2

Figure 1-26. Removing the Diskette (Model 8050)

Model 8050 Unload

Never remove a diskette when the LED is lit for that particular drive.

1. The disk drive lever should already be in the down position. With two fingers, give the lever a quick press downward and release the lever. The diskette should pop up from inside the drive (Figure 1-26a).

2. To eject the diskette, place your forefinger under the lever and gently push it upward and forward. This will eject the diskette out of the drive (Figure 1-26b).

3. Grab the diskette with your thumb and forefinger and gently withdraw the diskette. *Do not bend or force the diskette.*

4. Insert the diskette into its envelope.

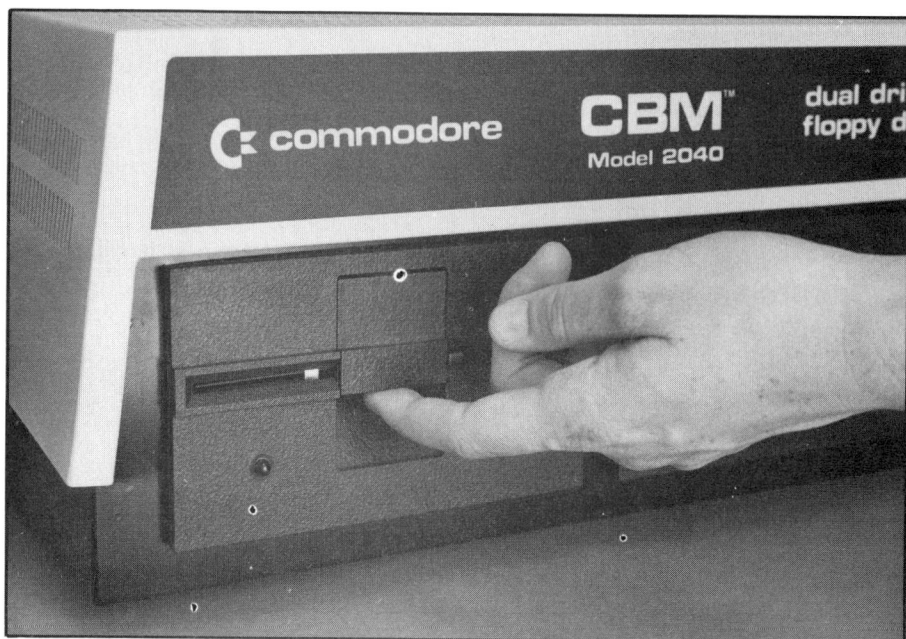

Figure 1-27. Opening Disk Drive Door (Model 2040)

Model 2040 Load

1. Hold the diskette by the plastic jacket. *Do not touch the exposed sections of the diskette.* The diskette should be facing up with the write-protect notch on the left edge.

2. Place the forefinger of your free hand under the drive door and gently pull your finger forward until the door springs open (Figure 1-27).

3. Carefully guide the diskette into one of the slots as illustrated in Figure 1-17 until you hear a faint click. Do not push the diskette further in. If it doesn't slide in smoothly, immediately withdraw it and try again. *Do not force the diskette* or you may damage both the diskette and the disk drive.

4. Close the drive door by pressing down on the door until it shuts completely.

Model 2040 Unload

Never remove a diskette when the LED is lit for that particular drive.

1. Place your forefinger under the drive door and gently pull your finger forward until the door springs open (see Figure 1-27).

2. Grab the diskette with your thumb and forefinger, and gently withdraw the diskette. *Do not bend or force the diskette.*

3. Close the drive door by pressing down on the door until it shuts completely.

4. Insert the diskette into its envelope.

FLOPPY DISKS

Care of the Diskettes

You must handle diskettes with care. All of your information will be stored on them. Once a disk is damaged, there is no way to recover data stored on it. Follow the hints below to protect your diskettes:

1. After removing the diskette from the disk drive, return it promptly to its storage envelope.
2. *Do not remove the diskette from its plastic jacket.*
3. When labeling a diskette, use the labels provided with the diskette. Do not write on the label with a lead pencil or ball point pen; use only a felt tip pen.
4. Do not touch or try to clean the diskette surface or you will damage the diskette.
5. Do not smoke when using diskettes. Tobacco ash or smoke residue on the diskette surface may damage it.
6. *Keep diskettes away from magnetic fields.* Exposure to a magnetic field will destroy the stored data.
7. Do not expose diskettes to heat or sunlight.

Diskette Write-Protect

You can prevent any diskette from being written on by "write-protecting" it. Each diskette has a write-protect notch on its outer edge, as illustrated in Figure 1-15. **When the write-protect notch is covered, the diskette cannot be written on.** You can use scotch tape to write-protect a diskette, but special adhesive tapes are available, and they are preferable. **If you remove the notch cover, you can write on the diskette again.**

THE CBM PRINTER

Two printers are available for the CBM computer: the CBM 2022 Tractor Feed (Figure 1-28) and the CBM 2023 Matrix or Friction Feed (Figure 1-29). The difference between the two models lies in their paper feed mechanisms. The Model 2022 has a tractor feed mechanism that pulls the paper through using sprocket holes on the paper edges. The Model 2023 uses a friction feed mechanism similar to a typewriter. Any type of paper may be used with this model.

Both models print characters using a 7×6 dot matrix (similar to the way characters are generated by the CRT display). Both printers print a maximum of 80 characters per line, at a speed of one line per second (60 lines per minute). Both printers have a ribbon mechanism and use purple or black nylon ribbon with stop eyelets that reverse ribbon direction. **Table 1-4 provides printer specifications.**

Figure 1-28. Model 2022 Printer

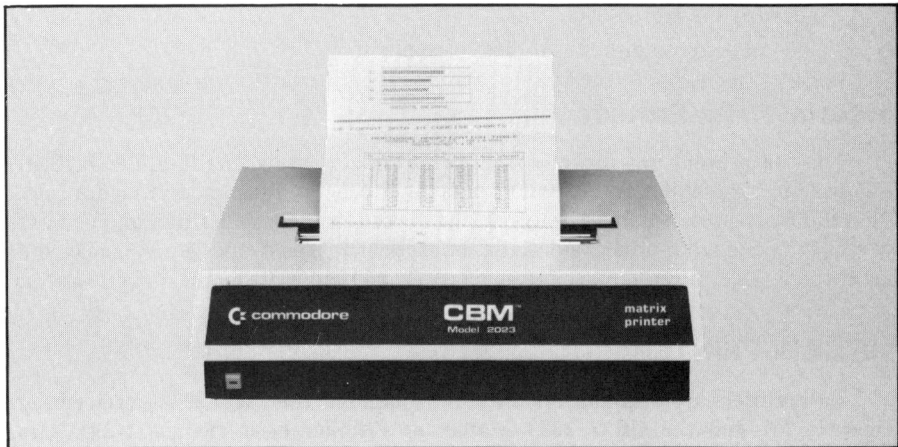

Figure 1-29. Model 2023 Printer

Connecting the Printer to Your CBM Computer

Connect your printer to the computer as follows:

1. Disconnect the computer's AC power cord from the electrical outlet.
2. For *direct* hookup of the printer to the CBM computer follow these steps:
   a. Using a CBM to IEEE cable, plug the small end (standard IEEE connector) into the right interface slot in the back of the printer (see Figure 1-5). Secure the connector by turning the two screws clockwise until tight.
   b. Gently push the "flared" connector into the center interface slot on the back of the CBM computer console. Make sure the connector side with "Commodore" stamped on it is facing up. The hookup is illustrated in Figure 1-30.

Table 1-4. Model 2022 and 2023 Printer Specifications

Model 2022 Printer Specifications

Printing Method	Serial Impact Dot Matrix
Print Rate	70 lpm or 150 cps (Maximum)
Print Direction	Unidirectional
Column Capacity	80
Character Font	6 × 7
Column Spacing	1/10'' 10 characters per inch
Line Spacing	Programmable
Character Size	0.11'' high 0.10'' wide
Copies	3 - including original
Ribbon Type	Nylon-fibered with eyelets
Ribbon Life	2×10^6 characters
Ribbon Spool Type	Underwood
Paper Width	10'' computer folded paper
Forms	8.5 + 0.5 × 2 (Sprocket margins)
	Pin to pin distance: 0.5'' longitudinally
	9.0'' laterally
	5/32'' diameter

Model 2023 Printer Specifications

The specifications for the Friction Feed Model 2023 are the same as for the Tractor Feed Model 2022, except for the following items:

Line Spacing	1/6'' six lines per inch
Forms	Not applicable

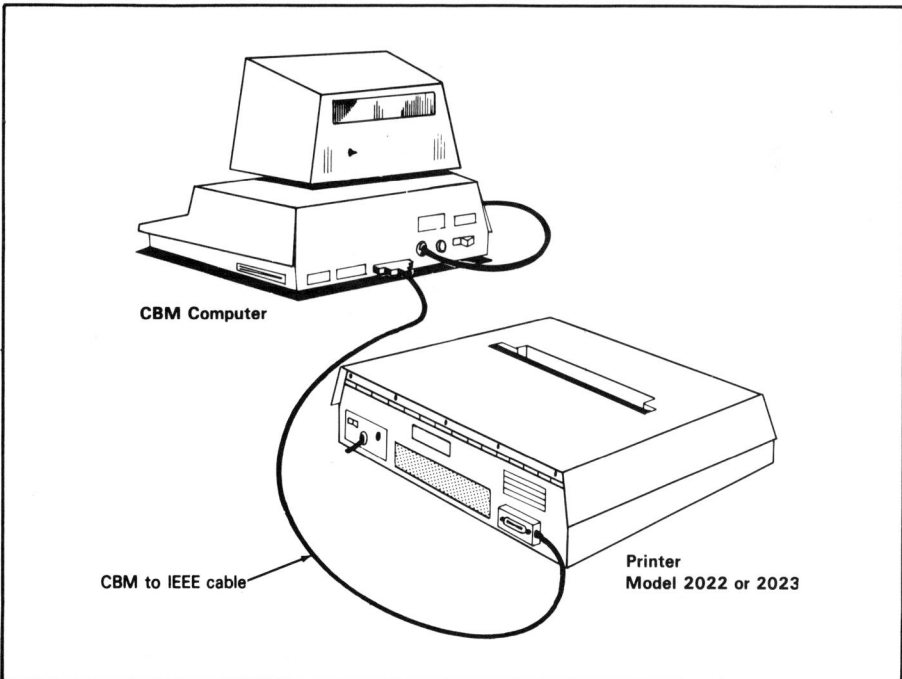

Figure 1-30. Printer to Computer Connection

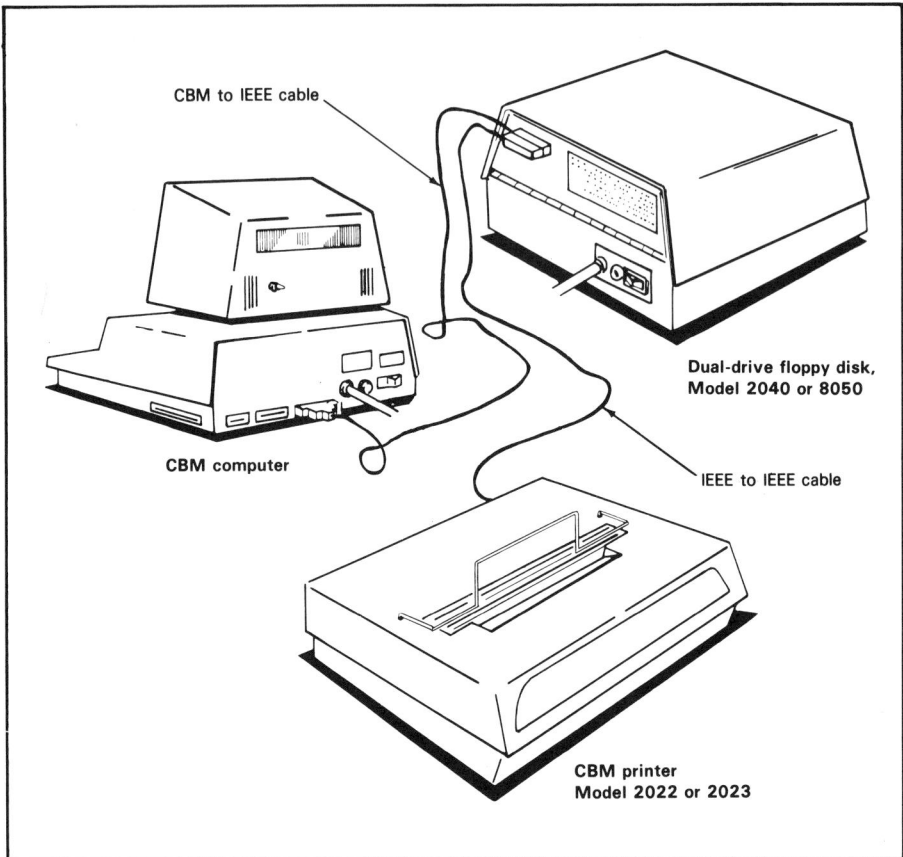

Figure 1-31. Multiple Hookup: Printer to Disk Unit to Computer

3. *Multiple* peripherals hookup: Because the CBM has only one IEEE interface slot to connect the peripherals, if you use both a disk drive and printer you must connect the printer to the disk drive and the disk drive to the CBM computer. Follow these steps:

   a. Using an IEEE to IEEE cable, plug one end into the right rear interface slot of the printer. Secure the connector by turning the two screws clockwise until tight.

   b. Plug the other end of the cable into the connector already attached to the back of the disk drive from the CBM computer as shown in Figure 1-31. This "daisy-chaining" passes the data from the CBM computer through the two-cable connection to the printer. Secure the connector by turning the two screws clockwise until tight.

   c. Plug the printer's AC power cord into an electrical outlet.

   d. Plug the CBM computer's AC power cord into an electrical outlet.

   e. Turn the CBM computer power on. Make sure the console is working correctly.

   f. Turn on power to the printer by pressing the rocker switch on the right back side of the printer, so that the white dot is visible. When the printer receives power, the print head moves all the way to the right and back again.

       If the print head does not move, turn off both the CBM computer and printer. Re-check all connections to make sure they are securely connected into the correct interface slots. Turn on the power to the CBM computer and try again. If nothing happens, contact your Commodore dealer.

Installing the Ribbon

1. Lift up the printer cover until its inner mechanisms are exposed.
2. Hold the ribbon so that the empty reel with stop eyelet is in your right hand and the full reel is in your left (Figure 1-32).
3. Push the right ribbon reel onto the right sprocket (position number 1 in Figure 1-33) until it clicks firmly into place.
4. With the left reel, unroll enough ribbon to guide the ribbon through positions 2, 3 and 4. At this point, stop and make sure that the ribbon stop eyelet is situated between position 2 and the reverse gate (position 3). Continue guiding the ribbon through positions 5 and 6. *Do not twist the ribbon.*
5. Unroll the ribbon past the print head, dropping the ribbon down behind the print head and around position 7. It is very easy to accidentally twist the ribbon at this step, so be very careful not to do so.
6. Guide the ribbon around positions 8, 9, 10, and 11.
7. Turning the ribbon reel until the ribbon is taut, push the left reel onto the left sprocket until it clicks firmly into place (position 12). Make sure the ribbon and reel are not loose.
8. Close the printer lid. The ribbon is now ready.

Loading Printer Paper

Each printer has a different load procedure due to its different paper feed mechanism.

Loading Paper Into Printer Model 2022

The tractor drive accepts standard fan-folded pin feed paper of various widths. The largest width acceptable is 10''.

To load the paper follow these steps:

1. With both hands, hold the tractor feed housings (see Figure 1-34) and gently pull them forward. This will move the tractor feed mechanism out of the way.
2. Guide the paper into the top of the printer behind the roller and along the inner plate. Figure 1-35 shows the paper path. Push the paper in gently as it moves down under a bottom roller and back up in front of the main roller and sprockets.
3. With the tractor feed housings, push the tractor feed mechanism back.
4. Pull the sprocket retainers on each sprocket up to the open position.

Figure 1-32. Installing the Ribbon

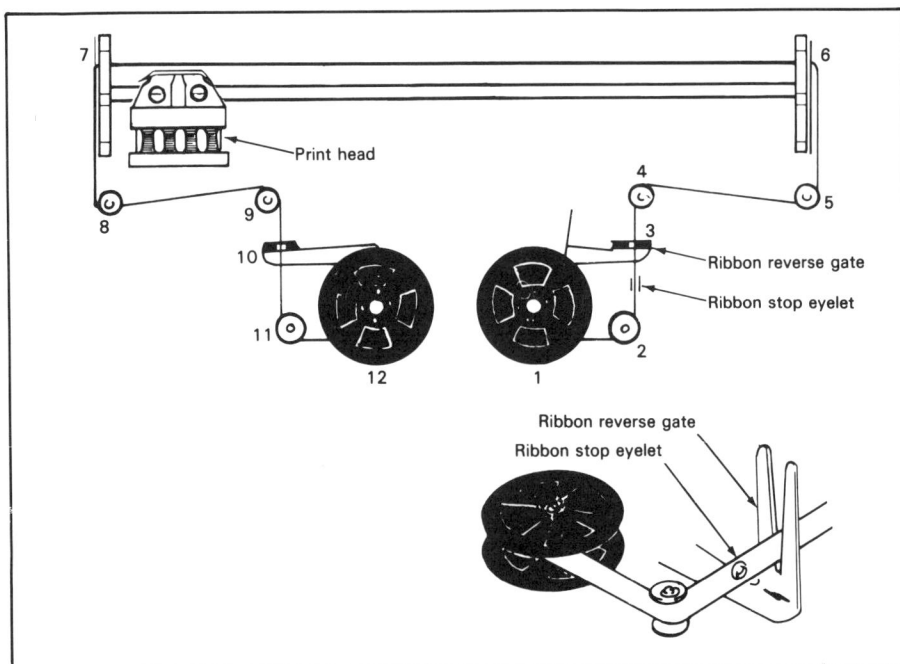

Figure 1-33. Printer Ribbon Path

Figure 1-34. CBM 2022 Printer

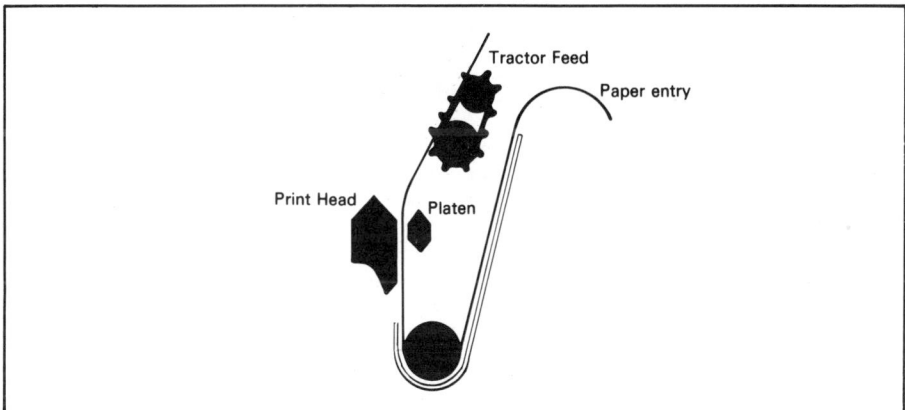

Figure 1-35. CBM 2022 Printer Paper Path

5. Pull the paper over the sprockets until the sprocket holes in the paper fit over the sprockets. If the sprockets do not match the paper sprocket holes, adjust the sprockets by:
    a. Lifting the lever to the side of the sprocket mechanism towards you.
    b. Sliding it to fit the tractor sprocket to the paper sprocket holes.
    c. Locking the lever by pushing it back to the original position.

6. When the paper sprocket holes fit snugly over the sprockets, push the sprocket retainers down to hold the paper in place.

7. Turn the printer power on. The power switch is on the lower right back panel.

8. The paper may be advanced by either:
    a. Pressing the paper feed button at the lower left front of the printer.
    b. Manually rolling the paper up with the roller knobs on each side of the tractor mechanism.

Figure 1-36. Loading Paper into Model 2023 Printer

Loading Paper Into Printer Model 2023

The friction feed model accepts paper up to 10" wide. No sprocket holes are needed. Paper may be the long fan-folded type or individual sheets of paper.

To load the paper follow these steps:

1. Turn the printer power on. The power switch is on the lower right back panel.

2. Guide the paper into the paper feed (on the top inside of the printer) as far as it will go.

3. While guiding the paper into the paper feed, press the paper feed button on the lower left front of the printer until the top of the paper has rolled out of the printer (see Figure 1-36).

4. To adjust or remove the paper, lift the paper release bar to loosen the friction feed mechanism (see Figure 1-37). Remove or adjust the paper, and push the bar back to its original position.

Print Head Test

Once the ribbon and paper have been properly installed, you should perform a print head test to make sure that everything is working correctly. *Do not perform this test or print anything if paper is not loaded;* you may damage the print head. To do the test follow these steps:

1. Turn printer power *off.* The power switch is located on the lower right back panel.

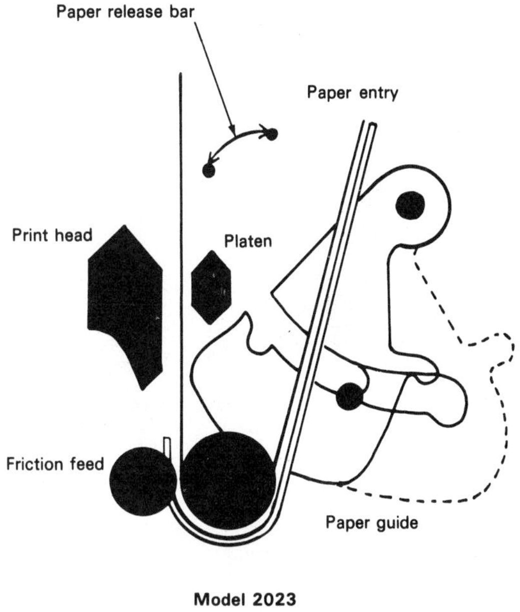
Paper release bar
Paper entry
Print head
Platen
Friction feed
Paper guide
Model 2023

Figure 1-37. CBM 2023 Printer Paper Path

```
 !"#$%&'()*+,-./0123456789:;<=>?@ABCDEFGHIJKLMNOPQRSTUVWXYZ[\]↑←  !"#$%&'()*+,-.
/0123456789:;<=>?@ABCDEFGHIJKLMNOPQRSTUVWXYZ[\]↑←  !"#$%&'()*+,-./0123456789:;<=
>?@ABCDEFGHIJKLMNOPQRSTUVWXYZ[\]↑←  !"#$%&'()*+,-./0123456789:;<=>?@ABCDEFGHIJKL
MNOPQRSTUVWXYZ[\]↑←  !"#$%&'()*+,-./0123456789:;<=>?@ABCDEFGHIJKLMNOPQRSTUVWXYZ[
\]↑←  !"#$%&'()*+,-./0123456789:;<=>?@ABCDEFGHIJKLMNOPQRSTUVWXYZ[\]↑←  !"#$%&'()
*+,-./0123456789:;<=>?@ABCDEFGHIJKLMNOPQRSTUVWXYZ[\]↑←  !"#$%&'()*+,-./012345678
9:;<=>?@ABCDEFGHIJKLMNOPQRSTUVWXYZ[\]↑←  !"#$%&'()*+,-./0123456789:;<=>?@ABCDEFG
HIJKLMNOPQRSTUVWXYZ[\]↑←  !"#$%&'()*+,-./0123456789:;<=>?@ABCDFFGHIJKLMNOFQRSTUV
WXYZ[\]↑←  !"#$%&'()*+,-./0123456789:;<=>?@ABCDEFGHIJKLMNOPQRSTUVWXYZ[\]↑←  !"#$
%&'()*+,-./0123456789:;<=>?@ABCDEFGHIJKLMNOPQRSTUVWXYZ[\]↑←  !"#$%&'()*+,-./0123
456789:;<=>?@ABCDEFGHIJKLMNOPQRSTUVWXYZ[\]↑←  !"#$%&'()*+,-./0123456789:;<=>?@AB
CDEFGHIJKLMNOPQRSTUVWXYZ[\]↑←  !"#$%&'()*+,-./0123456789:;<=>?@ABCDEFGHIJKLMNOPQ
RSTUVWXYZ[\]↑←  !"#$%&'()*+,-./0123456789:;<=>?@ABCDEFGHIJKLMNOPQRSTUVWXYZ[\]↑←
```

Figure 1-38. Print Head Test

2. Turn printer power back *on while pressing the paper feed button* (lower left front corner). The printer should rapidly print out a repeating sequence of all special symbols, numbers and letters available (no graphics). An example of the test is shown in Figure 1-38.
3. To stop the test, turn the printer off.

If the printer malfunctioned, or the printout has defects, contact your Commodore dealer. Otherwise, your printer is ready for use.

Chapter 2

Operating the CBM Computer

This chapter explains how you use the keyboard to operate the computer, disk drive unit, cassette unit, and printer.

You tell a CBM computer what to do using "statements." Statements are instructions to the computer. The computer "executes" statements in order to do their bidding. The CBM computer understands statements written in CBM BASIC (Beginning All-purpose Symbolic Instruction Code).

When you enter a BASIC statement, the statement line can be up to 80 characters in length. Eighty characters is equal to two lines on the screen display for the CBM graphic and business model computers, and one display line for the CBM 8000 series computer. When entering a statement line, type in the characters and terminate the line by pressing the RETURN key. If you type in 40 or more characters on the small-screen CBM computer without pressing the RETURN key, the cursor automatically drops down to the next display line, and you can continue entering up to 80 characters. If you continue typing past the 80th character on either the small- or the large-screen CBM computer, the CBM computer will respond with a ?SYNTAX ERROR message when you press the RETURN key.

You must press the RETURN key in order to terminate every BASIC statement. The CBM computer uses the RETURN character as a signal that the line is complete and ready to be analyzed.

BASIC statements may be entered in two ways: immediate mode or program mode. Immediate mode statements are executed immediately: hence the name "immediate mode." These statements are generally short, and are *not* stored in the computer's memory. Statements entered in program mode *are* stored in computer memory. But program mode statements are not executed until you explicitly instruct the computer to do so.

IMMEDIATE MODE

When powered up, the CBM computer is in immediate mode. Immediate mode is indicated by a flashing cursor on the screen.

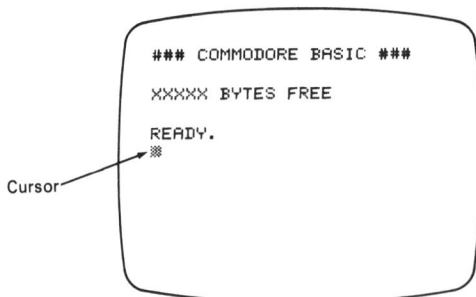

```
                    ###  COMMODORE  BASIC  ###

                    XXXXX  BYTES  FREE

                    READY.
              ┌─────── ▓
   Cursor─────┘
```

The computer remains in immediate mode until you execute a BASIC program. After the program has executed, the computer returns to immediate mode.

KEYBOARD INPUT IN IMMEDIATE MODE

The flashing cursor is displayed on the screen at the character position where the next character input from the keyboard will appear. As each character entered appears on the screen, the cursor advances one space to the right and waits for the next character, as shown in Figure 2-1. Some keys move the cursor without displaying any character. If a CURSOR key is pressed, the cursor moves one space in the direction of the arrow on the CURSOR key and waits for further input. Pressing the RETURN key drops the cursor down to the first position on the line below.

You can input any sequence of characters via the CBM computer keyboard, but in immediate mode the CBM computer assumes any input to be part of a BASIC statement and interprets the input by the rules of the CBM BASIC language. That is, the CBM computer tries to interpret all input as BASIC statements.

Figure 2-2 illustrates valid statement input in immediate mode. After the RETURN key is pressed, the statement is executed immediately, and results (if any) are displayed on the line below. Non-statement entry is shown in Figure 2-3. In the first two screens, upon pressing the RETURN key the display responds with a ?SYNTAX ERROR message.

A ?SYNTAX ERROR message signals that the CBM computer cannot interpret the input as a valid BASIC statement. If you are not trying to enter a statement, simply ignore the syntax error message. An exception is shown in the third screen of Figure 2-3. Graphic characters and cursor control characters do not generate a syntax error *unless mixed with* alphabetic or numeric characters. This allows you to "draw" directly onto the screen using graphic symbols.

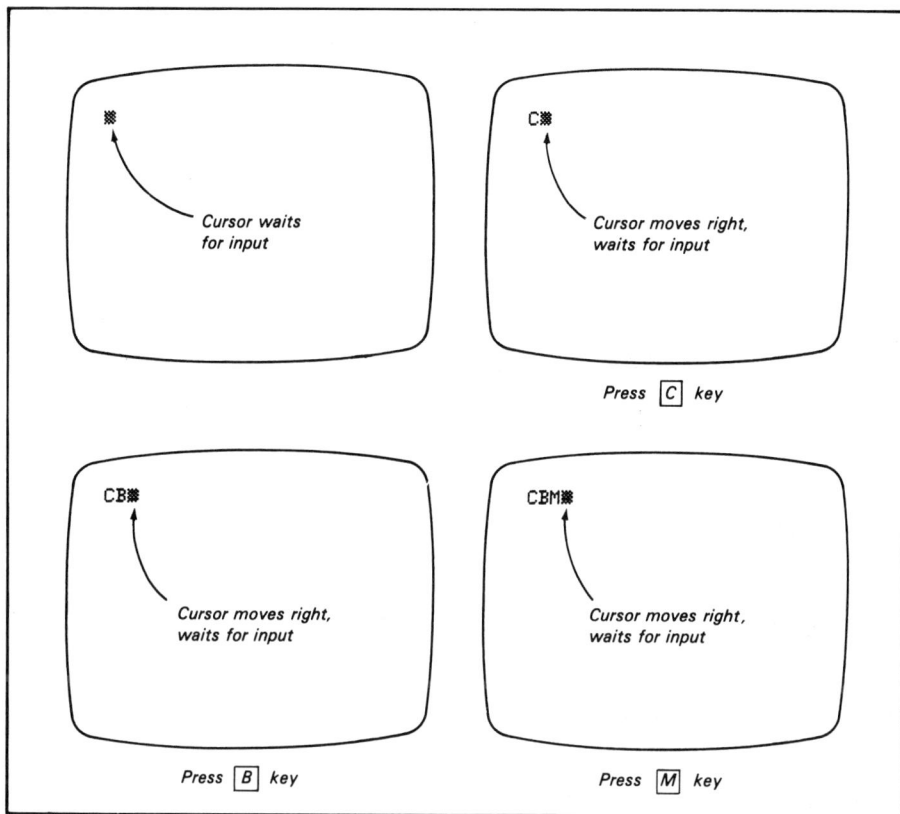

Figure 2-1. Keyboard Input in Immediate Mode

Statements in Immediate Mode

Statements entered in immediate mode do not, and cannot, **begin with line numbers**. Later we will examine exactly what you can include in an immediate mode statement. For the discussion at hand you only need to know how to input a few elementary statements, therefore we will explain how to write statements that print characters, solve arithmetic equations, and move the cursor.

The PRINT Statement

$$\left\{ \begin{array}{c} \text{PRINT} \\ ? \end{array} \right\} \text{ data}$$

The PRINT statement shown above is the most frequently used in immediate mode statements. The PRINT statement instructs the computer to display data on the screen. Upon pressing the RETURN key, the display appears on the line below the PRINT statement. If the word PRINT (or its abbreviation '?') is not placed before the data item to be displayed, no display will appear on the screen.

```
?"GOOD MORNING"
GOOD MORNING

READY.
▓
                              Press RETURN
```

PRINT statement (Alphabetic)

```
?2+2
4

READY.
▓
                              Press RETURN
```

PRINT statement (Numeric)

```
A=1
READY.
?A
  1

READY.
▓              Press RETURN
```

Assign variable: PRINT variable statement

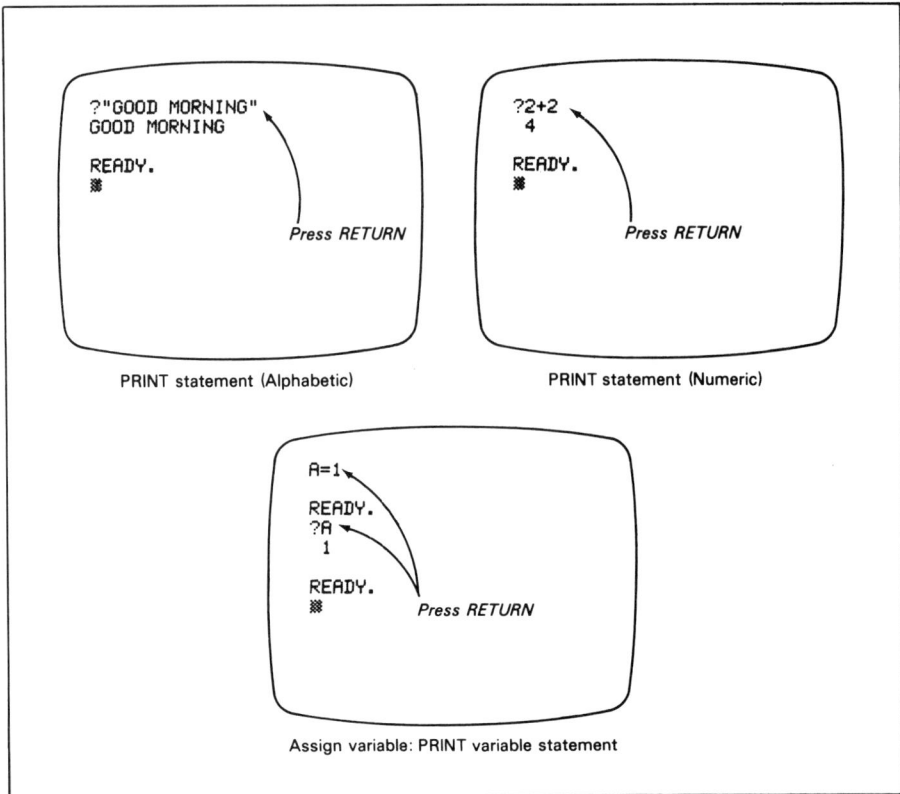

Figure 2-2. Valid Immediate Mode Statement Input

Printing Strings

CBM computers can recognize simple sequences of characters that have no "special" meaning. The word "string" is the computer jargon that describes such text.

A string is a sequence of one or more characters enclosed in double quotation marks. Here are some examples of strings:

```
"HI!"
"SYNERGY"
"12345"
"10.44 IS THE AMOUNT"
"22 UNION SQUARE, SAN FRANCISCO, CA"
```

All data keys (alphabetic, numeric, special symbols, and graphics), as well as the cursor control keys and the REVERSE ON/OFF key, can be included in a string. The only keys that cannot be used within a string are RUN/STOP and RETURN.

A string may be displayed, directly or indirectly, by assigning the string to a "string variable" and then printing the contents of the string variable.

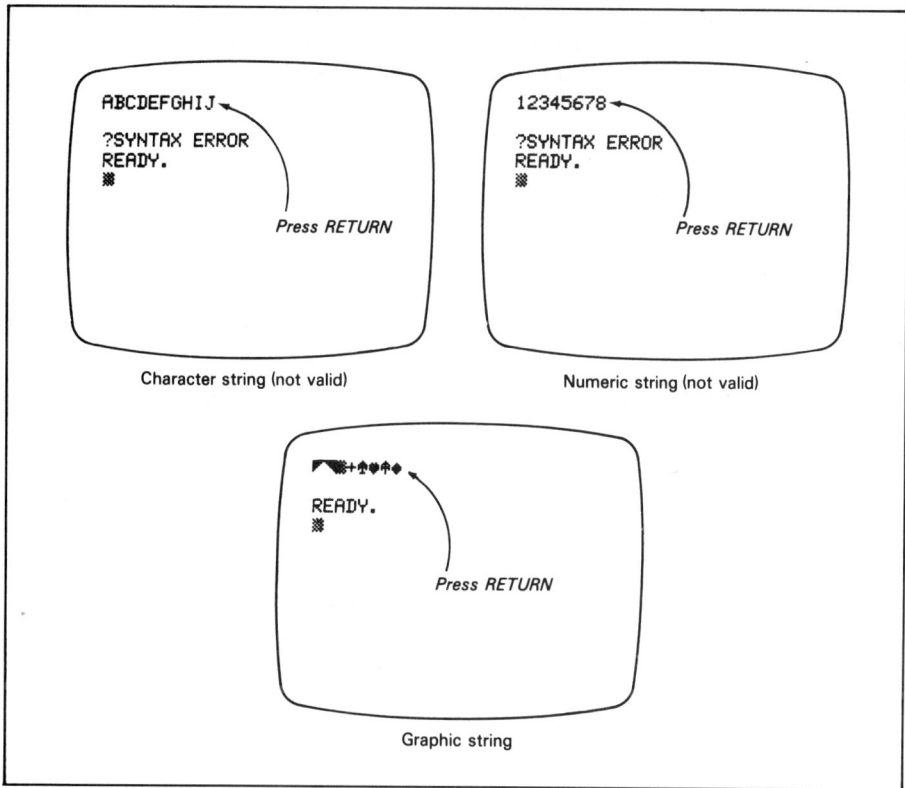

Figure 2-3. Non-statement Immediate Mode Input

To print a string directly, key in PRINT (or its abbreviation '?') followed by the string to be printed. The string must be enclosed within quotation marks.

PRINT "string"

where:

string   is a string of text

Upon pressing the RETURN key, the string is displayed on the following line. Some examples are shown below. The shaded characters designate your input, unshaded characters are the computer's response.

```
PRINT "MONDAY"
MONDAY

READY.

PRINT "MAY 12, 1980"
MAY 12,1980

READY.

PRINT "12345"
12345

READY.
```

Try inputting a couple of your own PRINT statements to display strings. When you press the RETURN key, if you get a ?SYNTAX ERROR message, you probably misspelled PRINT. If you get a zero (0) answer instead of your string, you have forgotten the set of quotation marks that precede the string. Keep trying until you can successfully print a string in immediate mode.

A string is printed indirectly by assigning the string to a "string variable," and then printing the contents of the variable. A string variable is an identifier, or a name, that can represent any text string. A string variable's identifier, or name, has a letter, optionally followed by another letter or a number. A "$" character must end the string variable name. Here are some examples of string variable names:

```
A$
M1$
F6$
```

You need two statements to print a string indirectly. The first statement assigns the string to a variable name as follows:

```
V$ = "string"
```

where:

```
V$          is the string variable name
string      is a string text
```

A PRINT statement comes next; it displays the contents of the string variable on the screen:

```
PRINT V$
```

where:

```
V$          is the string variable name
            assigned to a string of text
```

Here are a few examples:

```
A$="TAKE THE PROGRAM AND RUN!"

READY.
PRINT A$
TAKE THE PROGRAM AND RUN!

READY.
DY$="TUESDAY"

READY.
PRINT DY$
TUESDAY

READY.
B1$="♠ ♥ ♦ ♣"

READY.
PRINT B1$
♠ ♥ ♦ ♣

READY.
▓
```

Try telling the CBM computer to print your name indirectly, using a variable name. Type in a string name (don't forget the dollar sign!), an equals sign, and your name enclosed in quotation marks. Press the RETURN key, as shown below:

```
NM$="JIMMY OLSON ◄─── RETURN key pressed

READY.
▓
```

If you get a ?TYPE MISMATCH ERROR message, either your name is not enclosed in quotation marks, or the string variable name is incorrect (missing a dollar sign?). Now, type PRINT, followed by the string variable name. Press the RETURN key. Your name should be displayed on the line below:

```
NM$="JIMMY OLSON ◄─── RETURN key pressed

READY.
PRINT NM$ ◄─────────── RETURN key pressed
JIMMY OLSON

READY.
▓
```

If something other than your name is displayed, there is a mistake in your PRINT statement. If a ?SYNTAX ERROR message appears, you probably misspelled the word PRINT. If you used the wrong string variable name, you will get no display, since the new name describes a variable that has no contents. If the dollar sign was omitted from the string variable name, a '0' will be displayed. If any of these errors occur, go back and try it again.

ARITHMETIC CALCULATIONS

CBM BASIC can handle arithmetic. Leaving the complicated stuff for Chapter 4, we will now look at some simple addition, subtraction, multiplication and division. An arithmetic equation appearing in a PRINT statement instructs the computer to solve an equation and display the result immediately.

If you put an arithmetic equation into the PRINT statement, 'PRINT' or '?' must precede the arithmetic equation which is to be evaluated. An equals sign *cannot* appear in the statement:

$$\left\{ {\text{PRINT} \atop ?} \right\} \text{equation}$$

Here are some examples:

```
PRINT 2 + 2
PRINT 5/10
? 2.5
? (100/20) − 16.334
```

Upon pressing the RETURN key, the CBM computer calculates the equation and displays the answer.

Try an example: Type in PRINT or ?. Next, enter the arithmetic expression 2 + 2. Press the RETURN key. The answer should be displayed on the line below, as shown:

```
PRINT 2+2 ◄─────────── Press RETURN key
 4

READY.
▓
```

Below are some more examples you may want to try. Type in the shaded characters; the unshaded characters are the computer's response.

```
PRINT 2+2
 4

READY.
PRINT 5/10
 .5

READY.
? 2.5
 2.5

READY.
? (100/20)+16.334
 21.334

READY.
```

Arithmetic Calculations using Variables

Just as a string variable can represent a string, so a numeric variable can represent a number. A numeric variable's name has a letter, optionally followed by another letter or a number. Numeric variable names are *not* terminated by a dollar sign.

You must use two statements to print a number via a numeric variable. The first statement assigns the number to the numeric variable as follows:

V = n

where:

V	is the numeric variable name
n	is a number of numeric equation assigned to the variable

The second statement is a PRINT statement. It displays the value of the numeric variable on the screen:

PRINT V

where:

V	is the numeric variable name assigned to a number or numeric equation

Here are some sample statements assigning numbers to numeric variables:

```
A = 1
NM = 2.56
B1 = 1000/10
```

Notice that the numbers and equations are *not* enclosed within quotation marks.

Here are some examples of numeric assignment and PRINT statements:

```
C=100

PRINT C
 100

READY.
F1=1234.78

PRINT F1
 1234.78

READY.
```

CURSOR MOVEMENT

Cursor movement in immediate mode allows you to move the cursor and alter the screen display instantly. **When a cursor key is pressed, the cursor moves in the direction shown by the arrow on the key.** The cursor keys move the cursor around the screen, and over existing characters, without altering the display. These cursor keys include CURSOR HOME, CURSOR UP/DOWN, and CURSOR LEFT/RIGHT.

Cursor keys that move and alter the screen display include CLEAR SCREEN and INSERT/DELETE. CLEAR SCREEN wipes out the screen display and puts the cursor in the first character position of the top row; this is called the "home" position. INSERT/DELETE inserts spaces to the right of the cursor, or deletes the characters to the left of the cursor.

Whenever a cursor key is pressed after a quotation mark (or any *odd* number of quotation marks), the cursor movement is treated as part of a string. The cursor key is treated as a string character, and a special character appears in the string to represent that cursor movement, as shown in Table 2-1.

Table 2-1. String Representations of Cursor Keys

Function		Key	String Symbol
DELETE		INST DEL	(Reverse shifted T)
INSERT	Shifted	INST DEL	Not programmed
Home Cursor		CLR SCREEN HOME	◪ (Reverse S)
Clear Screen	Shifted	CLR SCREEN HOME	◳ (Reverse Shifted S)
Cursor Down		CURSOR	◲ (Reverse Q)
Cursor Up	Shifted	CURSOR	◱ (Reverse Shifted Q)
Cursor Right		CURSOR	▮▮ (Reverse])
Cursor Left	Shifted	CURSOR	▮▮ (Reverse Shifted])

Here are some examples of cursor movement keys appearing within character strings:

```
PRINT "1<CRSR→>2<CRSR→>3<CRSR→>4<CRSR→>5"
1 2 3 4 5

READY.
```

```
PRINT "♠<CRSR←><CRSR→>♥<CRSR←><CRSR→>♦<CRSR←><CRSR→>♠"
♠
♥
♦
♠

READY.
```

```
PRINT "*<CLR SCREEN><CRSR↓><CRSR←><CRSR↓><CRSR↓>* <CRSR↑>* <CRSR↓>*<CRSR↑>*
        <CRSR↓>* <CRSR↓><CRSR↓><CRSR↓><CRSR↓><CRSR↓>"
    *
      *
    *
  *
*

READY.
```

PROGRAM MODE

When you enter statements in program mode, they are stored in computer memory. Such statements must begin with a line number.

PROGRAM ENTRY

A program consists of one or more BASIC statements which, when executed in the proper sequence, cause the computer to perform a required task.

Programs may be entered via the keyboard. Programs may also be loaded into computer memory from an external peripheral (such as a cassette or diskette drive).

If entered from the keyboard, each statement is typed in with an initial line number. When the RETURN key is pressed at the end of the statement, the statement is stored in memory for later use, although it remains displayed on the screen. Program statements remain in memory until deleted, or until power is switched off. To avoid losing your program, you must save it either on cassette tape or on a diskette. Once the program has been saved on either medium, it can be loaded back into computer memory at any time.

At this point you need not know how to "write" a BASIC program; writing BASIC programs is the subject of Chapter 4. However, you now know enough about your CBM computer to **type in the short prewritten program called BLANKET, shown below.**

```
10 FOR I=1 TO 800
20 PRINT "A";
30 NEXT I
40 PRINT "PHEW!"
50 END
```

If you don't understand BASIC or this BLANKET program don't worry about it; you do not need to understand how or why it works. We will be using this program to illustrate computer operations.

When you type in this program, if you make a mistake, hit the RETURN key and then reenter the statement. If you get a ?SYNTAX ERROR message just retype the statement. Stop after you have typed the entire program correctly.

We will now look at how you can edit a program that is in the computer's memory.

Program LIST

The LIST statement displays the program which is currently in computer memory. After listing a program you can examine it for errors. The format for the LIST statement is:

	(blank)	List entire program.
	line	List one line.
LIST	line$_1$-line$_2$	List from line$_1$ to line$_2$.
	-line	List from start to line.
	line-	List from line to end.

where:

line   is a line number. Line$_1$ is a lower number than line$_2$. All line numbers are inclusive. The line numbers do not need to be actual line numbers in the program. In the case of listing one non-existent line, a blank line is printed.

If the program is longer than 23 lines, LIST will "scroll" the beginning lines of the program up off the screen. Use the line parameters in this case to display only the desired program lines.

Here are some examples:

LIST	List entire program.
LIST 50	List line 50.
LIST 60-100	List all lines in the program between lines 60 and 100, beginning with line 60 and ending with line 100.
LIST -140	List all lines in the program from the beginning of the program through line 140.
LIST 20000-	List all lines in the program from line 20000 to the end of the program.

List the program you entered previously. Type LIST, press RETURN, and your program should be displayed on the screen:

```
LIST

10 FOR I=1 TO 800
20 PRINT "A";
30 NEXT I
40 PRINT "PHEW!"
50 END
READY.
```

Notice that the cursor disappears while the program is being listed on the screen, to reappear at the end of the program list at the bottom of the program, waiting in immediate mode for further input.

Now practice listing only a portion of the program. To display line number 10, type in LIST and the number 10. Press the RETURN key:

```
LIST 10

10 FOR I=1 TO 800

READY.
▓
```

To see line numbers 20 through 40 type in LIST 20-40:

```
LIST 20-40

20 PRINT "A";
30 NEXT I
40 PRINT "PHEW!"
READY.
▓
```

Practice listing the program in many different ways until you understand the LIST statement completely.

Program RUN

The RUN statement executes the program currently stored in computer memory. As soon as you enter the RUN statement and press the RETURN key the program executes. The format for the RUN statement is:

$$\textbf{RUN} \begin{cases} \text{(blank)} \\ \text{line} \end{cases} \quad \begin{matrix} \text{Begin execution at the lowest-numbered line.} \\ \text{Begin execution at the specified line.} \end{matrix}$$

Try executing the example program. Enter RUN, then press the RETURN key Sit back and watch. The screen should rapidly fill up with 800 A's beginning on the line directly below the RUN statement, and end with a PHEW!. Notice that while the program is executed, the CBM computer is in program mode and the cursor disappears.

When the program has completed its execution, the computer drops out of program mode and returns to immediate mode; a READY message is displayed and the cursor flashes at the bottom of the program output.

```
RUN
AAAAAAAAAAAAAAAAAAAAAAAAAAAAAAAAAAAAAAAAAAAA
AAAAAAAAAAAAAAAAAAAAAAAAAAAAAAAAAAAAAAAAAAAA
AAAAAAAAAAAAAAAAAAAAAAAAAAAAAAAAAAAAAAAAAAAA
AAAAAAAAAAAAAAAAAAAAAAAAAAAAAAAAAAAAAAAAAAAA
AAAAAAAAAAAAAAAAAAAAAAAAAAAAAAAAAAAAAAAAAAAA
AAAAAAAAAAAAAAAAAAAAAAAAAAAAAAAAAAAAAAAAAAAA
AAAAAAAAAAAAAAAAAAAAAAAAAAAAAAAAAAAAAAAAAAAA
AAAAAAAAAAAAAAAAAAAAAAAAAAAAAAAAAAAAAAAAAAAA
AAAAAAAAAAAAAAAAAAAAAAAAAAAAAAAAAAAAAAAAAAAA
AAAAAAAAAAAAAAAAAAAAAAAAAAAAAAAAAAAAAAAAAAAA
AAAAAAAAAAAAAAAAAAAAAAAAAAAAAAAAAAAAAAAAAAAA
AAAAAAAAAAAAAAAAAAAAAAAAAAAAAAAAAAAAAAAAAAAA
AAAAAAAAAAAAAAAAAAAAAAAAAAAAAAAAAAAAAAAAAAAA
AAAAAAAAAAAAAAAAAAAAAAAAAAAAAAAAAAAAAAAAAAAA
AAAAAAAAAAAAAAAAAAAAAAAAAAAAAAAAAAAAAAAAAAAA
AAAAAAAAAAAAAAAAAAAAAAAAAAAAAAAAAAAAAAAAAAAA
AAAAAAAAAAAAAAAAAAAAAAAAAAAAAAAAAAAAAAAAAAAA
AAAAAAAAAAAAAAAAAAAAAAAAAAAAAAAAAAAAAAAAAAAA
AAAAAAAAAAAAAAAAAAAAAAAAAAAAAAAAAAAAAAAAAAAA
AAAAAAAAAAAAAAAAAAAAAAAAAAAAAAAAAAAAAAAAAAAA
PHEW!

READY.
▓
```

You can tell the computer to begin program execution at any line in the program by specifying the line number. For instance, you can tell the computer to execute the example program starting at line 40, as follows:

```
RUN 40
PHEW!

READY.
▓
```

You should use caution when beginning program execution at a specified line. Often a program will not run correctly if it is not executed from the beginning. Were you to start the example program from line 20 or 30, the computer would respond with a syntax error because the program cannot begin execution on those lines.

Stopping Program Execution

A program may be stopped during execution. This is called a program "break." **A break will occur if you press the STOP key while the program is executing.** Following a break, a break message is displayed identifying the line at which the break occurred:

```
RUN
AAAAAAAAAAAAAAAAAAAAAAAAAAAAAAAAAAAAAAAAAAAAA
AAAAAAAAAAAAAAAAAAAAAAAAAAAAAAAAAAAAAAAAAAAAA
AAAAAAAAAAAAAAAAAAAAAAAAAAAAAAAAAAAAAAAAAAAAA
AAAAAAAAAAAAAAAAAAAAAAAAAAAAAAAAAAAAAAAAAAAAA
AAAAAAAAAAAAAAAAAAAAAAAAAAAAAAAAAAAAAAAAAAAAA
AAAAAAAAAAAAAAAAAAAAAAAAAAAAAAAAAAAAAAAAAAAAA
AAAAAAAAAAAAA ◄─────────────────────── STOP key pressed
BREAK IN 40 ◄─────────────────────── Break message displayed
READY.
▓
```

During a program break the CBM computer returns to immediate mode allowing you to LIST, LOAD, SAVE, and VERIFY programs, and perform any immediate mode operations using CBM BASIC statements — including changing the values of program variables — before continuing program execution.

Continuing a Stopped Program

The "continue" statement, CONT, resumes program execution following a break. Execution continues at the exact point where the break occurred:

```
RUN
AAAAAAAAAAAAAAAAAAAAAAAAAAAAAAAAAAAAAAAAAA
AAAAAAAAAAAAAAAAAAAAAAAAAAAAAAAAAAAAAAAAAA
AAAAAAAAAAAAAAAAAAAAAAAAAAAAAAAAAAAAAAAAAA
AAAAAAAAAAAAAAAAAAAAAAAAAAAAAAAAAAAAAAAAAA
AAAAAAAAAAAAAAAAAAAAAAAAAAAAAAAAAAAAAAAAAA
AAAAAAAAAAAAAAAAAAAAAAAAAAAAAAAAAAAAAAAAAA
AAAAAAAAAAA ←————————————————————————————— STOP key pressed
BREAK IN 40
READY.
CONT ←—————————————————————————————————————— CONT command entered
AAAAAAAAAAAAAAAAAAAAAAAAAAAAAAAAAAAAAAAAAA
AAAAAAAAAAAAAAAAAAAAAAAAAAAAAAAAAAAAAAAAAA
AAAAAAAAAAAAAAAAAAAAAAAAAAAAAAAAAAAAAAAAAA
AAAAAAAAAAAAAAAAAAAAAAAAAAAAAAAAAAAAAAAAAA
AAAAAAAAAAAAAAAAAAAAAAAAAAAAAAAAAAAAAAAAAA
AAAAAAAAAAAAAAAAAAAAAAAAAAAAAAAAAAAAAAAAAA
3AAAAAAAAAAAAAAAAAAAAAAAAAAAAAAAAAAAAAAAAA
AAAAAAAAAAAAAAAAAAAAAAAAAAAAAAAAAAAAAAAAAA
AAAAAAAAAAAAAAAAAAAAAAAAAAAAAAAAAAAAAAAAAA
AAAAAAAAAAAAAAAAAAAAAAAAAAAAAAAAAAAAAAAAAA
AAAAAAAAAAAAAAAAAAAAAAAAAAAAAAAAAAAAAAAAAA
AAAAAAAAAAAAAAAAAAAAAAAAAAAAPHEW!

READY.
※
```

CONT cannot continue program execution if an error occurred and an error message is displayed.

Deleting a Program from Memory

You can delete a program.

To delete program from computer memory, type in NEW and press the RETURN key. The current program is erased from computer memory, though it does not alter the screen display. Be careful when using the NEW statement; you may lose a program accidentally. Test the NEW statement now to delete the example program:

```
LIST ←———————————— LIST the program

10 FOR I=1 TO 800
20 PRINT "A";
30 NEXT I
40 PRINT "PHEW!"
50 END
READY.
NEW ←———————————— Delete program from memory

READY.
LIST ←———————————— Re-LIST the program
     ←———————————— No program in memory
READY.
※
```

Always erase an old program using the NEW statement before entering a new program. Otherwise you will end up with a hodgepodge of the new and old program statements.

STANDARD AND ALTERNATE CHARACTER SETS

Recall that every CBM computer has a "standard" and an "alternate" character set. These character sets are summarized in Appendix A for different models of CBM computers.

When powered up, PET models select the standard character set; CBM models select the alternate character set. To change character sets you change the value in memory location 59468. If 59468 is 12, the standard character set is selected. If 59468 is 14, the alternate set is selected. The following commands change location 59468:

POKE 59468,12   *Activate the standard*
                                 character set

POKE 59468,14   *Activate the alternate*
                                 character set

Programming with the Alternate Character Set

Never use the SHIFT key to select upper-case letters within BASIC statements when using the CBM computer alternate character set.

All CBM computers assume that the standard character set is present. When you press a key in shifted mode the interpreter assumes that the shifted standard character has been used.

This can cause you a lot of trouble when keying in programs using the alternate character set.

When using a CBM computer you may be tempted to select upper-case letters, using the SHIFT key, for the first letter of a word, or for the entire word. Consider the following statement:

```
10 For I=1 To 10 Step 2
```

Were this statement entered as illustrated in alternate character mode on a CBM computer, every upper-case letter would have to be generated by pressing the SHIFT key. Since the CBM computer assumes that the standard character set is present, this is how the BASIC statement illustrated above would be interpreted:

```
10 —OR ╲=1 |0 10 ●TEP 2
```

The CBM computer would reject this statement and report a syntax error.

Within a printed text string shifted letters will not cause a syntax error.

OPERATING THE CASSETTE UNITS

Small CBM computer systems use cassette drives to store programs and data. Larger CBM computer systems use diskette drives for the same purpose. We will now give you step-by-step instructions to operate CBM computer cassette drives. Diskette drive operations are described next.

Before attempting to operate a cassette drive, make sure that the correct cassette tape is loaded in the drive. We are going to use drive 1, therefore load appropriate cassettes into drive 1, as described in Chapter 1. If the tape is not positioned at the beginning, press the REWIND button on the cassette unit; this will rewind the tape to its beginning. When rewound, press the STOP key. Make sure all of the cassette unit keys are in the off position (up).

The examples in this section will use the BLANKET program to illustrate the cassette operations. **Shaded portions of the examples designate your input; unshaded portions are the computer's response.**

Program SAVE

Saving a program on a cassette tape prevents it from being lost when the console's power is turned off. The SAVE statement writes the program which is currently in memory onto a cassette tape. Here is the SAVE statement format:

SAVE "program name"	*Save program on cassette unit # 1*
SAVE "program name",**1**	*Save program on cassette unit # 1*
SAVE "program name",**2**	*Save program on cassette unit # 2*

To save a program on cassette unit #1, use number 1 in the SAVE command. Use number 2 to save the program on cassette unit #2. When saving programs on cassette unit #1, the unit number is optional; you need not specify it. But, if you are saving a program on cassette unit #2, you must specify the unit number in the SAVE statement. In other words, #1 is the "default" cassette unit number, or the number selected when none is specified.

For practice, save the program BLANKET on a cassette tape. Load a blank cassette tape into cassette unit #1. Type in the program on the keyboard. To save the BLANKET program, enter the SAVE command and press the RETURN key. The computer responds by displaying the message PRESS PLAY & RECORD ON TAPE #*x*.

```
SAVE "BLANKET"

PRESS PLAY & RECORD ON TAPE #1
```

Simultaneously press the PLAY and RECORD buttons on the cassette unit. The cassette unit will move the tape forward as the BLANKET program is recorded onto the tape. Be careful to press both keys: if only the PLAY key is pressed, both you and the CBM computer will think that you are writing the program on the tape, but nothing will be written.

Once the PLAY and RECORD keys are pressed, the CBM computer responds with an OK and WRITING BLANKET message. When BLANKET has been successfully recorded the READY message and the cursor will appear on the screen. The entire screen display for a program save should look like this:

```
SAVE "BLANKET"

PRESS PLAY & RECORD ON TAPE #1
OK ◄─────────────────────────── PLAY pressed on cassette unit #2

WRITING BLANKET
READY.
※
```

Caution: If *any* of the three tape movement keys REW, FFWD, or PLAY are depressed when the SAVE statement is executed, the CBM computer will start "writing" to the tape. Be sure to press the tape STOP key before issuing a SAVE statement; this assures that the CBM computer will print the PRESS PLAY & RECORD ON TAPE #*x* message. **Remember to depress the RECORD and PLAY keys at the same time.**

Following a program SAVE is a program VERIFY.

Program VERIFY

The VERIFY statement checks for recording errors in a saved program. By simulating the processes of a program LOAD, it reads and compares the program on the tape to the program in memory without actually loading the program into memory. If an error is detected, the CBM computer displays a warning message. Always verify a program after saving it.

To VERIFY a program type in:

VERIFY	*Verify next program encountered on tape cassette unit #2*
VERIFY "program name"	*Verify program on cassette unit #1*
VERIFY "program name",**1**	*Verify program on cassette unit #1*
VERIFY "program name",**2**	*Verify program on cassette unit #2*

Follow these steps to verify a program that you have just saved on cassette tape:

1. Rewind to the beginning of the tape, or to a point that you know precedes the beginning (load point) of the program just saved.
2. Press the tape STOP key.
3. Type in the VERIFY statement. You do not need to specify the program name, or cassette drive #1. You must specify cassette drive #2.

To verify the BLANKET program you just saved on the cassette unit, rewind the cassette tape to the beginning of the tape. Enter the VERIFY statement and press the RETURN key:

```
SAVE "BLANKET"

PRESS PLAY & RECORD ON TAPE #1
OK

WRITING BLANKET
READY. ◄─────────────────────────── Rewind and position tape before
VERIFY "BLANKET"                     start of BLANKET program

PRESS PLAY ON TAPE #1
OK ◄─────────────────────────────── Press PLAY on cassette unit #1

SEARCHING FOR BLANKET
FOUND BLANKET
VERIFYING
OK

READY.
※
```

When the PRESS PLAY ON TAPE #1 message appears on the screen, press the PLAY key on the cassette unit. The cassette unit will search the tape for the BLANKET program as the OK and SEARCHING FOR BLANKET comments are displayed on the screen. When found, the FOUND BLANKET message is displayed. The VERIFYING message appears on the screen as the BLANKET program on the tape is compared to the BLANKET program in the CBM computer memory. If the two compare with no errors, the screen displays an OK message, followed by a READY message and the cursor. If there are problems in the recording, the message ?VERIFY ERROR will appear. Rewind the tape and try to verify it again. If the error persists, rewind the tape back to the load point, save the program again, and verify the program. If the error still persists, try using another portion of the tape, or use another tape.

Program LOAD

The LOAD statement loads programs into computer memory. To load a program off cassette unit #1, type in either of the following two statements:

LOAD "program name"

LOAD "program name",1

When loading a program off of a cassette tape, the program name is optional. If the name is specified, the computer will load only the named program. If the program name is omitted, the computer will load the next program found on the cassette tape.

The optional number following the program name tells the computer which cassette unit to use. Cassette unit #1 (the built-in cassette unit on the PET 2001 or the external cassette unit attached in the rear interface on all other models) is assigned device number 1. The optional, second cassette unit is assigned device number 2.

If only cassette unit #1 is in use, you need not specify the device number; the LOAD statement automatically defaults to cassette unit #1. For example, if you want to load program BLANKET off a tape in cassette unit #1 you type in:

```
LOAD "BLANKET"
```

or: ```LOAD "BLANKET",1```

Because cassette unit #1 is the default device, if you want to load a program off cassette unit #2 you must specify the #2, otherwise the computer will automatically search the tape in cassette unit #1.

The example below shows how the CBM computer responds to a LOAD statement. The shaded characters designate user input; unshaded characters are computer response:

```
LOAD "BLANKET"

PRESS PLAY ON TAPE #1◄——Press PLAY on cassette unit # 1
OK

SEARCHING FOR BLANKET
FOUND BLANKET
LOADING
READY.
▓
```

As soon as the LOAD statement is input, the computer checks to see if the PLAY button is depressed and the tape is moving. If not, the message: PRESS PLAY ON TAPE #x is displayed. Once the PLAY button is pressed, the tape starts moving and the CRT responds with an OK message. The SEARCHING FOR message is displayed on the screen as the computer searches the tape for the program. Every time it finds a program, the word FOUND and the program name are displayed on the CRT. If the "found" program is not the correct program, the computer continues to search the tape, displaying the "found" program names until the correct program is found. Once found, LOADING is displayed as the program is loaded into computer memory. When the loading process is complete, the READY message is displayed.

After the first program has been loaded from a tape, you can for convenience leave the PLAY key depressed if you will be loading again from the tape. However, do not leave the PLAY key depressed if you will subsequently be saving a program. The computer can sense that a tape control key is depressed, but it cannot distinguish between them. A common error is to LOAD, then subsequently attempt to SAVE, with only the PLAY key depressed.

Sometimes you may have trouble loading a program from tape into memory. Often the CBM computer will find the program name but does not load the program correctly or does not load it at all. If this happens try to load the program again. Rewind the tape and reload (several times if necessary). If this does not work, there may have been a problem when saving the program (SAVE statement) or in the cassette unit itself.

Before issuing a LOAD statement, make sure the cassette tape is rewound to a point preceding the program you want to load. Otherwise the computer would search to the end of the tape without finding the program. If the program to be loaded is located at the end of the tape, and the computer searches from the beginning of the tape, the computer will find and load that program, but the operation will take a long time. If you want to save loading time, devise a scheme to locate approximately where the desired program is on the tape, and position the tape at a point just prior to the program. Then a LOAD statement will find the program quickly.

One scheme to locate information, rather than have the CBM computer search at its PLAY speed, is to use the measuring scale on the tape cassette; the one below goes from 0 to 100 in units of 10, with the beginning of the tape at 30:

As the tape moves forward, the tape radius, measured on the scale, goes from 30 up to 100. 100 is the end of the tape. By keeping a record of information stored on a tape, using the radius numbers, you can Fast Forward to a point just before the desired location.

After the program is loaded into computer memory, list it on the screen using the LIST statement, which was described earlier in this chapter.

Input the RUN statement in immediate mode to execute the program loaded off the cassette tape.

Program LOAD & RUN

"LOAD & RUN" automatically loads and executes the next program found on cassette tape #1. Pressing the shifted RUN/STOP key executes this operation, providing a quick way to load and run the next program stored on the cassette tape.

LOAD & RUN works only on CBM computer models with BASIC < 3.0 (releases 1.x, 2.x, and 3.x).

To LOAD & RUN a program, position the cassette tape in cassette unit #1 before the beginning of the program to be loaded. Program names cannot be specified, therefore LOAD & RUN is usually used with cassette tapes that hold one program only. Press the shifted RUN key. The computer automatically loads and executes the next program found on the cassette tape, displaying all the regular LOAD messages. Here is an example of this method.

```
Lг ◄─────────────────────────────── Press shifted RUN/STOP key

PRESS PLAY ON TAPE #1 ◄──────────── Press PLAY on cassette unit #1
OK

FOUND BLANKET
LOADING
AAAAAAAAAAAAAAAAAAAAAAAAAAAAAAAAAAAAAAAAAAAA ◄── Automatic program execution
AAAAAAAAAAAAAAAAAAAAAAAAAAAAAAAAAAAAAAAAAAAA
AAAAAAAAAAAAAAAAAAAAAAAAAAAAAAAAAAAAAAAAAAAA
......
```

The shifted RUN key can only be pressed while the CBM computer is in immediate mode. If pressed during execution of another program, it acts like a STOP and breaks program execution.

OPERATING THE DISK UNIT

We will now explain how you load and execute programs that were previously stored on a diskette. We will also describe how you save new programs on a diskette.

No knowledge of BASIC programming is required to perform either of these tasks. Chapter 6 explains all disk operations and statements in detail. For now, just enter statements by rote.

By the end of this section you will know how to initialize both disk drives, list the diskette directory, and load, execute and save programs on diskette.

DOS RELEASES 1.x AND 2.x

A set of programs that come with your CBM computer control all disk operations. These programs are referred to collectively as a "Disk Operating System," or DOS.

There are currently several different releases of the CBM disk operating system. The first release, DOS 1.x (*x* is a number between 1 and 9 representing a subrelease of the DOS revision), is compatible with some CBM 2040 disk drive models and is used with BASIC<3.0. Major changes came with DOS release 2.x. Disk system statements were radically simplified, data storage and manipulation were improved, and the bugs in release 1.x were corrected. DOS 2.x works will all releases of BASIC. DOS 1.x works with BASIC<3.0. DOS 1.x will also work with BASIC 4.0 but some BASIC 4.0 disk commands will produce a disk syntax error.

All CBM 8050 disk drive models use the DOS release 2.x with BASIC 4.0. CBM 2040 model units use either DOS 1.x with BASIC<3.0 or 2.x with BASIC 4.0.

LOADING A PROGRAM FROM A DISKETTE USING BASIC<3.0

The following steps are involved when loading a program from a diskette:

1. **Open a logical file and device.**
2. **Initialize the disk drive(s).**
3. **List the directory. This step is optional. It lets you check on the exact spelling of the program name.**
4. **Load the program.**

To demonstrate the steps, we will use the TEST/DEMO diskette supplied by Commodore Business Machines with the disk unit.

Begin by inserting the TEST/DEMO diskette in drive 0 following the diskette loading procedure described in Chapter 1.

Opening a Logical File and Device

Before loading a program off a diskette, the communication line from the computer to the disk drive must be opened and readied for data transfer. The OPEN statement, input in immediate mode, opens the communication line.

To open a disk drive type in the following OPEN statement:

```
OPEN 1,8,15
```

Initializing the Disk Drive (BASIC < 3.0)

The next step is to initialize the disk drive. **When using BASIC < 3.0 the disk drive must be reinitialized every time a diskette is inserted in a drive, or when diskettes are switched between the two drives.** A disk drive must house a diskette before it is initialized.

You initialize the disk drive with the INITIALIZE statement. "I" is the abbreviation for INITIALIZE. Either may be used.

$$\text{PRINT} \# \text{file,"} \quad \left\{ \begin{array}{c} \text{Initialize} \\ \text{I} \end{array} \right\} \text{dr"}$$

where:

> file   is the logical file number used in the OPEN
>   command
>
> dr   is the disk drive number 0 or 1

To initialize drive 0 containing the TEST/DEMO diskette, type in:

```
PRINT#1,"I0"
```

You should see the drive 0 LED indicator light light up while the drive 0 motor runs briefly. When the motor stops and the drive indicator light goes out the drive is initialized.

To initialize drive 1, insert a diskette into drive 1 and type in:

```
PRINT#1,"I1"
```

To initialize both drives type in:

```
PRINT#1,"I"
```

Loading the Diskette Directory (DOS 1.x)

Step 3 loads and lists the disk directory into memory. This is an optional step; you can skip this step if you already know the name of the program you want to load.

The diskette directory serves the same function as the table of contents of a book: it names the programs stored on the diskette.

To load the directory off the diskette in drive 0 using BASIC < 3.0, type in:

```
LOAD "$0",8
```

To load a directory off a diskette in drive 1 using BASIC < 3.0, type in:

```
LOAD "$1",8
```

If the drive number is not specified, both drives are searched and each diskette's directory is loaded.

```
LOAD "$",8
```

The following messages are displayed on the screen as the directory is loaded:

```
LOAD"$0",8

SEARCHING FOR $0
LOADING
READY.
```

When the READY message appears, type in LIST and press the RETURN key. LIST will list the directory contents on the screen; the cursor will disappear as the directory appears on the screen. If the directory is longer than 25 lines, initial lines will scroll off the top of the screen. To slow down the scrolling, hold down the REVERSE key or the ← key on the business keyboard while the directory is listing. To stop the list, press the STOP key.

You may list the directory as often as you want by retyping the LIST statement.

Here is an example of the TEST/DEMO diskette directory for a CBM 2040 model disk unit:

```
LIST

0  ████████████████████████████
6     "DOS SUPPORT 4.0"   PRG
27    "DUM 3.4"           PRG
1     "  DISK DATA  "     SEQ
15    "DIAGNOSTIC BOOT"   PRG
10    "COPY DISK FILES"   PRG
4     "CHECK DISK"        PRG
10    "PET DISK"          PRG
10    "DISK DISPLAY"      PRG
3     "DISK COMM"         PRG
2     "DISK COMM2"        PRG
3     "DISK COMM3"        PRG
4     "DISK WRITE"        PRG
4     "DISK READ"         PRG
2     "DISK OVERLAYS"     PRG
5     "DISK DIR"          PRG
7     "  PET DATA  "      SEQ
34    "RANDOM 1.00"       PRG
27    "PRINTER DEMO"      PRG
12    "SEQUENTIAL 1.00"   PRG
484 BLOCKS FREE.
```

The top row of the directory is the "header." The header, displayed in reverse mode, shows the diskette name and identification number. The center column of the directory lists the program names. The quotation marks are not actually a part of the program name. The left column shows how many "blocks" of space on the diskette are filled by the program (a block is a unit of measure on the diskette). The number at the bottom of the column is the total number of unused blocks on the diskette. The rightmost column signals whether the information is saved as a program (PRG) or data. Do not worry about the left or right columns; they are of no importance at this time.

Once the directory is displayed scan the center column to find the program you wish to load.

Program LOAD (BASIC < 3.0)

The LOAD statement, input in immediate mode, loads the specified program from the diskette and stores it in computer memory.

To load any program from a diskette in drive 0, type in:

LOAD "0: program name ",8

The disk drive number precedes the program name; the two are separated by a colon. Together they are enclosed within quotation marks. If the disk drive number is not specified as 0 or 1, the disk operating system will search both drives for the program, providing both disk drives have previously been initialized.

To load the first program from the TEST/DEMO diskette in drive 0 using BASIC < 3.0, type in:

```
LOAD "0:DOS SUPPORT 4.0",8
```

Upon pressing RETURN the following messages appear on the screen, while the drive indicator light lights up and the disk drive makes a soft humming noise:

```
LOAD "0:DOS SUPPORT 4.0",8

SEARCHING FOR 0:DOS SUPPORT 4.0
LOADING
READY.
▓
```

The disk drive number and program name are always displayed following the SEARCHING FOR message. When the LED light goes out and the humming noise stops, the READY message appears on the screen with the flashing cursor. The program is now loaded and ready to be listed and run.

Program LIST (BASIC < 3.0)

Once a program is loaded into computer memory it may be listed on the display screen with the LIST statement, which we have already described. LIST displays the entire program. LIST with line parameters displays the specified portions of the program.

Program RUN (BASIC < 3.0)

To execute the program just loaded off the diskette, type the RUN statement. Upon pressing the RETURN key, the program is executed.

Preparing a Blank Diskette for BASIC < 3.0

A blank diskette cannot be used in the disk unit until it has been prepared, or "formatted." Following is the procedure to format a blank diskette, or to reformat an old diskette. Type in the statements by rote — you do not need to fully understand each step at this point.

OPEN the disk drive as follows:

```
OPEN 1,8,15
```

To format the diskette and intialize the disk drive the NEW statement is used. The format for the NEW statement is:

PRINT#file," $\left\{ \begin{matrix} \text{N} \\ \text{NEW} \end{matrix} \right\}$ dr:diskname,id"

where:

file	is the logical file number used in the OPEN command
dr	is the disk drive number 0 or 1
diskname	is the name assigned to the entire disk
id	is a unique two-character identifier.

Because your diskette is in drive 0, the disk drive number specified must be 0. Our example diskname is YAK, and the identification number is 01. Type in the following OPEN and NEW statements to format your diskette:

```
OPEN 1,8,15
PRINT#1,"N0:YAK,01"
```

Press the RETURN key. The drive 0 indicator light illuminates as the disk drive formats the diskette. The cursor disappears briefly, but then reappears with the READY message before the diskette format is complete; this allows you to do other things on the screen while the diskette is formatting. Once the operation is complete, type in:

```
LOAD "$0",8
```

$0 is the diskette directory for drive 0. $1 is the directory for drive 1. Directories display the diskette's "table of contents" on the screen. Each directory begins with a "header" with the diskname and identification number. When the directory is loaded, enter:

```
LIST
```

The directory will be displayed. Because the diskette is blank, only the header, shown here, is displayed:

```
LIST

0 ▒▓▒▓▓████████████████▓██ ▓▓ ███
670 BLOCKS FREE.
READY.
▒
```

Once the diskette is formatted you can store programs and data on it.

Program SAVE (BASIC < 3.0)

Recording a program on a diskette with the SAVE statement is similiar to recording onto a cassette tape. However, there are some differences in the syntax of the SAVE statement. A program SAVE for a diskette looks like this:

SAVE"dr:file name",8

where:

dr   is the disk drive number, 0 or 1

file   is the name assigned to the program

The number within the quotes and preceding the program name specifies the disk drive number, 0 or 1. It may not be omitted. The number following the program name, number 8, tells the computer to direct the program to the disk drive. If the number 8 is omitted the computer will try to save the program on the cassette unit O1.

Try saving the BLANKET program on a diskette in drive 0. Insert any formatted diskette into drive 0, then OPEN and INITIALIZE the drive, if not already done. Enter the BLANKET program on the keyboard. To save the program, enter the following SAVE statement and press the RETURN key.

```
OPEN 1,8,15 ◄─────── OPEN disk drive
PRINT#1,"I0" ◄─────── Initialize disk drive 0

10 FOR I=1 TO 800
20 PRINT "A"
30 NEXT I                Enter BLANKET program
40 PRINT "PHEW!"
50 END

SAVE "0:BLANKET",8 ◄─── Save BLANKET program on disk drive 0

READY.
▒
```

As BLANKET is saved, the cursor will disappear from the screen and the indicator light on the disk drive will light up briefly. When the program has been completely recorded, the cursor and a READY message will appear on the screen. After saving a program, verify it.

Program VERIFY (BASIC <3.0)

Diskette and cassette programs are verified in the same way. The computer compares the saved program on the diskette against the program in memory. If an error is detected, an error message is displayed.

You should always VERIFY a program immediately after saving it.

The specifications for the VERIFY statement are identical to the SAVE statement. A program VERIFY for a diskette looks like this:

VERIFY"dr:filename",8

where:

dr   is the disk drive number, 0 or 2

filename   is the name of the program just saved

When the RETURN key is pressed, the verify messages (SEARCHING FOR BLANKET, VERIFYING, and OK) are displayed on the screen. If an error message appears instead of OK, then re-verify the program. If an error message appears again, resave the program, then re-verify.

```
SAVE "0:BLANKET",8◄───────SAVE BLANKET program

READY.

VERIFY "0:BLANKET",8◄──────Verify BLANKET program

SEARCHING FOR 0:BLANKET
VERIFYING◄─────────────────Program verified
OK

READY.
▓
```

Another way to VERIFY the program just saved on the diskette uses this statement:

VERIFY"*",8

The asterisk (*) signals the CBM computer to verify the program just saved on the diskette without having to specify the program name.

LOADING A PROGRAM FROM DISKETTE USING BASIC 4.0

There are two steps to loading a program from a diskette using BASIC 4.0:

1. List the directory.
2. Load the program.

To demonstrate these steps use any available prepared diskette or the DEMO diskette supplied by Commodore. The examples in this section will use the programs from the 8050 DEMO diskette.

Insert the diskette in drive 0 following the diskette loading procedure described in Chapter 1.

The BASIC 4.0 system automatically initializes the diskette drive before a program is loaded. However, **if you switch diskettes that have the same identification number** (the number following the diskette name on the directory header) then **you should manually initialize the drive,** otherwise the computer will not know that the diskettes have been switched. Drives are initialized when you load the directory.

Loading the Diskette Directory (BASIC 4.0)

The DIRECTORY statement loads the diskette directory and displays it on the screen.

To load the diskette directory type in:

DIRECTORY D0	*Load and list the directory of disk drive 0*
DIRECTORY D1	*Load and list the directory of disk drive 1*
DIRECTORY	*Load and list the directory of disk drives 0 and 1*

If the disk drive is not specified, both directories are loaded and listed. A directory may *not* be listed or run like a regular CBM BASIC program under BASIC 4.0.

A sample diskette directory in drive 0 appears as follows:

```
DIRECTORY D0

0  █8050 DEMO█          W0  2A
5     "UNIVERSAL WEDGE"   PRG
8     "UNIT TO UNIT"      PRG
3     "CHANGE 8050"       PRG
11    "COPY 2040 - 8050"  PRG
27    "PRINTER DEMO"      PRG
12    "SEQUENTIAL"        PRG
11    "PERFORMANCE TEST"  PRG
5     "CHECK DISK"        PRG
17    "LOGIC DIAGNOSTIC"  PRG
1953 BLOCKS FREE.
READY.
▓
```

Program LOAD (BASIC 4.0)

Programs are loaded from a diskette with the DLOAD statement in immediate mode. To load a program from a diskette type in:

DLOAD "program name" ⎫
DLOAD "program name",D0 ⎬ *Load program from disk drive 0*

DLOAD "program name",D1   *Load program from disk drive 0*

The program name is mandatory and must be enclosed within quotation marks. If the disk drive is not specified the drive number defaults to 0 and only drive 0 is searched. If a program is not found, a ?FILE NOT FOUND error results.

Try these statements on your disk system. Load the directory of the DEMO diskette or your own diskette in drive 0. Type in:

```
DIRECTORY D0
```

The cursor should disappear briefly while the diskette is initialized and the directory is loaded into memory and displayed.

Next, load the second program listed on the directory. (In the following example, the program name may differ from your program name — don't worry about it.) Type in:

```
DLOAD "UNIT TO UNIT"
```

The normal load messages appear on the screen as the diskette is searched and the UNIT TO UNIT program is loaded into memory.

```
DLOAD "UNIT TO UNIT",D0

SEARCHING FOR UNIT TO UNIT
LOADING
READY.
▓
```

Program LIST (BASIC 4.0)

To list the program, use the LIST statement, which we described earlier.

The LIST statement is used in the same way by BASIC 4.0 and BASIC < 3.0. The LIST statement description given earlier applies to all DOS releases.

Program RUN (BASIC 4.0)

To execute the program, type in the RUN statement:

        RUN

Program LOAD & RUN (BASIC 4.0)

The LOAD & RUN function automatically loads and executes the first program found on disk drive 0. Pressing the shifted RUN/STOP key executes this operation, providing a quick way to load and run the first program on the drive 0 diskette.

The disk drive LOAD & RUN works only on CBM models with BASIC 4.0 (release 4.x).

To LOAD & RUN a program, simply press the shifted RUN key. The screen displays the following messages before the program begins execution:

                                    ─────────*Shifted RUN key pressed*
        DL"*

        SEARCHING FOR 0:*
        LOADING
                          ─────────*Program execution begins*

To perform a LOAD & RUN, the shifted RUN key can only be pressed while the CBM computer is in immediate mode. If pressed during execution of another program, it acts like a STOP and breaks program execution.

Preparing a Blank Diskette for BASIC 4.0

A blank diskette cannot be used in the disk unit until it has been prepared, or "formatted." **Following is the procedure to format a blank diskette, or to reformat an old diskette.** Type in the commands by rote — you do not need to fully understand each step at this point.

Insert a diskette in drive 0.

Diskettes are formatted with the HEADER statement:

        HEADER "diskname",Dx,I22

    where:

        diskname   is the name to be assigned to the disk

        x   is the disk drive number, 0 or 1

        22   is the two-character identification number

Type in the following HEADER statement to format your diskette:

        HEADER "YAK", D0, I01

Our example disk name is YAK. Because the diskette is in drive 0, the disk drive number specified must be D0. If the diskette is in drive 1, then D1 is specified. The identification number we will use is 1, although any unique two-letter combination of letters or numbers may be used.

When you press the RETURN key, the computer will respond with an ARE YOU SURE? message. Press the 'Y' key for yes, or the 'N' key for no. Press the RETURN key. 'N' will cause an exit from the format procedure. If 'Y' is pressed, the drive 0 indicator light illuminates as the disk drive formats the diskette. The cursor disappears for a short time, reappearing with a READY message when the format operation is complete.

```
HEADER "YAK", D0, I01
ARE YOU SURE ?Y ◄────────Y key pressed for "yes"
READY.
▓
```

Once the diskette is formatted you can write program and data files on it.

Program SAVE (BASIC 4.0)

Programs are saved on a diskette using the DSAVE statement in immediate mode. To save a program on a diskette type in:

> **DSAVE "filename",Dx**

where:

> filename   is the name of the program
>
> x   is the disk drive number 0 or 1

The program name is mandatory and must be enclosed within quotation marks. If the disk drive number is not specified, the program is automatically saved on the diskette in drive 0.

Try this statement by saving the BLANKET program on a formatted diskette in drive 0. Enter the BLANKET program on the keyboard. Then type in the following DSAVE statement:

```
DSAVE "BLANKET", D0
```

Upon pressing the RETURN key, the indicator light on the disk drive will light up briefly and the cursor will disappear from the screen. Upon completion of the save, a READY message and the cursor will return to the screen as shown:

```
DSAVE "BLANKET", D0

READY.
▓
```

The BLANKET program should now be verified.

Program VERIFY (BASIC 4.0)

The BASIC 4.0 and BASIC < 3.0 VERIFY statements are the same. Refer to the VERIFY statement under BASIC < 3.0 for the description.

OPERATING THE CBM PRINTER

The CBM printer can be used to list program statements and to print results. Like disk and tape units, the printer can be controlled by statements entered in immediate mode via the keyboard, or using statements within a program. We are going to describe immediate mode printer control. Chapter 6 explains how to control a printer using program statements. **Printer operations are identical using BASIC 4.0 or BASIC < 3.0.**

The OPEN Statement

Prior to sending data to the printer, you must open a communication line from the computer to the printer. This is done using an OPEN statement, as follows:

OPEN x,4

where:

x   is any integer from 1 to 255

Here are some examples of OPEN statements:

```
OPEN 1,4
OPEN 4,4
OPEN 250,4
```

The CMD Statement

Once the printer has been opened, output is directed to the printer using the CMD statement. This is optional.

CMD 1

The CMD number must match the first number of the OPEN statement. If the numbers do not match, the message ?FILE NOT OPEN ERROR will be displayed. If this occurs, the printer will have to be reopened by retyping the OPEN and CMD statements.

Here are some examples with PRINT statements:

```
OPEN 1,4:CMD 4
PRINT ".TISHNICK"


OPEN 2,4
CMD 2, "MY PET BITES"


OPEN 3,4
PRINT#3, "54321"
```

Printing to the Printer

Once the printer has been properly opened, it is ready to receive and print data. We will use the PRINT# statement, entered in immediate mode, to print data at the printer.

First make sure the printer is connected to the computer and powered up, with ribbon and paper properly installed.

Open the printer by typing in OPEN and CMD statements:

```
OPEN 1,4:CMD 1
```

Upon pressing RETURN, the printer executes a line feed (prints one blank line). The printer is now open and ready to print data input from the keyboard. Type in the following PRINT statement, placing your name between the quotation marks:

```
PRINT "KIT CARSON"
```

When you press RETURN, the cursor will disappear from the screen as your name is printed at the printer:

```
READY.
KIT CARSON
```

When printing in immediate mode, the first line printed is a READY message. The following line is your output; in this case, your name. At the end of the output the printer automatically executes a carriage return and another line feed. When the cursor reappears on the screen, you can input more data.

Below are some more sample inputs and printer outputs.

Screen Display   **Printer Output**

```
                                              KIT CARSON
OPEN 1,4:CMD 1
PRINT "KIT CARSON"                            READY.
PRINT "1234567890"                            1234567890
PRINT "MY NAME BACKWARDS IS TIK NOSRAC"
                                              READY.
                                              MY NAME BACKWARDS IS TIK NO RAC
```

Listing a Program on the Printer

To list a program on the printer, type in the OPEN and CMD statements, followed by the LIST statement.

```
OPEN 1,4:CMD 1
LIST
```

LIST line parameters may also be used.

The example below shows the BLANKET program listed by the printer:

```
OPEN 1,4:CMD 1
LIST

10 FOR I=1 TO 800
20 PRINT "A";
30 NEXT I
40 PRINT "PHEW!"
50 END
READY.
```

The CLOSE Statement

You must CLOSE the printer after using it. The printer is closed with a CLOSE statement, as follows:

CLOSE 1

The number following CLOSE must be the first number in the OPEN statement.

OPEN 1, 4   OPEN 15, 4
.   .
.   .
.   .
CLOSE 1   CLOSE 15

You must precede the CLOSE statement with a PRINT# statement to properly close the printer. Below are examples of correct and incorrect ways to close the printer:

	Right		**Wrong**
	OPEN 5, 4		
	PRINT#5,"HELLO THERE"		
	CLOSE 5		
	OPEN 5, 4		OPEN 5, 4
	CMD 5,"HELLO THERE"	not	CMD 5, "HELLO THERE"
	PRINT#5:CLOSE 5		CLOSE 5
	OPEN 5,4		OPEN 5,4
	CMD 5,"HELLO THERE"	not	CMD 5,"HELLO THERE"
	PRINT#5,"HELLO THERE"		PRINT#5,"HELLO THERE"
	CLOSE 5		PRINT#5:CLOSE 5
	OPEN 5, 4		OPEN 5, 4
	PRINT#5,"HELLO THERE"	not	PRINT#5,"HELLO THERE"
	CMD5,"HELLO THERE"		CMD5,"HELLO THERE"
	PRINT#5:CLOSE 5		CLOSE 5

Chapter 3

Screen Editing

CBM computers display characters on the video screen as they are input via the keyboard. Anything displayed on the screen may be edited or modified in immediate mode.

Screen editing is one of the most significant capabilities of your CBM computer. You can change your input simply and efficiently using a built-in screen editor, described in this chapter. Try all the examples provided in this chapter. If you do not understand these editing concepts read Chapter 4, "Programming the CBM Computer," and then reread this chapter. Chapter 4 will give you a fundamental understanding of the BASIC language.

The screen editor allows the cursor to be moved around the screen in four directions. Characters can be inserted or deleted anywhere on the screen. Cursor keys were described in Chapter 1 under "CBM Key Groups": The CLEAR SCREEN/HOME key moves the cursor to the beginning of the top screen line and/or blanks the screen. The CURSOR UP/DOWN, and CURSOR LEFT/RIGHT keys skip the cursor over text. The INSERT/DELETE key adjusts space on the screen to insert or delete single characters.

EDITING TEXT ON THE CURRENT DISPLAY LINE

Often while entering text you may notice a mistake on the line currently being entered. You can correct the mistake immediately. Backspace the cursor to the mistake using either the CURSOR LEFT key or the DELETE key.

We will use the following statement to illustrate editing:

MY PET BYTES

BITES is misspelled; we want to change the Y to an I.

You can use the CURSOR LEFT key to backspace the cursor back to the Y without altering the text, or you can use the DELETE key to backspace and erase text up to the Y. The choice depends upon whether you want text to the right of the Y to remain. If the error is many characters back, you are better off using the CURSOR LEFT key, which backspaces the cursor, so that you will not have to retype the remainder of the line, possibly introducing new errors.

Backspacing with the CURSOR LEFT Key

Enter the following text, leaving the cursor at the end of the text. Do not press the RETURN key:

MY PET BYTES▓

The cursor must be moved back to the Y, which must be changed to an I. BYTES then becomes BITES. To move the cursor left, press the CURSOR LEFT key and the SHIFT key simultaneously one time for each screen position to be moved. Stop pressing the cursor keys when the cursor is positioned at the Y character.

On the CBM 8000 models the cursor will move automatically if the cursor key is held down. You need not repeatedly press the cursor keys. Just hold the key down until the cursor is positioned on the Y character.

```
MY PET BYTES▓ ◄—Press CUROSR LEFT
MY PET BYTES◄—Press CURSOR LEFT
MY PET BYTES ◄—Press CURSOR LEFT
MY PET BYTES ◄—Press CURSOR LEFT
MY PET BYTES
```

To change the Y character to an I, press the I key on the keyboard. Replacing the Y with an I, the cursor moves one position to the right. This is called "typeover," because the cursor types over the existing character with a new character. Typeover changes the screen display to:

MY PET BITES ◄—Y character typed over with I key.

You can move the cursor past the end of the text with multiple pressings of the CURSOR RIGHT key (unshifted) to continue entering more text on the line. Or you can simply press the RETURN key to complete the line. Experiment with both methods.

As each screen line is edited, the change(s) become permanent when you press the RETURN key. Do not move the cursor off the line by pressing either the HOME, CLEAR SCREEN, or CURSOR UP/DOWN key. Although the screen display shows the modification, the change will not be registered in the computer's memory until the RETURN key is pressed.

Backspacing with the DELETE Key

Type in the example text again, leaving the cursor at the end of the text. Do not press the RETURN key.

```
MY PET BYTES▓
```

Press the DELETE key one time for each position to be moved. Stop the cursor when the Y character has been erased.

```
MY PET BYTES▓ ◄── Press DELETE
MY PET BYTE▓ ◄──── Press DELETE
MY PET BYT▓ ◄───── Press DELETE
MY PET BY▓ ◄────── Press DELETE
MY PET B▓
```

The cursor should be positioned over the Y character. Press the I key to enter the I character.

To complete the statement you must retype the remainder of the text that was deleted. When completed, press the RETURN key to make the change permanent in computer memory.

```
MY PET B▓
MY PET BI▓ ◄──────── Press I key
MY PET BIT▓ ◄─────── Press T key
MY PET BITE▓ ◄────── Press E key
MY PET BITES▓ ◄───── Press S key
```

Shifting and Deleting Text with the DELETE Key

The DELETE key can also be used to shift text one position to the left, while simultaneously deleting the character to the cursor's left.

The example statement has been altered to include an extra character in the text, as shown below:

```
MY PET BITTES▓
```

Type in this statement, leaving the cursor at the end of the line. Our task is to delete the extra T in BI(T)TES. We will arbitrarily choose to delete the first T. Instead of deleting the text back to the first T, move the cursor over the text with the CURSOR LEFT key. Move the cursor to the second T, because DELETE deletes the character to the immediate left of the cursor, not the character under the cursor.

```
MY PET BITTES
```

With the cursor on the second T, press the DELETE key. The first T is deleted and the text to its right is shifted one position to the left, filling its space.

```
MY PET BITTES ◄── Position of cursor before DELETE key pressed
MY PET BITES ◄── DELETE key pressed
```

Either press the CURSOR RIGHT key several times to move beyond the text before pressing the RETURN key, or simply press the RETURN key to exit the text.

Shifting Text with the INSERT Key

The INSERT key opens a space in the text at the current cursor position, moving all the text beyond the cursor position one space to the right. An additional character may be inserted into this new space.

To demonstrate the INSERT key, we will omit one character from our example text. Type in the statement below, leaving the cursor at the end of the statement:

```
MY PET BTES
```

The missing I may be added to the text in several different ways.

You can use the DELETE key to delete the text back to the error, then enter the omitted character and the remainder of the line, as previously described. But if you delete more than a couple of characters, you may make mistakes retyping the line. You do not have to retype if you use the INSERT key.

Before using the INSERT key, move the cursor to the character position where you want the insertion to begin. Place the cursor on the character that ultimately becomes the first character *beyond* the insertion.

```
MY PET BTES ←—Position of cursor before INSERT key pressed
        ↑——————INSERT I character here
```

To insert an I between the B and the T, backspace the cursor by pressing the CURSOR LEFT key until the cursor is on top of the T character:

```
MY PET BTES ←—Press CURSOR LEFT
MY PET BTES ←—Press CURSOR LEFT
MY PET BTES ←—Press CURSOR LEFT
MY PET BTES
```

Press the INSERT key once to insert one space between the B and the T. The TES text moves one space to the right while the cursor remains stationary.

```
MY PET B TES ←—INSERT key pressed
```

Type in the I character:

```
MY PET BITES ←—I character pressed
```

If you want to add text at the end of the line, press the CURSOR RIGHT key to move the cursor beyond the S, add new text, then press RETURN. Or just press the RETURN key to drop the cursor to a lower line if no new text is to be added.

This time we will insert an entire word into a line of text. Type in the following new text, leaving the cursor at the end of the statement:

```
NOW IS THE TIME
```

Suppose we want to insert the word NOT, to change the meaning of the statement.

```
NOW IS THE TIME
    ‿‿
    NOT
```

Press CURSOR LEFT repeatedly until the cursor backspaces to the T of THE.

```
NOW  IS  THE  TIME※
NOW  IS  THE  TIME
NOW  IS  THE  TIME
NOW  IS  THE  TIME
NOW  IS  THE  TIME
NOW  IS  THE TIME
NOW  IS  THE  TIME
NOW  IS  THE  TIME
NOW  IS  THE  TIME
```

Press the INSERT key four times to make room for the word NOT, plus a space.

```
NOW  IS  THE  TIME ◀────── Press INSERT key
NOW  IS  ※THE  TIME ◀────── Press INSERT key
NOW  IS  ※  THE  TIME ◀────── Press INSERT key
NOW  IS  ※    THE  TIME ◀────── Press INSERT key
NOW  IS  ※     THE  TIME
```

Type in the word NOT and a space:

```
NOW  IS  ※     THE  TIME
NOW  IS  N※    THE  TIME
NOW  IS  NO※  THE  TIME
NOW  IS  NOT※THE  TIME
NOW  IS  NOT  THE  TIME
```

Press the RETURN key to exit the cursor from the text.

There are a couple of rules that must be observed when using the INSERT key. Always move the cursor to the position where you want the insertion to *begin*. The character under the cursor will be moved to the right of the cursor, becoming the first character beyond the insertion. When entering in additional characters, press as many character keys, including spaces, as you did INSERT keys.

EDITING TEXT WITHIN QUOTATION MARKS

Editing text enclosed within quotation marks calls for different procedures, because quotation marks signal the beginning or the end of a text string.

Recall from Chapter 2 that any text entered after an odd number of quotation marks becomes a text string; this includes cursor keys. If you press a cursor control key to edit the string, the cursor will not move. Instead, a symbolic representation of the cursor key will be displayed as part of the string. **Before the string can be edited, it must be completed with a second set of quotation marks, or by pressing the RETURN key. Once out of the string, the cursor keys function normally. The CBM 8000 ESC key cancels the effect of an odd number of quotation marks.**

The example text we will use to demonstrate editing within a string is:

```
PRINT "MY PET BITES"
```

This is a PRINT statement which will display the character string MY PET BITES on the next line when the RETURN key is pressed.

When entering this statement we discover the I of BITES was accidentally entered as a Y.

```
PRINT "MY PET BYTES"※
```

To edit the Y character without altering the rest of the text, your first inclination is to press the CURSOR LEFT key three times and type over the Y with an I character. This will not work. The three CURSOR LEFTs will be incorporated into the text string instead of moving the cursor left. The incorporated CURSOR LEFTs, shown by their symbolic representations in the string, cause cursor movement when the PRINT statement is executed.

PRINT "MY PET BYTE█ █ █ ※ ◄── *CURSOR LEFT pressed three times*

Table 3-1 shows the string representations of all the cursor keys. To avoid "programming" the cursor keys in the string, type a second set of quotation marks before you start editing.

Returning to the original statement, to avoid entering the CURSOR LEFT keys as text, enter the remainder of the string, and the second set of quotation marks which end the string:

```
PRINT "MY PET BYTE※
PRINT "MY PET BYTES※
PRINT "MY PET BYTES"※ ◄── Cursor positioned after second
                            set of quotation marks
```

Table 3-1. String Representation of Cursor Keys

Function		Key	String Symbol
DELETE		INST DEL	(Reverse shifted T)
INSERT	Shifted	INST DEL	Not programmed
Home Cursor		CLR SCREEN HOME	◙ (Reverse S)
Clear Screen	Shifted	CLR SCREEN HOME	◘ (Reverse Shifted S)
Cursor Down		↑ CURSOR ↓	◙ (Reverse Q)
Cursor Up	Shifted	↑ CURSOR ↓	◘ (Reverse Shifted Q)
Cursor Right		← CURSOR →	▐ (Reverse])
Cursor Left	Shifted	← CURSOR →	██ (Reverse Shifted])

Then use the CURSOR LEFT key to move the cursor back to the Y.

```
PRINT "MY PET BYTES"▓ ◄──Press CURSOR LEFT
PRINT "MY PET BYTES"◄──Press CURSOR LEFT
PRINT "MY PET BYTES"◄──Press CURSOR LEFT
PRINT "MY PET BYTES"◄──Press CURSOR LEFT
PRINT "MY PET BYTES"◄──Press CURSOR LEFT
PRINT "MY PET BYTES"
```

Type over the Y with an I, and press the RETURN key to exit the statement. The corrected string is displayed on the following line:

```
PRINT "MY PET BYTES"◄──Type I over Y
PRINT "MY PET BITES"◄──Press RETURN
MY PET BITES ◄───────PRINT statement displayed on screen

READY.
▓
```

An alternative method when editing text within quotation marks is to press the RETURN key, which removes the cursor from the current display line. This places the cursor in the first character position of the next line. (The computer may respond in various ways, depending on the statement. Do not concern yourself with the computer response just yet — your task is to edit the string text.) Move the cursor up to the line using CURSOR UP, and move the cursor left to the character to be edited.

Type in this statement:

```
PRINT "MY PET BYTES"
```

Press the RETURN key to drop the cursor down to a lower line.

```
PRINT "MY PET BYTES"◄──Press RETURN key
MY PET BYTES

READY.
▓
```

Ignoring the screen response, press the CURSOR UP key (shifted) repeatedly to move the cursor up to the original statement line.

```
CURSOR UP key pressed    ┌►PRINT "MY PET BYTES"
CURSOR UP key pressed    ├►MY PET BYTES
CURSOR UP key pressed    ├►
CURSOR UP key pressed    └►READY.
                           ▓
```

Press the CURSOR RIGHT key several times to move the cursor rightward to the Y character. Type over the Y character with an I.

```
PRINT "MY PET BYTES"
PRINT "MY PET BITES"◄── Y typed over with I character
```

Press the RETURN key. Upon pressing the RETURN key the statement is executed. The string is displayed with the new I character replacing the corrected I.

```
PRINT "MY PET BITES"◄──Type I over Y
MY PET BITES ◄─────────RETURN key pressed

READY.
▓
```

Like the CURSOR LEFT key, the CURSOR RIGHT and the CURSOR UP/ DOWN become part of the string text when entered following an odd-numbered set of quotation marks.

But the INSERT/DELETE keys respond a little differently.

The INSERT key, when entered following an odd-numbered set of quotation marks, becomes a character in the text string. It is represented on the screen by the INSERT symbol (⬚). But when the PRINT statement is executed and the string is displayed, the INSERT character has no effect on the display.

The DELETE key is the only cursor key not affected by the presence of quotation marks. To edit our example statement with the DELETE key, simply press the DELETE key to delete text back to the position which must be edited.

```
PRINT "MY PET BYTES"▒ ◄──Press DELETE key
PRINT "MY PET BYTES▒ ◄──Press DELETE key
PRINT "MY PET BYTE▒ ◄──Press DELETE key
PRINT "MY PET BYT▒ ◄──Press DELETE key
PRINT "MY PET BY▒ ◄──Press DELETE key
PRINT "MY PET B▒
```

EDITING PROGRAM STATEMENTS

Do not read this section until you understand programming.

This section explains how to duplicate and edit similar BASIC statements using line numbers.

Line Duplication

Many programs have several similar or identical statements. It is often efficient to duplicate several statements from one original statement, rather than re-entering the statement many times. On the CBM computer, each program statement must be assigned a unique line number. **By changing the line number of a statement you can create a new statement without erasing the original.**

Enter the following program statement:

```
10 PRINT "*"
```

Suppose we need to enter five more identical statements, just like the one above. We could type in the statement five times, assigning each statement a unique line number. Or we could duplicate the statement five times by changing the line number of the original statement five times, as described below.

Enter the program statement to be duplicated. (If the program statement is already entered, list it using the LIST command, specifying the line number.) Press the CURSOR UP key until the cursor is positioned at the start of the line number. To change the statement line number, type over the number 10 with a new line number:

```
20▒PRINT "*" ◄── Type over line number 10 with line number 20
```

When the new line number has been entered, press the RETURN key to create a new statement from the original. The RETURN key must be pressed after each line number change. If you list the program, both statements are displayed:

```
20 PRINT "*"
LIST

10 PRINT "*"
20 PRINT "*"
READY.
▓
```

Editing Similar Program Statements

Editing similar program statements follows the same procedure described in duplicating program statements. LIST the statement to be duplicated, specifying its line number. Move the cursor up to the program statement and type over the line number with a new line number. Then using the CURSOR RIGHT, INSERT or DELETE keys, move the cursor to edit the statement as needed. Press the RETURN key, and the new statement created from the original statement is sent to memory. Do not worry if the original statement is not displayed on the screen. It is still in memory and will be displayed if you LIST the program.

Ultimately we want to create a short example program that looks like this:

```
10 PRINT "*"
20 PRINT " *"
30 PRINT "  *"
40 PRINT "   *"
50 PRINT "    *"
```

Because all five lines are similar, we will duplicate and edit the first statement four times to avoid redundant typing of identical text.

Enter program statement 10 and press the RETURN key. To create the program statement on 20, move the cursor up to line number 10 and type over the 10 with a 20. Press the CURSOR LEFT key repeatedly until the cursor is positioned on top of the asterisk (*). Press the INSERT key once to move the asterisk over one space to the right, leaving a blank space at the current cursor position. Press the RETURN key to send the new program statement to memory. Although line number 10 is not displayed on the screen, it is still in computer memory, as shown by a program LIST:

```
20 PRINT " *"  ◄── Statement 20 created from
LIST                  statement 10

10 PRINT "*"
20 PRINT " *"
READY.
▓
```

Statements 30, 40, and 50 are created in the same manner as statement 20 by moving the cursor up to the statement, then editing the line number and text. After entering all five statements, the screen should look like this:

```
50 PRINT "    *"
▓
```

Type in LIST to display the entire program:

```
50 PRINT "      *"
LIST

10 PRINT "*"
20 PRINT " *"
30 PRINT "  *"
40 PRINT "   *"
50 PRINT "      *"
READY.
```

As you can see, duplicating and editing similar program statements is an efficient means of entering similar statements.

BASIC 4.0 SCREEN EDITING EXTENSIONS

BASIC 4.0 has a number of screen editing capabilities not available with earlier releases of CBM BASIC. These added capabilities are generally used within programs; they are not used to edit screen data in immediate mode, therefore they are described in Chapter 5.

Chapter 4

Programming the CBM

This chapter teaches you how to start writing your own BASIC programs.

BASIC is a programming language. BASIC, like any programming language, consists of a set of statements, which you combine to create programs. A program defines the task you want the computer to perform.

We could teach you BASIC by forcing you first to learn BASIC statements, one by one. But you would probably give up, since individual statements are not very meaningful. A study of individual BASIC statements quickly degenerates into learning a number of arbitrary syntax rules that tell you nothing about programming or good programming practice. Therefore **rigorous definitions of all BASIC statements have been relegated to Chapter 8. Look up individual statements in Chapter 8 when you need to,** but do not try to read Chapter 8 before you read this chapter.

IMMEDIATE AND PROGRAMMED MODES

When the CBM computer is powered up it is in immediate mode. In immediate mode you can use the CBM computer as you would a calculator; it executes BASIC statements as soon as you press the RETURN key to signal the end of the statement entry. Try these arithmetic examples:

`?4.5+6.42` `  10.92`	Addition

`READY.`
`?500-410`
`  90`
	Subtraction

`READY.`
`?π*2`
`  6.28318531`
	Multiplication

`READY.`
`?100/3`
`  33.3333333`
	Division

`READY.`
`?6/2*4-1`
`  11`
	Combination

Results are displayed immediately on the next line of the display.

In programmed mode the computer accepts and stores your entries, but does not perform any operations until specifically instructed to do so by a RUN statement.

Programs and Statements

Each of the five immediate mode statements shown above is a miniature program.

A program provides the CBM computer with an exact and complete definition of the task which the computer is to perform.

A program consists of one or more statements. In each of the five immediate mode illustrations, the entire program consists of a single statement. These are trivial cases. Most programs have tens, hundreds, or even thousands of statements.

Program Execution

A computer is said to execute a program (or RUN the program) when it performs the operations which the program specifies.

An immediate mode program is executed as soon as you press the RETURN key.

In programmed mode you must issue a special RUN statement to execute a program; we described the RUN statement in Chapter 1.

Program Lines

In programmed mode every program line has a unique line number. The CBM computer assumes an immediate mode program if the line does not begin with a line number.

A program line can be up to 80 characters long. On an 80-column display, therefore, a program line corresponds to a display line. On a 40-column display a program line is equivalent to two display lines.

If a program line is less than 80 characters long, then it is terminated when you press the RETURN key. The CBM computer lets you continue beyond the 80th character, but subsequently the line does not execute correctly. To be safe you should end every line before the 80th character by pressing the RETURN key.

A line can contain more than one program statement, providing, of course, the entire line length is less than 80 characters. This holds true in program mode and in immediate mode.

ONE-LINE IMMEDIATE MODE PROGRAMS

In immediate mode the entire program must fit on a single line, since the immediate mode program is executed as soon as you press the RETURN key. A single line can contain more than one statement, therefore some interesting immediate mode programs can be created. Let us examine some possibilities.

A question mark appearing at the beginning of a BASIC statement causes the CBM computer to display something; the question mark is an abbreviated form of the PRINT statement. Although the illustrations of immediate mode statements shown earlier all begin with a question mark, this is by no means a requirement for an immediate mode program. Consider the following examples:

```
A=π*2

READY.
?A
 6.28318531
```

There are two immediate mode statements. Each becomes an independent, immediate mode program. When you type in the first statement, $A = \pi \cdot 2$, the result is not displayed, since the statement does not begin with ?; but the calculation is performed nevertheless. The result is displayed by the second immediate statement, ?A.

When statements are grouped together on one line, each is separated from the next with a colon (:). Thus, the two statements:

```
A=π*2
?A
```

can be condensed into one line as follows:

```
A=π*2:?A
```

The two statements have become a single, immediate mode program.

Since a line can have up to 80 characters, you can put a lot of program on one line, and execute it all in immediate mode. For example, consider the following line:

```
FOR I=1 TO 800:?"A";:NEXT:?"PHEW!"
```

Ignoring the meaning of this ''mini-program'' for now, type it in exactly as shown, ending with a RETURN. If you type it in successfully, you will see the letter A displayed across the next 20 lines of a 40-column screen, followed by the message PHEW! on the 21st line:

```
FOR I=1 TO 800:?"A";:NEXT:?"PHEW!"
AAAAAAAAAAAAAAAAAAAAAAAAAAAAAAAAAAAAAAAA
AAAAAAAAAAAAAAAAAAAAAAAAAAAAAAAAAAAAAAAA
AAAAAAAAAAAAAAAAAAAAAAAAAAAAAAAAAAAAAAAA
AAAAAAAAAAAAAAAAAAAAAAAAAAAAAAAAAAAAAAAA
AAAAAAAAAAAAAAAAAAAAAAAAAAAAAAAAAAAAAAAA
AAAAAAAAAAAAAAAAAAAAAAAAAAAAAAAAAAAAAAAA
AAAAAAAAAAAAAAAAAAAAAAAAAAAAAAAAAAAAAAAA
AAAAAAAAAAAAAAAAAAAAAAAAAAAAAAAAAAAAAAAA
AAAAAAAAAAAAAAAAAAAAAAAAAAAAAAAAAAAAAAAA
AAAAAAAAAAAAAAAAAAAAAAAAAAAAAAAAAAAAAAAA
AAAAAAAAAAAAAAAAAAAAAAAAAAAAAAAAAAAAAAAA
AAAAAAAAAAAAAAAAAAAAAAAAAAAAAAAAAAAAAAAA
AAAAAAAAAAAAAAAAAAAAAAAAAAAAAAAAAAAAAAAA
AAAAAAAAAAAAAAAAAAAAAAAAAAAAAAAAAAAAAAAA
AAAAAAAAAAAAAAAAAAAAAAAAAAAAAAAAAAAAAAAA
AAAAAAAAAAAAAAAAAAAAAAAAAAAAAAAAAAAAAAAA
AAAAAAAAAAAAAAAAAAAAAAAAAAAAAAAAAAAAAAAA
AAAAAAAAAAAAAAAAAAAAAAAAAAAAAAAAAAAAAAAA
AAAAAAAAAAAAAAAAAAAAAAAAAAAAAAAAAAAAAAAA
AAAAAAAAAAAAAAAAAAAAAAAAAAAAAAAAAAAAAAAA
PHEW!

READY.
*
```

The program line is conveniently left at the top of the screen. This is because the program displays just enough lines to scroll the program line to the top of a 40-column screen, but not off it.

The letter A will be displayed across 10 lines of an 80-column screen, with the program above the top line of A's.

Re-executing in Immediate Mode

When the one-line program described above completes execution in immediate mode, the READY message is displayed and the cursor is left at the beginning of the bottom display line.

An important feature of CBM BASIC is that **anything displayed on the screen is "live." You can edit any line on the screen and re-execute the edited statements,** providing they are still displayed.

Use CURSOR UP or, more conveniently, press the HOME key to move the cursor up to the F in FOR. Move the cursor right 15 positions to the A. Press a graphic key, say the DIAGONAL QUARTER-BLOCK SOLID (shift of ? key). Press RETURN. The new symbol now overwrites and replaces all the A's across the 20-row display. On completion, the cursor again rests at the beginning of the bottom line.

```
FOR I=1 TO 800:?""; :NEXT:?"PHEW!"
```

PHEW!

READY.
※

Modifying a Program

Before trying any more characters, make one editing modification to the line to make changing characters easier. The new line, with the display character changed to a W, will look like this:

```
C$="W":FOR I=1 TO 800:?C$; :NEXT:?"PHEW!"
```

To modify the current line, perform the following steps:

1. Home the cursor so it is blinking at the F in FOR (※ indicates position of cursor).

   ```
   FOR I=1 TO 800:?""; :NEXT:?"PHEW!"
   ```

2. Press the INSERT key seven times.

   ```
         FOR I=1 TO 800:?""; :NEXT:?"PHEW!"
   ```

3. Type in the seven characters *C$="W":*

   ```
   C$="W":FOR I=1 TO 800:?""; :NEXT:?"PHEW!"
   ```

4. CURSOR RIGHT 14 times to the first quotation mark.

   ```
   C$="W":FOR I=1 TO 800:?""; :NEXT:?"PHEW!"
   ```

5. Type in the two characters *C$*

   ```
   C$="W":FOR I=1 TO 800:?C$"; :NEXT:?"PHEW!"
   ```

6. Remove the other quotation mark by pressing one CURSOR RIGHT:

   ```
   C$="W":FOR I=1 TO 800:?C$"; :NEXT:?"PHEW!"
   ```

   Followed by one DELETE:

   ```
   C$="W":FOR I=1 TO 800:?C$; :NEXT:?"PHEW!"
   ```

The changes have all been made; press RETURN to print the new character. Now you can HOME the cursor, then move it right just four positions to change the display character. Display any other characters you want. The graphics are especially interesting.

SPACES ARE NOT NEEDED

Are you struggling with the question of where to put spaces in the line and where not to? Don't worry. **CBM BASIC interprets a line by the elements in it. Spaces, or blanks, are irrelevant.** For example, the line:

```
120 FOR I=1 TO 210
```
could read:
```
120 FOR I=1 TO210
```
or:
```
120 FORI=1TO210
```

You can put extra spaces anywhere, except within reserved words or other BASIC statements. In BASIC 3.0, GOTO may be written as either GOTO or GO TO, but in BASIC 4.0, it must be entered as one word. The only place you must put spaces is within quotation marks, where you want spaces to be part of the text string. Blanks in a statement improve readability of the program; use them for this purpose.

ELEMENTS OF A
PROGRAMMING LANGUAGE

Program statements must be written following a well defined set of rules. These rules, taken together, are referred to as "syntax."

There are many different sets of rules, or syntax, that define the way in which program statements are written. Each different set of rules applies to a different programming language. **CBM computers use** just one programming language; it is called **BASIC.** All of the syntax rules described in this book apply only to CBM BASIC.

Programming languages are as varied as spoken languages. In addition to BASIC, other common programming languages are PASCAL, FORTRAN, COBOL, APL, PL/M, PL-1, and FORTH. Uncommon program languages number in the hundreds.

Unfortunately, programming languages, like spoken languages, have dialects. **A BASIC program written for your CBM computer will not run on any other computer,** even if the other computer also claims to be programmable in BASIC. Dialects manifest themselves as minor variations in the language syntax used by one computer as compared to another. However, having learned how to program your CBM computer in BASIC, you will have little trouble learning any other computer's BASIC.

Some programming language syntax rules are obvious. The addition and subtraction examples at the beginning of this chapter use obvious syntax. You do not have to be a programmer to understand these two statements. But most syntax rules are utterly arbitrary; they are meaningless unless you have learned the syntax. You should not try to seek justification for syntax rules; usually there is none. For example, why use "*" to represent multiplication? One would normally use a "×" sign for multiplication; but the computer would have no way of differentiating between the use of the "×" sign to represent multiplication, or to represent the letter "x". Therefore nearly all computer languages have opted for the asterisk (∗) to represent multiplication. Division is universally represented by the "/" sign. There is no real justification for this selection; the standard division sign (÷) is not present on computer or typewriter keyboards, so some other character must be selected.

BASIC statement syntax deals separately with line numbers, data, and instructions to the computer. We will describe each in turn.

LINE NUMBERS

As we have already stated, in program mode **every line of a BASIC program must have a unique line number.** Moreover, the first line of the BASIC program must have the smallest line number, while the last line of the BASIC program must have the largest line number. In between, line numbers must be in ascending order. The CBM computer forces this upon you: **irrespective of where you enter a line on the display, the CBM computer will move it to its proper sequential position.** Consider an existing program with the following line numbers:

```
120
130
140
150
160
170
180
190
```

If you enter a new statement with line number 165, then the new statement initially appears below the existing program, but the CBM computer will automatically insert this statement between line numbers 160 and 170. This may be illustrated as follows:

Displayed line numbers when you entered line 165	Lines stored and re-displayed thus
120	120
130	130
140	140
150	150
160	160
170	165
180	170
190	180
	190
165	

If the line number for a new statement duplicates an existing line number, then the old statement will be replaced.

CBM BASIC allows line numbers to range between 0 and 63999. The CBM computer interprets digits appearing at the beginning of any line as the line number. If more than five digits appear at the beginning of the line then an error is flagged: it is referred to as a syntax error, since you have violated the syntax rules for CBM BASIC.

All BASIC dialects require line numbers to be assigned in ascending order as described above. However, the largest allowed line number varies from one dialect of BASIC to the next.

Computer languages other than BASIC do not require every line to begin with a line number, nor do they require line numbers, where present, to have any particular order.

You use line numbers as addresses, identifying locations within a program. This is an important concept, since every program will contain two types of statements:

1. Statements which create or modify data, and

2. Statements which control the sequence in which operations are performed.

The idea that operations specified by a program must be performed in some well defined sequence is a simple enough concept. Normally program execution begins with the first statement in the program, and continues sequentially. This may be illustrated as follows:

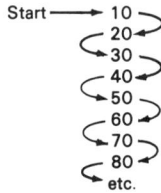

```
Start ──────► 10 ─┐
             ┌ 20 ◄┘
             └►30 ─┐
             ┌ 40 ◄┘
             └►50 ─┐
             ┌ 60 ◄┘
             └►70 ─┐
             ┌ 80 ◄┘
             └► etc.
```

But we will soon discover that most programs contain some non-sequential execution sequences. That is when line numbers become important, because you use the line number to identify a change in execution sequence. This may be illustrated as follows:

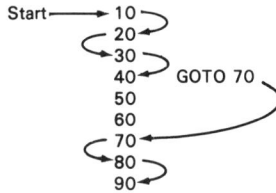

```
Start ──────► 10 ─┐
             ┌ 20 ◄┘
             └►30 ─┐
               40 ◄┘  GOTO 70 ─┐
               50               │
               60               │
             ┌ 70 ◄─────────────┘
             └►80 ─┐
               90 ◄┘
```

DATA

The statement (or statements) following a line number specify operations that the computer is to perform, as well as data that must be used while performing these operations. We will now describe the types of data you may encounter in a CBM BASIC program.

There are two kinds of numbers that can be stored in CBM computers: floating point numbers (also called real numbers) and integers.

Floating Point Numbers

Floating point is the standard number representation used by CBM computers. All arithmetic is done using floating point numbers. **A floating point number can be a whole number, or a fractional number preceded by a decimal point.** The number can be negative (−) or positive (+). If the number has no sign it is assumed to be positive. Here are some examples of floating point numbers that are equivalent to integers:

```
5
-15
65000
161
0
```

Here are examples of floating point numbers that include a decimal point:

```
0.5
0.0165432
-0.0000009
1.6
24.0055
-64.2
3.1416
```

Note that if you put commas in a number, you will get a SYNTAX ERROR message. For example, use 65000, not 65,000.

Roundoff

Numbers always have at least eight digits of precision; they can have up to nine, depending on the number. CBM BASIC rounds off additional significant digits. Usually it rounds up when the next digit is five or more, and it rounds down when the next digit is four or less, but there are some roundoff quirks.

Here are some examples:

Scientific Notation

Large floating point numbers are represented using scientific notation. **CBM BASIC automatically converts numbers less than .01 or greater than 10^8 in magnitude to scientific notation.** Here are some examples:

```
READY.
?1111111114
1.11111111E+09

READY.
?1111111115
1.11111112E+09
```

A number in scientific notation has the form:

numberE+ee

where:

number	is an integer, fraction, or combination, as illustrated above. The "number" portion contains the number's significant digits; it is called the "coefficient." If no decimal point appears, it is assumed to be to the right of the coefficient.
E	is always the letter E. It substitutes for the word "exponent."
+	is an optional plus sign or minus sign.
ee	is a one-digit or two-digit exponent. The exponent specifies the magnitude of the number, that is, the number of places to the right (positive exponent) or to the left (negative exponent) that the decimal point must be moved to give the true decimal point location.

Here are some examples:

Scientific Notation	Standard Notation
2E1	20
10.5E+4	105000
66E+2	6600
66E−2	0.66
−66E−2	−0.66
1E−10	0.0000000001
94E20	9400000000000000000000

Scientific notation is a convenient way of expressing very large or very small numbers. CBM BASIC prints numbers ranging between 0.01 and 999,999,999 using standard notation; but numbers outside of this range are printed using scientific notation. Here are some examples:

```
?.009
 9E-03

READY.
?.01
 .01

READY.
?999999998.9
 999999999

READY.
?999999999.6
 1E+09
```

Even using scientific notation there is a limit to the size of a number that CBM BASIC can handle. The limits are:

Largest floating point number: +1.70141183E+38
Smallest floating point number: +2.93873588E−39

Any number of larger magnitude will give an overflow error. Here are some examples of overflow error:

```
?1.70141183E+38    ⎫
 1.70141183E+38    ⎪
                   ⎬ No Overflow error
READY.             ⎪
?-1.70141183E+38   ⎪
-1.70141183E+38    ⎭

READY.             ⎫
?1.70141184E+38    ⎪
                   ⎬ Overflow error
?OVERFLOW ERROR    ⎪
READY.             ⎪
?-1.70141184E+38   ⎭

?OVERFLOW ERROR
```

A number that is smaller than the smallest magnitude will yield a zero result. This may be illustrated as follows:

```
?2.93873588E-39    ⎫
 2.93873588E-39    ⎪
                   ⎬ These numbers are OK
READY.             ⎪
?-2.93873588E-39   ⎪
-2.93873588E-39    ⎭

READY.             ⎫
?2.93873587E-39    ⎪
 0                 ⎬ These numbers are too small;
                   ⎪  they are replaced by 0
READY.             ⎪
?-2.93873587E-39   ⎭
 0
```

Integers

An integer is a number that has no fraction or decimal point. The number can be negative (−) or positive (+). An unsigned number is assumed to be positive. Integer numbers must have values in the range −32767 to +32768. The following are examples of integers:

```
0
1
44
32699
-15
```

Any integer can also be represented as a floating point number, since integers are a subset of floating point numbers. **CBM BASIC automatically converts integer numbers to floating point representation before using them in arithmetic.**

Strings

The word "string" is used to describe data that consists of words. This is non-numeric data; it is text.

We have already used strings as messages to be displayed on the CBM computer screen. **A string consists of one or more characters enclosed in double quotation marks.** Here are some examples of strings:

```
"HI!"
"SYNERGY"
"12345"
"$10.44 IS THE AMOUNT"
"22 UNION SQUARE, SAN FRANCISCO, CA"
```

Within a string you can include any alphabetic or numeric characters, special symbols or graphic characters, cursor control characters (CLEAR SCREEN/HOME, CURSOR UP/DOWN, CURSOR LEFT/RIGHT) and the REVERSE ON/OFF key. The only keys that cannot be used within a string are RUN/STOP, RETURN, and INSERT/DELETE.

All characters within the string are displayed as they appear. The cursor control and REVERSE ON/OFF keys, however, normally do not print anything themselves; to show that they are present in a string, certain reverse field symbols are used, as shown in Table 4-1.

Strings are entered as part of a statement. Since a statement must fit within an 80-character line, the longest string you can enter at a keyboard will have less than 80 characters; the statement needs some character positions for the line number, and required statement syntax.

Strings of up to 255 characters can be stored in CBM computer memory. Long strings are generated by concatenating shorter strings. We will describe how this is done later.

Variables

Earlier, when describing immediate mode, we illustrated the two-statement program:

```
A=π*2
?A
```

We rewrote the program using one statement:

```
A=π*2:?A
```

In these programs, A is a variable name.

The concept of a variable is easy to understand. Consider the two statements:

```
100 A=B+C
200 ?A
```

These two statements cause the sum of two numbers to be displayed. But what are the two numbers that get summed? They are whatever B and C represent at the time the statements are executed. In the following example:

```
90 B=4.65
95 C=3.72
100 A=B+C
200 ?A
```

B is assigned the value 4.65, while C is assigned the value 3.72. Therefore A equals 8.37.

Table 4-1. Special String Symbols

Function	Key	String Symbol*
Reverse On	OFF RVS ON	◨ (Reverse R)
Reverse Off	Shifted OFF RVS ON	▦ (Reverse Shifted R)
Home Cursor	CLR SCREEN HOME	◙ (Reverse S)
Clear Screen	Shifted CLR SCREEN HOME	⊓ (Reverse Shifted S)
Cursor Down	⬆ CURSOR ⬇	◙ (Reverse Q)
Cursor Up	Shifted ⬆ CURSOR ⬇	⊓ (Reverse Shifted Q)
Cursor Right	⬅ CURSOR ➡	▮▮ (Reverse])
Cursor Left	Shifted ⬅ CURSOR ➡	▮▮ (Reverse Shifted])

* The graphic symbol shown in this column may vary from one CBM computer
to the next, depending on the computer's keyboard options. But the key
description is accurate in every case.

Variable names can be used to represent string data or numeric data.

If you have studied elementary algebra, you will have no trouble understanding
the concept of variables and variable names. If you have never studied algebra, then
think of a variable name as a name which is assigned to a mail box. Anything which is
placed in the mail box becomes the value associated with the mail box name.

Variable Names

**A variable name can have one, two or three characters. The following character
options are allowed:**

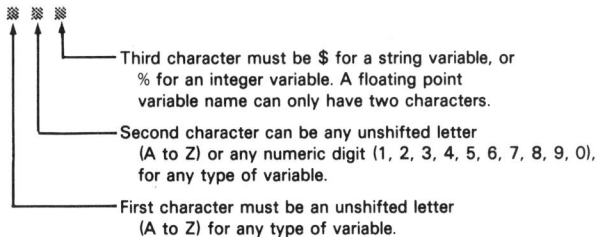

▨ ▨ ▨

Third character must be $ for a string variable, or
% for an integer variable. A floating point
variable name can only have two characters.

Second character can be any unshifted letter
(A to Z) or any numeric digit (1, 2, 3, 4, 5, 6, 7, 8, 9, 0),
for any type of variable.

First character must be an unshifted letter
(A to Z) for any type of variable.

**Thus the last character of the variable name tells CBM BASIC which type of
data the variable represents.**

Note that unshifted letters of the alphabet are used for the first and second label character. Depending on the model of CBM computer, the unshifted letter may be upper case or lower case. But in either case it is the letter displayed when the SHIFT key is not being depressed.

Floating point variables are the ones most frequently used in CBM BASIC. Here are some examples of floating point variable names:

```
A
B
C
A1
AA
Z5
```

Here are some examples of integer variable names:

```
A%
B%
C%
A1%
MN%
X4%
```

Remember, **floating point variables can have values that are equivalent to integers.** Here are examples of string variable names:

```
A$
M$
MN$
M1$
ZX$
F6$
```

Variable names can have more than two alphanumeric characters, but only the first two characters count. Therefore BANANA and BANDAGE are interpreted as the same name, since both begin with BA. CBM BASIC allows variable names to have up to 255 characters. Here are some examples of variable names with more than two characters:

MAGIC$	*interpreted as*	MA$
N123456789	*interpreted as*	N1
MMM$	*interpreted as*	MM$
ABCDEF%	*interpreted as*	AB%
CALENDAR	*interpreted as*	CA

If you use variable names with more than two characters, keep the following points in mind:

1. Only the first two characters, plus the identifier symbol ($ or %) are significant. Do not use extended names like LOOP1 and LOOP2; these are interpreted as the same variable: LO.

2. CBM BASIC has a number of "reserved words," which have special meaning within a BASIC statement. No variable name can contain a reserved word embedded anywhere in the name. Reserved words are listed in Table 4-4.

3. Additional characters need extra memory space, which you might need for longer programs. But the advantage of using longer variable names is that they make programs easier to read. PARTNO, for example, is more meaningful than PA as a variable name describing part numbers in an inventory program.

OPERATORS

The BASIC statement:

```
100 ?10.2+4.7
```

tells the CBM computer to add 10.2 and 4.7, and then display the sum. The statement:

```
250 C=A+B
```

tells the CBM computer to add the two floating point numbers represented by the variable names A and B, and to assign the sum to the floating point number represented by the variable name C.

The plus sign (+) specifies addition. Standard computer jargon refers to the plus sign an "operator." + is an arithmetic operator, because it specifies addition, which is an arithmetic operation.

Arithmetic operators are easy enough to understand; we all learn to add, subtract, multiply, and divide in early childhood. But there are two other types of operators: relational operators and Boolean operators. These are also easily understood, but they take a little more explanation, since they do not reflect day to day experiences.

Table 4-2 summarizes the BASIC operators. We will examine each group of operators in turn, beginning with arithmetic operators.

Table 4-2. Operators

	Precedence	Operator	Meaning
	High 9	( )	Parentheses denote order of evaluation
Arithmetic Operators	8 7 6 6 5 5	↑ — • / + —	Exponentiation Unary Minus Multiplication Division Addition Subtraction
Relational Operators	4 4 4 4 4 4	= < > < > < = or = < > = or = >	Equal Not equal Less than Greater than Less than or Equal Greater than or Equal
Boolean Operators	3 2 1 Low	NOT AND OR	Logical complement Logical AND Logical OR

Arithmetic Operators

An arithmetic operator specifies addition, subtraction, multiplication, division, or exponentiation. Arithmetic operations are performed using floating point numbers. Integers are automatically converted to floating point numbers before an arithmetic operation is performed; the result is automatically converted back to an integer, if an integer variable represents the result.

The data operated on by any operator is referred to as an "operand." Arithmetic operators each require two operands, which may be numbers and/or numeric variables.

Addition (+). The plus sign specifies that the data (or operand) on the left of the + sign must be added to the data (or operand) on the right. For numeric quantities this is straightforward addition. Examples:

```
2+2
A+B+C
X%+1
BR+10E-2
```

The plus sign (+) is also used to "add" strings; but rather than adding their values, they are joined together, or concatenated, to form one longer string. The difference between numeric addition and string concatenation can be visualized as follows:

```
Addition of Numbers:
   num1+num2=num3

Addition of Strings:
   string1+string2=string1string2
```

Via concatenation, strings containing up to 255 characters can be developed. Examples:

"FOR"+"WARD"	results in "FORWARD"
"HI"+" "+"THERE"	results in "HI THERE"
A$+B$	results in concatenation of the two strings represented by string variable labels A$ and B$
"1" + CH$+E$	results in the character "1," followed by concatenation of the two strings represented by string variable labels CH$ and E$

In the illustrations above, if A$ is set equal to "FOR" and B$ is set equal to "WARD," then A$ + B$ would generate the same results as "FOR" + "WARD."

Subtraction (−). The minus sign specifies that the data (or operand) to the right of the minus sign is to be subtracted from the data (or operand) to the left of the minus sign. Examples:

4−1	results in 3
100−64	results in 36
A−B	results in the variable represented by label B being subtracted from the variable represented by label A
55−142	results in −87

In the example above, if A is assigned the value 100, and B is assigned the value 64, then the second and third examples are identical.

The minus operator is also used to identify a negative number. Examples:

```
-5
-9E4
-B
4--2      Note that 4--2
          is the same as 4+2
```

Multiplication (*). An asterisk specifies that the data (or operand) on the right of the asterisk is multiplied by the data (or operand) on the left of the asterisk. Examples:

```
100•2     results in 200
50•0      results in 0
A•X1      results in multiplication of
          two floating point numbers
          represented by floating point
          variables labeled A and X1
R%•14     results in an integer
          represented by integer variable
          label R% being multiplied by 14
```

In the examples above, if variable A is assigned the value 4.2, and variable X1 is assigned the value 9.63, then the illustrated multiplication would generate 40.446. A and X1 could hold integer values 100 and 2 to duplicate the first example; however the two numbers would be held in the floating point format as 100.0 and 2.0, since A and X1 are floating point variables. In order to multiply 100 by 2, representing these numbers as integers, the example would have to be A%*X1%.

Division (/). The slash specifies that the data (or operand) on the left of the slash is to be divided by the data (or operand) on the right of the slash. Examples:

```
10/2      results in 5
6400/4    results in 1600
A/B       results in the floating point
          number assigned to variable
          A being divided by
          the floating point number
          assigned to variable B
4E2/XR    results in 400 being divided
          by the floating point number
          represented by label XR
```

The third example, A/B, can duplicate the first or second example, even though A and B represent floating point numbers. But the integer numbers would be held in floating point form. A%/B% could exactly duplicate either of the first two examples, however.

Exponentiation (↑). The up arrow specifies that the data (or operand) on the left of the up arrow is raised to the power specified by the data (or operand) on the right of the up arrow. If the data (or operand) on the right is 2, the number on the left is squared; if the data (or operand) on the right is 3, the number on the left is cubed, etc. The exponent can be any number, variable, or expression, as long as the exponentiation yields a number in the allowed floating point range. Examples:

2↑2	results in 4
12↑2	results in 144
1↑3	results in 1
A↑5	results in the floating point number assigned to variable A being raised to the 5th power
2↑6.4	results in 84.4485064
NM↑−10	results in the floating point number assigned to variable NM being raised to the negative 10th power
14↑F	results in 14 being raised to the power specified by floating point variable F

Order of Evaluation

An expression may have multiple arithmetic operations, as in the following statement:

A+C·10/2↑2

When this occurs, there is a fixed sequence in which operations are processed. **First comes exponentiation (↑), followed by sign evaluation, followed by multiplication and division (*/), followed by addition and subtraction (+ −).** Operations of the same hierarchy are evaluated from left to right. **This order of operation can be overridden by the use of parentheses. Any operation within parentheses is performed first.** Examples:

4+1·2	results in 6
(4+1)·2	results in 10
100·4/2−1	results in 199
100·(4/2−1)	results in 100
100·(4/(2−1))	results in 400

When parentheses are present, CBM BASIC evaluates the innermost set first, then the next innermost, etc. Parentheses can be nested to any level, and may be used freely to clarify the order of operations being performed in an expression.

Relational Operators

Relational operators represent the conditions: greater than (>), less than (<), equal (=), not equal (<>), greater than or equal (>=), and less than or equal (<=).

1=5−4	results in true (−1)
14>66	results in false (0)
15>=15	results in true (−1)
A<>B	the result will depend on the values assigned to floating point variables A and B

CBM BASIC arbitrarily assigns a value of 0 to a "false" condition; a value of -1 is assigned to a "true" condition. These 0 and -1 values can be used in equations. For example, in the expression $(1=1)*4$, $(1=1)$ is true. True equates to -1, therefore the expression is the same as $(-1)*4$, which results in -4. You can include any relational operators within a CBM BASIC expression. Here are some more examples:

25+(14>66)	is the same as	25+0
(A+(1=5−4))•(15>=15)	is the same as	(A−1)•(−1)

Relational operators can be used to compare strings. For comparison purposes, the letters of the alphabet have the order $A<B$, $B<C$, $C<D$, etc. Strings are compared one character at a time, starting with the leftmost character. Examples:

"A"<"B"	results in true (−1)
"X"="XX"	results in false (0)
C$=A$+B$	the result will depend
	on the string values assigned
	to the three string variables
	C$, B$, and A$

When operating on strings, as for numbers, CBM BASIC generates a value of -1 if a relational operator specifies a "true" condition; a value of 0 is generated for a "false" condition. Here are some examples:

("JONES">"DOE")+37	is the same as	−1+37
("AAA"<"AA")•(Z9−("OTTER">"AB"))	is the same as	0•(Z9−(−1))

Boolean Operators

Boolean operators give programs the ability to make logical decisions. There are four standard Boolean operators: AND, OR, EXCLUSIVE OR, and NOT. **CBM BASIC supports** three of these operators: **AND, OR, and NOT.**

If you do not understand Boolean operators, then a simple supermarket shopping analogy will serve to illustrate Boolean logic.

Suppose you are shopping for breakfast cereals with two children.

The AND Boolean operator says that a cereal is selected if child A *and* child B select the cereal.

The OR Boolean operator says that a cereal will be selected if either child A *or* child B selects the cereal.

The NOT operator generates an opposite. If child B insists on disagreeing with child A, then child B's decision is always the *not* of child A's decision.

Computers do not work with analogies; they work with numbers. Therefore Boolean logic reduces all variables and results to 0 or 1. **Table 4-3 summarizes the way in which Boolean operators handle numbers. This table is referred to as a "truth table."**

Boolean operators are used to control program execution logic; here are some examples:

```
IF A=100 AND B=100 GOTO 10
   If both A and B are equal to 100, branch to line 10

IF X < Y AND B >=44 THEN F=0
   If X is less than Y, and B is greater than or equal to 44,
   then set F equal to 0

IF A=100 OR B=100 GOTO 20
   If either A or B has a value of 100, branch to line 20.

IF X<Y OR B>=44 THEN F=0
   F is set to 0 if X is less than Y, or B is greater than 43

IF A=1 AND B=2 OR C=3 GOTO 30
   Take the branch if both A=1 and B=2; also take
   the branch if C=3
```

A single operand can be tested for "true" or "false." An operand appearing alone has an implied "$<>0$" following it. Any non-zero value is considered true; a zero value is considered false.

```
IF A THEN B=2
IF A<>0 THEN B=2
   The above two statements are equivalent

IF NOT B GOTO 100
   Branch if B is false, i.e., equal to zero. This is
      probably better written as:
      IF B=0 GOTO 100
```

All Boolean operations use integer operands. If you perform Boolean operations using floating point numbers, then the numbers are automatically converted to integers; therefore the floating point numbers must fall within the allowed range of integer numbers.

You cannot perform Boolean operations using string operands.

If you are a beginning programmer, you are unlikely to use Boolean operators in the manner which we are about to describe. If you find you do not understand the discussion, then skip to the next section.

Table 4-3. Boolean Truth Table

```
The AND operation results in a 1 only if both bits are 1
                    1 AND 1 = 1
                    0 AND 1 = 0
                    1 AND 0 = 0
                    0 AND 0 = 0

The OR operation results in a 1 if either bit is 1
                    1 OR 1 = 1
                    0 OR 1 = 1
                    1 OR 0 = 1
                    0 OR 0 = 0

The NOT operation logically complements each bit
                    NOT 1 = 0
                    NOT 0 = 1
```

Boolean operators operate on integer operands one binary digit at a time. CBM BASIC stores all numbers in binary format, using two's complement notation to represent negative numbers. Therefore we can illustrate an AND operation as follows:

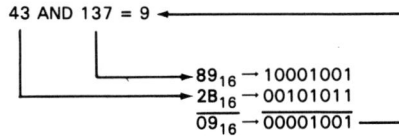

```
43 AND 137 = 9
        ┌──────────────────────────────────┐
        │   ┌──► 89₁₆ → 10001001            │
        └───┼──► 2B₁₆ → 00101011            │
            └──► 09₁₆ → 00001001 ───────────┘
```

Here is an OR operation:

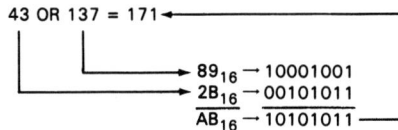

```
43 OR 137 = 171
        ┌──────────────────────────────────┐
        │   ┌──► 89₁₆ → 10001001            │
        └───┼──► 2B₁₆ → 00101011            │
            └──► AB₁₆ → 10101011 ───────────┘
```

Here are two NOT operations:

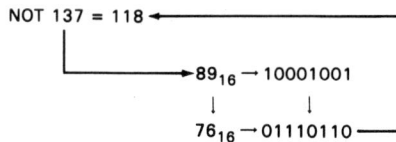

```
NOT 43 = 212
        ┌──────────────────────────────────┐
        └──► 2B₁₆ → 00101011                │
                  ↓        ↓                │
             D4₁₆ → 11010100 ───────────────┘
```

```
NOT 137 = 118
        ┌──────────────────────────────────┐
        └──► 89₁₆ → 10001001                │
                  ↓        ↓                │
             76₁₆ → 01110110 ───────────────┘
```

Boolean operations of this type are used in engineering applications.*

If operands are not integers, they are converted to integer form; the Boolean operation is performed, and the result is returned as a 0 or 1.

If a Boolean operator has relational operands, then the relational operand is evaluated to -1 or 0 before the Boolean operation is performed. Thus the operation:

$$A=1 \text{ OR } C<2$$

is equivalent to:

$$\left\{ \begin{matrix} -1 \\ \text{or} \\ 0 \end{matrix} \right\} \text{ OR } \left\{ \begin{matrix} -1 \\ \text{or} \\ 0 \end{matrix} \right\}$$

Consider this more complex operation:

$$\text{IF } A=B \text{ AND } C<D \text{ GOTO } 40$$

First the relational expressions are evaluated. Assume that the first expression is true and the second one is false. In effect, the following Boolean expression is evaluated as follows:

$$\text{IF } -1 \text{ AND } 0 \text{ GOTO } 40$$

---

*If you wish to learn more about binary arithmetic and Boolean operations, see *An Introduction to Microcomputers: Volume 0 — The Beginners Book* by A. Osborne, Osborne/McGraw-Hill, 1977.

Performing the AND yields a 0 result:

```
IF 0 GOTO 40
```

Recall that a single term has an implied "$<>0$" following it. The expression therefore becomes:

```
IF 0 <> GOTO 40
```

Thus, the branch is not taken.

In contrast, a Boolean operation performed on two variables may yield any integer number:

```
IF A% AND B% GOTO 40
```

Assume that A%=255 and B%=240. The Boolean operation 255 AND 240 yields 240. The statement, therefore, is equivalent to:

```
IF 240 GOTO 40
```

or, with the "$<>0$":

```
IF 240 <> 0 GOTO 40
```

Therefore the branch will be taken.

Now compare the two assignment statements:

```
A = A AND 10
A = A <10
```

In the first example, the current value of A is logically ANDed with 10 and the result becomes the new value of A. A must be in the integer range -32767 to $+32768$. In the second example, the relational expression $A<10$ is evaluated to -1 or 0, so A must end up with a value of -1 or 0.

ARRAYS

Arrays are used frequently, in every type of computer program. If you do not understand arrays, then you must learn about them. The information that follows will be very important to your programming efforts.

Conceptually, arrays are very simple. When you have two or more related data items, instead of giving each data item a separate variable name, you give the collection of related data items a single variable name. Then you select individual items using a position number, which in computer jargon is referred to as a subscript, an index, or a dimension.

A grocery list, for example, may have six items from the meat and poultry department, four fruit and vegetable items, three dairy products, etc. These three groups of items could each be represented by a single variable name as follows:

```
MP$(0) = "CHOPPED SIRLOIN"      FV$(0) = "ORANGES"
MP$(1) = "CHUCK STEAK"          FV$(1) = "APPLES"
MP$(2) = "NEW YORK STEAK"       FV$(2) = "BEANS"
MP$(3) = "CHICKEN"              FV$(3) = "CARROTS"
MP$(4) = "SALAMI"
MP$(5) = "SAUSAGES"             DP$(0) = "MILK"
                               DP$(1) = "CREAM"
                               DP$(2) = "COTTAGE CHEESE"
```

MP$ is a single variable name that identifies all meat and poultry products.
FV$ identifies fruits and vegetables, while DP$ identifies dairy products.

A subscript (index or dimension) follows each variable name. Thus a specific data item is identified by a variable name and an index.

We could take the array concept one step further, specifying a single variable name for the entire grocery list, using two indexes. The first index (or dimension) specifies the product type and the second index (or dimension) specifies the item within the product type. This is one way in which a single grocery list variable array with two subscripts could replace the three arrays with single subscripts illustrated above:

GL\$(0,0) = MP\$(0)	GL\$(1,0) = FV\$(0)	GL\$(2,0) = DP\$(0)
GL\$(0,1) = MP\$(1)	GL\$(1,1) = FV\$(1)	GL\$(2,1) = DP\$(1)
GL\$(0,2) = MP\$(2)	GL\$(1,2) = FV\$(2)	GL\$(2,2) = DP\$(2)
GL\$(0,3) = MP\$(3)	GL\$(1,3) = FV\$(3)	
GL\$(0,4) = MP\$(4)		
GL\$(0,5) = MP\$(5)		

Arrays can represent integer variables, floating point variables, or string variables; however, a single array variable can only represent one data type. In other words, a single variable cannot mix integer and floating point numbers. One or the other can be present, but not both.

Arrays are a useful shorthand means of describing a large number of related variables. Consider, for example, a table of numbers containing ten rows of numbers, with twenty numbers in each row. There are 200 numbers in the table. How would you like it if you had to assign a unique name to each of the 200 numbers? It would be far simpler to give the entire table one name, and identify individual numbers within the table by their table location. That is precisely what an array does for you.

Arrays can have one or more dimensions. An array with a single dimension is equivalent to a table with just one row of numbers. The dimension identifies a number within the single row. (Engineers use the word "vector" to describe an array with a single dimension.) An array with two dimensions yields an ordinary table with rows and columns: one dimension identifies the row, the other dimension identifies the column. An array with three dimensions yields a "cube" of numbers, or perhaps a stack of tables. Four or more dimensions yield an array that is hard to visualize, but mathematically no more complex than a smaller-dimensioned array.

Let us examine arrays in detail.

A single-dimensional array element has the form:

    name(i)

where:

name	is the variable name for the array. Any type of variable name may be used.
(i)	is the array index to that element. i must start at 0.

A single-dimensional array called A, having five elements, can be visualized as follows:

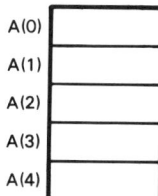

A(0)	
A(1)	
A(2)	
A(3)	
A(4)	

The number of elements in the array is equal to the highest index number, plus 1. This takes array elements 0 into account.

A two-dimensional array element has the form:

name(i,j)

where:

name	is the variable name of the array
i	is the column index
j	is the row index

A two-dimensional array called A\$, having three column elements and two row elements, might be visualized as follows:

A\$(0,0)			A\$(0,1)
A\$(1,0)			A\$(1,1)
A\$(2,0)			A\$(2,1)

The size of the array is the product of the highest row dimension plus 1, multiplied by the highest column dimension plus 1. For the array above, it is $3 \times 2 = 6$ elements.

Additional dimensions can be added to the array:

name (i,j,k,...)

Arrays of up to eleven elements (index 0 to 10 for a single dimensioned array) may be used routinely in CBM BASIC. Arrays containing more than eleven elements need to be "declared" in a Dimension statement. Dimension statements are described later in this chapter. An array (always with subscripts) and a single variable of the same name are treated as separate items by CBM BASIC.

BASIC COMMANDS

In Chapters 2 and 3 we describe a number of commands which you enter via the keyboard in order to control CBM computer operations. RUN is one such command. **Commands can all be executed as BASIC statements.**

You are unlikely to execute commands out of BASIC statements when you first start writing programs.

When you start writing very large programs you will run out of memory space. Then you must break a program up into a number of smaller modules and execute them one at a time. Each module must load the next module in turn. This is described in Chapter 6.

Reserved Words

All of the character combinations that define a BASIC statement's operations, and all functions, are called "reserved words." **Table 4-4 lists all CBM BASIC reserved words.** You will have encountered many of these reserved words in this chapter, but others are not described until Chapter 6.

Table 4-4. Reserved Words

WORD	Alternate Character Set	Standard Character Set	WORD	Alternate Character Set	Standard Character Set	WORD	Alternate Character Set	Standard Character Set	WORD	Alternate Character Set	Standard Character Set
ABS	aB	A I	DS$*	ds≢	DS≢	NEW	new	NEW	SCRATCH*	sC	S−
AND	aN	A⁄	DSAVE*	dS	D♥	NEXT	nE	N⌐	SGN	sG	SI
APPEND*	aP	A⅂	END	eN	E⁄	NOT	nO	N⌐	SIN	sI	S⟍
ASC	aS	A♥	EXP	eX	E↑	ON	on	ON	SPC(	sP	S⌐
ATN	aT	A I	FN	fn	FN	OPEN	oP	O⅂	SQR	sQ	S♥
BACKUP*	bA	B↑	FOR	fO	F⌐	OR	or	OR	ST	st	ST
CHR$	cH	C I	FROM	fR	F−	PEEK	⊳E	P−	STATUS	status	STATUS
CLOSE	c lO	CL⌐	GET	⅊E	G−	POKE	⊳O	P⌐	STEP	stE	ST−
CLR	cL	CL	GET #	⅊et#	GET#	POS	⊳os	POS	STOP	sT	SI
CMD	cM	C⟍	GOTO	⅊O	G⌐	PRINT	?	?	STR$	str$	STR≢
COLLECT*	coL	COL	GOSUB	⅊oS	GO♥	PRINT #	⊳R	P−	SYS	sY	S I
CONCAT*	conC	CON−	HEADER*	hE	H−	READ	rE	R−	TAB(	tA	T↑
CONT	cO	C⌐	IF	i f	IF	READ #	read#	READ#	TAN	tan	TAN
COPY*	coP	CO⅂	INPUT	input	INPUT	RECORD*	reC	RE−	THEN	tH	T I
COS	cos	COS	INPUT #	iN	I⁄	REM	rem	REM	TI	ti	TI
DATA	dA	D↑	INT	int	INT	RENAME*	reN	RE⁄	TIME	time	TIME
DCLOSE*	dC	D−	LEFT$	leF	LE−	RESTORE	reS	RE♥	TI$	ti$	TI$
DEF	dE	D⌐	LEN	len	LEN	RETURN	reT	REI	TO	to	TO
DIM	dI	D⟍	LET	lE	L−	RIGHT$	rI	R⟍	US	uS	U♥
DIRECTORY*	diR	DI−	LIST	lI	L⟍	RND	rN	R⁄	VAL	vA	V↑
DLOAD*	dL	DL	LOAD	lO	L⌐	RUN	rU	R⟍	VERIFY	vE	V−
DOPEN*	dO	D⌐	LOG	log	LOG	SAVE	sA	S↑	WAIT	wA	W↑
DS*	ds	DS	MID$	mI	M⟍						

* These are reserved words in BASIC versions 4.0 and higher only.

When executing BASIC programs, the CBM computer scans every BASIC statement, seeking out any character strings that constitutes a reserved word. The only exception is text strings enclosed in quotes. This can cause trouble if a reserved word is embedded anywhere within a variable name. The CBM computer is not smart enough to identify a variable name by its location in BASIC statement. **Therefore you should be very careful to keep reserved words out of your variable names;** this is particularly important with the short reserved words that can easily slip into a variable name.

Some reserved words are shown in Table 4-4 with an asterisk. These reserved words apply only to CBM BASIC versions 4.0 and higher. Nevertheless it is a good idea not to use these reserved words in any CBM BASIC program. You never know when you may wish to upgrade a program so that it runs on a newer CBM computer using BASIC 4.0.

BASIC Word Abbreviations

You learned early in this book that the BASIC statement PRINT could always be entered from the keyboard by the abbreviation ?, the question mark character. ? is expanded by the CBM BASIC interpreter to the full word PRINT.

Most BASIC commands, statements, and functions can be abbreviated using the first two characters of the keyword, with the second character entered in shifted mode. With the standard character set, the second character appears as a graphic character. For example, the abbreviation for LIST appears as:

L⟍

or   lI

Where a two-letter abbreviation is ambiguous (does ST mean STEP or STOP?) the two-letter abbreviation is assigned to the most frequently used keyword, and the other word (or words) are either not abbreviated or are abbreviated by the first three characters with the third entered in shifted mode. For STEP/STOP, STOP is abbreviated:

≤T
or ςι

STEP is abbreviated:

≤tE
or ςT⁻

To abbreviate STEP, type unshifted S (capital S), unshifted T (capital T), and shifted E (graphic 3/4 TOP LINE HORIZONTAL).

Following are a few sample input lines showing use of the two- and three-letter abbreviations wherever possible. All the abbreviated words are expanded to the full spelling when you list the programs.

```
ρO 59468,14          (after RETURN) Abbreviation for POKE
10 lE a=10
20 b=a aN 14+eX(2)
30 dI c(5)
40 fO i=0 to 5
50 rE c(i)
60 nE
70 dA 1,6,2,4,10,5,16
80 reS
90 eN
lI                   Abbreviation for LIST
10 let a=10
20 b=a and 14+exp(2)
30 dim c(5)
40 for i=0 to 5
50 read c(i)
60 next
70 data 1,6,2,4,10,5,16
80 restore
90 end
ρO 59468,12          (before RETURN) Abbreviation for POKE
```

After keying RETURN at the last POKE statement line (return to Standard Character Set), you will see the abbreviations show with graphics as the shifted characters, and the expanded listing will display upper case letters.

A list of reserved words is given in Table 4-4. Note that the expansions from abbreviations for the two functions SPC and TAB include the left parenthesis. This means that if you use the abbreviation for either of these, you must not type in the left parentheses. For example:

```
10 ?sP(5)
```

expands to:

```
10 print spc((5)
```
syntax error results from two left parentheses

The correct keyin is:

```
10 ?≤P5)
```

This parenthesis rule applies only to the SPC and TAB functions and is a format inconsistency you will have to watch for when abbreviating these function names. For all other functions, you key in both parentheses. For example:

```
10 ?rN(1)
```

BASIC STATEMENTS

The operation performed by a statement is specified using "reserved words" (see Table 4-4).

Remember, Chapter 8 provides a complete description of every statement recognized by CBM BASIC. This chapter introduces you to programming concepts, stressing the way statements are used. No statement is described in detail in this chapter. Read the statement description given in Chapter 8 if you do not understand how any statement is being used.

REMARKS

It is appropriate that any discussion of BASIC statements begins by describing the only BASIC statement which the computer will ignore: the remark. If the first three characters of a BASIC statement are REM, then the computer ignores the statement entirely. So why include such a statement? The answer is that remarks make your program easier to read.

If you write a short program with five or ten statements, you will probably have little trouble remembering what the program does — unless you leave it around for six months and then try to use it again. If you write a longer program with 100 or 200 statements, then you are quite likely to forget something very important the very next time you use the program. After you have written dozens of programs, you will stand no chance of remembering each program in detail. The solution to this problem is to document your program by including remarks that describe what is going on.

Good programmers use plenty of remarks in all of their programs. In all of this chapter's program examples we will include remarks that describe what is going on, simply to get you into the habit of doing the same thing yourself.

Remark statements have line numbers, like any other statement. A remark statement's line number can be used like any other statement line number.

ASSIGNMENT STATEMENT

Assignment statements let you assign values to variables. You will encounter assignment statements frequently, in every type of BASIC program. Here are some examples of assignment statements:

```
90 REM INITIALIZE VARIABLE X
100 LET X=3.24
```

  In statement 100, floating point variable
    X is assigned the value 3.24

```
150 X=3.24
```

  Equivalent to statement 100 above; the LET
   is optional in all assignment statements

```
215 A$="ALSO RAN"
```

  The string variable **A$** is assigned
   the two text words ALSO RAN

Here are three assignment statements that assign values to array variable DP$(I), which we encountered earlier when describing arrays:

```
200 REM DP$(I) IS THE DAIRY PRODUCTS SHOPPING
    LIST VARIABLE
210 DP$(0)="MILK"
220 DP$(1)="CREAM"
230 DP$(2)="COTTAGE CHEESE"
```

Remember, we can put more than one statement on a single line; therefore the three DP$ assignments could be placed on a single line as follows:

```
200 REM DP$(I) IS THE DAIRY PRODUCTS SHOPPING
    LIST VARIABLE
210 DP$(0)="MILK":DP$(1)="CREAM":DP$(2)=
    "COTTAGE CHEESE"
```

Recall that a colon must separate adjacent statements appearing on the same line.

Assignment statements can include any of the arithmetic or relational operators described earlier in this chapter. Here is an example of such an assignment statement:

```
90 REM THIS IS A DUMB WAY TO ASSIGN A VALUE TO V
100 V=3.24+7.96/8.5
```

This statement assigns the value 4.17647059 to floating point variable V; it is equivalent to these three statements:

```
90 REM X AND Y NEED TO BE INITIALIZED SEPARATELY
    FOR LATER USE
100 X=7.96
110 Y=8.5
120 V=3.24+X/Y
```

which could be written on one line as follows:

```
100 X=7.96:Y=8.5:V=3.24+X/Y
```

Here are assignment statements that perform the Boolean operations given earlier in this chapter:

```
90 REM THESE EXAMPLES WERE DESCRIBED EARLIER IN THE
   CHAPTER
100 A%=43 AND 137
200 B%=43 OR 137
```

The following example shows how a string variable could have its value assigned using string concatenation:

```
100 V$="COTTAGE"
200 W$="CHEESE"
300 DP$(2)=V$+" "+W$
400 REM DP$(2) IS ASSIGNED THE STRING VALUE "COTTAGE CHEESE"
```

DATA and READ Statements

When a number of variables need data assignments, the DATA and READ statements should be used rather than the LET statement. Consider the following example:

```
5 REM INITIALIZE ALL PROGRAM VARIABLES
10 DATA 10,20,-4,16E6
20 READ A,B,C,D
```

The statement on line 10 specifies four numeric data values. These four values are assigned to four floating point variables by the statement on line 20. After statements on lines 10 and 20 have been executed, $A = 10$, $B = 20$, $C = -4$ and $D = 16 \times 10^6$.

If you have one or more DATA statements in your program, then you can visualize them as building a "column" of numbers. For example, a DATA statement that contains a list of 10 numbers would build a ten-entry column. Two DATA statements each specifying five of the ten data entries would build exactly the same column. This may be illustrated as follows:

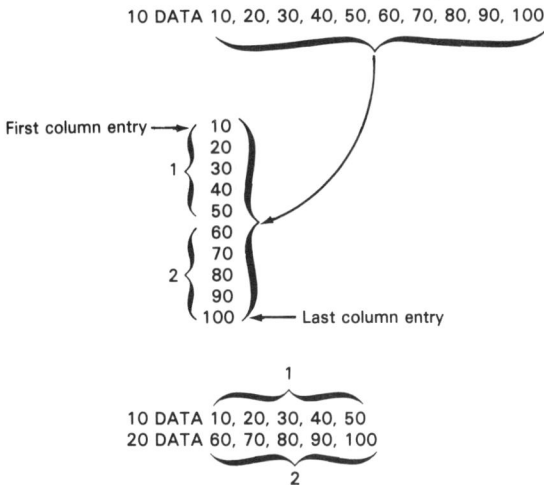

The first READ statement in the program starts at the first column entry and takes numbers sequentially, assigning them to variables named in the READ statement. The second (and subsequent) READ statements take values from the column, starting at the point where the previous READ statement left off. This may be illustrated as follows:

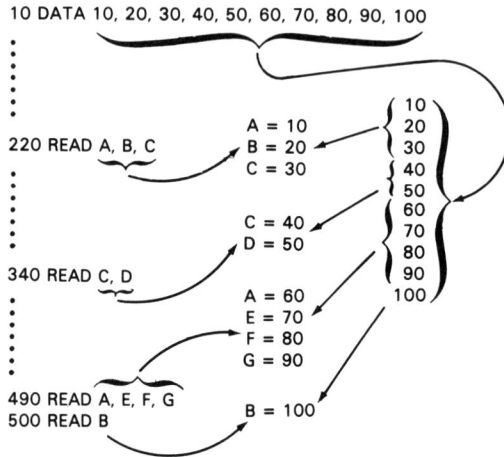

RESTORE Statement

You can at any time send the pointer back to the beginning of the numeric column by executing a RESTORE statement. Here is an example of the use of RESTORE:

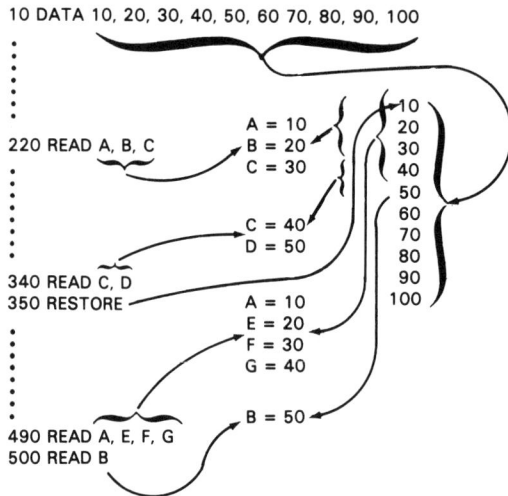

DIMENSION STATEMENT

CBM BASIC normally assumes an array variable has a single dimension, with index values of 0 through 10. This generates an eleven-element array. **If you want a single dimension with more, or less, than eleven elements, then you must include the array variable in a dimension statement. You must include the array in a dimension statement if it has two or more dimensions, whatever number of elements the array may have.** The following example provides dimensions for the three single-indexed variables MP$, FV$, and DP$. We used these variables in our earlier discussion of arrays.

```
DIM MP$(5),FV$(3),DP$(2)
```

The double-dimension grocery list variable would be dimensioned as follows:

```
DIM GL$(3,5)
```

A dimension statement can provide dimensions for any number of variables, providing the statement fits within an 80-column line.

The number (or numbers) following a variable name in a DIM statement is equal to the largest index value that can occur in that particular index position. But remember indexes begin at 0. Therefore MP$(5) dimensions the variable MP$ to have six values, not five, since indexes 0, 1, 2, 3, 4, and 5 will be allowed. GL$ (3,5), likewise, specifies a double-dimension variable with 24 entries, since the first dimension can have values 0, 1, 2, and 3, while the second dimension can have values 0 through 5.

Once you have specified an array variable in a dimension statement, you must subsequently reference the variable with the specified number of indexes; each index must have a value between 0 and the number specified in the dimension statement. If any of these syntax rules are broken a syntax error will be reported.

BRANCH STATEMENTS

Statements within a BASIC program are normally executed in ascending order of line numbers. This execution sequence was explained earlier in this chapter when we described line numbers. Branch statements change this execution sequence.

GOTO Statement

GOTO is the simplest branch statement; it **allows you to specify the statement which will be executed next.** Consider the following example:

```
20 A=4.37
30 GOTO 100
40
50
60
70
80
90
100
110
 .
 .
```

The statement on line 20 is an assignment statement; it assigns a value to floating point variable A. The next statement is a GOTO; it specifies that program execution must branch to line 100. Therefore the instruction execution sequence surrounding this part of the program will be line 20, then line 30, then line 100.

Of course, some other statement must branch back to line 40, otherwise the statement on line 40 would never be executed by program logic as illustrated above.

You can branch to any line number, even if the line has nothing but a remark on it. However, the computer ignores the remark, so the effect is the same as branching to the next line. For example, consider the following branch:

```
20 A=4.37
30 GOTO 70
40
50
60
70 REM THERE IS A REMARK, AND NOTHING ELSE ON THIS LINE
80
90
 .
 .
```

Program execution branches from line 30 to line 70; there is nothing but a remark on line 70, therefore the computer moves on to line 80, executing statements on this line. Therefore, even though you can branch to a remark, you might as well branch to the next line. This may be illustrated as follows:

```
20 A=4.37
30 GOTO 80
40
50
60
70 REM THERE IS A REMARK, AND NOTHING ELSE ON THIS LINE
80
90
 .
 .
```

Computed GOTO Statement

There is also a computed GOTO statement that lets program logic branch to one of two or more different line numbers, depending on the current value of a variable. Consider the following illustration:

```
          10
A% = 1    20
          30 A%=B%-2
          40 ON A% GOTO 10,70,150
          50
          60
A%=2      70
          80
          90
          100
          110
A%=3      120
          130
          140
          150
          160
           .
           .
```

The statement on line 40 is a computed GOTO. When this statement is executed, program logic will branch to statement 10 if variable A%=1, the branch will be to statement 70 if variable A%=2, while A%=3 causes a branch to statement 150. If A% has any other value than 1, 2, or 3, the next sequential instruction will be executed. Notice that variable A% is assigned a value in statement 30. The value assigned to A% depends on the current value of variable B%. The illustration does not show how variable B% is computed; however, so long as B% has a value of 3, 4, or 5, the statement on line 40 will cause a branch to be taken.

To test the computed GOTO statment, key in the following program:

```
10 B%=4
20 ?B%
30 A%=B%-2
40 ON A%GOTO 10,70,150
70 ?B%
80 B%=5
90 GOTO 30
150 ?B%
160 B%=3
170 GOTO 20
```

Now execute this program by typing RUN on any blank line. Do not type RUN on any line that already is displaying something. If you do, you will get a syntax error and the program will not be executed.

Can you account for the sequence in which digits are displayed? Try rewriting the program so that each number is displayed once, in the sequence: 345345345...

LOOPED CONTROL STATEMENTS

FOR-NEXT Statement

GOTO and computed GOTO statements let you create any type of statement execution sequence that your program logic may require. But **suppose you want to re-execute an instruction, (or a group of instructions) many times.** For example, suppose array variable A(I) has 100 elements and each element needs to be assigned a value ranging from 0 to 99. Writing a hundred assignment statements would be very tedious. It is far simpler to re-execute one statement one hundred times. **This can be done using the FOR and NEXT statements** as follows:

```
10 DIM A(99)
20 FOR I=0 TO 99 STEP 1
30 A(I)=I
40 NEXT I
```

Statement(s) between FOR and NEXT are executed repeatedly. In this case a single assignment statement appears between FOR and NEXT; therefore this single statement is re-executed repeatedly.

In order to test the workings of FOR-NEXT loops, we will display A(I) values created within the loop. Key in the following program:

```
10 DIM A(99)
20 FOR I=0 TO 99 STEP 1
30 A(I)=I
35 ?A(I);
40 NEXT I
50 REM IF YOU HAVE A GOTO STATEMENT THAT BRANCHES TO ITSELF, THE
70 REM COMPUTER EXECUTES AN ENDLESS LOOP; IN EFFECT, IT WAITS
80 GOTO 80
```

Now key in RUN. The program is executed. One hundred numbers are displayed, starting at 0 and ending at 99. Press the STOP key to stop program execution.

Statements between FOR and NEXT are re-executed the number of times specified by the index variable appearing directly after FOR; in the illustration above this index variable is I. I is specified as going from 0 to 99 in increments of 1. I also appears in the assignment statement. Therefore the first time the assignment statement is executed, I will equal 0 and the assignment statement will be executed as follows:

```
30 A(0)=0
```

I is increased by the step, or increment, size, which is specified on line 20 as 1; I therefore equals the second time the assignment statement on line 30 is executed. The assignment statement has effectively become:

```
30 A(1)=1
```

I continues to be incremented by the specified STEP until the maximum value of 99 is reached or exceeded.

STEP does not have to be 1; it can have any integer value. Change step to 5 on line 20 and re-execute the program. Now the assignment statement is executed just 20 times, since incrementing I by 5 nineteen times will take it to 95; the 20th increment will take it to 100, which is more than the maximum value of 99. Keeping STEP at 5, we could allow the assignment statement to be executed 100 times by increasing the maximum value of I to 500. Can you make this change? (Remember to change the dimension statement as well.)

The step size does not have to be positive. But if the step size is negative, then the initial value of I must be larger than the final value of I. For example if the step size is −1, and we want to initialize 100 elements of AC(I) with values ranging from 0 to 99, then we would have to rewrite the statement on line 20 as follows:

```
10 DIM A(99)
20 FOR I=99 TO 0 STEP -1
30 A(I)=I
35 ?A(I);
40 NEXT I
80 GOTO 80
```

Execute this program to test the negative STEP.

The initial and final values for I, and the step size, are evaluated as integers; but no other restrictions are placed on these three values. You can specify these three values using floating point variables or expressions. Expressions will be evaluated to a floating point result. Then the floating point result will be converted to an integer using the round-off rules described earlier in this chapter.

Because round-off rules can cause problems, you are strongly urged to specify beginning, ending and step sizes as integers. Do not use expressions since this unnecessarily complicates the program. If you must calculate one of these values, it is simpler and faster to do so in a separate statement.

If the step size is 1 (and this is frequently the case), **you do not have to include a step size definition.** In the absence of any definition, CBM BASIC assumes a step size of 1. Therefore we could rewrite the statement on line 20 as follows:

```
10 DIM A(99)
15 REM USE A STEP SIZE OF 1
20 FOR I=0 TO 99
30 A(I)=I
35 ?A(I);
40 NEXT I
80 GOTO 80
```

Also, you do not need to specify the index variable in the NEXT statement. But if you do, it will make your program easier to read.

Nested Loops

The FOR-NEXT structure is referred to as a "program loop" since statement execution loops around from FOR to NEXT, and back to FOR. This loop structure is very common; almost every BASIC program that you write will include one or more such loops. Loops are so common that they are frequently nested. **The statement sequence occurring between FOR and NEXT can be of any length; frequently it can run to tens or hundreds of statements. And within these tens or hundreds of statements, additional loops may occur.** The following illustration shows a single level of nesting:

```
10 DIM A(99)
20 FOR I=0 TO 99
30 A(I)=I
40 REM DISPLAY ALL VALUES OF A(I) ASSIGNED THUS FAR
50 FOR J=0 TO I
60 ?A(J)
70 NEXT J
80 NEXT I
90 GOTO 90
```

Complex loop structures appear frequently, even in relatively short programs. Here is an example, showing the FOR and NEXT statements, but none of the intermediate statements:

```
50 FOR I=1 TO 10
60 FOR X=25 TO 347 STEP 3
.
100 FOR A=9 TO 0 STEP -1
.
140 NEXT A
200 FOR B=25 TO 100 STEP 5
.
280 NEXT B
300 NEXT X
.
500 FOR Y=1 TO 20 STEP 2
.
600 FOR P=10 TO 20
.
650 NEXT P
700 NEXT Y
.
1000 FOR Z=1 TO 10
.
1090 NEXT Z
1200 NEXT I
```

The outermost loop uses index I; it contains three nested loops that use indexes X, Y, and Z. The first loop contains two additional loops which use indexes A and B. The second loop contains one nested loop using index P. The third loop contains no nested loops. **Each nested loop must have a different index variable name.** Statement execution sequences may be illustrated as follows:

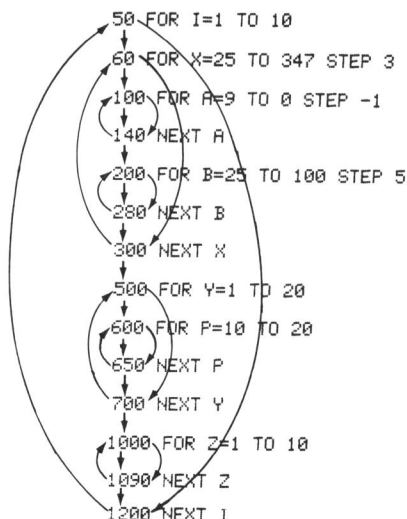

```
50 FOR I=1 TO 10
60 FOR X=25 TO 347 STEP 3
100 FOR A=9 TO 0 STEP -1
140 NEXT A
200 FOR B=25 TO 100 STEP 5
280 NEXT B
300 NEXT X
500 FOR Y=1 TO 20
600 FOR P=10 TO 20
650 NEXT P
700 NEXT Y
1000 FOR Z=1 TO 10
1090 NEXT Z
1200 NEXT I
```

Loop structures are very easy to visualize and use. There is only one common error which you must avoid: **Do not terminate an outer loop before you terminate an inner loop.** For example, the following loop structure is illegal:

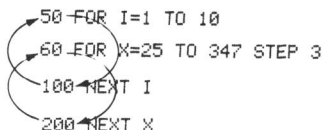

```
50 FOR I=1 TO 10
60 FOR X=25 TO 347 STEP 3
100 NEXT I
200 NEXT X
```

If you do not include the index variable in the NEXT statement, then program logic will automatically terminate loops correctly, since there is only one possible correct loop termination each time a NEXT statement is encountered. If you do not believe this, look again at the complex example illustrated earlier. Then work out some additional complex examples.

Every program must have the same number of FOR and NEXT statements, since every loop must begin with a FOR statement and end with a NEXT statement. For example, suppose there are two FOR statements, but only one NEXT statement. The second FOR statement constitutes an inner loop which will execute correctly. But the outer loop has no NEXT statement to terminate it and the program will execute incorrectly. If you have too many NEXT statements a syntax error will also be generated.

SUBROUTINE STATEMENTS

Once you start writing programs that are more than a few statements long, you will quickly find short routines that get used repeatedly. For example, suppose you have an array variable (such as A(I)) which is reinitialized frequently at different points in your program. Would you simply repeat the three instructions that constitute the FOR-NEXT loop that we described earlier? Since there are just three instructions, you may as well do so.

But suppose you have to initialize the array and then execute ten or eleven instructions that process array data in some fashion. If you had to use this loop many times within one program, rewriting ten to fifteen statements each time you wished to use the loop would take time; but more importantly it would waste a lot of computer memory. This may be illustrated as follows:

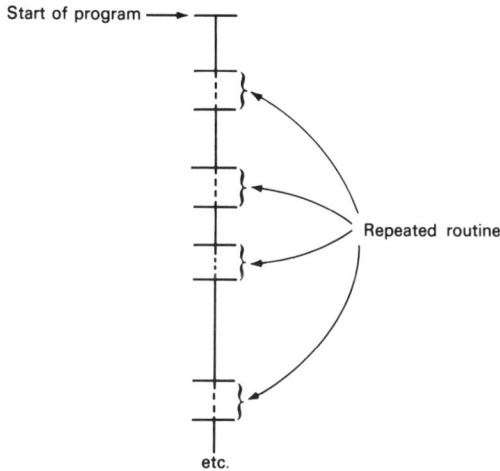

How about separating out the repeated statements and branching to them? That is precisely what we will do; the group of statements is then referred to as a "subroutine."

But a problem arises. Branching from your program to the subroutine is simple enough; the subroutine has an entry line number. But at the end of the subroutine, where do you branch back to? You *could* execute a GOTO statement whenever you wish to branch to a subroutine.

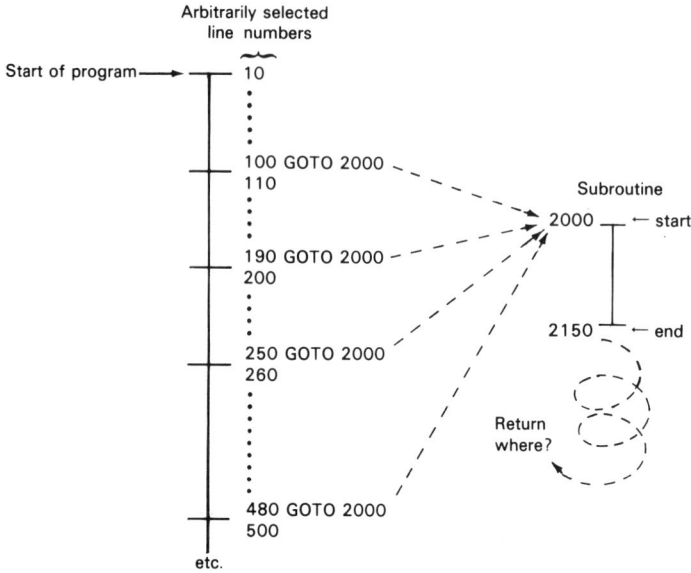

GOSUB Statement

At the end of the subroutine, where do you return to? If two GOTO statements branch to the subroutine, there are two different places to which you will wish to return after the subroutine has completed execution. The solution is to use special subroutine statements. **Instead of branching to the suboutine using a GOTO, use a GOSUB statement. This statement branches in the same way as a GOTO, but in addition it remembers the next line number.** This may be illustrated as follows:

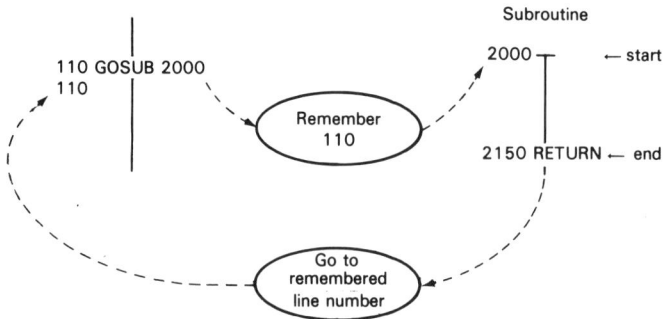

End the subroutine with a RETURN statement. This statement causes a branch back to the line number which the GOSUB statement remembered. The three-statement loop which initializes array A(I) would appear as follows if it were converted into a subroutine:

```
10 REM MAIN PROGRAM
20 REM YOU CAN DIMENSION A SUBROUTINE'S VARIABLE IN THE MAIN
30 REM PROGRAM.  IT IS A GOOD IDEA TO DIMENSION ALL VARIABLES
50 REM AT THE START OF THE MAIN PROGRAM.
60 DIM A(99)
70 GOSUB 2000
80 REM DISPLAY SOMETHING TO PROVE THE RETURN OCCURRED
90 ?"RETURNED"
100 GOTO 100
2000 REM SUBROUTINE
2010 FOR I=0 TO 99
2020 A(I)=I
2030 ?A(I);
2040 NEXT I
2050 RETURN
```

Nested Subroutines

Subroutines can be nested. That is to say, a subroutine can itself call another subroutine, which in turn can call a third subroutine, and so on. You do not have to do anything special in order to use nested subroutines. Simply branch to the subroutine using a GOSUB statement and end the subroutine with a RETURN statement. CBM BASIC will remember the correct line number for each nested return. The following program illustrates nested subroutines:

```
10 REM MAIN PROGRAM
20 REM YOU CAN DIMENSION A SUBROUTINE'S VARIABLE IN THE MAIN
30 REM PROGRAM.  IT IS A GOOD IDEA TO DIMENSION ALL VARIABLES
50 REM AT THE START OF THE MAIN PROGRAM.
60 DIM A(99)
70 GOSUB 2000
80 REM DISPLAY SOMETHING TO PROVE THE RETURN OCCURRED
90 ?"RETURNED"
100 GOTO 100
2000 REM FIRST LEVEL SUBROUTINE
2010 FOR I=0 TO 99
2020 A(I)=I
2030 GOSUB 3000
2040 NEXT I
2050 RETURN
3000 REM NESTED SUBROTINE
3010 ?A(I)
3020 RETURN
```

This program moves the ?A(I) statement out of the subroutine and puts it into a nested subroutine. Nothing else changes.

Computed GOSUB Statement

GOTO and GOSUB statement logic is very similar. The only difference is that GOSUB remembers the next line number. It will therefore not come as any surprise that **there is a computed GOSUB statement akin to the computed GOTO statement.** The computed GOSUB statement allows you to branch to one of two or more subroutines depending on the value of an index. Consider the following statement:

```
90
100 ON A GOSUB 1000,500,5000,2300
110
```

When the statement on line 100 is executed, if $A=1$ the subroutine beginning at line 1000 is called. If $A=2$ the subroutine beginning at line 500 is called. If $A=3$ the subroutine beginning at line 5000 is called. If $A=4$ the subroutine beginning at line 2300 is called. If A has any value other than 1, 2, 3, or 4, the next sequential instruction will be executed. The computed GOSUB statement remembers the next line number (in this case 110). It does not matter which of the subroutines gets called, the called subroutine's RETURN statement will cause a branch back to the "remembered" line number, in this case line 110.

You can nest subroutines using computed GOSUB statements, just as you can nest subroutines using standard GOSUB statements.

IF-THEN Statement

The arithmetic and relational operators which we described earlier in this chapter are frequently used in **IF-THEN** statements. This **gives a BASIC program decision-making capabilities. Following IF you enter any expression. If the expression is "true," then the statement(s) following THEN are executed. However if the expressio is "false" the statement(s) following THEN are not executed.** Here are three simple examples of IF-THEN statements:

```
10 IF A=B+5 THEN PRINT MSG1
40 IF CC$<"M" THEN IN=0
50 IF Q<14 AND M<>M1 GOTO 66
```

The word THEN is optional if it is followed by a GOTO; it may be omitted, as in the third example.

The statement on line 10 causes a PRINT statement to be executed if the floating point variable A value is five more than the floating point variable B value. The PRINT statement will not be executed otherwise.

The statement on line 40 sets floating point variable IN to 0 if string variable CC$ is any letter of the alphabet in the range A through L.

The statement on line 50 causes program execution to branch to line 66 if floating point variable Q is less than 14, and floating point variable M is not equal to floating point variable M1. Otherwise program execution will continue with the statement on the next line. If you do not understand the evaluation of expressions following IF, then refer to the discussion of such expressions given at the beginning of this chapter.

INPUT AND OUTPUT STATEMENTS

From the beginning of this chapter we have been using the question mark (?) to create displays. In fact the question mark is a shorthand version of the PRINT statement.

There are a variety of **BASIC statements that control the transfer of data to and from the computer. Collectively these are referred to as input/output statements. The simplest input/output statements control data input from the keyboard and data output to the display.** We are going to discuss these simple input/output statements in the paragraphs that follow. But there are also more complex input/output statements that control data transfer between the computer and peripheral devices such as cassette units, diskette units, and printers. These more complex input/output statements are described in Chapter 6. Since we have already encountered the PRINT statement, let us discuss this statement first.

PRINT Statement

You can use the word PRINT or a question mark (?) to create a PRINT statement.

Why use PRINT instead of DISPLAY or some abbreviation of the word display? The answer is that in the early sixties, when the BASIC programming language was being created, displays were very expensive and generally unavailable on medium- or low-cost computers. The standard computer terminal had a keyboard and a printer. Information was printed where today it is displayed; hence the use of the word "print" to describe a statement which causes a display.

The PRINT statement will display text or numbers. Text must be enclosed in quotes. For example, the following statement will display the single word "text":

```
      10 PRINT "TEXT"
or:
      10 ?"TEXT"
```

To display a number, you place the number, or a variable name, after PRINT. This may be illustrated as follows:

```
10 A%=10
20 ?5,A%
```

The statement at line 20 displays the number 5, and then the number 10 on the same line.

You can display a mixture of text and/or numbers by listing the information to be displayed after PRINT. Use commas to separate individual items. The following PRINT statement displays the words "one", "two", "three", "four" and "five", followed by the numeral for each number:

```
10 ?"ONE",1,"TWO",2,"THREE",3,"FOUR",4,"FIVE",5
```

If you separate variables with commas, as we did above, **then the CBM computer automatically assigns 10 character spaces for each variable displayed.** Try executing the statement illustrated above in immediate mode to prove this to yourself. **If you want the display to take out empty spaces, separate the variables with semicolons,** as follows:

```
10 PRINT "ONE";1;"TWO";2;"THREE";3;"FOUR";4;"FIVE";5
```

Enter this statement in immediate mode and display it to understand how the semicolon works.

A PRINT statement automatically inserts a carriage return at the end of the display, unless you suppress it. You can suppress the carriage return by putting a comma or a semicolon after the last variable. A comma occurring after the last variable will continue the display at the next 10-character space boundary. To illustrate this, enter the following three-statement program and run it by typing in RUN:

```
10 PRINT "ONE",1,"TWO",2
20 PRINT "THREE",3,"FOUR",4
30 GOTO 30
```

Now add a comma to the end of the statement on line 10 and again execute the program by typing RUN. You will see the two lines of display occur on a single line. Remember to type RUN on a blank line or you will get a syntax error.

Now replace the comma at the end of line 10 with a semicolon and again run the program. The display occurs on a single line, but the space between the numeral "2" and the word "three" has been removed. By changing other commas to semicolons you can selectively remove additional spaces.

We have been illustrating the numerals by inserting them directly into the PRINT statement. You can, if you wish, display the contents of variables instead. The following program reproduces the first PRINT statement, but uses variable A%(I) to create digits. Try entering this program and running it:

```
10 FOR I=1 TO 5
20 A%(I)=I
30 NEXT
40 PRINT "ONE";A%(1);"TWO";A%(2);"THREE";A%(3);"FOUR";A%(4);
   "FIVE";A%(5)
50 GOTO 50
```

We can put the displayed words into a string array and move the PRINT statement into the FOR-NEXT loop by changing the program as follows:

```
10 DATA "ONE","TWO","THREE","FOUR","FIVE"
20 FOR I=1 TO 5
30 A%(I)=I
40 READ N$(I)
50 PRINT N$(I);A%(I);
60 NEXT
70 GOTO 70
```

The program shown above is not well written. A%(I) can be eliminated, and N$ need not be an array variable. Can you rewrite the program using N$ and removing A$(I) entirely?

PRINT Formatting Functions

We use the word "formatting" to describe the process of arranging information on a display (or a printout) so that the information is easier to understand, or more pleasing to the eye. Given the PRINT statement and nothing else, formatting could become a complex and painful chore. For example, suppose you want to display a heading in the middle of the line at the top of the display. Does that mean displaying space codes until you reach the first heading character position? Not only would that be tedious and error prone, it would also waste a lot of memory, since each space code must be converted into an appropriate computer instruction. Fortunately, **CBM BASIC provides three PRINT formatting aides: the SPC, TAB, and POS functions.**

SPC Function

SPC is a space over function. You include SPC as one of the terms in a PRINT statement; after the letters SPC you must include (in parentheses) the number of character positions that you wish to space over. For example, we could display a heading beginning at the left-most character position of the display as follows:

```
10 ?"HEADING"
```

But to center the heading on a 40-column screen display you would first space over 16 character positions as follows:

```
10 ?SPC(16);"HEADING"
```

Notice the semicolon after the SPC function. A comma after SPC will start displaying text at the next 10-character boundary following the number of spaces specified by SPC.

Any time you include the SPC function in a PRINT statement you simply cause the next printed or displayed character to be moved over by the number of positions specified after SPC; no other PRINT statement syntax is changed.

TAB Function

TAB is a tabbing function similiar to typewriter tabbing.

Suppose you want to print or display information in columns. You must first calculate the character position of the line where each column is to begin. This may be illustrated as follows:

COLUMN NUMBER

0	16	32	48
JONES, P. J	431-25-6277	1420.00	258.74
BURKE, P. L	447-71-7614	2025.00	467.64
ROBINSON, L. W	231-80-8421	2150.00	477.04
etc.	etc.	etc.	etc.

In the illustration above, columns begin at character positions 0, 16, 32 and 48. (Obviously the computer has an 80-column display or is printing on 80-column paper.) Now instead of computing space codes as you go from line to line, following each column entry you simply insert a TAB function in the PRINT statement.

Consider one line of the display illustrated above; counting character positions, we could display the line without tab stops, as follows:

```
10 ?"JONES,P.J          431-25-6277        1420.00           258.74"
```

Instead of inserting space codes, we could use the space function and shorten the statement as follows:

```
10 ?"JONES, P.J";SPC(17);"431-25-6277";SPC(5);"1420.00";SPC(9);"258.74"
```

But tabbing is easier because you tab to a known column number instead of counting spaces:

```
10 ?"JONES,P.J";TAB(16);"431-25-6277";TAB(32);"1420.00";TAB(48);"258.74"
```

Note that the entries in the third and fourth columns are numbers which we have entered as text. Try rewriting the PRINT statement to display these as numbers. The numbers no longer align as they did when they were displayed as characters (in Chapter 5 we discuss the quirks associated with display formatting). In this case, numbers leave a space for a negative sign, and they do not display zeros occurring after the decimal point. That is why there are differences.

POS Function

POS is the last of the PRINT formatting functions. POS returns the current cursor position. The position is returned as a number, equal to the column number where the cursor is blinking. You always include a dummy argument of 0 after POS, written as POS(0).

The following statement demonstrates the capability of POS:

```
10 ?"CURSOR POSITION IS";POS(0)
```

Execute this statement in immediate mode. The display will appear as follows:

```
?"CURSOR POSITION IS";POS(0)
CURSOR POSITION IS 18
```

The cursor was at character position 18 after displaying "CURSOR POSITION IS." If you add some spaces after "IS," and before the closing quotes, you will change the number 18 to some larger number.

INPUT Statement

When an INPUT statement is executed, the computer waits for input from the keyboard; until the computer gets the input it requires, nothing else will happen.

An input statement begins with the word INPUT, which is followed by a list of variable names. Entered data is assigned to the named variables. The variable name type determines the form in which data must be entered. A string variable name (ending with a $) can be satisfied only by text input; any number of text characters can be entered for a string variable. To demonstrate string input, key in the following short program and run it:

```
10 INPUT A$
20 ?A$
30 GOTO 10
```

Upon executing an INPUT statement, the computer displays a question mark, then waits for your entry. The program illustrated above displays any text which you enter, as you enter it; but the text is displayed again because of the PRINT statement on the next line. The first display occurs when the INPUT statement on line 10 is executed. The second display is in response to the PRINT statement on line 20.

You input integer or floating point numeric data by listing the appropriate variable names following INPUT. Separate individual entries with commas. The comma has no punctuation significance in an INPUT statement. The following example inputs a text word, an integer number and a floating point number, then displays these three inputs. Enter the program and run it:

```
10 INPUT A$,A,A%
20 ?A$,A,A%
30 GOTO 10
```

You must enter a text word followed by a comma, then an integer number followed by a comma, then a floating point number followed by a carriage return. Any departure from this input sequence will cause an error; following an error the computer displays two question marks. You will have to re-enter the data in the correct format. If the computer then displays a question mark with the message "re-do from start," enter the correct data again.

Now rewrite the PRINT statement so that A$, A and A% are in an order that differs from the INPUT statement. Rerun the program.

As we discussed earlier, any integers can be represented using a floating point number. Therefore you can input an integer value for a floating point variable. But you cannot input a floating point value for an integer variable. You cannot enter text for an integer or a floating point number, but you can enter a number for a text variable; the number will be interpreted as characters rather than a numeric value. Try these variations to satisfy yourself that you understand the data entry options.

The INPUT statement is very fussy; its syntax is too demanding for any normal human operator. Just imagine the office worker who knows nothing about programming; on encountering the types of error message which can occur if one comma happens to be out of place, s/he will give up in despair. You are therefore likely to spend a lot of time writing "idiot-proof" data entry programs; these are programs which are designed to watch out for every type of mistake that an operator can make when entering data. An idiot-proof program will cope with errors in a way that the operator can understand. Chapter 5 describes data entry programming in detail.

One simple trick worth noting, however, is the INPUT statement's ability to display data. Therefore you can precede each item of data entry with a short message telling the operator what to do. The message appears in the INPUT statement as text between quotes. A semicolon must occur after the text to be displayed, and before the first input variable name. Here is an example:

```
10 INPUT "ENTER THE NUMBER 1";N
20 IF N<>1 THEN GOTO 50
30 ?"OK"
40 GOTO 40
50 ?"NO, DUMMY."
60 GOTO 10
```

This program prints a message, then waits for a single data entry. This certainly beats sticking a bunch of variables into a single INPUT statement, with only your memory reminding you what to enter next.

GET Statement

The GET statement inputs a single character. No carriage return is needed. The single character input can be any character that the CBM computer recognizes, or it may be a numeric value between 0 and 9. Entry will be interpreted as a character if a string variable name follows GET. Type in the following program and run it:

```
10 GET A$
20 ?A$
30 GOTO 10
```

When you run this program, everything will race off the top of the display. Each time you press a key, it too will race off the top of the screen. That is because GET does not wait for a character entry, it assumes the entry is there. **We can make GET wait for a specific character** by testing for the character as follows:

```
10 GET A$
20 IF A$<>"X" THEN GOTO 10
30 ?A$
40 GOTO 10
```

This program waits for the letter *X* to be entered. Nothing else will do.

GET can also be programmed to wait for any keyboard entry. This program logic uses the fact that the GET statement string variable is assigned a null character code until a character is input at the keyboard. The null code is 00 which cannot be entered from the keyboard, but can be specified within a program, using two adjacent quotation marks """. Here is the necessary program logic:

```
10 GET A$
20 IF A$="" THEN GOTO 10
30 ?A$
40 GOTO 10
```

If the GET statement specifies an integer or floating point variable, then the input is interpreted as a numeric digit. The integer of floating point variable appearing in a GET statement is assigned a value of 0 until it receives data input. But you can enter 0 at the keyboard. Therefore **program logic has no way of knowing whether the 0 represents a valid entry, or a lack of any entry.** This can present problems to programming logic that checks for an entry, as shown above. **GET statements therefore usually receive string characters.**

Programs use the GET statement most frequently when generating dialogue with an operator. For example, a program may wait for an operator to prove that he or she is there by entering a specific character (e.g. 'Y' for 'yes'). Here is appropriate program logic:

```
10 PRINT "OPERATOR! ARE YOU THERE? TYPE Y FOR YES"
20 GET A$
30 IF A$<>"Y" THEN GOTO 20
40 PRINT "OK, LET'S GET ON WITH IT"
```

Notice that this sequence never displays the character entered at the keyboard. Try rewriting the program so that any character entered for the GET statement is displayed.

PEEK AND POKE STATEMENTS

PEEK and POKE are two CBM BASIC statements that rightfully belong in Chapter 7; however we will mention them here since we have already encountered the POKE statement in the course of operating the CBM computer. We used it to access the computer's alternate character set.

CBM computers can have up to 65,536 individually addressable locations, each of which can store a number ranging between 0 and 255. (This strange upper bound is in fact $2^8 - 1$.) All programs and data are converted into sequences of numbers which are stored in this fashion.

A PEEK statement lets you read the number stored in any CBM computer memory location. Consider the following PEEK statement:

```
10 A%=PEEK(200)
```

This statement assigns the content of memory location 200 to variable A%. The PEEK argument may be a number, as shown, an integer variable name, or an integer expression, but it must evaluate to the address of a memory location.

The POKE statement writes data into a memory location. For example the statement:

```
20 POKE 8000,A%
```

takes the content of variable A% and stores it in memory location 8000. Each POKE argument may be a number, a variable or an expression with a value between 0 and 255. A floating point value is converted to an integer.

You can PEEK into read/write memory or read-only memory. But you can only POKE into read/write memory. This is self-evident; read-only memory, as its name implies, can have its contents read, but cannot be written into.

END AND STOP STATEMENTS

The END and STOP statements halt program execution. You can continue execution by typing CONT at the keyboard. You do not have to include END or STOP statements in your program; however these statements do make for tidy programming.

In many of the programming examples given in this chapter we use a GOTO statement that branches to itself in order to stop program execution. For example the statement:

```
50 GOTO 50
```

will execute endlessly since the GOTO statement selects itself for the execution. We could replace this statement with a STOP statement. When a STOP statement is executed, the following message will appear:

```
BREAK IN XXXX
READY
```

Then execution stops. XXXX is the line number of the STOP statement. If you have more than one STOP statement in your program, use XXXX to identify which statement was executed.

FUNCTIONS

Another element of CBM BASIC is the function, which in some ways looks like a variable, but in other ways acts more like a BASIC statement.

Perhaps the simplest way of understanding what a function is is to look at an example in an assignment statement:

```
10 A=SQR(B)
```

The variable A has been set equal to the square root of the variable B. SQR specifies the square root function. Here is a string function:

```
20 C$=LEFT$(D$,2)
```

In this example the string variable C$ is set equal to the first two characters of string variable D$.

Functions can substitute for variables or constants anywhere in a BASIC statement, except to the left of an equal sign. In other words, you can say that $A = SQR(B)$, but you cannot say that $SQR(A) = B$.

We have already used four functions. **SPC, TAB, and POS are system functions used with the PRINT statements to format displays. Also, PEEK is a function.**

The discussion which follows shows you how to use functions. An incomplete summary of the available CBM BASIC functions is presented here but **complete descriptions of all functions are given in Chapter 8.**

You specify a function using appropriate letters (such as SQR for square root), followed by arguments enclosed in parentheses. In the case of $A = SQR(B)$, SQR requires a single argument, which in this case is the variable B. For C = LEFT$(D$,2)$, LEFT$ specifies the function; the two arguments D$ and 2 are enclosed in brackets.

Generally stated, any function will have one of these two formats:

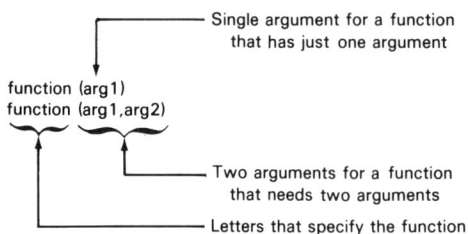

A few functions need three arguments.

Each function argument can be a constant, a variable, or an expression.

A function appearing in a BASIC statement is evaluated before any operators.
Each and every function in a BASIC statement is reduced to a single numeric or string
value before any other parts of the BASIC statement are evaluated. For example in the
following statement:

```
10 B=24.7*(SQR(C)+5)-SIN(0.2+D)
```

SQR and SIN functions are evaluated first. Suppose $SQR(C) = 6.72$ and
$SIN(0.2+D) = 0.625$. The statement on line 10 will first be reduced to:

```
10 B=24.7*(6.72+5)-0.625
```

Then this simpler statement is evaluated.

ARITHMETIC FUNCTIONS

Here is a list of the arithmetic functions that you can use with CBM BASIC:

INT	Converts a floating point argument to its integer equivalent by truncation.
SGN	Returns the sign of an argument: +1 for a positive argument, −1 for a negative argument, 0 for 0 argument.
ABS	Returns the absolute value of an argument. A positive argument does not change; a negative argument is converted to its positive equivalent.
SQR	Computes the square root of the argument.
EXP	Raises the natural logarithm base e to the power of the argument (e^{arg}).
LOG	Returns the natural logarithm of the argument.
RND	Generates a random number. There are some rules regarding use of RND; they are described in Chapter 5.
SIN	Returns the trigonometric sine of the argument, which is treated as a radian quantity.
COS	Returns the trigonometric cosine of the argument, which is treated as a radian quantity.
TAN	Returns the trigonometric tangent of the argument, which is treated as a radian quantity.
ATN	Returns the trigonometric arctangent of the argument, which is treated as a radian quantity.

You should start using functions as soon as possible, but do not bother with functions you do not already understand. For example, if you do not understand trigonometry, you are unlikely to use SIN, COS and TAN functions in your programs.

Here is an example that uses an arithmetic function:

```
10 A=2.743
20 B=INT(A)+7
30 ?B
40 STOP
```

When you execute this program, the result displayed is 9, since the integer value of A is 2. As an exercise, change the statement on line 10 to an INPUT. Change line 40 to GOTO 10. Now you can enter a variety of values for A and watch the integer function at work.

Here is a more complex example using arithmetic functions:

```
10 INPUT A,B
20 IF LOG(A)<0 THEN A=1/A
30 ?SQR(A)*EXP(B)
40 GOTO 10
```

If you understand logarithms, then as an exercise change the statement on line 20, replacing the LOG function with arithmetic functions that perform the same operation.

The argument of a function can be an expression; the expression may contain functions. For example, change line 30 to the following statement and rerun the program:

```
30 ?SQR(A*EXP(B)+3)
```

Now experiment with arithmetic functions by creating immediate PRINT statements that make complex use of arithmetic functions.

STRING FUNCTIONS

String functions allow you to manipulate string data in a variety of ways. You may not need to use arithmetic functions that you do not understand, but you must make the effort to learn every string function.

Here is a list of the string functions that you can use with CBM BASIC:

STR$	Converts a number to its equivalent string of text characters.
VAL	Converts a string of text characters to their equivalent number (if such a conversion is possible).
CHR$	Converts an 8-bit binary code to its equivalent ASCII character.
ASC	Converts an ASCII character to its 8-bit binary equivalent.
LEN	Returns the number of characters contained in a text string.
LEFT$	Extracts the left part of a text string. Function arguments identify the string and its left part.
RIGHT$	Extracts the right part of a text string. Function arguments identify the string and its right part.
MID$	Extracts the middle section of a text string. Function arguments identify the string and the required mid part.

String functions let you determine the length of a string, extract portions of a string, and convert between numeric, ASCII, and string characters. These functions take one, two, or three arguments. Here are some examples:

```
STR$(14)

LEN("ABC")

LEN(A$+B$)

LEFT$(ST$,1)
```

SYSTEM FUNCTIONS

In the interest of completeness, CBM BASIC system functions are listed below. They perform operations which you are unlikely to need until you are an experienced programmer. Perhaps the only system function you are likely to use fairly soon is the time of day function. If you print many variations of a report (or any other material) in a single day, it is often a good idea to print the time of day at the top of the report. Then you can tell the sequence in which these reports were generated.

Here is a list of system functions available with CBM BASIC:

PEEK	Fetches the contents of a memory byte.
TI\$, T1	Fetches system time, as maintained by a program clock.
FRE	Returns available free space — the number of unused read/write memory bytes.
SYS	Transfers to subsystem.
USR	Transfers to user assembly language program.

USER-DEFINED FUNCTIONS

In addition to the many functions which are a standard part of CBM BASIC, **you can define your own arithmetic functions,** providing they are not very complicated. User-defined string functions are not allowed. Here is an example of a short program that uses a DEF FN statement:

```
10 DEFFNP(X)=100*X
20 INPUT A
30 ?A,FNP(A)
40 GOTO 20
```

Following the DEF FN entry you can have any valid floating point variable name. In this case we have entered P, therefore the function name becomes FNP. If the varia-. ble name was AB, then the function name would be FNAB.

In a DEF FN statement, a single variable name must follow the function name, and must be enclosed in parentheses. This variable name is local to the function definition; its value is known only inside the DEF FN statement. You can use the same variable name outside the function, but it refers to a different variable value which is known to the program at large. The local variable receives its value when the function can, and usually does, appear in the expression on the right side of the DEF FN statement equals sign. Other variable names can appear there too. When the function is used via the FN statement, the expression is evaluated using the newly assigned value of the local variable and the latest values of any of the variables. The resulting value is used where the FN statement appeared.

Chapter 5

Making the Most of CBM Features

This chapter describes CBM computer hardware characteristics and programming techniques.

HARDWARE FEATURES

KEYBOARD ROLLOVER

If you press two or more keys simultaneously, or if you press a second key before the first character is displayed, a keystroke will be ignored — unless your keyboard has "rollover." Rollover "remembers" a keystroke until it is displayed. Fortunately, CBM computer keyboards have rollover.

Rollover remembers incoming keystrokes while a preceding keystroke is being processed. The "remembered" keystrokes are stored in a buffer until they are processed. Without this buffer, rapidly incoming keystrokes would be lost. For example, if keystroke #2 occurs before keystroke #1 has been processed, the CBM computer stores keystroke #2 in the buffer until keystroke #1 has been processed. Then keystroke #2 is taken from the buffer and processed in turn.

Rollover is a very useful feature of the CBM computer keyboard; it allows you to type in data very fast without the loss of occasional keystrokes.

KEYBOARD BUFFER

All CBM computers have a 10-character buffer that holds characters when keys are pressed at the keyboard.

To illustrate, load and run the final version of the BLANKET program, listed in Figure 5-1. Press a key. While the first display is generated, press up to ten more keys, then sit back and relax. Each of the ten keyed-in characters will be fetched from the buffer in turn and displayed by the BLANKET program.

Let us look at this process in more detail.

Whenever you press a key, it goes into the first storage location in the 10-character keyboard buffer. If you press the A key, this is what happens:

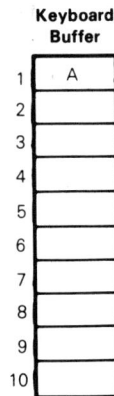

Keyboard
Buffer

```
 1 | A |
 2 |   |
 3 |   |
 4 |   |
 5 |   |
 6 |   |
 7 |   |
 8 |   |
 9 |   |
10 |   |
```

The CBM computer keeps track of the number of characters in the buffer and the location of the next character to be displayed. Each time the GET statement fetches another character, a buffer pointer is incremented to select the next buffer location.

If you press additional keys while the A is being displayed, the additional characters are stored in the keyboard buffer beginning at the next available location. Suppose you type in A, and while A is being displayed you type in B, C, D, and E. These characters are all stored in the keyboard buffer:

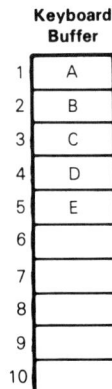

Keyboard
Buffer

```
 1 | A |
 2 | B |
 3 | C |
 4 | D |
 5 | E |
 6 |   |
 7 |   |
 8 |   |
 9 |   |
10 |   |
```

```
10 REM ******* B L A N K E T *******
20 REM CONTINUOUS-LINE DISPLAY OF ONE
30 REM   CHARACTER ENTERED FROM THE
40 REM   KEYBOARD
50 REM ********************************
90 PRINT"HIT A KEY OR <R> TO END";
100 GET C$:IF C$="" GOTO 100
105 IF C$=CHR$(13) GOTO 170
110 PRINT"⌧";          :REM CLEAR SCREEN
120 FOR I=1 TO 920     :REM 920/40=23 LINES
130 PRINT C$;
140 NEXT
150 PRINT"PHEW!"
160 GOTO 90
170 END
```

Figure 5-1. Program BLANKET

If you let the BLANKET program continue to run, it will successively display all the letters stored in the keyboard buffer. After A is finished, the program fetches B and displays it across 20 lines, then it fetches C and displays it, etc.

If you type in more than ten characters, then for any model with the exception of the 8000 series, the buffer pointer wraps around, returning to buffer position 1. For example, if you type in the first 11 letters of the alphabet (A-K), the first ten letters are stored in the ten buffer locations, then the letter K is stored in the first buffer location, overlaying the A:

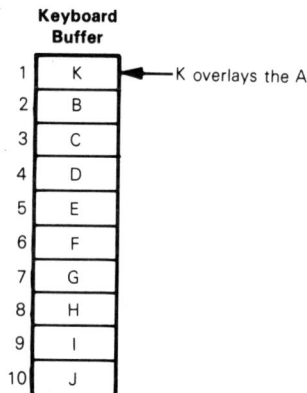

Keyboard Buffer

1	K	◀── K overlays the A
2	B	
3	C	
4	D	
5	E	
6	F	
7	G	
8	H	
9	I	
10	J	

When the program finishes displaying the A, it returns to fetch another character. But the CBM computer has already fetched the character in location 1, so it considers the buffer empty. Keying in exactly eleven characters, or multiples of eleven characters, produces no additional automatic displays in program BLANKET.

Typing in 12 to 20 characters displays the first character, and then a string of characters beginning with character 12. For example, type in A. While A is being displayed type in B, C, D, E, F, G, H, I, J, K, L, M, N, O, P, Q, R, S, and T.

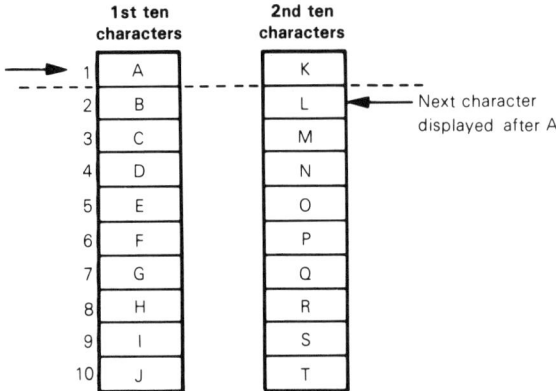

	1st ten characters	2nd ten characters	
1	A	K	
2	B	L	← Next character displayed after A
3	C	M	
4	D	N	
5	E	O	
6	F	P	
7	G	Q	
8	H	R	
9	I	S	
10	J	T	

The order of display is: A, L, M, N, O, P, Q, R, S, T.

This logic holds true for additional multiple characters. Type in A, and while A is being displayed type in the rest of the alphabet. (You will have to be quick to do this.)

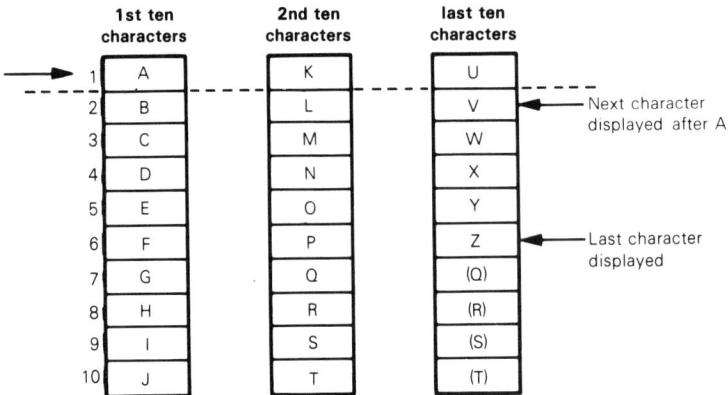

	1st ten characters	2nd ten characters	last ten characters	
1	A	K	U	
2	B	L	V	← Next character displayed after A
3	C	M	W	
4	D	N	X	
5	E	O	Y	
6	F	P	Z	← Last character displayed
7	G	Q	(Q)	
8	H	R	(R)	
9	I	S	(S)	
10	J	T	(T)	

A negating effect occurs every 11 characters. For instance, type in A and B, and let A display completely. Then, while B is displaying, type in C, D, E, F, G, H, I, J, K, and L. The additional ten characters are cancelled out, just as the additional ten characters B through K were when entered while A was being displayed.

The CBM 8000 discards input characters which other models wrap around within the input buffer.

Emptying the Buffer Before a GET

The keyboard buffer is a mild surprise, usually a pleasant one. For program BLANKET you can save up the characters you want displayed rather than keying them in one at a time in response to the HIT A KEY message. But the keyboard buffer can also come as a rude shock. **Accidentally pressing a key may cause a program to fetch an unwanted character from the keyboard buffer. To avoid this, you can program a loop to empty the keyboard buffer** before fetching an intended response character as follows:

```
95 FOR I=1TO10:GET C$:NEXTI: REM EMPTY KYBD BFR
100 GET C$:IF C$="" GOTO 100
```

The statements on line 95 empty the keyboard buffer by getting all ten possible buffer characters.

Edit program BLANKET by adding line 95 as shown above. Now press any combination of keys while a character is being displayed. Any stored characters are fetched and discarded by the GET loop, so you will not have any automatic continuous display.

STRING CONCATENATION

Within strings the CBM computer will accept alphabetic, graphic, and numeric characters, or combinations of these. While handling strings, it may be useful to create a single string by linking shorter strings end to end in a chain-like fashion:

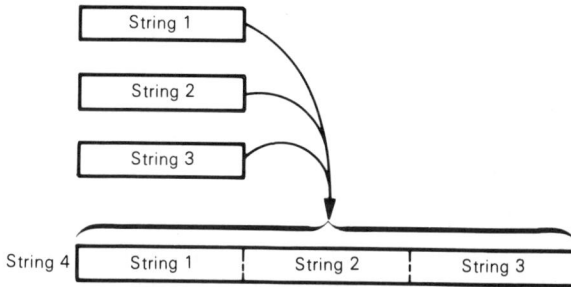

Suppose, for example, we want to create one large string, Z$, containing the alphabet A through Z. To do this we can link together the last character of A$, shown below, to the first character of J$, and the last character of J$ to the first character of S$, as follows:

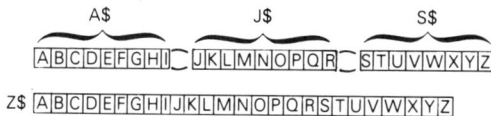

The arithmetic operator "+" adds the contents of numeric variables, but when used with strings the "+" concatenates the strings. Table 5-1 summarizes the effect of the "+" operator on strings and numbers.

Table 5-1. Addition (+) Operations

Sign	Type	Example Statement.	Operation	Result
+	numbers	P = 2 + 3	2 + 3	P = 5
+	numeric variables	Q = T + S T = |1|2|3|4|5| S = |1|1|1|1|1|	12345 +11111 23456	Q = 23456
+	alphabetic strings	R$ = A$ + F$ A$ = |A|B|C|D|E| F$ = |F|G|H|I|J|	|A|B|C|D|E|⌣|F|G|H|I|J|	R$ = |A|B|C|D|E|F|G|H|I|J|
+	numeric strings	Q$ = T$ + S$ T$ = |1|2|3|4|5| S$ = |1|1|1|1|1|	|1|2|3|4|5|⌣|1|1|1|1|1|	Q$ = |1|2|3|4|5|1|1|1|1|1|

A word of caution: strings cannot be separated or broken apart in the same fashion as they are concatenated; they cannot be "subtracted" the way they are "added." For instance, to create string X$ containing the contents of J$ and S$ from our original strings A$, J$, S$, and Z$, it would be incorrect to type:

```
X$=Z$-A$ ◄────── Incorrect
```

Try it yourself. Enter the values of A$, J$, S$, and X$=Z$−A$ into the CBM computer as shown below. The computer will respond with a ?TYPE MISMATCH ERROR IN LINE 50.

```
10 A$="ABCDEFGHI"
20 J$="JKLMNOPQR"
30 S$="STUVWXYZ"
40 Z$=A$+J$+S$
50 X$=Z$-A$ ◄────── Incorrect attempt to get J through Z string
60 PRINT X$

RUN

?TYPE MISMATCH ERROR IN LINE 50
```

The only valid arithmetic operator for strings is the addition sign (+). The other arithmetic operators (−,*,/) will not work, although the Boolean operators (<, >, =) may be used for string comparison.

The correct method of extracting part of a larger string is to use string functions. With the LEFT$, MID$, and RIGHT$ functions it is possible to extract any desired portion of a string. In our example, the letters J through Z can be extracted as follows:

```
50 X$=RIGHT$(Z$,17)
X$ = RIGHT$(|A|B|C|D|E|F|G|H|I|J|K|L|M|N|O|P|Q|R|S|T|U|V|W|X|Y|Z|,17)
X$ = |J|K|L|M|N|O|P|Q|R|S|T|U|V|W|X|Y|Z|
```

or the string may be built by concatenating J$ and S$:

```
50 X$=J$+S$
X$ = |J|K|L|M|N|O|P|Q|R|+|S|T|U|V|W|X|Y|Z|
X$ = |J|K|L|M|N|O|P|Q|R|S|T|U|V|W|X|Y|Z|
```

Printer/Screen Concatenation

If you want to concatenate strings for screen or printer output only, **use the PRINT statement with semicolon separators (;)** between the strings:

```
PRINT A$;J$;S$

ABCDEFGHIJKLMNOPQRSTUVWXYZ
```

The screen result (A through Z) is not retained anywhere in CBM computer memory.

GRAPHIC STRINGS

Graphic strings are concatenated in the same way as alphabetic strings. This is a useful way of creating pictures and diagrams.

NUMERIC STRINGS

A numeric string is a string whose contents can be evaluated as a number. Numeric strings may be created in two different ways, each yielding slightly different results.

When numeric variables are assigned to numeric strings using the STR$ function, the sign value preceding the number (blank if positive, " − " if negative) is transferred along with the number. This is shown in the short program below:

```
10 AB=12345
20 T$=STR$(AB)
30 PRINT"AB=";AB
40 PRINT"T$=";T$

RUN

AB= 12345
T$= 12345
```

However, **if a number is entered enclosed within quotation marks, or if the number is entered as a string with an INPUT, GET or READ statement,** then the numeric string is treated like any other alphabetic or graphic string. **No blank for a positive sign value is inserted before the number.** This is demonstrated in the following program:

```
10 AB=12345
20 T$="12345"
30 PRINT"AB=";AB
40 PRINT"T$=";T$

RUN

AB= 12345 ◄─────Space inserted
T$=12345 ◄─────No space inserted
```

Let us now concatenate two numeric strings, T$ and Q$, to make a new numeric string W$. W$ is to contain the ten digits 1, 2, 3, 4, 5, 6, 7, 8, 9, 0. Here is one possibility:

```
10 T=12345
20 Q=67890
30 T$=STR$(T)
40 Q$=STR$(Q)
50 W$=T$+Q$ ◄──────── Create new string W$
60 PRINT"W$=";W$

RUN

W$= 12345 67890
```

Why the blanks before the 1 and 6? T$ and Q$ were originally positive numeric variables T and Q; when T and Q were converted from numbers into strings, the blank sign position was transferred along with the number.

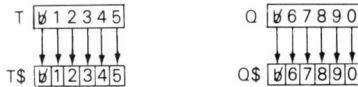

T │ ␢ 1 2 3 4 5 │   Q │ ␢ 6 7 8 9 0 │
     ↓ ↓ ↓ ↓ ↓ ↓   ↓ ↓ ↓ ↓ ↓ ↓
T$ │␢│1│2│3│4│5│   Q$ │␢│6│7│8│9│0│

Therefore, when T$ and Q$ are concatenated, the new string W$ contains a first-digit blank, and an embedded blank before the first digit of Q$.

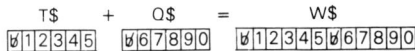

T$ +   Q$ =   W$
│␢│1│2│3│4│5│ │␢│6│7│8│9│0│ │␢│1│2│3│4│5│␢│6│7│8│9│0│

To get rid of the embedded blanks go back to the separate strings T$ and Q$. Look again at the contents of T$ and Q$ above. The only values we want in W$ are the numbers to the right of the sign value in both T$ and Q$. With the LEFT$, MID$, and RIGHT$ commands you can select any character or group of characters from within a given string. We want all the characters to the right of the first character, the first character being the sign value (either blank or "−"). T$=RIGHT(T$,LEN(T$)−1) does the trick:

Before: After:

T$ │␢│1│2│3│4│5│ ⟶   T$ │1│2│3│4│5│

Since the first digit needed is in the second position of the string, we tell the CBM computer to use only the values starting in position #2. We can concatenate T$ and Q$ and drop the leading blanks all in one statement:

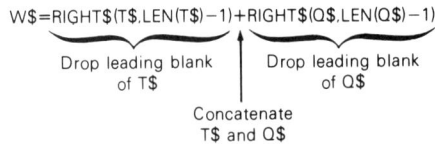

W$=RIGHT$(T$,LEN(T$)−1)+RIGHT$(Q$,LEN(Q$)−1)
    └──────┬──────┘   ↑   └──────┬──────┘
     Drop leading blank │   Drop leading blank
         of T$ │   of Q$
                   Concatenate
                   T$ and Q$

Our example program, amended to eliminate the sign digits, appears as follows:

```
10 T=12345
    T = |b|12345|

20 Q=67890
    Q = |b|67890|

30 T$=STR$(T)
    T$ = |b|1|2|3|4|5|

40 Q$=STR$(Q)
    Q$ = |b|6|7|8|9|0|

50 W$=RIGHT$(T$,LEN(T$)-1)+RIGHT$(LEN(Q$)-1)
    W$ = RIGHT$(T$,6-1)          +RIGHT$(Q$,6-1)
    W$ = RIGHT$(T$,5)            +RIGHT$(Q$,5)
    W$ = T$ |1|2|3|4|5|          +Q$ |6|7|8|9|0|
    W$ = |1|2|3|4|5|6|7|8|9|0|

60 PRINT "W$=";W$

RUN

W$=1234567890
```

In the example above, note that line 50 does not check for negative numbers. If both numbers are negative, then the leading character of T$ should not be dropped; this allows the negative sign to appear in front of the entire number W$. If the two strings have different signs, they should not be concatenated.

INPUT AND OUTPUT PROGRAMMING

The beginning programmer quickly discovers that the input and output sections of a program are its trickiest parts.

Nearly every program uses data which must be entered at the keyboard. Will a few INPUT statements suffice? In most cases the answer is no. What if the operator accidentally presses the wrong key? Or worse, what if the operator discovers that he or she input the wrong data — after entering two or three additional data items? **A usable program must assume that the operator is human, and will likely make every conceivable human error.**

Results, likewise, cannot simply be displayed, or printed, by executing a bunch of PRINT statements. A human being will have to read this output. Unless the output is carefully designed, it will be very difficult to read; as a consequence information could be misread, or entirely overlooked.

Fortunately CBM BASIC has many capabilities that make it easy to program input and output correctly. We will describe some of these capabilities before looking specifically at good input and output programming practices.

PRINT STATEMENT

Semicolon Punctuation

Normally a PRINT statement ends its display with a RETURN. This causes the next PRINT statement to begin displaying in the first character position of the next line. Thus the following immediate mode program displays a column of 20 characters in the first character position of 20 rows:

```
C$="W":FOR I=1 TO 20:? C$:NEXT:?"PHEW!"
W
W
W
W
W
W
W
W
W
W
W
W
W
W
W
W
W
W
W
W
PHEW!

READY.
▓
```

A semicolon (;) appearing after any variable in the PRINT statement causes the next display to begin immediately at the next available character position. A semicolon following the last (or only) variable in the PRINT statement parameter list suppresses the RETURN. Therefore the following program will display 800 characters across 20 rows of a 40-column display.

```
C$="W":FOR I=1 TO 800:? C$;:NEXT:?"PHEW!"
WWWWWWWWWWWWWWWWWWWWWWWWWWWWWWWWWWWWWWWWWW
WWWWWWWWWWWWWWWWWWWWWWWWWWWWWWWWWWWWWWWWWW
WWWWWWWWWWWWWWWWWWWWWWWWWWWWWWWWWWWWWWWWWW
WWWWWWWWWWWWWWWWWWWWWWWWWWWWWWWWWWWWWWWWWW
WWWWWWWWWWWWWWWWWWWWWWWWWWWWWWWWWWWWWWWWWW
WWWWWWWWWWWWWWWWWWWWWWWWWWWWWWWWWWWWWWWWWW
WWWWWWWWWWWWWWWWWWWWWWWWWWWWWWWWWWWWWWWWWW
WWWWWWWWWWWWWWWWWWWWWWWWWWWWWWWWWWWWWWWWWW
WWWWWWWWWWWWWWWWWWWWWWWWWWWWWWWWWWWWWWWWWW
WWWWWWWWWWWWWWWWWWWWWWWWWWWWWWWWWWWWWWWWWW
WWWWWWWWWWWWWWWWWWWWWWWWWWWWWWWWWWWWWWWWWW
WWWWWWWWWWWWWWWWWWWWWWWWWWWWWWWWWWWWWWWWWW
WWWWWWWWWWWWWWWWWWWWWWWWWWWWWWWWWWWWWWWWWW
WWWWWWWWWWWWWWWWWWWWWWWWWWWWWWWWWWWWWWWWWW
WWWWWWWWWWWWWWWWWWWWWWWWWWWWWWWWWWWWWWWWWW
WWWWWWWWWWWWWWWWWWWWWWWWWWWWWWWWWWWWWWWWWW
WWWWWWWWWWWWWWWWWWWWWWWWWWWWWWWWWWWWWWWWWW
WWWWWWWWWWWWWWWWWWWWWWWWWWWWWWWWWWWWWWWWWW
WWWWWWWWWWWWWWWWWWWWWWWWWWWWWWWWWWWWWWWWWW
WWWWWWWWWWWWWWWWWWWWWWWWWWWWWWWWWWWWWWWWWW
PHEW!

READY.
▓
```

The FOR-NEXT loop index 1 is used as a counter to indicate the number of W's to be displayed, in this case 800. On the first PRINT, a new line is begun and the character W is displayed. The semicolon prevents a RETURN to the next line, so the cursor remains at the character position following the first W. The second W is then displayed and the cursor is left in the next character position. This sequence continues up to the end of the first line, then the cursor moves to the beginning of the next line. This sequence continues for 20 lines (of a 40-column display).

Why does PHEW! print on a new line? It doesn't really; it appears to start a new line because the last character is displayed in the last position of the previous line. Change 800 to 780 and PHEW! is displayed at the end of the line of characters. This may be illustrated as follows:

```
C$="-":FOR I=1 TO 780:?C$;:NEXT:?"PHEW!"
----------------------------------------
----------------------------------------
----------------------------------------
----------------------------------------
----------------------------------------
----------------------------------------
----------------------------------------
----------------------------------------
----------------------------------------
----------------------------------------
----------------------------------------
----------------------------------------
----------------------------------------
----------------------------------------
----------------------------------------
----------------------------------------
----------------------------------------
----------------------------------------
----------------------------------------
-------------------PHEW!

READY.
▓
```

The semicolon concatenates string data, displaying items right next to each other, with no spaces in between. **Numeric data is also displayed in a continuous line format, but with a single space between negative numbers and two spaces between positive numbers** (since the + sign is not displayed).

To illustrate this, change the string variable to a single-digit numeric variable. Three character positions are needed to display each number, so change the ending index to 800/3 = 267. The number 5 is displayed as follows:

```
C=+5:FOR I=1 TO 267:?C;:NEXT:?"PHEW!"
 5  5  5  5  5  5  5  5  5  5  5  5  5  5
 5  5  5  5  5  5  5  5  5  5  5  5  5  5
    5  5  5  5  5  5  5  5  5  5  5  5  5
    5  5  5  5  5  5  5  5  5  5  5  5  5
 5  5  5  5  5  5  5  5  5  5  5  5  5  5
    5  5  5  5  5  5  5  5  5  5  5  5  5
 5  5  5  5  5  5  5  5  5  5  5  5  5
 5  5  5  5  5  5  5  5  5  5  5  5  5  5
    5  5  5  5  5  5  5  5  5  5  5  5  5
    5  5  5  5  5  5  5  5  5  5  5  5  5
 5  5  5  5  5  5  5  5  5  5  5  5  5  5
    5  5  5  5  5  5  5  5  5  5  5  5  5
 5  5  5  5  5  5  5  5  5  5  5  5  5  5
    5  5  5  5  5  5  5  5  5  5  5  5  5
 5  5  5  5  5  5  5  5  5  5  5  5  5
 5  5  5  5  5  5  5  5  5  5  5  5  5  5
    5  5  5  5  5  5  5  5  5  5  5  5  5
    5  5  5  5  5  5  5  5  5  5  5  5  5
 5  5  5  5  5  5  5  5  5  5  5  5  5  5
 PHEW!

READY.
```

Note the single space between the last number displayed and the word PHEW! This is because numbers are displayed using the following format:

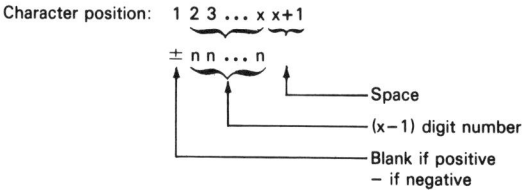

Character position: 1 2 3 ... x x+1

$$\pm\, n\, n\, ...\, n$$

- Space
- (x−1) digit number
- Blank if positive
  − if negative

which for a single digit becomes:

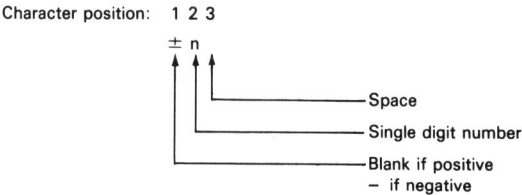

Character position: 1 2 3

$$\pm\, n$$

- Space
- Single digit number
- Blank if positive
  − if negative

Multiple-digit numbers will scroll the display off the screen unless the TO index is adjusted. If C is changed to 2001, a 6-digit display field is needed; you should adjust the TO index from 267 to 800/6 = 134:

```
C=2001:FOR I=1 TO 134:?C;:NEXT:?"PHEW!"
 2001  2001  2001  2001  2001  2001  200
1  2001  2001  2001  2001  2001  2001  2
001  2001  2001  2001  2001  2001  2001
 2001  2001  2001  2001  2001  2001  200
1  2001  2001  2001  2001  2001  2001  2
001  2001  2001  2001  2001  2001  2001
 2001  2001  2001  2001  2001  2001  200
1  2001  2001  2001  2001  2001  2001  2
001  2001  2001  2001  2001  2001  2001
 2001  2001  2001  2001  2001  2001  200
1  2001  2001  2001  2001  2001  2001  2
001  2001  2001  2001  2001  2001  2001
 2001  2001  2001  2001  2001  2001  200
1  2001  2001  2001  2001  2001  2001  2
001  2001  2001  2001  2001  2001  2001
 2001  2001  2001  2001  2001  2001  200
1  2001  2001  2001  2001  2001  2001  2
001 PHEW!

READY.
※
```

Numbers are broken across the end of lines. This is because the semicolon (;) generates a continuous display and nothing but an end of line can cause a return.

Comma Punctuation

Commas appearing after a variable, or at the end of a PRINT statement, treat the display as though it were tabbed at ten-character intervals. For a 40-column display this may be illustrated as follows:

```
1              11             21             31
↑
└──────── Leftmost position=1
```

In the display program change the semicolon in the PRINT statement to a comma. This causes numbers to be displayed in four columns on a 40-column display. At four numbers per line, the TO index will be 4*20 = 80. When you run this program, note that the first position in each field is reserved for the sign.

```
C=2001:FOR I=1 TO 80:?C,:NEXT:?"PHEW!"

2001        2001        2001        2001
2001        2001        2001        2001
2001        2001        2001        2001
2001        2001        2001        2001
2001        2001        2001        2001
2001        2001        2001        2001
2001        2001        2001        2001
2001        2001        2001        2001
2001        2001        2001        2001
2001        2001        2001        2001
2001        2001        2001        2001
2001        2001        2001        2001
2001        2001        2001        2001
2001        2001        2001        2001
2001        2001        2001        2001
2001        2001        2001        2001
2001        2001        2001        2001
2001        2001        2001        2001
2001        2001        2001        2001
PHEW!

READY.
▓
```

Using commas between PRINT statement variables is a convenient way to tab. Now change the value of C from 2001 to 44. Change the TO index from 134 to 200. Press RETURN and (surprise!) you will get the display shown below.

```
C=44:FOR I=1 TO 200:?C;:NEXT:?"PHEW!"
440 442 44   440 442 44   440 442 44   440
442 44   440 442 44   440 442 44   440 442
44   440 442 44   440 442 44   440 442 44
440 442 44   440 442 44   440 442 44   440
442 44   440 442 44   440 442 44   440 442
44   440 442 44   440 442 44   440 442 44
440 442 44   440 442 44   440 442 44   440
442 44   440 442 44   440 442 44   440 442
44   440 442 44   440 442 44   440 442 44
440 442 44   440 442 44   440 442 44   440
442 44   440 442 44   440 442 44   440 442
44   440 442 44   440 442 44   440 442 44
440 442 44   440 442 44   440 442 44   440
442 44   440 442 44   440 442 44   440 442
44   440 442 44   440 442 44   440 442 44
440 442 44   440 442 44   440 442 44   440
442 44   440 442 44   440 442 44   440 442
44   440 442 44   440 442 44   440 442 44
440 442 44   440 442 44   440 442 44   440
442 44   440 442 44   440 442 44   440 442
PHEW!HEW!

READY.
▓
```

Some of the digits from the previous 2001 display were not blanked out. **CBM BASIC uses a skip (cursor right) character, not blanks, between fields. When you display over existing data, characters between fields — or characters in tabbed format — are not erased.** Also note that there is a remaining "HEW!"; CBM BASIC displays the "PHEW!" but leaves the remaining positions of the line just as they were; it does not blank the rest of the line. **This can be a great advantage when you are adding to data already on the screen, and you should bear this capability in mind.** For the display program line, however, it is leaving extraneous characters in the display.

To remove extraneous characters from the display, you can have the program clear the screen before beginning a new display. To do this, insert a PRINT CLEAR SCREEN statement ahead of the FOR-NEXT loop:

```
C=44:?"⌧":FOR I=1 TO 200:?C$;:NEXT:?"PHEW!"
        ↖Clear Screen (shift of CLR/HOME key)
```

Now when you press RETURN, you will see the screen blank and the numbers displayed on the *second* line.

To begin displaying on the *first* line, insert a semicolon after the PRINT CLEAR SCREEN statement.

```
C$="A":?"⌧";:FOR I=1TO840:?C$;:NEXT:?"PHEW!"
```

With the extra line of forty characters, the program can display 840 characters without scrolling any off the top.

Commas also work when printing strings. As an example, enter the following immediate mode program to display twenty lines of tabbed character data:

```
A$="HUP!":B$="TWO!":C$="THREE!":D$="FOUR!"
FOR I=1 TO 20:?A$,B$,C$,D$:NEXT:?"PHEW!"
```

CURSOR MOVEMENT

In Chapter 3 we discussed the screen editing capabilities provided by the cursor control keys: CLEAR SCREEN/HOME, CURSOR UP/DOWN, CURSOR LEFT/RIGHT, INSERT/DELETE, and RETURN.

The CLEAR SCREEN/HOME, CURSOR UP/DOWN, CURSOR LEFT/RIGHT, and REVERSE keys can be included within PRINT statement strings. The INSERT/DELETE key and the RETURN key cannot be used within a PRINT statement.

Cursor control keys are interpreted as characters within a string until the PRINT statement is executed. Consider the PRINT statement:

```
100 PRINT"*▮▮*"
```

- Quotation set #2: change program mode to immediate mode
- Programmed representation of cursor right
- Quotation set #1: change immediate mode to program mode

When this PRINT statement is executed, you can see the cursor has moved right by the placement of the asterisks:

```
RUN

* *
```

To practice simple programmed cursor movement, type in the following program:

```
10  PRINT"<CLEAR SCREEN>";
20  PRINT"<CURSOR↓>* <CURSOR↓>* <CURSOR↓>* <REVERSE> <CURSOR↓>*
    <CURSOR↓>* <CURSOR↓>*"
30  PRINT"<CURSOR↓> <CURSOR↓> <CURSOR↓> <CURSOR↓>";
```

The program should look like this on your screen:

```
10 PRINT"⊐";
20 PRINT"▉*▉*▉*⊠⊐*⊐*⊐*";
30 PRINT"▉▉▉▉"
40 END
```

Upon execution, the output should appear as follows:

```
        ⊐
  *     ⊐
    *  ⊐
      *
```

This may or may not have been what you expected. If you expected the character sequence:

```
20 PRINT "▉*▉*▉*            "
```

to display the asterisks in a vertical line:

```
      *

      *

      *
```

or if you expected the character sequence:

```
20 PRINT "         ⊠⊐*⊐*⊐*"
```

to display three asterisks back up over the original three:

```
    ⊐

    ⊐

    ⊐
```

you forgot about the **automatic right movement of the cursor following every keystroke.** The programmed cursor control causes the CBM computer to move the cursor directly up or directly down, but the asterisks will be displayed in a diagonal line due to the cursor's automatic advance. Each time a character is displayed, the cursor is automatically advanced one space to the right. This prevents the last character from being overwritten. The following diagram shows the cursor movement of the previous program:

Automatic cursor advance

To display a vertical line you must compensate for the advance by moving the cursor back one space to the left before moving it up one space or down one space. For example, the following program statement displays a vertical descending line of three asterisks followed by a vertical line of three ascending, adjacent asterisks:

```
20 PRINT "<CURSOR↓>*<CURSOR←><CURSOR↓>*<CURSOR←><CURSOR↓>*
         <REVERSE>*<CURSOR←><CURSOR↑>*<CURSOR←><CURSOR↑>*";
```

This will be displayed as follows:

```
20 PRINT"▉*▉*▉*⊠⊐*⊐*⊐*";
```

If you attempt to program the INSERT/DELETE and the RETURN keys, you will encounter some surprising results.

The INSERT key is programmable. When you press the INSERT key between a set of quotes, a reverse capital T displays. Of course the CBM will not appear to insert a space if the entire line the cursor is on is blank.

The DELETE key remains in immediate mode. Trying to program the DELETE key in a PRINT statement will merely erase the previous character, unless the DELETE key occurs within a sequence of inserted characters. The DELETE key is programmable following an insert, but do not use it in this fashion. It will simply get you into trouble. There are simpler ways of achieving the same objective in a program.

The RETURN character in a PRINT statement will immediately move the cursor out of the statement and to the next line.

CHR$ FUNCTION: PROGRAMMING CHARACTERS IN ASCII

If you cannot press a key to include a character within a text string, you can still select the character by using its ASCII value.

The CHR$ function translates an ASCII code number into its character equivalent. The format of the CHR$ function is:

```
PRINT CHR$(xx)
             ┊
             └──────ASCII number from 0 to 255 of
                    desired character or control
```

To obtain the correct ASCII code for the desired character, refer to Appendix A. Scan the columns until you find the desired character or cursor control, then note the corresponding ASCII code number. Insert this number between the two parentheses of the CHR$ function. For example, to create the symbol "$" from its ASCII code, find the ASCII code for "$." "$" has two ASCII values: 36 and 100. Which value should you use? Either number works just as well. But for good programming technique, once you select one number over the other, use that number consistently throughout the program. We will use 36 and insert it into the CHR$ function as follows:

```
PRINT CHR$(36)
```

Try displaying this character in immediate mode:

```
PRINT CHR$(36)
$
```

Now, try displaying ASCII code 100:

```
PRINT CHR$(100)
$
```

The result is the same. Experiment in immediate mode using any ASCII code from 0 to 255.

You can use the CHR$ function in a PRINT statement as follows:

```
10 PRINT CHR$(36);CHR$(42);CHR$(166)

RUN
$*▒
```

The **CHR$ function lets you include otherwise unavailable characters such as RETURN, INSERT/DELETE, and the quote character (")** among a PRINT statement's parameters. **You may also use the CHR$ function to do comparison checking for cursor controls such as RETURN and INSERT/DELETE.** Suppose a program must check characters input at the keyboard, looking for a RETURN key. You could check for a RETURN (which has an ASCII code of 13) as follows:

```
10 GET X$ IF X$<>CHR$(13) THEN 10
```

This test would be impossible if you tried to put RETURN between quotation marks:

```
20 IF X$<>" RETURN "THEN 10
                ↑
            Impossible
```

This is impossible because when you depress the RETURN key following a set of quotes, it automatically moves the cursor to the next line:

```
20 IF X$<>"  ◄────── Press RETURN key
```

Cursor Controls (CBM 8000)

The screen editor release 4.1, available on the CBM 8000, has two new key functions and some new edit/control capabilities. The key functions are provided by the TAB and ESCAPE keys. The edit/control capabilities include a programmable bell, line insert and delete, screen erase, graphic/text switching, and scrolling within a programmable screen window.

The TAB Key and Tabbing Function. **The TAB key operates much like a typewriter TAB key. The tabbing capabilities of the TAB key are equivalent to the TAB function. Up to 80 TABs may be set per line.** To set a TAB in immediate mode, move the cursor to the desired screen column, then press the TAB and SHIFT keys simultaneously. When all tabs have been set, press the RETURN key:

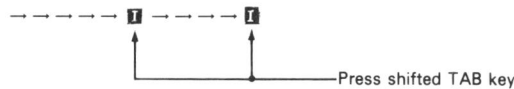

```
→ → → → ▉ → → → → ▉
        ↑         ↑
        └────┬────┘── Press shifted TAB key
```

You can **program the TAB SET using a PRINT statement.** The text string to be printed must move the cursor to the required column, then execute a TAB SET. The TAB SET character is generated by pressing the shifted TAB key. This may be illustrated as follows:

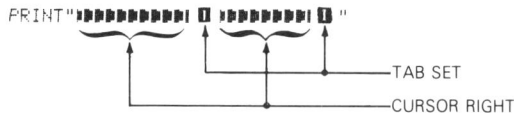

```
PRINT"▐▶▶▶▶▶▶▶▶▶ ▉ ▐▶▶▶▶▶▶▶ ▉ "
                ↑     ↑   ↑
                │     ↑   │──── TAB SET
                └─────┴───┴──── CURSOR RIGHT
```

A reverse upper-case I is displayed for the TAB SET.

The TAB SET is represented by ASCII value 137, therefore TAB SET can be programmed using the CHR$ function:

```
PRINT"▐▶▶▶▶▶▶";CHR$(137)
```

The TAB key advances the cursor to the next tabbed column on the screen. To tab the cursor in immediate mode, simply press the TAB key. If TAB is pressed beyond the last tab position on the screen, the cursor jumps to the end of the display line.

When included in a PRINT statement, the tab will occur at the point where the TAB character is encountered. Here is an immediate mode example:

```
PRINT" MY□PET BITES"
```
⌐————————————Programmed TAB
```
MY PET BITES
```

TAB CLEAR clears a TAB SET position. In immediate mode move the cursor to the column whose tab set is to be cleared, then press the TAB and SHIFT keys simultaneously. Following the last TAB CLEAR, press the RETURN key.

TAB CLEAR and TAB SET are both generated by the shifted TAB key. Therefore **if you try to clear a tab in a column where none was set, you will set a tab instead.**

Tabs are cleared in program mode using a PRINT statement that moves the cursor to the required column, then executes a TAB CLEAR character:

```
PRINT"▮▮▮▮▮▮▮▮▮▮▮▮▮▮▮▮▮▮▮▮"
```
————TAB CLEAR
————CURSOR RIGHT

TAB CLEAR, like TAB SET, is displayed as a reverse upper-case I character.

TAB CLEAR can be programmed using the CHR$ function as follows:

```
PRINT"▮▮▮▮▮";CHR$(137)
```

CHR$(137) represents the TAB SET and TAB CLEAR characters.

Escape. The ESCAPE key on the CBM 2001/B business keyboard generates an ASCII code, but has no editing capabilities. **On the CBM 8000 keyboard the ESCAPE key has two functions: pressed in immediate mode it cancels an insert, reverse, or text entry condition. ESCAPE also allows certain character strings to be interpreted as screen editing control functions.**

ESCAPE can be included in a PRINT statement by using the CHR$ function. Enter:

```
PRINT CHR$(27)
```

Control Functions (CBM 8000)

Control functions summarized below are available only on the CBM 8000 computers with the 80-column screen. These functions are defined in detail in Chapter 8. Some examples of their use are given later in this chapter.

All of these control functions are desgined to improve displays and data entry; although they can be used in immediate mode, they should not be used to edit programs. Many of these functions modify the display without simultaneously changing memory content.

To use one of these functions, its character must appear in a PRINT statement's parameter list. The function character can be specified within a text string using a control character, or it may be specified outside of a text string using a CHR$ function. The control character is generated by pressing the ESCAPE key, then the REVERSE key, then the appropriate unshifted letter key.

Bell. The Bell function works only on a CBM 8000 computer that is equipped with a bell. The bell will ring automatically on power-up, and whenever the cursor moves through column 75. If the screen window has been narrowed (using the scrolling window function) the bell will sound as the cursor passes through the fifth column from the right edge of the window. The bell is also sounded by a Control-g character, or a CHR$(7) function in a PRINT statement.

Delete Line and Insert Line. These functions delete or insert a display line. The Delete Line function deletes the line on which the cursor is located; all lower lines on the display are scrolled up one line position. The Insert Line function inserts a line at the cursor screen location, scrolling all lower lines down; the bottom line is scrolled off the screen. Neither the Delete nor the Insert Line function modifies computer memory; only the display changes. The Delete Line function is generated by a Control-u character or the CHR$(21) function in a PRINT statement parameter list. The Insert Line function is generated by a Control-M character or a CHR$(149) function in the PRINT statement parameter list.

Erase Begin and Erase End. These functions erase part of the line on which the cursor is currently positioned. The Erase Begin function erases all text to the left of the cursor; the Erase End function erases all text to the right of the cursor. Neither function moves remaining text. Neither function modifies memory. The Erase Begin function is generated by a Control-V character or a CHR$(150) function occurring in a PRINT statement parameter list. The Erase End function is generated by a Control-v character or a CHR$(22) function appearing in a PRINT statement parameter list.

Graphic or Text. The Graphic function selects graphic characters from the standard character set, while text characters select upper- and lower-case letters. Also, spaces between graphic characters are eliminated in order to improve the quality of graphics. The graphic function is selected by a Control-N character or a CHR$(142) function appearing in a PRINT statement parameter list.

The Text function is the inverse of the Graphic function. The Text function selects the alternate character set for graphic characters, while text characters continue to select upper- and lower-case letters. The Text function is selected by a Control-n character or the CHR$(14) function appearing in a PRINT statement parameter list.

Screen Window Functions. There are four functions which allow a window to be defined in the CBM 8000 display, with text scrolled up or down within the defined window. The **Set Top function** takes the current cursor location as the top left-hand corner of the display window; the **Set Bottom function** takes the current cursor location as representing the bottom right-hand corner of the window. This window can be canceled at any time by pressing the HOME key twice, or by executing a PRINT statement with two contiguous HOME characters in its parameter list. Set Top is selected by the CHR$(15) function and Set Bottom is set by the CHR$(143) function; these CHR$ functions should appear in a PRINT statement parameter list following cursor move characters that correctly position the cursor to define the top left and right bottom corners of the window.

The **Scroll Up function** moves text up one line within a window defined by the Set Top and the Set Bottom functions. A blank line is inserted at the bottom of the window. The **Scroll Down function,** likewise, moves text down one line within the window, inserting a blank line at the top of the window. Scroll Up is selected by a Control-q character or the CHR$(25) function. Scroll Down is selected by a Control-Q or the CHR$(153) function. The control character or CHR$ function must appear in a PRINT statement parameter list.

POKE to the Screen

You can use a POKE statement to display any character anywhere on the screen. Simply **POKE the character value into the correct screen location in memory.**

The CBM computer screen is like a grid of 1000 (or 2000) squares, organized as 25 rows and 40 (or 80 columns). A 40-column display may be illustrated as follows:

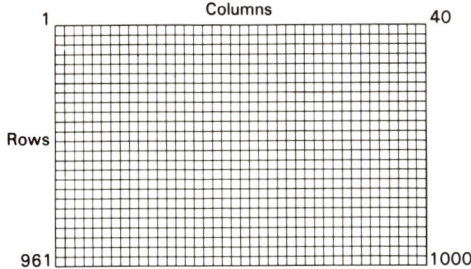

One character may be displayed in each square. **Every screen location is assigned an address and space in memory.** Memory screen space begins at address 32768 for square 1 (row 1, column 1) and ends at address 33767 for square 1000 (row 25, column 40), or at address 34767 for square 2000 (row 25, column 80). Memory address 32768 is screen location (1,1), address 32769 is screen location (1,2), etc. Figure 5-2 shows the correlation between screen locations and their corresponding memory spaces and addresses.

To find the screen address in memory for any screen location, use the following equations:

40 Column Screen   **80 Column Screen**

32768+(column-1)+(40•(row-1))   32768+(column-1)+(80•(row-1))

Enter the column and row numbers of any screen position into the equation to find its memory address. To demonstrate, enter the values 5 and 3 to find the memory address for the screen location at column 5, row 3:

```
=32768+(COL-1)+(40•(ROW-1))
=32768+(5-1)+(40•-1))
=32768+4+(40•2)
=32768+4+80
=32852
```

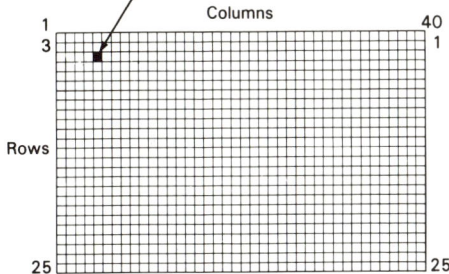

The memory address for screen location (5,3) is 32852.

This equation makes it possible to POKE characters to the screen without knowing any more than the column and row number of the location to be POKEd. Recall the format of the POKE statement:

POKE A,X

where:

A   is the screen address.

X   is the character or variable to be POKEd into A.

Replace A with the screen equation and the computer will calculate the screen address for you:

POKE 32768+(COL-)+(40•ROW-1),X

POKE   A   ,X

For instance, if COL (C) and ROW (R) is input as 5,3, and X is input as ♠, then a spade will be POKEd at screen location (3,5), address 32852.

Try entering and executing this program:

```
10 INPUT C,R,X
20 POKE 32768+(C-1)+(40*(R-1)),X
```

=32768+(COL-1)+(40•(ROW-1)),X
=32768+(5-1)+(40•(ROW-1)),X
=32768+4+(40•2),X
=32768+4+80,X
=32852,X

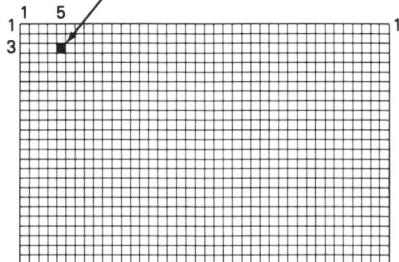

X is entered as a number in the range 0 to 255.

Variables may be used in POKE statements, but the variable must evaluate to a number within the allowed limits:

POKE 32768+A,X

where: A is a number between 0 and 999
             inclusive (32768+999=33767) for
             a 40 column screen

POKE A, X

where: A is a number between 32768 and 33767 inclusive for
             a 40 column screen

Using a variable to represent the screen address is wise when POKEing to a repeating sequence of screen spaces. For example, the program below POKEs the value of X ten spaces apart across the screen:

```
10 A=32768
20 POKE A,X
30 A=A+10
40 IF A<=33767 GOTO 20
```

DATA ENTRY (INPUT)

Data entry should be programmed in functional units.

A mailing list program, for example, requires names and addresses to be entered as data. You should treat each name and address as a single functional unit. In other words, your program should ask for the name and address, allowing the operator to enter all of this information and then change any part of it; when the operator is satisfied that the name and address are correct, the program should process the entire name and address as a single functional unit. Then the program should ask for the next name and address.

It is bad programming practice to break up data input into its smallest parts. In the case of a mailing list program it would be bad programming practice to ask for the name, process this data as soon as it has been entered, then ask for each line of the address, treating each piece of the name and address as a separate and distinct functional unit.

The goal of any data entry program should be to make it easy for an operator to spot errors and to give the operator as many chances as possible to fix errors.

Suppose a program requires a long list of short, identical data items to be input. Such a list may consist of names, social security numbers, or perhaps dates. It is a good idea to write a program which accepts such input in blocks. For example, if names must be entered, the program might allow the operator to enter as many names as will fit in one vertical column, so that any entry can be corrected while it is still being displayed. The program would accept and process names as they scroll off the top of the screen. The alternative would be to write an input program that accepts and processes one name at a time. But this program would reduce an operator's chances of spotting and correcting mistakes.

There is one set of circumstances when entering data in blocks is not the best way to go, and this set of circumstances is a surprising one: it occurs when a very large amount of data must be entered by keyboard operators. For example, suppose a keyboard operator must enter hundreds of names and addresses a day. Experience has shown that the highest volume of accurate data entry can be achieved by having the keyboard operator ignore all errors on first entry. The data entry program should not allow for the correction of any errors, even if the errors are detected as data is being entered. Operators should be trained to ignore errors and carry on entering data as fast as possible. Such data should be entered twice, preferably by different operators. The data entry should be compared. The chances of both operators making the same error are so small that you can count on all errors being flagged as differences between the two sets of data entry. A subsequent program should allow incorrect data to be corrected.

164   *PET/CBM Personal Computer Guide*

Interactive Data Input

To demonstrate the value of good, interactive data input we will begin with a very simple example. Starting with an early version of program BLANKET we will discuss, step by step, the changes that improve data entry, thereby making the program easier to use.

Start with the program listed below; we will finish with the program as it appears in Figure 5-1.

```
100 C$="A"
110 PRINT ""
120 FOR I=1 TO 840
130 PRINT C$;
140 NEXT
150 PRINT "PHEW!"
```

The program above will display 800 A's followed by the exclamation PHEW!

Suppose we want to display X's instead of A's.

First eliminate the assignment statement in the program. To delete a program statement, type the line number followed immediately by a RETURN.

```
LIST 100


    100 C$="A"

READY.
100 ◄─────────────────────────Type line number, then key RETURN.
LIST

    110 PRINT "";
    120 FOR I=1 TO 840
    130 PRINT C$;
    140 NEXT
    150 PRINT "PHEW!"
READY.
▓
```

Line 100 is no longer in the program. Type in the statement C$="X" in immediate mode, then run the program.

Before RETURN	After RETURN
C$="X"	PHEW!
READY.	READY.
RUN▓	▓

The screen blanks and the word PHEW! is printed, but the X's are not printed. Obviously the value of C$ is not being transmitted to the program.

RUN clears all variables to 0 and all strings to null before beginning execution of a program. So C$ was set to null, and a null character was printed in the program loop (a "null" is "nothing": it does not print nor does it move the cursor).

Is there a way to transmit the value of C$, entered in immediate mode, to the program? Instead of using RUN, which initializes variables, use GOTO 110 (110 being the line number of the first line of the program). This does not change any variable values.

```
Before RETURN

C$="X"

READY.
GOTO 110
```

After RETURN

```
XXXXXXXXXXXXXXXXXXXXXXXXXXXXXXXXXXXXXX
XXXXXXXXXXXXXXXXXXXXXXXXXXXXXXXXXXXXX
XXXXXXXXXXXXXXXXXXXXXXXXXXXXXXXXXXXXX
XXXXXXXXXXXXXXXXXXXXXXXXXXXXXXXXXXXXX
XXXXXXXXXXXXXXXXXXXXXXXXXXXXXXXXXXXXXX
XXXXXXXXXXXXXXXXXXXXXXXXXXXXXXXXXXXXX
XXXXXXXXXXXXXXXXXXXXXXXXXXXXXXXXXXXXX
XXXXXXXXXXXXXXXXXXXXXXXXXXXXXXXXXXXXX
XXXXXXXXXXXXXXXXXXXXXXXXXXXXXXXXXXXXX
XXXXXXXXXXXXXXXXXXXXXXXXXXXXXXXXXXXXX
XXXXXXXXXXXXXXXXXXXXXXXXXXXXXXXXXXXXX
XXXXXXXXXXXXXXXXXXXXXXXXXXXXXXXXXXXXX
XXXXXXXXXXXXXXXXXXXXXXXXXXXXXXXXXXXXX
XXXXXXXXXXXXXXXXXXXXXXXXXXXXXXXXXXXXX
XXXXXXXXXXXXXXXXXXXXXXXXXXXXXXXXXXXXX
XXXXXXXXXXXXXXXXXXXXXXXXXXXXXXXXXXXXX
XXXXXXXXXXXXXXXXXXXXXXXXXXXXXXXXXXXXX
XXXXXXXXXXXXXXXXXXXXXXXXXXXXXXXXXXXXX
XXXXXXXXXXXXXXXXXXXXXXXXXXXXXXXXXXXXX
XXXXXXXXXXXXXXXXXXXXXXXXXXXXXXXXXXXXX
XXXXXXXXXXXXXXXXXXXXXXXXXXXXXXXXXXXXX
PHEW!

READY.
※
```

Now the procedure for running the program is as follows:

1. In immediate mode enter the assignment C$="y" where y is any display character.
2. Enter the immediate statement GOTO 110.

There are only two steps in running the program, but the procedure is awkward. You must type in a line (the assignment statement), and if you enter RUN instead of GOTO, you must start all over. **But the program could fetch the display character while it is running,** using the GET statement. Type in the following line:

```
100 GET C$:IF C$="" GOTO 100
```

List the program and make sure you entered the line correctly. Then run the program. The screen blanks and the cursor disappears. Press any data key. The character you enter is displayed 800 times. Run the program again. Press any data key. The display appears with the new character.

Here is the new procedure for running program BLANKET:

1. Enter the RUN command.
2. Press any key.

This is a real improvement over the original program. However, it is a little disconcerting to have the screen completely blank out while it waits for you to press a key. Add a prompt line to the beginning of the program, asking for key to be pressed. Type in the line:

```
90 ?"HIT A KEY"
```

List the program and check the new line for errors.

Now the program gives operating instructions. Run the program several times to display different characters and note how much easier the program is to use.

There is one important modification left to make. If you want **to run the program more than once,** go back to the beginning of the program instead of ending it. Then you won't have to type in RUN to reexecute the program. Add the following line:

```
160 GOTO 90
```

Again, list the program and check the new line. It should look like this:

```
LIST

90 PRINT "HIT A KEY"
100 GET C$:IF C$="" GOTO 100
110 PRINT "J";
120 FOR I=1 TO 840
130 PRINT C$;
140 NEXT
150 PRINT "PHEW!"
160 GOTO 90
READY.
※
```

Now it is even easier to use the program. Enter RUN and follow directions.

Of course, you have to use the STOP key to exit from the program. This can be eliminated by programming one particular key **to terminate program execution.** For example, the RETURN key could be programmed to terminate execution.

Let us see how this is done.

All data keys and cursor control keys can be checked as string characters. For example, the following statements check for a 'Y' character:

```
100 GET C$:IF C$="" GOTO 100
105 IF C$="Y" GOTO 200
```

RETURN presents a special problem. You cannot reference RETURN as a string literal:

This is because any time RETURN is pressed, CBM BASIC stores the program line in memory and goes to the beginning of the next line. You can, however, use the CHR$ function to check for a RETURN key entry. CHR$ allows you to assign an ASCII code value to a string variable and treat it as a string. The ASCII code value for a RETURN is 13.

Before programming to check for a carriage return, consider what must be done if there is one. The last line of the program branches back to the beginning of the program. To terminate program execution, you need to branch beyond the last line. Add the following line:

```
170 END
```

Now add the check for RETURN for program termination at line 105:

```
105 IF C$=CHR$(13) GOTO 170
```

Note that we could have written, in place of line 170 and line 105:

```
105 IF C$=CHR$(13) THEN END ◄── Option
```

If you choose this option, it is generally good programming practice to have the program termination point at the physical end of the program. It is more difficult to find termination points embedded in the program.

Without the READY message being printed each time, there are two additional lines available on the screen. This allows 80 more characters (at 40 characters per line) to be printed. Change the number of characters on line 120 from 840 to 840 + 80 = 920. Line 120 will read:

```
120 FOR I=1 TO 920
```

When you run the program, you will find that it is scrolling up one line, leaving a blank line at the bottom of the screen. This is because CBM BASIC executes a RETURN after displaying HIT A KEY; it does this to select a new line in preparation for the next display. We can demonstrate this by making the cursor blink.

Normally you cannot see the cursor because its blinking is inhibited before a program is run. However, you can make the cursor blink by adding the following statement to the beginning of the program:

```
80 POKE 548,0 ←───── Enable cursor
```

This is a system location that is discussed further in Chapter 7. Run the program with this line added and you will see the cursor blinking at the bottom line.

```
        .
        .
        .
PHEW!
HIT A KEY
▓
```

This program does not really need the cursor, so delete line 80.

To prevent the blank line at the bottom of the screen, add a semicolon to the PRINT statement in line 90. We should also add a prompt that RETURN is used to exit from the program. To incorporate these changes, line 90 should now be edited as follows:

```
90 ?"HIT A KEY OR <R> TO END";
```

As a final task, you might read over the program and add remarks. Comment on how the number 920 was devised; you can optionally put the remark on the same line, using a colon to separate statements:

```
120 FOR I=1 TO 920    :REM 920/40=23 LINES
```

Add a reminder that the screen is cleared; optionally align the remarks:

```
110 PRINT"⊐";        :REM CLEAR SCREEN
```

Finally, add a few lines at the beginning of the program to describe it. The final program BLANKET is shown in Figure 5-1. Save it on tape or diskette.

Prompting Messages

Any program that requires data entry should prompt the operator by asking questions. Questions are usually displayed on a single line and demand a simple response such as "yes," "no," a word, or a number. For example the following message might be displayed:

```
DO YOU WANT TO MAKE ANY CHANGES?
```

An operator must respond to this message by entering the word YES or the word NO. Frequently just the letter Y or N suffices. Another common example may give the operator a number of options. The message:

```
WHICH ENTRY DO YOU WISH TO CHANGE?
```

may allow the operator to enter a number which identifies an entry.

Programs that control this type of dialogue should be written as stand-alone subroutines which do not depend on knowledge of the calling program. This has three implications:

1. You cannot assume that the row on which the message will be displayed is blank. If the row is not blank, then the message will overwrite whatever was previously there; but worse, the remainder of the line, beyond the message, will be interpreted as part of the response. This is ugly from the operator's viewpoint, but it can also be troublesome. Depending on how your program is written, remaining characters beyond the message may be interpreted as part of the data input.

2. The subroutine must receive parameters from the calling program. For example, if a message asks the operator to enter a number, then the calling program should pass the minimum and maximum allowed numbers to the subroutine as parameters.

3. The subroutine must return the operator's response to the calling program. This variable may be a character (e.g., Y or N), it may be a word (e.g., yes or no), or it might be a number.

Subroutine logic cannot deduce on which screen row the message is to appear. It is therefore fair to demand that the calling program position the cursor on the correct row. You can clear the selected row and position the cursor at column 0 of the row using the following statements:

```
2000 REM CLEAR THE ROW ON WHICH THE CURSOR IS CURRENTLY POSITIONED
2010 PRINTCHR$(13);"⌐";:REM MOVE CURSOR TO COLUMN 0
2020 FOR I=1 TO 39:PRINT" ";:NEXT
2030 PRINTCHR$(13);"⌐";
2040 STOP
```

For an 80-column screen the statements on line 2020 should write 79 blanks, rather than 39 blanks as illustrated.

Enter this program into your computer; position the cursor on a blank line between two lines of text, then type RUN <CR> to execute the program. If all the text scrolls off the top of the screen then you forgot the semicolon that must terminate the PRINT statement on line 2020.

Frequently the statements illustrated above will be called as a subroutine, in which case a RETURN statement must occur on line 2040.

Alternatively you can use the **CBM 8000 Erase Begin and Erase End** functions:

```
2000 REM CLEAR THE ROW ON WHICH THE CURSOR IS CURRENTLY POSITIONED
2010 PRINTCHR$(150);CHR$(22);CHR$(13);"⌐";
2030 STOP
```

The routine collapses to a single statement. Calling this single statement as a subroutine would be pointless.

Now look at the subroutine needed to ask a question that requires a reply of Y for yes, or N for no. We will use a PRINT statement to ask the question, followed by a GET to receive a one-character response. Clear the row on which the question is to be asked by calling the clear row subroutine. Here is the program and the called subroutine:

```
2000 REM CLEAR THE ROW ON WHICH THE CURSOR IS CURRENTLY POSITIONED
2010 PRINTCHR$(13);"⊐";:REM MOVE CURSOR TO COLUMN 0
2020 FOR I=1 TO 39:PRINT" ";:NEXT
2030 PRINTCHR$(13);"⊐";
2040 RETURN
3000 REM ASK A QUESTION AND RETURN A RESPONSE OF Y OR N IN YN$
3010 GOSUB 2000
3020 PRINT"DO YOU WANT TO MAKE ANY CHANGES? ";
3030 GET YN$:IF YN$<>"N" AND YN$<>"Y" THEN 3030
3040 PRINTYN$;
3050 RETURN
```

You can use the program illustrated above to ask any question that requires a "yes" or "no" response. The message to be displayed, whatever it may be, must occur in the PRINT statement on line 3020.

Next consider dialogue which allows an operator to enter a number. We will assume that the subroutine receives the smallest number in integer variable LO% and the largest number in integer variable HI%. The subroutine will return the entered number in NM%. Here is the necessary program:

```
2000 REM CLEAR THE ROW ON WHICH THE CURSOR IS CURRENTLY POSITIONED
2010 PRINTCHR$(13);"⊐";:REM MOVE CURSOR TO COLUMN 0
2020 FOR I=1 TO 39:PRINT" ";:NEXT
2030 PRINTCHR$(13);"⊐";
2040 RETURN
3000 REM ASK FOR A NUMERIC SELECTION
3001 REM RETURN SELECTION IN NM%
3002 REM NM% MUST BE LESS THEN HI% AND MORE THAN LO%
3003 REM CALLING PROGRAM MUST SET HI% AND LO%
3010 GOSUB 2000
3020 PRINT"WHICH DO YOU WANT TO CHANGE? ";
3030 GET NM$:IF NM$="" THEN 3030
3040 NM%=VAL(NM$)
3050 IF NM%<LO% OR NM%>HI% THEN 3030
3060 PRINTNM$;
3070 RETURN
```

Write a short program that sets values for HI% and LO%, then goes to subroutine 3000. Add the subroutine illustrated above and run it. A CBM 8000 version of this program will replace the GOSUB statement on line 3010 with the PRINT statement on line 2010 of the previous program.

Can you change the subroutine so that it accepts two-digit inputs? Try to write this modified program for yourself. If you cannot do it, then wait until the next section, where you will find the necessary subroutine in the program which controls input of a date.

There is another simple modification you can make to both of the dialogues we have described; the message printed on line 3020 in both programs could be supplied by the calling program via a string variable. This would make the subroutines more general purpose. Can you rewrite the programs to accept a message provided by the calling program?

Entering a Valid Date

Most programs at some point need relatively simple data input: more than a simple yes or no, but less than a full screen display. Consider a date.

You must take more care with such simple data entry than might at first appear necessary. In all probability the date will be just one item in a data entry sequence. By carefully designing data entry for each small item, you can avoid having to restart a long data entry sequence whenever the operator makes an error in a single entry.

We will assume that the date is to be entered as follows:

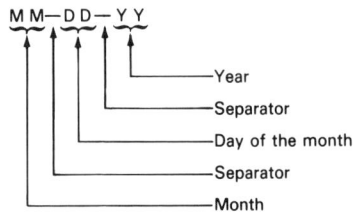

```
M M — D D — Y Y
                    ──────Year
                 ───────Separator
              ────────Day of the month
           ─────────Separator
        ──────────Month
```

Depending on your personal preferences, the dash separating two digit entries might be a slash, or any other visually pleasing character. In Europe the day of the month precedes the month.

Program data entry so that it is pleasing to the operator's eye. The operator should be able to see immediately where data is to be entered, what type of data is required, and how far the data entry process has proceeded. A good way of showing where data is to be entered is to reverse the data entry field. For example, the program that asks for a date to be entered might create the following reverse field display:

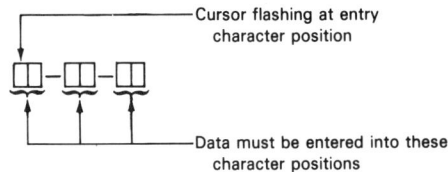

```
                            ─Cursor flashing at entry
                             character position

  ☐─☐─☐

                            ─Data must be entered into these
                             character positions
```

You can create such a display very simply using the following PRINT statement:

```
10 PRINT "<Clear><Cursor↓><Cursor↓>";TAB(20);"<Reverse>ЫЫ
   <Reverse off>-<Reverse>ЫЫ<Reverse off>-<Reverse>
   ЫЫ<Reverse off>";CHR$(13);"<Cursor↑>";TAB(20);

   Ы represents a space code.
```

The PRINT statement above includes cursor controls that position the date entry beginning at column 21 on row 3. Also, the PRINT statement clears the screen so that residual garbage display does not surround the request for a date. After displaying the date entry field, the PRINT statement moves the cursor back to the first character position of the first entry field by executing a carriage return, CURSOR UP and tab.

Try using an INPUT statement to receive entry of the month. This could be done as follows:

```
20 INPUT M$;
```

Enter statements on lines 10 and 20, as illustrated above, and execute them. The INPUT statement will not work. Apart from the fact that a question mark displaces the first reverse field character, the INPUT statement picks up the rest of the line following the question mark. Unless you overwrite the entire data entry display — and that requires entering a very large number — you will get a RE-DO FROM START message each time you press the RETURN key.

This is an occasion to use the GET statement:

```
10 PRINT"꒯꒯꒯";TAB(20);"▉ ▉-▉ ▉-▉ ▉";CHR$(13);"꒯";TAB(20);
20 GET C$:IF C$="" THEN 20
30 PRINTC$;:MM$=C$
40 GET C$:IF C$="" THEN 40
50 PRINTC$;:MM$=MM$+C$
60 STOP
```

These statements accept a two-digit input. The input is displayed in the first reverse field of the date. The two-digit input needs no carriage return or other terminating character; the program automatically terminates the data entry after two characters have been entered.

Three two-digit entries are needed: one each for the month, the day, and the year. Rather than repeating statements on lines 20 through 50, we will put these statements into a subroutine and branch to it three times, as follows:

```
10 PRINT"꒯꒯꒯";TAB(20);"▉ ▉-▉ ▉-▉ ▉";CHR$(13);"꒯";TAB(20).
20 GOSUB 1000:MM$=TC$:PRINTTAB(23)
30 GOSUB 1000:DD$=TC$:PRINTTAB(26)
40 GOSUB 1000:YY$=TC$
50 STOP
1000 REM TWO CHARACTER INPUT SUBROUTINE
1010 GET C$:IF C$="" THEN 1010
1020 PRINTC$;
1030 GET CC$:IF CC$="" THEN 1030
1040 PRINTCC$;
1050 TC$=C$+CC$
1060 RETURN
```

If you have a CBM 8000 computer, try rewriting the program above to use the TAB SET and TAB functions provided by the Editor release 4.1.

A CBM 8000 version of this program is much simpler because you can use the **CBM 8000 Erase End** function, as follows:

```
3000 REM ASK A QUESTION AND RETURN A RESPONSE OF Y OR N IN YN$
3005 REM CBM 8000 VERSION
3010 PRINTCHR$(150);CHR$(22);CHR$(13);"꒯";
3020 PRINT"DO YOU WANT TO MAKE ANY CHANGES? ";
3030 GET YN$:IF YN$<>"N" AND YN$<>"Y" THEN 3030
3040 PRINTYN$;
3050 RETURN
```

The variables MM$, DD$, and YY$ hold the month, day, and year entries, respectively. Each entry is held as a two-character string. As described earlier in this chapter, you should empty the ten-character input buffer before accepting the first input, otherwise any prior characters in the input buffer will be read by the first GET statement in the two-character input subroutine. You only need to empty the buffer once, before the first GET statement.

There are two ways in which we can help the operator recover from errors while entering a date.

1. The program can automatically test for valid month, day, and year entries.

2. The operator can be given a means of restarting the data entry.

The program can check that the month lies between 01 and 12. The program will not bother with leap year, but otherwise it will check for the maximum number of days in the specified month. Any year from 00 through 99 will be allowed. Any invalid entry will cause the entire date entry sequence to restart.

If the operator presses the RETURN key, then the entire date entry sequence restarts.

Our final date entry program now appears as follows:

```
5 REM ROUTINE TO ACCEPT AND VERIFY A DATE
10 PRINT"_____",TAB(20);"_ _-_ _-_ _";CHR$(13);"_";TAB(20);
50 GOSUB 1000:REM GET MONTH
60 IF C$=CHR$(13) OR CC$=CHR$(13) THEN 10
70 DT$=TC$:PRINTTAB(23);
80 REM CHECK FOR VALID MONTH
90 M%=VAL(TC$)
100 IF M%<1 OR M%>12 THEN 10
110 REM GET NUMBER OF DAYS IN MONTH
120 D%=31
130 IF M%=2 THEN D%=28
140 IF M%=4 OR M%=6 OR M%=9 OR M%=11 THEN D%=30
150 GOSUB 1000:REM GET DAY
160 IF C$=CHR$(13) OR CC$=CHR$(13) THEN 10
170 DT$=DT$+"-"+TC$:PRINT TAB(26);
190 REM CHECK FOR VALID DAY
200 IF VAL(TC$)<1 OR VAL(TC$)>D% THEN 10
210 GOSUB 1000:REM GET YEAR
220 DT$=DT$+"-"+TC$
230 IF C$=CHR$(13) OR CC$=CHR$(13) THEN 10
240 REM CHECK FOR VALID YEAR
260 IF VAL(TC$)<0 OR VAL(TC$)>99 THEN 10
270 STOP
1000 REM TWO CHARACTER INPUT SUBROUTINE
1005 FOR I=1 TO 10:GET C$:NEXT:REM CLEAR OUT INPUT BUFFER
1010 GET C$:IF C$="" THEN 1010
1015 IF C$=CHR$(13) THEN 1050
1016 IF C$<"0" OR C$>"9" THEN 1010
1020 PRINTC$;
1030 GET CC$:IF CC$="" THEN 1030
1035 IF CC$=CHR$(13) THEN 1050
1036 IF CC$<"0" OR CC$>"9" THEN 1030
1040 PRINTCC$;
1050 TC$=C$+CC$
1060 RETURN
```

Notice that the date is built up in eight-character string DT$, as month, day, and year are entered.

These three checks are made on data as it is entered:

1. Is the character a RETURN?

2. If the character is not a RETURN, is it a valid digit?

3. Is the two-character combination a valid month for the first entry, a valid day for the second entry, or a valid year for the third entry?

The carriage return has been selected as an abort (restart) character. By replacing CHR$(13) on lines 60, 160, 230 and 1035 you can select any other abort character. When the operator presses the selected abort key the entire date entry sequence restarts. We must check for the abort character in the two-character input subroutine (at line 1035) since we want to abort after the first or second digit has been entered. The main program also checks for an abort character in order to branch back to the statement on line 10 and restart the entire date entry sequence. You could branch out of the two-character input subroutine directly to the statement on line 10 in the calling program, thereby eliminating the abort character test in the calling program. But this is a bad practice and we strongly discourage it. Every subroutine should be treated as a logical module, with specified entry point(s) and standard subroutine returns. Branching between the subroutine and the calling program is likely to be a source of programming errors. If you branch out of the subroutine and back to the calling program without going through the return, you are laying yourself open to all kinds of subtle errors that you will not even understand until you are a very experienced programmer.

Program logic that tests for non-digit characters can reside entirely in the two-character input subroutine. We have chosen to ignore non-digit characters. Statements on lines 1016 and 1036 test for non-digit characters by performing comparisons between the ASCII value for the input character and the ASCII values for the allowed numeric digits.

Logic to check for valid month, day, and year must exist within the calling program since each of these two-character values have different allowed limits.

The statement on line 100 tests for a valid month.

Statements on lines 120, 130, and 140 compute the maximum allowed day for the detected month. The statement on line 200 checks for a valid day. The check for a valid year on line 260 is very simple.

Note that we generate an integer representation of the month on line 90, but we do not bother to generate integer representations of the day or the year. This is because the day and year are not used very often, but the month is used on lines 90 through 140.

It takes more time to write a good data entry program that displays information in a pleasing manner and checks for valid data input, allowing the operator to restart at any time. Is the time worth spending? By all means yes. You will write a program once; an operator may have to run the program hundreds or thousands of times. Therefore you spend extra programming time once, in order to save operators hundreds or thousands of delays.

Forms Data Input

The best way of handling multi-item data entry is to display a form, and then fill in the form as data is entered. Consider a name and address. First display a form as follows:

```
ENTER NAME AND ADDRESS
 1   NAME:
 2  STREET:
 3   CITY:
 4  STATE:                                    5 ZIP:
```

Notice that each entry has been assigned a number. The form displays the number in a reverse field.

The operator enters data sequentially, starting with item 1 and ending with item 5. The operator can then change any specific data entry.

The following program will clear the screen and display the initial form:

```
10 REM NAME AND ADDRESS DATA ENTRY
20 REM DISPLAY THE DATA ENTRY FORM
30 PRINT"    ENTER NAME AND ADDRESS"
40 PRINT" 1     NAME:"
50 PRINT" 2   STREET:"
60 PRINT" 3    CITY:"
70 PRINT" 4   STATE:";TAB(28);" 5 ZIP:"
```

As each data item is entered, create a reverse field to identify the character field where data will appear as it is entered. Then as each character is entered, display it. The CURSOR LEFT key is used to restart data entry into the current field. The RETURN key ends data entry into the current field. The following instruction sequence provides us with necessary program logic:

```
80 REM GET 20 CHARACTER NAME
90 LN%=20
100 PRINT"        ";TAB(10);
110 GOSUB 8000:NA$=CC$
120 REM GET 20 CHARACTER STREET
130 PRINTCHR$(13);TAB(10);
140 GOSUB 8000:SR$=CC$
150 REM GET 20 CHARACTER CITY
160 PRINTCHR$(13);TAB(10);
170 GOSUB 8000:CI$=CC$
180 REM GET 18 CHARACTER STATE
185 LN%=18
190 PRINTCHR$(13);TAB(10);
200 GOSUB 8000:ST$=CC$
210 REM GET 5 CHARACTER ZIP CODE
220 LN%=5
230 PRINTTAB(34);
240 GOSUB 8000:ZI$=CC$
250 STOP
8000 REM ENTER STRING DATA INTO A FIELD WITH LN% CHARACTERS
8010 REM THE CURSOR MUST BE IN THE FIRST CHARACTER POSITION OF THE FIELD
8020 REM THE RETURN KEY WILL END DATA ENTRY INTO THE FIELD
8030 REM THE ← KEY WILL RESTART DATA ENTRY INTO THE FIELD
8040 REM NO VALIDITY CHECKS ARE MADE ON ANY ENTERED DATA
8050 REM THE ENTERED STRING IS RETURNED IN STRING VARIABLE CC$
8060 ST%=POS(X):REM GET FIELD FIRST CHARACTER POSITION
8070 PRINT"▓";:REM REVERSE ENTRY FIELD
8080 FOR I=1 TO LN%:PRINT" ";:NEXT
8090 PRINT"■";CHR$(13);"⌐";TAB(ST%);
8100 REM ENTER DATA AND DISPLAY AS ENTERED
8110 CC$="":J%=0
8120 FOR I=1 TO LN%
8125 J%=J%+1
8130 GET C$:IF C$="" THEN 8130
8140 IF C$="←" THEN PRINTCHR$(13);"⌐";TAB(ST%);:GOTO 8070
8150 IF C$=CHR$(13) THEN 8200
8160 PRINTC$;:CC$=CC$+C$
8170 NEXT
8190 REM FILL THE REST OF CC$ WITH BLANKS AND DISPLAY IT
8200 IF J%=LN% THEN 8300
8210 FOR I=J% TO LN%
8220 CC$=CC$+" "
8230 NEXT
8300 PRINTCHR$(13);"⌐";TAB(ST%);CC$;
8310 RETURN
```

Key in the entire program (statement 10 to statement 8310) and run it. Remember, if you still have statements 10 through 70 keyed into your computer you do not need to reenter these statements.

If your program does not run correctly, check your entry carefully. In particular, check for semicolons in PRINT statements.

When you run the program each of the five fields in turn will be highlighted by a reverse field. As you enter characters they will be displayed in the field. When you press the RETURN key the entire reverse field is replaced by the data you entered. Try pressing the CURSOR LEFT key to restart data entry.

Carefully read through the data entry subroutine, beginning at line 8060 and ending at line 8310. Before going any further you should clearly understand this program logic.

Note how easy it is for an operator to see what he or she is entering, and how simple it is to restart any entry to correct errors.

After the complete name and address has been entered, the program should ask the operator if he or she wishes to make any changes; then the program should ask which field needs to be changed. Subroutines to ask both of these questions were given earlier in this chapter. We are going to use modified versions of these subroutines, where the calling program provides the question to be asked of the operator. Here is the complete program with added statements beginning at line 250:

```
10 REM NAME AND ADDRESS DATA ENTRY
20 REM DISPLAY THE DATA ENTRY FORM
30 PRINT"⬛ ENTER NAME AND ADDRESS"
40 PRINT" ⬛1⬛   NAME:"
50 PRINT" ⬛2⬛ STREET:"
60 PRINT" ⬛3⬛   CITY:"
70 PRINT" ⬛4⬛  STATE:";TAB(28);"⬛5⬛ ZIP:"
80 REM GET 20 CHARACTER NAME
90 LN%=20
100 PRINT"⬛⬛⬛";TAB(10);
110 GOSUB 8000:NA$=CC$
120 REM GET 20 CHARACTER STREET
130 PRINTCHR$(13);TAB(10);
140 GOSUB 8000:SR$=CC$
150 REM GET 20 CHARACTER CITY
160 PRINTCHR$(13);TAB(10);
170 GOSUB 8000:CI$=CC$
180 REM GET 18 CHARACTER STATE
185 LN%=18
190 PRINTCHR$(13);TAB(10);
200 GOSUB 8000:ST$=CC$
210 REM GET 5 CHARACTER ZIP CODE
220 LN%=5
230 PRINTTAB(34);
240 GOSUB 8000:ZI$=CC$
250 REM ASK IF ANY CHANGES ARE TO BE MADE
260 QU$="DO YOU WANT TO MAKE ANY CHANGES? "
270 PRINT"⬛⬛⬛⬛⬛⬛⬛⬛⬛";
280 GOSUB 3000
290 IF YN$="N" THEN STOP
300 REM ASK WHICH FIELD IS TO BE CHANGED
310 QU$="ENTER CHANGE FIELD NUMBER (1 TO 5): "
320 LO%=1:HI%=5
330 GOSUB 3500
340 ON NM% GOTO 400,450,500,550,600
400 REM CHANGE NAME
410 PRINT"⬛⬛⬛";TAB(10);:LN%=20
420 GOSUB 8000:NA$=CC$
430 GOTO 260
450 REM CHANGE STREET
460 PRINT"⬛⬛⬛⬛";TAB(10);:LN%=20
470 GOSUB 8000:SR$=CC$
480 GOTO 260
500 REM CHANGE CITY
510 PRINT"⬛⬛⬛⬛⬛";TAB(10);:LN%=20
520 GOSUB 8000:CI$=CC$
530 GOTO 260
550 REM CHANGE STATE
560 PRINT"⬛⬛⬛⬛⬛⬛";TAB(10);:LN%=18
570 GOSUB 8000:ST$=CC$
580 GOTO 260
600 REM CHANGE ZIP
610 PRINT"⬛⬛⬛⬛⬛⬛";TAB(34);:LN%=5
620 GOSUB 8000:ZI$=CC$
630 GOTO 260
2000 REM CLEAR THE ROW ON WHICH THE CURSOR IS CURRENTLY POSITIONED
2010 PRINTCHR$(13);"⬛";:REM MOVE CURSOR TO COLUMN 0
2020 FOR I=1 TO 39:PRINT" ";:NEXT
2030 PRINTCHR$(13);"⬛";
2040 RETURN
3000 REM ASK A QUESTION AND RETURN A RESPONSE OF Y OR N IN YN$
3010 GOSUB 2000
3020 PRINTQU$;
3030 GET YN$:IF YN$<>"N" AND YN$<>"Y" THEN 3030
3040 PRINTYN$;
```

```
3050 RETURN
3500 REM ASK FOR A NUMERIC SELECTION
3510 REM RETURN SELECTION IN NM%
3520 REM NM% MUST BE LESS THAN HI% AND MORE THAN LO%
3530 REM CALLING PROGRAM MUST SET HI%,LO% AND QU$,THE QUESTION ASKED
3540 GOSUB 2000
3550 PRINTQU$;
3560 GET NM$:IF NM$="" THEN 3560
3570 NM%=VAL(NM$)
3580 IF NM%<LO% OR NM%>HI% THEN 3560
3590 PRINTNM$;
3600 RETURN
8000 REM ENTER STRING DATA INTO A FIELD WITH LN% CHARACTERS
8010 REM THE CURSOR MUST BE IN THE FIRST CHARACTER POSITION OF THE FIELD
8020 REM THE RETURN KEY WILL END DATA ENTRY INTO THE FIELD
8030 REM THE ← KEY WILL RESTART DATA ENTRY INTO THE FIELD
8040 REM NO VALIDITY CHECKS ARE MADE ON ANY ENTERED DATA
8050 REM THE ENTERED STRING IS RETURNED IN STRING VARIABLE CC$
8060 ST%=POS(X):REM GET FIELD FIRST CHARACTER POSITION
8070 PRINT"▣";:REM REVERSE ENTRY FIELD
8080 FOR I=1 TO LN%:PRINT" ";:NEXT
8090 PRINT"■";CHR$(13);"⌝";TAB(ST%);
8100 REM ENTER DATA AND DISPLAY AS ENTERED
8110 CC$="":J%=0
8120 FOR I=1 TO LN%
8125 J%=J%+1
8130 GET C$:IF C$="" THEN 8130
8140 IF C$="←" THEN PRINTCHR$(13);"⌝";TAB(ST%);:GOTO 8070
8150 IF C$=CHR$(13) THEN 8200
8160 PRINTC$;:CC$=CC$+C$
8170 NEXT
8190 REM FILL THE REST OF CC$ WITH BLANKS AND DISPLAY IT
8200 IF J%=LN% THEN 8300
8210 FOR I=J% TO LN%
8220 CC$=CC$+" "
8230 NEXT
8300 PRINTCHR$(13);"⌝";TAB(ST%);CC$;
8310 RETURN
```

Enter the entire name and address program and run it. If it does not work, check for program errors. Here are some tips when looking for errors:

1. If the display scrolls off the top of the screen, you forgot to terminate the PRINT statement with a semicolon in the subroutine that clears a line.
2. If a reverse field is displayed in the wrong place, you have the wrong number of CURSOR DOWN shifts in a PRINT statement, or you have tabbed to the wrong column, or you have forgotten to separate two items in a PRINT statement with a semicolon.
3. If no message appears at the bottom of the display, make sure that the label you used in the main program to create the display is exactly the same as the label referenced in the subroutine which asks a question.

You should study the name and address program carefully and understand the data entry aids which have been included. They are:

1. By reversing the field into which data must be entered, you clearly indicate to the operator what data is expected, and how many characters are available.
2. When an operator enters a change field number, the reverse field display again quickly tells the operator whether the correct selection was made.
3. An operator does not have to fill in all the characters of a field; when the operator presses the RETURN key the balance of the field is filled with blank characters.
4. At any time the operator can restart entry into a field by pressing the CURSOR LEFT key.

5. When questions are asked, only meaningful character responses are recognized: Y or N for "yes" and "no," or a number between 1 and 5 to select a field. It is very bad programming practice to recognize any key other than a meaningful one. For example to recognize Y for "yes" and any other character for "no" could be disastrous, since accidentally tapping a key could take the operator out of the current data entry prematurely. Conversely, recognizing N for "no" and any other character for "yes" would cause the operator to unnecessarily reenter data into some field, just because the operator accidentally touched the wrong key.

Here are some data entry precautions which we have not taken but could add:

1. Check the ZIP code for any non-digit entry. Similar codes outside the USA do allow alphanumeric entries, however.

2. Many cautious programmers will ask the question ARE YOU SURE? when an operator types "no" in response to the question DO YOU WANT TO MAKE ANY CHANGES? This gives the operator a second chance in the event that he or she accidentally touched the wrong key.

3. We might add an additional key which aborts a current data entry and restores the prior value. For example, if the operator presses the wrong number to select a field which must be changed, the current program forces the operator to re-enter the field. We could easily add another key which aborts the current data entry and retains the previous entry.

Try modifying the name and address entry program yourself to add the additional safety features described above. Also, if you have a CBM 8000 computer, try using its TAB SET capabilities instead of the TAB functions.

PROGRAMMING DISPLAYS AND PRINTOUTS

When you power up a CBM computer, output is directly to the display. You must execute appropriate statements to send the output to the printer or any other device capable of receiving output.

There are a number of differences in the programming techniques required to create a screen display as compared to a hard copy printout. For example, the printer may be wider than the display, in which case output which will fit on a printed line will run over the display line. But there are also significant differences in programming logic which you must use to format a printout as compared to a screen display. This is because cursor control keys can be used to move the cursor around the screen display, but they cannot be used to move a print head around a piece of paper.

There are also many similarities in the programming techniques used to create printouts and displays. **The discussion that follows applies to displays only. If you are planning to write programs that generate output at a printer you should read the discussion of display outputs given in this chapter, and then proceed to the discussion of printer programming given in Chapter 6.**

Programming display output is much simpler than programming data input, since there is no operator interaction to worry about. You must make sure that the display is easy to read, and that is all. Here are a few rules to follow:

1. Avoid crowding too much information into a very small space.

2. If numbers or character strings are listed in columns, align the data so that the eye can quickly run down the column.

3. Use reverse fields on displays to highlight key information, top heading, and/ or side headings. Do not reverse fields on printouts; the printer generates very illegible reverse fields.

Below are some common mistakes which you should be aware of, and therefore avoid, when programming displays:

1. Remember to follow individual items in a PRINT statement with a semicolon(;) unless you specifically want the spacing provided by commas (,). This is the most common source of errors in output programming.

2. You will save a lot of programming time if you first get a piece of graph paper, section off rows and columns, then draw the display before attempting to program it. This will allow you to compute rows and columns accurately. The alternative is to use trial and error, which in the end will take a lot more time than drawing the display first.

3. Watch for array subscripts which do not divide evenly into columns. For example, suppose you have 25 items in array N$(I) which you are printing in 3 columns. You might be tempted to generate the display as follows:

```
100 FOR I=1 TO 25 STEP 3
200 REM PROCESS COLUMN 1
    .
    .
300 REM PROCESS COLUMN 2
    .
    .
400 REM PROCESS COLUMN 3
    .
    .
500 NEXT I
```

But on the final pass of the FOR-NEXT loop, indexes 26 and 27 will be computed, although they do not exist. You can easily check for the end of an array in a FOR-NEXT loop as follows:

```
100 FOR I=LO TO HI STEP ST
    .
    .
350 I=I+1
360 IF I>HI THEN 500
    .
    .
500 NEXT
```

An important warning applies to data which you read from a disk file (using techniques which we will describe in Chapter 6). **CBM computers have a nasty habit of adding blank characters onto the end of string variables which are read from a disk file.** For example, if you write names to a disk file, knowing in advance that no name has more than 20 characters, you might assume that when you read these names back from the disk file, each name will still have 20 characters or less. That is not necessarily the case. Some variable number of additional blank characters may get tacked onto the end of the string variable. This can distort your display or printout by extending a field beyond the column to which you will next tab. You can avoid this problem by using the LEFT$ function. Therefore a PRINT statement such as:

```
100 PRINT TAB(5);N$(I);TAB(30);N$(I+1)
```

would have to be rewritten as follows:

```
100 PRINT TAB(5);LEFT$(N$(I),29);TAB(30);LEFT$(N$(I+1),20)
```

If a list of variables has unknown string lengths, and you want to convert all variables to some fixed length, then you must add blank characters to the end of short strings, and truncate long strings. This is easily done by the following subroutine:

```
10 REM STRING VARIABLE N$ IS TO BE 20 CHARACTERS LONG
20 REM IF LESS THAN 20 CHARACTERS, ADD TRAILING BLANKS
30 REM IF MORE THAN 20 CHARACTERS, TRUNCATE EXCESS CHARACTERS
40 L%=LEN(N$):REM L%=NUMBER OF CHARACTERS IN N%
50 B$="                    ":REM B$ IS A DUMMY 20 BLANK CHARACTER VARIABLE
60 IF L%>20 THEN N$=LEFT$(N$,20):RETURN:REM N$ IS TRUNCATED
70 IF L%=20 THEN RETURN:REM N$ HAS CORRECT LENGTH
80 N$=N$+LEFT$(B$,20-L%):REM N$ IS SHORT, ADD BLANKS
90 RETURN
```

When dealing with large quantities of data, a very common technique is to create a "window" in which to enter the data. In order to provide a simple demonstration, we will create a double-dimensioned 14×50-integer array variable. Each integer in the array will contain a four-digit number which identifies the array coordinates as follows:

$$X\%(I,J) = OIOJ$$

For example:

```
X%(3,2) = 0302
X%(10,8) = 1008
X%(11,12) = 1112
etc.
```

We can create this integer array very simply, as follows:

```
10 DIM X%(14,50)
20 FOR I=1 TO 14
30 FOR J=1 TO 50
40 X%(I,J)=I*100+J
50 NEXT
60 NEXT
```

Now we will display some portion of this array. We will use the top two rows and columns 1 through 10 to create header displays as follows:

XX represents a number in the range 1 through 14
YY represents a number in the range 1 through 50

Here are the necessary program statements to create reverse field row and column headers as illustrated above:

```
1000 REM CREATE ROW AND COLUMN HEADERS
1010 PRINTTAB(9);
1020 FOR I=1 TO 3
1030 PRINT"█    COLUMN█";
1040 NEXT
1050 PRINT CHR$(13);TAB(9);
1060 FOR I=C% TO C%+2
1070 S%=7:IF I<10 THEN S%=8
1080 PRINTSPC(S%);"█";STR$(I);"█";
1090 NEXT
1095 PRINTCHR$(13);
1110 FOR I=R% TO R%+9
1120 S%=1:IF I<10 THEN S%=2
1130 PRINTTAB(2);"█ROW";SPC(S%);STR$(I);"█"
1140 NEXT
1150 RETURN
```

We deliberately create a window that is smaller than the entire screen so that we can better illustrate the concept of a window on data. There is nothing to stop you creating a window that occupies your entire display, however there will be occasions when you want a small window so that concurrent data can appear on the screen.

The STR$ function creates a display that is one character longer than the integer number. This extra character represents the sign. We could remove the sign, but we choose instead to display this extra character in reverse field. But we must account for its presence when counting character positions in order to set the tab on line 1130.

We will now add instructions that ask the operator to enter two numbers representing the smallest column and row of the array. The array element with this column and row number will appear in the top left-hand display position. The display will be filled with adjacent column and row elements, up to the end of the display. Add these lines to your program:

```
5 REM WINDOW ON A TABLE DISPLAY PROGRAM
10 DIM X%(14,50)
20 FOR I=1 TO 14
30 FOR J=1 TO 50
40 X%(I,J)=I*100+J
50 NEXT
60 NEXT
64 PRINT"█";
65 PRINT"█████████████████████";
70 INPUT "ENTER COLUMN (1 TO 12):";C%
80 IF C%<1 OR C%>12 THEN PRINT"█";:GOTO 70
90 INPUT "ENTER ROW (1 TO 41):";R%
100 IF R%<1 OR R%>41 THEN PRINT"█";:GOTO 90
105 PRINT"█";:GOSUB 1000
110 PRINT"███";
120 FOR I=R% TO R%+9
130 PRINT TAB(9);
140 FOR J=C% TO C%+2
150 X$=STR$(X%(J,I))
155 PRINTSPC(10-LEN(X$));X$;
160 NEXT
165 PRINTCHR$(13);
170 NEXT
180 PRINT"████CONTINUE? ENTER Y OR N ";
190 GET C$: IF C$<>"Y" AND C$<>"N" THEN 190
200 IF C$="Y" THEN 65
210 STOP
```

Run the program. If you entered it correctly, the first thing you will notice is that the computer stops and appears to do nothing for a while; it is executing the nested FOR-NEXT statements occurring on lines 20 through 60. It takes 10 or 15 seconds to fill array X% with numbers.

The PRINT statement on line 64 clears the screen so that any prior garbage is eliminated before INPUT statements on lines 70 and 90 ask you to enter the beginning row and column numbers. We do not put this clear command into the PRINT statement on line 65, since the program returns to line 65 in order to ask for new column and row numbers, at which time we do not want to erase the prior display.

Note that column numbers from 1 through 12 are allowed; there are three columns, therefore any column number up to 12 will stay within the limit of 14 columns. Column numbers from 1 to 41 are allowed, likewise, since ten columns are displayed, which means that the highest ten column numbers would be 41 through 50.

The integer value from array X% is converted into an ASCII string on line 150 before being printed on line 155. This conversion has been made to simplify display formatting. It is easy to compute the number of spaces between columns, as shown by the PRINT statement on line 155. It is not so easy to align numbers correctly when displaying integers. To prove this for yourself, remove line 150 and change line 155 as follows:

```
155 PRINT SPC(5);X%(J,I);
```

Numbers will align providing you do not display any four-digit numbers, in which case the display will overflow a 40-character screen. If you display three-digit numbers the rows are all shifted over one column to the right. You could correct this discrepancy by increasing the tab on line 130 from 9 to 10. Try it. When you next run the program it will overflow the 40-column display line and give you a lot of extra carriage returns.

Notice that the statements which ask for input on lines 70, 90, and 180 are all followed by program steps that disallow all invalid inputs. Even in this simple demonstration program we take the time to program safe input.

A useful refinement to a program that displays a window on an array is to provide the operator with a means of moving the window up or down, left or right. This is easily done. Using available symbols on a CBM standard keyboard, we will use the spade sign (♠) to move up one row, which means that the beginning row number is decreased by 1. We will use the heart sign (♥) to move down one row, which means that the beginning row number is increased by 1. We will use the less than sign (<) to move the table one column to the left (decrease the beginning column number by 1), and use the greater than sign (>) to move the table one column to the right (increase the beginning column number by 1). To accomplish this task we must replace statements on lines 180 through 210 with the following statements:

```
180 PRINT"XXXXCONTINUE? ENTER ♠,♥,<,>,Y OR N ";
190 GET C$: IF C$="" THEN 190
200 REM IF C$=ATN THEN DECREASE ROW BY 1
210 IF C$="♠" THEN R%=R%-1:PRINTCHR$(13);"X";:GOTO 100
220 REM IF C$=COPY THEN INCREASE ROW BY 1
230 IF C$="♥" THEN R%=R%+1:PRINTCHR$(13);"X";:GOTO 100
240 REM IF C$=< THEN DECREASE COLUMN BY 1
250 IF C$="<" THEN C%=C%-1:GOTO 300
260 REM IF C$=> THEN INCREASE COLUMN BY 1
270 IF C$=">" THEN C%=C%+1:GOTO 300
280 REM IF C$=Y,ENTER NEW ROW AND COLUMN IF C$=N,STOP
290 IF C$="Y" THEN 65
295 IF C$="N" THEN STOP
296 GOTO 190:REM REJECT ANY OTHER C$ INPUT
300 IF C%<1 OR C%>12 THEN PRINTCHR$(13);:GOTO 70
310 GOTO 105
```

Notice how straightforward the logic is, even though we are still checking for operator errors. Any entry other than one of the six allowed characters is rejected. If changing the row or column number puts it out of the allowed range, then program logic simply asks for new row and column numbers. (The CBM 8000 window and scrolling functions are not very useful in this example since we want to scroll left and right, as well as up and down.)

An untidy aspect of the program shown above is the fact that, following an out of range *row* number, only a new row is allowed to be entered; this results from the GOTO 100 on lines 210 and 230. Following an out of range *column* number the GOTO 70 on line 300 allows new column *and* row numbers to be entered (since in the main body of the program, column number entry precedes row number entry). Can you rewrite the program to get rid of this small untidiness (select whether only the row or column will be reentered, or if both the row *and* column will be reentered when either is out of range)?

Another undesirable feature of the display program is the time taken to fill the array X%. This has nothing to do with the display itself, but in many programs such delays are likely to occur. An operator may well assume that the computer is not working properly. Whenever such periods of inactivity are encountered it is a good idea to display a prominent message telling the operator that the computer is working, and to please wait. This is easily done. You simply precede the computation statements with an appropriate PRINT statement. In our case the following PRINT statement could be used:

```
15 PRINT ":PLEASE WAIT WHILE I FILL THE ARRAY WITH DATA"
```

Our program takes great care to terminate the display on the 39th column of the display, rather than the 40th and last column. **When using a CBM computer with a 40-column display, it is not wise to run displays out to the 40th column. You will run afoul of the wrap around logic whereby lines that are more than 40 characters long automatically continue on the next line.** You are best off not tangling with the display formatting nightmare that can result from carriage returns generated as part of line continuation interacting with your own formatting carriage returns.

40-Column Screen Wrap Around Logic. The following paragraphs explain how 40-column wrap around logic works.

When the cursor is on any 40-character screen line, the CBM computer assumes that it is a 39-character line until a character has been displayed in the 40th character position; then the CBM computer assumes it is in the first half of a 79-character line. If a character has been displayed in the 40th column of the preceding line (i.e., the cursor has moved to the next line), then the CBM computer assumes it is in the second half of a 79-character line.

When a program encounters a carriage return, it executes a carriage return to the next logical line. When the CBM thinks it is in the first half of a 79-character line (a character has been displayed at the 40th character position) and it executes a carriage return, it moves the cursor to the next logical line, which is two display lines below.

If you POKE into the 40th character position of a 40-character display then the computer does not assume a 79-character line. This can be done using the statement:

```
POKE 32767+(L-1)*40,ASC(CH$)
where:

    L      is the line number
    CH$    is the POKEd character
```

If you have a 40-column display, then as an exercise it is worth modifying the complete table display program so that it does go out to the 40th column. To do this you must change the TABs on line 30 and line 1010 from 9 to 10; the TAB on line 1050 must change from 13 to 14, the TAB on line 1130 goes from 2 to 3. Now try running the program; the columns of numbers line up, but you have too many carriage returns and they force the top of the display to scroll off the screen. Now try eliminating the extra carriage returns and generating the correct display. This is a very difficult programming task.

MATHEMATICAL PROGRAMMING

CBM computers can add, subtract, multiply, and divide with full accuracy using numbers that have up to nine digits. Numbers with more digits have to be rounded off to nine digits. Thus 123456789.12 is rounded to 123456789. Although this limit poses no problem in many applications, business and scientific applications can require more digits of accuracy. The CBM cannot keep track of dollars and cents (to the nearest cent) for amounts over $9,999,999.99, for example.

Two programming methods can overcome the CBM computer's numeric accuracy limitations. The first method uses numeric strings. The second method uses multiple integer math, where a large number is separated into smaller segments, and each segment is handled separately.

ADDITION

Numeric string and multiple integer techniques can both be used to add integer numbers that have more than nine digits. The *augend* is the first number in the equation. The *addend* is the second number. The addend is added to the augend.

Addition using Numeric Strings

The steps involved are:

1. Input the augend and addend as two positive numeric strings.
2. Right justify the strings.
3. Add the corresponding digits of the strings separately, including carry.
4. Concatenate the answer into a one-string result.
5. Print the answer string.

Let us examine each step in turn:

Step 1: Input the augend and addend as positive numeric strings using an INPUT statement.

Screen Display	Representation of Memory Contents
10 PRINT"⊃***ADDITION***":PRINT	A$ [1][2][3][4][5][6][7][8][9][0][1][2][3][4][5][6]
20 INPUT A$,B$	B$ [5][7][9][4][3][5][7][2]
RUN	
ADDITION	
?1234567890123456	
??57943572	

A$ is the augend and B$ is the addend. The INPUT statement allows either to exceed the 9-digit numeric length limit. For simplicity we will allow only positive integer numbers to be input. Once you are familiar with the basic concepts of the addition program, you should experiment and alter the program to accommodate negative and fractional numbers.

Step 2: Right justify the strings. Before performing arithmetic operations, the numbers should be right-justified, because in BASIC alphabetic and numeric strings are automatically left-justified. If the contents of numeric strings are added without first being right-justified, the answer will be incorrect, as shown below:

Left Justified - Incorrect	Right Justified - Correct
1234567890123456	1234567890123456
+57943572	+ 57943572
7028925090123456	1234565948067028

The following statements right-justify the shorter of the two numeric strings A$ and B$. The shorter string is filled with leading zeros until it equals the length of the longer string. X is assigned the length of A$. Y is assigned the length of B$:

```
30 BLANK$="                "
40 X=LEN(A$):Y=LEN(B$)
50 IF X<Y THEN A$=LEFT$(BLANK$,Y-X)+A$
60 IF Y<X THEN B$=LEFT$(BLANK$,X-Y)+B$
```

BLANK$ on line 30 is a buffer string that is used to fill the shorter numeric string with blanks. BLANK$ has 16 blank spaces, since we are going to simplify our problem by imposing a 16-digit limit on the size of numbers.

Statements on lines 50 and 60 use the LEN function to compare X (the length of A$) to Y (the length of B$), and subtract the length of the smaller string from the length of the larger string. In our example B$ is shorter than A$, so the length of B$ is subtracted from the length of A$.

```
60 IF Y<X THEN B$=LEFT$(BLANK$,X-Y)+B$
```
Length of smaller string subtracted
from length of larger string

If the length of A$ is 16 digits and the length of B$ is eight digits, the difference is eight digits:

A$ [1][2][3][4][5][6][7][8][9][0][1][2][3][4][5][6]   X = 16   [X-Y = 8]
B$ [5][7][9][4][3][5][7][2]   Y = 8   [16-8 = 8]

The number of blanks concatenated onto the front of B$ is the difference between the two lengths. Since the difference is eight, eight blanks are taken from BLANK$ to fill the shorter string. Blanks are added to the front of the shorter string B$ with the following statement:

```
LEFT$(BLANK$(X-Y)+B$
```

The procedure is as follows:

```
B$=LEFT$(BLANK$,X−Y)            +B$
B$=LEFT$(BLANK$,16−8)           +B$
B$=LEFT$(BLANK$,8)              +B$
B$=LEFT$( ｜ｷｷｷｷｷｷｷｷｷｷｷｷｷｷｷ ,8)   +B$
B$= ｷｷｷｷｷｷｷｷ                    + 57943572
B$= ｷｷｷｷｷｷｷｷ57943572
```

A$= `1234567890123456`   B$= `ｷｷｷｷｷｷｷｷ57943572`
   16 digits   16 digits

Step 3: Add the corresponding digits of the strings. At first glance, you might assume that A$ and B$ can now be added using the following statement:

```
C$=A$+B$
```

This is incorrect. When a plus sign is used with strings they are not added, but are concatenated:

```
C$=A$+B$
```

C$= `1234567890123456` + `ｷｷｷｷｷｷｷｷ57943572`
C$= `1234567890123456ｷｷｷｷｷｷｷｷ57943572`

We want to add the digits in the strings, not concatenate the strings. **To add the contents of numeric strings, each digit must be extracted separately from the string, converted into a numeric digit, then added to one digit from the other string.** This is done using the two string functions VAL and MID$.

```
1020 FOR I=LEN(A$) TO 1 STEP-1
1030 A=VAL(MID$(A$,I,1))
1050 B=VAL(MID$(B$,I,1))
1100 NEXT I
```

A is the digit extracted from A$. B is the digit extracted from B$. I is a counter initialized to the length of the INPUT strings (either A$ or B$ may be used). With each FOR-NEXT loop iteration, the value of I is decremented by 1. As I decrements, it allows the string contents to be extracted one by one, right to left, using the MID$ function:

I	MID$(B$,I,1)
16	ｷｷｷｷｷｷｷｷ5794357**2**
15	ｷｷｷｷｷｷｷｷ579435**7**2
14	ｷｷｷｷｷｷｷｷ57943**5**72
13	ｷｷｷｷｷｷｷｷ5794**3**572
12	ｷｷｷｷｷｷｷｷ579**4**3572
11	ｷｷｷｷｷｷｷｷ57**9**43572
10	ｷｷｷｷｷｷｷｷ5**7**943572
9	ｷｷｷｷｷｷｷｷ**5**7943572
8	ｷｷｷｷｷｷｷ**ｷ**57943572
7	ｷｷｷｷｷｷ**ｷ**ｷ57943572
6	ｷｷｷｷｷ**ｷ**ｷｷ57943572
5	ｷｷｷｷ**ｷ**ｷｷｷ57943572
4	ｷｷｷ**ｷ**ｷｷｷｷ57943572
3	ｷｷ**ｷ**ｷｷｷｷｷ57943572
2	ｷ**ｷ**ｷｷｷｷｷｷ57943572
1	**ｷ**ｷｷｷｷｷｷｷ57943572

The VAL function converts each extracted string literal into a numeric value:

When I = 16,

B=VAL(MID$(B$,16,1))

B=VAL($ |ø|ø|ø|ø|ø|ø|ø|ø|5|7|9|4|3|5|7|2|)

B= |ø|2|

When I = 15,

B=VAL(MID$(B$,15,1)) . . .

After both numeric string digits have been converted into an integer, they are added and the sum is returned in C$. Here are the necessary program steps:

```
1000 N=1                        Initialize string pointer N.

1010 D=0                        Initialize carry value.

1020 FOR I=LEN(A$) TO 1 STEP -1  Initialize decrement counter I.

1030 A=VAL(MID$(A$,I,1))        Extract digits separately. Convert
                                to non-string numeric.

1040 A=A+D:D=0                  Add tens value from carry (D) to A.

1050 B=VAL(MID$(B$,I,1))        Extract digits separately. Convert
                                to non-string numeric.

1060 C=A+B                      Add extracted digits of A$ and B$.

1070 IF C>=10 THEN D=1          Carry tens value into D if C>=10.

1080 IF D=1 AND I=1 THEN N=2

1090 C$=RIGHT$(STR$(C),N)+C$    Link sums into string answer.

1100 NEXT I
```

Variable D is initialized to zero at line 1010; D is then used as a carry value in lines 1040, 1070, and 1080. During addition, if the value of C is greater than or equal to 10, a tens value is *carried over* to the next left position. The tens value carried over is stored in D:

$$123^{+1}4^{+1}5^{+1}6\ \ ^17^{+1}89012$$
$$+\ \ \ \ \ \ \ \ \ \ \ 5\ \ 7\ \ 9\ \ \ 43572$$
$$\overline{123\ \ 5\ \ 1\ \ 4\ \ 7\ \ \ 32584}$$

If C is greater than or equal to 10, the carry variable D is incremented to 1 at line 1070; otherwise it remains 0:

```
1070 IF C>=10 THEN D=1
```

A |ø|6|

+B |ø|9|

C |ø|15| ⟶ 15>=10 → D|ø|1|

or

A |ø|3|

+B |ø|0|

C |ø|3| ⟶ 3<10 → D|ø|0| (no change)

D will be either 0 or 1, but never greater than 1, because the maximum possible sum of any two single-digit numbers is 18, thus the maximum tens value that can be carried over is 1.

To prevent losing the carry in D, line 1040 resets the value of A to A + D on the next loop iteration:

```
1040 A=A+D:D=0
```

If this statement were omitted, the carry would never be carried out, and the value of A would be incorrect. When D is added to A, D is reset to 0 in preparation for the next loop iteration.

Step 4: Link the individual sums (C) and convert the total sum into a string. Just as the augend and addend were entered as strings to avoid the 9-digit length limit the sums must be converted back into a string to avoid the length limit.

Line 1090 links the individual sums of C and converts the final answer back into string form.

The STR$(C) function converts C into a string. The RIGHT$ function extracts the rightmost N characters from STR$(C). N is set to 1 at line 1000 to indicate that we want only the rightmost character to be extracted; the leftmost character of C is unnecessary because it is the sign value ("0" if positive and " −" if negative) and would be concatenated between each number of C$ if we did not exclude it.

```
1000 N=1
     N 0 1
1060 C=A+B
     C 0 8 = A 0 6 + B 0 2
1090 C$=RIGHT$(STR$(C),N)+C$
     C$=RIGHT$(STR$(C),1)+C$
     C$=RIGHT$( 0 8 ,1)+C$
     C$= 8 + C$
```

Even if C is a two-digit number, only the rightmost digit is concatenated onto C$. The tens value has already been assigned to D and will be added during the next loop iteration.

N is set to 2 to include the last carry only if D=1 and I=1 (signaling a carry on the last loop iteration). This is important, because if both conditions are true the loop will *not* iterate again to add D's carry into A in line 1040, thereby losing the last carry value in D. By setting N to 2 on the last loop iteration, both digits of C are included in C$, and the last carry over is not lost.

```
1070 IF C>=10 THEN D=1
     C 0 12 >=10    D 0 1
1080 IF D=1 AND I=1 THEN N=2
     D 0 1        I 0 1        N 0 2
1090 C$=RIGHT$(STR$(C),N)+C$
     C$=RIGHT$( 0 1 2 ,2)+C$
     C$= 1 2 +C$
     C$= 1 2 x x x x x x x
```

The entire FOR-NEXT loop routine at lines 1020 through 1100 does as follows:

1. It extracts individual digits from a numeric string and assigns numeric values to them (statements 1030, 1050).

2. The digits from both strings are added together one digit at a time (statement 1060) and checked for a carry value (statement 1070). The carry is added to A in the next column (line 1040).

3. The individual sums are then linked and converted back into a numeric string (line 1090).

Step 5: Display the answer string. To complete this addition routine, the input and length test statements are inserted at the beginning of the FOR-NEXT loop (statements 10 to 1010). PRINT and CLEAR statements are added (statements 1110 to 1130). The final program now reads as follows:

```
10 PRINT"⌂***ADDITITON***":PRINT        Clear screen
20 INPUT A$,B$                          Input numeric strings
30 BLANK$="                    "
40 X=LEN(A$):Y=LEN(B$)
50 IF X<Y THEN A$=LEFT$(BLANK$,Y-X)+A$ ⎫
60 IF Y<X THEN B$=LEFT$(BLANK$,X-Y)+B$ ⎬ Right justify strings
1000 N=1
1010 D=0
1020 FOR I=LEN(A$) TO 1 STEP-1          ⎫
1030 A=VAL(MID$(A$,I,1))                ⎪
1040 A=A+D:D=0                          ⎪
1050 B=VAL(MID$(B$,I,1))                ⎪
1060 C=A+B                              ⎬ Addition loop
1070 IF C>=10 THEN D=1                  ⎪
1080 IF D=1 AND I=1 THEN N=2            ⎪
1090 C$=RIGHT$(STR$(C),N)+C$            ⎭
1100 NEXT I
1110 PRINT:PRINT"ANSWER= ";C$            Print C$
1120 C$="":PRINT:GOTO 20                 Clear C$
1130 END
```

Two sample runs of the program give the following output:

```
***ADDITION***

?12345
??579

ANSWER=  12924

?1234567890123456
??57943572

ANSWER=  1234567948067028
```

This addition routine overcomes the 9-digit numeric length limit. Try modifying this program to receive inputs as dollars and cents, and to display results in the same format.

Multiple Integer Addition

Another way to overcome the 9-digit length limit during addition is to use multiple integer addition.

Multiple integer math reorganizes a large number into smaller segments. Each segment is handled independently. The individual answers are joined together into one final answer, as follows:

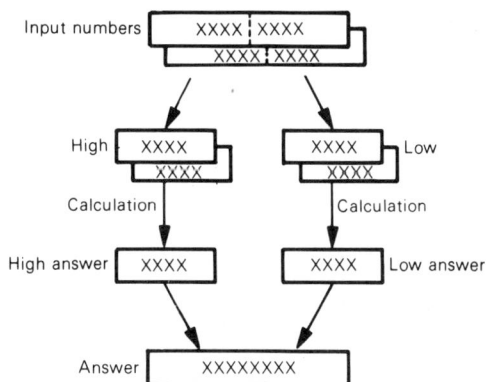

The steps involved in multiple integer addition are as follows:

1. Input the augend and addend as two positive numeric strings.
2. Divide the number into two equal high and low parts.
3. Separately calculate the sums of the high-order and low-order parts.
4. Concatenate the sums into one answer string.
5. Display the answer string.

Step 1: Input the augend and addend as two positive numeric strings:

```
10 PRINT"⊃***MULTIPLE INTEGER ADDITION***":PRINT
20 INPUT A$,B$

RUN

***MULTIPLE INTEGER ADDITION***

?1234567890123456
??57943572
```

A$ is the augend and B$ is the addend. The numbers are input as numeric strings because: 1) the numeric length limit is avoided, and 2) string functions can be used to divide the numbers into smaller segments.

Step 2: Determine the maximum length of numeric input, and the number of segments into which the numeric input must be divided. For example, if the maximum length of numeric input is 16 digits, numbers must be divided into two segments, with a maximum of eight digits per segment.

To keep our sample program simple, the maximum input length is assumed to be 16 digits. Input is divided into high and low segments of eight digits each.

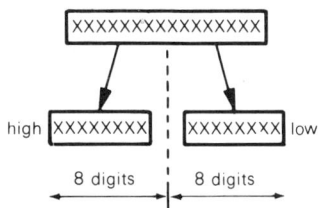

First we must determine which input string is longer. The lengths of A$ and B$ are assigned to variables X and Y respectively.

```
1000 X=LEN(A$):Y=LEN(B$)
```

Next, the lengths are compared. If X>Y (length of A$ is larger than length of B$) then variable F, the divider variable, is set to one-half of X. But if X<Y, then F is set to one-half of Y.

```
1002 IF X>Y THEN F=X/2:GOTO 1006
1004 F=Y/2
```

Here is another method of assigning a value to F:

```
1002 F=Y/2:IF X>Y THEN F=X/2
```

In this example, A$="1234567890123456" and B$="57943572." Let us run this through:

```
1000 X=LEN(A$):Y=LEN(B$)
     X = 16        Y = 8
1002 IF X>Y THEN F=X/2:GOTO 1006
     16>8 true statement, therefore
       F = 16/2
       F = 8
     program continues at line 1006
```

Once the value of F is set, the program continues at line 1006. The statement on line 1006 looks for a fractional value of F. If F is larger than its integer value, then F is assigned its integer value, plus 1. This rounds F up to the nearest integer. For example, if the value of F is 7.5, the statement on line 1006 rounds it up to 8:

```
1006 IF F>INT(F) THEN F=INT(F)+1
     If 7.5>7 then F = 7+1
       F = 8
```

To obtain the high (H) and low (L) parts of the sum of A$ and B$, use the following statements:

```
1000 X=LEN(A$):Y=LEN(B$)
1002 IF X>Y THEN F=X/2:GOTO 1006
1004 F=Y/2
1006 IF F>INT(F) THEN F=INT(F)+1
1010 IF X<=F THEN AH=0:AL=VAL(A$):GOTO 1040
1020 AH=VAL(LEFT$(A$,X-F))
1030 AL=VAL(RIGHT$(A$,F))
1040 IF Y<=F THEN BH=0:BL=VAL(B$):GOTO 1070
1050 BH=VAL(LEFT$(B$,Y-F))
1060 BL=VAL(RIGHT$(B$,F))
```

Statements 1010 and 1040 compare the string lengths with the divider F, which in this case is 8. If the string is shorter than eight, AH (or BH) is assigned a zero value, leaving only AL (or BL) equal to A$ or B$. If the string is longer than eight, it must be divided into high and low segments. AH or BH, the high segments, are assigned the value of the leftmost LEN(X or Y), minus eight digits, at 1020 and 1050.

```
1020 AH=VAL(LEFT$(A$,X-F))
```

AH=VAL(LEFT$(A$,16−8))

AH=VAL(LEFT$(|1|2|3|4|5|6|7|8|9|0|1|2|3|4|5|6| ,8))

AH=VAL(|1|2|3|4|5|6|7|8|)

AH= |b12345678|

To obtain AL, the rightmost eight digits are extracted from A$:

```
1030 AL=VAL(RIGHT$(A$,F))
```

AL=VAL(RIGHT$(|1|2|3|4|5|6|7|8|9|0|1|2|3|4|5|6| ,8))

AL=VAL(|9|0|1|2|3|4|5|6|)

AL= |b90123456|

The same procedure is used to extract BH and BL. Notice that *the VAL function converts the strings into numbers.*

Step 3: Once the large strings are divided into segments small enough for the CBM computer to handle, addition can begin. With multiple integer addition, you **add corresponding groups of numbers.** AH and BH are added. AL and BL are added. When a number is handled as a group of digits and not as a numeric string, the addition of each number does not have to be done digit by digit as with the numeric string method. The CBM computer can add *numbers,* whereas it is unable to add *numeric strings.*

```
  AH  ⌀12345678          AL  ⌀90123456
+ BH  ⌀00000000        + BL  ⌀57943572
  CH  ⌀12345678          CL  ⌀148067028
```

First, the low segments AL and BL are added using the following statement:

```
1070 CL$=STR$(AL+BL)
```

The sum of AL and BL is converted into a numeric string when assigned to CL$. It is not necessary that the sum be in string form, but it is much simpler to test for carry-over using the LEN function.

Line 1075 truncates the leading blank from the front of CL$. Remember that when a number is converted into a string the leading blank is included. We do not want this leading blank as part of CL$ when we concatenate the high and low segments together; therefore we truncate it with the MID$ function.

Line 1080 tests the length of sum CL$ against the segment length F. If the length of CL$ is greater than F, the leftmost digit is carried over and added to the sum CH$. (The value of D is equal to either 0 or 1.)

CH$ is obtained by adding AH, BH, and the carry D.

```
1070 CL$=STR$(AL+BL)
     CL$=STR$(⌀90123456 + ⌀57943572)
     CL$=STR$(⌀148067028)
     CL$=⌀148067028

1075 CL$=MID$(CL$,2,LEN(CL$)-1)
     CL$=MID$(⌀148067028,2,10-1)
     CL$=MID$(⌀148067028,2,9)
     CL$=148067028

1080 IF LEN(CL$)>F THEN D=1
     LEN(CL$)=9  ;F=8
     9>8→D=1

1090 CH$=STR$(AH+BH+D)
     CH$=STR$(⌀12345678 + ⌀00000000 + ⌀1)
     CH$=STR$(⌀12345679)
     CH$=⌀12345679

1095 CH$=MID$(CH$,2,LEN(CH$)-1)
     CH$=MID$(⌀12345679,2,10-1)
     CH$=MID$(⌀12345679,2,9)
     CH$=12345679
```

Step 4: Next we **concatenate the two sums** into one answer by linking CH$ to the front of CL$. The preceding space and carry are truncated from CL$ by selecting the rightmost eight digits from that string.

```
1100 C$=CH$+RIGHT$(CL$,F)
```

C$=CH$▯123456│79│ + RIGHT$(CL$▯│1│4│8│0│6│7│0│2│8│,8)

C$=▯│1│2│3│4│5│6│7│9│ + │4│8│0│6│7│0│2│8│

C$=▯│1│2│3│4│5│6│7│9│4│8│0│6│7│0│2│8│

Step 5: Print the answer C$.

```
1110 PRINT:PRINT"ANSWER=";C$:PRINT
```

The program is now complete. This Multiple Integer Addition program accepts two positive integer numbers that can be up to 16 digits long. The numbers are divided into high and low segments of eight digits each. The high and low segments are added and the two sums are concatenated into a single string answer with a maximum length of 17 digits. This Multiple Integer Addition program allows you eight more digits than the CBM computer's maximum.

Below is the listing of the complete program with a sample run.

```
10 PRINT"⊐***MULTIPLE INTEGER ADDITITON***":PRINT
20 INPUT A$,B$
1000 X=LEN(A$):Y=LEN(B$)
1002 IF X>Y THEN F=X/2:GOTO 1006
1004 F=Y/2
1006 IF F>INT(F) THEN F=INT(F)+1
1010 IF X<=F THEN AH=0:AL=VAL(A$):GOTO 1040
1020 AH=VAL(LEFT$(A$,X-F))
1030 AL=VAL(RIGHT$(A$,F))
1040 IF Y<=F THEN BH=0:BL=VAL(B$):GOTO 1070
1050 BH=VAL(LEFT$(B$,Y-F))
1060 BL=VAL(RIGHT$(B$,F))
1070 CL$=STR$(AL+BL)
1075 CL$=MID$(CL$,2,LEN(CL$)-1)
1080 IF LEN(CL$)>F THEN D=1
1090 CH$=STR$(AH+BH+D)
1095 CH$=MID$(CH$,2,LEN(CH$)-1)
1100 C$=CH$+CL$
1110 PRINT:PRINT"ANSWER=";C$:PRINT
1120 AH=0:AL=0:BH=0:BL=0:D=0:CH$="":CL$="":C$="":GOTO 20
1130 END


***MULTIPLE INTEGER ADDITION***

?1234567890123456
??57943572

ANSWER= 1234567948067028
```

Try modifying this program to receive inputs and display results as dollars and cents.

SUBTRACTION

As with addition, you can subtract numbers with more than nine digits by using numeric strings, or by using multiple integer math.

Subtraction using Numeric Strings

This subtraction program contains many sections of the "Addition using Numeric Strings" program. The steps involved are as follows:

1. Input the minuend and subtrahend as two positive numeric strings.
2. Right justify the strings.
3. Determine the larger numeric string.
4. Subtract corresponding digits of the strings separately, with borrowed carries.
5. Concatenate the answer into a one-string result.
6. Eliminate leading zeros in the answer string.
7. Print the answer string.

Step 1: The first step is to **input the minuend and subtrahend** as two positive numeric strings using an INPUT statement:

```
10 PRINT"***SUBTRACTION***":PRINT
20 INPUT A$,B$

RUN

***SUBTRACTION***

?123456789012
??57943572
```

A$ ⬚1⬚2⬚3⬚4⬚5⬚6⬚7⬚8⬚9⬚0⬚1⬚2⬚
B$ ⬚5⬚7⬚9⬚4⬚3⬚5⬚7⬚2⬚

A$ is the *minuend* (the first or top number entered, from which another number is subtracted). B$ is the *subtrahend* (the number subtracted from the minuend).

Step 2: Align the minuend and subtrahend by right-justifying both numeric strings. This is the same as was presented in step 2 of the "Addition using Numeric Strings" program.

```
30 BLANK$="                          "
40 X=LEN(A$):Y=LEN(B$)
50 IF X<Y THEN A$=LEFT$(BLANK$,Y-X)+A$
60 IF Y<X THEN B$=LEFT$(BLANK$,X-Y)+B$
```

Step 3: For subtraction, we must **determine which numeric string has a larger value.** Although the input strings may be equal in length, their values can be quite different.

The values of A$ and B$ are compared using the VAL function in statements 65 and 70:

```
65 IF VAL(A$)=VAL(B$) THEN C$="0":GOTO 1150
70 IF VAL(A$)>VAL(B$) GOTO 1000
```

We are going to subtract B$ from A$.

If A$ is larger than B$, we have a simple subtraction problem, and the program drops to line 1000. If B$ is larger than A$, we are subtracting a larger number from a smaller number, the program prepares for a negative answer.

If the subtrahend is larger than the minuend (B$ is larger than A$), the answer will be negative. To subtract two numbers that yield a negative answer, we switch the contents of A$ and B$ so that the value of A$ is larger than B$. Subtract B$ from A$, and the difference is C$. To make C$ negative, a negative sign, " − ", is concatenated onto the front of C$: C$ = " − " + C$.

Let us subtract 5 from 3, for example. This presents a subtraction problem where VAL(B$)>VAL(A$), or the subtrahend is larger than the minuend.

```
A$ 3
B$ 5
```
Switch A$ and B$
```
        A$ 5    B$ 3   →   A$ 5    B$ 3
```
Subtract: VAL(A$)−VAL(B$)=C$
```
        A$ 5  −  B$ 3   →   C$ 2
```
Convert to negative
```
        C$ = "−" + C$
        "−" + C$  2   →   C$  −2
```
Answer:
```
        C$  −2
```

The variables are switched at line 80.

```
80  X$=A$ : A$=B$ : B$=X$
```

Program Statement	Memory		
	X$	A$	B$
⋮	0	3	5
X$=A$	3	3	5
A$=B$	3	5	5
B$=X$	3	5	3

X$ acts as a storage string. Without X$, the original contents of A$ would be written over and the contents of B$ would be written back into itself:

Program Statement	Memory		
	A$	B$	
⋮	3	5	
A$=B$	5	5	Incorrect
B$=A$	5	5	

Later in the program we will need to know if the variables have been switched. We therefore set a marker to signal that A$ and B$ have been switched. Use variable S for this: S remains 0 if the variables have not been switched. If the variables are switched, set S=1. Line 90 sets S=1 if the values of A$ and B$ have been switched.

```
90  S=1
```

Remember that after the strings are properly switched, a value of 1 is assigned to S to signal that the numbers have been switched and a negative answer is needed. The negative answer is obtained by concatenating a negative sign to the front of the answer before it is printed. This occurs at statement 1140.

```
1140  IF S=1 THEN C$="−"+C$
```

Step 4: Whether the final answer is negative or positive, the value of A$ is now larger than B$. We can now **perform simple subtraction** at lines 1000 and 1080. The routine is taken directly from lines 1020 to 1100, step 3 of the "Addition using Numeric Strings" program, because the digits are extracted from the strings in the same manner. However, at line 1050, the carry variable D is now used as a "borrow" variable. If (A−B)<0, then a tens digit must be borrowed from the adjacent left column, increasing the value of A by 10. D is set to −1 because a "1" is being borrowed, thereby decreasing the value of the adjacent left column. The result is C:

```
1000 REM**SUBTRACTION ROUTINE**
1010 FOR I=LEN(A$) TO 1 STEP-1
1020 A=VAL(MID$(A$,I,1))
1030 A=A+D:D=0
1040 B=VAL(MID$(B$,I,1))
1050 IF (A-B)<0 THEN D=-1:A=A+10
1060 C=A-B
```

```
                                 +9
            +10 +10 +10      +10 +10
  A   1  2  3  3̸4 4̸5 5̸6 7  8  8̸9 9̸0  1  2
 −B   0̸  0̸  0̸  0̸  5  7  9  4  3  5  7  2
  C   1  2  3  3  9  8  8  4  5  4  4  0
```

Step 5: Concatenate the answer into a one-string result. This function is taken directly from line 1090 of the "Addition using Numeric Strings" program, except that N is not used since there will never be a final carry. In our subtraction program, concatenation of the individual answers into one result occurs at line 1070.

```
1070 C$=RIGHT$(STR$(C),1)+C$
```

Step 6: Subtraction can generate leading zeros in the answer. We eliminate these leading zeros before printing the answer. The FOR-NEXT loop in lines 1090 to 1120 **checks and eliminates all leading zeros,** using the VAL function and variable L as a counter.

```
1090 FOR I=1 TO LEN(C$)
1100 IF VAL(MID$(C$,I,1))=0 THEN L=L+1
1110 IF VAL(LEFT$(C$,I))<>0 THEN I=LEN(C$)
1120 NEXT I
```

The FOR-NEXT loop, which iterates from 1 to the length of the answer C$, searches for leading zeros or blanks by extracting each digit from C$ and comparing it to zero. It compares digits from left to right. If it identifies a zero or blank, counter variable L is incremented by 1 (statement 1100). As soon as the first non-zero or non-blank character is encountered, loop counter L is set to the length of the string so the program may drop out of the loop immediately.

Once we have determined the number of leading zeros in the answer, we separate the leading zeros from the remainder of the answer C$. At line 1130, the RIGHT$ function takes the LEN(C$) − L rightmost digits and stores them in the answer variable C$.

C$ = $\boxed{0}\boxed{0}\boxed{1}\boxed{2}\boxed{3}\boxed{5}\boxed{7}$ LEN(C$) = 7

I	MID$(C$,I,1)		
1	0 0 1 2 3 5 7	= 0	L = 1
2	0 0 1 2 3 5 7	= 0	L = 2
3	0 0 1 2 3 5 7	< > 0	I = LEN(C$)
7			I = 7 drop out of loop

```
1130 C$=RIGHT$(C$,LEN(C$)-L)
```

C$=RIGHT$ ($\boxed{0}\boxed{0}\boxed{1}\boxed{2}\boxed{3}\boxed{5}\boxed{7}$,7−2)

C$=RIGHT$ ($\boxed{0}\boxed{0}\boxed{1}\boxed{2}\boxed{3}\boxed{5}\boxed{7}$,5)

C$=$\boxed{1}\boxed{2}\boxed{3}\boxed{5}\boxed{7}$

Step 7: Print the answer string C$. But before we print C$, we check to see if the answer is to be negative by testing variable S at line 1140. If S=1, that means that originally A$<B$, and the final answer is to be negative, so a negative sign is added to C$. If S=0, the answer is positive, so nothing is added. Line 1150 prints C$:

```
1140 IF S=1 THEN C$="-"+C$
1150 PRINT:PRINT"ANSWER=";C$:PRINT
```

The last lines, 1160 through 1180, clear all strings and variables to zero or null, and return the program to the beginning for the next input numbers. The total program is listed below.

```
10 PRINT"⊃***SUBTRACTION***":PRINT        Clear screen
20 INPUT A$,B$                            Input numeric strings
30 BLANK$="                "          ⎫
40 X=LEN(A$):Y=LEN(B$)                ⎬   Right justify strings (from lines
50 IF X<Y THEN A$=LEFT$(BLANK$,Y-X)+A$⎟   20-60 of the addition program)
60 IF Y<X THEN B$=LEFT$(BLANK$,X-Y)+B$⎭
```

```
65 IF VAL(A$)=VAL(B$) THEN C$="0":GOTO 1150
70 IF VAL(A$)>=VAL(B$) GOTO 1000
80 X$=A$:A$=B$:B$=X$                          } If A$<B$, switch strings
90 S=1
1000 REM**SUBTRACTION ROUTINE**
1010 FOR I=LEN(A$) TO 1 STEP-1
1020 A=VAL(MID$(A$,I,1))
1030 A=A+D:D=0                                   Subtraction loop (based on
1040 B=VAL(MID$(B$,I,1))                         lines 1020-1100 of the addition
1050 IF (A-B)<0 THEN D=-1:A=A+10                 program)
1060 C=A-B
1070 C$=RIGHT$(STR$(C),1)+C$
1080 NEXT I
1090 FOR I=1 TO LEN(C$)
1100 IF VAL(MID$(C$,I,1))=0 THEN L=L+1     } Truncate leading zeros
1110 IF VAL(LEFT$(C$,I))<>0 THEN I=LEN(C$) } and blanks
1120 NEXT I
1130 C$=RIGHT$(C$,LEN(C$)-L)
1140 IF S=1 THEN C$="-"+C$
1150 PRINT:PRINT"ANSWER=";C$:PRINT              Print answer
1160 C$="":A$="":B$="":X$=""
1165 A=0:B=0:C=0:D=0:S=0:X=0:Y=0          } Clear strings and variables
1170 GOTO20
1180 END
***SUBTRACTION***
?123456789012
??57943572
ANSWER= 123398845440
```

The string subtraction program illustrated above has one problem: it generates a zero result if the subtrahend and minuend have the same number of digits, and in addition are identical in their nine most significant digits. For example, try subtracting 123456789000 from 123456789012. The answer is reported inaccurately as 0. This error results from the statements on line 65. The VAL function computes a 9-digit value for strings A$ and B$. If these two numeric strings are identical in their nine most significant digits, then the equivalence test on line 65 will be true whatever values the two numeric strings may have in lower significant digits. Can you correct this problem by separately testing the upper and lower halves of the numeric strings?

Multiple Integer Subtraction

Recall from the previous discussion of multiple integer addition that the multiple integer method divides a large number into smaller segments, calculates the segments separately, and joins the answers into one string. This method evades the 9-digit length limit.

Multiple Integer Subtraction has these steps:

1. Input the minuend and subtrahend as two positive numeric strings.
2. Determine which string has the larger value.
3. Divide the numbers into high and low parts.
4. Calculate the difference for the low-order and high-order halves.
5. Concatenate the differences into a one-string answer.
6. Truncate leading zeros.
7. Print the answer string.

Step 1: Input the minuend and the subtrahend as two positive numeric strings:

```
10 PRINT"♥***MULTIPLE INTEGER SUBTRACTION***":PRINT
20 INPUT A$,B$

RUN

***MULTIPLE INTEGER SUBTRACTION***

?123456789012
??57943572
```

A$, the minuend, and B$, the subtrahend, are entered as strings to avoid the 9-digit length limit.

Like multiple integer addition, A$ and B$ are divided into smaller segments. The maximum input length is arbitrarily set at 16 digits, so that we can divide the largest possible string into equal segments of eight digits each.

Step 2: Determine which input string has the larger value. If A$ is equal to B$ then the program drops down to line 1190 to print a zero answer. If B$ is larger than A$ the difference is negative and extra steps are needed.

If the answer is to be negative, the contents of the two strings are switched to put the larger value in A$ and the smaller value in B$. They are then subtracted, and a negative sign ("−") is concatenated onto the front of the difference (C$) as was demonstrated in line 70 of "Numeric String Subtraction." Line 30 is used here to direct the program past the switching routine if switching is not needed.

```
30 IF VAL(A$)>VAL(B$) THEN 1000
40 X$=A$:A$=B$:B$=X$
50 S=1
```

If the value of B$ is larger than the value of A$, the contents of A$ and B$ are switched at lines 40 to 50. This ensures that the smaller number is subtracted from the larger one. A marker is set to indicate that the variables have been switched.

For a detailed explanation of this routine, refer to step 3 of "Numeric String Subtraction."

Step 3: Divide A$ and B$ into two smaller segments, high and low.

```
1000 X=LEN(A$):Y=LEN(B$)
1002 IF X>Y THEN F=X/2:GOTO 1006
1004 F=Y/2
1006 IF F>INT(F) THEN F=INT(F)+1
1010 IF X<=F THEN AH=0:AL=VAL(A$):GOTO 1040
1020 AH=VAL(LEFT$(A$,X-F))
1030 AL=VAL(RIGHT$(A$,F))
1040 IF Y<=F THEN BH=0:BL=VAL(B$):GOTO 1070
1050 BH=VAL(LEFT$(B$,Y-F))
1060 BL=VAL(RIGHT$(B$,F))
```

Statements on lines 1010 and 1040 compare the string lengths with the divider point F. F is determined at lines 1002 and 1006. These lines are identical to lines 1002 and 1006 of the "Multiple Integer Addition" program. If the string is shorter than F, AH (or BH) is assigned a zero value, leaving AL (or BL) with the entire string as its value. If the string is longer than F it must be divided into high and low segments. AH is assigned the leftmost LEN(AH), minus F digits.

```
A$ 1 2 3 4 5 6 7 8 9 0 1 2
B$        5 7 9 4 3 5 7 2
AH Ø123456      AL Ø789012
BH ØØØØØ57      BL Ø943572
```

Lines 1000 through 1060 are also similar to lines 1000 through 1060 of the "Multiple Integer Addition" program, which divides A$ and B$ into AH, AL, BH, and BL. Refer to step 2 of "Multiple Integer Addition" for further explanation.

Step 4: Calculate differences for the high-order and low-order segments. BL is subtracted from AL, and BH is subtracted from AH:

AH |Ø123456| AL |Ø789012|

−BH |ØØØØØ57| −BL |Ø943572|

Before the segments are subtracted, the minuend and subtrahend must be compared. If the value of BL is larger than AL the difference is negative. This creates problems because a negative CL cannot be concatenated onto CH:

CH |Øxxxxxx| ⌒ CL |− xxxxxx| = C |Øxxxxxx−xxxxx| Incorrect

Therefore, **we must borrow from AH to increase the value of AL so that the difference will be positive.** Lines 1070 to 1090 borrow from AH and increase AL before BL is subtracted from AL:

```
1070 IF AL>=BL THEN 1100
1080 AL=AL+10↑F
1090 AH=AH-1
```

If AL is larger than BL we bypass 1080 and 1090 and jump directly to the subtraction. But if BL is larger than AL we must borrow a one million value from AH to increase the value of AL:

−1 ——————→ +1000000

AH |xxxxx|x| AL |_|xxxxxx|

−BH |xxxxx| −BL |xxxxxx|

CH |xxxxxx| CL |xxxxxx|

A ten is added to the leftmost digit of AL. The easiest way to add the ten in the correct position is to raise ten to the Fth power.

```
AL=AL+10↑F
```

In our sample program, AL is smaller than BL, as tested in line 1070.

AL |Ø789012| < BL |Ø943572|

Therefore we must borrow 1000000 (10↑F=10↑6=1000000) from AH to increase the value of AL:

```
1080 AL=AL+10↑F
```

AL=AL+10↑6

AL=AL+1000000

AL= |789012| + 1000000

AL= |1789012|

After AL is been increased, AH must be decremented by 1, since we borrowed from it.

```
1090 AH=AH-1
```

AH= |Ø123456| − |Ø1|

AH= |Ø123455|

Once AH, AL, BH, and BL have been set up properly, segments are subtracted. CL$ is the difference between AL and BL, and CH$ is the difference between AH and BH.

Statements on lines 1100 through 1102 compute CL$:

```
1100 CL$=STR$(INT(AL-BL))
     CL$=STR$(ø1789012-ø943572)
     CL$=STR$(ø845340)
     CL$=ø345540
```

Using the MID$ function at line 1101, the leftmost character (a blank representing a positive sign value) is truncated:

```
1101 CL$=MID$(CL$,2,LEN(CL$)-1)
```

CL$=MID$(|ø|8|4|5|4|4|0|,2,6)

CL$=　　　|8|4|5|4|4|0|

At 1102, if the length of CL$ is shorter than F, zeros from ZERO$ are concatenated onto the front of CL$. An assignment statement assigns a string of 0s to variable ZERO$ on line 15. In this case, the length of CL$ is equal to F, therefore no leading zeros are needed.

```
15 ZERO$="0000000000000000"
1102 CL$=LEFT$(ZERO$,F-LEN(CL$))+CL$
     CL$=LEFT$ (ZERO$,6-6)+CL$
     CL$=LEFT$ (ZERO$,0)+CL$
```

At line 1110, CH$ is assigned the string integer value of AH−BH:

```
1110 CH$=STR$(INT(AH-BH))
     CH$=STR$(ø123455-ø57)
     CH$=STR$(ø123398)
```

CH$=|ø|1|2|3|3|9|5|

Using the MID$ function, the leftmost blank character is truncated:

```
1111 CH$=MID$(CH$,2,LEN(CH$)-1)
```

CH$=MID$(|ø|1|2|3|3|9|8|,2,6)

CH$=|1|2|3|3|9|8|

The subtraction routine looks like this:

```
1070 IF AL>=BL GOTO 1100
```

789012 >=943572 ──────────→ False statement
Program continues at next line

```
1080 AL=AL+10↑F
```

AL=789012+1000000

AL=1789012

```
1090 AH=AH-1
```

AH=123456-1

AHø123455

```
1100 CL$=STR$(INT(AL-BL))
     CL$=STR$(ø1789012-ø943572)
     CL$=STR$(ø845540)
```

CL$=|8|4|5|5|4|0|

```
1101 CL$=MID$(CL$,2,LEN(CL$)-1)
```

CL$=MID$(|ø|8|4|5|5|4|0|,2,7-1)

CL$=MID$(|ø|8|4|5|5|4|0|,2,6)

CL$=|8|4|5|5|4|0|

```
1102 CL$=LEFT$(ZERO$,F-LEN(CL$))+CL$
     CL$=LEFT$(ZERO$,6-6)+CL$
     CL$=LEFT$(ZERO$,0)+8 4 5 5 4 0
     CL$=8 4 5 5 4 0
1110 CH$=STR$(INT(AH-BH))
     CH$=STR$(b123455-b57)
     CH$=STR$(b123398)
     CH$=b 1 2 3 3 9 8
1111 CH$=MID$(CH$,2,LEN(CH$)-1)
     CH$=MID$(b 1 2 3 3 9 8,2,7-1)
     CH$=MID$(b 1 2 3 3 9 8,2,6)
     CH$=1 2 3 3 9 8
```

Step 5: Concatenate the answer strings, CH$ and CL$, together by numeric string concatenation. They are concatenated in statement 1120:

```
1120 C$=CH$+CL$
```

$$C\$=CH\$\boxed{}+CL\$\boxed{}$$
$$C\$=\boxed{}$$

Only the rightmost "F" numbers from CL$ are concatenated onto CH$ to avoid concatenating any leading blanks in CL$ (see the "Subtraction using Numeric Strings" section for further discussion).

Step 6: Truncate leading zeros in C$ before C$ is printed. Leading zeros are subtracted in the same way for Multiple Integer Subtraction as for Numeric String Subtraction (see step 5 of "Subtraction using Numeric Strings"). Lines 1130 through 1170 truncate leading zeros just prior to printing C$:

```
1130 FOR I=1 TO LEN(C$)
1140 IF VAL(MID$(C$,I,1))=0 THEN L=L+1
1150 IF VAL(LEFT$(C$,I))<>0 THEN I=LEN(C$)
1160 NEXT I
1170 C$=RIGHT$(C$,LEN(C$)-L)
1180 IF S=1 THEN C$="-"+C$
```

If A$ and B$ had been switched, S would have been set to 1, signaling a negative answer, and thus a negative sign would be concatenated onto the front of C$ at 1180.

Step 7: Print the answer and clear out variable strings before allowing another problem to be input.

```
1190 PRINT:PRINT"ANSWER= ",C$:PRINT
1200 A$="":B$="":C$="":CH$="":CL$=""
1205 AH=0:AL=0:BH=0:BL=0:F=0:S=0:X=0:Y=0
1210 GOTO 20
1220 END
```

The finished program appears as follows:

```
10 PRINT"]***MULTIPLE INTEGER SUBTRACTION***":PRINT
15 ZERO$="0000000000000000"
20 INPUT A$,B$
25 IF VAL(A$)=VAL(B$) THEN C$="0":GOTO 1190
30 IF VAL(A$)>VAL(B$) GOTO 1000
40 X$=A$:A$=B$:B$=X$
50 S=1
1000 X=LEN(A$):Y=LEN(B$)
1002 IF X>Y THEN F=X/2:GOTO 1006
1004 F=Y/2
```

```
1006 IF F>INT(F) THEN F=INT(F)+1
1010 IF X<=F THEN AH=0:AL=VAL(A$):GOTO 1040
1020 AH=VAL(LEFT$(A$,X-F))
1030 AL=VAL(RIGHT$(A$,F))
1040 IF Y<=F THEN B=0:BL=VAL(B$):GOTO 1070
1050 BH=VAL(LEFT$(B$,Y-F))
1060 BL=VAL(RIGHT$(B$,F))
1070 IF AL>=BL GOTO 1100
1080 AL=AL+10↑F
1090 AH=AH-1
1100 CL$=STR$(INT(AL-BL))
1101 CL$=MID$(CL$,2,LEN(CL$)-1)
1102 CL$=LEFT$(ZERO$,F-LEN(CL$))+CL$
1110 CH$=STR$(INT(AH-BH))
1111 CH$=MID$(CH$,2,LEN(CH$)-1)
1120 C$=CH$+CL$
1130 FOR I=1 TO LEN(C$)
1140 IF VAL(MID$(C$,I,1))=0 THEN L=L+1
1150 IF VAL(LEFT$(C$,I))<>0 THEN I=LEN(C$)
1160 NEXT I
1170 C$=RIGHT$(C$,LEN(C$)-L)
1180 IF S=1 THEN C$="-"+C$
1190 PRINT:PRINT"ANSWER= ";C$:PRINT
1200 A$="":B$="":C$="":CH$="":CL$=""
1205 AH=0:AL=0:BH=0:BL=0:F=0:S=0:X=0:Y=0
1210 GOTO 20
1220 END

***MULTIPLE INTEGER SUBTRACTION***

?123456789012
??57943572

ANSWER= 123398845440

?1234567890123456
??57943572

ANSWER= 1234567832179884

?9999999999999999
??1234567890

ANSWER= 9999998765432109
```

You now know two methods of subtraction. The first method used numeric strings. The second uses multiple integer math. By comparing their outputs, you can see that both methods work equally well at getting around the 9-digit length limit.

MULTIPLICATION

A 9-digit length limit may be easily exceeded by multiplication because a product may be very large, even when the multiplier and multiplicand are small. This numeric length limit prohibits products longer than nine digits from being displayed without exponential notation. You can get around this limitation by writing a program that displays products with more than nine digits of precision. Displaying products exceeding nine digits without exponential notation is most easily done using Multiple Integer Multiplication. **The following program and discussion will enable you to display products up to 16 digits in length without exponential notation.**

Multiple Integer Multiplication

Using virtually the same steps as Multiple Integer Addition and Subtraction, Multiple Integer Multiplication separates the multiplicand and multiplier into smaller segments, multiplies all segments, and adds the multiple products together into one final product, which can have from one to 16 digits.

The steps for Multiple Integer Multiplication are as follows:

1. Input the multiplicand and the multiplier as two positive numeric strings.
2. Divide the strings into high and low segments.
3. Multiply the corresponding segments.
4. Add the segment products to create one product string. Truncate any leading zeros.
5. Print the product string.

Step 1: Input the multiplicand and the multiplier as two positive numeric strings, where A$ is the multiplicand and B$ is the multiplier. As with the other math programs, the numbers are input as strings to avoid the 9-digit length limit.

This program limits the length of the product to 16 digits. Since the maximum product length equals the sum of the lengths of the multiplicand and multiplier, *the sum of the lengths of the input numbers cannot exceed 16.* Changing the program to accept larger numbers requires several alterations which will not be discussed; you should be able to make such changes yourself. For this program:

$$\text{(length of A\$)} + \text{(length of B\$)} \leq 16$$
$$\begin{array}{ccccc} \text{Examples:} & 12 & + & 4 & \leq 16 \\ & 2 & + & 3 & \leq 16 \\ & 8 & + & 8 & \leq 16 \end{array}$$

The example program will multiply two input numbers with equal lengths of eight digits: 99999999 and 99999999, to give us a 16-digit product.

$$\begin{array}{rr} 99999999\leftharpoonup & 8 \text{ digits} \\ \times 99999999\leftharpoonup \quad + & 8 \text{ digits} \\ \hline 9999999800000001\leftharpoonup & 16 \text{ digits} \end{array}$$

Input the multiplier and multiplicand as two positive numeric strings, A$ and B$:

```
10 PRINT ":]***MULTIPLE INTEGER MULTIPLICATION***":PRINT
20 INPUT A$,B$
RUN
***MULTIPLE INTEGER MULTIPLICATION***
?99999999
??99999999
```

Step 2: Separate both input strings into two segments: high (H) for the leftmost digits and low (L) for the rightmost digits. The dividing point, variable F, specifies where to divide A$ and B$ into segments. The value of F is set at lines 1002 and 1006 (for explanation refer to "Multiple Integer Addition").

```
1000 X=LEN(A$):Y=LEN(B$)
     X=8          Y=8
1002 IF X>Y THEN F=X/2:GOTO 1008
1004 F=Y/2
     F=8/2
     F=4
1006 IF F>INT(F)THEN F=INT(F)+1
```

Once F is set, the program divides the numbers into high and low segments. This routine was presented in the "Multiple Integer Addition" program. Lines 1010 through 1060 divide the two strings into high and low segments.

```
1010 IF X<=F THEN AH=0:AL=VAL(A$):GOTO 1040
1020 AH=VAL(LEFT$(A$,X-F))
1030 AL=VAL(RIGHT$(A$,F))
1040 IF Y<=F THEN BH=0:BL=VAL(B$):GOTO 1070
1050 BH=VAL(LEFT$(B$,Y-F))
1060 BL=VAL(RIGHT$(B$,F))
```

The routine above divides A$ into AH and AL (four digits) and B$ into BH and BL (four digits):

A$ 9 9 9 9 9 9 9 9   B$ 9 9 9 9 9 9 9 9

AH 9 9 9 9   AL 9 9 9 9   BH 9 9 9 9   BL 9 9 9 9

Step 3: Multiply AH, AL, BH, and BL into four product strings: P1$, P2$, P3$, and P4$. The rules of algebraic multiplication multiply each variable as if it were a single number. A$ and B$ are multiplied as follows:

$$\begin{array}{cc} \text{AH} & \text{AL} \\ \times \text{BH} & \text{BL} \end{array}$$

Think of A$ and B$ as two sets of 4-digit numbers (H and L) joined in the middle, and not as eight individual digits: A$ is not eight 9s, but two sets of four 9s each. Thus AL and BL are multiplied as:

$$\begin{array}{cc} \text{AL} & 9999 \\ \times \text{BL} & 9999 \end{array}$$

Multiplying A$ and B$ is a four-step process. To begin, multiply BL by AL:

$$\begin{array}{cc} \text{AH} & \text{AL} \\ \text{BH} & \text{BL} \end{array}$$

and then multiply BL by AH:

$$\begin{array}{cc} \text{AH} & \text{AL} \\ \text{BH} & \text{BL} \end{array}$$

Next, move over to BH and multiply BH by AL:

$$\begin{array}{cc} \text{AH} & \text{AL} \\ \text{BH} & \text{BL} \end{array}$$

and finally multiply BH by AH:

$$\begin{array}{cc} \text{AH} & \text{AL} \\ \text{BH} & \text{BL} \end{array}$$

Here is the four-step process:

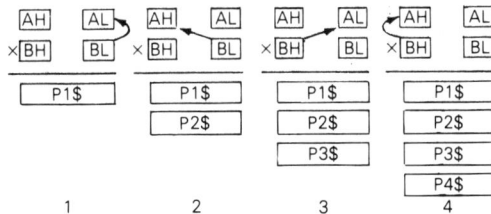

AH AL	AH AL	AH AL	AH AL
×BH BL	×BH BL	×BH BL	×BH BL
P1$	P1$	P1$	P1$
	P2$	P2$	P2$
		P3$	P3$
			P4$
1	2	3	4

Let's look step by step at how the multiplication works, using the values of AH, AL, BH, and BL from our example:

AH ⌷9999   AL ⌷9999

BH ⌷9999   BL ⌷9999

The first multiplication is BL times AL:

```
    AH    ⌷9999
 ×  BH    ⌷9999
    ────────────
          89991
          89991
          89991
          89991
        ────────
        99980001
```

The second multiplication is BL times AH, as shown in the diagram below:

```
  AH 9999         AL
 ×      BH    BL 9999
  ──────────────────
           99980001
       999800010000
```

Notice that P2 is not directly beneath P1, but four spaces to the left (recall the rules for lining up the products of 2-digit multiplication problems). To continue in the same manner, the third multiplication should be as follows:

```
      AH    AL 9999
  BH 9999       BL    ·
  ──────────────────
      999800010000
```

The fourth and final multiplication should be as follows:

```
  AH 9999     AL
  BH 9999     BL
  ──────────────────
  9998000100000000
```

Remember that only the values of the four segments are multiplied; this means that the actual multiplication done by AL × BH, etc. yields the same number, 99980001, for all four products. In the program the products are aligned by converting the products into strings and concatenating the necessary number of zeros onto the end of the strings. This aligns the strings correctly. Statements on lines 1070 through 1100 perform this alignment:

```
1070 P1$=STR$(BL*AL)
1080 P2$=STR$(BL*AH)+F$
1090 P3$=STR$(BH*AL)+F$
1100 P4$=STR$(BH*AH)+F$+F$
```

Without alignment the answers would be computed incorrectly as follows:

P1 ⌷99980001⌷

P2 ⌷99980001⌷   Incorrect

P3 ⌷99980001⌷

P4 ⌷99980001⌷

instead of:

```
                            99980001
                      99980001  0000
                      99980001  0000     Correct
                     99980001  00000000
                    ┌─────────────────────┐
                    │                     │
                    └─────────────────────┘
```

The number of zeros to be concatenated onto the end of the product strings is assigned to F$. F$ contains F zeros. F equals the number of digits in each half of the multiplier and multiplicand.

```
 40 ZERO$="0000000000000000"
1008 F$=LEFT$(ZERO$,F)

     F$=LEFT$(ZERO$,4)

     F$= 0 0 0 0 0 0 0 0 0 0

     F$="0000"
```

When P1$, P2$, P3$, and P4$ are computed (lines 1070 through 1100), the correct number of zeros are simultaneously concatenated to the end of the string to align the products correctly. The products are now aligned and ready to be added:

```
        AH 0 9 9 9 9      AL 0 9 9 9 9
      × BH 0 9 9 9 9      BL 0 9 9 9 9
      ─────────────────
                 99980001     P1
             999800010000     P2
             999800010000     P3
         9998000100000000     P4
                 F$   F$
```

At the end of step 3, the program looks like this:

```
  20 INPUT A$,B$                          Input values for A$, B$
  30 IF VAL(A$)=0 OR VAL(B$)=0 THEN     ⎫ If multiplicand or
     C$="0":GOTO 1190                   ⎬  multiplier = 0 then
  40 ZERO$="0000000000000000"           ⎭  answer (C$) = 0
1000 X=LEN(A$):Y=LEN(B$)               ⎫
1002 IF X>Y THEN F=X/2:GOTO 1006       ⎪
1004 F=Y/2                             ⎬ Set divider point, F
1006 IF F>INT(F)THEN F=INT(F)+1        ⎪
1008 F$=LEFT$(ZERO$,F)                 ⎭
1010 IF X<=F THEN AH=0:AL=VAL(A$):GOTO 1040 ⎫
1020 AH=VAL(LEFT$(A$,X-F))                  ⎪ Divide A$ and B$
1030 AL=VAL(RIGHT$(A$,F))                   ⎬  into parts:
1040 IF Y<=F THEN BH=0:BL=VAL(B$):GOTO 1070 ⎪ high and low
1050 BH=VAL(LEFT$(B$,Y-F))                  ⎭
1060 BL=VAL(RIGHT$(B$,F))
1070 P1$=STR$(BL*AL)                   ⎫
1080 P2$=STR$(BL*AH)+F$                ⎬ Multiply A$ and B$
1090 P3$=STR$(BH*AL)+F$                ⎪  and align products
1100 P4$=STR$(BH*AH)+F$+F$             ⎭
```

Step 4: Add the four products together. This is the most complicated part of the "Multiple Integer Multiplication" program because parameters are passed back and forth from the main program to an addition subroutine. We will use a portion of the

"Addition using Numeric Strings" program as a subroutine to add the products together. Below is the portion of the addition program we will be using as a subroutine:

```
2000 REM**ADD PRODUCTS**
2010 BLANK$="                    "
2020 X=LEN(A$):Y=LEN(B$)
2030 IF X<Y THEN A$=LEFT$(BLANK$,Y-X)+A$
2040 IF X>Y THEN B$=LEFT$(BLANK$,X-Y)+B$
2050 D=0:N=1:C$=""
2060 FOR I=LEN(A$) TO 1 STEP-1
2070 A=VAL(MID$(A$,I,1))
2080 A=A+D:D=0
2090 B=VAL(MID$(B$,I,1))
2100 C=A+B
2110 IF C>=10 THEN D=1
2120 IF D=1 AND I=1 THEN N=2
2130 C$=RIGHT$(STR$(C),N)+C$
2140 NEXT I
```

At line 1110 the contents of P1$ and P2$ are passed to the parameters A$ and B$, which are used in the addition subroutine (lines 2000 and 2140).

```
1110 A$=P1$:B$=P2$
```

A$ | 9 | 9 | 9 | 8 | 0 | 0 | 0 | 1 |

B$ | 9 | 9 | 9 | 8 | 0 | 0 | 0 | 1 | 0 | 0 | 0 | 0 |

Notice that the contents of A$ and B$ are not the same as those input at line 20. The same variable names are used to allow program compatibility between all four math programs. Only two parameters are passed at a time because the addition subroutine adds only two numbers at a time.

Once the values for P1$ and P2$ are passed to A$ and B$ the addition subroutine is called:

```
1120 GOSUB 2000
```

A$ and B$ are right-justified and equated in length for addition by adding blanks from BLANK$ to the shorter string (if there is one) in lines 2010 to 2040:

```
2010 BLANK$="                    "
2020 X=LEN(A$):Y=LEN(B$)
2030 IF X<Y THEN A$=LEFT$(BLANK$,Y-X)+A$
2040 IF X>Y THEN B$=LEFT$(BLANK$,X-Y)+B$
```

Statements 2050 to 2140 add the corresponding digits of A$ and B$ and convert the sum C into the numeric string C$. (A full explanation of this process is given in the "Addition using Numeric Strings" section.)

```
2050 D=0:N=1:C$=""
2060 FOR I=LEN(A$) TO 1 STEP-1
2070 A=VAL(MID$(A$,I,1))
2080 A=A+D:D=0
2090 B=VAL(MID$(B$,I,1))
2100 C=A+B
2110 IF C>=10 THEN D=1
2120 IF D=1 AND I=1 THEN N=2
2130 C$=RIGHT$(STR$(C),N)+C$
2140 NEXT I
```

The sum, C$, is passed through a FOR-NEXT loop to truncate any leading blanks or zeros at lines 3000 to 3060. This truncation routine is from "Subtraction using Numeric Strings."

```
3000 REM***TRUNCATE LEAD ZEROS***
3001 L=0
3010 FOR I=1 TO LEN(C$)
3020 IF VAL(MID$(C$,I,1))=0 THEN L=L+1
3030 IF VAL(LEFT$(C$,I))<>0 THEN I=LEN(C$)
3040 NEXT I
3050 C$=RIGHT$(C$,LEN(C$)-L)
3060 RETURN
```

C$, the sum of P1$ and P2$, is returned to the main program and converted to M1$:

```
1130 M1$=C$
```

The contents of C$ must be transferred to M1$ because C$ must be cleared before the addition subroutine is called again at line 1150 to add P3$ and P4$.

To add P3$ and P4$ together, the values of P3$ and P4$ are passed to the parameters A$ and B$ before calling the addition subroutine 2000:

```
1132 A$=P3$:B$=P4$:GOSUB 2000
```

A$ `9 9 9 8 0 0 0 0 0 0 0 0`

B$ `9 9 9 8 0 0 0 1 0 0 0 0 0 0 0 0`

The addition subroutine adds the corresponding digits of P3$ and P4$, truncates any leading zeros, and returns sum C$ to the main program, where C$ is converted to M2$:

```
1135 M2$=C$
```

The addition subroutine is called a third time to add M1$ and M2$ together to get the final answer, C$.

```
1140 A$=M1$:B$=M2$
```

A$ `9 9 9 8 9 9 9 9 0 0 0 1`

B$ `9 9 9 8 9 9 9 9 0 0 0 1 0 0 0 0`

```
1150 GOSUB 2000
```

Step 5: After the third return from the addition subroutine, C$ equals the sum of all four products. Step 5 **prints the answer.** The GOTO 20 allows another multiplication problem to be solved.

```
1190 PRINT:PRINT"ANSWER=";C$:PRINT:GOTO 20
1200 END
```

The flow of the program looks like this:

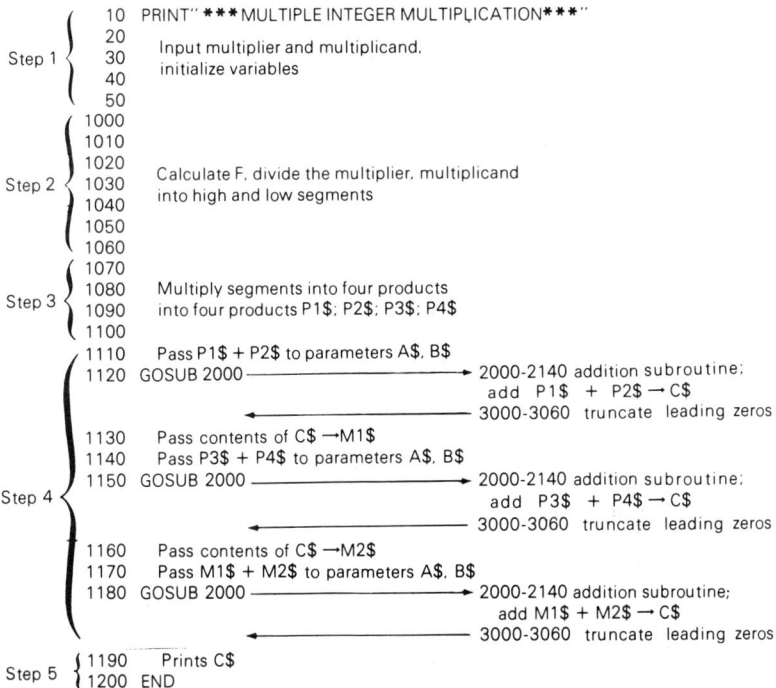

```
           ( 10   PRINT"***MULTIPLE INTEGER MULTIPLICATION***"
           { 20
  Step 1  <  30   Input multiplier and multiplicand,
           { 40   initialize variables
           ( 50
           ( 1000
           { 1010
           { 1020
  Step 2  <  1030  Calculate F, divide the multiplier, multiplicand
           { 1040  into high and low segments
           { 1050
           ( 1060
           ( 1070
  Step 3  <  1080  Multiply segments into four products
           {  1090  into four products P1$; P2$; P3$; P4$
           ( 1100
           / 1110  Pass P1$ + P2$ to parameters A$, B$
           | 1120  GOSUB 2000 ─────────────────────→ 2000-2140 addition subroutine;
           |                                            add P1$ + P2$ → C$
           |                        ←─────────────── 3000-3060 truncate leading zeros
           |
           | 1130  Pass contents of C$ →M1$
           | 1140  Pass P3$ + P4$ to parameters A$, B$
  Step 4  <  1150  GOSUB 2000 ─────────────────────→ 2000-2140 addition subroutine;
           |                                            add P3$ + P4$ → C$
           |                        ←─────────────── 3000-3060 truncate leading zeros
           |
           | 1160  Pass contents of C$ →M2$
           | 1170  Pass M1$ + M2$ to parameters A$, B$
           \ 1180  GOSUB 2000 ─────────────────────→ 2000-2140 addition subroutine;
                                                        add M1$ + M2$ → C$
                                    ←─────────────── 3000-3060 truncate leading zeros

           { 1190   Prints C$
  Step 5  { 1200   END
```

Here is the multiplication program listing and sample run:

```
10 PRINT"⊃***MULTIPLE INTEGER MULTIPLICATION***":PRINT
20 INPUT A$,B$
30 IF VAL(A$)=0 OR VAL(B$)=0 THEN C$="0":GOTO 1190
40 ZERO$="0000000000000000"
1000 X=LEN(A$):Y=LEN(B$)
1002 IF X>Y THEN F=X/2:GOTO 1008
1004 F=Y/2
1006 IF F>INT(F)THEN F=INT(F)+1
1008 F$=LEFT$(ZERO$,F)
1010 IF X<=F THEN AH=0:AL=VAL(A$):GOTO 1040
1020 AH=VAL(LEFT$(A$,X-F))
1030 AL=VAL(RIGHT$(A$,F))
1040 IF Y<=F THEN BH=0:BL=VAL(B$):GOTO 1070
1050 BH=VAL(LEFT$(B$,Y-F))
1060 BL=VAL(RIGHT$(B$,F))
1070 P1$=STR$(BL*AL)
1080 P2$=STR$(BL*AH)+F$
1090 P3$=STR$(BH*AL)+F$
1100 P4$=STR$(BH*AH)+F$+F$
1110 A$=P1$:B$=P2$
1120 GOSUB 2000
1130 M1$=C$
1132 A$=P3$:B$=P4$:GOSUB 2000
1135 M2$=C$
1140 A$=M1$:B$=M2$
1150 GOSUB 2000
1190 PRINT:PRINT"ANSWER=";C$:PRINT:GOTO 20
1200 END
2000 REM**ADD PRODUCTS**
2010 BLANK$="                "
2020 X=LEN(A$):Y=LEN(B$)
2030 IF X<Y THEN A$=LEFT$(BLANK$,Y-X)+A$
2040 IF X>Y THEN B$=LEFT$(BLANK$,X-Y)+B$
2050 D=0:N=1:C$=""
2060 FOR I=LEN(A$) TO 1 STEP-1
2070 A=VAL(MID$(A$,I,1))
2080 A=A+D:D=0
2090 B=VAL(MID$(B$,I,1))
2100 C=A+B
2110 IF C>=10 THEN D=1
2120 IF D=1 AND I=1 THEN N=2
2130 C$=RIGHT$(STR$(C),N)+C$
2140 NEXT I
3000 REM***TRUNCATE LEAD ZEROS***
3001 L=0
3010 FOR I=1 TO LEN(C$)
3020 IF VAL(MID$(C$,I,1))=0 THEN L=L+1
3030 IF VAL(LEFT$(C$,I))<>0 THEN I=LEN(C$)
3040 NEXT I
3050 C$=RIGHT$(C$,LEN(C$)-L)
3060 RETURN


*** MULTIPLE INTEGER MULTIPLICATION***

?99999999
??99999999

ANSWER= 9999999800000001
```

GRAPHICS

Computer graphics is a unique subject. Whole books are devoted to this subject. Of necessity, the discussion that follows is brief.

The standard graphic character set includes 64 graphic symbols. Select graphics by issuing a POKE 59468,12 if you are using the alternate character set, which has very few graphic characters. **If you have a CBM 8000 computer, select graphics using the Graphic editing function,** as follows:

100 print chr$(142):rem select graphics

The graphic characters are all located in the upper-case positions on the keys, so they must be entered in shifted mode.

Many graphic characters are referenced and illustrated on the following pages. Refer to Table 1-1 or Appendix A for easy reference to graphic character keys, names, and symbols.

GRAPHICS IN IMMEDIATE MODE

Sketching in immediate mode requires no line numbers, no PRINT statements, and no quotation marks. In immediate mode the cursor may be moved freely up, down, right, or left to any spot on the screen without pressing the RETURN key after each directional change. Below is an example of a square drawn in immediate mode. Starting with the cursor in home position, the square was drawn left to right, top to bottom, right to left, and bottom to top, in one continuous movement. No line numbers, program statements, or carriage returns were needed.

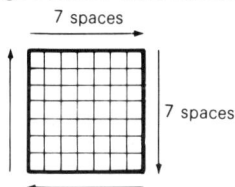

7 spaces

7 spaces

We will use the square shown above as the basic graphic design to illustrate elementary graphics. Though simple in its design, sketching this square uses all CBM computer graphic drawing techniques.

Draw a Square

There are nine steps to drawing a 7 × 7 square. They are:

Step 1: HOME the cursor. The top left corner of the HOME position space becomes the top left corner of the square (Figure 5-3a).

Step 2: Type the upper left corner of the square. This is done by using the TOP LEFT CORNER □ (Figure 5-3b).

Step 3: Draw the top line of the square. Because we will use a CORNER key for the top right corner, type five TOP LINE HORIZONTAL □ characters in this step (Figure 5-3c).

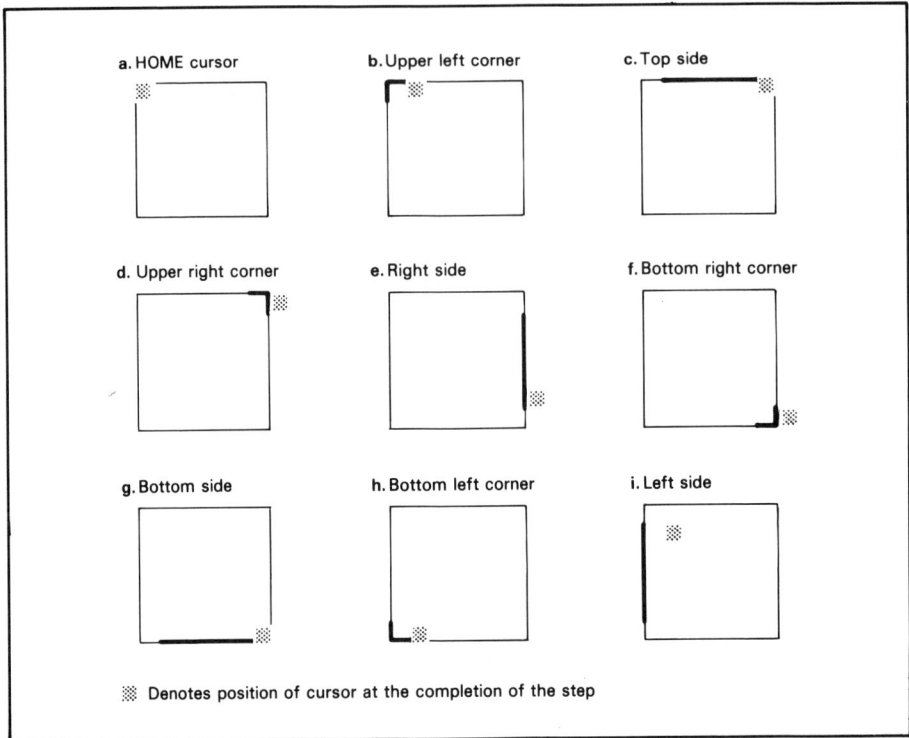

Figure 5-3. Draw the Square

Step 4: Type the upper right corner of the square using the TOP RIGHT COR-
NER character ▢ (Figure 5-3d).

Step 5: Draw the vertical right side of the square. To allow space for the corner
key, type five RIGHT LINE VERTICAL ▢ .

We all know what this part of the square should look like, but does your screen
look like this instead?

    ┌──────────┐ l l l l l

If so, this happened because the cursor is automatically moved one space to the right
after any character is displayed. To enter characters vertically, the cursor must be reposi-
tioned both vertically and horizontally to compensate for the automatic cursor movement to the right.

To print the vertical line of the square, then, repeat the sequence of CURSOR
DOWN, CURSOR LEFT, and RIGHT LINE VERTICAL. Do this five times, and you
should have printed the right side of the square (Figure 5-3e).

Step 6: Type the bottom right corner of the square using the BOTTOM RIGHT
CORNER character ▢ . Before you type this, look to see where your cursor is; if you
haven't already done so, use CURSOR DOWN and CURSOR LEFT to position the cursor at the corner of the square; then press the corner key (Figure 5-3f).

Step 7: Draw the bottom line. Because we are using CORNER keys, we need just
five BOTTOM LINE HORIZONTAL characters ▢ (Figure 5-3g).

One method is to enter the line from right to left. After each character entry on the bottom line, two CURSOR LEFT movements will be needed to correctly position the cursor for the next entry.

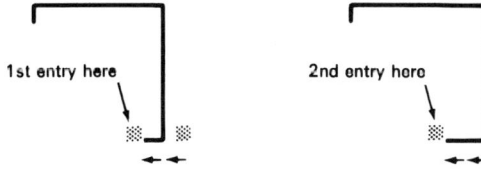

A second, and possibly more natural, method of drawing the bottom line is from left to right. To do this, position the cursor to the leftmost space of the bottom line (one space to the right of the left edge of the screen); this can be done using six CURSOR LEFTs. You can then easily enter five BOTTOM LINE HORIZONTALs to create the bottom line of the square.

Step 8: Type the bottom left corner. Depending on which method you used to enter the bottom line, you will need to use CURSOR LEFT two times (method 1) or six times (method 2) to position the cursor at the bottom left corner, then use the BOTTOM LEFT CORNER character □ to complete this step (Figure 5-3h).

Step 9: Complete the square by drawing the left vertical side. You should be able to type five LEFT LINE VERTICAL characters □ to complete the square (Figure 5-3i). You will need to position the cursor before each entry, using CURSOR LEFT and CURSOR UP.

PROGRAMMING GRAPHICS

Any graphics sketched directly onto the screen will be lost when you execute a NEW statement or turn the power off, unless you first convert the graphics into a program. **You can convert any design sketched onto the screen into a program simply by making each line on the screen a string which is to be printed as part of a program.**

After you have sketched the square, move the cursor to the HOME position. *Do not* press the CLEAR or RETURN key. If you press CLEAR you will lose your picture forever. If you press RETURN, "READY" will be written through the middle of the square as shown below:

Or, if you had made your square so large that the horizontal lines of the square were printed on the top and bottom rows of the screen, and the cursor was positioned on the bottom line, a RETURN would cause the display to scroll up one line in order to write the READY message on the next line, losing the top of the picture.

Before RETURN   **After RETURN**

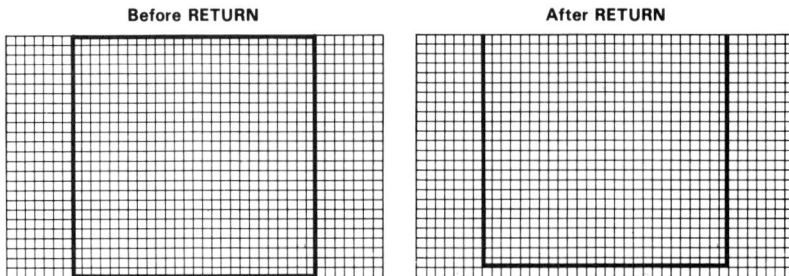

For this reason, pictures larger than 39 characters wide or 24 characters long should never be drawn in immediate mode.

Once the cursor is homed, the next step is to move each line of the picture to the right in order to insert line numbers, question marks (shorthand for **PRINT**) and quotes. This converts each line from immediate mode to program mode so it may be saved on a cassette tape or diskette.

When the cursor has been homed, it should be at the upper left corner of the square (Figure 5-4a). Press INSERT five times so that the top line of the square is shifted five spaces to the right (Figure 5-4b). Now there is enough room to type a line number (100), ?, and opening string quotes (Figure 5-4c). Then press **RETURN** (Figure 5-4d). The top line of the square is now a programmed statement. Continue doing this for each line, incrementing each line number by 100 until the entire square has been converted into program statements (Figure 5-4e, f).

Be sure to number the lines in sequential order to avoid distorting the picture. Also, you do not need to move the cursor past the graphics to insert a second set of quotation marks at the end of each line. After the first set of quotes is typed, merely press RETURN. Your final program listing should appear as follows:

```
100 PRINT"┌───────┐
200 PRINT"│       │
300 PRINT"│       │
400 PRINT"│       │
500 PRINT"│       │
600 PRINT"│       │
700 PRINT"└───────┘
```

Instead of creating graphics in immediate mode and converting them to a program, you can skip immediate mode completely. To draw the picture in program mode, each line of the picture is entered as part of a **PRINT** statement.

```
100 ?"┌───────┐
200 ?"│       │
300 ?"│       │
```

The space directly to the right of the quotation marks becomes column number 1 on th : screen. If you do not program with this in mind, your picture may end up shifted to the left-hand side of the screen.

If you PRINT a string that has exactly 40 characters, you must include a second set of quotes, and a semicolon at the end of the line. If you do not include the semicolon, an extra line will be displayed since the cursor automatically positions to the next line after a display in column 40.

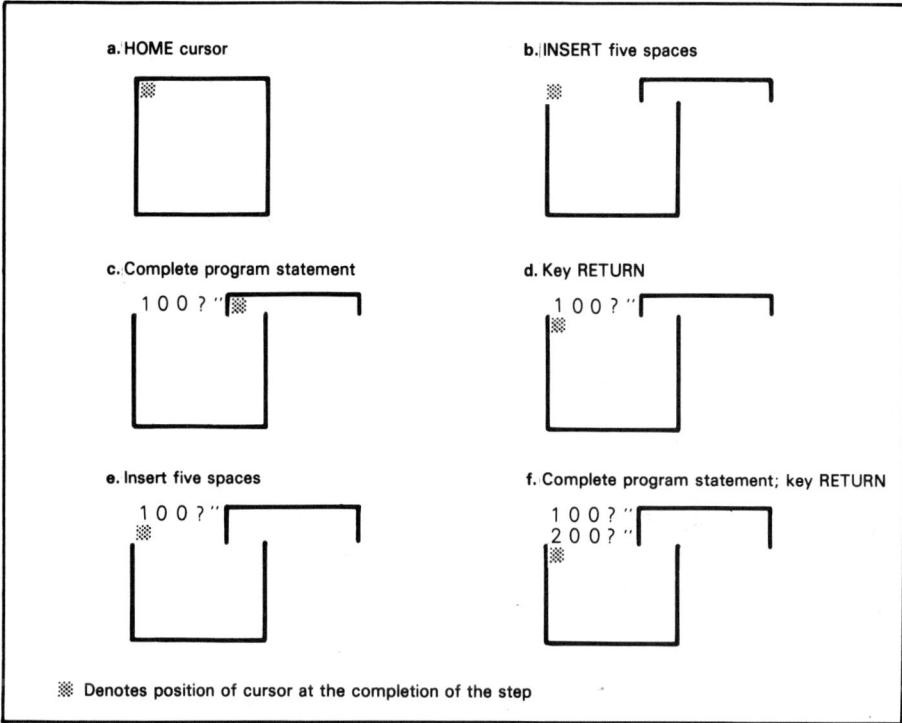

Figure 5-4. Make Program Statement from Graphics

A hint before moving to the next aspect of graphics: it is advisable to draw your picture or diagram on a piece of paper before drawing it on the screen. Map out on a piece of graph paper an area 40 squares wide by 25 squares long, using one square on paper for each space on the screen. Be sure to include space for the line numbers if you are going to convert the picture to program mode. Once everything is ready, type the program from the paper onto the screen.

ANIMATION

Any graph, number, design, word or picture may be programmed to move sideways, up, down, or diagonally, flash on and off, or display more slowly. These changes may be programmed in almost any combination.

To demonstrate animation, we will begin by animating the small square programmed in the previous section. **Instead of seeing the square appear instantaneously on the screen, animation will allow a viewer to watch each element of the square slowly appear on the screen.**

The program to animate the square looks very different from the previous program because the line segments are programmed as BASIC statements, rather than as picture segments. There is no large square within quotation marks; the square is broken down into individual graphic characters.

Time Delay

The animation program slowly moves the cursor so that the square appears to be drawn on the screen. The display begins at the top left corner of the screen and proceeds clockwise, as follows:

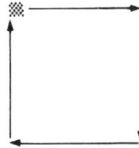

The first step, as always, is to clear the screen. This also puts the cursor in the home position.

```
5 PRINT"⊐";
```

The second step is to type the left corner. However, do not draw the whole top line as you did in the previous program, just the corner.

```
10 PRINT"Γ";
```

In order to see each element of the square being displayed, it is necessary to slow down statement execution. This can be done by using a time delay loop. This statement represents one way of creating a time delay:

```
100 FOR J=1 TO 100:NEXT J:RETURN
```

The FOR-NEXT loop increases the time that separates display of adjacent characters. It forces the computer to count from 1 to 10 each time the statement is executed as a subroutine. The TO index for J can be increased or decreased to lengthen or shorten the delay. The larger the TO index, the longer the time separating the display of each character.

For our animation program, then, we must include this time delay loop after displaying each element. Since the programmed time delay loop remains the same for each element, we call it as a subroutine. Therefore, after displaying the upper left corner of the square, call the time delay loop as subroutine 100.

Programming Character Placement

The third phase is to print the top line of the square. Instead of programming PRINT " ⁻ " we will use a FOR-NEXT loop:

```
15 FOR I=1 TO 5:PRINT"⁻";:GOSUB 100:NEXT I
```

Statement 15 uses a FOR-NEXT loop so that the subroutine time delay can be called between each printing of " ⁻ ". If the computer is to sketch the square slowly, the time delay must be called after *each* character is displayed. It would be useless to program:

```
15 PRINT"⁻⁻⁻⁻⁻";:GOSUB 100 ◄── Incorrect
```

because the whole line would be printed instantaneously without any time delay.

To complete the top line, type the upper right corner. Again, include the time delay subroutine call:

```
20 PRINT"⊓";:GOSUB 100
```

So far, the program looks like this:

```
5 PRINT"⊐";
10 PRINT"Γ";:GOSUB 100
15 FOR I=1 TO 5:PRINT"⁻";:GOSUB 100:NEXT I
20 PRINT"⊓";:GOSUB 100
30 END
100 FOR I=1 TO 100:NEXT J:RETURN
```

Run the program. You should see the following display grow progressively, from ⌐ to ⌐────⌐ .

Hopefully, this is what you saw. If not, go back and find out what went wrong. Did you forget the semicolons after each PRINT statement?

End all PRINT statements in this program with a semicolon (;). The semicolon concatenates graphic strings together when printed. This allows the " ⌐ " and the top line "────" to be concatenated together on the same line. Without the semicolons, the CBM computer performs a carriage return after each statement, and the top line will look like this:

```
          ⌐
          —
          —
          —
          ⌐
          ▒
```

The other three sides are drawn using a similar sequence. Line 20 begins the next sequence, to create the right side vertical line. Note the use of cursor control inside the FOR-NEXT loops to compensate for the automatic right cursor movement.

Here are the PRINT statements that must appear within FOR-NEXT loops to generate the right side, bottom and left side of the square:

```
                          PRINT<RIGHT LINE VERT. ><CURSOR L.>
PRINT" ▮◻"    right side   <CURSOR DOWN>
                          PRINT<BOTTOM LINE HORIZ.><CURSOR L.>
PRINT"⎽▮◻"    bottom      <CURSOR L.>
                          PRINT<LEFT LINE VERT. ><CURSOR L.>
PRINT"▮ ▮◻"   left side    <CURSOR UP>
```

The complete program listing looks like this:

```
5  PRINT"⤓";
10 PRINT"⌐"; :GOSUB 100
15 FOR I=1TO 5:PRINT"⁻"; :GOSUB 100:NEXT I
20 PRINT"⌐"; :GOSUB 100
25 FOR I=1TO 5:PRINT" ▮◻"; :GOSUB 100:NEXT I
30 PRINT"⌐"; :GOSUB 100
35 FOR I=1TO 5:PRINT"⎽▮▮"; :GOSUB 100:NEXT I
40 PRINT"L"; :GOSUB 100
45 FOR I=1TO 5:PRINT"▮ ▮◻"; :GOSUB 100:NEXT I
50 END
100 FOR J=1 TO 10:NEXT J:RETURN
```

Now try a trial run. Does your square look like this?

```
        ⌐────⌐ |
        READY. |
        |      |
        |      |
        |      |
        L |────
```

If this design appears instead of a perfect square, some of the cursor controls were left out. The computer did exactly what it was programmed to do, so where is the problem? Take a closer look at the program. We included cursor controls within the FOR-NEXT loops for all four sides of the square. Now look at the screen. The problem is not with the sides; therefore the problem must be in the corners. Look at statements 20, 30, and 40.

We forgot the cursor controls after each corner position. Make the proper changes, and the program should look like this:

```
5 PRINT"J";
10 PRINT"Г";:GOSUB 100
15 FOR I=1 TO 5:PRINT"¯";:GOSUB 100:NEXT I
20 PRINT"▀▐█";:GOSUB 100
25 FOR I=1 TO 5:PRINT" █▐█";:GOSUB 100:NEXT I
30 PRINT"▃█▌";:GOSUB 100
35 FOR I=1 TO 5:PRINT"▃█▌";:GOSUB 100:NEXT I
40 PRINT"L▐▛";:GOSUB 100
45 FOR I=1 TO 5:PRINT"I █▛";:GOSUB 100:NEXT I
50 END
100 FOR I=1 TO 100:NEXT J:RETURN
```

Now try another trial run. Your picture should look like this:

```
┌─────────┐
│READY.   │
│▓        │
│         │
│         │
└─────────┘
```

You should have been able to watch the computer slowly sketch the square on the screen in a clockwise direction. Remember, you may change the print speed by changing the TO index value for variable J in the time delay loop.

One last problem: how to avoid destroying the square with the READY message.

When the square has been drawn, the cursor is on line 2; when the program ends, the READY message is displayed on the next line, which happens to be within the square. Therefore, before ending the program, you must compensate for this by moving the cursor below the square; the READY message will be written underneath the square and not across it. This is done by printing several CURSOR DOWNs before the END statement.

```
50 PRINT"▧▧▧▧▧▧▧▧":END
```

This will move the cursor down below the square and the square will not be destroyed:

```
┌─────────┐
│         │
│         │
│         │
│         │
└─────────┘
READY.
▓
```

Enlarging the Square

Let's take the small square we just animated and enlarge it so that it forms a boundary one space from the perimeter of a 40-column screen:

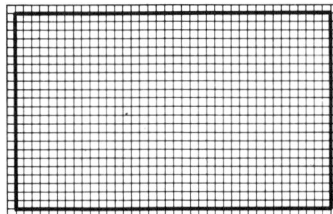

If the screen is 40 spaces wide by 25 spaces long, the rectangle's sides should be 38 spaces wide by 23 spaces long:

```
40─2   (1 space for each side) = 38
25─2   (1 space for each side) = 23
```

With just a few changes to the animated small square program we can draw a larger rectangle that forms a screen boundary. FOR-NEXT loops were used in the previous animation program to print a string of graphics for each side. To enlarge the square, change the value of the TO index to 36 for the horizontal sides and 21 for the vertical sides, leaving spaces for the corners.

```
15 FOR I=1 TO 36:?"‾";          ──────── Horizontal sides
25 FOR I=1 TO 21:?" ▌▐";  ╲  ╱
35 FOR I=1 TO 36:?"▟▛";   ╱  ╲
45 FOR I=1 TO 21:?"▌▐";   ──────── Vertical sides
```

Make these changes in your program and try a trial RUN.

That was simple. But, because you have created a boundary around the edge of the screen, the last statement of the program (to move the cursor out of the square) is unwanted. Instead, delete line 50 and program the cursor to move inside of the box and print something; you do not want a boundary surrounding an empty screen. Be sure not to program the cursor to go beneath the square, because the screen will scroll up, and you will lose the top of the square. Program something to be printed inside the box, type RUN and watch it go!

THE REAL TIME CLOCK

Another CBM computer feature is the real time clock. The CBM computer clock keeps real time in a 24-hour cycle by hours, minutes, and seconds. The reserved string variable TIME$ or TI$ keeps track of the time.

Setting the Clock

To set the clock, use the following format:

```
TIME$ = "hhmmss"
```

where: hh is the hour between 0 and 23
           mm is the minutes between 0 and 59
           ss is the seconds between 0 and 59

For hh, enter the hour of the day from 00 (12 AM) to 23 (11 PM). The CBM computer is on a 24-hour cycle so that you can distinguish between AM and PM, unlike 12-hour clocks. The hours from 00 to 11 designate AM, and the hours from 12 to 23 designate PM, returning to 00 at midnight. At midnight, when one 24-hour cycle ends and another begins, hh, mm, and ss are all equal to zero.

When initializing TIME$ to the actual time, type in a time a few seconds in the future. When that actual time is reached, press the RETURN key to set the clock.

```
TIME$="120150"
```

Accessing the Clock

To retrieve the time, type the following in immediate or program mode:

```
?TIME$
```

and the computer will display the time in hhmmss:

```
?TIME$
120200
```

The CBM computer clock keeps time until it is turned off. The clock needs to be reset when the computer is powered up again.

Real Time Clock Operation

The CBM computer actually keeps track of time in "jiffies." A "jiffy" is 1/60 of a second. TIME, or TI, is a reserved numeric variable which is automatically incremented every 1/60 of a second. TIME is initialized to zero on start-up, and is reset back to zero after 51,839,999 jiffies. TIME$ is a string variable that is genered from TIME. When TIME$ is called, the computer displays time in hours, minutes, and seconds (hhmmss), but in fact converts jiffy time to real time. Notice that TIME$ and TI$ are not the string representations of TIME and TI; they are numbers representing real time, calculated from jiffy time (TIME, TI). The conversion is done as follows. Each second is divided into 60 jiffies. One minute is composed of 60 seconds. One hour is made up of 60 minutes. Therefore one second is 60 jiffies, one minute is 3600 jiffies, and one hour is 216,000 jiffies, as illustrated below:

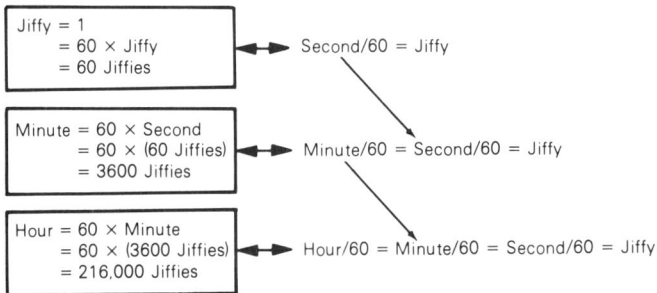

```
Jiffy = 1
      = 60 × Jiffy          Second/60 = Jiffy
      = 60 Jiffies

Minute = 60 × Second
       = 60 × (60 Jiffies)  Minute/60 = Second/60 = Jiffy
       = 3600 Jiffies

Hour = 60 × Minute
     = 60 × (3600 Jiffies)  Hour/60 = Minute/60 = Second/60 = Jiffy
     = 216,000 Jiffies
```

The following statements convert jiffy time (J) into real time, shown as hours (H), minutes (M), and seconds (S). A complete program follows the statement descriptions.

```
10 J=TI                          Calculate hours.
20 H=INT(J/216000)               Integer function takes only whole
                                 number.

30 IF H<>0 THEN J=J-H*21600      If any hours, subtract number of
                                 jiffies in one hour by H to leave
                                 remaining jiffies.

40 M=INT(J/3600)                 Calculate minutes.
                                 Integer function takes only whole
                                 number.

50 IF M<>0 THEN J=J-M*3600       If any minutes, subtract number of
                                 jiffies in minutes by 7 to leave
                                 remaining jiffies.

60 S=INT(J/60)                   Calculate seconds. Integer function
                                 takes only whole number.
```

```
5 PRINT"⌂REAL TIME":PRINT:PRINT:
10 J=TI
15 T$=TIME$
20 H=INT(J/21600)
30 IF H<>0 THEN J=J-H*21600
```

```
40 M=INT(J/3600)
50 IF M<>0 THEN J=J-M*3600
60 S=INT(J/60)
70 H$=RIGHT$(STR$(H),2)
80 M$=RIGHT$(STR$(M),2)
90 S$=RIGHT$(STR$(S),2)
100 PRINT"H:M:S: ";H$;":";M$;":";S$,"TIME$: ";T$
110 PRINT"█████";:GOTO10
```

In the program above, statements 70 through 90 convert the numeric answers into proper string form for tidy printing. Statement 100 prints both the real time calculated from the program, and TIME$, the real time calculated automatically by the computer. Notice that the result is the same in both cases.

To get an idea of jiffy speed and the conversion from the jiffy to the standard clock, type in the following program; it displays the running time of both TIME$ and TIME (TI):

```
5 REM **RUNNING CLOCKS**
10 PRINT ":REAL TIME: ":PRINT:PRINT "JIFFY TIME: "
20 FOR I=1 TO 235959
30 PRINT"█";TAB(13);TIME$
40 FOR J=1 TO 60 STEP 2
50 PRINT"█████";TAB(12);TI
60 NEXT J
70 NEXT I
```

The FOR-NEXT loop for TIME in line 40 increments by STEP 2 (every two jiffies) for two reasons:

1. Displaying 60 jiffies a second is too fast to read.
2. Displaying each jiffy takes longer than incrementing the jiffy. This delays the loop, so the TIME$ display is slower than it should be. By incrementing and printing every other jiffy we can minimize this delay problem. Run this program and you will see that jiffies increment to 60 within each second. Run this program without STEP 2 in line 40 and see the time delay when printing TIME$.

Real time: 006704
Jiffy time: 25500

Keeping time in jiffies is useful for timing program speed. This lets you test the efficiency of a program. Consider this short program:

```
10 PRINT":**KEYBOARD TEST**":PRINT
20 FOR I=32 TO 127
30 PRINT CHR$(I);
40 NEXT I
50 FOR J=161 TO 255
60 PRINT CHR$(J);
70 NEXT J
80 PRINT:PRINT:PRINT"**END TEST**"
```

We can compute execution time for this program as follows:

1. TI (or TIME) is assigned to a variable constant at the start of the time test.
2. TI (or TIME) is reassigned to a different variable constant at the end of the time test.
3. Subtract the first TI variable from the second. This will give you the amount of jiffy time it took to process the program that lies in between.

The listing below shows the three added steps:

```
Step 1   10 PRINT"⊃**KEYBOARD TEST**":PRINT
         15 A=TI
         20 FOR I=32 TO 127
         30 PRINT CHR$(I);
         40 NEXT I
         50 FOR J=161 TO 255
         60 PRINT CHR$(J);
         70 NEXT J
         75 B=TI
Step 2   80 PRINT:PRINT:PRINT"**END TEST**"
Step 3  100 PRINT:PRINT"TI = ";B-A
```

At line 15, variable A is set to the current value of TI.

```
        15 A=TI
```

A = TI 6001762

A 6001762

Then, as the program is processed, TI increments 60 times every second. At line 75, B is set to the current value of TI.

```
        75 B=TI
```

B=TI 6001953

B= 6001953

Line 100 subtracts the first value of TI (A) from the second (B).

```
        100 PRINT:PRINT"TI=";B-A
```

```
        B 6001953
      - A 6001762
        ─────────
            191
```

The example shows that it took 191 jiffies to print the keyboard characters on the screen. Dividing jiffy time (191 jiffies) by 60 (the number of jiffies in a second):

$$191/60=3.1833$$

shows it took 3.1833 seconds (191 jiffies) to process the program. Below is a sample run of the program.

```
**KEYBOARD TEST**

 !"#$%&'()*+,-./0123456789:;<=>?@ABCDEFG
HIJKLMNOPQRSTUVWXYZ[\]↑← !"#$%&'()*+,-./
0123456789:;<=>?▎▖▔◢ ▗ ◣ ├▮┴▂◤▐▌ ┌
▄▖ ▙▝◥├─┐─◣ ▏╲◿┌▌◢◖▂◖ ╱X◎◆ ◖┼▓ |π◥
▐▄┐※◢ ├┼◦┴▂◤┐◢│ ┌▄▖ ▙ π

**END TEST**

TI = 191
```

Digital Display Clock

The following program is a fun program. It is a variation of the CBM digital clock using enlarged numbers 0 through 9, created with the graphic characters. The program prints out only the hour and minutes due to the size of the screen. The program is long, as you can see, but it is made up almost entirely of PRINT statements to print the numbers. After keying in the program, watch it run.

```
100 PRINT"⬛⬛⬛⬛⬛⬛⬛⬛";
110 S=INT(TIME/60)
120 M=INT(S/60)
130 H=INT(M/60)
140 M=M-H*60
150 T=H
160 GOSUB500
170 PRINT"⬛⬛⬛⬛ ⬛⬛ ⬛⬛⬛⬛ ⬛⬛ ⬛⬛⬛⬛⬛⬛ ";
180 T=M
190 GOSUB500
200 PRINT"⬛⬛⬛";
210 GOTO110
500 U=T-10*INT(T/10)
510 T=INT(T/10)
520 D=T+1
530 GOSUB600
540 D=U+1
550 GOSUB600
560 RETURN
600 ON D GOSUB 1000,1100,1200,1300,1400,1500,1600,
    1700,1800,1900
610 RETURN
1000 PRINT"  ⬛       ⬛ ⬛⬛⬛⬛⬛⬛⬛⬛⬛";
1001 PRINT"  ⬛       ⬛⬛⬛⬛⬛⬛⬛⬛⬛";
1002 PRINT"⬛ ⬛     ⬛ ⬛⬛⬛⬛⬛⬛⬛⬛⬛";
1003 PRINT"⬛ ⬛     ⬛ ⬛⬛⬛⬛⬛⬛⬛⬛⬛";
1004 PRINT"⬛ ⬛     ⬛ ⬛⬛⬛⬛⬛⬛⬛⬛⬛";
1005 PRINT"⬛ ⬛     ⬛ ⬛⬛⬛⬛⬛⬛⬛⬛⬛";
1006 PRINT"⬛ ⬛     ⬛ ⬛⬛⬛⬛⬛⬛⬛⬛⬛";
1007 PRINT"⬛ ⬛     ⬛ ⬛⬛⬛⬛⬛⬛⬛⬛⬛";
1008 PRINT"⬛⬛      ⬛⬛⬛⬛⬛⬛⬛⬛⬛⬛";
1009 PRINT" ⬛⬛     ⬛  ⬛⬛⬛⬛⬛⬛⬛⬛";
1010 RETURN
1100 PRINT"   ⬛  ⬛  ⬛⬛⬛⬛⬛⬛⬛⬛⬛";
1101 PRINT"   ⬛  ⬛  ⬛⬛⬛⬛⬛⬛⬛⬛⬛";
1102 PRINT"    ⬛ ⬛  ⬛⬛⬛⬛⬛⬛⬛⬛⬛";
1103 PRINT"    ⬛ ⬛  ⬛⬛⬛⬛⬛⬛⬛⬛⬛";
1104 PRINT"    ⬛ ⬛  ⬛⬛⬛⬛⬛⬛⬛⬛⬛";
1105 PRINT"    ⬛ ⬛  ⬛⬛⬛⬛⬛⬛⬛⬛⬛";
1106 PRINT"    ⬛ ⬛  ⬛⬛⬛⬛⬛⬛⬛⬛⬛";
1107 PRINT"    ⬛ ⬛  ⬛⬛⬛⬛⬛⬛⬛⬛⬛";
1108 PRINT"  ⬛     ⬛ ⬛⬛⬛⬛⬛⬛⬛⬛⬛";
1109 PRINT"  ⬛     ⬛  ⬛⬛⬛⬛⬛⬛⬛⬛";
1110 RETURN
1200 PRINT"  ⬛       ⬛ ⬛⬛⬛⬛⬛⬛⬛⬛⬛";
1201 PRINT"  ⬛       ⬛⬛⬛⬛⬛⬛⬛⬛⬛";
1202 PRINT"⬛ ⬛     ⬛ ⬛⬛⬛⬛⬛⬛⬛⬛⬛";
1203 PRINT"⬛ ⬛     ⬛ ⬛⬛⬛⬛⬛⬛⬛⬛⬛";
1204 PRINT"      ⬛ ⬛⬛⬛⬛⬛⬛⬛⬛⬛⬛";
1205 PRINT"    ⬛ ⬛ ⬛⬛⬛⬛⬛⬛⬛⬛⬛";
1206 PRINT"  ⬛ ⬛ ⬛⬛⬛⬛⬛⬛⬛⬛⬛";
1207 PRINT" ⬛ ⬛ ⬛⬛⬛⬛⬛⬛⬛⬛⬛";
1208 PRINT"⬛ ⬛     ⬛⬛⬛⬛⬛⬛⬛⬛⬛";
1209 PRINT"⬛ ⬛     ⬛  ⬛⬛⬛⬛⬛⬛⬛⬛";
1210 RETURN
1300 PRINT"  ⬛       ⬛ ⬛⬛⬛⬛⬛⬛⬛⬛⬛";
1301 PRINT"  ⬛       ⬛⬛⬛⬛⬛⬛⬛⬛⬛";
1302 PRINT"⬛ ⬛     ⬛ ⬛⬛⬛⬛⬛⬛⬛⬛⬛";
1303 PRINT"       ⬛ ⬛⬛⬛⬛⬛⬛⬛⬛⬛";
1304 PRINT"     ⬛ ⬛⬛⬛⬛⬛⬛⬛⬛⬛";
1305 PRINT"     ⬛ ⬛⬛⬛⬛⬛⬛⬛⬛⬛";
1306 PRINT"      ⬛ ⬛⬛⬛⬛⬛⬛⬛⬛⬛";
1307 PRINT"⬛ ⬛   ⬛ ⬛⬛⬛⬛⬛⬛⬛⬛⬛";
```

```
1308 PRINT"◥◪        ◤██████████◨";
1309 PRINT" ◥◪     ◤   ▯▯▯▯▯▯▯▯▯▯]";
1310 RETURN
1400 PRINT"      ◢▘ ▉  ██████████◨";
1401 PRINT"     ◢▘ ▉  ██████████◨";
1402 PRINT"    ◢▘  ▉  ██████████◨";
1403 PRINT"   ◢▘   ▉  ██████████◨";
1404 PRINT"◢▘  ◢▘◪ ▉   ██████████◨";
1405 PRINT"◪  ◢▘ ◪ ▉   ██████████◨";
1406 PRINT"◪       ██████████◨";
1407 PRINT"◪       ██████████◨";
1408 PRINT"    ◪ ▉  ██████████◨";
1409 PRINT"    ◪ ▉   ▯▯▯▯▯▯▯▯▯▯]";
1410 RETURN

1500 PRINT"◪       ██████████◨";
1501 PRINT"◪       ██████████◨";
1502 PRINT"◪ ▉      ██████████◨";
1503 PRINT"◪       ◥██████████◨";
1504 PRINT"◪       ◥██████████◨";
1505 PRINT"    ◥◪  ██████████◨";
1506 PRINT"      ◪ ██████████◨";
1507 PRINT"◪ ◥  ◢▘  ██████████◨";
1508 PRINT"◥◪     ◤██████████◨";
1509 PRINT" ◥◪   ◤   ▯▯▯▯▯▯▯▯▯▯]";
1510 RETURN
1600 PRINT" ◢▘   ◥ ██████████◨";
1601 PRINT"◢▘      ◥██████████◨";
1602 PRINT"◪ ◢▘  ◥◪ ██████████◨";
1603 PRINT"◪ ▉     ██████████◨";
1604 PRINT"◪   ◥ ██████████◨";
1605 PRINT"◪      ◥██████████◨";
1606 PRINT"◪ ◢▘  ◥◪ ██████████◨";
1607 PRINT"◪ ◥  ◢▘ ██████████◨";
1608 PRINT"◥◪     ◤██████████◨";
1609 PRINT" ◥◪   ◤   ▯▯▯▯▯▯▯▯▯▯]";
1610 RETURN
1700 PRINT"◪       ██████████◨";
1701 PRINT"◪       ██████████◨";
1702 PRINT"       ◢▘ ██████████◨";
1703 PRINT"      ◢▘ ◤██████████◨";
1704 PRINT"     ◢▘ ◤ ██████████◨";
1705 PRINT"    ◢▘ ◤  ██████████◨";
1706 PRINT"    ◪ ◢▘  ██████████◨";
1707 PRINT"    ◪ ▉   ██████████◨";
1708 PRINT"    ◪ ▉   ██████████◨";
1709 PRINT"    ◪ ▉    ▯▯▯▯▯▯▯▯▯▯]";
1710 RETURN
1800 PRINT" ◢▘   ◥ ██████████◨";
1801 PRINT"◢▘      ◥██████████◨";
1802 PRINT"◪ ◢▘  ◥◪ ██████████◨";
1803 PRINT"◪ ◥  ◢▘ ██████████◨";
1804 PRINT"◥◪     ◤██████████◨";
1805 PRINT"◢▘      ◥██████████◨";
1806 PRINT"◪ ◢▘  ◥◪ ██████████◨";
1807 PRINT"◪ ◥  ◢▘ ██████████◨";
1808 PRINT"◥◪     ◤██████████◨";
1809 PRINT" ◥◪   ◤   ▯▯▯▯▯▯▯▯▯▯]";
1810 RETURN
1900 PRINT" ◢▘   ◥ ██████████◨";
1901 PRINT"◢▘      ◥██████████◨";
1902 PRINT"◪ ◢▘  ◥◪ ██████████◨";
1903 PRINT"◪ ◥  ◢▘ ██████████◨";
1904 PRINT"◥◪      ◤██████████◨";
```

```
1905 PRINT"  ◥◪      ■■■■■■■■◘";
1906 PRINT"      ◪ ■■■■■■■◘";
1907 PRINT"◪  ◥◣  ◢▶ ■■■■■■◘";
1908 PRINT"◥◪   ◢▶■■■■■■◘";
1909 PRINT" ◥◪   ◢▶   ⊓⊓⊓⊓⊓⊓";
1910 RETURN
```

RANDOM NUMBERS

Random numbers are generated by the CBM computer using an algorithm that depends on a starting number, or seed. The same seed always generates the same sequence of random numbers.

RANDOM NUMBER SEED

Every CBM computer has a constant initial seed number which it generates when power is first turned on. This initial seed number will probably differ from one CBM computer to the next, but for any single CBM computer the same seed is generated whenever power is turned on. Therefore, for any single CBM computer, the same initial sequence of random numbers will be generated each time the computer is powered up. The display below shows the first five numbers of a typical sequence, as it might appear when the RANDOM function RND(arg) is executed after power-up:

```
### COMMODORE BASIC ###

7167 BYTES FREE

READY.

FOR I=1 TO 5:? RND(1):NEXT
RUN
 .880969862
 .355265655
 .659512252
 .803285178
 .546991144
READY.
```

CBM computer random function logic is best visualized as accessing a large number of fixed random number sequences. These random number sequences will vary from one CBM computer to the next, but they will always be the same for any given CBM computer.

Each random number sequence is identified by a seed, which is a negative number. This may be illustrated as follows:

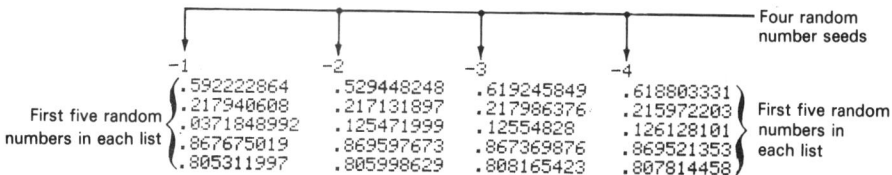

```
                                                    ┌── Four random
        │          │          │          │          │   number seeds
        ▼          ▼          ▼          ▼
       -1         -2         -3         -4
      ⎛.592222864  .529448248  .619245849  .618803331 ⎞
      ⎜.217940608  .217131897  .217986376  .215972203 ⎜ First five random
First five random⎜.0371848992 .125471999  .12554828   .126128101 ⎬ numbers in
numbers in each list⎜.867675019 .869597673  .867369876  .869521353 ⎜ each list
      ⎝.805311997  .805998629  .808165423  .807814458 ⎠
```

Every negative number seeds a different random number list. There are innumerable negative numbers, therefore there are innumerable lists of random numbers which can be accessed by any CBM computer.

You select any random number sequence by executing any BASIC statement that includes the RND function with a negative argument. You can use a simple assignment statement such as:

```
20 X=RND(-2)
```

Executing a BASIC statement that includes an RND function with a negative argument has the effect of resetting a pointer to the first random number in that negative argument's random number list. For example, on one particular CBM computer, executing the assignment statement on line 20 above will reset the random function pointer to the number .271819872, the first number in the list seeded by −2. This reset will occur every time the RND(−2) function is encountered. The CBM computer that was used to generate this particular example selects the number .271819872, but another CBM computer will have a totally different fixed random number sequence initialized by the (−2) seed. If you have three CBM computers, each will have a different random number sequence initialized by the (−2) seed; however, each CBM computer will initialize to the same random number sequence on encountering an RND(−2) function.

Random Number Sequences

Having initialized the random number generator to the first number in a particular list, you access sequential random numbers in the list by executing any BASIC statement that includes an RND function with a positive argument. Here, for example, is a program that will display the first six numbers of five random number sequences, seeded by the negative functions −1 through −5:

```
30 FOR I=-1 TO -5 STEP -1
35 X=RND(I):PRINTI
40 FOR J=1 TO 5
50 PRINT RND(1)
60 NEXT J
70 NEXT I
100 STOP
```

The random function on line 35 occurs in the outer FOR-NEXT loop; it resets the random function generator pointer to the first element of five different sequences for the five negative values of I: −1, −2, −3, −4, and −5. The inner FOR-NEXT loop (lines 40, 50, and 60) displays the first six elements in each of these five random number sequences.

```
-1
.592222864
.217940608
.0371848992
.867675019
.805311997
-2
.529448248
.217131897
.125471999
.869597673
.805998629
```

```
-3
.619245849
.217986376
.12554828
.867369876
.808165423
-4
.618803331
.215972203
.126128101
.869521353
.807814458
-5
.529738186
.216918235
.128416908
.868422708
.717787951
```

To demonstrate the existence of a fixed number sequence in each random list, stop the generation of numbers for a list and then restart it. Look at the following modification of the random number generator program:

```
30 FOR I=-1 TO -5 STEP -1
35 X=RND(I):PRINTI
40 FOR J=1 TO 3
50 PRINT RND(1)
60 NEXT J
70 FOR K=10 TO 11
75 PRINT RND(1)
80 NEXT K
90 NEXT I
100 STOP
```

This program again references the first six elements in five random number lists, but it does so in two separate FOR-NEXT loops. Nevertheless, when you execute this program you will get exactly the same display as the earlier program. In other words, it does not matter where or how a random function with a positive argument is executed, it will always access the next element of the fixed random number list identified by the most recent negative seed. Moreover, any time this negative seed is encountered in a subsequent random function, the list pointer immediately returns to the first element of the sequence. For example, add this statement to the program shown above:

```
65 X=RND(I)
```

Now when you execute the program, you will access the first three numbers in each list, then the first two numbers in each list will be re-accessed.

Now experiment by keying in the programs illustrated above. Vary both the negative seed numbers specified by the I index in the outer FOR-NEXT loop, and the number of elements selected by J and K in the inner FOR-NEXT loops. Experiment in this fashion until you are completely satisfied that you understand the manner in which random numbers are generated.

Printing Random Numbers

In order to better compare random numbers, you should print results rather than displaying them (assuming you have a printer). Although printer programming is described in Chapter 6, necessary additional statements are shown below in order to select a printer.

```
10 OPEN 4,4
20 CMD 4
30 FOR I=-1 TO -5 STEP -1
35 X=RND(I):PRINTI
40 FOR J=1 TO 5
50 PRINT RND(1)
60 NEXT J
70 NEXT I
80 PRINT#4
90 CLOSE 4
100 STOP
```

Statements on lines 10 and 20 select the printer; statements on lines 80 and 90 deselect it. Make sure the printer power is turned on, and that it is connected correctly to your CBM computer; then use variations of the program illustrated above to experiment with random numbers. The hard copy printed with each experiment will make it easier for you to compare the numbers generated by different variations of your program.

If you execute a statement that contains an RND function with a 0 argument, then the random number generated depends on the system clock. But there are similarities in random number patterns generated by sequences of RND functions with a 0 argument. To prove this to yourself, change the argument of the RND function on line 50 from 1 to 0 and reexecute the random number generator program a few times. You will see that no two sequences of numbers are identical, but they certainly are quite close.

Random Seeds

To generate a totally different random number you need to have some way of generating a totally random seed. This can be done using the current jiffy count, TI:

```
10 X=RND(-TI): REM START SEED
```

Now you will get a different random sequence started each time statement 10 is executed.

A more nearly pure random seed can be obtained by using RND $(-RND(0))$, but only if your CBM computer has the new BASIC ROMs. For example:

```
10 X=RND(-RND(0))
```

Here again you will get a different random sequence started each time statement 10 is executed.

In the programs that follow, $-TI$ is used, as it is compatible with both the old and new ROMs. If you have the new ROMs, you can use $-RND(0)$ in place of $-TI$.

Generating Random Dice Throws

Random numbers are initially generated in the range 0 through 1. You will have to convert the random number to whatever range you require. Suppose numbers must range from 1 to 6 (as in one die number of a dice game). You will need to multiply the random number by 6:

```
6•RND(1)
```

This gives a floating point number in a range just greater than 0 but just less than 6 $(0<n<6)$. Add 1 to get a number in the range $1<n<7$:

```
6•RND(1)+1
```

Then convert the number to an integer, which discards any fractional part of a number, returning the number in the range 1 to 6 but in integer form:

INT(6•RND(1)+1)

or:

A%=6•RND(1)+1

The general cases for converting the RND fraction to whole number ranges are shown below. Note that the INT function will only handle numbers in the integer range ±32767.

INT((n+1)•RND(1))	Range 0 to n
INT(n•RND(1)+1)	Range 1 to n
INT((n−m+1)•RND(1)+m	Range m to n

Now experiment with a variety of different random number ranges by modifying the statement(s) illustrated above.

The program below shows −TI being used to generate a random seed. This program calculates numbers in the range m to n; in this program, the values of m and n are set in line 10 for a given program run. Note that these values can be negative. In the following example, the display is an unending sequence of random numbers between −50 and +50. (Press the STOP key to end the program.) A different sequence of numbers will be printed each time the program runs, since −T1 provides a random seed. Note that the X value returned from RND(−TI) is displayed instead of the TI value.

```
10 M=-50:N=50
20 X=RND(-TI):PRINT X
30 FOR I=1 TO 8
40 C%=(N-M+1)*RND(1)+M
50 PRINT C%;:NEXT I
60 PRINT:GOTO 30
RUN
 8.27633085E-06
-14   9 -34 -35 -47 -44  28  31
 29  -8 -36 -28 -42 -28  15  14
  7 -13   3  -8   8  41  19 -43
 35  12  24  -7  -7 -21 -47   1
-32 -49   7 -49  28 -22 -17 -24
-12   7  27   1  11   9 -18  35
 48  49   1  34 -46 -29 -43  29
-18   5 -30   2   8 -28 -13 -23
 48 -15 -12 -45  26  44 -25   2
 -9   4  27  50  33 -16 -43 -15
 20  20  17  43 -18 -48 -38  24
-16  43 -50  36 -38   5  11  25
-30   6 -25 -47  32  10  42 -21
-47 -38 -28  -8  16 -20  42  -4
-34  36 -17  27  -8 -49  -6 -35
-19  19 -35  48 -42  36 -25   2
-49  37  47  38 -20 -25  32 -50
 -5 -35 -35  17 -41  36 -19   4
 33 -20  45  -7  48  -4 -33 -10
  1  27 -39 -14 -38  -6   4  10
 -5  17   2  49   0 -40  -5  32
-50  32 -24 -37 -38  22 -13 -27
-24 -30  35  10   6  16 -50  49
-49  50  43  38 -21  47 -43  28
 32 -35 -18  -5  27 -46 -14  23
-49 -45  27   7 -35   1  46 -25
 -8  20  -8 -12 -46 -31 -17 -18
-47  47 -49  18  47  17  40 -13
-40  48 -41 -33   5 -14 -46  45
-29 -37  22  17  42  33 -31  49
  8  -4  36  37  11  18  29  25
  0  -1   2 -16  32 -29 -31  33
 -9 -41  -4  47  12 -22   9 -48
-40  32  15  32 -50   3  -9  19
```

To illustrate different number ranges, change the values of M and N in line 10 of the above program. For example, make M=1 and N=6; this will generate and unending sequence of random numbers between 1 and 6.

Random Selection of Playing Cards

A quick scan of the display above shows that numbers repeat within the first 100 generated. That is, every 101 numbers will not pick a number in the range −50 to +50 with every number present and no duplications. This is fine in, say, a dice game where you take the rolls as they come. For other random number uses, however, **you may need to develop random numbers in a certain range where every number is accounted for, and there are no duplications. An example is dealing from a deck of cards.** You need to pick a card, and when that card has been picked it cannot be picked again during the same deal.

The program below shows one way to program shuffling a deck of cards on the CBM computer. This program fills a 52-element table D% with the numbers 1 through 52 in a random sequence. (Element D%(0) is not used.) The cards can be pegged to the random numbers in any way, such as:

A=1, 2=2, 3=3, ..., Q=12, K=13
Spades=0, Hearts=13, Diamonds=26, Clubs=42

With this scheme the Ace of Spades=1+0=1, the Queen of Spades=12+0=12, the Three of Hearts=3+13=16, etc.

In the shuffle program, a 52-element flag table FL keeps track of whether a card has been picked or not. PRINT statements are inserted to display the seed value, followed by the numbers, in a continuous-line format. Note that exactly 52 numbers are displayed and that no number is repeated. Each program run will produce a new random sequence.

```
10 DIM FL(52),D%(52)
20 X=RND(-TI):PRINT X
30 FOR I=1 TO 52
40 C%=52*RND(1)+1
50 IF FL(C%)<>0 GOTO 40
60 D%(I)=C%:FL(C%)=1
70 PRINT C%;
80 NEXT I
RUN
 1.18586613E-05
 48  40  13  37  50  43  46  31  49  44
 23  38  25  11   9  35  32  30  24  41
 26   5   6   1  45  10  21  14  42  20  15
 34  18  52  47   7  16   8  19  33  36   4
 17   3  22  27  29  28  39   2  51  12
RUN
 1.01154728E-06
 14  35  52  50  26  48  27  36  34  25
 18  20  41  33  39   7  46  24  23  28   1
  9   3  12  43   2  31  44   4   1  32  37   3
  0  40  22  45  48  42  49  16  11   6  10
 29   9  51  17   8  15  38   5  21  13
```

But this program runs more slowly as it nears the 52nd number. It is especially slow on the last card. This is because the program has to fetch more and more random numbers to find one that has not already been picked. A simple routine such as this has much room for improvement, of course. It can be speeded up just by findng the last number in the program from the table rather than waiting until it is selected randomly.

RANDOM POKE TO THE SCREEN

The following program is a modification of program BLANKET. Instead of displaying a character in continuous-line format, this program fills the screen by randomly POKEing the character into the 1000 positions of the screen.

Here is the first version.

```
10 REM ******* B L A N K E T *******
20 REM RANDOM DISPLAY OF ONE
30 REM   CHARACTER ENTERED FROM THE
40 REM   KEYBOARD
50 REM ****************************
90 PRINT"HIT A KEY OR <R> TO END";
100 GET C$:IF C$="" GOTO 100
105 IF C$=CHR$(13) GOTO 170
110 PRINT"⊐";      :REM CLEAR SCREEN
120 X=RND(-TI)     :REM START NEW SEED
125 C=(ASC(C$)AND128)/2 OR (ASC(C$)AND63)
127 A=1000*RND(1)+32768
130 POKE A,C       :REM DISPLAY CHAR
140 GET D$:IF D$="" GOTO 127
150 C$=D$
160 GOTO 105
170 END
```

The program is the standard BLANKET program through line 110, where a new character is input and the screen is cleared. The statement on line 120 stores a new seed in preparation for a random display sequence on the screen. The statement on line 125 converts C$ to its equivalent POKE number. The statement on line 127 calculates a random screen address in the range 32768 to 33767; using the RND range formula with m = 32768 and n = 33767 as follows:

$(n-m+1) \cdot RND(1)+m$ Range formula
$(33767-32768+1) \cdot RND(1)+32768$ as used in line 127
$=1000 \cdot RND(1)+32768$

Neither the INT function nor an integer variable (which would have been A%) can be used, because the screen addresses begin just beyond the maximum integer value of 32767. Fortunately the POKE function, which is where the screen addresses will be used, simply discards any fractional portion of a real number address presented to it. (For other applications when you are dealing with random numbers outside the integer range, you will have to check that the floating point equivalent provides the intended range.)

The first version of the program above randomly fills the screen with the keyed-in character. It does this by simply POKEing to random screen locations. It may POKE many times to the same location when other locations are not yet filled, and it continues to POKE, even after the screen is filled, until a new character is keyed in.

When the program is run, about half the screen positions quickly fill with the character. Then character placement slows down more and more until at the end, when the screen is almost filled, and remaining positions are filled very slowly. It takes about three minutes to completely fill the screen with this version of the program.

The program is operating at the same speed throughout, but it does not get much work done towards the end, because many of the positions that it POKEs to are already filled. The program appears to slow down because displaying a character over the same character has no visible effect.

The program can be speeded up a good deal by eliminating the superfluous POKEs to screen positions that are already filled. A new version of program BLANKET does this.

Rather than calculating a number in the same range all the time and discarding, or in this case re-POKEing, the duplicate numbers, the new program decreases the range of numbers generated to correspond with the number of items left to operate on. It does this by keeping track in a table of the screen positions remaining to be filled, and generating a random number within the range of table indexes yet to be POKEd to. The POKE address itself is retrieved from the contents at the table index.

```
5 REM RANDOM VERSION 2
10 REM ******* B L A N K E T *******
20 REM RANDOM DISPLAY OF ONE
30 REM   CHARACTER ENTERED FROM THE
40 REM   KEYBOARD
50 REM *******************************
70 DIM T(999)
80 GOSUB 200     :REM INITIALIZE TABLE
90 PRINT"HIT A KEY OR <R> TO END";
100 GET C$:IF C$="" GOTO 100
105 IF C$=CHR$(13) GOTO 170
110 PRINT"[]";       :REM CLEAR SCREEN
120 X=RND(-TI)       :REM START NEW SEED
125 C=(ASC(C$)AND128)/2 OR (ASC(C$)AND63)
126 FOR N=999 TO 0 STEP -1
127 A%=(N+1)*RND(1) :REM PICK AN ELEM
128 A=T(A%)+32768 :REM FORM POKE ADDR
129 TP=T(A%):T(A%)=T(N):T(N)=TP:REM SWAP ELEMENTS
130 POKE A,C         :REM DISPLAY CHAR
140 NEXT N
160 GOTO 100
170 END
199 REM **SUBR TO INITIALIZE TABLE**
200 FOR I=0 TO 999:T(I)=I:NEXT
210 RETURN
```

In this program, the table holds the 1000 screen position indicators; it is dimensioned on line 70.

At line 80 an initialization subroutine is called that places the numbers 0 through 999 into corresponding elements of Table T. T(0) will contain 0, T(1) will contain 1,. . .T(999) will contain 999. The elements do not have to be filled with consecutive numbers since they are to be picked randomly, but this is the easiest way to program the fill loop. In fact, the table will be in order only the first time the program is run after loading. Lines 90 through 125 hold exactly the same program statements as in the earlier version.

Lines 126 through 140 hold a FOR-NEXT loop that fills the 1000 screen locations with the keyed-in character. The statement on line 127 picks a random table index A% from the remaining unfilled range of 0 to N. The expression $(N+1)*RND(1)$ performs this task. The statement on line 128 forms the POKE address A as the sum of the T table element whose index was picked on line 127, plus the beginning screen memory address of 32768. The statement on line 129 exchanges the chosen table element T(A%) with the highest active table element T(N) via a temporary location TP. The statement on line 130 displays the character at the random screen location. The NEXT N at line 140 decrements the pointer N so that the used screen address just swapped into T(N) is not picked again during the current program run.

Chapter 6

Peripheral Devices: Tape Cassette Drives, Diskette Drives and Printers

A computer system contains more than a keyboard, a screen, and the computer itself. To avoid keying in a program every time you want to run it, you will store the program on a floppy disk or magnetic tape cassette. As described in Chapter 2, you can then load the program into memory and run it, thus avoiding repeated key entry.

You will also store data on magnetic tape cassettes or floppy disks. Consider a mailing list program. This program will be stored on a cassette or floppy disk. A mailing list program is used to create a list of names and addresses. The list of names and addresses is also stored on cassette or floppy disk. Later the names and addresses are read off the cassette or floppy disk in order to print mailing labels. But that requires a printer.

Most computer systems include a line printer. Line printers are used to print output, such as mailing labels. Also, a line printer is indispensable if you want to write programs. The most efficient way of changing or correcting a program is to print a listing of the program as it currently exists, mark intended changes to this printed listing, then enter the changes that you have written down.

In this chapter we are going to describe CBM BASIC program logic needed to handle cassette drives, floppy disk drives, and printers.

CBM computers have an IEEE 488 bus connector. This is an industry standard bus which is used by the floppy disk drives and the printer. The IEEE 488 bus is also used by instruments and sundry electronics in industrial applications. Although we describe floppy disk drives and printers, this book does not describe the IEEE 488 bus itself, or programming required by any instruments connected to it.*

---

* To learn about the IEEE bus, see *PET and the IEEE 488 Bus (GPIB)* by Eugene Fisher and C. W. Jensen, Osborne/McGraw-Hill, 1980.

STORING DATA ON MAGNETIC SURFACES

THE CONCEPT OF A FILE

Information is stored as "files" on cassettes or diskettes.

In order to understand the concept of a "file," think of a bookshelf. The cassette or diskette is the bookshelf; each book on the shelf is equivalent to a file.

To a computer user, a "file" is a very simple concept. When you "open" a file, all information stored within the file becomes accessible. The information remains accessible until you "close" the file. This is much like taking a book down off the bookshelf and opening it up. But unlike the book, writing to a file is as easy as reading from it. When the computer writes a program or data to a cassette or diskette, it creates a new file, or it adds to an old file.

A file can have any size, limited only by the capacity of the cassette or diskette. You can create a new file and put nothing in it, in which case the file is empty. This is equivalent to having a book with covers, but no content. A file must fit on a single tape cassette or floppy disk, therefore the maximum size of a file depends on the storage capacity of the cassette or floppy disk.

You can have up to 256 files per diskette; there is no limit per cassette. Of course, if many files are stored on a single diskette or cassette, the individual files will have to be very short.

The amount of memory in your CBM computer has no impact on the size of a data file. A data file may be much larger than available computer memory. Having "opened" a data file, you can read one character from it, or as much information as will fit in the available computer memory. When writing to a data file, information that you output from computer memory can be, and usually is, added to data already stored on the cassette or floppy disk.

Program Files

There are two types of files: program files and data files. A program file, as its name would imply, contains program statements.

You create a program file whenever you SAVE a program on diskette or cassette. You read a program file when you LOAD a program into memory. These operations were described in Chaper 2.

Every file can have a name assigned to it; the name which you assign to a program file will become the name of the program. **CBM computers recognize file names of up to 128 characters, but only the first 16 characters are displayed. Disk file names must have 16 or fewer characters. Therefore, it is a good idea to restrict all file names to 16 characters or less.**

The amount of memory in your CBM computer does affect the maximum size of a program file. This is because you create a single program file when you SAVE a program on cassette or diskette. When you load a program into memory, you load the entire contents of a program file. You cannot load part of a program file into memory. Therefore the maximum size of the program file must be less than the program memory capacity of your CBM computer. If you have a very long program, and it will not fit in the available computer memory, you can break it up into a number of files, each of which will fit in the available memory space. When each section of the program completes execution, you simply load the next section into memory and run it; in this fashion you get to execute the entire program. Later in this chapter we will describe the programming steps needed to execute large programs in this fashion.

An advantage of program files is that you do not need to know anything about their internal organization. When you save a program on diskette or cassette, it becomes a file which you can subsequently load back into memory. You must be able to identify the program file (via its file name or its location) in order to load the file back into memory, but that is all.

Data Files

A data file, as its name would imply, contains information which gets interpreted as data, in contrast to program statements. Data files are created, written, and read by programs.

Records and Fields

Data files are divided into "records," which in turn are subdivided into "fields."

A single field contains information which can be represented by a single variable name. Therefore a single field can contain an integer number, a floating point number, or a single string variable.

A record contains one or more fields. Records usually represent units of repeated information within the file, but this does not have to be the case.

Consider a mailing list. The entire mailing list will become a single data file. Each name and address within the mailing list will become one record within the file. If names and addresses are entered using the program described in Chapter 5, then each record will contain five fields: the name, the street, the city, the state, and the zip code. This file organization is illustrated in Figure 6-1.

A file may contain one or more records. Each record may contain one or more fields. The number of records in a file and the maximum length of a record varies with the type of file, as described later in this chapter. However, for all practical purposes the size of a file is limited only by the capacity of the diskette.

No restrictions are placed on the length of tape cassette records. A record can have any length that will fit on the tape cassette.

DATA TRANSFER TO AND FROM CASSETTE AND DISKETTE

A novice accessing tape or diskette data files is frequently mislead into thinking that something is wrong. One would instinctively expect the tape or disk unit to move in response to every statement that reads from the unit, or writes to it. A cassette drive should move the cassette; a disk drive should activate the diskette. Sometimes you will see such activity; at other times you will see no activity. This is because a small amount of memory acts as a data buffer connecting the computer with the cassette or disk drive.

When the computer reads from one of these drives, enough data is read to fill the buffer. You will see no further drive activity until a program accesses data that is not currently in the buffer.

	Part of a **Mailing list file**	
	⋮	
	Name (n − 1)	Field 1
	Street (n − 1)	Field 2
Record n − 1	City (n − 1)	Field 3
	State (n − 1)	Field 4
	ZIP (n − 1)	Field 5
	Name (n)	Field 1
	Street (n)	Field 2
Record n	City (n)	Field 3
	State (n)	Field 4
	ZIP (n)	Field 5
	Name (n + 1)	Field 1
	Street (n + 1)	Field 2
Record n + 1	City (n + 1)	Field 3
	State (n + 1)	Field 4
	ZIP (n + 1)	Field 5
	Name (n + 2)	Field 1
	Street (n + 2)	Field 2
Record n + 2	City (n + 2)	Field 3
	State (n + 2)	Field 4
	ZIP (n + 2)	Field 5
	Name (n + 3)	Field 1
	Street (n + 3)	Field 2
	⋮	

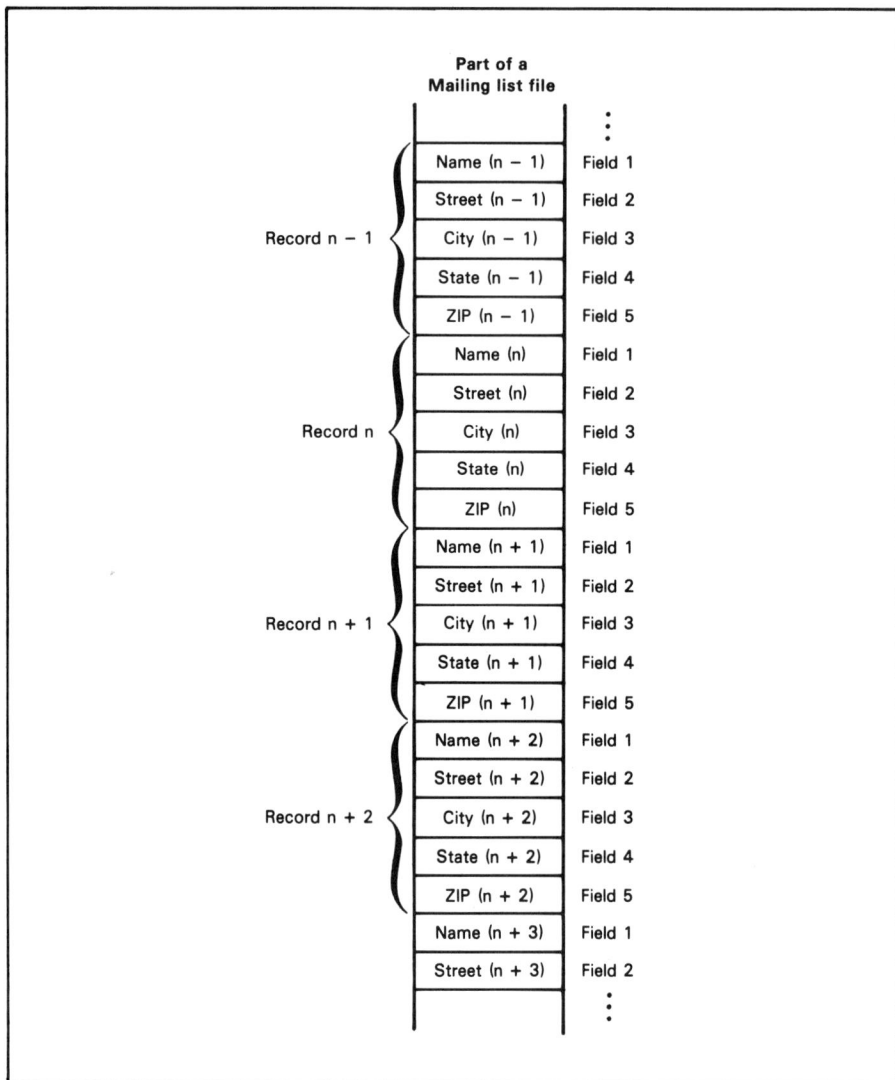

Figure 6-1. Conceptual Illustration of Four Records
in a Mailing List File

Data being written to a cassette or disk drive is first written to the data buffer. As soon as the data buffer is full, all the contents of the buffer are output to the cassette or diskette, at which time you will see some activity. You will see no further activity until the buffer is again filled.

The cassette drive buffer is located in CBM computer memory. It is 192 bytes long and holds 191 bytes of data. The diskette drive buffer is located in the diskette unit itself, not in CBM computer memory. Each diskette drive buffer is 256 bytes long and holds 254 bytes of data. The diskette and cassette buffers are relatively large. In consequence, drives are inactive for much of the time while the computer is accessing drive buffers to read or write data.

Logical Files and Physical Units

We use the term "input/output programming" to describe program logic that transfers data between the computer and external physical units. Disk drives, cassette drives and printers are all external physical units.

In order to perform any input/output operation, program logic must identify the external physical unit being accessed; that will come as no surprise to you. But what about the computer end of the data transfer? This end cannot simply be specified as "the computer." Think of the problem in programming terms; programs identify data as variables or constants within BASIC statements. Therefore, the computer end of the data transfer must be specified in similar program logic terms. This concept is easy to understand if you **think of the CBM computer keyboard and display as external physical units (which in fact they are). When an INPUT statement is executed, data which you input at the keyboard gets assigned to variable(s) whose name(s) are specified as INPUT statement parameter(s).** For example, when the statement:

10 INPUT A

is executed, some number which an operator enters at the keyboard is assigned to floating point variable A. **The PRINT statement, likewise, will output variables(s) or constant(s) to the display.** Thus the PRINT statement:

20 PRINT A

takes the value assigned to floating point variable A and outputs this value to the display.

Thus the INPUT and PRINT statements have specified the computer end of the data transfer using a variable name, in this instance floating point variable A. When an INPUT statement is executed, the external physical unit is assumed to be the keyboard. When a PRINT statement is executed, the external physical unit is assumed to be the display.

Input/output programming becomes more complex when data is transferred to or from cassette drives, disk drives, printers, and external physical units other than the keyboard and display. For these more complex input/output operations you must first open a "channel" between the program and the selected physical unit. After performing required input/output operations you must close the channel. **CBM BASIC identifies individual channels using a channel number which can range between 0 and 255.**

You OPEN a channel using the CBM BASIC OPEN statement; statement parameters identify the physical unit being accessed, and the nature of the access, as illustrated in Figure 6-2. Until the channel is closed, any input or output statement need only specify the channel number in order to fully describe the nature of the input or output operation.

Every physical unit has its own, unique physical unit number. This number is used as a parameter when opening a channel in order to identify the physical unit to be accessed. Channel numbers have no equivalent permanent assignments. **Channel numbers are** therefore **frequently referred to as "logical file" numbers, or "logical unit" numbers.**

The name "logical file" describes a channel very accurately, since a channel establishes a link between a program and a data file.

Logical file numbers are a programming concept. As illustrated in Figure 6-2, you initiate any input or output operation using an OPEN statement. One of the OPEN statement parameters is a channel, or logical file number; other OPEN statement parameters identify the physical unit, the data file being accessed, and the way in which the access is to occur. After the input or output operation has gone to completion, you execute a CLOSE statement which closes down the channel. The CLOSE statement requires just one parameter: a channel or logical file number. This logical file number links the CLOSE statement to an OPEN statement. In between the OPEN and CLOSE statements, all input and output statements use a channel or logical file number to identify the device being accessed, and the way in which the device is being accessed.

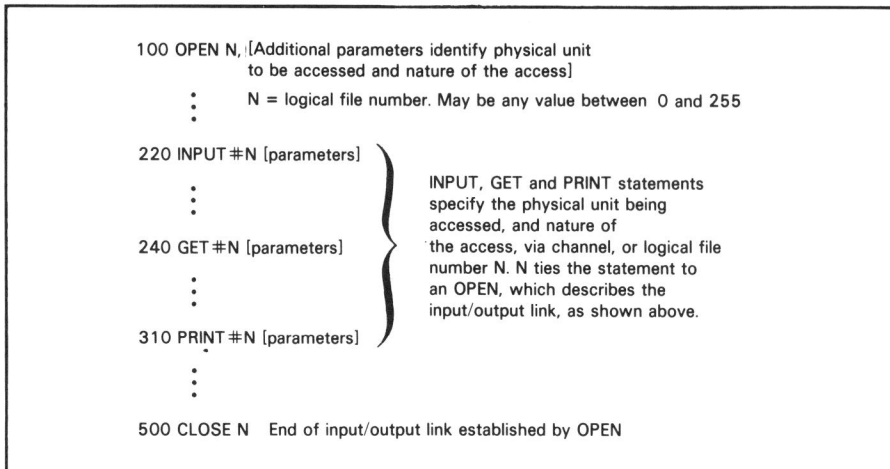

```
100 OPEN N, [Additional parameters identify physical unit
              to be accessed and nature of the access]
  :        N = logical file number. May be any value between 0 and 255
  :

220 INPUT#N [parameters]      ⎫
  :                           ⎪  INPUT, GET and PRINT statements
  :                           ⎬  specify the physical unit being
                              ⎪  accessed, and nature of
240 GET#N [parameters]        ⎪  the access, via channel, or logical file
  :                           ⎬  number N. N ties the statement to
  :                           ⎪  an OPEN, which describes the
                              ⎪  input/output link, as shown above.
310 PRINT#N [parameters]      ⎭
  :
  :

500 CLOSE N    End of input/output link established by OPEN
```

Figure 6-2. Conceptual Illustration of Logical Field Number
as Used in a BASIC Program

The logical file number relates OPEN, CLOSE, INPUT, GET, and PRINT statements with each other. Once you have used a logical file number in an OPEN statement, you cannot reuse the same logical file number to establish a different input or output channel until the logical file is closed. If you do, CBM BASIC will give you a syntax error. But otherwise no restrictions are placed on the way you assign logical file numbers within your program.

Device numbers identify the physical unit being accessed by the computer. The device number appears as a parameter in the OPEN statement. Every physical unit which can communicate with a CBM computer has a permanently assigned device number. Upon encountering a device number in an OPEN statement, the CBM computer activates appropriate electronic logic to establish communications with the specific physical unit identified by the device number. **Table 6-1 summarizes device number assignments** recognized by a CBM computer. 256 device numbers are available, ranging between 0 and 255. However, as shown in Table 6-1, only device numbers 0 through 30 are currently in use.

Table 6-1. Device Numbers with Secondary Addresses used by CBM Computers

Device	Device Number	Secondary Address	Operation Performed
Keyboard	0	None	
Cassette Drive #*	1 (Default)	0 1	Open for read Open for write
Cassette Drive #2	2	2	Open for write, but add End of Table mark (EOT) on close
Video Display	3	None	
Line Printer Models 2022 and 2023	4	0 1 2 3 4 5 6	Print data exactly as received Print data using previously defined format Received format to be used in subsequent formatted printout Receive lines per page specification Enable printer diagnostic message Create a special character Set spacing between lines (Model 2022 only)
Disk Drives (all models)	8	0 1 2-14 15	Load a program file to the computer Save a program file from the computer Unassigned Open command/status channel
Other devices connected to IEEE 488 Bus	5,6,7 and 9 through 31		Device numbers and secondary addresses are selected and assigned by the manufacturer of the device connecting to the IEEE 488 Bus.
	32|to|255 unavailable at this time		
* This is the cassette drive mounted			

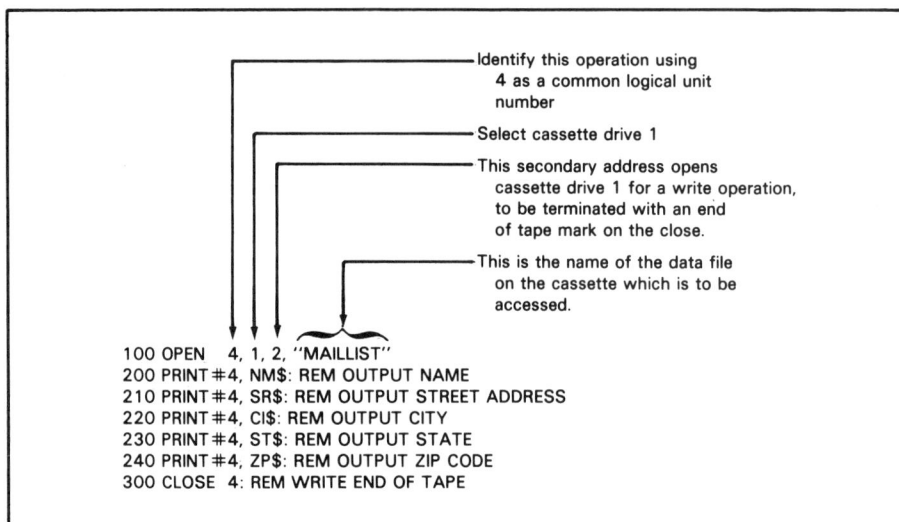

```
                                        ┌─── Identify this operation using
                                        │    4 as a common logical unit
                                        │    number
                               ┌────────┼─── Select cassette drive 1
                               │        │
                          ┌────┼────────┼─── This secondary address opens
                          │    │        │    cassette drive 1 for a write operation,
                          │    │        │    to be terminated with an end
                          │    │        │    of tape mark on the close.
                    ┌─────┼────┼────────┼─── This is the name of the data file
                    │     │    │        │    on the cassette which is to be
                    │     │    │        │    accessed.
100 OPEN    4, 1, 2, "MAILLIST"
200 PRINT#4, NM$: REM OUTPUT NAME
210 PRINT#4, SR$: REM OUTPUT STREET ADDRESS
220 PRINT#4, CI$: REM OUTPUT CITY
230 PRINT#4, ST$: REM OUTPUT STATE
240 PRINT#4, ZP$: REM OUTPUT ZIP CODE
300 CLOSE  4: REM WRITE END OF TAPE
```

Figure 6-3. Use of Parameters by Input/Output Statements

In addition to having a device number, most physical units respond to a variety of secondary addresses. Secondary addresses are best visualized as "commands" from the computer telling the physical unit what operations it is to perform. **Secondary addresses are summarized in Table 6-1** for the physical units that are commonly connected to a CBM computer. You should not bother studying secondary addresses at this time; later when we describe input and output programming in detail, the function of secondary addresses will become obvious through their frequent use.

Figure 6-3 fully illustrates the use of parameters in input/output statements. The five PRINT# statements occurring on lines 200 through 240 write the five parts of a name and address to a file named MAILLIST, located on a cassette in cassette drive 1. On encountering each PRINT# statement, the computer knows what to do, because it checks the logical file number appearing after #. In Figure 6-3 this logical file number is 4, therefore an OPEN statement specifying logical file number 4 describes the nature of the operation; this OPEN statement occurs on line 100. If the computer could not find an OPEN statement with the required logical unit number, it would not attempt to perform the input or output operation, since it would not know what to do. In Figure 6-3 there is an OPEN statement with logical file number 4. This OPEN statement specifies physical unit number 1, therefore cassette drive 1 is selected. The secondary address is 2, therefore (on this occasion) it will be possible to write to the cassette in drive 1, but it will not be possible to read from it. Moreover, when this operation is closed, an end of tape mark will be written to the cassette, preventing any further data from being added to it. The OPEN statement specifies that the data file to be accessed has the name MAILLIST.

On line 300 there is a CLOSE statement. This CLOSE statement specifies logical file number 4, therefore everything which the OPEN statement initiated on line 100 will be terminated by the CLOSE statement on line 300. Furthermore, since the OPEN statement on line 100 specified secondary address number 2, the CLOSE statement on line 300, when executed, will cause an end of tape mark to be written to the cassette.

Thus, logical file number 4, occurring in statements on lines 200 through 300, links these statements with the OPEN statement on line 100. Additional parameters appearing in the OPEN statement on line 100 describe the operation for all of the other statements appearing on lines 200 through 300.

Physical Unit Status

Line printers can receive output from a computer. You cannot input data to a computer from a line printer. Yet there is nothing to stop you from executing an INPUT statement that references the logical file number which an OPEN statement used to initialize printer output.

Although a cassette drive can receive data from the computer, or transmit data to it, the secondary address used in the OPEN statement which initializes the cassette drive will specify either a cassette read or a cassette write operation. Nevertheless, you could erroneously execute a statement which attempts to access the cassette drive in the wrong direction.

When you execute a PRINT, GET, or INPUT statement attempting to do something which the physical unit either is incapable of handling or has not been programmed to handle, the physical unit will register an error status. A physical unit will not attempt to perform an operation that was not allowed by the OPEN statement, even if it could perform the operation. For example, if you OPEN a cassette drive for write operations only, then an INPUT or GET statement accessing the cassette unit will not execute; an error status will be generated, and that is all.

Physical units return status information following every input or output operation, whether it executes successfully or unsuccessfully. An 8-bit status is returned. **To access status, simply reference the variable ST.** For example, the statement:

```
10 X=ST
```

assigns the current status value, whatever it may be, to variable X.

Table 6-2 summarizes the way statuses are generated by all of the devices commonly attached to a CBM computer. You should refer to Table 6-2 later when writing programs that access various physical units.

Do not use status to check for keyboard or display operations, even though the keyboard and display have external device numbers.

Standard status returned by the IEEE 488 bus is shown on Table 6-2 for completeness, but interfacing to this bus is not described in this book.

CASSETTE FILE HANDLING

We are now going to describe the program steps needed to handle cassette files. We will describe how data files are created, read, and modified under program control.

Some of the file handling BASIC statements we are about to use have not yet been introduced in this book. Remember that all CBM BASIC statements are described completely in Chapter 8. If you have difficulty following any discussion in this chapter because you do not understand the BASIC statement being used, then you should go to Chapter 8, read the complete description of the statement which is giving you trouble, return to this chapter and continue.

Table 6-2. Status Byte Returned by External Devices Via Variable ST

Device Operation	Status							
	00000001 Read as 1	00000010 Read as 2	00000100 Read as 4	00001000 Read as 8	00010000 Read as 16	00100000 Read as 32	01000000 Read as 64	10000000 Read as −128
Read from Cassette drive #1 or #2	Operation OK	Operation OK	Short Block. Data block read had fewer bytes than expected	Long Block Data block read had more bytes than expected	Unrecoverable read error	Checksum error. One or more data bits read incorrectly	End of file encountered	End of tape encountered
Verify cassette drive #1 or #2					Any verify mismatch		None	
Disk drives (all models)	Receiving device not available	Transmitting device not available	None	None	None	None	End of file	Disk drive not present
IEEE 488 Bus	Time out on listener	Time out on talker					End of Identify	Device not present

You can program the CBM computer to write data onto a cassette, or to read data off the cassette, but you cannot program physical cassette movement. It is important that you understand the way cassette drives operate; otherwise, you may attempt to perform operations which the cassette drives cannot handle.

Files are stored sequentially on cassette tape. A header precedes the first file, and an end-of-tape mark follows the last file. Each file ends with an end-of-file mark.

The header is written automatically at the beginning of cassette tape when you first write to it. At this time, you may notice cassette activity which you did not expect, but otherwise the existence of the header is of no concern to you.

The computer can find files while the tape is moving forward at PLAY speed, but not at FAST FORWARD speed. An end-of-file mark identifies the end of one file. The computer can also sense an end of tape mark. **A status of 64 is returned by an end-of-file mark. A status of −128 is returned by an end of tape mark.**

The computer cannot rewind a tape nor can it detect anything on the cassette while the cassette is being rewound.

You must start cassette movement manually by pressing appropriate keys on the cassette drive when instructed to do so by the CBM computer. Do not depress any cassette drive keys before being instructed to do so via a displayed message. Subsequently, the computer will automatically stop the cassette drive at the proper time, and providing you leave appropriate keys depressed (which you should do), the computer will automatically restart the cassette drive as needed by subsequent cassette accesses.

Let us examine the impact on cassette operations of these cassette drive capabilities.

When writing data to a cassette drive, the cassette must be correctly positioned when writing begins. This is the responsibility of the CBM computer operator. Previous data on the tape under the write head will be overwritten. If the transparent tape leader is under the write head, the tape drive will start writing nevertheless, but nothing will be recorded. The safest policy is to start writing on a blank cassette, or a cassette that contains data you no longer need, and **position the cassette at the beginning of its magnetic surface;** you can then write records and files one after another until you reach the end of the cassette. The cassette drive will make sure that sufficient space is left between the end of one record or file and the beginning of the next. You do not have to, and should not, space forward on the cassette tape after writing one record or file, and before beginning the next. **You cannot back up a cassette and re-record a record or file,** since your chances of precisely rewinding the tape to the correct position are not very good. Even a small error will cause the drive to write files which you subsequently cannot read back.

When reading prerecorded data files, you must make sure that the tape is rewound to a point preceding the first file that you wish to read. The CBM computer can find any named data file while playing the tape forward, but it cannot automatically rewind the tape to find a file occurring earlier on the tape.

Never attempt to rewrite a small portion of a file that was previously recorded on tape; the operation is simply too risky. For example, suppose you have ten names and addresses stored on a tape cassette and you wish to change the fifth name and address. In theory, you could read the first four names and addresses, which would leave the tape positioned at the beginning of the fifth name and address. Then you could write a new fifth name and address over the old one. In practice, this seldom works. The cassette drives are not very precise, and there is a strong probability that you will start writing the new name and address a little too soon or a little too late. Then a small piece of the old name and address will be left in front of the new one, or after it, but in either case you will not be able to read the new data.

To update cassette data files you *must* use two cassette drives. Read the old data off the cassette on one drive, and write the new updated data to the cassette in the other drive. You should use this procedure even if you want to change one data item among hundreds.

CBM BASIC has no statements that simply move a cassette or position it in any fashion.

PROGRAMMING CASSETTE DATA FILES

Three program steps are needed in order to access a cassette data file:

1.   OPEN the data file.
2.   INPUT from the data file, or PRINT to it.
3.   CLOSE the data file.

OPEN a Cassette Data File

You must use an OPEN statement to open a data file. You will get a syntax error if you attempt to access an unopened data file. When opening a cassette data file, you can use any one of these OPEN statement formats:

OPEN N	Open logical file N. Select the first file encountered on cassette drive 1 and allow a read operation.
OPEN N,D	Open logical file N. Select the first file encountered on device D and allow a read operation. D must be 1 for cassette drive 1, or 2 for cassette drive 2.
OPEN N,D,S	Open logical file N. Select the first file encountered on device D and allow the operation specified by secondary address S (see Table 6-1). D must be 1 for cassette drive 1, or 2 for cassette drive 2.
OPEN N,D,S,FILENAME	Open logical file N. Select the file named FILENAME on device D and allow the operation specified by secondary address S (see Table 6-1). D must be 1 for cassette drive 1, or 2 for cassette drive 2.

You can use the OPEN statement with a variety of other parameter combinations. N is the only parameter which must be present. D, if absent, is assumed to be 1. S, if absent, is assumed to be 0. If FILENAME is absent, the first file encountered is accessed.

When the OPEN statement is executed to open a tape cassette unit for a *read*, the CBM computer will display the following message if no tape control keys are pressed:

```
PRESS PLAY ON TAPE #1
OK ◄─────────────────── A tape control key is depressed; tape begins moving.
```

The CBM computer then reads the tape header. In immediate mode the messages continue as follows (bracketed items are shown only if a filename was specified by the OPEN statement):

SEARCHING [FOR filename]	Lists the first 16 characters of all files found, if any, between begin-
FOUND filename a	ning tape position and requested file location
FOUND filename b	
FOUND filename c	
FOUND filename d	Format for named file
FOUND	Format for unnamed file
FOUND [filename]	Found file
READY.	File is opened for read

In program mode this block of messages is not displayed.

When the OPEN statement is executed to open a tape cassette unit for a *write*, the CBM computer displays the following message if no tape control keys are pressed:

```
PRESS PLAY & RECORD ON TAPE #1
OK ◄─────────────────────────── A tape control key is depressed; tape begins moving
```

The CBM computer writes the tape header; tape movement then stops. Here are some sample OPEN statements:

OPEN 1	Open logical file 1. No physical unit is specified, so select cassette #1, the default physical unit. No secondary address is specified, so select a read operation (the default secondary address is 0). Since no filename is specified, read from the first cassette file encountered
OPEN 1,1	Same as above, since the second parameter has the default value.
OPEN 1,1,0	Same as above, since the second and third parameters have default values
OPEN 1,1,0,"DAT"	Same as above, but the file named DAT is accessed. The second and third parameters have default values
OPEN 3,1,2	Open logical file 3 for cassette #1. Write a new file and an End of Tape mark. The new file is unnamed
OPEN 3,1,2,"PENTAGRAM"	Same as above, but give the new file the name PENTAGRAM

CLOSE a Cassette Data File

Since file opening and closing are conceptually related, for the sake of clarity we are going to describe how to CLOSE a file before describing file access program logic. But remember, CLOSE must be the last statement in the file access sequence. You cannot access a file once you have CLOSEd it.

To CLOSE a file you execute the statement:

CLOSE N

where N is the logical file number appearing as the first parameter in the OPEN statement.

When you CLOSE a cassette file after reading from it, all further read accesses are inhibited. **No harm is done if you forget to CLOSE a file after reading from it, but you are indulging in sloppy programming practices.**

You *must* CLOSE a file after writing to it. Recall that data written to the cassette file is stored in a memory buffer. Whenever the buffer is filled, buffer contents is automatically written to the cassette. Any residual, partial buffer contents is written to the cassette when you close the file. If the file is not closed for any reason, then this residual, partial buffer contents will not be written out, and that can cause problems. Also, when you close a file after writing to it, an end-of-file mark is written on the tape cassette. The computer needs this end-of-file mark to separate one file from the next. Without the end-of-file mark, the computer would start reading the next file as though it were part of the previous file, and that would certainly cause errors.

When you close a cassette file after opening it with secondary address 2, an end-of-tape mark is written on the cassette. The end-of-tape mark tells the CBM computer that there is no more data on the cassette tape. If there is no end-of-tape mark, on the subsequent read the CBM computer would keep searching beyond recorded data files, and any previously recorded garbage will be interpreted as valid data, and that will generate read errors.

You do not have to execute CLOSE statements in order to close cassette data files. **The END statement closes cassette files logically but not physically. If you write to a file, you must close it with a CLOSE statement to avoid losing data.**

So why bother individually closing files that you don't write to? There are two reasons:

1. It makes you think through all file operations in a logical fashion, and that reduces programming errors.
2. A maximum of two cassette files can be open at one time.

Few programs need more than ten cassette files open at one time. However, if you do not bother to close files after accessing them, your program can finish up with a lot of open files that are no longer being used. That can cause problems, particularly in large programs which are written in small modules. If each module leaves a few files open, then ten open files can quickly accumulate, in which case the eleventh OPEN statement will cause an execution error. This is the worst kind of error to debug, since it will occur in a program which previously might have executed without error for a long time.

It takes very little program space, or execution time to CLOSE files individually after accessing them. And by doing so, you can avoid future execution errors.

CLOSE may be executed in either immediate or program mode. After writing to a file, if no tape control key is depressed when a CLOSE is issued, the CBM computer displays the following message:

```
PRESS PLAY & RECORD ON TAPE #1 ◄─── Press cassette keys
OK ◄──────────────────────────────── Tape begins moving to write tape buffer
```

No tape control keys need to be down for a CLOSE after a READ access. Here are some examples of CLOSE statements:

10	CLOSE 1	Close logical file 1
100	CLOSE 14	Close logical file 14
210	A=14	Same as above
220	CLOSE A	Same as above

Accessing Cassette Data Files

Having OPENed a cassette data file you can either read from it or write to it. The secondary address specified in the OPEN statement determines the allowed access. Accesses can continue until the file is CLOSEd. But remember, **whether you read from a cassette data file or write to it, you must do so sequentially.** The first cassette record written or read will always be the first record of the file. If you wish to read the tenth record of a file, you must first read records one through nine. Conversely, you cannot write the tenth record of a file without first writing records one through nine.

You must make sure that the proper tape cassette is loaded in every drive that is to be accessed by an executing program.

If you have just one cassette drive, the safest procedure is to mount the program tape in this drive, load the selected program into memory, remove the program tape and replace it with a data tape before executing the program. If you have two cassette drives, then make sure that data tape(s) are loaded in the correct drive(s). You may or may not have to remove the program tape after loading a program into memory, depending on which drive(s) the program needs for data tapes.

No cassette drive keys should be depressed prior to the first cassette access. The CBM computer will display a message telling you which keys to depress.

Remember, it is the operator's responsibility to make sure that a cassette tape is correctly positioned. The cassette drive will start writing immediately, wherever the tape happens to be positioned. When reading from tape, the drive will search forward for a data file, but it cannot find a file that has been recorded earlier on the tape.

You write data to cassette tape using the PRINT# statement:

PRINT#f,data

where:

f	is the logical file number. It must match f in the OPEN and CLOSE statements and must have a value ranging between 1 and 255.
data	is the data to be written.

PRINT# cannot be typed as ?#. PRINT# must be completely spelled out.

PRINT# transfers data to a cassette buffer in computer memory. When the cassette buffer reaches its maximum capacity of 191 data bytes, the data is written to tape as a "block." A block may contain a partial record, a single record, or several data records.

Either numbers or strings may be written to tape using the PRINT# statement.

Writing Numbers to Cassette Tape

When numbers are written to cassette tape, every number must be followed by a carriage return character.

We will write a program called NUM.PRINT# to write the numbers 1 through 10 on cassette tape.

First, the program displays a message stating its purpose, and providing load instructions:

NUM. PRINT#

```
10 PRINT"⊐** CREATE NUMERIC DATA TAPE **":PRINT
20 PRINT"** MOUNT TAPE; PRESS <RETURN> WHEN READY **":PRINT
30 GET A$:IF A$="" THEN 30
```

Line 20 instructs the user to insert a cassette tape in the cassette unit, rewind to the beginning of the tape, and press RETURN when ready. Statements on line 30 wait for any key to be pressed. If no keystroke is entered, the computer waits. This wait loop gives the user time to mount and rewind the cassette tape.

The wait loop created on line 30 is undesirable since it can be terminated by pressing any key. The operator's elbow brushing a key can end the wait loop, despite the instruction to press the RETURN key, which would lead an operator to the logical conclusion that no other key will do. A better wait loop is created by:

```
30 GET A$:IF A$<>CHR$(13) THEN 30
```

Once the RETURN key is pressed, the program drops down to the next line where an OPEN statement opens a cassette data file:

```
40 PRINT"** OPENING DATA FILE **":OPEN1,1,2,"NUMBERS"
```

This OPEN statement opens logical file #1, selects physical unit #1 (the cassette tape unit) with secondary address 2 (OPEN for write and EOT mark at close of file). The data file is named NUMBERS.

Next, we set up a FOR-NEXT loop to display the numbers 1 through 20 on the screen, and to write these numbers on cassette tape:

```
50 FOR N=1 TO 10
60 PRINT N ◄──────────Display N on screen
70 PRINT#1,N ◄────────Write N to data file #1 (NUMBERS)
80 NEXT N
```

PRINT N creates a screen display. PRINT#1,N writes to tape. Remember, PRINT# cannot be typed in as ?#. PRINT must be spelled out completely, with the number sign, file number, comma, and variable following respectively.

Incorrect	Correct
?#1,N	PRINT#1,N
PRINT N	
PRINT #1,N	
PRINT#1N	
PRINT1,N	

Any of the above incorrect entries will result in a syntax error, except PRINT N, which will display N on the screen.

If everything works correctly, lines 50 through 80 display numbers on the screen and write them to tape:

PET Screen

Representation of Data Tape

```
1
2
3
4
5
6
7
8
9
10
```

The PRINT# statement writes a carriage return character on cassette tape wherever a PRINT statement would display a carriage return. Thus the PRINT# statement on line 70 writes a carriage return after outputting N, just as the PRINT statement on line 60 causes a carriage return after displaying N. **To ensure that you write numbers correctly to cassette, use PRINT# statement parameter syntax which, with PRINT statement(s), would display a single, vertical column of numbers.**

After all data is written to the tape, the file is closed. You must CLOSE the file to be certain that all data is written to cassette tape.

```
90 PRINT"♦♦ CLOSING DATA FILE ♦♦":CLOSE1
100 END
```

Be sure that the same logical file number is used in the OPEN and CLOSE statements.

```
OPEN     1,1,2,"NUMBERS"
  .
  .
  .
CLOSE    1
```

Here is the complete listing for NUM.PRINT#:

```
10 PRINT"⊐♦♦ CREATE NUMERIC DATA TAPE ♦♦":PRINT
20 PRINT"♦♦ MOUNT TAPE; PRESS <RETURN> WHEN READY ♦♦":PRINT
30 GET A$:IF A$="" THEN 30
40 PRINT"♦♦ OPENING DATA FILE ♦♦":OPEN1,1,2,"NUMBERS"
50 FOR N=1 TO 10
60 PRINT N
70 PRINT#1,N
80 NEXT N
90 PRINT"♦♦ CLOSING DATA FILE ♦♦":CLOSE1
100 END
```

Here is a run of the program:

```
♦♦ CREATE NUMERIC DATA TAPE ♦♦

♦♦ MOUNT TAPE; PRESS <RETURN WHEN READY♦♦

♦♦ OPENING DATA FILE ♦♦

PRESS PLAY & RECORD ON TAPE #1
OK

1
2
3
4
5
6
7
8
9
10
♦♦CLOSING DATA FILE ♦♦
```

Writing Strings to Cassette Tape

Unlike numbers, **when you write string variables to cassette tape, you can separate variables using a comma or a carriage return.** But the effect of these two separators differs. When string variables are subsequently read off the cassette tape, each INPUT# statement will read all string variables up to the next carriage return separator. Therefore you can use commas only to separate string variables that will always be read back as a group, via a single INPUT# statement. You must use a carriage return following the last string variable to appear in an INPUT# statement.

Special programming techniques are required in order to separate string variables using commas. Moreover, the mixed use of commas and carriage returns as separators can become a source of great confusion, even to experienced BASIC programmers. Therefore make sure that you study examples carefully before attempting to write programs for yourself.

We will modify NUM.PRINT# to write the words "ONE" through "TEN" as strings. The new program is called WORD.PRINT#. The words can be supplied using either INPUT or READ/DATA statements. Our sample program uses READ/DATA statements. The READ statement is inserted in the FOR-NEXT loop at line 60. A DATA statement is added to the end of the program. The final program is listed below, followed by a sample run of the program.

WORD. PRINT #

```
10 PRINT"*♦♦CREATE WORD DATA FILE♦♦":PRINT
20 PRINT"♦♦MOUNT DATA TAPE; PRESS <RETURN> WHEN READY♦♦"
30 GET A$:IF A$="" THEN 30
40 PRINT"♦♦OPENING DATA FILE♦♦":OPEN1,1,2,"NUMWORD":PRINT
50 FOR N=1 TO 10
60 READ N$
70 PRINT N$
80 PRINT#1,N$
90 NEXT N
100 PRINT"♦♦CLOSING DATA FILE♦♦":CLOSE1
110 DATA ONE,TWO,THREE,FOUR,FIVE,SIX,SEVEN,EIGHT,NINE,TEN
120 END
```

```
♦♦CREATE WORD DATA FILE♦♦

♦♦MOUNT TAPE; PRESS <RETURN> WHEN READY♦♦

♦♦OPENING DATA FILE♦♦

PRESS PLAY & RECORD ON TAPE #1
OK·

ONE
TWO
THREE
FOUR
FIVE
SIX
SEVEN
EIGHT
NINE
TEN
♦♦CLOSING DATA FILE♦♦
```

As each string variable is written to cassette tape, this program terminates the string variable with a carriage return.

Let us now look at the use of commas to separate string variables that are written to cassette tape. Commas must be inserted; they are not taken from the PRINT statement parameter list. For example, when the statement:

```
10 PRINT#1,F$,M$,L$
```

is executed, contents of the three string variables F$, M$ and L$ will be concatenated into a single string variable which will be written to cassette tape as follows:

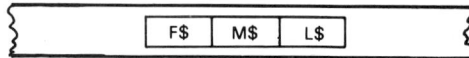

A comma can be inserted between fields using one of these two methods:

1. Enclose the separator within quotes:

```
PRINT#1,F$;",";M$;",";L$
```

2. Use the CHR$( ) function:

```
PRINT#1,F$;CHR$(44);M$;CHR$(44);L$
```

CHR$(44) is the CHR$ function representation of the comma character.

Here is the illustration of F$, M$ and L$ written to cassette tape with commas separating F$-M$ and M$-L$:

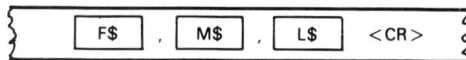

The program below, called NAMES.PRINT#, forces separators to keep F$, M$, L$ name strings (first, middle, last) from running together:

NAMES. PRINT #

```
10 PRINT":**CREATE NAME DATA FILE**":PRINT
20 PRINT"**MOUNT DATA TAPE; PRESS <RETURN> WHEN READY**"
30 GET A$:IF A$="" THEN 30
40 PRINT"**OPENING DATA FILE**":OPEN1,1,2,"NAME":PRINT
50 FOR J=1 TO 4
60 INPUT F$,M$,L$
70 PRINT F$,M$,L$
80 PRINT#1,F$;CHR$(44);M$;CHR$(44);L$
90 NEXT J
100 PRINT"**CLOSING DATA FILE**":CLOSE1
110 END
```

The rule to follow when writing to cassette tape is that **characters written to cassette tape will be the same characters that a PRINT statement would display on the screen.** A carriage return is written to cassette tape where it would force a carriage return on the display. To create a comma separating two cassette variables, you will require the same PRINT# statement parameter list needed to display a comma between two string fields on the screen.

The next sample program shows how mailing list data is written to tape. A new program MAIL.PRINT# writes a mailing list named MAIL onto a cassette tape. MAIL is read by another program called MAIL.INPUT#.

In this sample program we want to demonstrate program steps needed to write cassette records. We do not want to demonstrate good data entry program design. The mailing list data entry program described in Chapter 5 illustrated good data entry program design. The mailing list program we are now about to describe has very simple (and inadequate) data entry logic, but it is short and easy to follow, allowing the discussion to focus on cassette handling.

Each name and address is written to cassette tape as one record with these five fields: 1) record number 2) name 3) street address 4) city 5) state and ZIP code. This may be illustrated as follows:

```
◆◆ RECORD #6 ◆◆        Field 1  ⎫
                                 ⎪
WIDGETS SUPPLY CO.     Field 2  ⎬
555 BOGUS AVE.         Field 3  ⎬  One record
GERTIE                 Field 4  ⎪
TENNESSEE 38901        Field 5  ⎭
```

Of course, this is not how the data will appear on cassette tape. The data on the tape may be illustrated conceptually as follows:

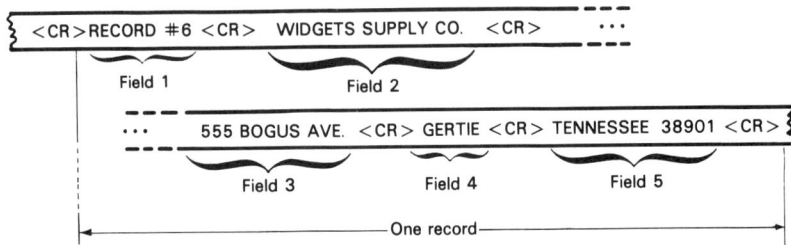

Below is a program listing of MAIL.PRINT#. Type MAIL.PRINT# into your computer and save it on a cassette tape. Then list the program. (This listing assumes the standard keyboard characters.)

```
10 PRINT"⊃↑↑↑↑↑↑↑↑↑↑↑↑↑↑↑↑↑↑↑↑↑↑"
20 PRINT"↑                      ↑"
30 PRINT"↑ MAILING LIST ENTRY ↑"
40 PRINT"↑                      ↑"
50 PRINT"↑↑↑↑↑↑↑↑↑↑↑↑↑↑↑↑↑↑↑↑↑↑"
60 PRINT"⬛↑↑ MOUNT TAPE; <RETURN> WHEN READY ↑↑"
70 GET A$:IF A$="" THEN GOTO 70
80 PRINT"⬛↑↑ OPENING MAIL FILE ↑↑":OPEN 1,1,2,"MAIL"
85 I=0
90 I=I+1
100 PRINT"⊃  ↑↑  MAILING LIST ENTRY ITEM";I;" ↑↑"
110 PRINT"                             ⬛⬛"
120 PRINT"   (IF NO MORE ENTRIES, ENTER ";CHR$(34);"END";CHR$(34);")"
130 PRINT"⬛⬛⬛":INPUT "1) NAME        ";NM$
140 IF NM$="END" THEN CLOSE 1:PRINT "⊃";"↑↑ END OF PROGRAM ↑↑":END
150 INPUT "2) ADDR LINE 1";A1$
160 INPUT "3) ADDR LINE 2";A2$
170 INPUT "4) ADDR LINE 3";A3$
180 INPUT "⬛⬛⬛⬛    ENTER FIELD # TO CHANGE (0=SAVE)";X
190 IF X=0 THEN 220
200 IF X>=1 AND X<=4 THEN GOSUB 280
210 GOTO 180
220 PRINT#1,I
230 PRINT#1,NM$
240 PRINT#1,A1$
```

```
250 PRINT#1,A2$
260 PRINT#1,A3$
270 GOTO 90
280 PRINT"▒▒▒":ON X GOTO 290,300,310,320
290 INPUT "1) NAME        ";NM$:RETURN
300 PRINT:INPUT "2) ADDR LINE 1";A1$:RETURN
310 PRINT"▒▒":INPUT "3) ADDR LINE 2";A2$:RETURN
320 PRINT"▒▒▒":INPUT "4) ADDR LINE 3";A3$:RETURN
```

The first five lines (10 to 50) display a brief description of the program function. The next segment instructs the user to mount the data tape (lines 60 and 70).

The statement on line 80 OPENs the data file:

```
80 PRINT"▒♠♠ OPENING MAIL FILE ♠♠":OPEN 1,1,2,"MAIL"
```

MAIL is opened as logical file #1 on the cassette unit, with an EOT (End of Tape) mark to be written at the CLOSE of the file. The message "OPENING MAIL FILE" is displayed on the screen prior to the actual OPEN command. The operator is given this message since it takes a few seconds to open the file.

Now the tape is ready to accept data. Before data is written to the tape it should be displayed on the screen so the data may be checked for mistakes.

Statements on lines 130 through 170 input data from the keyboard and display the data on the screen.

Variable "I" on line 90 is the incrementing record counter; it is displayed at line 100. Statements on lines 130 to 170 accept variables NM$ (name) and A1$, A2$, and A3$ (addresses) as separate fields. The end of each field is signaled by a carriage return. After all four fields have been entered, the statement on line 180 instructs the operator to either change a field or save the record. If a field is incorrect, the operator types the field number (1-4) and the program jumps to a field correction routine at line 280.

Using the field number input (variable X), the cursor is placed at the specified field, allowing the operator to change the selected field. The program returns to line 180 so the operator can specify another field change. When all the fields are correct, the operator inputs 0 and the program continues at lines 220 through 270. Statements on these lines write the record to the cassette data file as follows:

6 <CR> WIDGET SUPPLY CO. <CR> 555 BOGUS AVE. <CR> GERTIE

Be sure the logical file number referenced by the PRINT# statement is the same one specified in the OPEN statement.

After the record is saved, the program returns to line 90 to prepare for input of another record. The operator types "END" for NM$ when there are no more records to enter. The statements on line 140 close the data file and write an EOT mark (specified in the OPEN command) when NM$ = "END".

Notice that the tape does not move after each record is saved. As described earlier, the CBM computer stores all cassette data in a buffer. When the buffer is full, the entire buffer contents is written as a block to the tape. A block may contain a partial record, a single record, or several records. The CBM computer leaves interblock gaps between each block of data as follows:

	Block	Gap	Block	Gap	

Reading Data from Cassette Tape

These are the three program steps needed to read data from cassette tape:

1. OPEN the data file
2. Read the data file
3. CLOSE the data file

A data file must be opened for a read with the file name it was assigned when written. A different logical file number may be assigned. The secondary address code must be 0 for the READ option.

```
        Write Program           Read Program
     OPEN 1,1,2,"DATA"        OPEN 1,1,0,"DATA"
         ↑   ↑  physical device no ↑        ↑
         └───┴──────────┬──────────┴────────┘
                     file name
```

Two statements read data from cassette tape: INPUT# and GET#. To read numeric and string fields from a data file use the INPUT# statement. The GET# statement reads one character at a time.

CLOSE the file after data has been read. CLOSE the same logical file that you OPENed.

```
OPEN   1,1,0,"DATA"
 ·                ↑
 ·                │
 ·          ,     ↓
CLOSE  1
```

A good way to CLOSE a file that is being read is to test for an end-of-file (EOF) via the status word (ST). When a data file is written, an EOF mark is written at the end of the file. When an EOF mark is read, the file status equals 64 and the file may be closed. You may test for an EOF mark and close the file using this one statement:

```
IF ST=64 THEN CLOSE 1
```

When ST equals 64, the file is CLOSEd.

Previously we wrote the program NUM.PRINT# to write the numbers 1 through 10 in a cassette data file named NUMBERS. Now we will write a program called NUM.INPUT# to read the ten numbers from the NUMBERS data file, and display them on the screen.

The INPUT# statement is used to read numbers and strings from cassette tape. INPUT# reads one field at a time.

The first few statements of NUM.INPUT# instruct the user to load the data tape. These statements are identical to the first three statements of NUM.PRINT#. At line 30 there is a wait loop which gives the operator time to mount the data tape. After mounting the tape, key RETURN; the program continues at the next line.

```
10 PRINT"⊃●● READ NUMERIC DATA TAPE ●●":PRINT
20 PRINT"●● MOUNT TAPE ; PRESS <RETURN> WHEN READY ●●":PRINT
30 GET A$:IF A$="" THEN 30
```

Before any data can be read, the data file must be opened. Statements on line 40 open file #1, physical device #1, with secondary address 0 (OPEN for read) and filename NUMBERS.

```
40 PRINT"●● OPENING DATA FILE ●●":OPEN 1,1,0,"NUMBERS":PRINT
```

Next, a FOR-NEXT loop reads the first ten data items from the tape and displays them on the screen:

```
50 FOR I=1 TO 10
60 INPUT#1,N ◄─────── Read N from tape
70 PRINT N ◄────────── Print N on screen
80 NEXT I
```

The INPUT#1 statement on line 60 reads one number per execution. The FOR-NEXT loop ensures the correct number of executions. Program execution may be illustrated as follows:

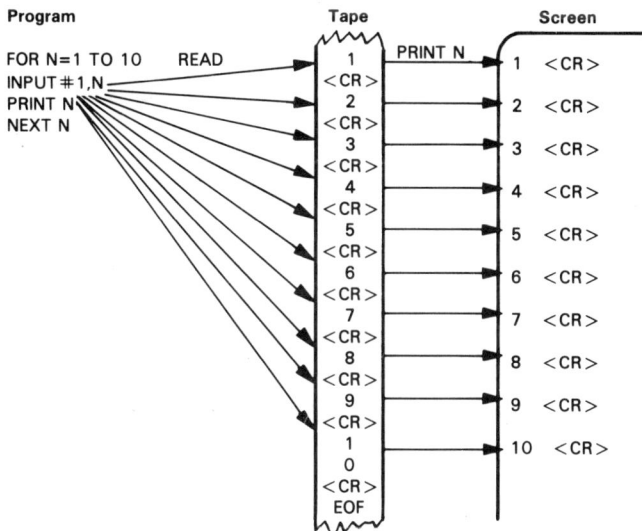

After the data is read, the file must be closed.

```
90 PRINT"●● CLOSING DATA FILE ●●":CLOSE1
100 END
```

A complete listing of NUM.INPUT# is given below, followed by a sample run of the program.

NUM.INPUT#

```
10 PRINT"J** READ NUMERIC DATA FILE **":PRINT
20 PRINT"** MOUNT TAPE;PRESS <RETURN> WHEN READY":PRINT
30 GET A$:IF A$="" THEN 30
40 PRINT"** OPENING DATA FILE **":OPEN 1,1,0,"NUMBERS":PRINT
50 FOR I=1 TO 10
60 INPUT#1,N
70 PRINT N
80 NEXT I
90 PRINT"** CLOSING DATA FILE **":CLOSE1
100 END

** READ NUMERIC DATA TAPE **

** MOUNT TAPE; PRESS <RETURN> WHEN READY **

** OPENING DATA FILE **

PRESS PLAY ON TAPE #1
OK

 1
 2
 3
 4
 5
 6
 7
 8
 9
 10
** CLOSING DATA FILE **
```

The INPUT# statement also reads fields that contain string variables. The program WORD.PRINT# wrote ten string variables to cassette tape. The data file created was named NUMWORD. NUMWORD looks like this:

```
{ <CR>ONE<CR>TWO<CR>  ······   <CR>NINE<CR>TEN<CR> }
```

To read fields from NUMWORD, use INPUT# with a string variable parameter. With only slight modification, you can change the READ NUMERIC DATA TAPE program to read NUMWORD. The changes occur at line 40 (name the data file), and line 60 (INPUT variable). The complete changed listing appears below, followed by a sample run of the program.

```
10 PRINT"J** READ NUMWORD DATA FILE **":PRINT
20 PRINT"** MOUNT TAPE;PRESS <RETURN> WHEN READY":PRINT
30 GET A$:IF A$="" THEN 30
40 PRINT"** OPENING DATA FILE **":OPEN 1,1,0,"NUMWORD":PRINT
50 FOR I=1 TO 10
60 INPUT#1,N$
70 PRINT N$
80 NEXT I
90 PRINT"** CLOSING DATA FILE **":CLOSE1
100 END
```

```
** READ NUMWORD DATA FILE **

** MOUNT TAPE; PRESS <RETURN> WHEN READY

** OPENING DATA FILE **

PRESS PLAY ON TAPE #1
OK

ONE
TWO
THREE
FOUR
FIVE
SIX
SEVEN
EIGHT
NINE
TEN

** CLOSING DATA FILE **
```

Returning to the NAMES.PRINT# program, recall that the names in data file NAME are written as three separate string fields: F$, M$, L$. Each string field has a comma separating it from the next string field. The data tape looks like this:

HEADLY, GEORGE, JOYCE<CR>CAROL, A. , SMITH<CR>

If commas do not separate the fields, they will be read as a single string variable, and the three fields will be displayed on the screen as follows:

```
HEADLYGEORGEJOYCE
CAROLA.SMITH
```

A program to read data from the NAME file is listed below. The INPUT# statement on line 60 will read all fields up to the next carriage return separator. Fields lying between carriage returns are separated by commas. Since three fields lie between carriage returns, separated by commas, three string variable names appear in the INPUT# statement parameter list. The PRINT statement on line 70 displays the three string variables on a single line, with a space inserted between adjacent strings.

```
10 PRINT"]** READ NAME DATA FILE **":PRINT
20 PRINT"** MOUNT TAPE;PRESS <RETURN> WHEN READY":PRINT
30 GET A$:IF A$="" THEN 30
40 PRINT"** OPENING DATA FILE **":OPEN 1,1,0,"NAME":PRINT
50 FOR J=1 TO 4
60 INPUT#1,F$,M$,L$
70 PRINT F$;" ";M$;" ";L$
80 NEXT J
90 PRINT"** CLOSING DATA FILE **":CLOSE1
100 END
```

```
** READ NAME DATA FILE **

** MOUNT TAPE; PRESS <RETURN> WHEN READY **

** OPENING DATA FILE **

PRESS PLAY ON TAPE #1
OK
```

```
ARNOLD J. SIMPSON
BETTY S. CLARK
HEADLY GEORGE JOYCE
CAROL ANNE SMITH

** CLOSING DATA FILE **
```

The next program demonstrates how to read mailing list data which was written to data file MAIL by program MAIL.PRINT#. Each record contains five fields: record number, customer name, street, city, state and ZIP code. Below is an example of a MAIL file record:

```
** RECORD #6 **      Field 1 ⎫
                             ⎪
WIDGETS SUPPLY CO.   Field 2 ⎪
555 BOGUS AVE.       Field 3 ⎬ One record
GERTIE               Field 4 ⎪
TENNESSEE 38901      Field 5 ⎭
```

Below is a program listing of MAIL.INPUT#. Type in MAIL.INPUT# and save it on a cassette tape. Then LIST the program to follow the step-by-step discussion.

MAIL. INPUT #

```
10 PRINT"⊃↑↑↑↑↑↑↑↑↑↑↑↑↑↑↑↑↑↑↑↑↑↑↑↑↑↑↑↑"
20 PRINT"↑                          ↑"
30 PRINT"↑ READ MAIL FILE W/ INPUT# ↑"
40 PRINT"↑                          ↑"
50 PRINT"↑↑↑↑↑↑↑↑↑↑↑↑↑↑↑↑↑↑↑↑↑↑↑↑↑↑↑↑":PRINT:PRINT
60 PRINT"↑↑ PRESS <RETURN> WHEN TAPE IS LOADED ↑↑█"
70 GET A$:IF A$="" THEN 70
80 PRINT"↑↑ OPENING MAIL FILE ↑↑":OPEN1,1,0,"MAIL"
90 PRINT"█↑↑ READING MAIL FILE ↑↑"
100 IF ST=64 THEN 9999
110 INPUT#1,I$
120 INPUT#1,NM$
130 INPUT#1,A1$
140 INPUT#1,A2$
150 INPUT#1,A3$
160 PRINT"⊃↑↑ RECORD #";I$;" ↑↑"
170 PRINT"█████NAME:";TAB(9);NM$
180 PRINT"ADDR:";TAB(9);A1$
190 PRINTTAB(9);A2$
200 PRINTTAB(9);A3$
210 PRINT"█████"
220 INPUT"ENTER 'Y' TO READ NEXT RECORD";A$:IF A$="Y" GOTO 100
9999 PRINT"█↑↑ END OF MAIL FILE--PROGRAM TERMINATED":CLOSE1:END
```

Statements on the first five lines display a brief program description. Statements on lines 60 and 70 instruct the user to mount the data tape; the program is then ready to begin reading customer addresses. First the data file must be OPENed. MAIL is OPENed as logical file #1 on the cassette unit #1. The secondary address must be 0 for READ.

```
80 PRINT"↑↑ OPENING MAIL FILE ↑↑":OPEN1,1,0,"MAIL"
```

The statement on line 100 uses the status word (ST) to check for an end-of-file mark. If ST=64 (indicating an end-of-file mark is found), then the file is closed at line 9999. ST should be checked before data is read so that you do not attempt to read data when there is no more.

Statements on lines 110 to 150 read data using INPUT#. Each field was written to tape separated by a carriage return, so each field is read with an individual INPUT#. The variable or string names used to read data may differ from names used when the data was written. For instance, data may be written to the tape as X$ and read back from the tape as A$. The computer will not know the difference because data variable names are neither saved nor passed from one program to another.

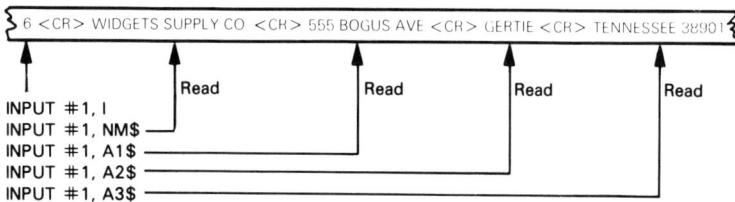

Data is stored in the input buffer (memory) when read. Nothing is displayed on the screen unless the display is programmed. This is done by statements on lines 160 to 200, where tabs and leaders were inserted. Line 210 moves the cursor down four lines.

```
160 PRINT"♥♠♠ RECORD #";I$;" ♠♠"
170 PRINT"▨▨▨▨▨NAME:";TAB(9);NM$
180 PRINT"ADDR:";TAB(9);A1$
190 PRINTTAB(9);A2$
200 PRINTTAB(9);A3$
210 PRINT"▨▨▨▨▨":
```

The screen output looks like this:

```
♦♦ RECORD #6 ♦♦

NAME:     WIDGETS SUPPLY CO.
ADDR:     555 BOGUS AVE.
          GERTIE
          TENNESSEE  38901
```

After all four fields have been displayed, the operator is asked whether the next record is desired:

```
220 INPUT"ENTER 'Y' TO READ NEXT RECORD";A$:IF A$="Y" GOTO 100
```

If the user wants the next record, the program goes to line 100 and repeats program execution until the status word (ST) signals an EOF. If the user does not wish to continue, or if an EOF is encountered, the file is closed and the program ends.

Figure 6-4 provides a flowchart of the MAIL.INPUT# program. A sample run of the program follows:

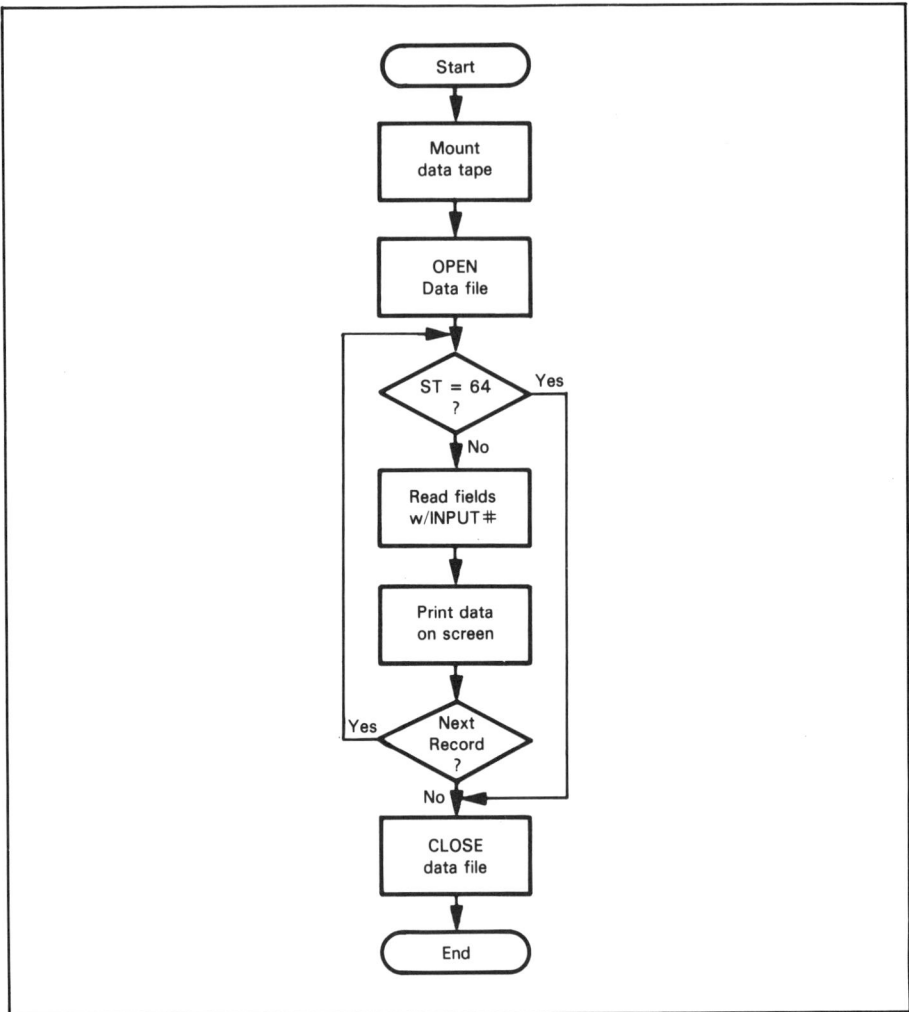

Figure 6-4. MAIL. INPUT#

```
♠♠♠♠♠♠♠♠♠♠♠♠♠♠♠♠♠♠♠♠♠♠♠♠♠♠♠♠♠♠
♠                            ♠
♠ READ MAIL FILE W/ INPUT# ♠
♠                            ♠
♠♠♠♠♠♠♠♠♠♠♠♠♠♠♠♠♠♠♠♠♠♠♠♠♠♠♠♠♠♠

♠♠ PRESS <RETURN> WHEN TAPE IS LOADED ♠♠

♠♠ OPENING MAIL FILE ♠♠

PRESS PLAY ON TAPE #1
OK
```

```
♠♠ READING MAIL FILE ♠♠

♠♠ RECORD # 1 ♠♠

NAME:           ACME MANUFACTURING CO.
ADDR:           1235 MAIN ST.
                DOWNTOWN
                IL   62501

ENTER 'Y' TO READ NEXT RECORD

♠♠ RECORD # 2 ♠♠

NAME:           BENJAMIN FRANKLIN
ADDR:           12 LIBERTY TOWER
                PHILADELPHIA
                PA   16524

ENTER 'Y' TO READ NEXT RECORD

♠♠ RECORD # 3 ♠♠

NAME:           NEIL ARMSTRONG
ADDR:           597 SEA OF TRANQUILITY AVE.
                EARTHVIEW
                LUNAR   000000

ENTER 'Y' TO READ NEXT RECORD

♠♠ RECORD # 4 ♠♠

NAME:           MAMMOTH DISTRIBUTION CO.
ADDR:           INDUSTRIAL PARK
                CITY OF INDUSTRY
                CA   92425

ENTER 'Y' TO READ NEXT RECORD

♠♠ RECORD # 5 ♠♠

NAME:           HENRY MUSCATEL
ADDR:           819 OAK ST.
                NAPA
                CA   95303

ENTER 'Y' TO READ NEXT RECORD

♠♠ RECORD # 6 ♠♠

NAME:           WIDGET SUPPLY CO.
ADDR:           555 BOGUS
                GERTIE
                TENNESSEE   38901

ENTER 'Y' TO READ NEXT RECORD
♠♠ END OF MAIL FILE--PROGRAM TERMINATED ♠♠
```

When you run MAIL.INPUT#, do not panic if the computer appears to stop for a few seconds. Look at the cassette drive and you will see the cassette tape moving. What is happening is that the computer is reading the next 191 bytes of data into the input buffer before continuing with the program. Once the buffer is full the computer will come to life again.

Note that **statements on line 220 do not represent good programming practice.** This program logic will cause another name and address to be read and displayed if the operator depresses the Y key. But if the operator depresses any other key, or accidentally bumps the keyboard, the program will shut down. A well-written program will respond to just two keys, perhaps "Y" for "yes" and "N" for "no". The prompt message will tell the operator to depress one of these two keys. Any other key input should be ignored. Can you rewrite the statements on line 220 to operate in this fashion?

Another method of reading data files uses the GET# statement:

GET#f,var

where:

>   f   is the logical file number (1-255, matching the file
>   number in the OPEN and CLOSE statements).
>
>   var   is the variable name of the data to be read.

GET# reads one character at a time from the data file. It is similar to GET, which accepts one character at a time from the keyboard.

GET# reads characters, file delimiters and anything else on the tape. This is especially useful when you want to read everything that is written on a bad data tape to find the cause of any problem. GET# allows individual characters to be compared with specific values as a means of character identification.

Two sample programs will demonstrate how to read and display an entire file, including all file delimiters, and how to display the MAIL data file separated into records.

The following program, MAIL.GET#1, reads data file MAIL one character at a time and displays the contents of MAIL on the screen:

MAIL.GET#1

```
10 PRINT"?**************************"
20 PRINT"*                          *"
30 PRINT"*  READ MAIL FILE W/ GET#  *"
40 PRINT"*                          *"
50 PRINT"***************************":PRINT:PRINT
60 PRINT"** PRESS <RETURN> WHEN TAPE IS LOADED **"
70 GET A$:IF A$="" THEN 70
80 PRINT"*** OPENING MAIL FILE **":PRINT:OPEN1,1,0,"MAIL"
90 PRINT"*** MAIL FILE **"
100 IF ST=64 THEN 9999
110 GET#1,X$
120 IF X$=CHR$(13) THEN X$="*"
130 PRINT X$;
140 GOTO 100
9999 PRINT"****** END OF MAIL FILE--PROGRAM TERMINATED**"
    :CLOSE1:END
```

Statements on lines 10 through 90 are similar to the beginning lines of MAIL.INPUT#. These statements introduce the program, give instructions for mounting the data tape, and then open the data file.

Statements on lines 100 through 140 read data from file MAIL and display data on the screen.

The statement on line 100 checks for an end-of-file (EOF) status. If an EOF is not encountered, the next character is read by the GET# statement on line 110. #1 is the file number and X$ is the variable name assigned to the data strings. This statement will read the next character in the file.

The statement on line 120 compares the current value of X$ to a carriage return (CHR$(13)). If the value of X$ is CHR$(13), then the value of X$ is changed to a FULL GRID ■. This change avoids printing a carriage return, which would push the cursor to the next line; with the FULL GRID substituting for a carriage return, the whole file appears as one continuous line, as a good conceptual representation of the data tape. An example of this is shown in the sample run.

Make sure that a semicolon follows the variable in the PRINT statement on line 130, otherwise characters will be displayed vertically down the first column of the screen.

After each character is read from tape and displayed on the screen, the program returns to check status and GET# another character. This process repeats until ST=64 (the end-of-file). When the end-of-file is encountered at line 100, the job of MAIL.GET#1 is complete. At line 9999 the program closes the data file and ends.

Here is a sample run of MAIL.GET#1, using MAIL as the data file.

```
********************************
*                              *
*    READ MAIL FILE W/ GET#    *
*                              *
********************************


** PRESS <RETURN> WHEN TAPE IS LOADED **

** OPENING MAIL FILE **

PRESS PLAY ON TAPE #1
OK

** MAIL FILE **

 1 *ACME MANUFACTURING CO.*1235 MAIN ST.
*DOWNTOWN*IL   62501* 2 *BENJAMIN FRANKL
IN*12 LIBERTY TOWER*PHILADELPHIA   16524
* 3 *NEIL ARMSTRONG*597 SEA OF TRANQUILI
TY*EARTHVIEW*LUNAR   00000* 4 *MAMMOTH D
ISTRIBUTION CO.*INDUSTRIAL PARK*CITY OF
INDUSTRY*CA   92425* 5 *HENRY MUSCATEL*8
19 OAK ST.*NAPA*CA   95303* 6 *WIDGET SU
PPLY CO.*555 BOGUS AVE.*GERTIE*TENNESSEE
   38901*


** END OF MAIL FILE--PROGRAM TERMINATED**
```

Next program MAIL.GET#2 reads MAIL and displays data on the screen, divided into records. Here is a program listing of MAIL.GET#2:

```
10 PRINT":♠♠♠♠♠♠♠♠♠♠♠♠♠♠♠♠♠♠♠♠♠♠♠♠♠♠♠"
20 PRINT"♠                             ♠"
30 PRINT"♠ READ MAIL FILE W/ GET# ♠"
40 PRINT"♠                             ♠"
50 PRINT"♠♠♠♠♠♠♠♠♠♠♠♠♠♠♠♠♠♠♠♠♠♠♠♠♠♠♠":PRINT:PRINT
65 PRINT"♠♠ PRESS <RETURN> WHEN TAPE IS LOADED ♠♠":PRINT:
70 GET A$:IF A$="" THEN 70
80 PRINT"♠♠ OPENING MAIL FILE ♠♠":PRINT:OPEN 1,1,0,"MAIL"
90 PRINT:PRINT":♠♠ MAIL FILE ♠♠":PRINT:
95 F=0:R=0
100 IF ST=64 THEN 9999
110 GET#1,X$
120 IF X$=CHR$(13) THEN F=F+1
130 PRINT X$;
140 IF F>=5 THEN GOSUB 160
150 GOTO 100
160 PRINT
170 R=R+1
180 IF R>2 THEN PRINT "PRESS /Y/ FOR NEXT SET OF RECORDS";:INPUT A$
185 IF A$="Y" THEN R=0
190 F=0:PRINT:RETURN
9999 PRINT"♠♠♠♠♠♠ END OF MAIL FILE--PROGRAM TERMINATED♠♠":CLOSE1:END
```

Type in MAIL.GET#2. SAVE and VERIFY the program on a cassette tape. Then LIST it.

Statements on the first ten lines (10 through 100) of MAIL.GET#2 are identical to MAIL.GET#1. This part of the program informs the user of the program's functions and procedures, and opens the MAIL data file in preparation for reading the data.

The difference between MAIL.GET#2 and MAIL.GET#1 is at line 120. If X$=CHR$(13), instead of changing the value of X$ from a carriage return to FULL GRID ▦ , variable F (a carriage return counter) is incremented by +1. When MAIL.PRINT# wrote to the data file, a carriage return marked the end of each field. There are five fields in each record. MAIL.GET#2 counts fields. The conditional statement on line 140 calls a subroutine if five records have been read.

The statement on line 160 inserts a blank line between records. On line 170, variable R serves as a record counter. Statements on line 180 test to see if more than two name and address records have been read. When three records have been read, the screen is full, and the operator is asked if a new set of records is desired. If yes, the record counter R and field counter F are initialized to zero before returning to read the next set of records at line 100. This continues until the user inputs something other than a Y character or ST=64; at that time the file is closed and the program ends. Figure 6-5 illustrates program logic.

Although GET# is similar to INPUT# in some ways, it is more difficult to format the printout when using GET# if titles and indentation or spacing are desired. Just as X$ is compared with CHR$(13), so other field delimiters or characters would have to be conditionally tested in order to create a formatted display.

Following is a sample run of MAIL.GET#2 reading MAIL.

```
♠♠♠♠♠♠♠♠♠♠♠♠♠♠♠♠♠♠♠♠♠♠♠♠♠♠♠♠
♠                            ♠
♠ READ MAIL FILE W/ GET#  ♠
♠                            ♠
♠●♠♠♠♠♠♠♠♠♠♠♠♠♠♠♠♠♠♠♠♠♠♠♠♠♠♠♠
♠♠ PRESS <RETURN> WHEN TAPE IS LOADED ♠♠
♠♠ OPENING MAIL FILE ♠♠
PRESS PLAY ON TAPE #1
OK

♠♠ MAIL FILE ♠♠

 1
ACME MANUFACTURING CO.
1235 MAIN ST.
DOWNTOWN
IL    62501


 2
BENJAMIN FRANKLIN
12 LIBERTY TOWER
PHILADELPHIA
PA    16524


 3
NEIL ARMSTRONG
597 SEA OF TRANQUILITY
EARTHVIEW
LUNAR   00000

PRESS 'Y' FOR NEXT SET OF RECORDS?Y
 4
MAMMOTH DISTRIBUTION CO.
INDUSTRIAL PARK
CITY OF INDUSTRY
CA    92425


 5
HENRY MUSCATEL
819 OAK ST.
NAPA
CA    95303


 6
WIDGET SUPPLY CO.
555 BOGUS AVE.
GERTIE
TENNESSEE    38901

PRESS 'Y' FOR NEXT SET OF RECORDS?Y

♠♠ END OF MAIL FILE--PROGRAM TERMINATED♠♠
```

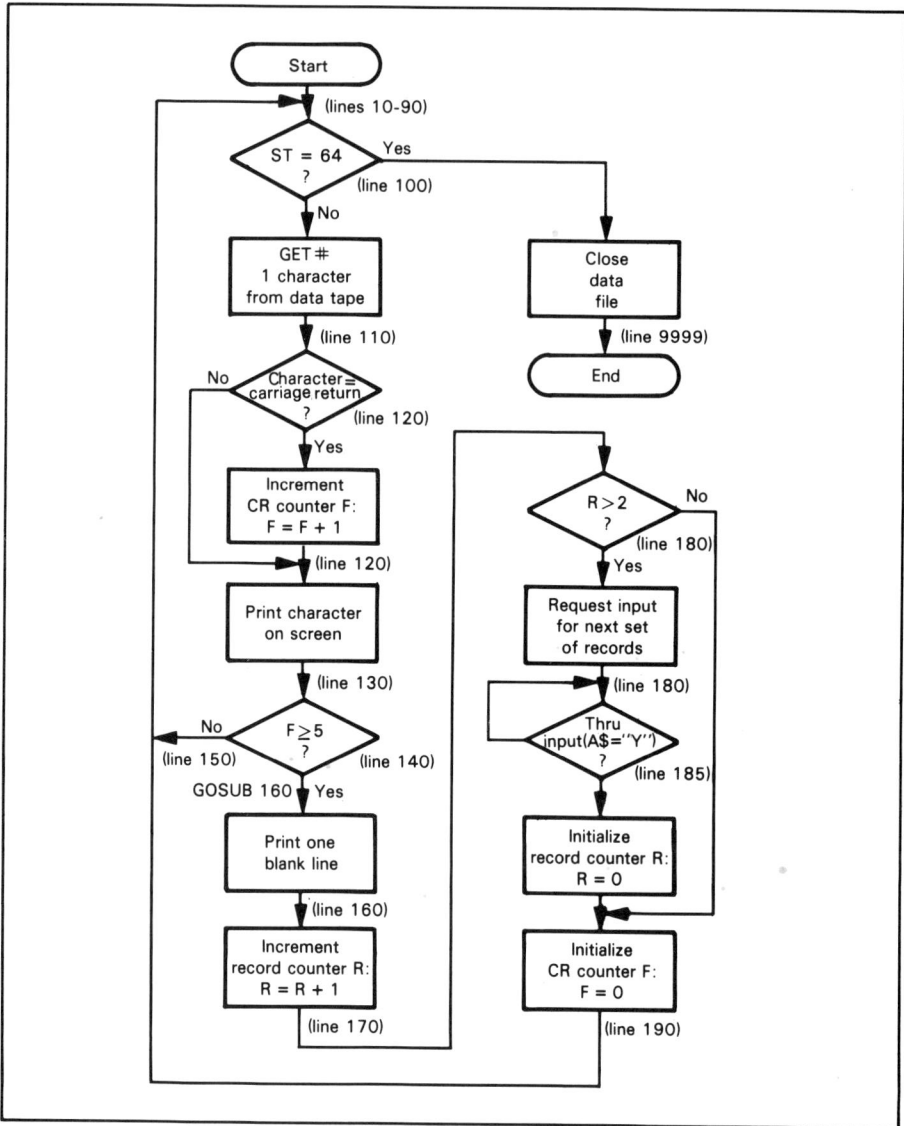

Figure 6-5. Format Printing using GET #

CASSETTE FILE FORMATS

The description of data files given at the beginning of this chapter is a conceptually accurate description of the way data is structured by computer systems in general. Data files are subdivided into records and fields. You can maintain this classical organization using appropriate CBM BASIC program logic, and we recommend that you do so. But **the actual organization of CBM cassette data files has little to do with fields and records** — as should be clear by now.

Every numeric field must be followed by a carriage return character (CHR$(13)). Therefore, a file consisting of numeric fields only could be looked upon as a sequence of numbers separated by carriage return characters. This may be illustrated as follows:

N < CR > N < CR > N < CR > N < CR > N < CR >

Nothing within the numeric file partitions fields into records, or distinguishes one record from another. It is entirely up to your program logic to keep track of records as repeating field sequences — if indeed such repeating field sequences exist.

String variables can optionally be divided into fields and records. You can use commas (CHR$(44)) to separate fields within a record, while a carriage return (CHR$(13)) follows the last field of the record. Thus, a file containing string variables only, with five fields per record, might be illustrated as follows:

< CR > S < , > S < , > S < , > S < , > S < CR > S < , > S < , > S < , > S < , > S < CR >

If you use comma and carriage return separators to divide string files into fields and records as illustrated above, then all the fields of each record must be read by a single INPUT# statement.

You are not required to use comma and carriage return separators with string variables. **You will likely be better off separating all string variable fields using carriage returns. As for numeric data, rely on program logic to group fields into records.**

Program logic needed to organize files into records and fields is usually self-evident; take the example of a mailing list. It takes no training as a programmer to see that each name and address becomes a record, while parts of the name and address must be treated as individual fields. There are a number of ways in which the parts of a name and address could be divided into fields; each option would probably do as well as any other. File organization is likely to be dictated on the needs of your program rather than the structure of CBM cassette data files. Programming difficulties, if any, will surround the PRINT# and INPUT# statement syntax.

Now we will take a simple program and, by looking at variations, identify syntax that is and is not allowed.

Key in the following program:

```
10 OPEN 1,1,1
20 FOR I=1 TO 10
30 PRINT#1,I+100
40 NEXT
50 CLOSE 1
60 STOP
70 OPEN 1
80 FOR I=1 TO 10
90 INPUT#1,J
100 PRINT J
110 NEXT
120 CLOSE 1
132 STOP
```

The OPEN statement on line 10 opens logical file 1, selecting cassette drive 1 for a write operation. **The FOR-NEXT loop on lines 20, 30, and 40 writes ten numbers to cassette tape. Numbers are followed by carriage return characters because the PRINT# statement on line 30 forces a carriage return on each execution,** just as an identical PRINT statement would cause a screen carriage return after displaying each number. The logical file is closed on line 50. Thus the ten numbers can be visualized on cassette tape as follows:

Statements on lines 70 through 120 read and display the ten numbers that were written to cassette tape by statements on lines 20 through 50.

Let us execute this program and see what happens.

Get a blank cassette tape; wind the tape forward until magnetic surface appears in front of the read gap, then mount the tape in cassette drive 1. Make sure that no cassette drive keys are depressed.

LIST the program to make sure that it is in memory and correctly entered. Now type RUN. The following message will be displayed:

```
PRESS PLAY AND RECORD ON TAPE #1
```

Depress these two keys on cassette drive 1. The CBM computer will respond by displaying OK:

```
PRESS PLAY AND RECORD ON TAPE #1
OK
```

The tape cassette will wind forward while the ten numbers 101 through 110 are written on tape cassette. After these ten numbers have been written, the drive stops moving and the following message is displayed:

```
BREAK IN 60
READY
```

The cursor flashes below the message. The STOP statement on line 60 caused the break. Now depress the STOP key on drive 1 to raise the PLAY and RECORD keys. Press the REWIND key to fully rewind the tape cassette, then press the STOP key again to raise the REWIND key. Now execute the second half of the program by typing:

```
GOTO 70
```

The message PRESS PLAY ON TAPE 1 will be displayed. Press the PLAY key on cassette drive 1. The computer will respond by displaying OK:

```
PRESS PLAY ON TAPE 1
OK
```

Nothing will happen for a while; the tape drive will move forward until the ten numbers previously written are located. Then these ten number will be displayed in a vertical column on the screen as follows:

```
101
102
103
104
105
106
107
108
109
110
BREAK IN 130
READY
```

The ten numbers are displayed in a vertical column because the PRINT statement on line 100 causes one number to be displayed per execution.

The final message is caused by execution of the STOP statement on line 130.

```
BREAK IN 130
READY
```

If you forget to rewind the tape cassette before typing GOTO 70, then the drive will search the cassette endlessly looking for data which occurred earlier on the tape. You must now stop the tape cassette and stop program execution. Rewind the tape cassette, but before you restart program execution, you will have to close file 1 in immediate mode by typing:

```
CLOSE 1
```

Then restart with:

```
GOTO 70
```

Now list the program again; end the PRINT statement on line 100 with a semi-colon:

```
100 PRINT J;
```

Rewind the tape cassette; then type GOTO 70.

Once again the message PRESS PLAY ON TAPE #1 will be displayed. When you press the PLAY key, OK will follow. After a short pause **the ten numbers read off the tape cassette will be displayed on a single line as follows**:

```
101  102  103  104  105  106  107  108  109  110
BREAK IN 130
READY
```

As an experiment we will now **change statements on lines 80 through 110 so that the ten numbers are input using a single INPUT statement**, as follows:

```
10 OPEN 1,1,1
20 FOR I=1 TO 10
30 PRINT#1,I+100
40 NEXT
50 CLOSE 1
60 STOP
70 OPEN 1
80 INPUT#1,N(1),N(2),N(3),N(4),N(5),N(6),N(7),N(8),N(9),N(10)
90 FOR I=1 TO 10
100 PRINT N(I);
110 NEXT
120 CLOSE 1
130 STOP
```

Again rewind the cassette and execute the second part of the program by typing GOTO 70.

Once again you will be told to PRESS PLAY ON TAPE #1, and when you do so, ten numbers will be read from the tape cassette and displayed on a single line, as illustrated previously. Thus it makes no difference whether you read the ten numbers from tape cassette by executing one INPUT# statement with ten variables in its parameter list, or by executing one INPUT# statement, with one variable, ten times.

Experimenting further with field separation punctuation, modify the first part of the program, where data is written to the tape cassette as follows:

```
10 OPEN 1,1,1
20 FOR I=1 TO 10
30 PRINT#1,I+100
40 NEXT
45 C$=CHR$(59)
46 PRINT#1,M(1);C$;M(2);C$;M(3);C$;M(4);C$;M(5)
47 PRINT#1,M(6);C$;M(7);C$;M(8);C$;M(9);C$;M(10)
50 CLOSE 1
60 STOP
70 OPEN 1
80 FOR I=1 TO 10
90 INPUT#1,J
100 PRINT J
110 NEXT
120 CLOSE 1
130 STOP
```

CHR$(59) represents a semicolon. Rewind the tape cassette, advance the tape until magnetic surface appears below the read gap and mount the tape in the tape drive. With all keys up type RUN. When instructed to do so, press the PLAY and RECORD keys. The data will record successfully and the following message will appear.

```
BREAK IN 60
READY
▓
```

Rewind the cassette tape and type GOTO 70.

When instructed to do so, press the PLAY key on tape drive 1. Data is not read successfully; an error message is displayed.

```
FILE DATA ERROR IN 90
READY
```

You cannot use any punctuation other than carriage returns to separate numeric data fields. You can use commas or carriage returns to separate string fields. To prove this change the program as follows:

```
5 DATA ONE,TWO,THREE,FOUR,FIVE,SIX,SEVEN,EIGHT,NINE,TEN
10 OPEN 1,1,1
20 FOR I=1 TO 10
30 READ M$(I)
40 NEXT
45 C$=CHR$(44)
46 PRINT#1,M$(1);C$;M$(2);C$;M$(3);C$;M$(4);C$;M$(5)
47 PRINT#1,M$(6);C$;M$(7);C$;M$(8);C$;M$(9);C$;M$(10)
50 CLOSE 1
60 STOP
70 OPEN 1
80 FOR I=1 TO 10
90 INPUT#1,J$
100 PRINT J$
110 NEXT
120 CLOSE 1
130 STOP
```

Rewind the data cassette, advance the tape until magnetic surface appears below the read gap, mount the tape in drive 1 and type RUN. When instructed to do so, depress the PLAY and RECORD keys of tape 1. Data will record successfully on the cassette. When the message:

```
BREAK IN 60
READY
```

appears, rewind the cassette tape and type GOTO 70.

Press the PLAY key when told to do so. You will see the string variables 1 and 6 displayed, followed by the error message:

```
STRING TOO LONG ERROR IN 90
READY
```

What went wrong? The problem is in the INPUT# statement on line 90. An INPUT# statement will read all string fields up to the first carriage return. Therefore M$(1) through M$(5) is input on the first execution of the line 90 INPUT# statement; however, only M$(1) has its value assigned to J$ since the comma is interpreted as a field separator, not a record terminator. The second time the line 90 INPUT# statement is executed, M$(6) through M$(10) is input, since these are the fields lying between two carriage returns. Once again only M$(6) is assigned to J$, since the comma is interpreted as a field terminator. The third time the line 90 INPUT# statement is executed there is no data left to read and a file error is reported. This explains the observed display. In order to resolve the problem we must **execute INPUT# statements with the same number of variables as there were in the PRINT# statement.** Consider the following program:

```
5 DATA ONE,TWO,THREE,FOUR,FIVE,SIX,SEVEN,EIGHT,NINE,TEN
10 OPEN 1,1,1
20 FOR I=1 TO 10
30 READ M$(I)
40 NEXT
45 C$=CHR$(44)
46 PRINT#1,M$(1);C$;M$(2);C$;M$(3);C$;M$(4);C$;M$(5)
47 PRINT#1,M$(6);C$;M$(7);C$;M$(8);C$;M$(9);C$;M$(10)
50 CLOSE 1
60 STOP
70 OPEN 1
80 INPUT#1 N$(1),N$(2),N$(3),N$(4),N$(5)
90 INPUT#1 N$(6),N$(7),N$(8),N$(9),N$(10)
100 FOR I=1 TO 10
105 PRINT N$(I);" ";
110 NEXT
120 CLOSE 1
130 STOP
```

If you repeat the execution steps for the two halves of this program, accurately manipulating the cassette tape as described for previous executions, then when the second half of the program is executed, you will obtain the display:

```
ONE TWO THREE FOUR FIVE SIX SEVEN EIGHT NINE TEN
BREAK IN 130
READY
```

There are a few more experiments worth trying on your own.

Can a single INPUT# statement read a number of string variables separated by carriage returns? To check this out, change line 45 in the final program so that C$ is assigned the value CHR$(13). Then re-execute the program.

How about mixing numeric and string fields in a single data file? To check this out, create the ten string variables M$(I) as shown in the final program illustration, but in addition, create ten numeric variables M(I) by adding the following statement on line 35:

```
35 M(I)=I+100
```

Now try various combinations of PRINT# character sequences on lines 46 and 47, and see what it takes to read these sequences back correctly with INPUT# statements on lines 80 and 90.

DISKETTE FILES

Program files and data files may be recorded on diskettes. Program files store BASIC programs. Data files store numeric and string data.
There are three types of diskette data files:

1. **Sequential files**, which store data in a very compact way, but have restricted file access capabilities.
2. **Relative files**, which require more diskette surface than sequential files to store the same amount of data, but allow data to be accessed and manipulated more efficiently.
3. **Random files**, which rely on your program logic for their structure.

Program files, sequential data files and relative data files are described in this chapter. Random data files are described in Chapter 7.

A Comparison of Diskette and Cassette File Handling

Diskette file handling differs markedly from cassette file handling for these two reasons:

1. Data can be accessed off a diskette very quickly, as compared to cassette file access times.
2. There is no "beginning" or "end" to a diskette surface, as there is to a cassette tape. A diskette drive can access any point on the diskette surface with equal ease. In contrast, cassette tape has a beginning and an end.

Cassette and diskette file handling differ markedly because they use totally different data storage formatting and access methods. Mechanical speed has very little to do with it; the speed at which a diskette is rotated is comparable to the speed at which cassette tape is moved.

Cassette tape stores data on a continuous track down the length of the tape; the cassette drive moves the tape past stationary read and write heads in order to access any part of the tape.

In contrast, diskettes store data on a large number of concentric circular tracks. The diskette drive read and write heads are on a moving arm that can position over any track. The diskette is rotated to bring the required section of the selected track under the read or write head.

In order to use diskettes you do not have to understand how information is stored on the diskette surface, but some knowledge will help you program diskette files more efficiently. Therefore we will begin our discussion of diskette files by describing the way data is recorded on the diskette surface.

HOW DISKETTES STORE DATA

Diskettes store data on a number of concentric tracks. Tracks are divided into sectors.

In order to imagine a single track, draw a circle to represent the diskette, then draw a smaller concentric circle to represent one track on the diskette surface. This may be illustrated as follows:

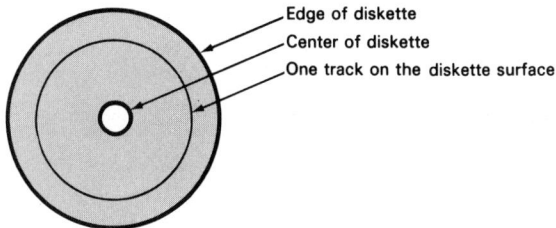

Edge of diskette
Center of diskette
One track on the diskette surface

Different diskette drives write different numbers of tracks on the surface of a diskette. Some drives write on both surfaces of the diskette; other drives write on one surface only. **The CBM 2040 and 8050 diskette drives write on one surface of the diskette; as summarized in Table 6-3, the 2040 drive writes 35 tracks, whereas the 8050 drive writes 77 tracks.**

The diskette drive does not write data across the entire length of a track. To do so would make diskette surface addressing very difficult. If data were recorded over the full length of the track, no two tracks would hold the same amount of information, since no two tracks have the same length. To resolve this problem, **tracks are divided into sectors**. Every sector holds exactly the same amount of information. In the case of the 2040 and 8050 drives, 256 characters (bytes) of data are stored on each sector. Figure 6-6 illustrates this organization.

Most diskette drives write the same number of sectors on every track, even though the track closest to the edge of the diskette is much longer than the track closest to the diskette center. The 2040 and 8050 diskette drives take advantage of the longer tracks closer to the edge of the diskette by writing more sectors on longer tracks. Table 6-3 identifies the number of sectors written on various tracks. Track numbers begin at 0 for the outermost track. The innermost track has the highest track number.

If you manually rotate a CBM diskette in its cardboard jacket, you will notice a single circular hole appear in the small circular window close to the center of the cardboard jacket. A diskette with a single hole is said to be soft-sectored. In contrast, there are hard-sectored disks which have as many holes as there are sectors. CBM diskette drives can use either kind of diskette; soft-sectored diskettes are most commonly used.

Diskette Directory and Block Availability Map (BAM)

Two tracks of every diskette are used to index the diskette on the 8050 disk. Only one track is used on the 2040/3040/4040 disks.

The Directory track contains the name you assign to the diskette, together with the names of all files, and their starting sector addresses.

The Block Availability Map identifies sectors which have, or have not, been allocated to files.

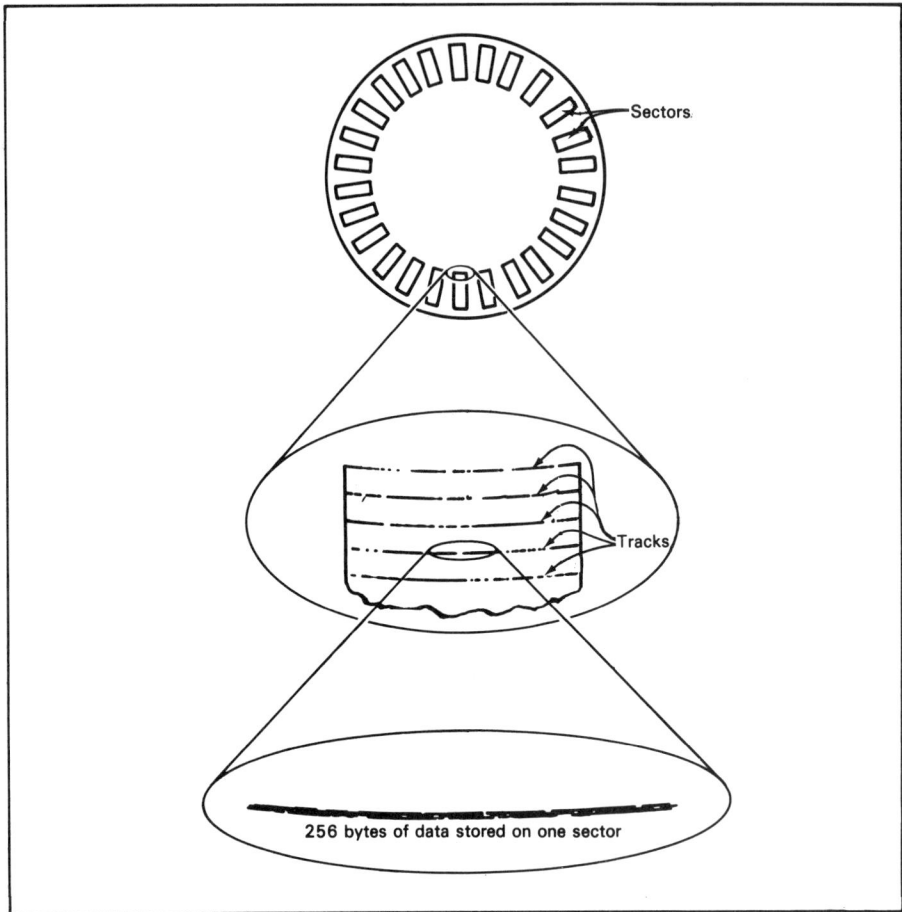

Figure 6-6. A Diskette's Recorded Surface

Files stored on cassette tape do not need a directory at the beginning of the tape. **If ten files are stored on a cassette tape, and a particular access specifies the sixth file,** having a directory at the beginning of the tape would not help the drive locate the sixth file any sooner. Since cassette files can have any length, there is no way of translating a cassette file number into a cassette tape position. You can take your chances winding the cassette tape forward to some position that precedes the file you want, thereby reducing cassette search time. Otherwise **the cassette drive must read past the first five files in order to locate the beginning of the sixth file**.

A diskette drive, in contrast, **can go directly to the beginning of any file** on the diskette surface, since every diskette sector is equally accessible. **To make this possible, every diskette has a directory** which lists the names and beginning sector addresses for all files stored on the diskette. The directory also records the file type and its current size. When a diskette data file is opened, the drive first reads the diskette directory, from which it obtains the sector address where the opened file begins. The drive can then go directly to the beginning of the opened file.

But what about the records of a diskette data file?

Table 6-3. Diskette Drive Specifications

Characteristics	2040 Drive		8050 Drive	
Total Capacity	176,640 bytes		534,272 bytes	
Usable Capacity — Sequential Files	170,180 bytes		527,812 bytes	
Usable Capacity — Relative Files			182,880 bytes	
Tracks	35		77	
Sectors per track	**Tracks**	**Sectors**	**Tracks**	**Sectors**
	0-16 17-23 24-29 30-34	21 20(or 19*) 18 17	0-38 39-52 54-65 66-76	29 27 25 23
Bytes per sector	256		256	
Total blocks (sectors)	690		2087	
Block Availability Map (RAM) track	17		38	
Directory track	18		39	
*Model 2				

Relative Data Files

All records in a relative file have the same length. It is easy to compute sector addresses for individual records of a relative file. Suppose the relative file records fit exactly two per sector. (This is unlikely to happen by chance, but it makes our illustration easy to follow.) The tenth record of this relative file will then be found on the fifth sector allocated to the file. **Relative data files are available with CBM BASIC versions 4.0 and higher, using DOS 2.0 and higher.**

Sequential Data Files

The records of a sequential file can have different lengths. We cannot compute the sector on which a particular sequential file record is to be found, since the lengths of individual sequential file records are unknown. The diskette drive can go directly to the beginning of a sequential file, since the beginning sector address is held in the diskette directory, but having gotten to the sequential file, it must access records sequentially, as a cassette drive would. For example, there is no way of reaching a sequential file's tenth record without first reading records 1 through 9. Figure 6-7 conceptually illustrates the distribution of ten records across sectors for relative and sequential files.

All versions of CBM BASIC support sequential data files.

A Relative File

Sector No.:	N		N + 1		N + 2		N + 3		N + 4	etc.
Record No.:	0	1	2	3	4	5	6	7	8	9 etc.

A Sequential File

Sector No.:	N			N + 1		N + 2			N + 3		N + 4	
Record No.:	0	1	2	3	4	5	6	7	8		9	

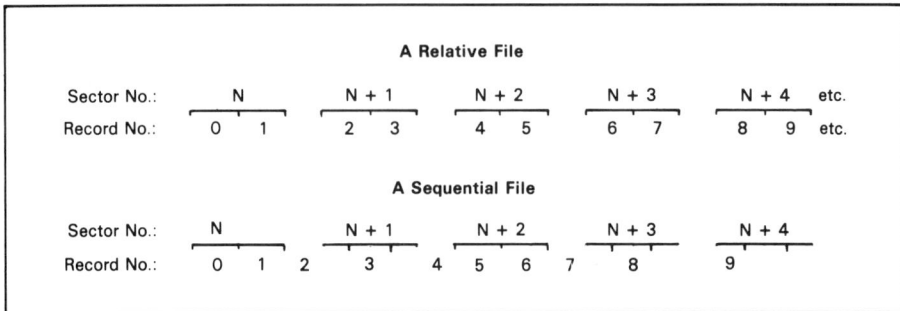

Figure 6-7. Record/Sector Correlation for Relative and Sequential Access Files

Relative versus Sequential Data Files

If sequential file records must be read sequentially, much of the diskette's random access capability is lost, so why bother with sequential files? The answer is that **sequential files store information more densely than relative files. Therefore, sequential files make better use of the diskette surface.** To illustrate this point, consider the following two names and addresses:

> Cornelius J. Winkleberger
> 257631 Avenue of the Americas
> Billinghampton
> California   92804

> Joe R. Smith
> 5 N St.
> York
> Iowa   50307

Suppose these two names and addresses are part of a mailing list data file. Each name and address will become one record within the data file. A relative data file must assign the same diskette space to every name and address. To avoid abbreviations the assigned diskette space must be sufficient to accommodate the longest name and address. Therefore, all shorter names and addresses will leave some space unused; and unused record space is wasted record space.

But a sequential file assigns each name and address the space it needs, however short or long this particular name and address may be. No diskette space is unused, and therefore none is wasted.

No restrictions are placed on the way you access or modify relative files. Since relative files have fixed length records that can be addressed individually, you can access a single record to read it or to change it. For example, you could rewrite the 10th name and address in a relative data file containing 20 names and addresses, leaving all other records unaltered. You can add records to a relative data file so long as the diskette has available space. You can delete any relative file record.

On the other hand **you must handle sequential files much as you would handle cassette files.** Records must be read sequentially, beginning with the first record of the file. You can append new records to the end of a sequential data file, but you cannot write new records into the middle of a sequential data file. Instead, you must rewrite the entire sequential file as a new file, modifying records in transit, as needed. **The trade-off is that sequential files make better use of the diskette surface, but they are harder to process.**

Sector Addressing

The sectors assigned to any diskette data file are unlikely to be physically sequential on the diskette surface. For example, when you add records to an existing data file, the new records may run into the beginning of the next file; therefore the file will have to be continued wherever unused sectors are available on the diskette surface. The file contracts when you erase records. Vacated sectors must be made available to other files. Therefore **diskette drive logic assumes that sectors assigned to any data file will be scattered all over the surface of the diskette. This presents no problem when dealing with sequential files.** So long as each sector points to the next sector, the drive can work its way across the diskette, sector by sector, reading the sequential file. But **for relative files** the problem is more complex, since drive logic must be able to compute addresses of individual records. **Therefore a record's displacement from the beginning of the file must be converted into a sector displacement.** Looking again at a file that has two records per sector, a request to access the 10th record becomes a request to access the 5th sector of the relative file. Since sectors are not sequential on the diskette surface, the relative file must maintain a sector index. This may be illustrated conceptually as follows:

Record number	Sequential sector number on which record begins	Actual track and sector address	
		Track no.	Sector no.
1	1	11	4
2	1		
3	2	11	5
4	2		
5	3	11	6
6	3		
7	4	13	9
8	4		
9	5		
10	5	13	10
11	6	9	3

Thus record number 6 is on the third sector assigned to the file. This sector is the sixth sector on track 11.

The term "side sector" is used to describe the relative file sector index. Currently, the 8050 diskette drive cannot use the entire diskette capacity for relative files because it runs out of space for side sectors. That is why Table 6-3 shows relative files using just 180,000 of the 8050 diskette's half million bytes. Future versions of the 8050 diskette drive will remove this restriction.

PROGRAMMING DISKETTE FILES

Different program logic is required by program files, sequential data files and relative data files. Moreover, program statements allow you to perform a variety of very necessary diskette "housekeeping" operations.

Diskette File Names

Diskette file names follow normal CBM BASIC label rules. Normally file names have 16 characters or less. Some file names are restricted to a maximum of 16 characters, but it is a good idea to observe this limit, even where it is not enforced.

DOS statements identify files via the file name. You can specify the complete file name, or you can provide the first few characters of the file name, followed by an asterisk (*) in which case the first file name encountered with matching leading characters will be selected. Here are some examples:

Specified filename:	PAR * ⎞
Selected filenames:	PARITY ⎟
	PARITY,SEC ⎟ The first file whose name
	PARITY,N12 ⎟ begins with PAR will be selected
	PARTITION ⎟
	etc. ⎠

Specified filename:	*
Selected filenames:	Any and all, since no characters
	precede the * . There the first
	file encountered is selected.

You can also search for file names by comparing some characters, but not others. Characters that are not to be compared are specified using question marks (?). Here is an example:

Specified filename:	N??,SEQ
Selected filenames:	NUM,SEQ ⎞
	NXY,SEQ ⎟ The first file whose name
	NAB,SEQ ⎟ is N??,SEQ, where ? can be any character,
	NRA,SEQ ⎟ is selected
	etc. ⎠

Instructions that specify file names can use question marks and asterisks together. Here is an example:

Specified filename:	NUM??*
Selected filenames:	Any filename with five
	or more characters, the
	first three being NUM.
	The first encountered
	filename is selected.

Versions of the Disk Operating System

CBM BASIC disk handling statements rely on a group of programs referred to collectively as a disk operating system (or DOS). There is very little you need to know about the disk operating system in order to use it, just as you need to know little or nothing about the BASIC interpreter in order to write BASIC programs. But you should be aware of the fact that **many CBM disk operating system versions have been released. The version is identified by a number following DOS. Currently, versions 2.1 through 2.5 are in use. These are the DOS versions we are going to describe.**

Versions of CBM BASIC

Recall that several versions of CBM BASIC are in general use. BASIC 3.0 and earlier versions were shipped with all CBM computers until March of 1980. Since then, BASIC 4.0 has been shipped on the 8000 series.

BASIC versions 1.0, 2.0 and 3.0 are very similar. As stated in the preface, we refer to these three versions of BASIC collectively as BASIC<3.0. Version 4.0 is referred to as BASIC 4.0.

BASIC<3.0 supports sequential and random files. BASIC 4.0 supports sequential, relative or random files.

BASIC 4.0 recognizes all statements from lower numbered versions of BASIC. It also has some additional disk handling statements not present in lower BASIC versions. Therefore, if your CBM computer has BASIC 4.0, you can use any disk handling BASIC statements. **The converse is not true.** For example, if your CBM computer has BASIC 1.0, you cannot use any BASIC 4.0 statements.

BASIC 4.0 does not allow the second cassette drive to be used if disk drives are present.

BASIC 4.0 disk statements assume that disk drives are the default physical unit; if no physical unit is specified, physical unit 8 is assumed. In contrast, BASIC<3.0 statements assume cassette drive 1 (physical unit 1) if no physical unit is specified.

Although BASIC 4.0 will execute all BASIC<3.0 statements, there are some file errond status incompatibilities that result when you use BASIC<3.0 file handling statements with BASIC 4.0. For example, BASIC<3.0 does not support relative files; however, if you open a file using BASIC<3.0 statements and you do not specify the file type, BASIC 4.0 will open a relative file. Also, if you execute a file operation using BASIC<3.0 statements and the file operation is illegal under BASIC<3.0, but legal under BASIC 4.0, then the error indicator will turn red at the diskette drive, the disk operation is not executed, but BASIC 4.0 will report an OK disk operation status.

OPENING A DISKETTE FILE

Twelve memory buffers in each diskette unit are used to access files on diskettes held in drives 0 and/or 1. As soon as you access any diskette file, two of these buffers are used to support overhead operations. That leaves ten buffers in each diskette unit (two drives) via which the data files themselves can be accessed.

Two buffers are needed for each open sequential file. Three buffers are needed for each open relative file. Therefore BASIC<3.0 can have up to five sequential files open simultaneously on each diskette unit (but see below). The number of files which can be held open simultaneously by BASIC 4.0 depends on the combination of sequential and random files being accessed. For each diskette unit, the following combinations are allowed:

> 0 Relative and 5 Sequential files
> 1 Relative and 3 Sequential files
> 2 Relative and 2 Sequential files
> 3 Relative and 0 Sequential files

You can increase the total number of files that can be open at one time by adding more diskette units, but only up to a point. Each open file requires a unique secondary address, and only 13 secondary addresses are available for data files.

Secondary Addresses (BASIC<3.0)

BASIC<3.0 uses 16 secondary addresses: 0 through 15. Every BASIC<3.0 OPEN statement must specify a secondary address. BASIC 4.0 automatically assigns secondary addresses.

BASIC<3.0 secondary addresses are used as follows:

1. Address 0 is used to load programs from diskette into CBM computer memory.
2. Address 1 is used to save programs from computer memory on a diskette program file.
3. Secondary addresses 2 through 14 are used to access data files. You can select any one of these secondary addresses, providing it is not being used by another OPEN data file.
4. **Secondary address 15 opens a special "command channel"** which is used to access diskette status and to perform any of the special diskette operations described later in this chapter, under "Diskette Housekeeping Operations."

The Command Channel (BASIC<3.0)

The command channel needs special mention since it is very important.

BASIC 4.0 automatically opens a command channel when any diskette file is opened. You do not have to execute any statement in order to open the command channel using BASIC 4.0.

Using BASIC<3.0 you should always OPEN the command channel before performing any diskette operation; you should leave the command channel open until you have completed all diskette operations. Use the command channel with BASIC<3.0 to interrogate diskette status, and to perform special diskette operations.

Opening Diskette Data Files (BASIC 4.0)

With BASIC 4.0 you OPEN diskette data files using the DOPEN# statement. (You can also use the OPEN statement since BASIC 4.0 includes all BASIC<3.0 statements.)

The DOPEN# statement must specify a logical file number and a file name. The diskette drive is assumed to be D0 unless you include the parameter D1 to specify drive 1.

If you specify a record length using the LX parameter, then a relative file is assumed. You can read from a relative file, or write to it; no parameter specifies a read or write operation.

If no record length is included in the DOPEN# parameter list, then a sequential file is assumed. For a sequential file you must add the parameter W if the file is to be opened for a write operation; a read operation is assumed as the default case.

The physical unit number is assumed to be 8 unless you add an ON UZ parameter. Here are some examples of BASIC 4.0 DOPEN# statements:

`10 DOPEN#1,"MAIL"`	Open logical file 1 to access a sequential file named MAIL for a read operation. The diskette is in drive 0.
`50 DOPEN#1,"MAIL",D1,W`	Open logical file 1 to access a sequential file named MAIL for a write operation. The diskette is in drive 1.
`230 DOPEN#5,"DATALIST",D0 ON U5`	Open logical file 5 to access a sequential file named DATALIST for a read operation. The diskette is in drive 0 of a diskette unit being accessed as physical unit 5.
`100 DOPEN#2,"MAIL",L100`	Open logical file 2 in order to access a relative file named MAIL. The diskette is in drive 0. If the relative file is new, then its records will each have 100 characters (bytes). If the file already exists, then it must have been assigned 100 characters (bytes) when it was first opened. Read and write accesses are both allowed.
`25 DOPEN#3,"SAMPLE",L20,D1`	Open logical file 3 to access a relative file named SAMPLE for a read or write operation. The diskette is in drive 1. If the file is being opened for the first time, then its records will have 20 characters (bytes) each. If the file already exists, then it must have been assigned 20-character (byte) records when it was first opened.

File names can be specified using a string variable instead of a string. For example, the last example could be replaced by:

```
20 S$="SAMPLE"
25 DOPEN#3,S$,L20,D1
```

Opening Sequential Diskette Data File (BASIC<3.0)

Using BASIC<3.0 you open diskette files using the OPEN statement. The OPEN statements below duplicate those DOPEN# statements shown opening sequential files above. Remember, BASIC<3.0 cannot open or handle relative files. Secondary addresses have been selected arbitrarily for the OPEN statements below.

```
10 OPEN 1,8,2 "MAIL,SEQ"
50 OPEN 1,8,7 "1:MAIL,SEQ,WRITE"
230 OPEN 5,5,3 "0:DATALIST,SEQ"
```

The string portion of the OPEN statement parameter list can be created using a string variable. For example, the OPEN statement on line 10 could be replaced by these two statements:

```
5 M$="MAIL,SEQ"
10 OPEN 1,8,2,M$
```

Here is a more complex example that replaces the OPEN statement on line 50:

```
45 M$="MAIL,SEQ"
50 OPEN 1,8,7,"1:"+M$+",WRITE"
```

File Opening Errors

These are the conditions that can cause errors when you open a data file:

1. You will get a FILE NOT FOUND error if you OPEN a new sequential data file for a read operation. The sequential file must exist, since a new file will be empty when created, and you cannot read data out of an empty file.

2. If you open an old file but specify the wrong file type, then you will get a FILE TYPE MISMATCH error. This occurs if you open an old relative file as a sequential file, or if you open an old sequential file as a relative file, or if you open a program file as any type of data file.

3. You cannot open an old sequential file for a write access. If you do, you will get a FILE EXISTS error. You can only write into new sequential data files.

Misspelling a file name in an OPEN statement is an error that can cause you a lot of trouble without generating a warning. The disk operating system will simply assume that the misspelled file is a new file. If opening the new file would otherwise be valid, no error is reported.

CLOSING A DISKETTE FILE

To close any diskette data file you execute the BASIC 4.0 statement:

DCLOSE#N

or the BASIC<3.0 statement:

CLOSE N

where N is the logical file number appearing as the first parameter in the OPEN or DOPEN# statement.

You must CLOSE a file after writing to it, otherwise some data written to the file may be lost.

You do not have to CLOSE a file after reading from it, but to do so is good programming practice.

All open files are automatically closed by the computer when you execute an END statement. (This assumes that the diskette drives are still turned on.) Nevertheless it is good programming practice to close files individually using CLOSE statements rather than using the END statement to close all files. This subject was discussed in detail earlier in this chapter for cassette data files. The discussion on closing cassette data files applies also to diskette data files.

DISKETTE ERRORS AND ERROR STATUS

There is a red warning light which acts as an error indicator on all CBM diskette drives. This error indicator lights up red when a diskette operation is not successful. No other diskette operation can be performed until this error indicator has been cleared. To clear the error indicator, stop program execution by pressing the STOP key, then read diskette error status.

It is a good idea to read status after every diskette operation, and to include status checking as a routine part of all diskette handling program logic.

Recall that you cannot write to a diskette if its write-protect slot is covered. The diskette is said to be write-protected. **If you try to copy a file to a diskette that is write-protected, then the CBM computer will hang up.** The computer will endlessly try to write, but the diskette will not send back an error status. This situation manifests itself when the computer seems to be doing nothing, but you cannot stop program execution by pressing the STOP key. When this happens, you must remove the diskette from its disk drive, turn power off at the CBM computer, then turn power on again.

Clearing Diskette Error Status (BASIC 4.0)

Using BASIC 4.0 you can clear diskette errors in immediate mode, or in program mode.

To clear error status in immediate mode, execute an immediate mode PRINT statement to display numeric variable DS or string variable DS$.

Numeric variable DS returns status as a decimal number which should be interpreted using Table 6-2.

DS$ displays four parameters as follows:

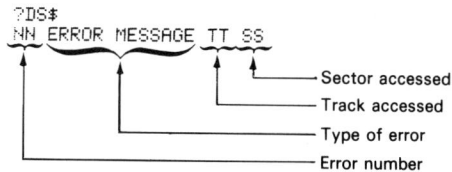

```
?DS$
NN ERROR MESSAGE TT SS
```
                                        ┌── Sector accessed
                                        ├── Track accessed
                                        ├── Type of error
                                        └── Error number

Diskette error messages are given in Appendix B.

A program written using BASIC 4.0 should **test diskette status by referencing variable DS** as follows:

```
20 IF DS <> 0 THEN PRINT "ERROR";
```

Following any diskette error this statement will clear the error status, stop program execution and display the message:

```
ERROR
BREAK IN XXXX
```

XXXX is the line number on which the STOP statement is located. A more informative variation displays DS$ to give the operator some idea what happened. Here are the necessary statements:

```
20 IF DS <> 0 THEN PRINT DS$:STOP
```

Following any diskette error, this statement will clear the error status, stop execution and display the message:

```
NN ERROR MESSAGE TT SS
BREAK IN XXXX
READY
▨
```

NN is the error number; see Appendix B for a summary of error numbers and what they mean. When the error occurred the sector being accessed is identified by TT (track) and SS (sector).

Diskette Errors (BASIC<3.0)

Using BASIC<3.0 you cannot access variables DS or DS$. To examine error status, **you must OPEN a logical file specifying physical unit 8 with secondary address 15. You must then input four string variables and display them.** In program mode this may be illustrated as follows:

```
10 OPEN 1,8,15
20 INPUT#1,A$,B$,C$,D$
30 PRINT A$,B$,C$,D$
40 CLOSE 1
```

The INPUT#1 statement will not execute in immediate mode.

A$, B$, C$ and D$ are the error message number (A$), the error message (B$), the track number (C$) and the sector number (D$) as illustrated above for DS$ using BASIC 4.0. A$, B$, C$ and D$ are arbitrarily selected string variable names. On lines 20 and 30 above you could use any four string variable names instead of A$, B$, C$ and D$.

When writing programs using BASIC<3.0 you should OPEN a logical file with physical unit address 8 and secondary address 15 before beginning any diskette access. Then test error status following every diskette operation by inputting the error message number. If this number is 0, the disk operation was successful. Here is necessary program logic:

```
10 OPEN 15,8,15
  .
150 Disk operation statement here
160 REM TEST DISKETTE STATUS
170 INPUT#15,A$,B$,C$,D$
180 IF VAL(A$)<>0 THEN PRINT A$,B$,C$,D$:ST
  .
  .
```

If a program contains numerous disk operations, then the statements shown on lines 170 and 180 above will reappear frequently. You may be tempted to put these statements into a subroutine. You can do so, but it will be more difficult to tell where the disk error occurred, since the STOP statement will always report a break on the same subroutine line. In contrast, if statements on 170 and 180 are repeated wherever they are needed, then by looking at the line where the break occurred, you can tell which STOP statement caused the break, and therefore which disk access caused the error.

DISKETTE HOUSEKEEPING OPERATIONS

In addition to reading and writing data files, file handling BASIC statements allow you to perform these operations:

1. Prepare a new diskette.
2. Erase an old diskette and prepare it for reuse.
3. Display a diskette's directory to see what files are stored on the diskette, and how much unused diskette space remains.
4. Check the diskette for sectors that have been allocated to a file but are still unused. Make these sectors generally available again, thereby increasing available diskette space.
5. Copy a file.
6. Copy an entire diskette.
7. Rename a file.
8. Delete a file from a diskette, or replace file contents.

Every BASIC<3.0 file or disk operation must begin with an OPEN statement. You can then read, write or perform one of the housekeeping operations described above. The operation must end with a CLOSE statement.

Using BASIC 4.0 you must OPEN a data file before reading from it or writing to it, and you must then CLOSE the data file. However the housekeeping operations described above are executed by special statements that do not need to be preceded by an OPEN, or followed by a CLOSE.

We will describe all of these housekeeping operations before looking at file handling program logic.

Although housekeeping operations are frequently performed in immediate mode, they can be executed in program mode.

BASIC statements used to perform housekeeping operations are described fully in Chapter 8. If you have trouble following any discussion because you do not understand a BASIC statement, read the BASIC statement description given in Chapter 8, then return and continue.

DISKETTE PREPARATION AND INITIALIZATION

You cannot take an unused diskette, load it into a disk drive and write data on it. First the diskette surface must be prepared. Sectors must be marked off on tracks, then the directory and block availability map must be written. The diskette is also assigned a name. You can prepare a used disk; this erases all prior data and readies the diskette for reuse.

You will usually prepare a diskette in immediate mode.

Diskette Preparation (BASIC 4.0)

Using BASIC 4.0 you prepare a new diskette using the HEADER statement, as follows:

HEADER "DISK NAME", DX, IYY

"DISK NAME" can be any string name with up to 16 characters. YY is a number which you must assign to the diskette. X is the drive number holding the diskette; it must be 0 or 1.

It takes approximately two minutes to prepare a diskette. If for any reason the diskette cannot be prepared, the following message is displayed:

?BAD DISK

This message will be displayed for any of these reasons:

1. You forgot to load a diskette into the selected drive.
2. You specified the wrong drive in the HEADER statement parameter list.
3. You forgot to specify a diskette number in the HEADER statement parameter list.
4. The diskette is write-protected (the write-protect notch is covered).
5. The diskette has a defective magnetic surface.

When preparing a used diskette you only need specify the drive number in the HEADER statement parameter list. If you specify a disk name, then it will replace the old disk name; if you do not, then the old disk name will be retained. If you specify a disk number, then it will replace the old disk number; if you do not, the old disk number will be retained. But you cannot specify a new disk number unless you also specify a new disk name. You will get a syntax error if you try it.

Recall that BASIC 4.0 assumes that the diskette drive is physical unit number 8. If for any reason you are initializing a diskette using a disk drive with a different physical unit number, then you must add this information to the HEADER statement parameter list using: ON UZ or, UZ, where Z is the physical unit number.

It takes just a few seconds to prepare a used diskette.

Below are some examples of immediate mode HEADER statements. Subsequent dialogue is not shown.

`HEADER "SAMPLE",D0, I01`	A diskette is prepared on drive 0. The diskette is given the name SAMPLE and the number 01.
`HEADER D0`	An old diskette is prepared on drive 0. The old name and diskette number are preserved.
`HEADER "NEW", D1`	An old diskette is prepared on drive 1. The diskette is given the new name NEW, but it retains its old diskette number.
`HEADER "SAMPLE", D0, I05, ON U7`	A diskette is prepared in drive 0 of a diskette drive with physical unit number 7. The diskette is given the name SAMPLE and the number 05.
`HEADER D1, I01` `$ SYNTAX ERROR`	The HEADER statement will not execute because a new diskette number has been specified without a new disk name.

Diskette Preparation (BASIC<3.0)

To prepare a diskette using BASIC<3.0 you must OPEN the diskette command channel, then execute a PRINT# statement using the logical file specified in the OPEN statement parameter list. The PRINT# statement must have the following character string enclosed in quotes:

"NEWX:DISKNAME,YY"

NEW may be replaced by N. X is the drive number; it must be 0 or 1. DISKNAME is the name which will be assigned to the diskette; it can be any valid 16 character string. YY is the diskette number.

The OPEN statement which opens the diskette command channel can specify any logical file number, but it must specify physical unit number 8 and secondary address 15.

Here are some examples of BASIC<3.0 diskette initialization statements:

`OPEN 1,8,15` `PRINT#1, "N0:SAMPLE,01"`	A diskette is initialized in drive 0. It is given the name SAMPLE and the number 01.
`OPEN 3,8,15` `PRINT#3,"NEW1:NEW,01"`	A diskette is initialized in drive 1 with the name NEW and the number 01.

BASIC<3.0 diskette preparation does not always work on a CBM computer that has BASIC 4.0. Sometimes the disk drive continues to spin the diskette after initialization has been completed.

BASIC<3.0 allows you to prepare an old diskette, in which case everything previously stored on the diskette is erased, and the surface is prepared for reuse. You do not have to specify a diskette number in the PRINT# parameter list when preparing an old diskette; the old diskette number will be used if no new number is specified.

Diskette Initialization (BASIC<3.0)

When using BASIC<3.0, you must initialize a diskette that has data stored on it before opening a file. To initialize the diskette you OPEN the command channel and execute a PRINT# statement with the letter "I" or the word "INITIALIZE", plus the drive number appearing as a string variable in the PRINT# statement parameter list. The drive number can be omitted, in which case diskettes in both drives will be initialized.

Diskettes are usually initialized in program mode.
When a diskette is initialized, no data on the diskette surface is changed.
Here are some examples of BASIC<3.0 diskette initialization statements:

```
10 OPEN 1,8,15          Initialize a diskette in drive 0.
20 PRINT#1,"I0"

5 OPEN 3,8,15           Initialize two diskettes in drives 0 and 1.
10 PRINT#1, "INITIALIZE"
```

You do not have to initialize a diskette that you have just prepared. Preparation also initializes the diskette.

DISPLAYING THE DISKETTE DIRECTORY

Displaying the Diskette Directory (BASIC 4.0)

Before accessing any diskette, it is advisable to display the diskette directory. Using BASIC 4.0 this is done using the DIRECTORY statement. The DIRECTORY statement is usually executed in immediate mode. Here are some examples of the directory statement:

DIRECTORY	Display directories for diskettes in drives 0 and 1.
DIRECTORY D1	Display directory for diskette in drive 1.
DIRECTORY D1 ON U8	This statement also displays the directory for the diskette in drive 1 since the physical unit 8 is the default physical unit.
DIRECTORY D0	Display the directory for the diskette in drive 0.

The word CATALOG can be used instead of DIRECTORY.
The directory is displayed as follows:

```
0       "Diskette name      "NNXX

BBBB    "Filename"      Type
BBBB    "Filename"      Type
              etc.

YYYY BLOCKS FREE
```

The diskette name and number appears at the top of the display in a reverse field. NN is the diskette number. XX is the DOS version number. Below a list of file names is displayed. These are the files recorded on the diskette. To the left of the file name is the number of blocks (sectors) assigned to the file. To the right of the file name is the file type: REL for a relative file, SEQ for a sequential file, or PRG for a program file. Finally, the number of unused blocks (sectors) is displayed. (There are also user files which are described in Chapter 7.)

There must be a diskette in every drive specified by the DIRECTORY statement. A very common error is to type DIRECTORY when you want to display the DIRECTORY for a diskette in drive 0. If there is no diskette in drive 1, then the error indicator will turn red and no directories will be displayed. Remember, you must clear the error indicator by reading diskette status (type ?DS$<CR>). You cannot use the diskette drive again until the error indicator has been cleared. You will also get an error indication if you specify the wrong drive in the DIRECTORY statement. For example, if there is a diskette in drive 1 but you enter the immediate statement:

DIRECTORY D0

then you will get an error indication, but no directory.

Displaying the Diskette Directory (BASIC<3.0)

Using BASIC<3.0 you display the directory using a LOAD statement as follows:

LOAD "$X",Y

X is the drive number (0 or 1) and Y is the physical unit number (usually 8). The dialogue that follows is standard program-loading dialogue. After the program is loaded, you list it in order to display the directory. The following example displays the directory for a diskette in drive 0.

```
LOAD "$0", 8
SEARCHING FOR $0
LOADING
READY
LIST
```

COLLECTING A DISKETTE

BASIC 4.0 has a COLLECT statement which you can use to "houseclean" a diskette.

The COLLECT statement identifies sectors that have been assigned to data files but are unused. These sectors are made available again, and the diskette directory is modified appropriately.

The COLLECT statement is usually executed in immediate mode, as follows:

COLLECT   *Collect diskettes on both drives.*

COLLECT D0   *Collect the diskette in drive 0.*

COPYING FILES AND DISKETTES

You should make backup copies of every file that you wish to keep permanently. At least one copy of the file should be on a different diskette. Keeping a copy of the file on the same diskette will not help if the entire diskette is erased by accident.

CBM BASIC statements allows you to copy an individual file or backup an entire diskette.

Copying Files (BASIC 4.0)

The BASIC 4.0 COPY statement lets you copy a single file or an entire diskette. But the COPY statement will only address one physical unit, therefore copies must be made on the same diskette, or using the two drives in a single diskette unit.

If a file name is specified in the COPY statement parameter list, then a single file is copied. If no file name is specified, then all files on the diskette are copied. Here are some immediate mode examples:

```
COPY D0 TO D1
```
Copy all files on the diskette in drive 0 to the diskette in drive 1.

```
COPY D0, "TESTDATA" TO D1, "TESTDATA"
```
Copy file "TESTDATA" from the diskette in drive 0 to the diskette in drive 1. Keep the filename.

```
COPY D1, "TESTDATA" TO D0, "NEWTEST"
```
Copy file "TESTDATA" from the diskette in drive 1 to the diskette in drive 0. Rename the file "NEWTEST."

Copying Files (BASIC<3.0)

In order to copy files using BASIC<3.0, use the PRINT# statement with the following string parameter:

"COPYM:NEWNAME=N:OLDNAME"

Instead of COPY you can have the letter C. N is the drive number holding the (old) source file diskette; OLDNAME represents the name of the source file. M is the drive number holding the (new) destination file diskette; NEWNAME represents the name which will be assigned to the new destination file.

Here are some examples:

```
OPEN 15,8,15
PRINT#15, "COPY1:MAILDATA=0:MAILDATA"
CLOSE 15
```
Copy a file named "MAILDATA" from the diskette in drive 0 to the diskette in drive 1. Keep the filename.

```
OPEN 15,8,15
PRINT#15, "C0:NEWTEST=1:TESTDATA"
CLOSE 15
```
Copy file "TESTDATA" from the diskette in drive 1 to the diskette in drive 0. Rename the file "NEWTEST."

Concatenating Files (BASIC<3.0)

In the course of copying files, the BASIC<3.0 PRINT# statement allows two, three, or four source files to be concatenated into a single destination file. The following immediate mode example concatenates data files DATA1 and DATA2, taken from the diskette in drive 0, and writes them to the diskette in drive 1, assigning the name DATAX to the concatenated data file:

```
OPEN 15,8,15
PRINT#15,"C1:DATAX=1:DATA1,1:DATA2"
CLOSE 15
```

Concatenated source files do not have to come from the same diskette, as shown above. DATAX could be concatenated from data files residing on the same diskette and/or the other diskette.

File Copying Errors

A copy operation cannot specify a destination file name that already exists. If it does, the COPY operation will not occur. The error light of the diskette drive will turn red; when you fetch error status, a FILE EXISTS error will be reported.

When copying all files from one diskette to another using the BASIC 4.0 COPY statement, if a source file name is found to exist on the destination diskette, then the COPY operation stops immediately. The error indicator at the diskette drive turns red. No files get copied if their names appear on the source diskette directory after the duplicated file name.

Duplicating a Diskette

You can copy all files from one diskette to another; you can also backup a diskette by making a duplicate of it. The two are not the same. The backup operation creates a destination diskette which is an exact duplicate of the source, with the same diskette name and number as well as the same files. In contrast, if you copy all files from a source diskette to the destination diskette, the destination diskette name does not change, nor do any files which were previously on the destination diskette. Thus the destination diskette will have a different name, and although it will have all of the source diskette files, it may also have additional files which the source diskette did not have.

Backup a Diskette (BASIC 4.0)

Use the BASIC 4.0 BACKUP statement to duplicate a diskette. You can copy from drive 0 to drive 1 or from drive 1 to drive 0 of any valid physical unit. Here are some examples of the BACKUP statement executed in immediate mode:

```
BACKUP D0 TO D1          Make a copy of the diskette in drive 0 on the diskette in drive 1.

BACKUP D1 TO D0 ON U5    Make a copy of the diskette in drive 1 on the diskette in drive 0.
                         The disk unit is addressed as physical unit 5.
```

The BACKUP statement lets you copy onto a diskette that has not been prepared. If necessary the destination diskette is prepared before the BACKUP operation begins.

Duplicating a Diskette (BASIC<3.0)

Use the PRINT# statement to copy a diskette using BASIC<3.0. You can copy from drive 1 to drive 0, or from drive 0 to drive 1. You cannot copy from a drive in one physical unit to a drive in another physical unit. The PRINT# statement must have the following string variable in its parameter list:

"DUPLICATEN=M"

Instead of DUPLICATE you can use D. N is the destination drive number; M is the source drive number.

Here is an immediate mode example:

```
OPEN 15,8,15      Make a copy of the diskette in drive 0 on the diskette in drive 1 .
PRINT#15, "D1=0"
CLOSE 15
```

RENAMING A FILE

You can rename any program or data file. Most frequently program files are renamed in the normal course of writing and correcting programs.

Renaming a File (BASIC 4.0)

Use the BASIC 4.0 RENAME statement to rename a single file. Here is an immediate mode example:

```
RENAME D0, "SEQ.NUM.B4" TO "SEQNUM"
```

Rename a File (BASIC<3.0)

To rename a single file using BASIC<3.0 use the PRINT# statement with the following string variable in its parameter list:

```
                      "RENAMEX:NEWNAME=OLDNAME"
```

Instead of RENAME you can have R. X is the drive number holding the diskette on which the file being renamed is stored. NEWNAME is the new file name; it replaces OLDNAME, the old file name.

Here is an immediate mode example:

```
OPEN 15,8,15                            The file on drive 0 named "SEQ. NUM. B4" is
PRINT#15, "R0:SEQNUM=SEQ.NUM.B4"            renamed "SEQNUM"
CLOSE 15
```

DELETING FILES

You can delete any file from a diskette. When you delete a file in immediate mode the CBM computer will always display the prompt message ARE YOUR SURE? You must respond by typing "YES", and then a carriage return, otherwise the file will not be deleted. If you delete a file in program mode, no prompt message is displayed.

Scratch a File (BASIC 4.0)

Using BASIC 4.0 you delete a file using the SCRATCH statement. Here is an immediate mode example:

```
SCRATCH D0, "REL.NUM.B4"         Delete file REL.NUM. B4 on drive D0
```

Here is the program mode version of the immediate mode example given above:

```
  .
  .
240 DCLOSE
250 SCRATCH D0, "REL.NUM.B4"
  .
  .
```

Some versions of BASIC 4.0 have a problem with the SCRATCH statement; it will not delete files that were not properly closed. You can solve this problem by collecting the diskette, and then scratching the file.

Scratch a File (BASIC<3.0)

Using BASIC<3.0 you can scratch one or more files using a single PRINT# statement. The PRINT# statement must have the following string variable in its parameter list:

"SCRATCHX:FILENAME"

Instead of SCRATCH you can use S. X is the drive number holding the diskette with the file being scratched. FILENAME is the name of the file being scratched. For a single file this may be illustrated as follows in immediate mode:

```
OPEN 15,8,15              Delete file REL. NUM. B4 on drive 0
PRINT#15, "S0:REL.NUM.B4"
CLOSE 15
```

To delete two or more files you simply add the drive number and file name to the parameter string. For example, you can modify the statements illustrated above and delete two files as follows:

```
OPEN 15,8,15                   Delete file REL. NUM. B4 on drive 0 and file
PRINT#15, "S0:REL.NUM.B4,1:REL.NUM.B<3"      REL.NUM.B<3 on drive 1
CLOSE 15
```

If you place an asterisk after one or more letters of a file name, then any file whose name has the letters preceding the asterisk will be deleted. Consider the following example:

```
OPEN 15,8,15
PRINT#15, "S0:NUM*"
CLOSE 15
```

Any file on drive 0 whose name begins with the three letters NUM will be deleted.

If you replace a character in a file name with a question mark, then the name of the file to be scratched can have any character in that position.

For example the following statements delete a file whose name begins with NUM, ends with .SEQ, and has four characters in between.

```
OPEN 15,8,15
PRINT#15, "S0:NUM????.SEQ"
CLOSE 15
```

Replace a File (BASIC<3.0)

Although BASIC<3.0 does not allow you to write into an old file, it does allow the contents of an old file to be replaced. The old file should be opened for a write operation with an @ sign appearing as the first character in the parameter list string variable. For example, the MAIL file opened on line 50 below could be an old file:

```
50 OPEN 1,8,7,"@1:MAIL,SEQ,WRITE"
```

SEQUENTIAL DATA FILES

BASIC 4.0 and BASIC<3.0 both support sequential data files.

A sequential data file is opened either for a read access or for a write access, never for both. When a new sequential file is opened, the process of opening the file also creates it. The new sequential file must be opened for a write operation; it cannot be opened for a read operation. An existing sequential file must be opened for a read operation; it cannot be opened for a write operation.

SEQUENTIAL FILE FIELD SEPARATORS

Numeric variables in a sequential data file must be terminated by carriage return characters. String variables may be terminated by comma characters or by carriage return characters.

We recommend that you **use carriage return characters to separate all fields in sequential data files.** Using comma characters to separate string variables offers no identifiable advantage and can cause unnecessary programming problems.

If all fields are terminated with a carriage return, then rules for writing to sequential data files are very simple: use the PRINT# statement with a parameter list which in a PRINT statement would display variables on the screen as a single vertical column. The data is read back using INPUT# or GET# statements. Using BASIC 4.0 with DOS 2.0, PRINT# statements automatically add a carriage return character at the end of a line if the logical file number is 128 or higher. No terminating carriage return character is output if the file number is 127 or less.

WRITING NUMERIC DATA TO A SEQUENTIAL FILE

Beginning with a very simple example, we will write a program that opens a sequential file, then writes ten records to the file, with ten numbers in each record, as follows:

Record 1:	1	2	3	4	5	6	7	8	9	10
Record 2:	101	102	103	104	105	106	107	108	109	110
Record 3:	201	202	203	204	205	206	207	208	209	210
Record 4:	301	302	303	304	305	306	307	308	309	310
Record 5:	401	402	403	404	405	406	407	408	409	410
etc.										

The program will read the records back and display them. Listings for BASIC 4.0 and BASIC<3.0 versions of this program are given below. The programs are named SEQ.NUM.B4 and SEQ.NUM.B3.

BASIC 4.0 Version

```
10 REM PROGRAM "SEQ.NUM.B4"
20 DOPEN#1,"TESTDATA",W
30 IF DS<>0 THEN PRINT DS$:STOP
40 REM WRITE TEN RECORDS
50 FOR R=1 TO 10
60 REM WRITE TEN FIELDS PER RECORD
70 FOR F=1 TO 10
80 PRINT#1,(R-1)*100+F
85 IF DS<>0 THEN PRINT DS$:STOP
90 NEXT F
100 NEXT R
```

```
110 DCLOSE#1
200 REM NOW READ BACK FILE CONTENTS AND DISPLAY IT
210 DOPEN#1,"TESTDATA"
215 IF DS<>0 THEN PRINT DS$:STOP
220 FOR R=1 TO 10
230 PRINT "RECORD";R;
240 REM INPUT CONTENTS OF NEXT RECORD AND DISPLAY IT
250 FOR F=1 TO 10
260 INPUT#1,N
265 IF DS<>0 THEN PRINT DS$:STOP
270 PRINTN;
280 NEXT F
290 PRINT
300 NEXT R
310 DCLOSE#1
320 SCRATCH D0,"TESTDATA"
330 STOP
```

BASIC< 3.0 Version

```
10 REM PROGRAM "SEQ.NUM.B<3"
20 OPEN 15,8,15:REM COMMAND CHANNEL
21 INPUT#15,A$,B$,C$,D$
22 IF VAL(A$)<>0 THEN PRINT A$,B$,C$,D$
23 PRINT#15,"I0"
24 OPEN 1,8,2,"0:TESTDATA<3,SEQ,W":REM DATA FILE
30 INPUT#15,A$,B$,C$,D$
31 IF VAL(A$)<>0 THEN PRINT A$,B$,C$,D$
40 REM WRITE TEN RECORDS
50 FOR R=1 TO 10
60 REM WRITE TEN FIELDS PER RECORD
70 FOR F=1 TO 10
80 PRINT#1,(R-1)*100+F
85 INPUT#15,A$,B$,C$,D$
86 IF VAL(A$)<>0 THEN PRINT A$,B$,C$,D$
90 NEXT F
100 NEXT R
110 CLOSE 1
120 CLOSE 15
200 REM NOW READ BACK FILE CONTENTS AND DISPLAY IT
210 OPEN 15,8,15:REM COMMAND CHANNEL
211 INPUT#15,A$,B$,C$,D$
212 IF VAL(A$)<>0 THEN PRINT A$,B$,C$,D$
213 OPEN 1,8,2,"0:TESTDATA<3,SEQ":REM DATA FILE
215 INPUT#15,A$,B$,C$,D$
216 IF VAL(A$)<>0 THEN PRINT A$,B$,C$,D$
220 FOR R=1 TO 10
230 PRINT "RECORD";R;
240 REM INPUT CONTENTS OF NEXT RECORD AND DISPLAY IT
250 FOR F=1 TO 10
260 INPUT#1,N
265 INPUT#15,A$,B$,C$,D$
266 IF VAL(A$)<>0 THEN PRINT A$,B$,C$,D$
270 PRINTN;
280 NEXT F
290 PRINT
300 NEXT R
310 CLOSE 1
320 SCRATCH D0,"TESTDATA<3"
330 CLOSE 15
340 STOP
```

Key in the version of the program that will work on your CBM computer, check it carefully for errors, save the program, then run it. You should get the display shown below when you run the program.

```
RECORD 1    1    2    3    4    5    6    7    8    9   10
RECORD 2  101  102  103  104  105  106  107  108  109  110
RECORD 3  201  202  203  204  205  206  207  208  209  210
RECORD 4  301  302  303  304  305  306  307  308  309  310
RECORD 5  401  402  403  404  405  406  407  408  409  410
RECORD 6  501  502  503  504  505  506  507  508  509  510
RECORD 7  601  602  603  604  605  606  607  608  609  610
RECORD 8  701  702  703  704  705  706  707  708  709  710
RECORD 9  801  802  803  804  805  806  807  808  809  810
RECORD 10 901  902  903  904  905  906  907  908  909  910
```

Let us examine program logic.

Statements on lines 10 through 120 create the sequential data file and write ten records into it. Statements on lines 200 through 320 read the contents of the sequential data file, record by record, and display data as it is read.

Look at how files have been opened and closed.

In the BASIC 4.0 version sequential data file TESTDATA is opened for a write operation by the DOPEN# statement on line 20. Logical file number 1 is used by the DOPEN# statement. The file is closed on line 110 before being reopened for a read operation by the DOPEN# statement on line 210. Logical file number 1 is used again by the DOPEN# statement on line 210; reusing the same logical file number for the same data file is not necessary. Logical file 1 is closed finally on line 310.

The BASIC<3.0 version of the program opens its sequential data file TESTDATA<3 for a write operation using the OPEN statement on line 24. Logical file number 1 is used with secondary address 2. The file is closed on line 110 before being reopened for a read operation by the OPEN statement on line 213. TESTDATA<3 is finally closed on line 310. The BASIC<3.0 program also opens the command channel via the OPEN statement on line 20 using logical file number 15, which is optional, and secondary address 15, which is necessary. It is common practice to use logical file #15 for the command channel in BASIC<3 programs since the secondary address associates this number with the command channel. The command channel is closed on line 120, it is reopened on line 210, and closed finally on line 330. The command channel does not have to be closed and reopened. Lines 120 and 210 could be eliminated. But closing and reopening the command channel establishes the two halves of the program as separate modules which can be executed independently.

Notice that the BASIC<3.0 program initializes the diskette on line 23. Strictly speaking, the diskette should be re-initialized after the command channel is reopened on line 210 if the two halves of the program are to be treated as separate modules.

The BASIC 4.0 and BASIC<3.0 programs both scratch the data file at the end of the program (on line 320). If the data file were not scratched you would not be able to re-execute the program. Try eliminating statement 320 and running the program twice. On the second execution you will get a FILE ALREADY EXISTS error when the data file is opened for a write operation (on line 20 in the BASIC 4.0 version and on line 24 in the BASIC<3.0).

You should scratch temporary data files at the end of a program if the data held in the file does not need to be saved. If the temporary data file is not scratched it cannot be reused when the program is re-executed.

Next look at the diskette status logic in the two programs; this logic is missing from most programs written by programmers who are in a hurry. (BASIC 4.0 and BASIC<3.0 statements needed to test diskette status were described earlier in this chapter.)

The BASIC 4.0 program tests diskette status on lines 30, 85, 215, and 265. In each case the status string variable DS$ is displayed to identify a problem when status is not 0. Program execution is then stopped.

The BASIC<3.0 program executes the same logic by inputting status via string variables A$, B$, C$, and D$. If the numeric value of A$ is not zero, then the four variables are displayed. The disk status testing statements can be found on lines 21 and 22, 30 and 31, 85 and 86, 210 and 211, 215 and 216, 265 and 266.

The BASIC 4.0 and BASIC<3.0 programs contain identical statements to write records to the sequential data file, to read records back, and to display data.

Records are written to the sequential data file by statements on lines 50 through 100. The outer FOR-NEXT loop, indexed by R, counts records; the inner FOR-NEXT loop, indexed by F, counts fields within records. The PRINT# statement on line 80 writes each field to the sequential data file. Since there is only one variable in the PRINT# statement parameter list, a carriage return is forced; you do not have to force one. Remember, if the PRINT# statement rewritten as PRINT statements would display fields in a single vertical column, then the fields will be written correctly to the diskette data file.

Statements on lines 220 through 300 read data back from the sequential file and display the data. The outer FOR-NEXT loop indexed by R reads records; the PRINT statement on line 230 starts each record display with the record number. The inner FOR-NEXT loop indexed for F read fields one at a time using the INPUT# statement on line 260. Fields for a single record are displayed on one line by the PRINT statement on line 270. The PRINT statement on line 290 forces a carriage return after each record has been displayed.

Although we have described the sequential data file as consisting of ten records with ten fields in each record, on the diskette surface the sequential file consists of 100 fields separated by carriage return characters. If you were to look at the data as stored on the diskette surface, you would find nothing to identify the end of one record or the beginning of the next. Program logic must keep track of records and fields.

To demonstrate the lack of any real file structure on the diskette, **change the second half of the program so that it assumes 12 records, with 8 fields per record.** Statements on lines 220 and 250 must change as follows:

```
220 FOR R=1 TO 12
250 FOR F=1 TO 8
```

Make these changes in your program, then run it. The following display will appear:

```
RECORD 1    1    2    3    4    5    6    7    8
RECORD 2    9   10  101  102  103  104  105  106
RECORD 3  107  108  109  110  201  202  203  204
RECORD 4  205  206  207  208  209  210  301  302
RECORD 5  303  304  305  306  307  308  309  310
RECORD 6  401  402  403  404  405  406  407  408
RECORD 7  409  410  501  502  503  504  505  506
RECORD 8  507  508  509  510  601  602  603  604
RECORD 9  605  606  607  608  609  610  701  702
RECORD 10 703  704  705  706  707  708  709  710
RECORD 11 801  802  803  804  805  806  807  808
RECORD 12 809  810  901  902  903  904  905  906
```

Each record begins reading fields wherever the previous record left off. No attention was paid to the field/record organization used when the file was written.

When a single PRINT# statement writes two or more numeric variables to a data file, you must force carriage return characters using the CHR$ function. Suppose on line 80 we output R, F and the computed expression. The PRINT# statement would have to be rewritten as follows:

```
80 PRINT#1,R,CHR$(13),F,CHR$(13),(R-1)*100+F
```

Usually the carriage return character is assigned to a string variable and the string variable is used in the PRINT# statement as follows:

```
15 C$=CHR$(13)
     .
     .
80 PRINT#1,R,C$,F,C$,(R-1)*100+F
```

There are now 30 numbers in each record, not 10. Therefore 30 numbers must be read and displayed for each record in the second half of the program. A simple (but inelegant) way of displaying 30 numbers would be to change the FOR statement on line 250, increasing the upper index of F from 10 to 30, as follows:

```
250 FOR F=1 TO 30
```

Make these changes, then run the program to assure yourself that three numbers were written out each time the PRINT# statement on line 80 was executed.

WRITING STRING DATA TO A SEQUENTIAL FILE

String variables can be separated using comma characters or carriage return characters. However, the use of comma character separators serves no useful purpose when string variables are stored in sequential files. Therefore **we will end all sequential file text variables using carriage return characters.**

There is no difference between program logic needed to write string variables or numeric variables to a sequential file.

We will write a simple mailing list program to illustrate string variables being stored in a sequential data file. Listings for BASIC 4.0 and BASIC<3.0 versions of this program are given below, followed by an illustration of program execution.

BASIC 4.0 Version

```
10 REM PROGRAM "SEQ.MAIL.B4"
20 REM MAILING LIST PROGRAM TO ILLUSTRATE DISKETTE FILE STRING HANDLING
30 DATA "   NAME: "," STREET: ","   CITY: "," STATE: ","    ZIP: "
40 DOPEN#1,"SEQ.MAILDATA",W
50 IF DS<>0 THEN PRINT DS$:STOP
60 PRINT"⊃ ENTER NAME AND ADDRESS:▨▨"
70 FOR I=1 TO 5
80 READ F$
90 PRINTF$;:INPUT AD$(I)
100 NEXT I
110 RESTORE
120 PRINT"ENTER Y TO RECORD,N TO RE-ENTER";
130 GET Y$:IF Y$<>"Y" AND Y$<>"N" THEN 130
135 PRINTY$
140 IF Y$="N" THEN 60
150 REM WRITE NAME AND ADDRESS TO SEQUENTIAL FILE
160 FOR I=1 TO 5
170 PRINT#1,AD$(I)
180 NEXT I
190 PRINT"ENTER Y FOR ANOTHER NAME AND ADDRESS,N TO END";
200 GET Y$:IF Y$<>"Y" AND Y$<>"N" THEN 200
205 PRINTY$
210 IF Y$="Y" THEN 60
220 DCLOSE#1
```

```
300 REM DISPLAY NAMES AND ADDRESSES ONE AT A TIME
310 DOPEN#1,"SEQ.MAILDATA"
330 IF DS<>0 THEN PRINT DS$:STOP
340 REM CLEAR SCREEN AND DISPLAY NAME AND ADDRESS
350 PRINT"█"
360 RESTORE
370 FOR I=1 TO 5
380 READ F$:PRINT F$;
390 INPUT#1,AD$
400 IF DS<>0 THEN PRINT DS$:STOP
410 PRINT AD$
420 NEXT I
430 PRINT"ENTER Y FOR ANOTHER NAME AND ADDRESS,N TO END";
440 GET Y$:IF Y$<>"Y" AND Y$<>"N" THEN 440
450 IF Y$="Y" THEN 350
460 DCLOSE#1
470 SCRATCH D0,"SEQ.MAILDATA"
480 STOP
```

BASIC<3.0 Version

```
10 REM PROGRAM "SEQ.MAIL.B<3"
20 REM MAILING LIST PROGRAM TO ILLUSTRATE DISKETTE FILE STRING HANDLING
30 DATA "    NAME: "," STREET: ","   CITY: ","  STATE: ","    ZIP: "
40 OPEN 15,8,15:REM COMMAND CHANNEL
41 INPUT#15,A$,B$,C$,D$
42 IF VAL(A$)<>0 THEN PRINT A$,B$,C$,D$
43 PRINT#15,"I0"
44 OPEN 1,8,2,"0:MAILDATA<3,SEQ,W"
50 INPUT#15,A$,B$,C$,D$
51 IF VAL(A$)<>0 THEN PRINT A$,B$,C$,D$
60 PRINT"█ ENTER NAME AND ADDRESS:██"
70 FOR I=1 TO 5
80 READ F$
90 PRINTF$;:INPUT AD$(I)
100 NEXT I
110 RESTORE
120 PRINT"ENTER Y TO RECORD,N TO RE-ENTER";
130 GET Y$:IF Y$<>"Y" AND Y$<>"N" THEN 130
135 PRINTY$
140 IF Y$="N" THEN 60
150 REM WRITE NAME AND ADDRESS TO SEQUENTIAL FILE
160 FOR I=1 TO 5
170 PRINT#1,AD$(I)
180 NEXT I
190 PRINT"ENTER Y FOR ANOTHER NAME AND ADDRESS,N TO END";
200 GET Y$:IF Y$<>"Y" AND Y$<>"N" THEN 200
205 PRINTY$
210 IF Y$="Y" THEN 60
220 CLOSE 1
300 REM DISPLAY NAMES AND ADDRESSES ONE AT A TIME
310 OPEN 1,8,2,"0:MAILDATA<3,SEQ"
320 INPUT#15,A$,B$,C$,D$
321 IF VAL(A$)<>0 THEN PRINT A$,B$,C$,D$
330 IF DS<>0 THEN PRINT DS$:STOP
340 REM CLEAR SCREEN AND DISPLAY NAME AND ADDRESS
350 PRINT"█"
360 RESTORE
370 FOR I=1 TO 5
380 READ F$:PRINT F$;
390 INPUT#1,AD$
400 INPUT#15,A$,B$,C$,D$
401 IF VAL(A$)<>0 THEN PRINT A$,B$,C$,D$
410 PRINT AD$
420 NEXT I
430 PRINT"ENTER Y FOR ANOTHER NAME AND ADDRESS,N TO END";
440 GET Y$:IF Y$<>"Y" AND Y$<>"N" THEN 440
450 IF Y$="Y" THEN 350
460 CLOSE 1
470 SCRATCH D0,"SEQ.MAILDATA"
480 STOP
```

```
ENTER NAME AND ADDRESS:


    NAME: JO BLOW
  STREET: 125 5TH. AVE
    CITY: NEW YORK
   STATE: NY
     ZIP: 10010
ENTER Y TO RECORD,N TO RE-ENTERY
ENTER Y FOR ANOTHER NAME AND ADDRESS,N TO ENDY
ENTER NAME AND ADDRESS:


    NAME: FRED SMITH
  STREET: 23 ROYAL RD.
    CITY: BERKELEY
   STATE: CA
     ZIP: 94708
ENTER Y TO RECORD,N TO RE-ENTERY
ENTER Y FOR ANOTHER NAME AND ADDRESS,N TO ENDN


    NAME: JO BLOW
  STREET: 125 5TH. AVE
    CITY: NEW YORK
   STATE: NY
     ZIP: 10010
ENTER Y FOR ANOTHER NAME AND ADDRESS,N TO END


    NAME: FRED SMITH
  STREET: 23 ROYAL RD.
    CITY: BERKELEY
   STATE: CA
     ZIP: 94708
```

Let us examine program logic.

Statements on lines 40 through 220 input names and addresses from the keyboard, then output the names and addresses to a sequential data file. Statements on lines 300 through 460 read names and addresses from the sequential data file and display them.

The sequential data file is named SEQ.MAILDATA in **the BASIC 4.0 program**. This sequential file is opened on line 40 for a write operation; it is closed on line 220. The file is reopened on line 310 for a read operation, and finally closed on line 460. In **the BASIC<3.0 version** of the program the sequential data file is named MAILDATA<3. The file is opened on line 44 for a write operation; it is closed on line 220. The file is reopened on line 310 for a read operation, and finally closed on line 460.

Both programs scratch the sequential data file on line 470 so that the program can be rerun. A real mailing list program would not scratch the file; mailing lists need to be preserved. Instead, additional names and addresses would be appended to the file. Appending data to sequential files is described next.

File status is tested in the BASIC 4.0 version of the program by statements on line 50, 330, and 400. In the BASIC<3.0 version file status is tested on lines 41 and 42, 50 and 51, 320 and 321, and 400 and 401. File status statement logic was described earlier in this chapter.

Notice that SEQ.MAIL.B<3 opens a command channel at the beginning of the program on line 40. The STOP statement on line 480 is allowed to close the command channel; this is not good programming practice, but it will work.

Identical statements are used by the BASIC 4.0 and BASIC<3.0 versions of the mailing list program to read data from the keyboard, write data to the sequential file, read data from the sequential file, and display data on the screen.

Statements on lines 60 through 140 input names and addresses from the keyboard. Names and addresses are input as five fields by the FOR-NEXT loop on lines 70 through 100. Notice that the operator's prompt message is identified by string variable F$ which is read from the DATA statement on line 30. The five fields of the name and address are input to string array AD$(I). The RESTORE statement on line 110 restores the data pointer to select the first string variable of the DATA statement.

Statements on lines 120 through 140 are standard operator dialogue which allow the operator to re-enter the entire name and address, or record it. This type of dialogue was described frequently in Chapter 5. Note that very primitive error recovery logic is provided since our goal is to demonstrate file handling; we are not trying to illustrate good data entry programming practice.

The name and address is written to the sequential data file by the FOR-NEXT loop on lines 160 through 180. Since one string variable is output each time the PRINT# statement on line 170 is executed, a carriage return is forced. We could replace statements on lines 160 through 180 with these two statements:

```
160 C$=CHR$(13)
170 PRINT#1,AD$(1),C$,AD$(2),C$,AD$(3),C$,AD$(4),C$,AD$(5)
```

The following INPUT# statement can be used optionally to read the data back:

```
200 INPUT#1,AD$(1),AD$(2),AD$(3),AD$(4),AD$(5)
```

Statements on lines 190 through 210 allow the operator to enter another name and address, or proceed to the display portion of the program.

The FOR-NEXT loop on lines 370 through 420 reads the five fields of each name and address from the sequential data file, then displays the name and address. Once again the DATA statement on line 30 is used to provide labels for each field that is displayed. On line 380 the READ statement takes the next string value from the DATA statement on line 30 and assigns it to F$; the PRINT statement then displays this string variable as a label. The INPUT# statement on line 390 reads the corresponding field from the sequential data file and the PRINT statement on line 410 displays it.

Operator dialogue on lines 430 through 450 allow the operator to display the next name and address, or terminate program execution.

Note that we have provided no protection against the operator asking for another name and address to be displayed when the end of file has been reached. We could solve this problem by adding the following statements on a new line 405:

```
405 IF DS=64 THEN PRINT "END OF FILE": I=5: GOTO 420
```

Mixed Sequential Data Files

No special program logic is needed in order to write numeric and string variables to the same sequential data file. However your program logic must keep track of field types. If a statement attempts to read a field from a sequential data file using a variable name of the wrong type, then an error will be reported.

Here is an example of a statement that writes two numeric variables and three string variables to a sequential data file:

```
10 DOPEN#1,"DATA",W
20 C$=CHR$(13)
30 PRINT#1,P$,C$,X,C$,Q$,C$,Y,C$,R$
```

These five variables would be read back correctly by the following INPUT# statement:

```
100 INPUT#1,A$(1),A$(2),A$(3),X(1),X(2),
```

The following INPUT# statement would not execute correctly since the variable types in its parameter list do not correspond with the variable types recorded in the sequential data file:

```
100 INPUT#1,A$(1),A$(2),A$(3),X(1),X(2)
```

There are now 30 numbers in each record, not 10. Therefore 30 numbers must be read and displayed for each record in the second half of the program. A simple (but inelegant) way of displaying 30 numbers would be to change the FOR statement on line 250, increasing the upper index of F from 10 to 30, as follows:

```
250 FOR F=1 TO 30
```

Make these changes, then run the program to assure yourself that three numbers were written out each time the PRINT# statement on line 80 was executed.

ADDING DATA TO SEQUENTIAL FILES

BASIC 4.0 allows you to add data to an existing sequential file using the APPEND# and CONCAT statements. The APPEND statement will write fields to the end of the existing file; the CONCAT statement will concatenate two files.

Appending Data To Sequential Files (BASIC 4.0)

To illustrate the APPEND# statement, we will modify program "SEQ.NUM.B4". The modified program, named "SEQ.NUMAPPEND", is listed below, with changed statements shaded.

```
10 REM PROGRAM "SEQ.NUMAPPEND"
20 DOPEN#1,"TESTDATA",W
30 IF DS<>0 THEN PRINT DS$:STOP
35 FOR J=1 TO 3
40 REM WRITE TEN RECORDS
50 FOR R=1 TO 10
60 REM WRITE TEN FIELDS PER RECORD
70 FOR F=1 TO 10
80 PRINT#1,(R-1)*100+F*J
85 IF DS<>0 THEN PRINT DS$:STOP
90 NEXT F
100 NEXT R
110 DCLOSE#1
200 REM NOW READ BACK FILE CONTENTS AND DISPLAY IT
210 DOPEN#1,"TESTDATA"
215 IF DS<>0 THEN PRINT DS$:STOP
220 FOR R=1 TO 10*J
230 PRINT "RECORD";R;
240 REM INPUT CONTENTS OF NEXT RECORD AND DISPLAY IT
250 FOR F=1 TO 10
260 INPUT#1,N
265 IF DS<>0 THEN PRINT DS$:STOP
270 PRINTN;
280 NEXT F
290 PRINT
300 NEXT R
310 DCLOSE#1
315 APPEND#1,"TESTDATA"
316 NEXT J
320 SCRATCH D0,"TESTDATA"
330 STOP
```

"SEQ.NUMAPPEND" is equivalent to three executions of "SEQ.NUM.B4". On the first execution 100 numeric fields are written to "TESTDATA". On each re-execution 100 fields are added to sequential data file TESTDATA. Therefore after the second execution "TESTDATA" will hold 200 numbers, and after the third execution "TESTDATA" will hold 300 numbers.

The three executions are enabled by a FOR-NEXT loop which uses the index J. The FOR statement is on line 35. The NEXT statement is on line 316.

In order to identify appended numbers, the field counter F is multiplied by the execution counter J on line 80. On line 220 the upper bound for the record counter R becomes 10 * J, since the number of records will increase by 10 on each re-execution.

You cannot APPEND to a file that does not exist. Therefore you cannot simply replace the DOPEN# statement on line 20 with an APPEND# statement, and open "TESTDATA" within the FOR-NEXT loop indexed by J. The DOPEN# statement on line 20 creates sequential file "TESTDATA" and opens it for a write operation. Ten records are written to "TESTDATA" on the first execution of statements 40 through 315; these ten records are read from the file and displayed. At the end of the first execution the APPEND# statement on line 315 reopens TESTDATA for the second execution of statements on lines 40 through 315. Ten additional records are added to TESTDATA. Similarly on the third execution of statements on lines 40 through 315, ten more records are added to TESTDATA, bring the total to 30 records.

Now run the program. On the first execution you will see exactly the same display that program SEQ.NUM.B4 created. There will be a pause, then on the second execution 20 records will be displayed; you will be able to identify the second set of ten records by the fact that the last digit of each number has been doubled. After another short pause you will see 30 records displayed when the program is executed a third time. You will be able to differentiate the first, second, and third set of ten records by the last digit of each number, which is doubled for the second set of ten records, and tripled for the third set of ten records.

Concatenating Sequential Data Files (BASIC 4.0)

BASIC 4.0 with DOS 2.0 allows you to concatenate files using the CONCAT statement. Program CONCATEST, listed below, provides a simple demonstration of file concatenation.

```
5 REM PROGRAM "CONCATEST", DEMONSTRATES CONCAT STATEMENT
10 DOPEN#1,"DATA1",W
20 DOPEN#2,"DATA2",W
30 FOR I=1 TO 20
40 PRINT#1,I
50 PRINT#2,I+10
60 NEXT I
80 DCLOSE
90 DOPEN#1,"DATA1"
100 DOPEN#2,"DATA2"
110 PRINT"⌧"
120 FOR I=1 TO 20
130 INPUT#1,X:PRINT X;
140 NEXT
145 PRINT
150 FOR I=1 TO 20
160 INPUT#2,X:PRINT X;
170 NEXT
175 PRINT
180 DCLOSE
190 CONCAT "DATA2" TO "DATA1"
```

```
200 DOPEN#1,"DATA1"
210 FOR I=1 TO 40
220 INPUT#1,X:PRINT X;
230 NEXT
235 PRINT
240 DCLOSE
250 STOP
```

This very simple program writes 20 numbers into sequential data files DATA1 and DATA2, then concatenates DATA2 to DATA1. Contents of DATA1 and DATA2 are displayed separately, then the contents of DATA1 are displayed after concatenation.

The two sequential data files DATA1 and DATA2 are opened on lines 10 and 20. The FOR-NEXT loop on lines 30 through 60 writes 20 numeric fields to each of the two files. Numbers one through 20 are written to DATA1. Numbers 11 through 31 are written to DATA2 so that the two numeric sequences can be distinguished, one from the other.

The two data files are closed by the single DCLOSE statement on line 80 so that they can be reopened for read accesses by the DOPEN# statements on lines 90 and 100. Two FOR-NEXT loops on lines 120 through 140 and 150 through 170 display the contents of DATA1 and DATA2 respectively. The PRINT statements on lines 145 and 175 force carriage returns.

DATA1 and DATA2 are both closed on line 180. DATA2 is concatenated to DATA1 by the CONCAT statement on line 190. DATA1 is then opened so that its contents can be displayed by the FOR-NEXT loop on lines 210 through 230. DATA1 is closed on line 240.

Note that CONCATEST does not scratch DATA1 and DATA2 at the end of the program. Before re-executing the program you must SCRATCH files DATA1 and DATA2 in immediate mode, or you must SCRATCH statements to the end of the program as follows:

```
245 SCRATCH "DATA1":SCRATCH "DATA2"
```

It is easy to misuse the CONCAT statement and get into a lot of trouble.

The two concatenated files must both contain data, and must both be closed when the CONCAT statement is executed.

If you concatenate data to an empty file, the computer will "hang up." You must turn power off at the computer, then turn power on again and restart whatever you were doing.

If you attempt to concatenate files that are open, or improperly closed, the computer may start appending a file to the diskette directory. If this happens, you will see diskette activity continue for a very long time after the CONCAT statement has been executed. It is possible to stop the diskette operation by pressing the STOP key at the keyboard. If you display the directory you will see a lot of garbage appear after the valid file names. In order to remove this garbage execute the COLLECT statement in immediate mode.

Appending Data to Sequential Files (BASIC< 3.0)

In order to append data to an existing sequential file using BASIC<3.0, you need two sequential files, which we will arbitrarily name DATA1 and DATA2. Suppose DATA1 contains data. In order to add data to DATA1 you must create a new file DATA2 using these steps:

1. If DATA2 exists scratch it.
2. OPEN DATA2 for a write access.
3. OPEN DATA1 for a read access.
4. Read records sequentially from DATA1 and write them sequentially to DATA2.
5. On detecting the end of the DATA1 file, start writing new records to DATA2.
6. Close DATA1.
7. Scratch DATA1.
8. Rename DATA2, giving it the new name DATA1.

The next time you wish to update the file, repeat the steps described above, switching DATA1 with DATA2.

END OF FILE

You can test for an end of file by looking for a value of 64 in ST. The following statement will stop program execution on detecting an end-of-file:

```
200 IF ST=64 THEN PRINT "END OF FILE":STOP
```

RELATIVE DATA FILES (BASIC 4.0)

Only BASIC 4.0 supports relative data files.

An open relative file can be read from or written to. However, you cannot read from an empty relative file; until you have written into the file, you cannot read from it.

RELATIVE FILE FIELD SEPARATORS

Comma and carriage return characters have different meanings as field separators in relative files; **the record length specified in a relative file DOPEN# statement identifies the number of characters (bytes) separating carriage return characters**. If all fields are separated using carriage return characters, then the relative file record length becomes a field length. Remember, BASIC 4.0 PRINT# statements do not transmit an automatic carriage return character at the end of a line if the file number is 127 or less.

Relative File Record Length

All numeric fields must be terminated with carriage return characters, therefore if a relative file holds numeric data, the record length specified for the relative file is also the field length. The number appearing after the L parameter in the relative file DOPEN# statement identifies the number of characters (bytes) that will be set aside for every numeric field in the file.

Since string variables can be terminated by comma characters or carriage return characters, you can place a number of string variables within a single relative file record. A name and address, for example, could have the following five fields:

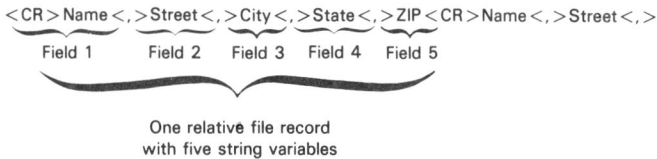

<CR>Name<,>Street<,>City<,>State<,>ZIP<CR>Name<,>Street<,>

Field 1   Field 2   Field 3   Field 4   Field 5

One relative file record
with five string variables

The record length specified for the relative file in its DOPEN# statement now applies to all five fields of the name and address record. This is useful since it accommodates records that have one or two very long fields. This may be illustrated as follows:

Number of Characters

| | Name | Street | City | State | ZIP | |
	Field 1	Field 2	Field 3	Field 4	Field 5	Total
Address 1	9	14	16	2	5	46
Address 2	13	12	8	2	5	40
Address 3	12	11	12	2	5	42
Address 4	17	8	11	2	5	43
Address 5	10	12	13	2	5	42
etc.						

If all five fields are stored in a single record, a record length of 50 characters (bytes) would probably be adequate.

If every string variable field ended with a carriage return, then the record length specified in the DOPEN# statement would apply to each field of the name and address. Every field would have to be long enough to accomodate the longest expected entry in any one of the five fields. To be safe we would probably select a 20-character (byte) field length. Now every field, including state and ZIP, will be allocated 20 characters. The total allocation for the name and address becomes 100 characters (bytes), since there are five fields with 20 characters per field. Therefore each name and address requires twice as much disk space as it would need if data were stored five fields per record.

Reading Relative File Records

INPUT# and GET# statements can be used to read fields from a relative file.

If commas are used to separate string variables, and INPUT# statements are used to read data from the relative file, then each INPUT# statement must read all of the variables occurring between two carriage return characters. We will illustrate this with programming examples on the following pages.

If a relative file has numeric and string variables, selecting a record length becomes more complicated. You can select a record length that allows a number of string variables separated by commas to be stored in each record, but numeric fields will still have to be stored one per long record. And that can prove very costly in terms of wasted diskette space. There are two solutions to this problem:

1. Select a record length based on the numeric variables. Store string variables one field per record, breaking up any long strings into smaller pieces.
2. Convert numeric variables into strings using the STR$ function, then store a number of numeric strings in each record.

WRITING NUMERIC DATA TO RELATIVE FILES

To explore numeric relative files we will modify program SEQ.NUM.B4, creating REL.NUM.B4, which is listed below.

```
10 REM PROGRAM "REL.NUM.B4"
20 DOPEN#1,"RELDATA",L10
30 IF DS<>0 THEN PRINT DS$:STOP
40 REM WRITE TEN RECORDS
50 FOR R=1 TO 10
60 REM WRITE TEN FIELDS PER RECORD
70 FOR F=1 TO 10
80 PRINT#1,(R-1)*100+F
85 IF DS<>0 THEN PRINT DS$:STOP
90 NEXT F
100 NEXT R
110 DCLOSE#1
200 REM NOW READ BACK FILE CONTENTS AND DISPLAY IT
210 DOPEN#1,"RELDATA",L10
215 IF DS<>0 THEN PRINT DS$:STOP
220 FOR R=1 TO 10
230 PRINT "RECORD";R;
240 REM INPUT CONTENTS OF NEXT RECORD AND DISPLAY IT
250 FOR F=1 TO 10
260 INPUT#1,N
265 IF DS<>0 THEN PRINT DS$:STOP
270 PRINTN;
280 NEXT F
290 PRINT
300 NEXT R
310 DCLOSE#1
320 SCRATCH D0,"RELDATA"
330 STOP
```

Load program SEQ.NUM.B4 into memory, then create program REL.NUM.B4 by making appropriate changes to statements on lines 10, 20, and 210. Run program REL.NUM.B4. If it executes correctly you will get the same display that program SEQ.NUM.B4 generated. Save program REL.NUM.B4 when it has executed correctly.

Record Length

Note the short record length of ten characters (bytes) specified by the REL.NUM.B4 program's DOPEN# statements. Since numeric data is written to relative file RELDATA, one field is written per record. This is because record length is always interpreted as the number of characters (bytes) separating carriage return characters; and every numeric variable must be terminated with a carriage return. Therefore just one numeric variable can be stored per record. Ten characters (bytes) is enough space for one numeric field.

There is no need to close relative file RELDATA on line 110 and then reopen it on line 210. We do so in order to separate the program into two modules, and examine how the two halves of the program interact.

Next change the record length in the DOPEN# statement on line 210 from L10 to L8. Now re-execute the program. The program will not execute; the following message will appear:

```
50,RECORD NOT PRESENT, 00,00
BREAK IN 215
READY
```

The wrong record length in the DOPEN# statement on line 210 has caused the problem. **BASIC 4.0 does not allow a relative file to be reopened with the wrong record length.**

WRITING STRING DATA TO RELATIVE FILES

When writing string variables to relative files you can end each variable with a comma or a carriage return character. If you end each field with a carriage return character, there will be one string variable field per record. You can include a number of string variables within a single record by using a comma character to separate fields within the record. The last field of the record must end with a carriage return character.

For our first example of writing string variables to a relative file, we will modify the sequential mailing list program SEQ.MAIL.B4. The modified program generates a relative file with the five fields of each name and address stored as a single record. This new program (named REL.MAIL.B4) is listed below; statements that differ from SEQ.MAIL.B4 are shaded.

```
10 REM PROGRAM "REL.MAIL.B4"
20 REM MAILING LIST PROGRAM TO ILLUSTRATE DISKETTE FILE STRING HANDLING
25 REM FOR RELATIVE FILES
30 DATA "   NAME: "," STREET: ","  CITY: "," STATE: ","   ZIP: "
40 DOPEN#1,"REL.MAILDATA",L50
50 IF DS<>0 THEN PRINT DS$:STOP
60 PRINT"⊃ ENTER NAME AND ADDRESS:▨▨"
70 FOR I=1 TO 5
80 READ F$
90 PRINTF$;:INPUT AD$(I)
100 NEXT I
110 RESTORE
120 PRINT"ENTER Y TO RECORD,N TO RE-ENTER";
130 GET Y$:IF Y$<>"Y" AND Y$<>"N" THEN 130
135 PRINTY$
140 IF Y$="N" THEN 60
150 REM WRITE NAME AND ADDRESS TO SEQUENTIAL FILE
160 CM$=CHR$(44)
170 PRINT#1,AD$(1);CM$;AD$(2);CM$;AD$(3);CM$;AD$(4);CM$;AD$(5)
171 IF DS<>0 THEN PRINT DS$:STOP
190 PRINT"ENTER Y FOR ANOTHER NAME AND ADDRESS,N TO END";
200 GET Y$:IF Y$<>"Y" AND Y$<>"N" THEN 200
205 PRINTY$
210 IF Y$="Y" THEN 60
220 DCLOSE#1
224 IF DS<>0 THEN PRINT DS$:STOP
300 REM DISPLAY NAMES AND ADDRESSES ONE AT A TIME
310 DOPEN#1,"REL.MAILDATA",L50
330 IF DS<>0 THEN PRINT DS$:STOP
340 REM CLEAR SCREEN AND DISPLAY NAME AND ADDRESS
350 PRINT"▨▨"
360 RESTORE
365 INPUT#1,AD$(1),AD$(2),AD$(3),AD$(4),AD$(5)
366 IF DS<>0 THEN PRINT DS$:STOP
370 FOR I=1 TO 5
380 READ F$:PRINT F$;
410 PRINT AD$(I)
420 NEXT I
430 PRINT"ENTER Y FOR ANOTHER NAME AND ADDRESS,N TO END";
440 GET Y$:IF Y$<>"Y" AND Y$<>"N" THEN 440
450 IF Y$="Y" THEN 350
460 DCLOSE#1
470 SCRATCH D0,"REL.MAILDATA"
480 STOP
```

Load program SEQ.MAIL.B4 from diskette, change statements on the shaded lines, then run the program. If you have entered the program correctly, it will execute exactly as described for SEQ.MAIL.B4. When program REL.MAIL.B4 is free of errors, save it.

Let us examine the changed statements in program REL.MAIL.B4.

The DOPEN# statements on lines 40 and 310 have been changed to specify a relative file with a 50-character record length and the name REL.MAIL.DATA.

Data is input from the keyboard and displayed on the screen as described for SEQ.MAIL.B4, but statements that write each name and address to the data file are completely different. The PRINT# statement on line 170 outputs a single record. CM$ has been assigned the numeric value of the comma character (CHR$(44)) by the assignment statement on line 160. Note the semicolons separating each variable in the PRINT# statement parameter list. The combination of semicolons separating parameters in the PRINT# statement and CM$ occurring between each field of the name and address will cause a relative file record to be created as follows:

```
170 PRINT#1,AD$(1);CM$;AD$(2);CM$;AD$(3);CM$;AD$(4);CM$;AD$(5)


       JO BLOW ,125 5TH AVE. , NEW YORK, NY ,10010
```

This illustration assumes that AD$(1) = "JO BLOW", AD$(2) = "125 5TH AVE.", AD$(3) = "NEW YORK", AD$(4) = "NY" and AD$(5) = "10010".

Note the statements on line 171, which test for diskette status after each record is written to the relative file. Strictly speaking, program SEQ.MAIL.B4 should have had statements to test status at this point; for SEQ.MAIL.B4 it would have represented good programming practice. But **it is vitally important after writing a record to a relative file, since you must check for record overflow.** Without the status testing statements on line 171, any name and address that did not fit into the allowed record length would be stored inaccurately; if your eye were fast you might notice the error indicator on the diskette drive flash red while the long record is written to the relative file. Otherwise you would have no idea that an overflow had occurred until a program read data back from the file, and found one or more fields of the record missing.

To demonstrate the need for the status testing logic on line 171, eliminate this line, then change the semicolons on line 170 to commas. Now re-execute the program. If you watch carefully you will see the error indicator at the diskette drive flash red when records are written to the diskette. When names and addresses are subsequently displayed, the first two or three fields of each name and address will be present; remaining fields will be absent.

What happened?

The commas in the parameter list of the PRINT# statement on line 170 have the same effect on display fields and relative file fields; each new field is written or displayed beginning at the next 10th character boundary. The PRINT# statement on line 170 has 9 variables in its parameter list (you must count the four CM$ variables). Therefore the record will require at least 90 characters. More characters will be needed if any of the five name and address fields has more than ten characters. You can see the effect of commas by adding the following statement to program REL.MAIL.B4:

```
PRINT AD$(1),CM$,AD$(2),CM$,AD$(3),CM$,AD$(4),CM$,AD$(5)
```

Each record will be displayed exactly as it will be written to file REL.MAIL.DATA. You can then count characters for yourself, and see where the name and address gets truncated by a 50 character record length.

Statements that read the name and address back from the relative data file are shown on lines 365 and 366. Statements that read names and addresses back for program SEQ.MAIL.B4 have been removed; hence the absence of lines 390 and 400.

An INPUT# statement reads one record from a diskette file. This is true for all INPUT# statements, reading from any type of diskette file. In other words, each INPUT# statement reads data from one carriage return character to the next. In program REL.MAIL.B4 there are five fields between each pair of carriage return characters, therefore the INPUT# statement on line 365 will read five fields each time the statement is executed. This is true whatever number of variables there may be in the INPUT# statement parameter list.

The INPUT# statement on line 365 has five string variables in its parameter list. If any variable in the parameter list were not a string variable, you would get a syntax error and the program would stop executing.

If there were less than five string variables in the parameter list, some variables at the end of the relative file records would not be read. You can demonstrate this for yourself by removing AD$(4) and AD$(5) from the INPUT# statement on line 365. When you re-execute the program, names and addresses read from the relative file will have their first three fields displayed correctly, with nothing in the last two fields.

Next add an additional variable to the INPUT# statement on line 365 by appending ,AD$(6) to the end of the INPUT# statement. When you execute the program, you will find that the presence of this additional variable in the INPUT# statement has no effect. Unlike sequential files, the additional variable has no data assigned to it, since the record has run out of fields.

POSITIONING TO RECORDS OF RELATIVE FILE

The RECORD# statement allows you to position to any character (byte) of any record in a relative file. To demonstrate the use of the RECORD# statement, add the following line to program REL.NUM.B4:

```
23 RECORD#1,((10-R)*10+1)
```

You will see ten records displayed, with 901 through 910 in the first record and 1 through 10 in the last record. This is the exact inverse of the record display given by REL.NUM.B4.

The record positioning factor is derived as follows:

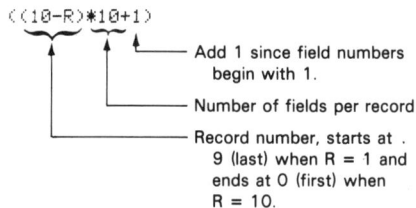

```
((10-R)*10+1)
```
— Add 1 since field numbers begin with 1.

— Number of fields per record

— Record number, starts at 9 (last) when R = 1 and ends at 0 (first) when R = 10.

Whether a relative record contains numeric or string data has no effect on the way the RECORD# statement works. Prove this to yourself by adding RECORD# statements to the REL.MAIL.B4 program to select names and addresses in any sequence.

Changing Records in a Relative File

Having positioned to any record in a relative file, you can write a single record. No special programming techniques are required. The same PRINT# statement that creates a record can be used to overwrite a record, once you have positioned to the record.

USING GET# WITH DISKETTE FILES

The GET# statement reads one character from a diskette data file, just as the GET statement reads one character from the keyboard buffer. The character read by the GET# statement is taken from the 256 byte diskette buffer. Characters are taken sequentially, beginning with the first character in the buffer. Blanks, punctuation characters and anything occupying a character position will be read.

When using the GET# statement to read from sequential files, you must read characters sequentially, beginning with the first character of the file. However, when reading from relative files you can use the RECORD# statement to select any character in any record; the GET# statement will then start reading at the selected character.

We will demonstrate use of the GET# statement by modifying programs SEQ.MAIL.B4 and REL.MAIL.B4, substituting a GET# statement for the INPUT# statement that reads back name and address fields. Changes apply also to SEQ.MAIL.B<3.

Using GET# with Sequential Files

First we will modify program SEQ.MAIL.B4 substituting GET# for the INPUT# statement on line 390. The GET# statement follows standard GET statement logic (which you should understand by now). Here is the new line 390:

```
390 GET#1,AD$:IF AD$="" THEN 390
```

The PRINT statement on line 410 will now print just one character; we must therefore add a semicolon to the end of the PRINT statement in order to suppress a carriage return.

We must test for a carriage return by adding this extra statement on a new line 415:

```
415 IF AD$<>CHR$(13) THEN 390
```

The IF statement on line 415 branches back to the GET# statement until a carriage return is detected. Then the FOR-NEXT loop is allowed to iterate once more. Since carriage return characters mark the end of each word, the carriage return is displayed by the PRINT statement on line 410 before the IF statement on line 415 causes program logic to move on to the next word.

Load program SEQ.MAIL.B4 into memory. Make the changes described and run the program. Execution should be identical.

In order to experiment with the GET# statement, try modifying your program to detect and change specific characters. For example, you could display a graphics character wherever a carriage return is detected.

Using GET# with Relative Files

Program REL.MAIL.GET#, listed below, shows program REL.MAIL.B4 modified to use the GET# statement; in addition, some characters have been modified so that we can examine the organization of relative file records.

```
10 REM PROGRAM "REL.MAIL.GET#"
20 REM MAILING LIST PROGRAM TO ILLUSTRATE DISKETTE FILE STRING HANDLING
25 REM FOR RELATIVE FILES
30 DATA "   NAME: "," STREET: ","  CITY: "," STATE: ","   ZIP: "
40 DOPEN#1,"REL.MAILDATA",L50
50 IF DS<>0 THEN PRINT DS$:STOP
60 PRINT"] ENTER NAME AND ADDRESS:▒▒"
70 FOR I=1 TO 5
80 READ F$
90 PRINTF$;:INPUT AD$(I)
100 NEXT I
110 RESTORE
120 PRINT"ENTER Y TO RECORD,N TO RE-ENTER";
130 GET Y$:IF Y$<>"Y" AND Y$<>"N" THEN 130
135 PRINTY$
140 IF Y$="N" THEN 60
150 REM WRITE NAME AND ADDRESS TO SEQUENTIAL FILE
160 CM$=CHR$(44)
170 PRINT#1,AD$(1);CM$;AD$(2);CM$;AD$(3);CM$;AD$(4);CM$;AD$(5)
171 IF DS<>0 THEN PRINT DS$:STOP
190 PRINT"ENTER Y FOR ANOTHER NAME AND ADDRESS,N TO END";
200 GET Y$:IF Y$<>"Y" AND Y$<>"N" THEN 200
205 PRINTY$
210 IF Y$="Y" THEN 60
220 DCLOSE#1
224 IF DS<>0 THEN PRINT DS$:STOP
300 REM DISPLAY NAMES AND ADDRESSES ONE AT A TIME
310 DOPEN#1,"REL.MAILDATA",L50
330 IF DS<>0 THEN PRINT DS$:STOP
340 REM CLEAR SCREEN AND DISPLAY NAME AND ADDRESS
350 PRINT"▒▒▒"
360 RESTORE
370 FOR I=1 TO 5
380 READ F$:PRINT F$;
390 GET#1,AD$:IF AD$="" THEN 390
395 IF DS<>0 THEN PRINT DS$:STOP
400 IF AD$=CHR$(32) THEN AD$="*"
405 IF AD$=CHR$(44) THEN PRINT AD$;:AD$=CHR$(13)
410 PRINT AD$;
415 IF AD$<>CHR$(13) THEN 390
420 NEXT I
430 PRINT"ENTER Y FOR ANOTHER NAME AND ADDRESS,N TO END";
440 GET Y$:IF Y$<>"Y" AND Y$<>"N" THEN 440
450 IF Y$="Y" THEN 350
460 DCLOSE#1
470 SCRATCH D0,"REL.MAILDATA"
480 STOP
```

Since the GET# statement reads characters one at a time, we do not need to worry about the different punctuation separating fields and records. The GET# statement will read punctuation like any other character, and carry on reading. Therefore the INPUT# and status test instructions on lines 365 and 366 of program REL.MAIL.B4 have been removed. A standard GET# statement has been added on line 390; status for this file access is tested by the IF statement on line 395.

In order to detect space codes, on line 400 space code characters are replaced by the more visible • character.

Line 405 checks for a comma. Commas are displayed, then replaced with a carriage return character.

On line 410 a semicolon has been added to the end of the PRINT statement since this statement will now display just one character. On line 415 logic branches back for the next character, unless the carriage return has been detected, at which point the next field is input. Remember, on line 405 commas have been converted to carriage returns, therefore on line 415 commas and carriage returns will both cause an advance to the next field.

Enter program REL.MAIL.B4 and make the modifications shown. Now run the program. You will find that REL.MAIL.GET# and REL.MAIL.B4 create identical displays, apart from asterisks appearing instead of blanks. Notice that no asterisks appear after the zip code. Therefore **a carriage return character must appear directly after the zip code, with unused disk space separating this record from the beginning of the next.**

Using the GET# and RECORD# Statements With Relative Files

The RECORD# statement will position to any character in any record of a relative file. To demonstrate the character positioning ability of the RECORD# statement add the following line to program REL.MAIL.GET#:

```
365 RECORD#1,2,5
```

The second half of program REL.MAIL.GET# will now start displaying names and addresses at the fifth character of the second record. Re-execute the program (making sure that you enter at least two names and addresses). You will find that the second name and address is displayed, beginning at its fifth character.

PROGRAM FILES

CBM computers handle program and data files in totally different ways. Each has its own set of file handling statements.

Loading and Saving Program Files

Program files are loaded into memory using the LOAD (for BASIC<3.0) or the DLOAD (for BASIC 4.0) statements.

Program files are written to diskette using the SAVE (for BASIC<3.0) or the DSAVE (for BASIC 4.0) statements.

Loading and saving programs is described first in Chapter 2.

Accessing Program Files as Data Files

You can OPEN and CLOSE program files as you would data files, and you can execute GET#, INPUT#, and PRINT# statements accessing program files as though they were data files. But until you have an intimate understanding of CBM computer system software, you will get results that are highly unpredictable;

moreover you will achieve nothing that could not be done more easily using standard program file statements and screen editing capabilities.

When using BASIC<3.0, remember that secondary address 0 is used to LOAD program files into memory, while secondary address 1 is used to SAVE program files on diskette. By specifying these secondary addresses in OPEN statements you get to access program files as though they were data.

Backup Program Files

It is imperative that you always have one or more copies of every program file. Wherever possible, at least one copy of the program file should be held on a different diskette. Having two copies of the same program file on one diskette serves no purpose if by some mischance the entire diskette is erased.

Use the BASIC 4.0 COPY statement to copy a single file. Use the COPY or the BACKUP statement to copy an entire diskette.

With BASIC<3.0 you must copy files and diskettes using a variation of the PRINT# statement, as described earlier in this chapter.

Program File Update Sequence

Programs constantly change as you make corrections or improvements. The safest way of changing a program is to keep a copy of the present version, and the two most recent versions, generally referred to as the "father" and "grandfather." When you change a program follow these steps:

1. LOAD the present "current" version into memory and make appropriate changes.
2. SCRATCH the current grandfather program.
3. RENAME the father program as the grandfather.
4. RENAME the current program as the father.
5. SAVE the new version as the new current program.

JOB QUEUING

Programmed use of the LOAD command allows you to execute very long programs and to perform various types of job queuing.

Suppose you have an application whose program will not fit in available memory. Try resolving the problem by splitting the program into two pieces. The two pieces must be completely independent, except for data which one piece can transmit to the other via an external data file. This may be illustrated as follows:

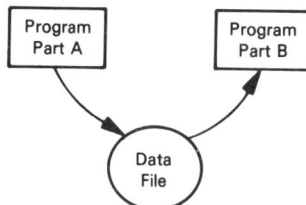

For this scheme to work, the original program must be divisible into two or more independent steps.

Let us call the two parts of the program Part A and Part B. **The entire program is loaded,** using the following steps:

1. Load Part A into memory via an immediate mode LOAD command.
2. Execute Part A via an immediate mode RUN command.
3. When Part A finishes, it loads part B.
4. Part B executes automatically.

Here is a BASIC 4.0 statement which will transfer from Part A to Part B:

```
60030 DLOAD D0,"PART B"
```

Part A must terminate execution by writing out a data file that contains all of the data needed by Part B. Part B must begin execution by loading the data file which Part A wrote out.

PROGRAMMING THE LINE PRINTER

Up to this point we have made very little use of the CBM computer system's line printer. All we have done is list programs; and that takes no programming effort. But most programs generate results in the form of printed reports. The format of a report is very important; reports get used if they are easy to read. A badly formatted report is discarded. Fortunately it is easy to program CBM line printers to generate well formatted reports.

Two printers are available with CBM computer systems: the Model 2022 and the Model 2023. Both printers contain their own internal microprocessors, which is why well formatted printouts are so easy to generate.

The Model 2022 and 2023 printers both print the PET keyboard character set, not the CBM keyboard character set.

Printers are accessed by opening a logical file specifying physical unit #4, and a secondary address whose value must range between 0 and 7. If no secondary address is specified, then 0 is assumed. As summarized in Table 6-4, secondary addresses provide these printer options:

1. Print data exactly as received.
2. Print output to a previously specified format.
3. Define the number of lines to be printed per page.
4. Specify the space separating printed lines (Model 2022 Printer only).
5. Print characters that are not part of the standard character set.
6. Enable special diagnostic messages to be printed.

Additional formatting can be specified using the special control characters summarized in Table 6-5.

PRINTING DATA EXACTLY AS RECEIVED

To print data exactly as received you must open a logical file specifying physical unit #4 and no secondary address, or a secondary address of 0. Then print data using PRINT# and/or CMD statements.

Printing with the PRINT# Statement

The PRINT# statement outputs data to the printer just as it would to a cassette or diskette file. For example, to print the word "MESSAGE", enter the following program and run it:

```
10 OPEN 2,4
20 PRINT#2,"MESSAGE"
30 CLOSE 2
40 STOP
```

Each time you run this program the single word "MESSAGE" is printed; then the following display appears:

```
BREAK IN 40
READY
```

This display is generated by the STOP statement on line 40.

You cannot use BASIC 4.0 DOPEN# and DCLOSE# statements to access the line printer. These statements will only work with diskette files.

Printing with the CMD Statement

Instead of using the PRINT# statement you can transmit data to the printer using the CMD statement. But the CMD statement must be followed by at least one PRINT# statement before the printer logical file is closed. To demonstrate the use of the CMD statement, enter and run the following program:

```
10 OPEN 2,4
20 CMD 2,"MESSAGE"
25 PRINT#2
30 CLOSE 2
40 STOP
```

Table 6-4. Printer Control Chaacters, used in Text Printed to Secondary Address 0 or 1

	Printer Function	C Code	Keyboard Entry	Comment
Necessary	End string field	CHR$ (29)	CRSR →	Every string field must be followed by CHR$ (29) except for the last variable in a PRINT # statement parameter list.
	Leading blanks in string	CHR$ (160)	SHIFT + SPACE	To insert leading space codes in a string variable you must use shifted space codes. Unshifted space characters will be deleted.
	Enhance	CHR$ (1)	NONE	Each occurance of CHR$ (1) in the parameter list of a PRINT # statement will double the width of subsequent string characters (initially 6 dots) printed on the same line. A carriage return nullifies character enhancement. CHR$ (1) characters have a cumulative effect on characters printed on a single line.
Optional	Line Feed	CHR$ (10)	NONE	The printer executes a carriage return and line feed on encountering this character.
	Carriage Return	CHR$ (13)	RETURN	
	Reverse on	CHR$ (18)	OFF RVS	Start printing reverse field characters. Reverse field is cancelled by a carriage return.
	Lower-case	CHR$ (17)	CRSR ↓	Start printing lower-case letters. Lower-case is cancelled by a carriage return or an upper-case specification.
	Paging off	CHR$ (19)	HOME	Execute a top of form if paging is on.
	Quote character	CHR$ (34)	NONE	Print all control characters.
	Unenhance	CHR$ (129)	NONE	Cancel character enhancement specified by preceding CHR$ (1) character(s)
	Carriage return with no line feed	CHR$ (141)	NONE	The printer executes a carriage return without a line feed, overprinting prior text, if any.
	Upper-case	CHR$ (145)	CRSR ↑	The printer returns to printing upper-case letters if it is printing lower-case letters following a CHR$ (17) control. CHR$ (145) has no effect if the printer is already printing upper-case letters.
	Reverse off	CHR$ (146)	SHIFT + OFF RVS	Cancel reverse character printing, if in effect.
	Paging on	CHR$ (147)	CLR	Print 66 lines per page until a subsequent output to secondary address 3 changes the lines per page specification.

Table 6-5. Printer Format Characters, Used in Format Statements Printed in Secondary Address 2

Data Type	Code	Specification	Use	Data	Format	Printed Result
Numeric Fields	9	A numeric digit with leading zeros suppressed.	Specify all characters to the left and/or right of a decimal point (if present).	23 124.756 124.756	999.9 9999.99 999	23.0 124.75 124
	Z	A numeric digit with leading zeros printed.	Specify all characters to the left of a decimal point (if present).	23 124.756 124.756	ZZZ.9 ZZZZ.99 ZZZ	023.0 0124.75 124
	.	Decimal point	Numbers are aligned on the decimal point, if present. Numbers are right justified otherwise		See below	
	$	Number is a dollar amount	Print $ in front of first non-blank character, or in first character of the field	23 124.756	$999.9 $$$$$.99	$23.0 $ 124.75
	S	A signed number. S must be first format character.	Sign (+ or −) is printed as first non-blank character	124.756 −23 −475.2	S$999.99 S$$$$.99 S9999.9	+$124.75 −$ 23.00 +475.2
	−	A signed number. − must be last format character	Negative numbers are identified by a − printed as the last non-blank character	124.756 −23 −475.2	$999.99− $$$$.99− 9999.9−	$124.75 $ 23.00− 475.2−
String Fields	A	Any string field character position	Use an A to specify each string field character position String variables are left adjusted within the string field	ABCDE ABC ABCDE	AAAAAA AAAAAA AA	ABCDE ABC AB
	b	Character spaces between fields	Use one blank for every character position separating fields			
Any	<RVS ON>	Print the next character literally	The character in the format specification is printed		<RVS ON> − <RVS ON> −A	− −

When you run this program the word "MESSAGE" will be printed followed by two carriage returns. The PRINT# statement on line 25 generates the second carriage return.

Printing With CMD and PRINT Statements

After a CMD statement has been executed, PRINT statements will output data to the printer rather than the display until the next PRINT# statement is executed. To demonstrate this, change the printer program as shown below and run it:

```
10 OPEN 2,4
20 CMD 2
21 PRINT "MESSAGE"
21 PRINT#2
26 PRINT "MESSAGE"
30 CLOSE 2
40 STOP
```

When you run this program, the printer will execute a carriage return, then it will print the word "MESSAGE" followed by two carriage returns, then the word "MESSAGE" is displayed. The CMD statement on line 20 generates the first carriage return; the PRINT statement on line 21 causes the word "MESSAGE" to be printed by a carriage return. The PRINT# statement on line 25 generates the additional carriage return. The PRINT statement on line 26 displays the word "MESSAGE".

Now remove the PRINT statement on line 21. When you run the program again, the printer will execute two carriage returns, but the word "MESSAGE" is displayed; it is not printed.

A Comparison of CMD and PRINT# Statements

To understand what happened we must examine the slight difference between the effect of a CMD statement, as compared to a PRINT# statement.

Visualize the printer as a substitute for the display. A single output channel goes from the CBM computer either to the display, or to the printer. When an OPEN statement is executed specifying physical unit 4, the CBM computer is told that a printer is present, but the single output channel still selects the display.

When a PRINT# statement is executed subsequently, the output channel is deflected from the display to the printer; data in the PRINT# statement parameter list is transmitted to the printer, then the output channel selects the display again.

When a CMD statement is executed, the output channel is deflected from the display to the printer, data in the CMD statement parameter list is transmitted to the printer, but the output channel is left selecting the printer; the display no longer has an output channel.

When a PRINT statement is executed after a CMD statement, data is printed, not displayed, because the CMD statement has deflected the output channel from the display to the printer. But as soon as a PRINT# statement is executed, the output channel is deflected back to the display at the end of the PRINT# statement's execution. A PRINT statement executed after the PRINT# statement will again cause data to be displayed.

The printer must be closed, like any other logical file. When the CLOSE statement is executed, the CBM computer is told that the printer is no longer present.

If the output channel is left selecting the printer rather than the display when the printer is closed, then subsequent PRINT statements will continue to select the printer. To demonstrate this, enter and run the following program:

```
10 OPEN 2,4
20 CMD 2
30 CLOSE 2
35 PRINT "MESSAGE"
40 STOP
```

When you run this program you will see the following printout:

```
MESSAGE
BREAK IN 40
READY
```

The BREAK and READY lines which were previously displayed are now printed since the output channel was left selecting the printer.

FORMATTED PRINTER OUTPUT

CBM computer system printers will automatically format output for you.

First you must specify the printer format. You do this by transmitting an appropriate text string to the printer, using secondary address 2. Text string characters used to specify printer format are summarized in Table 6-5.

Data which is to be printed using the specified format must be output via secondary address 1. Data output in this fashion is printed using the most recently transmitted format specification. If no format has been specified, then data output using secondary address 1 is printed as transmitted — as it would be if output via secondary address 0.

To program formatted printer output, OPEN two logical files: one file selects physical unit 4 with secondary address 2; the other file selects physical unit 4 with secondary address 1. Then transmit format specifications and data using the appropriate logical file numbers.

Printing Formatted Numeric Data

We will begin by examining how the printer can format numeric data.

Character positions for each numeric field are specified using the digit 9, the letter Z, and optionally, a decimal point.

The decimal point, if included, will be printed wherever it appears in the numeric field. Numbers are aligned on the decimal point.

The digit 9 and the letter Z both specify numeric character positions. However the letter Z forces all zeros to be printed, whereas the digit 9 prints blanks for leading zeros. Here are some examples:

Number	Format Specification	Result
123.456 6457 −128.1	999999.99	123.45 6457.00 128.10
123.456 6457 −128.1	ZZZZZ.9	00123.4 00123.4 00128.1

A number can be printed with a preceding sign, or a trailing sign.

The letter S appearing at the beginning of the number field specification will cause a + or − sign to be printed at the beginning of the numeric field.

A minus sign (−) appearing as the last character of the numeric field specification will cause negative numbers to be represented by a trailing minus sign; no trailing plus sign is printed.

When a number is to be treated as a $ value then the $ sign can directly precede the number, or it can be aligned at the beginning of the allotted number field. The sign can precede the $ sign, it can follow the number, or the number can be unsigned.

For the simplest specification, add a $ character at the beginning of the numeric field format. This will cause a $ to be printed in the first (leftmost) character position of the numeric field. If the $ amount is to be printed with a + or − sign preceding the number, then the format must begin with S$; this will cause a + or − sign, and then a $ character, to be printed in the first two character positions of the numeric field.

You can also print $ amounts with leading zeros suppressed and a $ character appearing in front of the first numeric digit. For this specification specify all digit positions preceding the decimal point using $ characters; add one more $ character to specify the $ sign. Once again you have the option of putting an S at the beginning of the format in which case a + or − sign will precede the $ character.

Here are some examples of formats that include a sign and/or $ specification:

Number	Format Specification	Printed Result
123.456 6457 −128.1	S9999	123 6457 −128
123.456 6457 −128.1	S$9999.99	$0123.45 $6457.00 −$0128.10
123.456 6457 −128.1	S$9999.99	$123.45 $6457.00 −128.10
123.456 6457 −128.1	$$$$$.99−	$123.45 $6457.00 $ 128.10−
123.456 6457 −128.1	$$$$$.99−	$0123.45 $6457.00 $0128.10−

Later we will describe how you can substitute any other character or symbol for the $ sign if you are programming in a country that does not use $'s.

In order to demonstrate formatted numeric printout, key in program NUM.FORM.PRINT as listed below. This program reads eight miscellaneous numbers from the DATA statement on line 30, then prints them using the format specified by the PRINT# statement on line 100. When you run the program, a single column of numbers will be printed, as shown below the listing.

```
10 REM PROGRAM "NUM.FORM.PRINT"
20 REM DEMONSTRATE FORMATTED NUMERIC PRINTOUT
30 DATA 1.75,-12300,0.74682,12,-456.832,23456.78,-100.798,4789326
70 OPEN 1,4,1:REM OUTPUT DATA VIA LOGICAL FILE 1
80 OPEN 2,4,2:REM OUTPUT DATA FORMATS VIA LOGICAL FILE 2
90 REM OUTPUT DATA FORMAT
100 PRINT#2,"999999.99"
110 FOR I=1 TO 8
```

```
120 READ N
130 PRINT#1,N
140 NEXT I
150 CLOSE 1
155 CLOSE 2
160 STOP


     1.75
 12300.00
      .74
    12.00
   456.83
 23456.78
   100.79
******.**
```

Notice that numbers have been aligned on the decimal point. The eighth number will not fit within the specified numeric field. **Asterisks are printed in all digit positions when a number is too large for the specified format.**

Now change the PRINT# statement on line 100, substituting Z's for the 9's preceding the decimal point; re-run the program. Numbers are printed as follows:

```
000001.75
012300.00
000000.74
000012.00
000456.83
023456.78
000100.79
******.**
```

Notice that the Z's cause leading zeros to be printed. The eighth number still overflows the numeric field and is printed as asterisks. Add one more numeric digit position preceding the decimal point and the eighth number will be printed. Try it and see it for yourself.

You cannot mix Z's and 9's in the pre-decimal point field specification. If you do the printer will stop interpreting the field specification at the character change. For example, change the PRINT# statement on line 100 as follows:

```
100 PRINT#2,"ZZZZ999.99"
```

Now run the program. Numbers will be printed as though the field specification were "ZZZZ". Now try changing the PRINT# statement on line 100 as follows:

```
100 PRINT#2,"9999ZZZ.99"
```

When you run the program, numbers are printed as though the specification were "9999".

Numbers have been printed unsigned. **In order to print a leading sign, change the PRINT# statement on line 100 as follows:**

```
100 PRINT#2,"S9999999.99"
```

Now run the program. Numbers are printed with a leading sign and suppressed leading zeros as follows:

```
+       1.75
-   12300.00
+        .74
+      12.00
-     456.83
+   23456.78
-     100.79
+4789326.00
```

To print a trailing sign, change the PRINT# statement on line 100 as follows:

```
100 PRINT#2,"9999999.99-"
```

Now run the program. A minus sign appears after negative numbers; positive numbers have no sign printed.

Notice that all numbers are truncated after the specified digit has been printed. The printer does not round up.

Now we will convert numbers to $ amounts by adding a $ sign to the front of the numeric specification. We will also print a leading sign; the PRINT# statement on line 100 must now change as follows:

```
100 PRINT#2,"S$9999999.99"
```

When you re-run the program you will get the following printout:

```
+$        1.75
-$    12300.00
+$         .74
+$       12.00
-$      456.83
+$    23456.78
-$      100.79
+$4789326.00
```

Note that S must precede the $ sign. If a $ precedes the S, unformatted numbers will be printed.

It is common in financial reports to identify negative $ amounts with a trailing minus sign. You can generate such a printout by removing the S and replacing it with a trailing minus sign. Change line 100 as follows:

```
100 PRINT#2,"$9999999.99-"
```

Now re-run the program; you will get the following printout:

```
$        1.75
$    12300.00-
$         .74
$       12.00
$      456.83-
$    23456.78
$      100.79-
$4789326.00
```

In any printout of $ amounts, **the $ sign can be printed directly in front of the first numeric digit; this requires all character positions preceding the decimal point to be filled with $ signs.** Change 100 as follows:

```
100 PRINT#2,"$$$$$$$.99-"
```

Now re-run the program; you will get the following printout:

```
$1.75
$12300.00-
$.74
$12.00
$456.83-
$23456.78
$100.79-
******.****
```

What went wrong? The eighth number was printed as asterisks. The problem is that the new line 100 has seven $ characters preceding the decimal point; it needs 8. **You need one $ for each character position preceding the decimal point, plus an additional $ to select the $ character printout.**

So far we have printed formatted numeric data in a single column. To print multi-column data, provide a separate numeric format specification for each column using blank spaces to separate numeric specifications. To illustrate multi-column printing consider the following 3-column output:

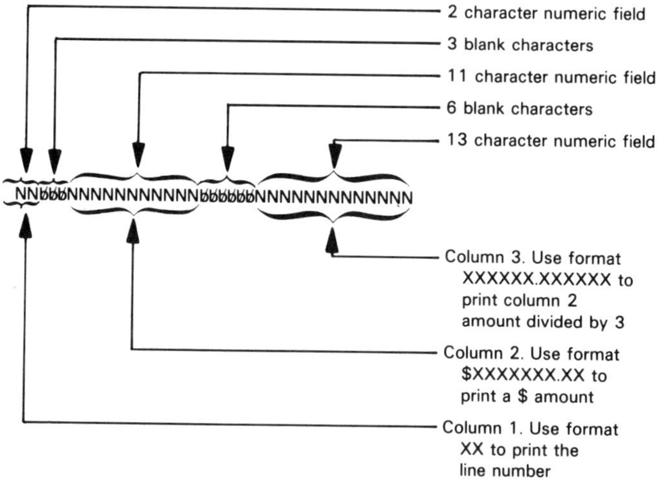

The PRINT# statement on line 100 must change as follows to specify the 3 column format illustrated above:

```
100 PRINT#2,"99    $$$$$$$$.99-    999999.999999"
```

We will change the PRINT# statement on line 130 to print line number I, N, and N/3. Here is the new line 130:

```
130 PRINT#1,I,N,N/3
```

When you run the program the following printout will be generated:

```
1           $1.75           .583333
2       $12300.00-      4100.000000
3            $.74           .248940
4          $12.00          4.000000
5         $456.83-       152.277333
6       $23456.78       7818.926670
7         $100.79-        33.599333
8     $4789326.00      ******.******
```

Each column of numbers has been printed according to the specification provided for that column in the formatting PRINT# statement. **The number of spaces separating printed columns is equal to the number of spaces separating the column formats in the PRINT# statement on line 100.**

Printing Formatted Strings

To print formatted strings you use the letter A to identify each string character position. Use space codes to separate fields, if necessary. The entire format is specified as a single string variable appearing in the parameter list of a PRINT# statement. As described earlier, this PRINT# statement must specify a logical file number which was opened to physical unit 4 with secondary address 2.

String variables which are to be printed using the specified format are output using another PRINT# statement whose logical file number was opened specifying physical unit 4 and secondary address 1. **String variables in the PRINT# statement parameter list must be separated by CHR$(29) characters, which may be generated using the CURSOR RIGHT key within a string. Strings are left-justified within the specified field; trailing character positions (if any) are filled with blanks. Leading space codes are truncated.**

Here are two PRINT# statements that print formatted strings:

```
100 PRINT#X,"AAAAAAAAAA      AAAAAAAAAAAA"
110 PRINT#Y,M$CHR$(29)N$
```

X represents any valid logical file number that has been opened specifying physical unit 4 with secondary address 2. Y represents any logical file number that has been opened specifying physical unit 4 with secondary address 1.

The PRINT#X statement specifies 10-character and 12-character string fields separated by five blank spaces.

The PRINT#Y statement specifies two string variables, M$ and N$, separated by the required separator CHR$(29). **Notice that commas have not been used to separate elements of the PRINT#Y statement parameter list.** You can use commas if you wish; the following alternate PRINT#Y statement is valid:

```
PRINT#Y,M$,CHR$(29),N$
```

You can replace M$ and N$ with actual string elements, with or without commas separating the string elements from the CHR$(29) separators. This may be illustrated as follows:

```
PRINT#Y,"ONE"CHR$(29)"TWO"
```

To illustrate formatted string printing, we will modify program NUM.FORM.PRINT to generate STR.FORM.PRINT. The program and sample run are listed below.

```
10 REM PROGRAM "STR.FORM.PRINT"
20 REM DEMONSTRATE FORMATTED STRING PRINTOUT
30 DATA  "MARY PERKINS","35 WEST ST.","BERKELEY","CALIFORNIA","94705"
35 DATA "345-67-8910","SPONSOR","AXC"
70 OPEN 1,4,1:REM OUTPUT DATA VIA LOGICAL FILE 1
80 OPEN 2,4,2:REM OUTPUT DATA FORMATS VIA LOGICAL FILE 2
90 REM OUTPUT DATA FORMAT
100 PRINT#2,"AAAAAAAAAA      AAAAAAAAAAAA"
105 SP$=CHR$(29)
110 FOR I=1 TO 4
120 READ M$,N$
130 PRINT#1,M$,SP$,N$
140 NEXT I
150 CLOSE 1
155 CLOSE 2
160 STOP

MARY PERKI      35 WEST ST.
BERKELEY        CALIFORNIA
94705           345-67-8910
SPONSOR         AXC
```

The PRINT#X statement appears on line 100 specifying logical file 2, which is opened on line 80. The PRINT#Y statement appears on line 130 specifying logical file 1, which is opened on line 70. Instead of using CHR$(29) in the PRINT#1 statement on line 130, we use SP$, which is equated to CHR$(29) on line 105.

The eight numeric data items which appeared in a single DATA statement in the NUM.FORM.PRINT program now occupy two DATA statements on lines 30 and 35. Eight string variables are specifed; they consist of an arbitrary address followed by a social security number and two code words, shown on line 35 as "SPONSOR" and "AXC".

Note that the first field (containing the name MARY PERKINS) has been truncated after the I of PERKINS. You must add three more A's to the first field specification in order to accommodate the entire name. Notice also that all fields are left justified. **In order to insert leading space codes you cannot use a normal space bar character; you must use CHR$(160), the upper case space bar character**. We can demonstrate this by adding leading blank characters to one string variable; we will choose AXC. Change the data statement on line 35 as follows:

```
35 DATA "345-67-8910","SPONSOR","  AXC"
```
                                   └─────── Press space bar twice

Now rerun the program. The printout does not change. The two blank characters preceding AXC were ignored. Now retype the modified data statement, holding the shift key down while you enter the two spaces in front of AXC. This time when you run the program AXC will be shifted two character positions to the right in the printout.

Using string concatenation you can shift string variables to the right within a string field. This is illustrated by the modification of program STR.FORM.PRINT shown below, followed by a sample run.

```
10 REM PROGRAM "STR.FORM.PRINT"
20 REM DEMONSTRATE FORMATTED STRING PRINTOUT
30 DATA  "MARY PERKINS","35 WEST ST.","BERKELEY","CALIFORNIA","94705"
35 DATA "345-67-8910","SPONSOR","AXC"
70 OPEN 1,4,1:REM OUTPUT DATA VIA LOGICAL FILE 1
80 OPEN 2,4,2:REM OUTPUT DATA FORMATS VIA LOGICAL FILE 2
90 REM OUTPUT DATA FORMAT
100 PRINT#2,"AAAAAAAAAA      AAAAAAAAAAAA"
105 SP$=CHR$(29)
106 BL$="            ":REM 12 UPPER CASE SPACE CODES
110 FOR I=1 TO 4
120 READ M$,N$
125 IF LEN(M$)<10 THEN M$=LEFT$(BL$,(10-LEN(M$)))+M$
126 IF LEN(N$)<12 THEN N$=LEFT$(BL$,(12-LEN(N$)))+N$
130 PRINT#1,M$SP$N$
140 NEXT I
150 CLOSE 1
155 CLOSE 2
160 STOP
```

```
MARY PERKI      35 WEST ST.
  BERKELEY       CALIFORNIA
     94705      345-67-8910
   SPONSOR              AXC
```

In order to right-justify string fields, statements on lines 125 and 126 check for string variables that are shorter than the specified field width. Lengths for shorter variables are increased to the field width by adding leading upper-case space characters. Leading upper-case space characters are taken from string variable BL$, which is defined on line 106. The number of upper-case space characters is computed as the difference between the field width and the length of the string variable. This number of characters is taken from BL$ using the LEFT$ function.

We will now modify program STR.FORM.PRINT to print data using a reasonable format. For example, the five name and address fields might be printed in a single vertical column (with no truncated characters), while the three additional fields are printed on a single line below the name and address. Program STR.FORM.PRINT1, listed below, generates the required printout. A sample run is shown after the listing.

```
10 REM PROGRAM "STR.FORM.PRINT1"
20 REM DEMONSTRATE FORMATTED STRING PRINTOUT
30 DATA   "MARY PERKINS","35 WEST ST.","BERKELEY","CALIFORNIA","94705"
35 DATA "345-67-8910","SPONSOR","AXC"
70 OPEN 1,4,1:REM OUTPUT DATA VIA LOGICAL FILE 1
80 OPEN 2,4,2:REM OUTPUT DATA FORMATS VIA LOGICAL FILE 2
90 REM OUTPUT DATA FORMAT
105 SP$=CHR$(29)
110 FOR I=1 TO 8
120 READ M$(I)
140 NEXT I
150 PRINT#2,"AAAAAAAAAAAAAA"
160 FOR I=1 TO 5
170 PRINT#1,M$(I)
180 NEXT I
190 PRINT#2,"AAAAAAAAAA   AAAAAA    AAA"
200 PRINT#1,M$(6)SP$M$(7)SP$M$(8)
210 CLOSE 1
220 CLOSE 2
230 STOP

MARY PERKINS
35 WEST ST.
BERKELEY
CALIFORNIA
94705
345-67-8910   SPONSOR   AXC
```

All eight string variables have been read into the string array M$(I) by the FOR-NEXT loop on lines 110 through 140, before any string data is printed out. Five fields are then printed in a single vertical column by the FOR-NEXT loop on lines 160 through 180, using the format specified by the PRINT# statement on line 150. A new format is then specified by the PRINT# statement on line 190; this new format is used to print out the last three string variables using the PRINT# statement on line 200.

Printing Mixed Formatted Data

You can mix numeric and string data in formatted printer output. A simple demonstration of such output is given by program STR.FORM.PRINT2, which is listed below together with a sample printout.

```
10 REM PROGRAM "STR.FORM.PRINT2"
20 REM DEMONSTRATE FORMATTED STRING PRINTOUT
30 DATA   "MARY PERKINS","35 WEST ST.","BERKELEY","CALIFORNIA","94705"
35 DATA "345-67-8910","SPONSOR","AXC"
70 OPEN 1,4,1:REM OUTPUT DATA VIA LOGICAL FILE 1
80 OPEN 2,4,2:REM OUTPUT DATA FORMATS VIA LOGICAL FILE 2
90 REM OUTPUT DATA FORMAT
105 SP$=CHR$(29)
110 FOR I=1 TO 8
120 READ M$(I)
140 NEXT I
150 PRINT#2,"99   AAAAAAAAAAAAAA"
160 FOR I=1 TO 5
170 PRINT#1,I,M$(I)
180 NEXT I
190 PRINT#2,"99   AAAAAAAAAA   AAAAAA    AAA"
200 PRINT#1,I,M$(6)SP$M$(7)SP$M$(8)
```

```
210 CLOSE 1
220 CLOSE 2
230 STOP

1   MARY PERKINS
2   35 WEST ST.
3   BERKELEY
4   CALIFORNIA
5   94705
6   345-67-8910   SPONSOR   AXC
```

This program is a minor variation of STR.FORM.PRINT1. A line number numeric followed by three blank spaces has been added to the two PRINT# statements on lines 150 and 190. The data output PRINT# statements on lines 170 and 200 each print the FOR-NEXT loop index.

A second program, PRINTDATE, is more interesting. It accepts the month, day and year entered at the keyboard as three separate numeric variables. Each date is printed with a dash separating month from day and day from year. Program PRINT-DATE is listed below together with a sample printout for three dates.

```
10 REM PROGRAM "PRINTDATE"
20 OPEN 1,4,1:REM OUTPUT DATA VIA LOGICAL FILE 1
30 OPEN 2,4,2:REM OUTPUT DATA FORMAT VIA LOGICAL FILE 2
40 PRINT"◼◼◼"
50 INPUT "ENTER MONTH:";M
60 INPUT "ENTER DAY  :";D
70 INPUT "ENTER YEAR :";Y
80 PRINT#2,"AAAAA   99A99A99"
90 SP$=CHR$(29)
100 PRINT#1,"DATE:"SP$,M,"-"SP$,D,"-"SP$,Y
110 PRINT"ANOTHER DATE? ENTER Y FOR YES OR N FOR NO";
120 GET YN$:IF YN$="" THEN 120
130 IF YN$="N" THEN PRINTYN$:STOP
140 IF YN$<>"Y" THEN 120
150 GOTO 40
```

```
DATE:     6-12-80
DATE:    12-25-81
DATE:     1- 1-70
```

Program PRINTDATE makes no validity checks on the numbers entered for month, day and year since we want to focus attention on printer formatting rather than good data entry programming practice. But the usefulness of formatted printout is obvious from the example below.

Including Literals in Formatted Printout

The printer format specification can include literal characters. A literal character is printed exactly as it appears in the printer format specification; it does not specify format for data occurring in a subsequent PRINT# statement. **A literal character must be preceded by the REVERSE ON (RVS) character.** The character coming directly after the REVERSE ON is printed normally. In consequence you cannot print reverse field literal characters.

Program PRINTDATEL1 makes very simple use of literals. A literal dash separates month from day and day from year, replacing the string used by program PRINT-DATE. To create program PRINTDATEL1, load program PRINTDATE from the previous section, then change the PRINT# statements on lines 80 and 100 as shown below. PRINTDATEL1 and PRINTDATE generate the same display and printout.

```
10 REM PROGRAM "PRINTDATEL1"
20 OPEN 1,4,1:REM OUTPUT DATA VIA LOGICAL FILE 1
30 OPEN 2,4,2:REM OUTPUT DATA FORMAT VIA LOGICAL FILE 2
40 PRINT"    "
50 INPUT "ENTER MONTH:";M
60 INPUT "ENTER DAY  :";D
70 INPUT "ENTER YEAR :";Y
80 PRINT#2,"AAAAA   99 -99 -99"
90 SP$=CHR$(29)
100 PRINT#1,"DATE:"SP$,M,D,Y
110 PRINT"ANOTHER DATE? ENTER Y FOR YES OR N FOR NO";
120 GET YN$:IF YN$="" THEN 120
130 IF YN$="N" THEN PRINTYN$:STOP
140 IF YN$<>"Y" THEN 120
150 GOTO 40
```

You can create forms, while printing output, by making appropriate use of literals in printer format statements. However, literals and text must come from the same character set. Moreover, the printers recognize the PET character sets. When using CBM computers, therefore, it is very difficult to generate forms using literals. But a program written on a 2001 computer can be run on a CBM computer in order to generate forms.

SPECIAL PRINTER CONTROL CHARACTERS

There are a number of special printer control characters which modify printer output when inserted in data. Printer control characters are summarized in Table 6-4.

Printer control characters are inserted in the data stream transmitted to the printer via secondary address 0 or 1. Printer control characters are not transmitted as part of the format specified using secondary address 2.

You can use printer control characters with formatted or unformatted printouts.

The first two entries in Table 6-4, CHR$(29) and CHR$(160), must be used with formatted printouts (as previously described); they are ignored in unformatted printouts.

Codes listed as optional in Table 6-4 can be used with formatted or unformatted printouts; their effect is the same in either case.

Enhanced Character Printout

CBM printers normally generate characters using a dot matrix that is seven dots high and six dots wide. If you include a CHR$(1) character within a data output PRINT# statements parameter list, all characters following the CHR$(1) are printed double-width: using a dot matrix that is seven dots high and 12 dots wide. More than one CHR$(1) character can appear in a single parameter list. Each CHR$(1) character takes the previous character width and doubles it. Following two CHR$(1) characters, therefore, 7 by 24 dot matrices will be used to print characters. After a third CHR$(1) character, 7 by 48 dot matrices would be used.

In order to demonstrate enchanced printout, load program STR.FORM.PRINT1 and add the following line:

```
125 M$(I)=CHR$(1)+M$(I)
```

When you run this modified program, the first printed column (including name, address and social security number) is printed using double-width characters. The word SPONSOR uses quadruple-width characters, while the letters AXC are printed using characters that are eight times normal width. Here is a sample printout:

```
MARY PERKINS
35 WEST ST.
BERKELEY
CALIFORNIA
94705
345-67-8910        SPONSOR         AXC
```

What happened?

Line 125 added an enchancement character to the beginning of each string varia-ble. Therefore the first string variable on any line is printed double-width, the second string variable is printed quadruple-width and the third variable is printed using charac-ters that are eight times standard width.

You do not have to concatenate CHR$(1) characters to strings. **You can insert CHR$(1) into the PRINT# statement parameter list, but you must not use commas to separate CHR$(1).** For example, reload program STR.FORM.PRINT1, and replace line 200 with these two lines:

```
195 E$=CHR$(1)
200 PRINT#1,E$M$(6)SP$E$M$(7)SP$E$M$(8)
```

When you run this program, the name and address are printed using standard character widths. The social security number is printed using double-character widths, the word SPONSOR is printed using quadruple-character width, while AXC is printed using characters that are eight times normal width. Here is a sample printout:

```
MARY PERKINS
35 WEST ST.
BERKELEY
CALIFORNIA
94705
345-67-8910        SPONSOR         AXC
```

You can print enhanced numeric variables. The numeric variable is included in the PRINT# statement parameter list, but it must have commas separating it from other variables. To demonstrate enhanced numeric printout we will again start with program STR.FORM.PRINT1. Modify lines 190 through 200 as follows:

```
190 PRINT#2,"AAAAAAAAAA    99999  AAAAAAA"
195 E$=CHR$(1)
196 N=12345
200 PRINT#1,E$M$(6)SP$,N,E$M$(7)
```

The final line printer format has been changed by the PRINT# statement on line 190; two string fields are printed with a numeric field appering between them. The PRINT# statement on line 200 specifies M$(6) and M$(7) as the two string fields, with the new numeric variable N between them. N is equated to 12345 on line 196. In the parameter list of the PRINT# statement on line 200 **notice that the numeric variable N is separated using commas, but commas are not used to separate string variables.**

These syntax rules are very specific and must be observed in order to generate successful mixed, enhanced numeric and string printout. Here is a sample of the printout generated by STR.FORM.PRINT1 with lines 190 through 200 modified as listed above:

```
MARY PERKINS
35 WEST ST.
BERKELEY
CALIFORNIA
94705
345-67-8910        12345       SPONSOR
```

You can cancel character enhancement using the CHR$(129) character. Subsequent characters revert to standard size until another CHR$(1) character is encountered.

Printing Reverse Field Characters

Reverse field characters can be included in a PRINT# statement parameter list using the RVS ON and RVS OFF keys. However, you should not print more than five consecutive lines of reverse field characters; if you do, the printhead will wear out very quickly.

Printing Control Characters

To print a quote character you must use CHR$(34).

If you print a single CHR$(34), or any odd number of quote characters in this fashion, then the printer will subsequently display all control characters via their graphic representation.

The only time you are likely to do this is when you are listing programs which include control characters that would not normally be printed.

PAGE FORMAT

Number of Lines per Page

Unless otherwise instructed, CBM printers pay no attention to page length. To enable paging, transmit the CHR$(147) character to the printer as data. The printer then assumes a 66-line page; it prints 60 lines, skips six lines, prints another 60 lines, and so on. Below is the listing for a simple program that turns paging on, then prints a line number followed by the character string ABCDEFG. If you enter and run this program, you will see paged printing in action.

```
10 REM PROGRAM "PAGING" TESTS PAGING OPTIONS
20 OPEN 1,4:REM OPEN UNFORMATTED PRINTOUT
30 REM SELECT PAGING
40 PRINT#1,CHR$(147)
50 FOR I=1 TO 100
60 PRINT#1,I,"ABCDEFG"
70 NEXT I
80 CLOSE 1
90 STOP
```

You can change the number of lines printed per page once paging has been enabled. To do this, you output the selected number of lines as numeric data to a logical file which must be opened specifying physical unit 4 with secondary address 3. The printer then assumes that the page length equals the number of lines specified, plus six. The specified number of lines are printed on each page, with six skipped lines between each page. Program PAGINL25, listed below, prints 25 lines per page.

```
10 REM PROGRAM "PAGINGL25" TESTS PAGING OPTIONS
20 OPEN 1,4:REM OPEN UNFORMATTED PRINTOUT
25 OPEN 3,4,3:REM OPEN FILE TO SELECT NUMBER OF LINES PER PAGE
30 REM SELECT PAGING
40 PRINT#1,CHR$(147)
45 PRINT#3,25:REM SELECT 25 LINES PER PAGE
50 FOR I=1 TO 100
60 PRINT#1,I,"ABCDEFG"
70 NEXT I
80 CLOSE 1
85 CLOSE 3
90 STOP
```

The PRINT# statement on line 45 specifies 25 lines per page. Logical file 3 is opened on line 25.

You can change the number of printed lines per page by outputting a new value to secondary address 3. The new value goes into effect at the beginning of the next page; the current page is printed using the old number of lines per page.

Add the following line to program PAGINGL25:

```
55 IF I=23 THEN PRINT#3,10
```

Run the program twice. The first time a 25-line page is printed, followed by a number of ten-line pages. But on the second execution something strange happens; a ten-line page is printed, followed by a 25-line page, and then a number of ten-line pages. The printer remembered the previously specified number of lines per page and used it for the first page of the new run.

Top of Form

While paging is in effect, if you print a CHR$(19) character, the printer will skip remaining lines on the current page, and position itself at the first print line of the next page. Printing continues from this new position. This is referred to as a top of form. If a page does not print to the last line (and this is the rule rather than the exception), you should end the page by printing a top of form; this will advance the printer to the next page. You do not have to count remaining lines and skip over them.

Space Between Lines (Model 2022)

The model 2022 printer allows you to change the space between printed lines. Printers divide each vertical inch into 144 steps. Normally each line is allotted 24 steps. Thus six lines are printed per vertical inch. **The model 2022 line printer allows you to change the number of lines that will be printed per vertical inch.** To do this, you must open a logical file specifying physical unit 4 with secondary address 6. Then output a CHR$ function to this logical file number, specifying the new number of steps per line as the CHR$ function's argument.

Suppose you want to print eight lines per inch; the number of steps per inch then becomes 144/8, which equals 18. Here are the statements needed to make this change:

```
10 OPEN 6,4,6
20 PRINT#6,CHR$(18)
```

If you have a model 2022 printer, load program PAGINGL25, insert these two lines, then run the program. Lines will be printed with no space in between them; the vertical width of characters does not change when you increase the number of lines per inch. Steps are removed (or inserted) between lines. By specifying appropriate steps per line you can print lines that overlap, or have a lot of space between them.

DEFINING YOUR OWN CHARACTERS

CBM printers allow you to define, or draw, your own printer characters.

All printer characters are generated using a 7 × 6 dot matrix. To create your own character draw 7 × 6 dot matrix as follows:

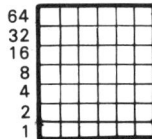

Each row in the dot matrix is represented by a number, ranging from 1 to 64. The top row has the value of 64, while the bottom row has the value 1. (Each row value is double the previous row value.)

Now generate your character by drawing dots in the 7 × 6 matrix. Here is an English pound character:

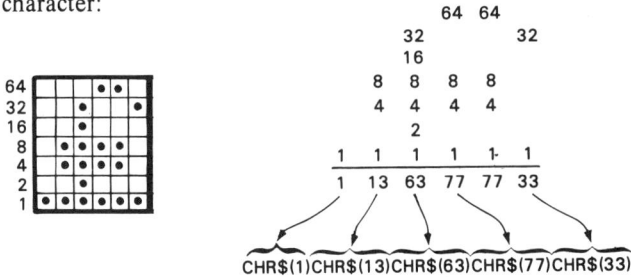

You must now convert the character into 6 numbers. Each number corresponds to 1 column of the 7 × 6 matrix and identifies the dots in that column. The first of the 6 numbers represents the left-most column and the last of the 6 numbers represents the right-most column.

To compute the number for any column, write down row values corresponding to each existing dot, then sum the row values, as illustrated above.

Next the six numbers must be converted into a six-character string; each character of the string is a CHR$ function, where the column total becomes the CHR$ function argument. Thus the English pound character becomes a six-character string where the first character has the value CHR$(1), the second character has the value CHR$(13), the third character has the value CHR$(63), the fourth and fifth characters both have the values CHR$(77), and the sixth character has the value CHR$(33). This string is output to the printer using a PRINT# statement that specifies a logical file opened with physical unit 4 and secondary address 5. The printer stores the special character; it does not print it. Subsequently any PRINT# statement that prints data specifies the special character using the function CHR$(254).

The steps needed to print a special character are illustrated by program POUNDCHAR listed below. This program, when executed, will print a column of ten English pound signs.

```
10 REM PROGRAM "POUNDCHAR"
20 REM DEMONSTRATE SPECIAL PRINTER CHARACTER GENERATION
30 DATA 1,13,63,77,77,33
35 EP$=""
40 OPEN 1,4:REM OPEN PRINTER
50 OPEN 5,4,5:REM OPEN SPECIAL CHARACTER GENERATION FILE
60 FOR I=1 TO 6
70 READ EP
80 EP$=EP$+CHR$(EP)
90 NEXT I
95 PRINT#5,EP$
100 FOR I=1 TO 10
110 PRINT#1,CHR$(254)
120 NEXT I
130 CLOSE 1
140 CLOSE 5
150 STOP
```

Let us examine how the pound sign is created and printed.

The data statement on line 30 specifies the number and location of dots in the character matrix, as illustrated previously.

The FOR-NEXT loop on lines 60 through 90 generate the six-character string representing the pound sign and assign this string to string variable EP$. Each number from the data statement is read into numeric variable EP by the READ statement on line 70; this numeric value is converted into a character, and a character is concatenated to EP$ on line 80. The assembled string is output to logical file 5 on line 95. Logical file 5 was opened on line 50 specifying physical unit 4 and secondary address 5. After the PRINT# statement on line 95 has been executed, the printer holds one special character, which it recognizes and prints on encountering a CHR$(254) function in the data string received from a PRINT# statement. This occurs each time the PRINT# statement on line 110 is executed.

Note that the CBM printer can only recognize one special character at any time. You can change the special character by creating a new 6 character string and outputting this string to the printer via secondary address 5. Although this technique is quite straightforward, it does not readily lend itself to the indiscriminate use of the many special characters.

Using Special Characters to Print Non-Dollar Monetary Data

The $ sign is not much use when printing financial data outside of the USA and Canada. Some other character must be substituted for the $ sign. This is easily done using formatted printout in conjunction with special character generation.

Program POUNDVAL, listed below, uses the English pound character which we just generated to print English financial data with a trailing sign. Two sample printouts are shown at the end of the listing.

```
10 REM PROGRAM "POUNDVAL"
20 REM PRINT A NUMERIC VALUE AS BRITISH POUNDS
30 REM CREATE THE POUND SIGN
40 DATA 1,13,63,77,77,33
50 OPEN 5,4,5
60 EP$=""
70 FOR I=1 TO 6
80 READ EP
90 EP$=EP$+CHR$(EP)
100 NEXT I
110 PRINT#5,EP$
```

```
120 OPEN 1,4,1:REM USE FORMATTED PRINTOUT
130 OPEN 2,4,2
140 REM OUTPUT ENGLISH POUND PRINT FORMAT
150 PRINT#2,"AAAAAA    A999999.99-"
160 INPUT "ENTER AMOUNT:";N
170 PRINT#1,"VALUE="CHR$(29)CHR$(254)CHR$(29),N
180 CLOSE 1
190 CLOSE 2
200 CLOSE 5
210 STOP

VALUE=   £  1234.56
VALUE=   £  1234.56-
```

The pound sign is created by statements on lines 40 through 110. These statements have been taken from program POUNDCHAR.

The OPEN statement on lines 120 and 130 open logical files 1 and 2 for formatted printout. The format is output by the PRINT# statement on line 150; a six-character string field if specified, followed by three blank spaces and then a numeric field with preceding single character string field. The numeric field has two places after the decimal point and a trailing sign

The INPUT statement on line 160 lets you enter a number which is assigned to numeric variable N. N is printed by the PRINT# statement on line 170.

Let us examine this PRINT# statement parameter list.

The string "VALUE=" is printed in the first 6 character string fields. This character is followed by the mandatory string separator CHR$(29). Three spaces are printed as required by the printer format. Next comes a single character string field. The character is CHR$(254); it is followed by the mandatory CHR$(29) string field terminator. CHR$(254) selects the special character. The pound sign is therefore printed in front of the numeric field. Numeric variable N is printed in the numeric field.

PRINTER DIAGNOSTIC MESSAGES

If you are having problems with printer output, enable a logical file selecting physical unit 4 with secondary address 6. This will cause the printer to output detailed diagnostic messages when it encounters identifiable errors in printout specifications. You do not have to execute any statements in order to generate error diagnostics; they are output automatically.

Programs in their final form will not normally use printer diagnostic messages. These diagnostic messages are used while you are writing a program, in order to find errors.

You can create a sample diagnostic message by loading program STR.FORM.PRINT1 into memory. Change one of the A format specifications on line 190 to some illegal character such as Q. Then add the following line:

```
85 OPEN 4,4,4
```

When you run the program an error message similar to the one shown below will be generated.

```
MARY PERKINS
35 WEST ST.
BERKELEY
CALIFORNIA
94705
345-6
AAAAAQAAAAA    AAAAAAA    AAA
     ↑
*****BAD FORMAT*****
PONSOR AXC
```

Chapter 7

System Information

CBM COMPUTER SYSTEM ORGANIZATION

The CBM computer uses a 6502 microprocessor. The display screen, cassette tape unit, keyboard diskette drives and printer are physical devices that have been described in Chapter 2. The three external I/O ports are interfaced through the 2K block of memory-mapped I/O. The organization of the CBM computer system is shown in Figure 7-1. On 4K/8K PETs, the cassette tape unit connects directly to the I/O block, and the Cassette Tape Interface is available for connecting a second cassette unit. On 16K/32K PETs the cassette tape unit is connected through the Cassette Tape Interface; additional tape units, if any are desired, must be interfaced through the IEEE 488 port. Such tape units would operate under different protocol than standard tape units. The six ROM, RAM, and I/O blocks are allocated from the total 65K bytes of available memory (1K = 1024).

Memory allocation by 4K blocks is shown in Table 7-1. Each portion of the memory is described in more detail in the following text.

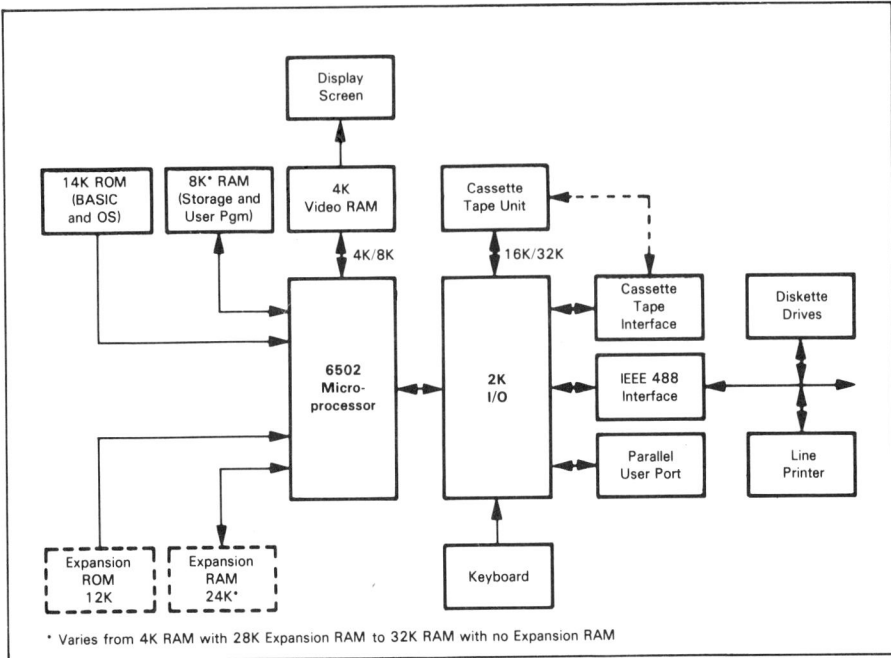

* Varies from 4K RAM with 28K Expansion RAM to 32K RAM with no Expansion RAM

Figure 7-1. PET Block Diagram

Table 7-1. Memory Allocation by 4K Blocks

Block	Memory Type	Start Address		Description
		Decimal	Hexadecimal	
0	RAM	0	0000	Working storage, start of text
1	RAM	4096	1000	Text and variable storage (8K only)
2	—	8192	2000	
3	—	12288	3000	
4	—	16384	4000	Expansion RAM
5	—	20480	5000	
6	—	24576	6000	
7	—	28672	7000	
8	RAM	32768	8000	Screen Memory (and I/O — BASIC 4.0 only)
9	ROM	36864	9000	
10	ROM	40960	A000	Expansion ROM
11	ROM	45056	B000	Start of BASIC 4.0
12	ROM	49152	C000	BASIC (principally statement interpreter)
13	ROM	53248	D000	BASIC (principally math package)
14	ROM	57344	E000	Screen Editor (2K)
	I/O	59392	E800	I/O Memory (2K)
15	ROM	61440	F000	Operating System (OS)

Addresses 0-8191: 8K RAM (Storage and User Program)

The first block of RAM is allocated to working storage, the stack, tape buffers, and storage of user programs. The amount of active RAM may be 4K (addresses 0-4095), 8K (addresses 0-8191), 16K (addresses 0-16384), or 32K (addresses 0-32767). The first 1K allocation (to 1024) is fixed; the larger the memory size, the more space is available in the user program area.

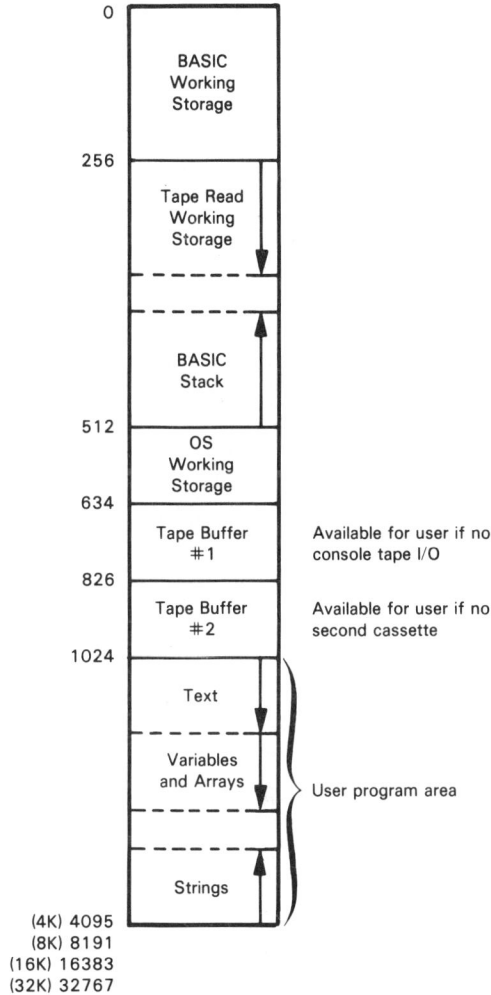

```
        0 ┌──────────────┐
          │    BASIC     │
          │   Working    │
          │   Storage    │
      256 ├──────────────┤
          │  Tape Read   │
          │   Working    │
          │   Storage    │
          ├ ─ ─ ─ ─ ─ ─ ─┤
          │              │
          │    BASIC     │
          │    Stack     │
      512 ├──────────────┤
          │     OS       │
          │   Working    │
          │   Storage    │
      634 ├──────────────┤   Available for user if no
          │ Tape Buffer  │   console tape I/O
          │     #1       │
      826 ├──────────────┤   Available for user if no
          │ Tape Buffer  │   second cassette
          │     #2       │
     1024 ├──────────────┤ ┐
          │    Text      │ │
          ├ ─ ─ ─ ─ ─ ─ ─┤ │
          │  Variables   │ ├ User program area
          │ and Arrays   │ │
          ├ ─ ─ ─ ─ ─ ─ ─┤ │
          │   Strings    │ │
(4K) 4095 └──────────────┘ ┘
(8K) 8191
(16K) 16383
(32K) 32767
```

Locations 0 through 255 are used by the BASIC interpreter as working storage locations. This area is detailed in Appendix F.

Locations 256 through 511 are used mainly by the BASIC Stack. A portion of the area beginning at location 256 and proceeding upward is used by the Tape Read routine for error correction and by BASIC as an expansion buffer. The stack begins at location 511 and proceeds downward. Storage is allocated dynamically as needed. An OUT OF MEMORY error occurs if the stack pointer reaches the end of available space in this area.

Locations 512 through 633 are used by the "Operating System" (OS) as working storage locations. This area is detailed in Appendix F.

Locations 634 through 825 form a 192-byte tape buffer for the console tape cassette. Locations 826 through 1023 form a second 192-byte tape buffer for the optional second cassette unit. User-written assembly language programs can be stored in tape buffers if there are no tape cassettes, or no second cassette in the system.

Locations 1024 through the end of available RAM are used to store user programs and variables. Programs begin at location 1024 and are stored upward toward the end of memory. Variable storage begins after the end of the program. Array storage begins at the end of variable storage. Strings are stored beginning at the end of memory and working downward. An OUT OF MEMORY error occurs if an upgoing pointer meets the downgoing pointer.

Addresses 8192-32767: Expansion RAM 24K

Memory addresses 8192 through 32767 are allocated for expansion of RAM to 32K.

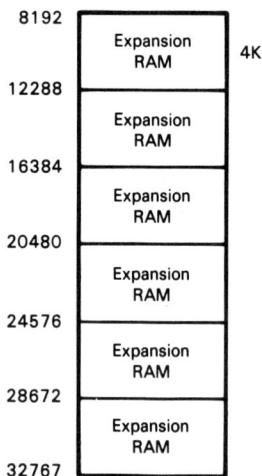

```
8192  ┌──────────────┐
      │  Expansion   │  4K
      │     RAM       │
12288 ├──────────────┤
      │  Expansion   │
      │     RAM       │
16384 ├──────────────┤
      │  Expansion   │
      │     RAM       │
20480 ├──────────────┤
      │  Expansion   │
      │     RAM       │
24576 ├──────────────┤
      │  Expansion   │
      │     RAM       │
28672 ├──────────────┤
      │  Expansion   │
      │     RAM       │
32767 └──────────────┘
```

32K of RAM address space is allocated between active RAM and expansion RAM, as follows:

Active RAM	Expansion RAM
4K (0-4095)	28K (4096-32767)
8K (0-8191)	24K (8191-32767)
16K (0-1638)	

Addresses 32768-36863: 4K Video RAM

The first thousand locations of this block, from addresses 32768 through 33767, are allocated to screen memory. A POKE to any of these locations displays the character in the appropriate screen position.

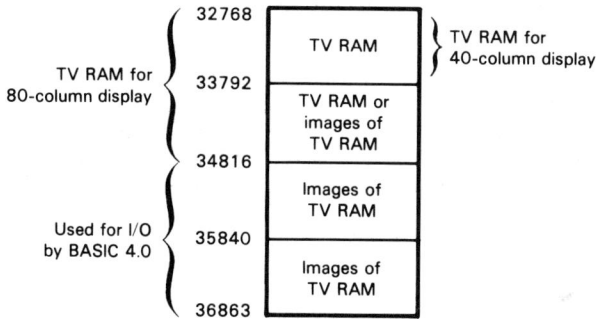

```
                        32768  ┌──────────────┐
                               │   TV RAM      │ ⎱ TV RAM for
TV RAM for              33792  │              │ ⎰ 40-column display
80-column display  ⎰           ├──────────────┤
                   ⎱           │ TV RAM or    │
                               │ images of    │
                               │ TV RAM       │
                        34816  ├──────────────┤
                               │ Images of    │
                               │ TV RAM       │
Used for I/O       ⎰    35840  ├──────────────┤
by BASIC 4.0       ⎱           │ Images of    │
                               │ TV RAM       │
                        36863  └──────────────┘
```

Addresses 36864-49151: Expansion ROM 12K

Memory addresses 36864 through 49151 are allocated for optional expansion of ROM to 26K.

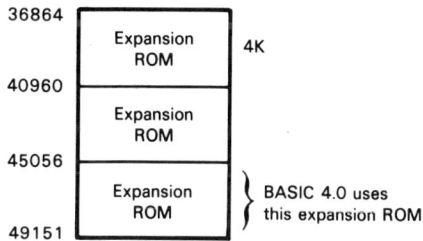

```
        36864  ┌──────────────┐
               │  Expansion   │  4K
               │    ROM       │
        40960  ├──────────────┤
               │  Expansion   │
               │    ROM       │
        45056  ├──────────────┤
               │  Expansion   │ ⎱ BASIC 4.0 uses
               │    ROM       │ ⎰ this expansion ROM
        49151  └──────────────┘
```

Addresses 49152-65535: 14K ROM and 2K I/O

Locations 49152 (45056 for BASIC 4.0) through 59391 and locations 61440 through 65535 hold the BASIC interpreter and OS diagnostics. Memory-mapped I/O locations are from 59392 through 61439.

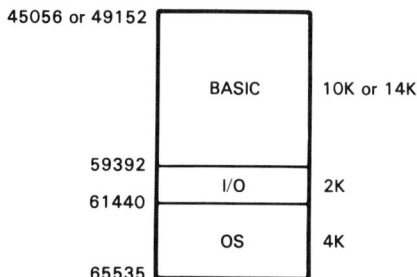

```
45056 or 49152  ┌──────────────┐
                │              │
                │    BASIC     │  10K or 14K
                │              │
        59392   ├──────────────┤
                │    I/O       │  2K
        61440   ├──────────────┤
                │    OS        │  4K
        65535   └──────────────┘
```

Location 65535 is the end of CBM memory.

MEMORY MAP

Detailed memory maps used by different versions of CBM BASIC are shown in Appendix F. Table F-1 describes the Revision Level 2 ROMs used in the original PET computers. Table F-2 shows the Revision Level 3 ROMs used in BASIC<3.0. Table F-3 shows the most recent memory map for BASIC 4.0.

Tables F-1 and F-2 show the memory address in decimal and hexadecimal. You should use the decimal value as the PEEK or POKE address. Tables F-1 and F-2 also show sample decimal and hexadecimal equivalent values in memory locations.

With the exception of pointers, these sample values are typical of what you might see if you PEEKed at the location; these are all byte values, in the range 0 to 255 ($0\text{-}FF_{16}$). **A pointer is a two-byte address, in the range 0 to 65535 ($0FFFF_{16}$), that is stored in the CBM in low-byte, high-byte order.** All two-byte locations in the table contain values stored in low-high order. Consider the first such location in the table:

Memory Address		Sample Value		Description
Decimal	Hexadecimal	Decimal	Hexadecimal	
1-2	0001-0002	826	033A	User address jump vector

If you PEEKed at these locations, the 16-bit address would be presented in two parts, first the low-order byte:

```
?PEEK(1)
58
```

and then the high-order byte:

```
?PEEK(2)
3
```

To convert the two values to the appropriate address, you can convert them separately to hexadecimal and then convert the hexadecimal address to decimal:

Low	High	Address
$58_{10}=3A_{16}$	$3_{10}=03_{16}$	$\longrightarrow$ $033A_{16}=826_{10}$

Note carefully that the sample value 033A means that the first memory byte $=3A$ and the second (higher) memory byte $= 03$.

Or you can multiply the high-order byte by 256 and add it to the low-order byte. The following is a PEEK statement that will do this for you:

```
?PEEK(1)+PEEK(2)
826
```

Conversely, to convert a 16-bit memory address into two separate bytes for POKEing (in low-byte, high-byte order), you can convert the decimal value to hexadecimal and then convert the separated byte digit pairs to decimal, e.g., to convert the address 59409:

	High	Low
$59409_{10}=E811_{16}$ $\longrightarrow$	$E8_{16}=232_{10}$ and	$11_{16}=17_{10}$

Or you can convert using decimal arithmetic by first dividing the address value by 256 and discarding any fractional remainder:

High

59409/256=232.06641=232

Then subtract the high value multiplied by 256 from the original value (59409 in this case) to get the remainder, which is the low-order byte value:

232·256=59392

Low

59409 − 59392=17

(Of course, if you do the division by longhand, the remainder is directly available.)

For a block of byte locations, only the first byte value is shown in the table.

The column labeled DESCRIPTION in Table F-1 gives a short description of the location's use. There are multiple uses for some locations, in which case the primary one is indicated. While not exhaustive, the table illustrates the overall makeup of the CBM memory.

Table F-3 compares the BASIC 4.0 memory map with the BASIC 3.0 revision shown in Table F-2. The DESCRIPTION column provides the location description as currently used by Commodore; the label column shows the assembly language label currently assigned to the location by Commodore. The BASIC 4.0 column gives the hexadecimal address of each location, while the BASIC 3.0 column gives the equivalent BASIC 3.0 hexadecimal address. To find any BASIC 4.0 location, first find the hexadecimal address given in Table F-2. Find this hexadecimal address in the BASIC 3.0 column of Table F-3 and the comparable BASIC 4.0 hexadecimal address is in the adjacent column.

With the exception of the first two entries in Table F-3 which actually represent memory address 0000, all subsequent 0000 addresses identify entries which do not exist in one version of BASIC or the other. For example, if you see an address in the BASIC 3.0 column with 0000 in the BASIC 4.0 column, then BASIC 4.0 has no equivalent location in its memory map. Conversely, a 0000 address in the BASIC 3.0 column identifies a new entry in the BASIC 4.0 memory map for which there is no BASIC 3.0 equivalent.

CBM BASIC INTERPRETER

The CBM BASIC interpreter executes a user program by decoding each source line. Source lines are stored in memory in a compacted form. When you enter a line from the keyboard, the Line Editor has control, allowing you to edit the line until you press the RETURN key. Program lines are stored in memory in ascending line number order. When the RETURN key is pressed, the BASIC interpreter searches memory for the same line number. If there is one, it replaces the current line with the new line. If there isn't one, it searches for the next higher line number. The BASIC interpreter then inserts the new line into memory and moves the reset of the program up.

Program lines are stored at the beginning of the user program area of memory, which starts at memory location 1024. Variables are stored in memory above the program lines, and arrays are stored above the variables. All three areas begin at lower addresses and build upwards to higher addresses. Strings are stored beginning at the top of memory and work downwards. The BASIC interpreter builds all four areas, moving them as necessary and adjusting pointers for insertions and deletions. Eight pairs of

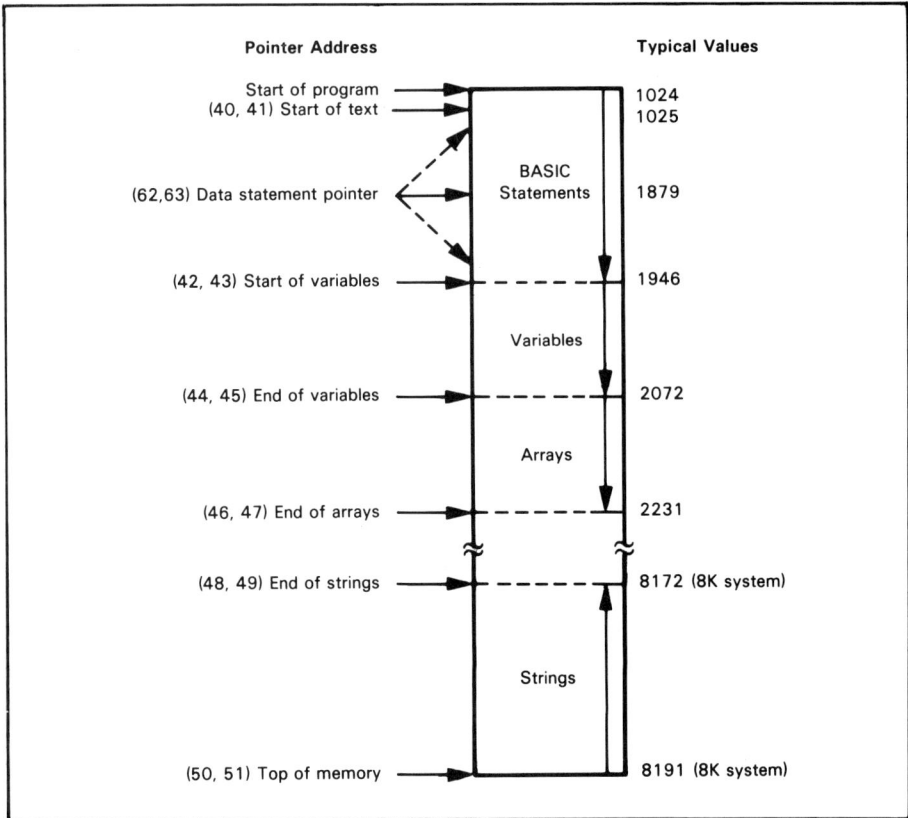

Figure 7-2. Principal Pointers In User Program Area

memory locations contain pointers to the division points in the user program area of memory. These are shown in Figure 7-2. (They are also listed in Appendix F tables).

The formats in which BASIC statements, variables, arrays, and strings are stored in their respective areas are discussed next.

BASIC STATEMENT STORAGE

BASIC statements are stored in the format shown in Figure 7-3.

Memory location 1024 always contains a zero byte.

The next two bytes contain a pointer to the beginning of the first BASIC statement. The pointer, like all other addresses, is stored in low-byte, high-byte order. The pointer is a link to the memory address of the next link. **A link address of zero denotes the end of the text;** i.e., there are no more links and no more statements. BASIC statements are stored in order of ascending line numbers, even though there are links to the next statements. Links are used to quickly search through line numbers.

Following the link address is the line number of the statement, stored in low-byte, high-byte order. Line numbers go from 1 (stored as 1 and 0) to 63999 (stored as 255 and 249).

After the line number, the BASIC statement text begins. Keywords consist of reserved words (listed in Table 4-4) and operators (listed in Table 4-2). Reserved words and logical operator keywords are stored in a compressed format. A one-byte token is used to represent a keyword. All keywords are encoded such that the high-order bit is set to 1. Other elements of the BASIC text are represented by their stored ASCII code; these elements include constants, variable and array names, and special symbols other than operators. All are coded just as they appear in the original BASIC statement. Table A-1 shows the byte codes for all values from 0 to 255 that may appear in the compressed BASIC text. Codes are interpreted according to this table except after an odd number of double quotation marks enclosing a character string; within a character string the standard ASCII codes prevail, as shown in Table A-4.

Note that the left parenthesis is stored as part of the one-byte token for the functions TAB and SPC, but that the other functions use a separate byte for this symbol. For example, the following line would be coded as bytes (in decimal) as illustrated below.

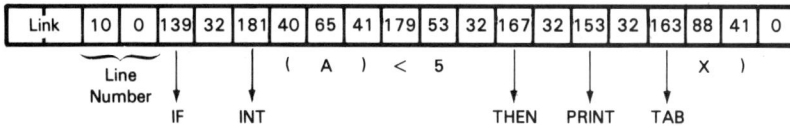

| Link | 10 | 0 | 139 | 32 | 181 | 40 | 65 | 41 | 179 | 53 | 32 | 167 | 32 | 153 | 32 | 163 | 88 | 41 | 0 |

Line Number — IF — INT — (A) < 5 — THEN — PRINT — TAB — X)

The operators (the symbols $+,-,*,/,<,=,>$ and the words AND, OR, and NOT) are given keyword codes (high-order bit set) since they "drive" the BASIC interpreter just as reserved words do (e.g., 179 for $<$). The standard ASCII codes for these symbols (e.g., 60 for $<$) appear only in the text of a string.

Spaces in the source line are stored except for the space between the line number and first keyword. This space is supplied on LISTing when a stored statement is expanded to its original form. **You can conserve memory storage space by eliminating blanks (but this makes the program harder to read). You can also conserve space by putting more than one statement on a line, since the five bytes of link, line number, and 0-end-byte are stored only once.**

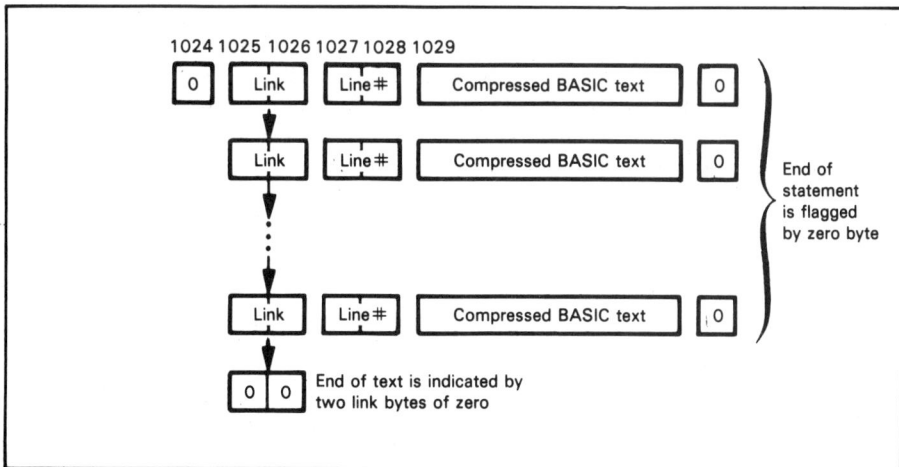

1024 1025 1026 1027 1028 1029

0 | Link | Line # | Compressed BASIC text | 0

Link | Line # | Compressed BASIC text | 0

Link | Line # | Compressed BASIC text | 0

End of statement is flagged by zero byte

0 | 0 — End of text is indicated by two link bytes of zero

Figure 7-3. BASIC Statement Storage

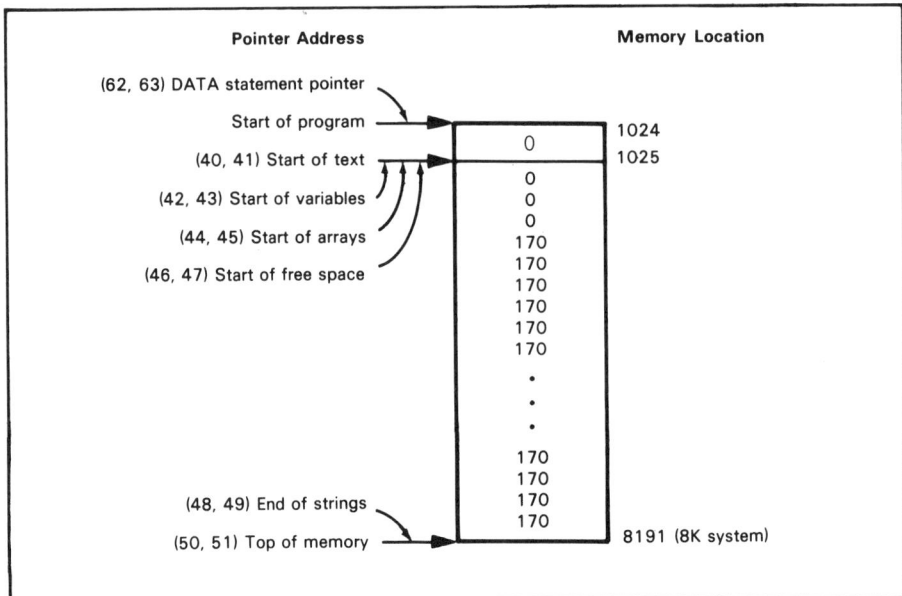

Figure 7-4. User Program Area on Power-Up

The size of each statement is variable and is terminated by a byte of zero to indicate the end of the statement. (A value of zero anywhere within the text is stored as 48.) 0-byte flags are used by the BASIC interpreter in executing a program when it goes through the compressed BASIC text from left to right picking out keywords and performing the indicated operations. A 0-byte indicates the end of the statement; the next four bytes are the link and the line number of the next statement. In contrast to searching through the text and using 0-byte indicators to locate the next statement, links are used when searching the statements for their line numbers. Three consecutive bytes of zero (the last statement's 0-byte followed by two zero link bytes) flag the end of text when executing the program.

A program is stored onto cassette tape in the same format as for memory storage (Figure 7-3). Thus, it is basically "dumped" onto tape in a continuous block, including link addresses and 0-end-bytes.

The use of tokens in place of keywords is not unique to the CBM BASIC, but there is no standard coding from one interpreter to another. Thus, **a BASIC source program SAVEd on tape by CBM BASIC is not compatible with other BASICs, nor can BASIC programs generated on other (non-CBM) machines normally be loaded by the CBM BASIC interpreter.**

USER PROGRAM AREA INITIALIZATION

On power-up, the user program area of memory is initialized to "+" characters (code 170) except for the first few beginning locations 1024 to 1026. Location 1024 is zero, the initial link in locations 1025 and 1026 is also zero. The pointers into the user area are initialized as shown in Figure 7-4.

As lines are entered and edited and new programs loaded, the contents of memory locations throughout the user program area change. They change, however, only as necessary for the current program. The user area is not continuously reinitialized (to "+" or any other code). It is the pointers into the user area that determine the extent of the current program, if any. The action of a NEW statement is simply to re-adjust the pointers to the initial values shown in Figure 7-4. A CLR does the same thing except that it adjusts the variable and array pointers from the end of the program rather than the start of the program as NEW does. In fact, **if you have accidentally cleared the program or variables, you can reinstate them by "reading" through the user program area as needed and restoring the pointer values.**

DATA FORMATS

Variables

Variables are stored in the Variable Area of user program memory (see Figure 7-2). These are simple (unsubscripted) variables; arrays are stored in a separate area. The variables may be floating point, integer, or string and are freely intermixed in the Variable Area. **Each variable, regardless of its type, occupies seven bytes of memory.** The first two bytes contain the variable name, and the remaining five bytes further define the variable. Variables are entered into the variable table as they are encountered during execution of the user program. A variable that is not in the table is assumed to have a value of zero for numeric variables or null for a string variable.

Floating Point Variable Format

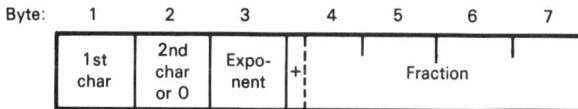

Byte:	1	2	3	4	5	6	7
	1st char	2nd char or 0	Expo-nent	+	Fraction		

Byte 1 contains the first character of the variable name. Byte 2 contains the second character of the variable name or, if there is no second character, byte 2 contains a zero. The characters are stored in standard ASCII codes (see Appendix A). For example, the name A is stored as 65, 0 whereas the name A0 is stored as 65, 48. **A floating point variable is denoted by variable names having stored ASCII values of 90 or below.**

Bytes 3 through 7 contain the value of the floating point variable. **Byte 3 contains the exponent in excess 128 format.** The exponent determines the magnitude of the number. In excess 128 format, 128 is added to the true exponent (after normalization of the significant digits) so that the smallest exponent representation contains all zeros. The largest exponent representable contains all ones. A true exponent of zero is represented by an exponent value of 128 (0+128). Excess 128 format eliminates having to consider a sign in the exponent. Here are some examples:

Actual Exponent	Stored Exponent	Approximate Value	
127	255	10^{38}	(maximum exponent)
34	162	10^{10}	
−1	127	10^{-1}	
−126	2	10^{-38}	
−128	0	10^{-39}	(minimum exponent — number is zero)

Bytes 4 through 7 contain the significant digits of the number. The number is
normalized such that the binary point is to the immediate left of the first non-zero binary digit. That is, it is represented as a fraction in the form:

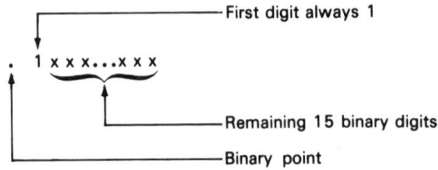

The binary point is always assumed and is not stored. Further, **the most significant 1 digit is always assumed** (since it is always 1) **and** is not stored either. **Its bit
position is used to hold the sign of the number,** 0=positive and 1=negative. To nor-
malize a number, the point is moved to the left and the exponent decremented (smaller
numbers), or the point is moved to the right and the exponent incremented (larger
numbers), until the number is a fraction in the form shown above. **The number zero is**
generally **represented by** all zeros in bytes 3 through 7, but the fraction may contain
roundoff errors; **an exponent of zero** is sufficient to make the number zero.

**Some examples of floating point number representations stored in the Variable
Area follow.** 1E+38 has the maximum exponent of 255. This decreases down to zero as
the numbers decrease to zero. Fractional floating point numbers (e.g., 5, .01, .006) have
exponents below 129. For negative numbers, the exponent increases from 0 to 255 as
the absolute value of the numbers increases. In byte 4 the high-order bit is the sign bit.
In this column, decimal numbers less than 127 have bit 7=0 (positive numbers), and
decimal numbers higher than this have bit 7=1 (negative numbers).

Byte: Number	3 Exponent	4 ±MSB	5 Fraction	6 	7 LSB
1E+38	255	22	118	153	83
1E+10	162	21	2	249	0
1000	138	122	0	0	0
1	129	0	0	00	
0.01	122	35	215	10	62
1E−4	115	81	183	23	90
1E	62	60	229	8	101
1E−39	0	32	0	0	0
0	0	0	0	0	0
−1	129	128	0	0	0
−1000	138	250	0	0	0
−1E+10	162	149	2	249	0
−1E+38	255	150	118	153	83

**The following short program allows you to examine floating point representa-
tions for any numbers.** Line 10 inputs a number that you enter from the keyboard, terminating with a RETURN key. Line 20 points to the beginning of variables +2 to go
past the two-byte variable name. Line 30 prints the number that was input, followed by
the five bytes PEEKed from the variable table. The program is continuous; to end, enter
a null line (RETURN key only).

```
10 INPUT A
20 X=PEEK(43)*256+PEEK(42)+2
30 PRINT A;"="PEEK(X);PEEK(X+1);PEEK(X+2);PEEK(X+3)PEEK(X+4)
40 GOTO 10
```

Integer Variable Format

Byte:	1	2	3	4	5	6	7
	1st char +128	2nd char +128 or 128	Value High	Low	0	0	0

Byte 1 contains the first character of the variable name shifted (+128). Byte 2 contains the second character of the variable name shifted (+128), or if there is no second character, byte 2 contains 128. An integer variable is denoted by variable names having ASCII values of 176 or higher. The % notation is dropped from the variable name. Bytes 3 and 4 contain the value of the integer in high-byte, low-byte order. (Note that this value is not an address and does not conform to the reverse standard for pointers). The value is stored in twos complement format so that the high-order bit (bit 7 of byte 3) represents the sign, 0=positive, and 1=negative. The remaining three bytes are not used and are set to zero.

The following are some examples of integer representations stored in the Variable Area. You can use the same program as above to look at integer number representations after changing A to A% in lines 10 and 30.

Byte Number	3	4
32767	127	255 (256·127+255=32767)
32766	127	254
14000	54	176
256	1	0
255	0	255
1	0	1
−1	255	255 (FFF$_{16}$)+1=1
−2	255	254
−32766	128	2
−32767	1281	1

String Variable Format

Byte:	1	2	3	4	5	6	7
	1st char	2nd char +128 or 128	Char count	Pointer High	Low	0	0

Byte 1 contains the first character of the variable name. Byte 2 contains the second character of the variable name shifted (+128), or if there is no second character, the second byte contains 128. This combination of ASCII ranges denotes a string variable entry. The $ notation is dropped from the variable name. Byte 3 contains a count of the number of characters in the string (0 to 255). This is the value fetched for the LEN function. Bytes 4 and 5 contain a pointer to the beginning of the string itself, stored elsewhere in memory. This pointer is in the standard 6502 low-byte, high-byte order. The remaining two bytes are not used and are set to zero.

String storage is optimized by using the copy of the string already in memory if there is one. If there is not, a string is created and stored in the String Area in upper memory. A few examples are given below.

Constants

Constants are stored in the BASIC statement itself. They are not placed into a separate area of memory, and they are not stored in the Variable Area. **Floating point, integer and string constants are all stored as ASCII character source codes,** as described previously under BASIC Statement Storage. For example, the line:

```
10 PRINT "HI!"
```

is stored **entirely in the BASIC Statement Area,** in the form:

```
| Link | 10 | 0 | 153 | 32 | 34 | 72 | 73 | 33 | 34 | 0 |
```

Line number — 10 0
P R I N T — 153
" — 32
" H I ! " — 34 72 73 33 34

whereas the statement

```
10 A$="HI!":PRINT A$
```

is stored in two areas. The original statement is stored in the BASIC Statement Area:

Memory Address → 1025   1033 1034   1042

```
| Link | 10 | 0 | 65 | 36 | 178 | 34 | 72 | 73 | 33 | 34 | 58 | 153 | 32 | 65 | 36 | 0 |
```

Line number — 10 0
A $ = " H I ! " : P R I N T A $

The illustrated memory addresses assume that this is the first statement in program memory, therefore it is stored at the beginning of the user program area (location 1025). In addition, when this statement is executed the following entry is made in the Variable Area:

Byte: 1   2   3   4   5   6   7

```
(42, 43) →  | 65 | 128 | 3 | 9 | 4 | 0 | 0 |   (String)
```

A — 65
Length of string — 3
No 2nd char — 128
4·256+9 =1033 — 9 4

The string in the BASIC Statement Area is pointed to (beginning at memory location 1033 in this program) rather than storing a copy of it in upper memory. However, when you create a new string, as in:

```
20 B$=A$+"HO"
```

the BASIC Program Area entry is:

```
| Link | 20 | 0 | 66 | 36 | 178 | 65 | 36 | 170 | 34 | 72 | 79 | 34 | 0 |
```

Line number — 20 0
B $ = A $ + " H O "

and the entry in the Variable Area is:

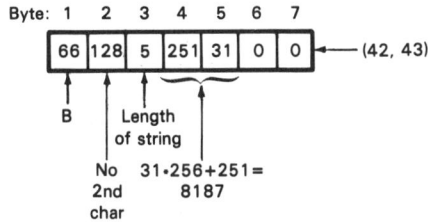

Byte: 1 2 3 4 5 6 7

| 66 | 128 | 5 | 251 | 31 | 0 | 0 | ◄—— (42, 43) |

B — Length of string

No 2nd char — $31 \cdot 256 + 251 = 8187$

This time the pointer addresses a location in upper memory (8187 in this program) that contains the string:

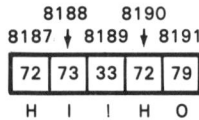

8188   8190
8187 ↓ 8189 ↓ 8191

| 72 | 73 | 33 | 72 | 79 |

H   I   !   H   O

The address 8187 assumes an 8K memory. The largest available address is then 8191.

ARRAY STORAGE FORMAT

Arrays are stored in the Array Area of user program memory (see Figure 7-2). Arrays may be floating point, integer, or string, and are stored in the order in which they are created by the program. The type of array is distinguished by the way in which the two-character array name is stored. Array names and variable names are encoded in exactly the same way. **An array is stored with a header, followed by the elements of the array,** as follows:

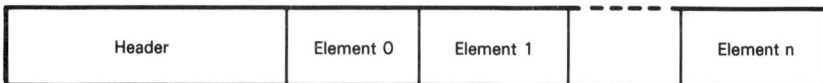

| Header | Element 0 | Element 1 | | Element n |

Elements are stored in reverse order for strings.

Array Header

All types of arrays have the same header format. The header contains seven bytes, plus two additional bytes for each array dimension beyond 1.

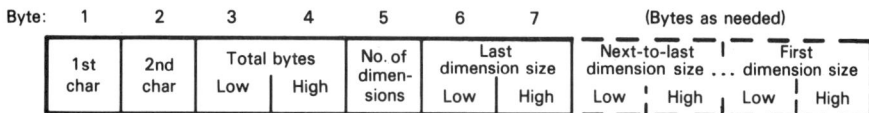

Byte: 1   2   3   4   5   6   7   (Bytes as needed)

| 1st char | 2nd char | Total bytes Low | Total bytes High | No. of dimen- sions | Last dimension size Low | Last dimension size High | Next-to-last dimension size Low : High | ... First dimension size Low : High |

Floating point array elements are encoded using floating point variable format, therefore each floating point array element occupies five bytes. But array integers require just two bytes, while array strings require three bytes; in each case the zero bytes are discarded.

In the array header, bytes 1 and 2 contain the array name. Bytes 3 and 4 contain a count of the number of memory locations that the array occupies. For example,

A(0) would occupy 12 bytes: 7 for the header and 5 for the single element. The byte count is **stored in low-byte, high-byte order. Byte 5 contains a count of the number of dimensions in the array.** Thus, A(5) has one dimension (byte 5=1) and A(10,10,2) has three dimensions (byte 5=3). **For a one-dimensional array (or vector), bytes 6 and 7 contain the dimension size** — this is the number specified between parentheses in the DIM statement +1. For example, the dimension size = 61 for DIM A(60), = 101 for DIM A(100), etc. If the array does not appear in a DIM statement, the dimension size defaults to 11. The dimension size is **stored in low-byte, high-byte order. For a multiple dimension array, the header contains additional bytes in which additional dimension sizes are stored. Two additional bytes are used for each additional dimension. The dimension sizes are stored in reverse order as compared to the order in which they appear in the DIM statement.** For example, for DIM A(10,5) the dimension sizes are stored as bytes 6,7=6 and bytes 8,9=11. For DIM X(2,1,3) the dimension sizes are stored as bytes 6,7=4, bytes 8,9=2 and bytes 10,11=3.

Array element formats for each type of array are shown below. Formats are as described for variables, with bytes deleted.

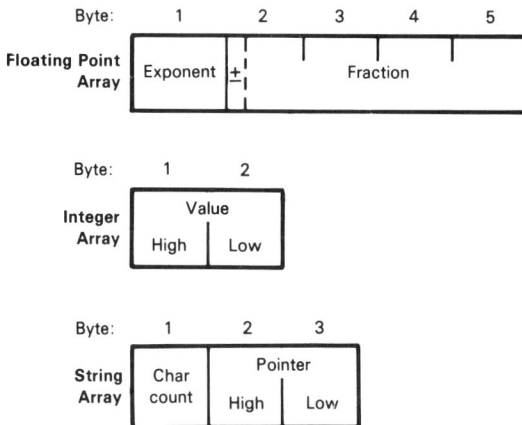

The size of the header may be calculated as five bytes plus twice the number of dimensions in the array. **Memory occupied by array elements may be calculated as the number of bytes per element (5 for floating point, 2 for integer, 3 for string) times the number of elements (the dimensions multiplied together + 1).** The total size of the array, header plus elements, is stored in byte 4 of the array header.

The following program examines Array Area entries:

```
10 DIM A(5),B%(2,2),C$(10): REM SAMPLE ARRAYS
20 FOR I=0 TO 5: A(I)=I: NEXT I
30 FOR I=0 TO 2: FOR J=0 TO 2: B%(J,I)=100+3*I+J: NEXT J,I
40 FOR I=0 TO 10: C$(I)=CHR$(ASC("A")+I): NEXT I
50 X=PEEK(45)*256+PEEK(44): REM POINT TO ARRAY AREA
60 Y=PEEK(47)*256+PEEK(46): REM END OF ARRAYS
70 FOR I=X TO Y
80 PRINT I,PEEK(I)
90 GET D$: IF D$="" GOTO 90
100 NEXT I
```

Each of the three types of array is dimensioned. Line 20 fills the floating point array A with the numbers 0 through 5. Line 30 fills the integer array C$ with the single strings A through K. Lines 50 and 60 fetch the pointers to the end of the Variable Area and the end of the Array Area. The display stops at each memory location; to print the next location, press any key (e.g., the RETURN key). You will need to locate the beginning of the arrays by the sequence for the first array shown below (the pointer addresses the end variable). **The memory locations will appear as shown below.**

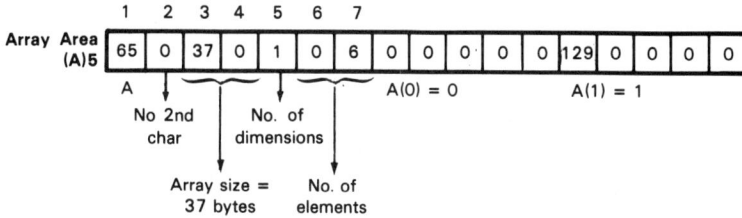

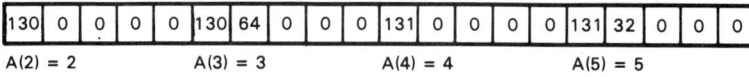

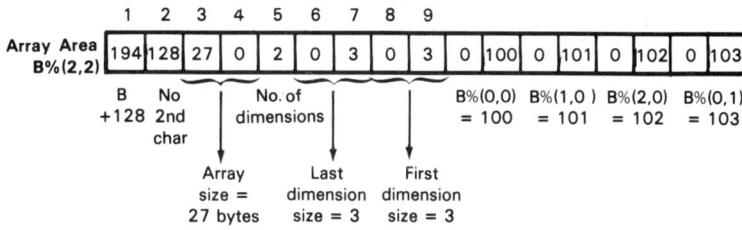

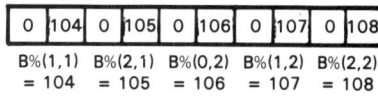

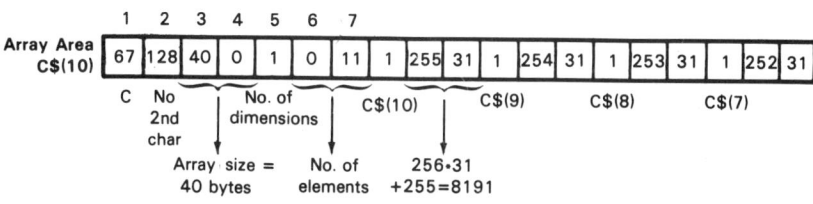

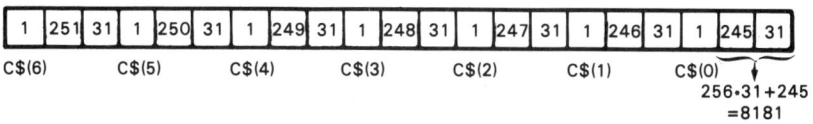

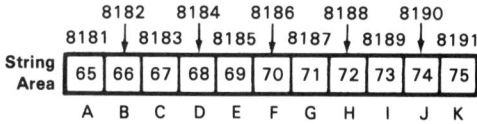

Array Area (A)5

1	2	3	4	5	6	7
65	0	37	0	1	0	6	0	0	0	0	0	129	0	0	0	0

A — No 2nd char; No. of dimensions; Array size = 37 bytes; No. of elements; A(0) = 0; A(1) = 1

| 130 | 0 | 0 | 0 | 0 | 130 | 64 | 0 | 0 | 0 | 131 | 0 | 0 | 0 | 0 | 131 | 32 | 0 | 0 | 0 |

A(2) = 2   A(3) = 3   A(4) = 4   A(5) = 5

Array Area B%(2,2)

1	2	3	4	5	6	7	8	9
194	128	27	0	2	0	3	0	3	0	100	0	101	0	102	0	103

B; No +128 2nd char; No. of dimensions; Array size = 27 bytes; Last dimension size = 3; First dimension size = 3; B%(0,0) = 100; B%(1,0) = 101; B%(2,0) = 102; B%(0,1) = 103

| 0 | 104 | 0 | 105 | 0 | 106 | 0 | 107 | 0 | 108 |

B%(1,1) = 104; B%(2,1) = 105; B%(0,2) = 106; B%(1,2) = 107; B%(2,2) = 108

Array Area C$(10)

1	2	3	4	5	6	7
67	128	40	0	1	0	11	1	255	31	1	254	31	1	253	31	1	252	31

C; No 2nd char; No. of dimensions; Array size = 40 bytes; No. of elements; 256·31 +255=8191; C$(10); C$(9); C$(8); C$(7)

| 1 | 251 | 31 | 1 | 250 | 31 | 1 | 249 | 31 | 1 | 248 | 31 | 1 | 247 | 31 | 1 | 246 | 31 | 1 | 245 | 31 |

C$(6)   C$(5)   C$(4)   C$(3)   C$(2)   C$(1)   C$(0)
256·31+245 =8181

String Area

8181	8182	8183	8184	8185	8186	8187	8188	8189	8190	8191
65	66	67	68	69	70	71	72	73	74	75
A	B	C	D	E	F	G	H	I	J	K

CHARACTER REPRESENTATION

ASCII (American Standard Code for Information Interchange) is a widely used code for representing character data. It is normally a 7-bit code, allowing 128 characters ($7F_{16} = 128_{10}$) to be represented. The standard ASCII 7-bit character set is shown in Table A-2 in Appendix A. Bits are numbered from 0 (least significant bit) to 6 (most significant bit):

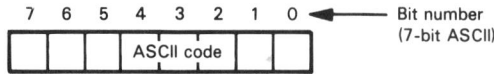

```
7  6  5  4  3  2  1  0  ◄──────  Bit number
┌──┬──┬──┬──┬──┬──┬──┬──┐        (7-bit ASCII)
│  │  │  │ ASCII code │  │  │
└──┴──┴──┴──┴──┴──┴──┴──┘
```

The first 32 codes are reserved for non-printable control characters, intended for message formatting and print format control.

CBM computers store characters in an extended, 8-bit version of ASCII format. With eight bits normally available, rather than just seven, up to 256 characters can be represented. Within compressed BASIC text, the 8-bit character codes are interpreted as shown in Table A-1, where bit 8 = 1 signifies a keyword. Elsewhere in main memory the 8-bit character codes are interpreted as shown in Table A-4.

The screen memory, occupying memory locations 32768 through 33767, uses a different ASCII character representation than main memory. It is a 7-bit code as shown in Table A-3. The eighth bit is a normal/reverse field indicator. Note that the characters are arranged such that bits 0 through 5 represent one key on the PET keyboard, with bit 6 = 0 being the unshifted character and bit 6 = 1 being the shifted character of the same key.

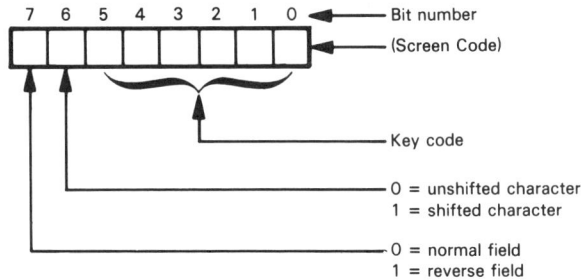

```
7  6  5  4  3  2  1  0  ◄────── Bit number
┌──┬──┬──┬──┬──┬──┬──┬──┐ ◄──── (Screen Code)
└──┴──┴──┴──┴──┴──┴──┴──┘
      └───────┬───────┘
              └────────────── Key code

          └────────────────── 0 = unshifted character
                               1 = shifted character

       └───────────────────── 0 = normal field
                               1 = reverse field
```

The complete character set for screen memory is shown in Table A- 4 under the PEEK/POKE column.

The screen memory ASCII code may be derived from the CBM ASCII code by moving bit 7 of the main code into bit 6 and dropping the previous value of bit 6. The examples below illustrate the four cases of a 0 or 1 in bit 7 going into a 0 or 1 in bit 6:

Character	Main Memory Representation	Screen Memory Representation
	01000001	00000001
Shifted A (♠)	11000001	01000001
1	00110001	00110001
Shifted 1 (⊞)	10110001	01110001

When PRINTing to the screen, the CBM computer automatically makes the conversion to screen codes. Only when you are PEEKing and POKEing in screen memory do you need to be concerned with character set differences.

Screen memory can be looked upon as having an additional bit that selects the alternate character set in response to a POKE 59468,14. POKE 59468,12 restores the standard set. The alternate set is also shown in Table A-4.

ASSEMBLY LANGUAGE PROGRAMMING

CBM BASIC can execute small programs written in 6502 assembly language. Assembly language programs execute faster and require less memory space for a given function than the equivalent BASIC program. **You might want to write an assembly language program to be run on the CBM computer if:**

1. The operation is not fast enough using a BASIC program.
2. The operation cannot be implemented in CBM BASIC.
3. The operation takes up too much memory space as a BASIC program.
4. Assembly language lends itself better to the task than the BASIC language. Some I/O operations probably fall into this category.

An assembly language program can be loaded into memory by POKEing the decimal values of the 6502 instructions that make up the program. There is no area set aside for use by assembly language programs. You have to make space, either by taking otherwise unused locations or by setting up a space in the user program area of memory. The following are possible locations:

1. **Cassette Buffers**. If you do not have a second cassette unit, then the 192-byte tape buffer for cassette #2 can be used to store an assembly language program. The buffer #2 extents are locations 826 to 1017 (see Appendix F). In addition, if the console cassette unit is not going to be used while the assembly language program is operating, then the other 192-byte tape buffer for cassette #1, at memory locations 634-825, is also available. No LOADs, SAVEs or other tape I/O can be performed accessing the particular cassette while its buffer is used by an assembly language program.

2. **Top of Memory**. Memory locations 52 and 53 contain the pointer to the top of memory. On 8K PETs this value is 8192. You can temporarily set the top-of-memory pointer to a lower address, thereby reserving a number of bytes from the new pointer value to the actual top of memory for storage of an assembly language program. To set the pointer, say, down 1000 bytes, you will need to store the value 7192 (8192−1000) converted into low address, high address order:

$$\text{High} \qquad\qquad \text{Low}$$
$$7192_{10} = 1C18_{16} \rightarrow \ 1C_{16} = 28_{10} \ \text{ and } \ 18_{16} = 24_{10}$$

So 24 is to be stored at location 52 (low byte), and 28 is to be stored at location 53 (high byte). The following instructions can be used:

```
10 AL=PEEK(52):AH=PEEK(53):REM SAVE CURRENT POINTER
20 POKE 52,24:POKE 53,28:REM TOP OF CORE = 7192
.
100 POKE 52,AL:POKE 53,AH:REM RESTORE POINTER
110 END
```

3. You may find usable locations in the **BASIC Statement Area**. You may create a block of dummy DATA statements and use those locations. There are generally a few locations free between the end of the program and the beginning of the Variable Area. But you must be very careful that your assembly language program and the BASIC interpreter do not get in each other's way.

The CBM BASIC interpreter can be used to load an assembly language program into the selected area of memory. The process is a rudimentary one, consisting of POKEing the decimal equivalents of the 6502 machine language instructions. To get the instructions in decimal, write your program in 6502 assembly language (reference manuals are listed in Appendix D), hand assemble it into hexadecimal, and then convert the hexadecimal codes to decimal. Commodore's Terminal Interface Monitor stores the hexadecimal codes directly. However, with the Monitor you must load the assembly language routine separately from the BASIC program, whereas by POKEing you can load the assembly language routine as part of executing the main program written in BASIC. DATA statements are used to define the machine language codes, which can be subsequently READ into the program and passed to a POKE loop.

Control is transferred to an assembly language program in one of two ways: the SYS or the USR function, which are more or less interchangeable. SYS is geared to turning control over to an assembly language program. USR is a true function reference that allows a value to be sent to the called assembly language routine and a value returned by it to the main program.

The assembly language program must return control to BASIC via a Return-from-Subroutine (RTS) assembly language instruction.

SYS

SYS is a system function that transfers program control to an independent subsystem.

Format:

SYS(address)

where:

    address   is a numeric constant, variable, or expression representing the starting
        address at which execution of the subsystem is to begin. The
        value must be in the range $0 \leq \text{address} \leq 65535$.

Unlike other functions, SYS can be specified alone in a direct or program statement.

Example:

SYS(826)   In immediate mode transfer control of the system to the 6402 assembly
        language program beginning at memory location 826
        (the 2nd cassette buffer)

55 SYS(826)   Same as above but executed in program mode. On return, execution
        proceeds with the first statement following the SYS statement

126 SYS(A+14)   Transfer control of the system to the computer address A+14

SYS is the assembly language subroutine equivalent of GOSUB, but with the important difference that the safeguards built in to CBM BASIC to protect the system from user program errors are no longer operable. The system will tend to crash even more frequently while debugging assembly language programs than it does debugging BASIC programs.

Use the RTS assembly language instruction to return to BASIC.

Values can be passed between the BASIC program and the SYS subroutine using PEEKs and POKEs.

USR

USR is a system function that passes a parameter to a user-written assembly language subroutine whose address is contained in memory locations 1 and 2 and fetches a return parameter from the subroutine.

Format:

USR(datan)

where:

datan   is the numeric parameter value passed to the subroutine.

Example:

```
?USR(60)
```
Displays in immediate mode the value returned by the USR subroutine when passed a value of 60

```
105 A=USR(60)
```
Same as above but in program mode

```
210 IF USR(X)<4 GOTO 50
```

```
510 SM=USR(XA)+USR(3.4)+SQR(Y)+π
```

Before making a USR reference, the beginning address of the assembly language subroutine must be placed into memory locations 1 and 2. For example, if the subroutine is located in the cassette #2 area, you would include the instructions:

```
10 POKE 1,58                   Low              High
20 POKE 2,3          826_{10}=033A_{16}=3A_{16}=58_{10}  and  03_{16}=3_{10}
```

The parameter value is passed to the USR subroutine in system locations that function as a floating point accumulator (FAC) for all functions. The FAC resides in six bytes, from memory locations 94 to 99 ($5E_{16}$-63_{16}). The FAC has the following format:

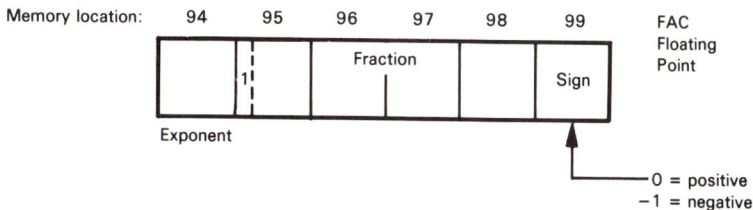

Like floating variables, the exponent is stored in excess 128 format and the fraction is normalized with the high-order bit of byte 95 (the high-order byte of the fraction) set to 1. The difference between this format and the variable format is that the high-drder 1 bit is present in byte 95 of the FAC. An extra byte (99) is used to hold the sign of the fraction. (This is done for ease of manipulation by the functions that use the FAC.)

The USR subroutine must fetch the value passed to it from the FAC locations. It must deposit the value being returned into the FAC before terminating. If the USR subroutine does not alter the FAC, then the same value is returned to the program as was passed from it.

RANDOM ACCESS FILES

Random access files are created by directly addressing diskette data blocks and memory buffers.

Diskette data blocks each occupy a single sector. Random access files directly address diskette data blocks via their actual track and sector address. Diskette memory buffers, likewise, are directly addressed and assigned to logical file secondary addresses. (Recall that each diskette unit has sixteen 256-byte memory buffers.)

Random access files are created by using a number of subroutines that directly access the diskette surface and memory buffers. These are the same subroutines used to implement sequential and relative file logic; however, your program creates the field/record/file structure, whatever it may be.

You should not use random access files unless you are a very experienced programmer. You will be working at the same level as the people who designed the sequential and relative file logic found in standard CBM BASIC. These individuals are professional system programmers. Unless you are an equally experienced programming professional, you are unlikely to have much success with the information presented in this section.

Diskette random access is programmed using PRINT# statements with appropriately coded text strings in their parameter list. The PRINT# statements access the command channel, via secondary address 15. Random access logical files are opened with specific diskette memory buffers assigned to each logical file via its secondary address. The PRINT# statement parameter list uses the secondary address to identify logical files and assigned buffers.

The following standard OPEN statement format is used when opening a random access logical file:

```
100 OPEN  lf,dev,sa,"#[bu]"
```

where:

lf	is the logical file number specified in the command channel OPEN statement
dev	is the device number (usually 8)
sa	is the secondary address, which should have a value between 2 and 14
bu,	if present, is the buffer number allocated to the specified secondary address. There are sixteen 256-byte buffers; the first three buffers are used by the disk operating system. Buffer numbers 3 through 15 are therefore available. If bu is not specified, then the next available buffer is assigned to the secondary address

You can execute a GET# statement immediately after opening a random access file in order to determine the assigned buffer number. However, the GET# statement must be executed before any other input or output statement accesses the logical file. Here is an example program:

```
5 REM ASSIGN BUFFER 5 TO SECONDARY ADDRESS 4, USED BY LOGICAL FILE 2
10 OPEN 2,8,4,"#5"
20 PRINT DS$:REM CHECK I/O OPERATION STATUS
30 GET#2,A$:PRINT ASC(A$):REM DISPLAY THE BUFFER NUMBER TO CHECK OPERATION
40 PRINTDS$:REM RECHECK I/O STATUS
50 CLOSE 2
60 STOP
```

Random access file commands are subsequently issued using PRINT# statements with the following general format:

```
10 OPEN lf,8,15
20 PRINT# lf, "parameter"
```

parameter identifies the random access file operation. parameter has two parts: a command and a parameter list. The command has a long form which must end with a colon, or a short form, in which case the parameter list is assumed to begin at the fourth character position of the string. Parameters can be separated by comma, space or skip characters. The following abbreviations are used to describe parameters:

sa	The secondary address specified in the data logical file OPEN statement
dr	The diskette drive number (0 or 1)
t	The diskette track number
s	The sector number within the selected track
p	The buffer pointer, or character position selector, which may have a value between 0 and 255
adl	The low-order byte of a memory address
adh	The high-order byte of a memory address
nc	Number of characters. This number must be between 1 and 34
data	A data string with nc characters

adl, adh and nc must be specified as parameters of CHR$ functions. For example, if adl has the value 123, it must be specified as CHR$(123).

Block Read

This statment reads any diskette sector into a buffer. The BLOCK READ statement has the following format:

```
PRINT# lf, "BLOCK-READ:sa,dr,t,s"
PRINT# lf, "B-Rsa,dr,t,s"
```

The following example opens logical file 2, assigning buffer 5 to secondary address 4, then reads sector 0 of track 18 on drive 1 into buffer 5:

```
10 REM OPEN LOGICAL FILE 2, ASSIGNING BUFFER 5 TO SECONDARY ADDRESS 4
20 OPEN 2,8,4,"#5"
30 REM READ SECTOR 0 OF TRACK 18 ON DRIVE 1 INTO BUFFER 5
40 OPEN 15,8,15
50 PRINT#15,"B-R4,1,18,0"
60 REM DISPLAY THE BUFFER CONTENTS TO PROVE THAT DATA WAS FETCHED
70 REM DISPLAY 256 BYTE BUFFER AS 8 ROWS OF 32 NUMBERS PER ROW
75 PRINT"";
80 FOR I=1 TO 8
90 FOR J=1 TO 32
100 GET#2,A$:IF A$="" THEN 100
110 PRINT ASC(A$);
120 NEXT J
130 PRINT
140 NEXT I
150 CLOSE 2
160 CLOSE 15
170 STOP
```

Block Write

This statement writes the contents of a buffer to a specified sector. It has the following format:

```
PRINT # If,"BLOCK-WRITE:sa,dr,t,s"
or  PRINT # If,"B-Wsa,dr,t,s"
```

The following statements open logical file 2, assigning buffer 8 to secondary address 7. The contents of buffer 8 are written to sector 10 of track 35 on drive 0:

```
200 OPEN 2,8,7,"#8"
210 OPEN 15,8 15
220 REM STATEMENTS THAT WRITE TO BUFFER 8 MUST FOLLOW HERE
300 PRINT#15,"B-W7,0,35,0"
310 CLOSE 2
320 CLOSE 15
330 STOP
```

Block Execute

This statement is the same as a BLOCK READ, except that data read from the sector is assumed to be an assembly language program's object code. As soon as the program is loaded it is executed. The program must end with a Return-from-Subroutine instruction (RTS). It has the following format:

```
PRINT # If,"BLOCK-EXECUTE:sa,dr,t,s"
or  PRINT # If,"B-Esa,dr,t,s"
```

Buffer Pointer

This statement moves the pointer from the beginning of the buffer to any character position within the buffer. It has the following format:

```
PRINT # If,"BUFFER-POINTER:sa,p"
or  PRINT # If,"B-Psa,p"
```

The statement on line 55, shown below, if added to the BLOCK READ example, moves the buffer pointer to character 24:

```
55 PRINT#15,"B-P4,26"
```

Block Allocate

This statement updates the Block Availability Map (BAM) to show how the current block has been used. The block availability map is written to the diskette when the logical file is closed. If the requested block (sector) has already been allocated, the error channel identifies the next available block, while specifying a NO BLOCK error. If no blocks are available, then 00 is returned for the track and sector parameters. It has the following format:

```
PRINT # If,"BLOCK-ALLOCATE:dr,t,s"
or  PRINT # If,"B-Adr,t,s"
```

Memory Write

The MEMORY WRITE statement writes data into a diskette buffer. It has the following format:

```
PRINT # If,"M-W"adl/adh/nc/data
```

Table 7-2. Starting Address for Model 2040 and Model 8050
256-Byte Diskette Buffers

Buffer No.	Model 2040/8050	
	Hexadecimal	Decimal
0	1000	4096
1	1100	4352
2	1200	4608
3	1300	4864
4	2000	8192
5	2100	8448
6	2200	8704
7	2300	8960
8	3000	12288
9	3100	12455
10	3200	12800
11	3300	13056
12	4000	13312
13	4100	13568
14	4200	13824
15	4300	14080

Diskette memory buffer addresses are summarized in Table 7-2 for the Model 2040 and 8050 diskette drives. Note that buffer addresses are somewhat scattered.

Suppose the four data bytes 32, 0, 17 and 96 are to be written into buffer 2 of a Model 2040 diskette drive. From Table 7-2, note that this buffer starting address is 1800_{10}. Therefore the following PRINT# statement is needed:

```
100 PRINT#15, "M-W"CHR$(00)CHR$(18)CHR$(32)CHR$(0)CHR$(17)CHR$(96)
```

Memory Read

This statement allows a byte of data to be read from a diskette buffer. It has the following format:

```
PRINT# lf,"M-R"adl/adh
```

The address of the byte to be read is specified by the parameter list using CHR$ functions. The byte itself is then read using a GET# statement, via the control channel (15). Subsequently an INPUT# statement will not execute correctly until a random access statement other than a MEMORY READ, MEMORY WRITE or MEMORY EXECUTE has been executed.

For example, the following statements read a data byte from buffer address 1808:

```
100 PRINT#15, "M-R"CHR$(8)CHR$(18)
110 GET#15,A$
```

Memory Execute

This statement executes an assembly language subroutine. It has the following format:

```
PRINT# lf,"M-E"adl/adh
```

adl and adh are the decimal low- and high-order halves of the subroutine starting address in diskette buffer memory. The subroutine which gets executed must end with the following Return-from-Subroutine instruction:

```
RTS, $60
```

Table 7-3. Random Access File User Statements

User Designation	Alternate User Designation	Function
U1	UA	BLOCK-READ replacement
U2	UB	BLOCK-WRITE replacement
U3	UC	jump to $1300
U4	UD	jump to $1303
U5	UE	jump to $1306
U6	UF	jump to $D008
U7	UG	jump to $D00B
U8	UH	jump to $D00E
U9	UI	jump to $D0D5
U:	UJ	power up $E18E

User

There are ten special "user" statements. The first two substitute for BLOCK READ and BLOCK WRITE; seven are JUMP TO subroutines, while the eighth enters the power-up routine. User statements are summarized in Table 7-3. For U3 through U9 see the revision 3 memory map given in Appendix F in order to identify the routines jumped to.

For U1 and U2 use the following format:

PRINT # If "Ux;sa,dr,t,s"

x is 1 for U1 or 2 for U2.

Chapter 8

CBM BASIC

This chapter describes the syntax for all CBM BASIC statements and functions. Statements are described first, listed in alphabetic order; then functions are described, also in alphabetic order.

This chapter serves as a reference for all statements and functions. Chapters 4, 5 and 6 describe programming concepts; these three chapters also give examples of statements and functions used in programs.

Immediate and Program Modes

Most statements can be executed in immediate or program mode. Unless otherwise stated, you can assume that a statement can be used in both modes. Exceptions are identified. Some statements can be used in one mode, but not the other; other statements can be used in both modes, but only one mode is practical.

BASIC Revisions

All statements and functions are identified as available with BASIC 4.0 only, or with all versions of BASIC. Statements and functions are cross referenced where an "all versions" statement or function has a BASIC 4.0 equivalent. All BASIC 4.0 statements need DOS 2.0, or higher releases of DOS.

Format Conventions

Consistent syntax is used when defining the format for all statements and functions. The following conventions have been adopted:

UPPER CASE	Upper case words and letters must appear exactly as shown.
lower case	Lower case words and letters are variable; the exact wording or value is supplied by the programmer.
{ }	Braces indicate a choice of items; braces do not appear in an actual statement.
[ ]	Brackets indicate that the parameter is optional; brackets do not appear in an actual statement.
...	Ellipses indicate that the preceding item can be repeated; ellipses do not appear in actual statements.
line number	A beginning line number is implied for all stored statements.

Terms are used as follows in statement and function format definitions:

access	the way in which a data file is to be accessed. Use WRITE for a write access and READ for a read access.
bno	the character number within a record of a relative data file.
byte	a numeric constant variable or expression which evaluates to a number in the range 0 through 255.
condition	a relational term or expression of the type:

$$\text{var} \begin{Bmatrix} < \\ > \\ = \\ <\,> \\ <\,= \\ >\,= \end{Bmatrix} \text{[expression]}$$

	If the expression to the right of the relational operator is absent then = 0 is implied.
constant	any numeric or string constant.
c$	a character string or CHR$ function representing a comma, carriage return, or other legal separator in a PRINT# statement parameter list.
<CR>	a carriage return character.
d	a destination diskette drive number (0 or 1).
data	any constant, variable or expression.
datan	any numeric constant, variable or expression.
data$	any string constant, variable or expression.
Dd	a destination diskette drive number which must be specified as D0 or D1.
destfile	the name of a destination file.
dev	a physical unit device number (see Table 8-1).

Table 8-1. Physical Device Numbers

Device Number	Device
0	Keyboard
1 (default)	Cassette tape unit #1
2	Cassette tape #2
3	Video display screen
4	Printer
5-7	IEEE port devices
8	Diskette unit
9-30	IEEE port devices
31-255	Currently unassignable

Table 8-2. Secondary Address Codes

Device	Secondary Address Code	Operation
CBM Cassette Tape Units	0 (default) 1 2	Open for read Open for write Open for write and end-of-file (EOF) tape mark Write end-of tape (EOT) mark when file is closed
CBM Line Printer	0 (default) 1 2 3 4 5 6 7* 8* 9* 10*	Normal Print Print under format statement control Store the formatting data Set number of lines per page Enable printer format diagnostic messages Define a programmable character Set spacing between lines (Model 2022 only) Select lower-case Select upper-case Turn off Unit 4 Reset
CBM Diskette Unit	0 1 2-14 15	Not defined Not defined Open for Read/Write as specified Access parameter
* New printer ROMs only		

diskname	the name assigned to a disk.
dr	a diskette drive number (0 or 1).
Ds	a source diskette drive number which must be specified as D0 or D1.
<ESC>	the escape key or character.
expression	an arithmetic expression containing any combination of operators, numeric constants and variables.
filename	any file name.
Ivv	a diskette number which may range between 00 and 99, and must be written as I00 through I99.
lf	a logical file number (an integer between 0 and 255).
line	any basic program line number.
line$_i$	one of many basic program line numbers.
Ly	relative file record length. y is the number of characters per record; it may range between 1 and 254. The record length must be specified using the format L1 through L254.
memadr	any memory address. Memory addresses may range from 0 to 65536.
message	any text string enclosed in quotes.
newname	a new data file name.
nvar	any numeric variable name.
oldname	any old data file name.
ON Uz	the standard BASIC 4.0 means of specifying a physical unit number. ON U must be present; z is the physical number. If this parameter is absent physical unit number 8 (the standard disk drive physical number) is assumed.
rno	the record number within a relative data file.
<RVS>	the unshifted REVERSE key.
s	a source diskette drive number (0 or 1).
sa	a secondary address (see Table 8-2).
sourcefile	the name of a source data file.
statement	any BASIC statement.
type	data file type specification. SEQ represents a sequential file, PRG represents the program file, and USR represents a random access file.
var	any numeric integer or string variable.
var(sub)	any subscripted integer, numeric, or string variable.
vv	a diskette number (between 00 and 99).
W	a parameter specifying the sequential file being opened for a write access.

BASIC STATEMENTS

APPEND # (BASIC 4.0)

The APPEND# statement opens an existing sequential diskette file and allows new data to be added at the end of the file. (See also PRINT# COPY.)

Format:

    APPEND #If,"filename"[,Dd][ON Uz]

The APPEND# statement opens sequential data file "filename" on the diskette on drive d and positions file pointers beyond the current end of file. Subsequent PRINT# statements referencing logical file If can then write additional data, which gets appended to the end of the file. If no disk drive is specified (d is absent) drive 0 is assumed.

Example:

    APPEND#1,"CALC"   *Open sequential file "CALC" as logical file #1 on drive 0. Write*
    PRINT#1,A   *variable A contents to the end of the file*

    APPEND#3,"TALK",D1   *Open sequential file "TALK" as logical file #3. The string "123" is*
    PRINT#3,"123"   *added to the end of the file*

BACKUP (BASIC 4.0)

The BACKUP statement duplicates an entire diskette. The duplicate and original have the same header, disk name, identification number, directory, and files. (See also PRINT# DUPLICATE.)

Format:

    BACKUP Ds TO Dd [ON Uz]

The diskette in drive s is duplicated. The duplicate diskette is generated in drive d. Duplicating the entire diskette takes a couple of minutes.

Example:

    BACKUP D0 TO D1   *Duplicate contents of diskette in drive 0 to diskette in drive 1*

    BACKUP D1 TO D0   *Duplicate contents of diskette in drive 1 to diskette in drive 0*

Caution: All files on the diskette must be properly closed before the diskette is backed up.

CLOSE

The CLOSE statement closes a logical file. (See also DCLOSE.)

Format:

    CLOSE If

The CLOSE statement closes logical file If. If If is not present, all open logical files are closed by BASIC < 3.0, but BASIC 4.0 gives a syntax error.

Every file should be closed after all file accesses have been completed. An open logical file may be closed only once. The particular operations performed in response to a CLOSE statement depend on the open file's physical device and the type of access that occurred. For details see Chapter 6.

Example:

```
CLOSE 1      Close logical file 1

CLOSE 14     Close logical file 14
```

CLR

The CLR statement sets all numeric variables to zero and assigns null values to all string variables. All array space in memory is released. This is equivalent to turning the CBM computer off, then turning it back on and reloading the program into memory. CLR closes all logical files that are currently open within the executing program.

Format:

```
CLR
```

A program will continue to run following execution of a CLR statement providing the effects of the CLR statement's execution do not adversely effect program logic.

Example:

```
100 CLR
```

CMD

The CMD statement sends to physical unit 4 (the printer) all output that would have gone to the display. Output goes to the printer, instead of the display, until a PRINT# statement specifying the same logical file number is executed. At least one PRINT# statement must follow a CMD statement.

Format:

```
CMD lf
```

The CMD statement assigns a line printer output channel to logical file lf. After execution of a CMD statement, PRINT and LIST both print data instead of displaying it. See Chapter 6 for a discussion of line printer programming.

Example:

The following sequence uses CMD to print program listings.

```
OPEN 5,4     Open logical file 5 selecting the printer

CMD 5        Direct subsequent output to the printer

LIST         Print the program listing

PRINT#5      Print a carriage return and deselect the printer

CLOSE 5      Close logical file 5
```

COLLECT (BASIC 4.0)

The COLLECT statement recreates a Block Availability Map (BAM) for all files on the diskette. Improperly closed files are closed or deleted.

Format:

COLLECT [Dd][ON Uy]

The diskette on drive d is collected. If the Dd parameter is absent, drive 0 is assumed.

Example:

COLLECT	*Collects space on diskette in last drive accessed*
COLLECT D0	*Collects space on diskette in drive 0*
COLLECT D1	*Collects space on diskette in drive 1*

CONCAT (BASIC 4.0)

The CONCAT statement concatenates two data files. (See also PRINT# COPY.)

Format:

CONCAT[Ds,]"sourcefile" TO [Dd,]"destfile"[ON Uz]

The contents of sourcefile on the diskette in drive s is concatenated onto the end of destfile on the diskette in drive d. The file named sourcefile does not change. The file named destfile keeps its original contents, with the contents of sourcefile tacked on at the end. If drive numbers s and/or d are not specified, then drive 0 is assumed.

Caution: Files must be closed before they are concatenated.

Example:

CONCAT "FIRST" TO "SECOND"	*The contents of file FIRST is concatenated on the end of file SECOND. Both files are on the diskette in drive 0*
CONCAT D1,"ABC" TO D0,"XYZ"	*The contents of file ABC on the diskette in drive 1 is concatenated on the end of file XYZ on the diskette in drive 0*

CONT

The CONT statement, typed at the keyboard in immediate mode, resumes program execution after a BREAK.

Format:

CONT

A break is caused by execution of a STOP statement or an END statement that has additional statements following it. Depressing the STOP key while a program is running also causes a break. Program execution continues at the exact point where the break occurred.

Pressing the RETURN key in response to an INPUT statement will also cause a break. Typing CONT after this break re-executes the INPUT statement.

Example:

CONT

COPY (BASIC 4.0)

The COPY statement copies a single diskette file, or all the files on a diskette. (See also PRINT# COPY.)

Format:

COPY [Ds,]["sourcefile"] TO [Dd,]["destfile"][ON Uz]

If the COPY statement is used to copy a single file, then the file named sourcefile on the diskette on drive s is copied to a new file named destfile on the diskette in drive d; the file names sourcefile and destfile must be present, but if Ds and/or Dd are absent, drive 0 is assumed.

The COPY statement can also be used to copy all files from the diskette in one drive to the diskette in the other drive. To use the COPY statement in this fashion, file names sourcefile and destfile must be absent, but drive numbers Ds and Dd must be present and different.

If the name of a source file that is being copied exists on the destination diskette, then the copy will be aborted at that file, and a FILE ALREADY EXISTS error will be reported.

COPY does not modify any files previously on the destination diskette.

Caution: A file must be closed before it is copied.

Example:

```
COPY D1 TO D0              Copy all files on the diskette in drive D1 to the
                           diskette in drive D0. (DOS 2.0 and higher
                           releases only)

COPY D1, "MAJOR" TO D1, "MINOR"   Create MINOR file on the diskette in drive D1
```

DATA

The DATA statement declares constants that are assigned to variables by READ statements.

Format:

DATA   constant[,constant,constant,...,constant]

DATA statements may be placed anywhere in a program.

The DATA statement specifies either numeric or string contents. String constants are usually enclosed in double quotation marks; the quotes are not necessary unless the string contains graphic characters, blanks (spaces), commas, or colons. Blanks, commas, colons and graphic characters are ignored unless the string is enclosed in quotes. A double quotation mark cannot be represented in a DATA string; it must be specified using a CHR$(34) function.

The DATA statement is valid in program mode only.

Example:

```
10 DATA NAME, "C.D."     Defines two string variables

50 DATA 1E6,-10,XYZ     Defines two numeric variables and one string variable
```

See the READ statement for a description of how DATA statement constants are used within a program.

DCLOSE (BASIC 4.0)

DCLOSE closes a single file or all the files currently open on a disk unit. (Also see CLOSE.)

Format:

DCLOSE#lf   [ON Uz]

The DCLOSE statement closes logical file lf. If the logical file number is not specified, all currently open diskette files are closed.

Example:

DCLOSE	*Closes all open diskette files*
DCLOSE#1	*Closes the diskette file identified by logical file 1*
DCLOSE ON U8	*Closes all open diskette files on physical unit #8*

DEF FN

The DEF function (DEF FN) allows special purpose functions to be defined and used within BASIC programs.

Format:

DEF FNnvar(arg)=expression

Floating point variable nvar identifies the function, which is subsequently referenced using the name FNnvar(data). (If nvar has more than five letters a syntax error is reported. A syntax error is also reported if nvar is a string or integer variable.)

The function is specified by expression, which can be any arithmetic expression, containing any combination of numeric constants, variables, and/or operators. arg is a dummy variable name which can (and usually does) appear in expression.

arg is the only variable in expression which can be specified when FNnvar(data) is referenced. Any other variables in expression must be defined before FNnvar(data) is referenced for the first time. FNnvar(data) evaluates expression using data as the value for arg.

The entire DEF FN statement must appear on a single 80 character line; however a previously defined function can be included in expression, so user-defined functions of any desired complexity can be developed.

The function name var can be re-used, and therefore redefined by another DEF FN statement appearing later in the same program.

The DEF FN definition statement is illegal in immediate mode. However, a user-defined function that has been defined by a DEF FN statement in the current stored program can be referenced in an immediate mode statement.

Example:

`10 DEF FNC(R)=π*R↑2`	*Defines a function that calculates the circumference of a circle. It takes a single argument R, the radius of the circle, and returns a single numeric value, the circumference of the circle*
`?FNC(1)`	*Prints 3.141159265 (the value of π)*
`A=FNC(14)`	*Assigns to A the value calculated by the user-defined function FNC, using an argument of 14*
`55 IF FNC(X)>60 GOTO 150`	*Uses the value calculated by the user-defined function FNC as a branch condition. The current contents of variable X is used when calculating the user-defined function*

DIM

The Dimension statement DIM allocates space in memory for array variables.

Format:

DIM var(sub)[,var(sub),. . .,var(sub)]

The DIM statement identifies arrays with one or more dimensions as follows:

var(sub$_i$)	Single-dimension array
var(sub$_i$,sub$_j$)	Two-dimension array
var(sub$_i$,sub$_j$,sub$_k$)	Multiple-dimension array

See Chapter 4 for a complete description of arrays.

Arrays with more than eleven elements must be dimensioned in a DIM statement. Arrays with eleven elements or less (subscripts 0 through 10 for a one-dimensional array) may be used without being dimensioned by a DIM statement; for such arrays, eleven array spaces are automatically allocated in memory when the first array element is encountered in the program. An array with more than eleven elements must occur in a DIM statement before any other statement references an element of the array.

If an array is dimensioned more than once, or if an array having more than eleven elements is not dimensioned, a ?REDIM'ED ARRAY error occurs and the program is aborted.

A CLR statement allows a DIM statement to be reexecuted.

Example:

`10 DIM A(3)`	Dimension a single-dimensional array of 3 elements.
`45 DIM X$(44,2)`	Dimension a two-dimensional array of 88 elements.
`1000 DIM MU(X,3*B),N(12)`	Dimension a two-dimensional array of X times 3*B elements and a single dimensional array of 12 elements. X and B must have been assigned values before the DIM statement is executed.

DIRECTORY (BASIC 4.0)

The DIRECTORY statement displays directories for diskettes in one or both drives. The word CATALOG may be used instead of DIRECTORY (also see LOAD"$dr").

Format:

DIRECTORY[Dd][ON Uz]

The directory for the diskette in drive d is displayed. If the Dd parameter is absent, directories for the diskettes in both drives are displayed.

If a selected drive contains no diskette an error status is reported.

The DIRECTORY statement is usually executed in immediate mode.

Example:

DIRECTORY   *Displays the directory of drive 0 and drive 1*

DIRECTORY D1   *Displays the directory of drive 1*

Printing a Directory

A directory can be printed instead of being displayed by opening a printer channel before executing the DIRECTORY statement. Here is the required immediate mode statement sequence:

OPEN 4,4   *Open the printer specifying logical file 4*

CMD 4   *Deflect display output to the printer*

DIRECTORY   *Print directories for diskettes in both drives*

PRINT#4   *Deflect output back to the display*
CLOSE 4

DLOAD (BASIC 4.0)

The DLOAD statement loads a BASIC program from a diskette into memory (also see LOAD).

Format:

DLOAD "filename"[Dd][ON Uz]

The DLOAD statement loads program file "filename" from the diskette in drive Dd into computer memory. If Dd is not present, drive 0 is assumed.

Example:

DLOAD "CALC"   *Load CALC file from drive 0*

DLOAD "TIME",D1   *Load TIME file from drive 1*

A$="PROG"   *Load PROG file from drive 0*
DLOAD A$

DLOAD"PROG",D0 ON U8   *Load PROG file from drive 0 on the disk unit*

Using BASIC 4.0, if you press the shifted RUN/STOP key, the next program encountered on the diskette is loaded and run.

DOPEN (BASIC 4.0)

DOPEN opens a data file for a read and/or write access.

Format:

DOPEN #lf,"filename"[,Ly][,Dd][ON Uz][,W]

The DOPEN statement opens data file filename on the diskette in drive d, assigning to it logical file number lf. If d is not specified then drive 0 is assumed. If Ly is not present then a sequential file is assumed. The sequential file is opened for a write access if W is not present; it is opened for a read access if W is present.

If Ly is present then a relative file is assumed with a record length of y bytes. Relative files are opened for read or write accesses, therefore the W parameter cannot be present.

Example:

DOPEN#1,"PRIZES"   *Opens the sequential file named PRIZES on drive 0 for a read access*

DOPEN#6,"SNAKE"L30,D1   *Opens the relative file named SNAKE, with a record length of 30, for read and write accesses. The file is on drive D1*

DSAVE (BASIC 4.0)

The DSAVE statement writes a BASIC program file from memory onto a diskette (also see SAVE).

Format:

DSAVE"filename"[,Dd][ON Uz]

The DSAVE statement saves the BASIC program currently in memory, writing it to a new file named filename, on the diskette in drive d. If Dd is not present, drive 0 is assumed.

Example:

DSAVE"TRUE"   *Write program file TRUE to diskette in drive 0*

DSAVE"FALSE",D1   *Write program file FALSE to diskette in drive 1*

END

The END statement terminates program execution and returns the computer to immediate mode.

Format:

END

The END statement can provide a program with one or more termination points, at locations other than the physical end of the program. END statements can be used to terminate individual programs when more than one program is in memory at the same time. An END statement at the physical end of the program is optional.

The END statement is used in program mode only.

Example:

20001 END

FOR-NEXT STEP

All statements between the FOR statement and the NEXT statement are re-executed the same number of times.

Format:

```
FOR nvar = start TO end STEP increment
[statements in loop]
NEXT[nvar]
```

where:

nvar	is the index of the loop. It holds the current loop count. nvar is often used by the statements within the loop.
start	is a numeric constant, variable or expression that specifies the beginning value of the index.
end	is a numeric constant, variable, or expression that specifies the ending value of the index. The loop is completed when the index value is equal to the end value, or when the index value is incremented or decremented past the end value.
increment	if present, is a numeric constant, variable, or expression that specifies the amount by which the index variable is to be incremented with each pass. The step may be incremental (positive) or decremental (negative). If STEP is omitted the increment defaults to 1.

The nvar may optionally be included in the NEXT statement. A single NEXT statement is permissible for nested loops that end at the same point. The NEXT statement then takes the form:

```
NEXT nvar₁,nvar₂...
```

The FOR-NEXT loop will always be executed at least once, even if the beginning nvar value is beyond the end nvar value. If the NEXT statement is omitted and no subsequent NEXT statements are found, the loop is executed once.

The start, end, and increment values are read only once, on the first execution of the FOR statement. You cannot change these values inside the loop. You can change the value of nvar within the loop. This may be used to terminate a FOR-NEXT loop before the end value is reached: set nvar to the end value, and on the next pass the loop will terminate itself. Do not jump out of the FOR-NEXT loop with a GOTO. Do not start the loop outside a subroutine and terminate it inside the subroutine.

FOR-NEXT loops may be nested. Each nested loop must have a different nvar variable name. Each nested loop must be wholly contained within the next outer loop; at most, the loops can end at the same point.

Example:

```
10 FOR IN = 0 TO 100
.
40 NEXT IN
100 FOR X = A + 14 TO C-64+D/2 STEP 4
.
150 NEXT X
60 FOR A1 = 50 TO 0 STEP -1
.
90 NEXT
100 FOR I = 0 TO 10 STEP 0.5
.
155 NEXT
250 FOR I = 1 TO 5
260 FOR J = A TO B
.
300 NEXT I,J    same as    300 NEXT I     same as    300 NEXT
                           310 NEXT J                310 NEXT
```

GET

The GET statement receives single characters as input from the keyboard.

Format:

GET var

The GET statement can be executed in program mode only.

When a GET statement is executed, var is assigned a 0 value if numeric, or a null value if a string. Any previous value of the variable is lost. Then GET fetches the next character from the keyboard buffer and assigns it to var. If the keyboard buffer is empty, var retains its 0 or null value.

GET is used to handle one-character responses from the keyboard. GET accepts the RETURN key as input and passes the value (CHR$(13)) to var.

If var is a numeric variable and no key has been pressed, 0 is returned. However, a 0 is also returned when 0 is entered at the keyboard.

If var is a numeric variable and the character returned is not a digit (0-9), a ?SYNTAX ERROR message is generated and the program aborts.

The GET statement may have more than one variable in its parameter list, but it is hard to use if it has multiple parameters:

GET var,var,. . .,var

Example:

```
10 GET C$

10 GET D

10 GET A,B,C
```

GET#

The GET External statement (GET#) receives single characters as input from an external storage device identified via a logical file number.

Format:

GET #lf,var

The GET# statement can only be used in program mode. GET# fetches a single character from an external device and assigns this character to variable var. The external device is identified by logical file number lf. This logical file must previously have been opened by an OPEN or DOPEN statement.

GET# and GET statements handle variables and data input identically. For details see the GET statement description.

Example:

```
10 GET#4,C$:IF C$="" GOTO 10     Get a keyboard character. Re-execute if no character
                                 is present
```

GOSUB

The GOSUB statement branches program execution to a specified line and allows a return to the statement following GOSUB. The specified line is a subroutine entry point.

Format:

GOSUB ln

The GOSUB statement calls a subroutine. The subroutine's entry point must occur on line ln. A subroutine's entry point is the beginning of the subroutine in a programming sense; that is to say it is the line containing the statement (or statements) which are executed first. The entry point need not necessarily be the subroutine line with the smallest line number.

Upon completing execution the subroutine branches back to the line following the GOSUB statement. The subroutine uses a RETURN statement in order to branch back in this fashion.

A GOSUB statement may occur anywhere in a program; in consequence a subroutine may be called from anywhere in the program.

Subroutines may be nested; that is to say subroutines may be called from within subroutines. Twenty-six levels of nesting are allowed; that means 25 GOSUB statements may be executed before the first RETURN statement.

Example:

```
100 GOSUB 2000        Branch to subroutine at line 2000
110 A = B*C
  .
  .                   Subroutine branches back here

2000                  Subroutine entry point
  .
  .

2090 RETURN           Branch back to line 110
```

GOTO

The GOTO statement branches unconditionally to a specified line.

Format:

GOTO ln

The GOTO statement causes program execution to branch to line ln.

Example:

```
10 GOTO 100
```

Executed in immediate mode, GOTO branches to the specified line in the stored program without clearing the current variable values. GOTO cannot reference immediate mode statements, since they do not have line numbers.

HEADER (BASIC 4.0)

The HEADER statement formats a diskette, assigning it a disk name and identification number. (See also PRINT# PREPARE.)

Format:

HEADER "diskname",Dd[,Ivv][ON Uz]

When formatting a diskette the HEADER statement marks off sectors on each track, then initializes the directory and Block Availability Map. The formatted diskette must be in drive d. The diskette is given the name diskname and the number vv. This name and number appears in the reverse field at the top of a diskette directory display.

The HEADER statement is usually executed in immediate mode.

The HEADER statement can be used to format a blank diskette or to reformat and clear a used diskette. Because the changes are permanent, this command requires caution in its use. If executed in immediate mode, the question ARE YOU SURE? is displayed. You must respond by typing YES (CR) to continue.

If a media error occurs when the HEADER statement is executed, a ?BAD DISK message is displayed on the screen. Media errors occur when a diskette is missing from the drive, the write protect tab is in place, or the diskette magnetic surface is defective.

Example:

HEADER "MASTER",D0,I02   *Prepare and format a diskette, giving it the name "MASTER"*
                           and the number 02. The diskette is in drive 0

IF-THEN

The IF-THEN statement provides conditional execution of statements based on a relational expression.

Format:

IF condition THEN statement[:statement. . .]   *Conditionally execute statement(s)*

IF condition $\begin{Bmatrix} \text{THEN} \\ \text{GOTO} \end{Bmatrix}$ line   *Conditionally branch*

If the specified condition is true, then the statement or statements following the THEN are executed. If the specified condition is false, control passes to the statement(s) on the next line and the statement or statements following the THEN are not executed. For a conditional branch, the branch line number is placed after the word THEN, or after the word GOTO. The compound form THEN GOTO is also acceptable.

IF A = 1 THEN 50   ⎫
IF A = 1 GOTO 50   ⎬ *Equivalent*
IF A = 1 THEN GOTO 50   ⎭

If an unconditional branch is one of many statements following THEN, then the branch must be the last statement on the line, and it must have "GOTO line" format. If the unconditional branch is not the last statement on the line, then statements following the unconditional branch can never be executed.

The following statements cannot appear in an immediate mode IF-THEN statement: DATA, GET, GET#, INPUT, INPUT#, REM, RETURN, END, STOP, WAIT.

If a line number is specified, or any statement containing a line number, there must be a corresponding statement with that line number in the current stored program.

The CONT and DATA statements cannot appear in a program mode IF-THEN statement.

If a FOR-NEXT loop follows the THEN, then the loop must be completely contained on the IF-THEN line. Additional IF-THEN statements may appear following the THEN as long as they are completely contained on the original IF-THEN line. However, Boolean connectors are preferred to nested IF-THEN statements. For example, the two statements below are equivalent, but the second is preferred.

```
10 IF A$ = "X" THEN IF B = 2 THEN IF C > D THEN 50
10 IF A$ = "X" AND B = 2 AND C > D THEN 50
```

Example:

```
400 IF X > Y THEN A = 1
500 IF M+1 THEN AG = 4.5:GOSUB 1000
```

INPUT

The INPUT statement receives data input from the keyboard.

Format:

$$\text{INPUT} \left\{ \begin{array}{l} \text{(blank)} \\ \text{"message";} \end{array} \right\} \text{var [,var,. . .,var]}$$

INPUT can be used in program mode only.

When the INPUT statement is executed, CBM BASIC displays a question mark on the screen requesting data input. The user must enter data items that agree exactly, in number and type, with the variables in the INPUT statement parameter list. If the INPUT statement has more than one variable in its parameter list, then keyboard entries must be separated by commas. The last entry must be terminated with a carriage return:

```
?1234<CR>                    Single data item response
?1234,567.89,NOW<CR>         Multiple data item response
```

If "message" is present, it is displayed before the question mark. "message" can have up to 80 characters.

If more than one but less than the required number of data items are input, CBM BASIC requests additional input with double question marks (??) until the required number of data items have been input. If too many data items are input, the message $EXTRA IGNORED is displayed. The extra input is ignored, but the program continues execution.

Example:

Statement	Operator Response	Result
10 INPUT A,B,C$	?123,456,NOW	A=123, B=456, C$="NOW"
10 INPUT A,B,C$	?123 ??456 ??NOW	A=123 B=456 C$="NOW"
10 INPUT A,B,C$	?NOW ?REDO FROM START ?123 ?456 ?789	 A=123 B=456 C="789"
10 INPUT "A= ";A	A= ?123	A=123

Note that you must input numeric data for a numeric variable, but you can input numeric or string data for a string variable.

Caution: If the RETURN key is pressed in response to an INPUT statement with no preceding data entry, then program execution ceases and the computer enters immediate mode. To restart execution type CONT in response to the READY message.

INPUT#

The Input External statement (INPUT#) inputs one or more data items from an external device identified via a logical file number.

Format:

INPUT#lf var[,var,. . .,var]

The INPUT# statement inputs data from the selected external device and assigns data items to variable(s) var. Data items must agree in number and kind with the INPUT# statement parameter list.

If an end of record is detected before all variables in the INPUT# statement parameter list have received data, then an OUT OF DATA error status is generated, but the program continues to execute.

INPUT# and INPUT statements execute identically, except that INPUT# receives its input from a logical file. Also, INPUT# does not display error messages; instead it reports error statuses which the program must interrogate and respond to.

Input data strings may not be longer than 80 characters (79 characters plus a carriage return) because the input buffer has a maximum capacity of 80 characters. Commas and carriage returns are treated as item separators by the computer when processing the INPUT# statement; they are recognized, but are not passed on to the program as data.

INPUT# is valid in program mode only.

Example:

1000 INPUT#10,A	*Input the next data item from logical file 10. A numeric data item is expected; it is assigned to variable A*
946 INPUT#12,A$	*Input the next data item from logical file 12. A string data item is expected; it is assigned to variable A$*
900 INPUT#5,B,C$	*Input the next two data items from logical file 5. The first data item is numeric; it is assigned to numeric variable B. The second data item is a string; it is assigned to string variable C$*

LET=

The Assignment statement, LET=, or simply =, assigns a value to a specified variable.

Format:

$$\begin{Bmatrix} \text{(blank)} \\ \text{LET} \end{Bmatrix} \text{ var=data}$$

Variable var is assigned the value computed by resolving data.
The word LET is optional; it is usually omitted.

Example:

```
10 A=2
450 C$="◥"

300 M(1,3)=SGN(X)
310 XX$(I,J,K,L)="STRINGALONG"
```

LIST

LIST displays one or more lines of a program. Program lines displayed by the LIST statement may be edited.

Format:

$$\text{LIST} \begin{cases} \text{(blank)} \\ \text{line} \\ \text{line}_1\text{-line}_2 \\ \text{-line} \\ \text{line-} \end{cases}$$

The entire program is displayed in response to LIST. Use line limiting parameters for long programs to display a section of the program that is short enough to fit on the screen.

Example:

LIST	*List entire program*
LIST 50	*List line 50*
LIST 60-100	*List all lines in the program from lines 60 to 100, inclusive*
LIST -140	*List all lines in the program from the beginning of the program through line 140*
LIST 20000-	*List all lines in the program from line 20000 to the end of the program*

Listed lines are reformatted as follows:

1. ?'s entered as a shorthand for PRINT are expanded to the word PRINT. Example:

?A	becomes	PRINT A

2. Blanks preceding the line number are eliminated. Example:

50 A=1	becomes	50 A=1
100 A=A+1	becomes	100 A=A+1

3. A space is inserted between the line number and the rest of the statement if none was entered. Example:

55A=B-2	becomes	55 A=B-2

4. The line is displayed beginning at column 2 instead of column 1.

LIST is always used in immediate mode. A LIST statement in a program will list the program, but then exit to immediate mode. Attempting to continue program execution via CONT simply repeats the LIST indefinitely.

Printing a Program Listing

To print a program listing instead of displaying it, OPEN a printer logical file and execute a CMD statement before executing the LIST statement. Here is the necessary immediate mode sequence:

```
OPEN 4,4        Open the printer specifying logical file 4
CMD 4           Deflect display output to the printer
LIST            Print the program listing
PRINT#4
CLOSE 4         Deflect output back to the display
```

LOAD

The LOAD statement loads a program from an external device into memory. (Also see DLOAD.)

Cassette Unit Format:

```
LOAD ["filename"][,dev]
```

The LOAD statement loads into memory the program file specified by filename from the cassette unit selected by device number dev. If no device is specified then device 1 is assumed by default; cassette unit 1 is then selected. If no filename is given then the next file detected on the selected cassette unit is loaded into memory.

For cassette unit operating instructions see Chapter 2.

Example:

```
LOAD              Load into memory the next program found on cassette unit #1. If
                  you start a LOAD when the cassette is in the middle of a program,
                  the cassette will read past the remainder of the current program,
                  then load the next program
LOAD "",2         Load into memory the next program found on cassette unit #2
LOAD "EGOR"       Search for the program named EGOR on tape cassette #1 and load
                  it into memory.
N$="WHEE!LS"      Search for the program named WHEE!LS on cassette unit #1 and
LOAD N$           load it into memory.
LOAD "X"          Search for a program named X on cassette unit #1 and load it
                  into memory
```

Diskette Drive Format:

LOAD "dr:filename",dev

The LOAD statement loads into computer memory the program file with the name filename on the diskette in drive dr. dev. The device number for the diskette drive unit is the value 8 in all standard CBM computer systems. If dev is not present, then the default value is 1 which selects the primary tape cassette unit.

A single asterisk can be included instead of the filename, in which case the first program found on the selected diskette drive is loaded into memory.

For diskette operating instructions see Chapter 2.

Example:

LOAD"0:*",8	*Load the first program found on disk drive 0*
LOAD"0:FIREBALL",8	*Search for the program named FIREBALL on disk drive 0, and load it into memory*
T$="0:METEOR"	*Search for the program named METEOR on disk drive 0 and load it*
LOAD T$,8	*into memory*

When a LOAD is executed in immediate mode, CBM BASIC automatically executes a CLR before the program is loaded. Once a program has been loaded into memory, it can be listed, updated, and/or executed.

The LOAD statement can also be used in program mode to build program overlays. A LOAD statement executed from within a program causes that program's execution to stop and another program to be loaded. In this case the CBM computer does not perform a CLR; therefore the old program can pass on all of its variable values to the new program.

When a LOAD statement accessing a cassette unit is executed in program mode, LOAD message displays are suppressed unless the tape PLAY key is up (off). If the PLAY key is off, the PRESS PLAY ON TAPE #1 message is displayed so that the load can proceed. All LOAD messages are suppressed when loading programs from a diskette in program mode.

Using LOAD to Display the Diskette Directory

The BASIC 4.0 DIRECTORY statement displays diskette directories. To display the diskette directory using earlier releases of BASIC, you must load and list a program file name $0 (for the diskette in drive 0) or $1 (for the diskette in drive 1).

Example:

```
LOAD "$0",8
SEARCHING FOR $0
LOADING
READY
LIST
```

NEW

The NEW statement clears the current program from memory.

Format:

NEW

When a NEW statement is executed, all variables are initialized to zero or null values and array variable space in memory is released. The pointers that keep track of program statements are reinitialized, which has the effect of deleting any program in memory; in fact the program is not physically deleted. NEW operations are automatically performed when a LOAD statement is executed.

If there is a program in memory, then you should execute a NEW statement in immediate mode before entering a new program at the keyboard. Otherwise the new program will overlay the old one, replacing lines if their numbers are duplicated, but leaving other lines. The result is a scrambled mixture of two unrelated programs.

Example:

NEW

NEW is always executed in immediate mode. If a NEW statement is executed from within a program, the program will "self destruct;" it will clear itself out.

ON...GOSUB

The ON...GOSUB statement provides conditional subroutine calls to one of several subroutines in a program, depending on the current value of a variable.

Format:

ON byte GOSUB line$_1$ [,line2,...,line$_n$]

ON...GOSUB has the same format as ON...GOTO. See the ON...GOTO statement description for branching rules. byte is evaluated and truncated to an integer number, if necessary.

For byte=1, the subroutine beginning at line$_1$ is called. That subroutine completes execution with a RETURN statement which causes program execution to continue at the statement immediately following ON...GOSUB. If byte=2, the subroutine beginning with line$_2$ is called, etc.

ON...GOSUB is normally executed in program mode. It may be executed in immediate mode as long as there are corresponding line numbers to branch to in the current stored program.

Example:

10 ON A GOSUB 100,200,300

ON...GOTO

The ON...GOTO statement causes a conditional branch to one of several points in a program, depending on the current value of a variable.

Format:

ON byte GOTO line$_1$ [,line$_2$,...,line$_n$]

byte is evaluated and truncated to an integer number, if necessary.

If byte = 1, a branch to line number line$_1$ occurs. If byte = 2, a branch to line number line$_2$ occurs, etc.

If byte = 0, no branch is taken. If byte is in the allowed range but there is no corresponding line number in the program, then no branch is taken. If a branch is not taken, program control proceeds to the statement following the ON...GOTO; this statement may be on the same line as the ON...GOTO (separated by a colon), or on the next line.

If index has a non-zero value outside of the allowed range, the program aborts with an error message. As many line numbers may be specified as will fit on the 80-character line.

ON...GOTO is normally executed in program mode. It may be executed in immediate mode as long as there are corresponding line numbers in the current stored program that may be branched to.

Example:

```
40 A=B<10              Branch to statement 100 if A is true (-1) or branch to
50 ON A+2 GOTO 100,200   statement 200 if A is false (0)

50 X=X+1               Branch to statement 500 if X=1, to statement 600 if X=2,
60 ON X GOTO 500,600,700  or to statement 700 if X=3. No branch is taken if X> 3.
```

OPEN

The OPEN statement opens a logical file and readies the assigned physical device. (Also see DOPEN.)

Cassette Tape Format:

OPEN lf[,dev][,sa][,"filename"]

The file named filename on the tape cassette unit identified by dev is opened for the type of access specified by the secondary address sa; the access is assigned the logical file number lf.

If no filename is specified then the next file encountered on the selected tape cassette is opened. If no device is specified then device number 1 is selected by default; this device number selects cassette unit 1. If no secondary address is specified then a default value of 0 is assumed and the file is opened for a read access only. A secondary address of 1 opens the file for a write access while a secondary address of 2 opens the file for a write access with an end-of-tape mark written when the file is subsequently closed.

Example:

OPEN 1	*Open logical file 1 at cassette drive #1 (default) for a read access (default) from the first file encountered on the tape (no filename specified)*
OPEN 1,1	*Same as above*
OPEN 1,1,0	*Same as above*
OPEN 1,1,0,"DAT"	*Same as above but access the file named DAT*
OPEN 3,1,2	*Open logical file 3 for cassette #1, for a write with EOT (End Of Tape) access. The new file is unnamed and will be written at the current physical tape location*
OPEN 3,1,2,"PENTAGRAM"	*Same as above but access the file named PENTAGRAM*

Disk Unit Format:

OPEN lf,dev,sa, "dr:filename,type[,access]"

The file named filename on the diskette in drive dr is opened and assigned logical file number lf. type identifies the file as sequential (SEQ), program (PRG), or random (USR). If the file is sequential then access must be WRITE to specify a write access or READ to specify a read access. access is not present for a program or random access file.

An existing sequential file can be opened for a write access if dr is preceded by an @ sign. The existing sequential file contents are replaced entirely by new written data.

dev, the device number, must be present; it is 8 for all standard disk units. If dev is absent then a default value of 1 is assumed and the primary tape cassette unit is selected.

For a data file the secondary address sa can have any value between 2 and 14, however every open data file should have its own unique secondary address. A secondary address of 15 selects the disk unit command channel. Secondary addresses of 0 and 1 are used to access program files. Secondary address 0 is used to load a program file; secondary address 1 is used to save a program file.

Example:

OPEN 1,8,2,"0:DAT,SEQ,READ"	*Open logical file 1 on a diskette in drive 0. Read from sequential file DAT*
OPEN 5,8,3,"1:NEWFILE,SEQ,WRITE"	*Open logical file 5 on a diskette in drive 1. Write to sequential file NEWFILE*
OPEN 4,8,4,"@1:NEWFILE,SEQ,WRITE"	*Open logical file 4 on diskette drive 1. Write to sequential file NEWFILE replacing prior contents*

See Chapter 6 for a discussion of files and file handling.

POKE

The POKE statement stores a byte of data in a specified memory location.

Format:

POKE memadr,byte

A value between 0 and 255, provided by byte, is loaded into the memory location with the address memadr.

Example:

10 POKE 1,A	*POKE value of variable A into memory at address 1*
POKE 32768,ASC("A")-64	*POKE 1 (the value of ASC ("A")-64) into memory at address 32768*

PRINT

The PRINT statement displays data; it is also used to print to the line printer.

Format:

$$\left\{ {\text{PRINT} \atop ?} \right\} \text{ data[} \left\{ {, \atop ;} \right\} \text{ data... } \left\{ {, \atop ;} \right\} \text{ data]}$$

Print Field Formats:

Numeric fields are displayed using standard numeric representation for numbers greater than 0.01 and less than or equal to 999999999. Scientific notation is used for numbers outside of this range. Numbers are preceded by a sign character and are followed by a blank character:

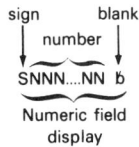

```
    sign        blank
     |  number    |
     ↓ ⌒⌒⌒⌒⌒⌒ ↓
    SNNN....NN  b
     ⌒⌒⌒⌒⌒⌒⌒⌒
    Numeric field
      display
```

The sign is blank for a positive number and minus sign (−) for a negative number.

Strings are displayed without additions or modifications.

PRINT Formats:

First data item. The first data item is displayed at the current cursor position. The PRINT format character (comma or semicolon) following the first data item specifies the location of the second data item's display. The location of each subsequent data item's display is determined by the punctuation following the preceding data item. Data items may be in the same PRINT statement, or in a separate PRINT statement.

New line. When no comma or semicolon follows the last data item in a PRINT statement, a carriage return occurs after the last data item is displayed.

Tabbing. A comma following a data item causes the next data item to be displayed at the next default tab column. Default tabs are at columns 1, 11, 21 and 31 for a 40 column display, continuing at 41, 51, 61 and 71 for an 80 column display. If a comma precedes the first data item, then a tab will precede the first item display.

Continuous. A semicolon following a data item causes the next display to begin immediately, in the next available column position. Numeric data always has one trailing blank character. For string data, items are displayed continuously with no forced intervening spaces.

Example:

```
40 PRINT A

40 PRINT A,B,C

40 PRINT A;B;C

40 PRINT, A;B;C

40 PRINT "NUMBERS",A;B;C

40 PRINT "NUM";"BER";

41 PRINT "S",A;B;C
```

PRINT#

The Print External statement (PRINT#) outputs one or more data items from the CBM computer to an external device (cassette tape unit, disk unit, or printer) identified by a logical file number.

Format:

PRINT #lf,data;c$;data;c$;...data

Data items listed in the PRINT# statement parameter list are written to the external device identified by logical unit number 1f.

Very specific punctuation rules must be observed when writing data to external devices. A brief summary of punctuation rules is given below but for complete details see Chapter 6.

PRINT# Output to Cassette Files

Every numeric or string variable written to a cassette file must be followed by a carriage return character. This carriage return character is automatically output by a PRINT# statement that has a single data item in its parameter list. But a PRINT# statement with more than one data item in its parameter list must include c$ characters that force carriage returns. For example, use CHR$(13) to force a carriage return, or a string variable which has been equated to CHR$(13) wherever c$ appears.

PRINT# Output to Diskette Files

The cassette output rules described above apply also to diskette files with one exception: groups of string variables can be separated by comma characters (CHR$(44)). The comma character separators, like the carriage return separators, must be inserted using c$. String variables written to diskette files with comma character separators must subsequently be read back by a single INPUT# statement. The INPUT# statement reads all text from one carriage return character to the next.

PRINT# Output to the Line Printer

When the PRINT# statement outputs data to a line printer c$ must equal CHR$(29). No punctuation characters should separate c$ from data items as illustrated in the PRINT# format definition.

Caution: The form ? #cannot be used as an abbreviation for PRINT#.

Using BASIC <3.0, the PRINT# statement terminates every line output with a carriage return character. Using BASIC 4.0, this occurs only for file numbers of 127 or less, no automatic carriage return is output. Some non-Commodore printers require a carriage return character to be output at the end of a line. If you have such a printer, then using BASIC 4.0, choose a file number greater than 127, or output the carriage return as a separate terminating character.

Example:

```
100 PRINT#1,A          Output numeric variable A and a RETURN code to logical file 1
200 PRINT#4,A$         Output string variable A$ and a RETURN code to logical file 4
300 PRINT#10,B%;",";C$ Output numeric variable B%, a comma, string variable C$, and a
                          RETURN code to logical file 10

10 OPEN 1,1,2          Open logical file #2 on cassette #1 for write
20 PRINT#1,"HI"        Output HI to logical file #1 on cassette #2
```

The PRINT# statement also performs a variety of disk-handling operations. These uses of PRINT# are summarized below. BASIC 4.0 has individual statements that perform the same operations.

Disk files must be closed before being subject to any disk-handling operation.

COPY

Use PRINT# to copy and/or merge files. (Also see BASIC 4.0 COPY and CON-CAT statements.

Format:

PRINT#lf,"C[OPY]d:destfile=s:sourcefile[,s:sourcefile....]"

Up to four source files can be concatenated and copied to a destination file. The source files are not changed. The source files are identified by their file name sourcefile and drive s. If more than one source file is specified then files are concatenated in the order in which they appear in the PRINT# statement. The newly created destination file is identified by its file name destfile and drive d.

Example:

```
OPEN 1,8,15                        Open the diskette command channel
PRINT#1,"C1:FILE1=C0:FILE0"        Copy FILE0 on drive 0 to a new file named
                                      FILE1 on drive 1

PRINT#1,"C0:NEWFIL=C1:FILEA,C0:FILEB"  A new file named NEWFIL is created on
                                      drive 0 by concatenating file FILEB on
                                      drive 0 at the end of file FILEA on drive 1
```

DUPLICATE

Use PRINT# to duplicate a diskette and thus generate a backup copy of it. (See also the BASIC 4.0 BACKUP statement.)

Format:

PRINT#lf,"D[UPLICATE]d=s"

The diskette in drive d becomes a duplicate of the diskette in drive s. Diskette name and number are copied, along with all data files.

Before duplicating a diskette it is wise to put write protect tabs on the diskette which is to be duplicated. Then if you put diskettes in the wrong drives, or if you mix the source and destination drive numbers in the PRINT# statement, you will simply get a diskette write error; you will not wipe out the diskette that you were trying to duplicate.

Example:

```
OPEN 1,8,15                Open the diskette command channel
 .
PRINT#1,"D0=1"             The diskette in drive 1 is duplicated; the duplicate is
 .                           generated in drive 0
PRINT#1,"DUPLICATE0=1"     Same as above
```

INITIALIZE

Use PRINT# to initialize a diskette before performing any operation on it. You do not need to initialize diskettes if you are using a DOS release 2.0 or higher, and BASIC 4.0.

Format:

PRINT #file,"I[NITIALIZE][dr]

The diskette in drive dr is initialized. If the dr parameter is not present, diskettes in both drives are initialized.

Versions of DOS preceding release 2.0 require diskettes to be initialized before any file on the diskette is opened. BASIC 3.0 and earlier versions were used with these revisions of DOS. DOS 2.0 and subsequent releases automatically initialize diskettes when they are loaded into drive. BASIC 4.0 should be used with DOS 2.0 and subsequent releases.

You do not need to initialize a diskette after preparing it; the preparation process also initializes the diskette.

Example:

```
OPEN 1,8,15                Open the diskette command channel
 .
PRINT#1,"I"                Initialize diskettes in drives 0 and 1
 .
PRINT#1,"INITIALIZE1"      Initialize the diskette in drive 1
```

NEW

Use PRINT# to prepare and format a new diskette, or to erase and reformat an old diskette. (See also the BASIC 4.0 HEADER statement.)

Format:

PRINT #lf,"N[EW]dr:diskname,vv"

The diskette in drive dr is prepared. When a diskette is prepared, sectors are laid out on the diskette surface. The diskette directory and Block Availability Map (BAM) are initialized. The diskette is assigned the name diskname and the number vv.

The diskette name and number is displayed in the reverse field at the top of a directory display.

Example:

```
OPEN 1,8,15                Open the diskette command channel
 .
PRINT#1,"N0:NEWDATA,02"    A diskette has been prepared for use in drive 0. The diskette is given
                             the name NEWDATA and the number 02
```

When preparing an old diskette, you can specify a new diskette name, while keeping the old diskette number; or you can keep the old diskette name and number. For example, suppose a diskette has the name NEWDATA and the number 02. The following preparation statements are legal:

```
OPEN 1,8,15              Open the diskette command channel
.
PRINT#1,"NEW0"          Prepare an old diskette in drive 0. Keep its old name and number.
PRINT#1,"N1:NEWDISK"   Prepare an old diskette in drive 1. Rename the diskette
                            NEWDATA but keep the old diskette number
PRINT#1,"N1:NEWDATA,01"  As above but give the diskette the number 01
```

The following statement is illegal:

```
PRINT#1,"N0:02"
```

This statement is attempting to give the old diskette a new number while keeping the old name.

RENAME

Use PRINT# to rename a diskette file. (See also the BASIC 4.0 RENAME statement.)

Format:

PRINT #lf,"R[ENAME]dr:newname=oldname"

A file on the diskette in drive dr has its name changed from oldname to newname.

Example:

```
OPEN 1,8,15                        Open the diskette command channel
.
PRINT#1,"R1:BACKUP=CURRENT"   The file on the diskette in drive 1 which was named
                                     CURRENT is renamed BACKUP
```

SCRATCH

Use PRINT# to scratch one or more files on a diskette. (See also the BASIC 4.0 SCRATCH statement.)

Format:

PRINT #lf,"Sdr:filename[,dr:filename]"

A single PRINT# statement can delete one file, many files or all files, on a single diskette, or on both diskettes.

To scratch one or more files, specify the drive number and file name for each file that is to be scratched.

When a number of similarly named files are to be scratched, use the asterisk (*) and question mark (?) characters to name the files.

The asterisk (*) is used to scratch a number of files whose names have the same beginning characters. Enter the common beginning file name characters, followed by an asterisk. For example the name "FILE*" will scratch all files whose names begin with the four letters FILE. The name "F*" will scratch all files whose names begin with the letter F. The name "*" will scratch all files on the diskette. The asterisk (*) may be used in the same way to specify names for OPEN, DOPEN and DLOAD statements.

Use the question mark (?) in file name character positions that are allowed to differ. For example the name "FILE?.SRC" will scratch all files named "FILEX.SCR" where X can be any character. The name "F???NO" will scratch any file whose name begins with an F, ends with NO and has any three characters in between. The name F???N∗ will scratch any file whose name has an F in the first character position and an N in the fifth character position.

Example:

```
OPEN 1,8,15                          Open the diskette command channel
  .
PRINT#1,"S0:FILENAME"                Scratch the file on drive 0 named FILENAME

PRINT#1,"S0:FILENAME,1:NEWFILE"      As above but also scratch the file on drive 1 named NEWFILE

PRINT#1,"S0:FILENAME,0:NEW∗"         As above but also scratch all files on drive 0 whose
                                       names begin with the letters NEW

PRINT#1,"S1:A???"                    Scratch all files on drive 1 whose names begin with A and
                                       have a total of 4 characters in the name

PRINT#1,"S0:∗"                       Scratch all files on the diskette in drive 0
```

VALIDATE

Use PRINT# to validate a diskette. (See also the BASIC 4.0 COLLECT statement.)

Format:

PRINT #If,"V[ALIDATE][dr]"

The diskette in drive dr is validated. If the dr parameter is absent, then the diskette in the most recently selected drive is validated.

When a diskette is validated, a new Block Availability Map is created for all valid data files on the diskette. Any files that were improperly closed, or were not closed become invalid files; they are deleted from the diskette and their diskette space is released.

Do not validate a diskette that contains random access files; validation will erase the random access file.

If a read error occurs during validation, the validation operation is aborted and the diskette is left in its initial state.

A diskette must be initialized after it is validated.

Example:

```
OPEN 1,8,15                          Open the diskette command channel

PRINT#1,"I0"                         Initialize the diskette in drive 0

PRINT#1,"V0"                         Validate the diskette in drive 0
```

READ

The READ statement assigns values from a DATA statement to variables named in the READ parameter list.

Format:

READ var[,var,. . .,var]

READ is used to assign values to variables. READ can take the place of multiple assignment statements (see LET=).

READ statements with variable lists require corresponding DATA statements with lists of constant values. The data constants and corresponding variables have to agree in type. A string variable can accept any type of constant; a numeric variable can accept only numeric constants.

The number of READ and DATA statements can differ, but there has to be an available DATA constant for every READ statement variable.

There can be more data items than READ statement variables, but if there are too few data items the program aborts with an ?OUT OF DATA error message.

READ is generally executed in program mode. It can be executed in immediate mode as long as there are corresponding DATA constants in the current stored program to read from.

Example:

```
10 DATA 1,2,3          On completion, A=1, B=2, C=3
20 READ A,B,C
150 READ C$,D,F$       On completion, C$="STR", D=14.5, F$="TM"
160 DATA STR
170 DATA 14.5,"TM"
```

RECORD (BASIC 4.0)

The RECORD statement adjusts a relative file pointer to select any byte (character) of any record in the relative file. The RECORD statement is used before GET#, INPUT# or PRINT# statements.

Format:

RECORD #lf,rno[,bno]

The RECORD statement selects byte number bno in record rno of the file identified by logical file lf.

If the RECORD statement sets the file pointer beyond the end of the file, and a PRINT# statement attempts to write another record, the file is extended to include these additional records. If an INPUT# statement is executed after the RECORD statement has set the record pointer beyond the last record, INPUT# will return null data and an end of file status is generated in ST, the status word variable.

Example:

```
10 DOPEN#1,"DATAFILE",L20,6: REM RELATIVE FILE DATAFILE HAS 20 BYTES PER RECORD
20 RECORD#1,20,6: REM SELECT THE 6TH BYTE RECORD NO. 20
30 GET#1,A$:IF A$= THEN 30: REM LOAD THIS BYTE INTO A$
40 STOP
```

REM

The Remark statement (REM) allows comments to be placed in the program for program documentation purposes.

Format:

REM comment

where:

comment   is any sequence of characters that will fit on the current 80 column line.

REM statements are reproduced in program listings, but they are otherwise ignored. A REM statement may be placed on a line of its own or it may be placed as the last statement on a multiple statement line.

A REM statement cannot be placed ahead of any other statements on a multiple-statement line, since all text following the REM is treated as a comment.

REM statements may be placed in the path of program execution, and they may be branched to.

Example:

```
10 REM *** * * * * * * * * * * * * * ****
20 REM ***PROGRAM EXCALIBUR***
30 GOTO 55:REM BRANCH IF OUT OF DATA
```

RENAME (BASIC 4.0)

The RENAME statement changes the name of a file on a diskette without altering the file. (See also PRINT# RENAME.)

Format:

RENAME[dr]"oldname" TO "newname"[ON Uz]

The file named oldname on the diskette in drive dr has its name changed to newname. If dr is absent, drive 0 is assumed.

If you have any trouble renaming a file, try to validate the file, then rename it. *Caution:* A file must be closed before it is renamed.

Example:

RENAME "PET" TO "CBM"   *Rename PET file on drive 0. The new file name is CBM*

RENAME D1, "ONE" TO "TWO"   *Rename ONE file on drive 1. The new file name is TWO*

RESTORE

The RESTORE statement resets the DATA statement pointer to the beginning of data.

Format:

RESTORE

RESTORE may be given in immediate or program mode.

Example:

```
10 DATA 1,2,N44
20 READ A,B,B$        A=1, B=2, B$="N44"
30 RESTORE
40 READ X,Y,Z$        X=1, Y=2, Z$="N44"
```

RETURN

The RETURN statement branches program control to the statement in the program following the most recent GOSUB call. Each subroutine must terminate with a RETURN statement.

Format:

```
RETURN
```

Example:

```
100 RETURN
```

Note that the RETURN statement returns program control from a subroutine, whereas the RETURN key moves the cursor to the beginning of the next display line. The two are not related in any way.

RUN

RUN begins execution of the program currently stored in memory. RUN closes any open files, and initializes all variables to 0 or null values.

Format:

```
RUN[line]
```

When RUN is executed in immediate mode, the CBM computer performs a CLR of all program variables and resets the data pointer in memory to the beginning of data (see RESTORE) before executing the program.

If RUN specifies a line number, the CBM computer still performs the CLR and RESTOREs the data, but execution begins at the specified line number.

RUN specifying a line number should not be used following a program break — use CONT or GOTO for that purpose.

The RUN may also be used in program mode. It restarts program execution from the beginning of the program with all variables cleared and data pointers re-initialized.

Example:

```
RUN              Initialize and begin execution of the current program

RUN 1000         Initialize and begin execution of the program starting
                 at line 1000
```

SAVE

The SAVE statement writes a copy of the current program from memory to an external device. (Also see DSAVE.)

Cassette Unit Format:

    SAVE ["filename"][,dev][,sa]

The SAVE statement writes the program which is currently in memory to the tape cassette drive specified by dev. If the dev parameter is not present then the assumed value is 1 and the primary cassette drive is selected. The filename, if specified, is written at the beginning of the program. If a non-zero secondary address (sa) is specified, then an end of file mark is written on the cassette after the saved program.

Although none of the SAVE statement parameters are required when writing to a cassette drive, it is a good idea to name all programs. A named program can be read off cassette tape either by its name, or by its location on the cassette tape. A program with no name can be read off cassette tape by its location only.

The SAVE statement is most frequently used in immediate mode, although it can be executed from within a program.

For cassette operating instructions when using the SAVE statement see Chapter 2.

Example:

SAVE	*Write the current program onto the cassette in drive 1, leaving it unnamed*
SAVE "RED"	*Write the current program onto the cassette in drive 1, assigning the file name of RED*
A$="RED" SAVE A$	*Same as above*
SAVE "BLACKJACK",2,1	*Write the current program onto the cassette in drive 2 naming the program BLACKJACK. Write and end of file mark after the program*

Diskette Drive Format:

    SAVE "dr:filename",dev

The SAVE statement writes a copy of the current program from memory to the diskette in the drive specified by dr. The program is given the name filename. dev must be present; in all standard CBM computer systems it has the value 8. If dev is absent, a default value of 1 is assumed and the primary cassette is selected.

The file name assigned to the program must be new. If a file with the same name already exists on the diskette, a syntax error is reported. However a program file can be replaced; if an @ sign precedes dr in the SAVE statement text string, then using DOS 2.0 or higher, the program replaces the contents of a current file named filename.

The diskette SAVE statement is also used primarily in immediate mode although it can be executed out of a program.

For diskette operating instructions see Chapter 2.

Example:

```
SAVE "0:BLACKJACK",8    Write the current program to the diskette on drive 0 and name the
                        program file BLACKJACK
SAVE "@0:BLACKJACK",8   Write the current program to the diskette on drive 0, replacing prior
                        contents of program file BLACKJACK
```

SCRATCH (BASIC 4.0)

The SCRATCH statement erases a single file from a diskette. (Also see PRINT#
SCRATCH.)

Format:

```
SCRATCH [Dd],"filename"[ON Uz]
```

The file named filename on the diskette in drive d is deleted. If the Dd parameter
is not present, drive 0 is assumed.

The SCRATCH statement is used in immediate mode and in program mode. In
immediate mode the statement is used to perform general diskette housekeeping operations. When executed the message ARE YOU SURE? is displayed. You must key the
response YES <CR> or Y <CR>, or the file will not be scratched.

When the SCRATCH statement is executed out of a program, no prompt
messages are displayed. Temporary data files are frequently created by a program to hold
transient data that will not fit in available memory. Temporary data files should be
scratched before the program completes execution; otherwise a FILE EXISTS syntax
error will be generated when the program is run next.

Files must be closed before they are scratched. If you attempt to scratch an open
file the CBM computer may perform complex, erroneous diskette operations.

If using DOS 2.0 it is a good idea to COLLECT the diskette in immediate mode
before scratching any files (see COLLECT).

Example:

```
SCRATCH D0,"DUMMY1"     Scratch file DUMMY1 on diskette drive 0

SCRATCH "DUMMY1"        Same as above

SCRATCH D1,"FILE1"      Scratch FILE1 on diskette drive 1
```

STOP

The STOP statement causes the program to stop execution and return control to
CBM BASIC. A break message is displayed on the screen.

Format:

```
STOP
```

Example:

```
655 STOP                Will cause the message BREAK IN 655 to be displayed
```

VERIFY

The VERIFY statement compares the current program in memory with the contents of a program file.

Cassette Unit Format:

VERIFY ["filename"][,dev]

The program currently in memory is compared with the program named filename on the cassette in the unit specified by dev. If dev is not present, a default of 1 is assumed and cassette unit 1 is selected. If filename is not present, the next file on the cassette in the selected unit is verified.

You should always verify a program immediately after saving it.

The VERIFY statement is almost always executed in immediate mode. For cassette operating instructions see Chapter 2.

Example:

VERIFY	*Verify the next program found on the tape*
VERIFY "CLIP"	*Search for the program named CLIP on cassette unit #1, and verify it*
A$="CLIP" VERIFY A$	*Same as above*

Diskette Drive Format:

VERIFY "dr:filename",dev

The program currently stored in memory is compared with the program file named filename on the diskette in drive dr. The dev parameter must be present and in all standard CBM computer systems it must have the value 8. If the dev parameter is absent a default value of 1 is assumed and the primary cassette drive is selected.

In order to verify the program most recently saved, use the following version of the VERIFY statement:

VERIFY "*",8

You should always verify programs as soon as you have saved them.

The VERIFY statement is nearly always executed in immediate mode. For diskette operating instructions see Chapter 2.

Example:

VERIFY "*",8	*Verify the program just saved*
VERIFY"0:SHELL",8	*Search for the program named SHELL on disk drive 0, and verify it*
C$="0:SHELL" VERIFY C$	*Same as above*

WAIT

The WAIT statement halts program execution until a specified memory location acquires a specified value.

Format:

```
WAIT memadr, mask[,xor]

where:

    mask    is a one-byte mask value
    xor     is a one-byte mask value
```

The WAIT statement executes as follows:

1. The contents of the addressed memory location are fetched.
2. The value obtained in step 1 is Exclusive-ORed with xor, if present. If xor is not specified, it defaults to 0. When xor is 0, this step has no effect.
3. The value obtained in step 2 is ANDed with the specified mask value.
4. If the result is 0, WAIT returns to step 1, remaining in a loop that halts program execution at the WAIT.
5. If the result is not 0, program execution continues with the statement following the WAIT statement.

The STOP key will not interrupt WAIT statement execution.

FUNCTIONS

CBM BASIC functions are described below in alphabetical order. Names and abbreviations used are described at the beginning of this chapter.

A few functions are available only on CBM 8000 series computers; these functions are described in the next section.

ABS

ABS returns the absolute value of a number. This is the value of the number withtions are described in the next section.

Format:

```
ABS(datan)
```

Example:

```
A=ABS(10)              Results in A=10

A=ABS(-10)             Results in A=10

PRINT ABS(X),ABS(Y),ABS(Z)
```

ASC

ASC returns the ASCII code number for a specified character.

Format:

ASC(data$)

If the string is longer than one character, ASC returns the ASCII code for the first character in the string. The returned argument is a number and may be used in arithmetic operations. ASCII codes are listed in Appendix A.

Example:

```
?ASC("A")       Prints 65
N=ASC(B$)
X=ASC("S").
$X              Prints the ASCII value of "S", which is 83
```

ATN

ATN returns the arctangent of the argument.

Format:

ATN(datan)

ATN returns the value in radians in the range ±17.

Example:

```
A=ATN(AG)
?180π*ATN(A)
```

CHR$

CHR$ returns the string representation of the specified ASCII code.

Format:

CHR$(byte)

CHR$ can be used to specify characters that cannot be represented in strings. These include a carriage return and the double quotation mark.

Example:

```
IF C$=CHR$(13) GOTO 10       Branch if C$ is a carriage return (CHR$(13))

?CHR$(34):"HOHOHO":CHR$(34)  Print the eight characters "HOHOHO" (where CHR$(34)
                             represents a double quotation mark)
```

COS

COS returns the cosine of the argument.

Format:

COS(datan)

Example:

```
AG=0.25
A=COS(AG)      A is assigned the value 0.968912422
```

DS (BASIC 4.0)

Whenever the variable DS is referenced by any BASIC statement, an integer number is returned specifying the status of the most recent disk access operation. See Table 8-1 for DS interpretations.

Example:

```
20 IF DS<>0 THEN PRINT "ERROR":STOP
```

DS$ (BASIC 4.0)

When the string variable named DS$ is referenced by any BASIC statement the status of the most recent disk access is returned with the following format:

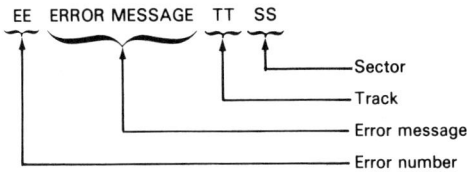

See Appendix B for a summary of diskette error messages.

Example:

```
20 IF DS>20 THEN PRINT DS$:STOP
```

If DS has a value of 1, a file has been scratched; any other value less than 20 is no error.

EXP

EXP returns the value e^{arg}. The value of e used is 2.71828183.

Format:

```
EXP(argn)
```

argn must have a value in the range ± 88.029691. A number larger than $+88.029691$ will result in an overflow error message. A number smaller than -88.029691 will yield a zero result.

Example:

?EXP(0)	*Prints 1*
?EXP(1)	*Prints 2.71828183*
EV=EXP(2)	*Results in EV=7.3890561*
EB=EXP(50.24)	*Results in EV=6.59105247E+21*
?EXP(88.0296919)	*Largest allowable number, yields 1.70141183E+38*
?EXP(-88.0296919)	*Smallest allowable number, yields 5.87747176E-39*
?EXP(88.029692)	*Out of range, overflow error message*
?EXP(-88.029692)	*Out of range, returns 0*

FRE

FRE is a system function that collects all unused bytes of memory into one block (called "garbage collection") and returns the number of free bytes.

Format:

FRE(arg)

arg is a dummy argument. It may be string or numeric.

FRE can be used anywhere a function may appear, but it is normally used in an immediate mode PRINT statement.

Example:

?FRE(1)   *Institute garbage collection and print the number*
                 of free bytes

INT

INT returns the integer portion of a number, rounding to the next lower signed number.

Format:

INT(argn)

For positive numbers, INT is equivalent to dropping the fractional portion of the number without rounding. For negative numbers, INT is equivalent to dropping the fractional portion of the number and adding 1. Note that INT does *not* convert a floating point number (5 bytes) to integer type (2 bytes).

Example:

A=INT(1.5)	*Results in A=1*
A=INT(-1.5)	*Results in A=-2*
X=INT(-0.1)	*Results in X=-1*

A caution here: Since floating point numbers are only close approximations of real numbers, an argument may not yield the exact INT function value you might expect. For instance, consider the number 3.89999999. The function *INT(3.89999999) would yield a 3 answer, not 4 as would be expected:

?INT(3.89999999)
3

LEFT$

LEFT$ returns the leftmost characters of a string.

Format:

> LEFT$(arg$,byte)

byte specifies the number of leftmost characters to be extracted from the arg$ character string.

Example:

>   ?LEFT$("ARG",2)   *Prints AR*
>
>   A$=LEFT$(B$,10)   *Prints leftmost ten characters of B$ string*

LEN

LEN returns the length of the string argument.

Format:

> LEN(arg$)

LEN returns a number that is the count of characters in the specified string.

Example:

>   ?LEN("ABCDEF")   *Displays 6*
>
>   N=LEN(C$+D$)   *Displays the sum of characters in strings C$ and D$*

LOG

LOG returns the natural logarithm, or log to the base e. The value of e used is 2.71828183.

Format:

> LOG(argn)

An ILLEGAL QUANTITY ERROR message is returned if the argument is zero or negative.

Example:

>   ?LOG(1)   *Prints 0*
>   A=LOG(10)   *Results in A=2.30258509*
>   A=LOG(1E6)   *Results in A=13.8155106*
>   A=LOG(X)/LOG(10)   *Calculates log to the base 10*

MID$

MID$ returns any specified portion of a string.

Format:

MID$(data$,byte₁ [,byte₂])

Some number of characters from the middle of the string identified by data$ are returned. The two numeric parameters $byte_1$ and $byte_2$ determine the portion of the string which is returned. String characters are numbered from the left, with the leftmost character having position 1. The value of $byte_1$ determines the first character to be extracted from the string. Beginning with this character, $byte_2$ determines the number of characters to be extracted. If $byte_2$ is absent then all characters up to the end of the string are extracted.

An ILLEGAL QUANTITY ERROR message is printed if a parameter is out of range.

Example:

```
?MID$("ABCDE",2,1)     Prints B
?MID$("ABCDE",3,2)     Prints CD
?MID$("ABCDE",3)       Prints CDE
```

PEEK

PEEK returns the contents of the specified memory location. PEEK is the function counterpart of the POKE statement.

Format:

PEEK(memadr)

Any memory location can be PEEKed except for system locations that contain the BASIC interpreter. These locations have been PEEK-protected to discourage examination of proprietary software. The protected area returns a PEEK value of 0. Locations of interest that you might want to PEEK at are discussed in Chapter 7.

Example:

```
?PEEK(1)               Prints contents of memory location 1
A=PEEK(20000)
```

POS

POS returns the column position of the cursor.

Format:

POS(data)

data is a dummy function; it is not used and therefore can have any value.

POS returns the current cursor position. If no cursor is displayed, the current character position within a program line or string variable is returned. Character positions begin at 0 for the leftmost character.

For a 40 column display POS will return a value between 0 and 39. For an 80 column display POS will return a value between 0 and 79.

Recall that program logic processes 80 character lines even if a CBM computer has a 40 character display. If program logic in such a computer is processing a character in the second half of the line, the POS function will return a value between 40 and 79, even though the computer only has a 40 character display.

By concatenation, string variables with up to 255 characters may be generated. If program logic is processing a long string, then the POS function will return the character position currently being processed. Under these circumstances the POS function will return a value ranging between 0 and 255.

Example:

```
?POS(1)                 At the beginning of a line, returns 0

?"ABCABC";POS(1)        With a previous POS value of 0, displays a
                        POS value of 6
```

RIGHT$

RIGHT$ returns the rightmost characters in a string.

Format:

```
RIGHT$(arg$,byte)
```

byte identifies the number of rightmost characters that are extracted from the string specified by arg$.

Example:

```
RIGHT$(ARG,2)           Displays RG

MM$=RIGHT$(X$+"#",5)    MM$ is assigned the last four characters of X$, plus the
                        character #.
```

RND

RND generates random number sequences ranging between 0 and 1.

Format:

```
RND(argn)               Return random number
RND(-argn)              Store new seed number
```

Example:

```
A=RND(-1)               Store a new seed based on the value -1
A=RND(1)                Fetch the next random number in sequence
```

An argument of zero is treated as a special case; it does not store a new seed, nor does it return a random number. RND(0) uses the current system time value TI to introduce an additional random element into play.

A pseudo-random seed is stored by the function:

```
RND(-TI)                Store pseudo-random seed
```

RND(0) can be used to store a new seed that is more truly random, by using the following function:

```
RND(-RND(0))          Store random seed
```

For a complete discussion of the RND function see Chapter 5.

SGN

SGN determines whether a number is positive, negative, or zero.

Format:

```
SGN(argn)
```

The SGN function returns +1 if the number is positive, non-zero; 0 if the number is zero; −1 if the number is negative.

Example:

```
?SGN(-6)          Displays -1
?SGN(0)           Displays 0
?SGN(44)          Displays 1
IF A>C THEN SA=SGN(X)
IF SGN(M)>= 0 THEN PRINT "POSITIVE NUMBER"
```

SIN

SIN returns the sine of the argument.

Format:

```
SIN (argn)
```

Example:

```
A=SIN(AG)
?SIN(45*π/180)     Displays the sine of 45 degrees
```

SPC

SPC moves the cursor right a specified number of positions.

Format:

```
SPC(byte)
```

The SPC function is used in **PRINT** statements to move the cursor some number of character positions to the right. Text which the cursor passes over is not modified.

The SPC function moves the cursor rightward from whatever column position the cursor happens to be at when the SPC function is encountered. This is in contrast to a TAB function which moves the cursor to some fixed column measured from the leftmost column of the display. (See TAB for examples.)

SQR

SQR returns the square root of a positive number. A negative number returns an error message.

Format:

SQR(argn)

Example:

A=SQR(4)	*Results in A=2*
A=SQR(4.84)	*Results in A=2.2*
?SQR(144E30)	*Displays 1.2E+16*

ST

ST returns the current value of the I/O status. This status is set to certain values depending on the results of the last input/output operation.

Format:

ST

ST values are shown in Table 8-3.

Status should be checked after execution of any statement that accesses an external device. See Chapter 6 for a complete discussion of I/O status.

Example:

10 IF ST <>0 GOTO 500	*Branch on any error*
50 IF ST=4 THEN ?"SHORT BLOCK"	

STR$

STR$ returns the string equivalent of a numeric argument.

Format:

STR$(argn)

STR$ returns the character string equivalent of the number generated by resolving argn.

Example:

A$=STR$(14.6)	*Displays 14.6*
?A$	
?STR$(1E2)	*Displays 100*
?STR$(1E10)	*Displays 1E+10*

Table 8-3. ST Values for I/O Devices

ST Bit Position	ST Numeric Value	Cassette Tape Read	Cassette Tape Verify and Load	IEEE Devices Read/Write
0	1			Time out write
1	2			Time out read
2	4	Short block	Short block	
3	8	Long block	Long block	
4	16	Unrecoverable read error	Any mismatch	
5	32	Checksum error	Checksum error	
6	64	End of file		EOI
7	−128	End of tape	End of tape	Device not present

SYS

SYS is a system function that transfers program control to an independent subsystem.

Format:

    SYS(memadr)

memadr is the starting address at which execution of the subsystem is to begin. The value must be in the range 0<address<65535. SYS is described in Chapter 7.

TAB

TAB moves the cursor right to the specified column position.

Format:

    TAB(argn)

TAB moves the cursor to the n+1 position, where n is the number obtained by resolving argn.

Example:

```
?"QUARK";SPC(10);"W"        These two examples show the difference between
QUARK            W              SPC and TAB.  SPC skips ten positions from
                                the last cursor location, whereas TAB skips to
                                the 10+1th position on the row
?"QUARK";TAB(10);"W"
QUARK          W
```

Using the TAB Key

Recent CBM computers have a TAB key. This key can be used within a PRINT statement's text string to set tabs, clear tabs, or move the cursor right to the next tab stop.

Tabs are set and cleared using the shifted TAB key, or the CHR$(9) function. A tab is cleared if the cursor is in a column where a tab was previously set; a tab is set otherwise.

Tabs may be set and cleared in immediate mode or in program mode. To set or clear tabs in immediate mode simply move the cursor to the desired screen column then press the shifted TAB key. In program mode execute a PRINT statement that moves the cursor to the required column position, then execute a shifted tab character.

Up to 80 tabs may be set. Execution of a carriage return makes tab settings permanent until cleared.

The unshifted TAB key or the CHR$(137) function moves the cursor right to the next tab column.

Example:

The following example sets tabs at columns 15, 25, and 50, then displays the words one, two, and three at these three column positions:

```
10 PRINT"▮▮▮▮▮▮▮▮▮▮▮▮▮▮▮▮▮▮▮▮▮▮▮▮▮▮▮▮▮▮▮▮▮▮▮▮▮▮▮▮▮▮▮▮▮▮▮▮▮▮▮"
20 PRINT"▮ONE▮TWO▮THREE"
```

TAN

TAN returns the tangent of the argument.

Format:

TAN(argn)

Example:

```
?TAN(3.2)              Displays 0.0584738547
XY(1)=TAN(180*π/180)
```

TI, TI$

TI and TI$ represent two system time variables.

Format:

TI	Number of jiffies since current startup
TI$	Time of day string

Example:

```
?TI
TI$="081000"
```

Usages of TI and TI$ are described in Chapter 5, under "Setting Time of Day."

USR

USR is a system function that passes a parameter to a user-written assembly language subroutine whose address is contained in memory locations 1 and 2. USR also fetches a return parameter from the subroutine.

Format:

USR(arg)

The USR function is described in more detail in Chapter 7.

VAL

VAL returns the numeric equivalent of the string argument.

Format:

VAL(data$)

The number returned by VAL may be used in arithmetic computations.

VAL converts the string argument by first discarding any leading blanks. If the first non-blank character is not a numeric digit (0-9), the argument is returned as a value of 0. If the first non-blank is a digit, VAL begins converting the string into real number format. If it subsequently encounters a non-digit character, it stops processing so that the argument returned is the numerical equivalent of the string up to the first non-digit character.

Example:

```
A=VAL("123")
NN=VAL(B$)
```

CBM 8000 EDITING FUNCTIONS

The CBM 8000 Computer also supports the following unique functions.

BELL

BELL rings the console bell of appropriately equipped CBM 8000 computers.

Format:

CHR$(7) or <ESC><RVS>g

The bell rings whenever BELL format characters appear in a PRINT statement parameter list. The bell rings automatically on power-up, or when the cursor moves through column 75 of the display. If the screen window has been narrowed using window scrolling functions, then the bell sounds when the cursor passes through the fifth column from the right edge of the window.

Example:

```
100 PRINT CHR$(7)
```

DELETE LINE (BASIC 4.0)

Delete a line on the display. Scroll up all text below the deleted line.

Format:

CHR$(21) or <ESC><RVS>u

To delete a line include one of the formats illustrated above in a PRINT statement parameter list. The line on which the cursor is currently located gets deleted. The line is deleted on the display only; memory is not modified. This function should be used in programs that create displays; it should not be used to erase data from memory.

Example:

```
PRINT"<HOME><CRSR↓><CRSR↓><CRSR↓><ESC><RVS>U"      Delete the fourth display line
```

ERASE BEGIN

ERASE BEGIN erases all text on the current cursor line from the beginning of the line up to the cursor position.

Format:

```
CHR$(150) or <ESC> <RVS>V
```

To access the ERASE BEGIN function, one of the formats illustrated above must appear in a PRINT statement parameter list. The display line on which the cursor is located is erased from the beginning of the line up to the cursor position but memory is not modified. This function should only be used in programs that are controlling screen displays.

Example:

```
100 PRINT TAB(20);CHR$(150)      Erase first 20 characters of line
```

ERASE END

ERASE END erases all text on the current cursor line from the cursor position up to the end of the line.

Format:

```
CHR$(22) or <ESC> <RVS>v
```

To access the ERASE END function, one of the formats illustrated above must appear in a PRINT statement parameter list. The display line on which the cursor is located is erased from the cursor position up to the end of the line, but memory is not modified. This function should only be used in programs that are controlling screen displays.

Example:

```
100 PRINT TAB(20);CHR$(22)      Erase line starting at character 20
```

GRAPHIC

The GRAPHIC function changes the screen display from text to graphic characters.

Format:

```
CHR$(142) or <ESC> <RVS>N
```

The GRAPHIC function is enabled when one of the formats illustrated above is encountered in a PRINT statement parameter list. The standard character set is selected for those characters which have a graphic symbol. Also, spacing between lines is eliminated to improve the quality of graphics.

The effect of the GRAPHIC function is cancelled by the TEXT function.

Example:

        PRINT CHR$(142)   *Select graphics display*

INSERT LINE

The INSERT LINE function inserts one blank line at the cursor position on the screen display.

Format:

    CHR$(149) OR <ESC> <RVS>m

A line is inserted in the screen display at the current cursor position when one of the character formats illustrated above is encountered in a PRINT statement parameter list. The display below the inserted line is scrolled down one line; the bottom display line is scrolled off the screen.

The insert line function modifies the screen display but does not alter memory. This function should be used only in programs that are creating and modifying displays.

Example:

        PRINT "<HOME><CRSR↓><CRSR↓><CRSR↓><ESC<RVS>M"   *Insert a line at display line 4*

SCROLL DOWN AND SCROLL UP

These two functions scroll text down one line, or up one line within a display window.

Format:

        Scroll Down: CHR$(153) or <ESC> <RVS>Q
        Scroll Up: CHR$(25) or <ESC> <RVS>q

The SET BOTTOM and SET TOP functions can be used to define a window on the CBM computer display. Within this window the SCROLL DOWN function will scroll text down one line; a blank line appears at the top of the window, while the bottom line of the window is scrolled off the screen. The SCROLL UP function scrolls text up one line within the window, scrolling the top line off the screen, while a blank line is inserted at the bottom of the window. These two functions are enabled when they appear in a PRINT statement parameter list.

The SCROLL UP and SCROLL DOWN functions modify the display, but do not change memory. These two functions should only be used in programs that create displays.

Example:

        10 PRINT CHRS$(25)   *Scroll up one line within window*

SET BOTTOM AND SET TOP

These two functions define a window on the CBM computer display.

Format:

Set Bottom: CHR$(143)
Set Top: CHR$(15)

The SET BOTTOM function defines the bottom righthand corner of the screen. The SET TOP function defines the top lefthand corner of the screen. In order to define the window a PRINT statement parameter list must move the cursor to the required bottom right and top left corners of the window and then execute the SET BOTTOM and SET TOP functions respectively.

To cancel a window, execute a PRINT statement with two consecutive HOME characters in its parameter list.

Example:

Suppose a display window is to be bounded by rows 5 and 15, and columns 10 and 60. The following PRINT statement would establish the required window:

```
10 PRINT"■■■■■■■";TAB(10);CHR$(15);"■■■■■■■■■■■";TAB(60);CHR$(143)
```

Subsequently the following PRINT statement would cancel the window:

```
100 PRINT "<HOME><HOME>"
```

TEXT

The TEXT function cancels the effect of the GRAPHIC function. Characters that have a graphic symbol in the standard character set are switched to the alternate character set representation.

Format:

CHR$(14) or <ESC> <RVS>n

The TEXT function is enabled by executing a PRINT statement with one of the formats illustrated above in its parameter list.

Example:

```
100 PRINT CHR$(14)       End graphics
```

CBM Character Codes

This appendix contains the following tables:

- CBM BASIC keywords (Table A-1)
- CBM ASCII 7-bit codes (Table A-2)
- CBM screen memory 7-bit codes (Table A-3)
- CBM standard and alternate character set 8-bit codes (Table A-4)

Tables A-1, A-2 and A-3 are self-explanatory; they are referred to frequently throughout the book. The standard and alternate character sets illustrated in Table A-4 are also referred to frequently throughout the book; however, being unique to CBM computers, information presented in this table is summarized below.

The first two columns of Table A-4 show the standard and alternate character sets for the PET and CBM computers. The right three columns show each character's corresponding ASCII code and PEEK/POKE number. The characters are arranged in ascending sequence by their CBM ASCII code number. If the character does not have a CBM ASCII code number, as in the case of reverse characters, they are arranged in ascending sequence of PEEK/POKE number. Many characters appear twice because they have two CBM ASCII code numbers.

Standard Character Set. The standard character set is in effect when the PET 2001 computer is powered up, or when a value of 12 is poked into memory location 59468 by a POKE 59468,12 statement on a PET or CBM computer. The standard character set has upper-case alphabetics, numbers, graphic characters and special symbols.

Alternate Character Set. The alternate character set is in effect when the CBM computer is powered up, or when a value of 14 is poked into memory location 59468 by a POKE 59468,14 statement on a PET or CBM computer. The alternate character set has upper- and lower-case alphabetics, numbers, and some special symbols.

CBM ASCII Code. ASCII stands for American Standard Code for Information Interchange. Commodore Business Machines developed its own ASCII code for the CBM Computer in order to include its unique characters.

The ASCII code column (and Table A-2) shows both the decimal and hexadecimal CBM ASCII codes for each character. To find a character's ASCII code column, find the desired character in the character column, then look across the chart for the corresponding CBM ASCII code. When using the ASC( ) or CHR$( ) function refer only to the decimal ASCII number.

The last portion of the chart, the reverse characters, do not have CBM ASCII codes. Therefore they are arranged by their PEEK/POKE numbers.

PEEK/POKE. The PEEK/POKE number is the number used when POKEing a character to the screen. It also represents the number of the character returned when PEEKing into memory to see what character is contained in a specified memory location. The PEEK/POKE numbers do not appear in strict ascending sequence until the reverse characters portion of the chart. At this point, the chart is arranged in ascending PEEK/POKE order because the reverse CBM characters lack CBM ASCII numbers, and can only be referenced with PRINT or PEEK/POKE statements.

Table A-1. CBM BASIC Keyboard Codes

Code (decimal)	Character/ Keyword	Code (decimal)	Character/ Keyword	Code (decimal)	Character/ Keyword	Code (decimal)	Character/ Keyword
0	End of line	70	F	141	GOSUB	181	INT
1-31	Unused	71	G	142	RETURN	182	ABS
32	space	72	H	143	REM	183	USR
33	!	73	I	144	STOP	184	FRE
34	''	74	J	145	ON	185	POS
35	#	75	K	146	WAIT	186	SQR
36	$	76	L	147	LOAD	187	RND
37	%	77	M	148	SAVE	188	LOG
38	&	78	N	149	VERIFY	189	EXP
39	'	79	O	150	DEF	190	COS
40	(	80	P	151	POKE	191	SIN
41	)	81	Q	152	PRINT#	192	TAN
42	*	82	R	153	PRINT	193	ATN
43	+	83	S	154	CONT	194	PEEK
44	,	84	T	155	LIST	195	LEN
45	—	85	U	156	CLR	196	STR$
46	.	86	V	157	CMD	197	VAL
47	/	87	W	158	SYS	198	ASC
48	0	88	X	159	OPEN	199	CHR$
49	1	89	Y	160	CLOSE	200	LEFT$
50	2	90	Z	161	GET	201	RIGHT$
51	3	91	[	162	NEW	202	MID$
52	4	92	\	163	TAB(	203	Unused
53	5	93	]	164	TO	204	CONCAT†
54	6	94	↑	165	FN	205	DOPEN†
55	7	95	←	166	SPC(	206	DCLOSE†
56	8	96-127	Unused	167	THEN	207	RECORD†
57	9	128	END	168	NOT	208	HEADER†
58	:	129	FOR	169	STEP	209	COLLECT†
59	;	130	NEXT	170	+	210	BACKUP†
60	<	131	DATA	171	—	211	COPY†
61	=	132	INPUT#	172	*	212	APPEND†
62	>	133	INPUT	173	/	213	DSAVE†
63	?	134	DIM	174	↑	215	CATALOG†
64	@	135	READ	175	AND	216	RENAME†
65	A	136	LET	176	OR	217	SCRATCH†
66	B	137	GOTO	177	>	218	DIRECTORY†
67	C	138	RUN	178	=	219	?SYNTAX ERROR†
68	D	139	IF	179	<	220-254	Unused
69	E	140	RESTORE	180	SGN	255	π

† For BASIC 4.0 only

Table A-2. ASCII Standard 7-Bit Codes

			6	0	0	0	0	1	1	1	1
	Bit →		5	0	0	1	1	0	0	1	1
3	2	1	0 4	0	1	0	1	0	1	0	1
0	0	0	0	NUL	DLE	SP	0	@	P	`	p
0	0	0	1	SOH	DC1	!	1	A	Q	a	q
0	0	1	0	STX	DC2	"	2	B	R	b	r
0	0	1	1	ETX	DC3	#	3	C	S	c	s
0	1	0	0	EOT	DC4	$	4	D	T	d	t
0	1	0	1	ENQ	NAK	%	5	E	U	e	u
0	1	1	0	ACK	SYN	&	6	F	V	f	v
0	1	1	1	BEL	ETB	`	7	G	W	g	w
1	0	0	0	BS	CAN	(	8	H	X	h	x
1	0	0	1	HT	EM	)	9	I	Y	i	y
1	0	1	0	LF	SUB	*	:	J	Z	j	z
1	0	1	1	VT	ESC	+	;	K	[	k	{
1	1	0	0	FF	FS	,	<	L	\	l	l
1	1	0	1	CR	GS	—	=	M	]	m	}
1	1	1	0	SO	RS	.	>	N	∧	n	~
1	1	1	1	SI	US	/	?	O	—	o	DEL

NUL	Null	FF	Form feed	ETB	End of transmission block
SOH	Start of heading	CR	Carriage return	CAN	Cancel
STX	Start of text	SO	Shift out	EM	End of medium
ETX	End of text	SI	Shift in	SUB	Substitute
EOT	End of transmission	DLE	Data line escape	ESC	Escape
ENQ	Enquiry	DC1	Device control 1	FS	File separator
ACK	Acknowledge	DC2	Device control 2	GS	Group separator
BEL	Bell, or alarm	DC3	Device control 3	RS	Record separator
BS	Backspace	DC4	Device control 4	US	Unit separator
HT	Horizontal tabulation	NAK	Negative acknowledge	SP	Space
LF	Line feed	STN	Synchronous idle	DEL	Delete
VT	Vertical tabulation				

Table A-3. CBM Screen Memory 7-Bit Codes

Table A-4. PET/CBM Standard and Alternate Character Sets (Continued)

Standard Character Set PET	CBM	Alternate Character Set PET	CBM	ASCII DEC	HEX	PEEK/POKE
				0	00	
				1	01	
				2	02	
STOP		STOP		3	03	
				4	04	
				5	05	
				6	06	
				7	07	
				8	08	
				9	09	
				10	0A	
				11	0B	
				12	0C	
RETURN		RETURN		13	0D	
				14	0E	
				15	0F	
				16	10	
CRSR↓		CRSR↓		17	11	
RVS		RVS		18	12	
HOME		HOME		19	13	
DELETE		DELETE		20	14	
				21	15	
				22	16	
				23	17	
				24	18	
				25	19	
				26	1A	
				27	1B	
				28	1C	
CRSR→		CRSR→		29	1D	
				30	1E	
				31	1F	
▨	▨	▨	▨	32	20	32
!		!		33	21	33
"		"		34	22	34
#		#		35	23	35
$		$		36	24	36
%		%		37	25	37
&		&		38	26	38
'		'		39	27	39
(		(		40	28	40
)		)		41	29	41
*		*		42	2A	42
+		+		43	2B	43
,		,		44	2C	44
-		-		45	2D	45
.		.		46	2E	46
/		/		47	2F	47
0		0		48	30	48
1		1		49	31	49
2		2		50	32	50
3		3		51	33	51
4		4		52	34	52
5		5		53	35	53
6		6		54	36	54
7		7		55	37	55
8		8		56	38	56
9		9		57	39	57
:		:		58	3A	58
;		;		59	3B	59
<		<		60	3C	60
=		=		61	3D	61
>		>		62	3E	62
?		?		63	3F	63
@		@		64	40	0

Standard Character Set PET	CBM	Alternate Character Set PET	CBM	ASCII DEC	HEX	PEEK/POKE
A	A	a	a	65	41	1
B	B	b	b	66	42	2
C	C	c	c	67	43	3
D	D	d	d	68	44	4
E	E	e	e	69	45	5
F	F	f	f	70	46	6
G	G	g	g	71	47	7
H	H	h	h	72	48	8
I	I	i	i	73	49	9
J	J	j	j	74	4A	10
K	K	k	k	75	4B	11
L	L	l	l	76	4C	12
M	M	m	m	77	4D	13
N	N	n	n	78	4E	14
O	O	o	o	79	4F	15
P	P	p	p	80	50	16
Q	Q	q	q	81	51	17
R	R	r	r	82	52	18
S	S	s	s	83	53	19
T	T	t	t	84	54	20
U	U	u	u	85	55	21
V	V	v	v	86	56	22
W	W	w	w	87	57	23
X	X	x	x	88	58	24
Y	Y	y	y	89	59	25
Z	Z	z	z	90	5A	26
[	[	[	[	91	5B	27
\	\	\	\	92	5C	28
]	]	]	]	93	5D	29
↑	↑	↑	↑	94	5E	30
←	←	←	←	95	5F	31
				96	60	32
!		!		97	61	33
"		"		98	62	34
#	#	#	#	99	63	35
$	$	$	$	100	64	36
%	%	%	%	101	65	37
&	&	&	&	102	66	38
'	'	'	'	103	67	39
(	(	(	(	104	68	40
)	)	)	)	105	69	41
*	*	*	*	106	6A	42
+	+	+	+	107	6B	43
,	,	,	,	108	6C	44
-	-	-	-	109	6D	45
.	.	.	.	110	6E	46
/	/	/	/	111	6F	47
0	0	0	0	112	70	48
1	1	1	1	113	71	49
2	2	2	2	114	72	50
3	3	3	3	115	73	51
4	4	4	4	116	74	52
5	5	5	5	117	75	53
6	6	6	6	118	76	54
7	7	7	7	119	77	55
8	8	8	8	120	78	56
9	9	9	9	121	79	57
:	:	:	:	122	7A	58
;	;	;	;	123	7B	59
<	<	<	<	124	7C	60
=	=	=	=	125	7D	61
>	>	>	>	126	7E	62
?	?	?	?	127	7F	63
				128	80	64

Table A-4. PET/CBM Standard and Alternate Character Sets (Continued)

Standard Character Set PET	CBM	Alternate Character Set PET	CBM	ASCII DEC	HEX	PEEK/POKE
				129	81	65
				130	82	66
RUN		RUN		131	83	67
				132	84	68
				133	85	69
				134	86	70
				135	87	71
				136	88	72
				137	89	73
				138	8A	74
				139	8B	75
				140	8C	76
Shifted RETURN		Shifted RETURN		141	8D	77
				142	8E	78
				143	8F	79
				144	90	80
CRSR↑		CRSR↑		145	91	81
RVS Off		RVS Off		146	92	82
CLR Screen		CLR Screen		147	93	83
INSERT		INSERT		148	94	84
				149	95	85
				150	96	86
				151	97	87
				152	98	88
				153	99	89
				154	9A	90
				155	9B	91
				156	9C	92
CRSR←		CRSR←		157	9D	93
				158	9E	94
				159	9F	95
Shifted ⌂		Shifted ⌂		160	A0	96
				161	A1	97
				162	A2	98
				163	A3	99
				164	A4	100
				165	A5	101
				166	A6	102
				167	A7	103
				168	A8	104
				169	A9	105
				170	AA	106
				171	AB	107
				172	AC	108
				173	AD	109
				174	AE	110
				175	AF	111
				176	B0	112
				177	B1	113
				178	B2	114
				179	B3	115
				180	B4	116
				181	B5	117
				182	B6	118
				183	B7	119
				184	B8	120
				185	B9	121
				186	BA	122
				187	BB	123
				188	BC	124
				189	BD	125
				190	BE	126
				191	BF	127
				192	C0	64

Standard Character Set PET	CBM	Alternate Character Set PET	CBM	ASCII DEC	HEX	PEEK/POKE
♠	♠	A	A	193	C1	65
		B	B	194	C2	66
		C	C	195	C3	67
		D	D	196	C4	68
		E	E	197	C5	69
		F	F	198	C6	70
		G	G	199	C7	71
		H	H	200	C8	72
		I	I	201	C9	73
		J	J	202	CA	74
		K	K	203	CB	75
		L	L	204	CC	76
		M	M	205	CD	77
		N	N	206	CE	78
		O	O	207	CF	79
		P	P	208	D0	80
●	●	Q	Q	209	D1	81
		R	R	210	D2	82
♥	♥	S	S	211	D3	83
		T	T	212	D4	84
		U	U	213	D5	85
		V	V	214	D6	86
		W	W	215	D7	87
		X	X	216	D8	88
		Y	Y	217	D9	89
♦	♦	Z	Z	218	DA	90
+	+	+	+	219	DB	91
				220	DC	92
				221	DD	93
π	π			222	DE	94
◤	◤			223	DF	95
				224	E0	96
				225	E1	97
				226	E2	98
				227	E3	99
				228	E4	100
				229	E5	101
				230	E6	102
				231	E7	103
				232	E8	104
				233	E9	105
				234		106
				235		107
				236		108
				237		109
				238		110
				239		111
				240		112
				241		113
				242		114
				243		115
				244		116
				245		117
				246		118
				247		119
				248		120
				249		121
				250		122
				251		123
				252		124
				253		125
				254		126
π	π			255		127

Table A-4. PET/CBM Standard and Alternate Character Sets (Continued)

Standard Character Set		Alternate Character Set		ASCII		PEEK/ POKE
PET	CBM	PET	CBM	DEC	HEX	
						128
		a	a			129
		b	b			130
		c	c			131
		d	d			132
		e	e			133
		f	f			134
		g	g			135
		h	h			136
		i	i			137
		j	j			138
		k	k			139
		l	l			140
		m	m			141
		n	n			142
		o	o			143
		p	p			144
		q	q			145
		r	r			146
		s	s			147
		t	t			148
		u	u			149
		v	v			150
		w	w			151
		x	x			152
		y	y			153
		z	z			154
						155
						156
						157
						158
						159
						160
						161
						162
						163
						164
						165
						166
						167
						168
						169
						170
						171
						172
						173
						174
						175
						176
						177
						178
						179
						180
						181
						182
						183
						184
						185
						186
						187
						188
						189
						190
						191

The center column is labeled "re–verse" (Standard set) and "reverse" (Alternate set).

Standard Character Set		Alternate Character Set		ASCII		PEEK/ POKE
PET	CBM	PET	CBM	DEC	HEX	
						192
						193
						194
						195
						196
						197
						198
						199
						200
						201
						202
						203
						204
						205
						206
						207
						208
						209
						210
						211
						212
						213
						214
						215
						216
						217
						218
						219
						220
						221
						222
						223
						224
						225
						226
						227
						228
						229
						230
						231
						232
						233
						234
						235
						236
						237
						238
						239
						240
						241
						242
						243
						244
						245
						246
						247
						248
						249
						250
						251
						252
						253
						254
						255

CBM Error Messages

Error messages may be displayed in response to just about anything you key in at the CBM keyboard or when your program is running. Both the CBM BASIC interpreter and the operating system issue error messages, listed separately below.

Whenever the CBM BASIC interpreter detects an error, it displays a diagnostic message, headed by a question mark, in the general form:

?message ERROR IN LINE number

where message is the type of error (listed alphabetically below) and number is the line number in the program where the error occurred (not present in immediate mode). Following any error message, BASIC returns to immediate mode and gives the READY prompt.

CBM BASIC error messages are listed below, with two descriptive paragraphs: The first describes the cause of the error, and the second discusses possible ways of correcting the error.

BASIC ERROR MESSAGES

Error Message	Cause and Suggested Remedies
BAD SUBSCRIPT	An attempt was made to reference an array element that is outside the dimensions of the array. This may happen by specifying the wrong number of dimensions (different from the DIM statement), using a subscript larger than specified in the DIM statement or using a subscript larger than 10 for a non-dimensioned array.

Correct the array element number to remain within the original dimensions, or change the array size to allow more elements.

CAN'T CONTINUE

A CONT command was issued, but program execution cannot be resumed because the program has been altered, added to or cleared in immediate mode, or execution was stopped by an error. Program execution cannot be continued past an error message.

Correct the error. The most prudent course is to type RUN and start over. However, you can attempt to reenter the program at the point of interruption by a directed GOTO.

DIVISION BY ZERO

An attempt was made to perform a division operation with a divisor of zero. Dividing by zero is not allowed.

Check the values of variables (or constants!) in the indicated line number. Change the program so that the divisor can never be evaluated to zero or add a check for zero before performing the division.

FORMULA TOO COMPLEX

This is not a program error but indicates that a string expression in the program is too intricate for CBM BASIC to handle.

Break the indicated expression into two or more parts and rerun the program (this will also tend to improve program readability).

ILLEGAL DIRECT

A command was given in immediate mode that is valid only in program mode. The following are invalid in immediate mode: DATA, DEF FN, GET, GET#, INPUT, INPUT#.

Enter the desired operation as a (short) program and RUN it.

ILLEGAL QUANTITY

A function is passed one or more parameters that are out of range. This message also occurs if the USR function is referenced before storing the subroutine address at memory locations 1 and 2.

Check the ranges given in Chapter 8 for the function in question. Change the program to be sure that the argument will always be within range, or add a check before the function reference to make sure that the argument is allowed. If USR error, insert statements to POKE the subroutine address before the USR reference.

NEXT WITHOUT FOR

A NEXT statement is encountered that is not tied to a preceding FOR statement. Either there is no FOR statement or the variable in the NEXT statement is not in a corresponding FOR statement.

The FOR part of a FOR-NEXT loop must be inserted or the offending NEXT statement deleted. Be sure that the index variables are the same at both ends of the loop.

OUT OF DATA

A READ statement is executed but all of the DATA statements in the program have already been read. For each variable in a READ statement, there must be a corresponding DATA element.

Add more DATA elements or restrict the number of READs to the current number of DATA elements. Insert a RESTORE statement to reread the existing data. Or add a flag at the end of the last DATA statement (any value not used as a DATA element may be used for the flag value) and stop READing when the flag has been read.

OUT OF MEMORY

The user program area of memory has been filled and a request is given to put more in, e.g., add a line to the program. This message may also be caused by multiple FOR-NEXT and/or GOSUB nestings that fill up the Stack; this is the case if ?FRE(0) shows considerable program area storage left.

Simplify the program. Pay particular attention to reducing array sizes. It may be necessary to restructure the program into overlays.

OVERFLOW

A calculation has resulted in a number outside the allowable range, i.e., the number is too big. The largest number allowed is $1.70141184E+38$.

Check your calculations. It may be possible to eliminate this error just by changing the order in which the calculations are programmed.

REDIM'D ARRAY

An array name appears in more than one DIM statement. This error also occurs if an array name is used (given a default size of 11) and later appears in a DIM statement.

Place DIM statements near the beginning of the program. Check to see that each DIM statement is executed only once. DIM must not appear inside a FOR-NEXT loop or in a subroutine where either may be executed more than once.

REDO FROM START

This is a diagnostic message during an INPUT statement operation and is not a fatal error. It indicates that the wrong type of data (string for numeric or vice versa) was entered in response to an INPUT request.

Reenter the correct type data. INPUT will continue prompting until an acceptable response is entered.

RETURN WITHOUT GOSUB

A RETURN statement was encountered without a previous matching GOSUB statement being executed.

Insert a GOSUB statement or delete the RETURN statement. The error may be caused by dropping into the subroutine code inadvertently. In this case correct the program flow. An END or STOP statement placed just ahead of the subroutine serves as a debugging aid.

STRING TOO LONG

An attempt was made by use of the concatenation operator (+) to create a string longer than 255 characters.

Break the string into two or more shorter strings as part of the program operation. Use the LEN function to check string lengths before concatenating them.

SYNTAX

There is a syntax error in the line just entered (immediate mode) or scanned for execution (program mode). This is the most common error message, and is caused by such things as misspellings, incorrect punctuation, unmatched parentheses, extraneous characters, etc.

Examine the line carefully and make corrections. Note that syntax errors in a program are diagnosed at run time, not at the time the lines are entered from the keyboard. You can eliminate many syntax error messages by carefully scrutinizing newly entered program lines before running the program.

TYPE MISMATCH

An attempt was made to enter a string into a numeric Assignment variable or vice versa, or an incorrect type was given as a function parameter.

Change the offending item to correct type. Refer to Chapter 8 for acceptable parameter types.

UNDEF'D STATEMENT

An attempt was made to branch to a nonexistent line number.

Insert a statement with the necessary line number or branch to another line number.

UNDEF'D FUNCTION

Reference was made to a user defined function that has not previously been defined by appearing in a DEF FN statement. The definition must precede the function reference.

Define the function. Place DEF FN statements near the beginning of the program.

OPERATING SYSTEM ERROR MESSAGES

BAD DATA

String data was input when numeric data was expected.

BAD DISK

Correct the input data to numeric, or change the program to accept string input.

A media failure on a HEADER command, due to either the diskette missing from the drive, a write protect tab, or a defective magnetic surface.

Check the disk drive to see if a diskette is properly inserted. Remove write protect tab if present. If magnetic surface is defective, use a different diskette (BASIC 4.0).

DEVICE NOT PRESENT

No device on the IEEE 488 Bus was present to handshake an attention sequence. The Status function will have a value of 2, indicating a timeout. This message may occur for any I/O command.

If the device identification is in error, correct the OPEN (or other) statement. If the statement is correct, especially if it has worked before, check the addressed device for malfunction, misconnection, or power off.

FILE ALREADY EXISTS

The name of the source file being copied with the COPY statement already exists on the destination diskette.

Delete the file on the destination diskette before attempting to COPY, or use a different diskette as the destination diskette.

FILE NOT FOUND

The filename given in the LOAD or OPEN statement was not found on the specified device.

Check that you have the correct tape or diskette in the device. Check the filenames on the tape or diskette for possible spelling error in the program statement.

FILE NOT OPEN

An attempt was made to access a file that was not opened via the OPEN statement.

Open the file.

FILE OPEN

An attempt was made to open a file that has already been opened via a previous OPEN statement.

Check the logical file number (first parameter in the OPEN statement) to be sure a different number is used for each file. Insert a CLOSE statement if you want to reopen the same file for a different I/O operation.

LOAD

An unacceptable number of tape errors were accumulated on a tape load (more than 31) that were not cleared on reading the redundant block. This message is issued in connection with the LOAD command (see Chapter 4).

NOT INPUT FILE   An attempt was made to read from a tape file that has been opened for output only.

Check the READ# and OPEN statement parameters for correctness. Reading requires a zero as the third parameter of the OPEN statement (this is the default option).

NOT OUTPUT FILE   An attempt was made to write to a tape file that has been opened for input only.

Check the PRINT# and OPEN statement parameters for correctness. Writing to a file requires a 1 (or a 2 if you want an EOT at the end of the file) as the third parameter in the OPEN statement.

VERIFY ERROR   The program in memory and the specified file do not compare. This message is issued in connection with the VERIFY command (see Chapter 8).

DOS ERROR MESSAGES

REQUESTING ERROR MESSAGES

To request error messages under BASIC 4.0, execute a PRINT statement to display numeric variable DS or string variable DS$.

DS$ displays four parameters as follows:

```
? DS$
```

```
NN   ERROR MESSAGE   TT   SS
 |_____     _____|    |    |_____ Sector accessed
          |   |             |_____ Track accessed
          |   |_____ Type of error
          |_____ Error number
```

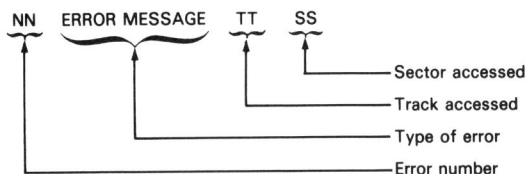

Using BASIC < 3.0 you cannot access variables DS or DS$. To examine error status, you must OPEN a logical file specifying physical unit 8 with secondary address 15. You must then input four string variables and display them. This may be illustrated as follows:

```
10 OPEN 1,8,15
20 INPUT#1, A$, B$, C$, D$
30 PRINT A$,B$,C$,D$
40 CLOSE 1
```

A$, is the error message number, B$ is the error message, C$ is the track number, and D$ is the sector number.

Table B-1 includes the track number and sector number for all DOS errors.

Table B-1. DOS Error Messages

	Error Number	Error Message	Track	Sector
Status Messages	00	OK	00	00
	01	FILES SCRATCHED	# FILES	00
Read Errors	20	READ ERROR (Block header not found)	T	S
	21	READ ERROR (No synch character)	T	S
	22	READ ERROR (Data block not present)	T	S
	23	READ ERROR (Checksum error in data block)	T	S
	24	READ ERROR (Byte decoding error)	T	S
	27	READ ERROR (Checksum error in header)	T	S
Write Errors	25	WRITE ERROR (Write-verify error)	T	S
	26	WRITE PROTECT ON	T	S
	28	WRITE ERROR (Long data block)	T	S
	29	DISK ID MISMATCH	T	S
Syntax Errors	30	SYNTAX ERROR (General syntax)	00	00
	31	SYNTAX ERROR (Invalid command)	00	00
	32	SYNTAX ERROR (Long line)	00	00
	33	SYNTAX ERROR (Invalid file name)	00	00
	34	SYNTAX ERROR (No file given)	00	00
	39	SYNTAX ERROR (Invalid DOS command)	00	00
	50	SYNTAX ERROR (Record not present)	00	00
	51	SYNTAX ERROR (Overflow in record)	T	S
	52	SYNTAX ERROR (File too large)	T	S
File Errors	60	WRITE FILE OPEN	00	00
	61	FILE NOT OPEN	00	00
	62	FILE NOT FOUND	00	00
	63	FILE EXISTS	00	00
	64	FILE TYPE MISMATCH	00	00
	65	NO BLOCK	T	S
	66	ILLEGAL TRACK AND SECTOR	T	S
	67	ILLEGAL SYSTEM TRACK AND SECTOR	T	S
System Errors	70	NO CHANNEL	00	00
	71	DIR ERROR	00	00
	72	DISK FULL	00	00
	73	DOS MISMATCH	00	00
	74	DRIVE NOT READY	00	00

READ ERRORS

Error Message Number	Error Message	Cause of Error
20	Block header not found	The disk controller is unable to locate the header of the requested data block. Caused by an illegal sector number, or the header has been destroyed.
21	No synch character	The disk controller is unable to detect a synch mark on the desired track. Caused by misalignment of the read/write head or no diskette is present. Can also indicate a hardware failure.

| 22 | Data block not present | The disk controller has been requested to read or verify a data block that was not properly written. This error message occurs in conjunction with the BLOCK commands and indicates an illegal track and/or sector request. |

| 23 | Checksum error in data block | This error message indicates that there is an error in one or more of the data bytes. The data has been read into the DOS memory, but the checksum over the data is in error. This message may also indicate grounding problems. |

| 24 | Byte decoding error | The data or header has been read into the DOS memory, but a hardware error has been created due to an invalid bit pattern in the data byte. This message may also indicate grounding problems. |

| 27 | Checksum error in header | The controller has detected an error in the header of the requested data block. The block has not been read into the DOS memory. This message may also indicate grounding problems. |

WRITE ERRORS

Error Message Number	Error Message	Cause of Error
25	Write-verify error	This message is generated if the controller detects a mismatch between the written data and the data in the DOS memory.
26	WRITE PROTECT ON	This message is generated when the controller has been requested to write a data block while the write protect switch is depressed. Typically, this is caused by using a diskette with a write protect tab over the notch.
28	Long data block	The controller attempts to detect the synch mark of the next header after writing a data block. If the synch mark does not appear within a predetermined time, the error message is generated. The error is caused by a bad diskette format (the data extends into the next block), or by hardware failure.
29	DISK ID MISMATCH	This message is generated when the controller has been requested to access a diskette which has not been initialized. This message can also occur if a diskette has a bad header.

SYNTAX ERRORS

Error Message Number	Error Message	Cause of Error
30	General syntax	The DOS cannot interpret the command sent to the command channel. Typically, this is caused by an illegal number of file names, or patterns are illegally used. For example, two file names may appear on the left side of the COPY command.
31	Invalid command	The DOS does not recognize the command. The command must start in the first position.
32	Long line	The command sent is longer than 40 characters.
33	Invalid file name	Pattern matching is invalidly used in the OPEN or SAVE command.
34	No file given	The file name was left out of a command or the DOS does not recognize it as such. Typically, a quotation mark ('') or colon (:) has been left out of the command.
39	Invalid DOS Command	An unrecognizable disk operating system command was received.
50	Record not present	An INPUT# or GET# statement selected a record beyond the current end of file. This is an error if you are attempting to read a record; it is not necessarily an error if you are positioning to the end of a file in order to add new records to an old file.
51	Overflow in Record	A PRINT# statement attempted to write more than the allowed number of characters to a relative file. The terminating carriage return is counted as one character when computing record length.
52	File too large	The current record position will result in disk overflow on the next write-to-disk operation.

FILE ERRORS

Error Message Number	Error Message	Cause of Error
60	WRITE FILE OPEN	This message is generated when a write file that has not been closed is being opened for reading.
61	FILE NOT OPEN	This message is generated when a file is being accessed that has not been opened in the DOS. Sometimes, in this case, a message is not generated; the request is simply ignored.
62	FILE NOT FOUND	The requested file does not exist on the indicated drive.
63	FILE EXISTS	The file name of the file being created already exists on the diskette.
64	FILE TYPE MISMATCH	The file type does not match the file type in the directory entry for the requested file.
65	NO BLOCK	This message occurs in conjunction with the B-A command. It indicates that the block to be allocated has been previously allocated. The parameters indicate the next higher in number available track and sector. If the parameters are zero (0), then all blocks higher in number are in use.
66	ILLEGAL TRACK AND SECTOR	An attempt has been made to access a sector that does not physically exist. The track and/or sector number specified is outside of the allowed range for the current diskette. Unless you are using random access files, you should never see this error code.
67	ILLEGAL SYSTEM TRACK AND SECTOR	When accessing program or data files, an attempt has been made to access a sector that is reserved for use by the disk operating system.

SYSTEM ERRORS

Error Message Number	Error Message	Cause of Error
70	NO CHANNEL (available)	The requested channel is not available, or all channels are in use. A maximum of five sequential files may be opened at one time to the DOS. Direct access channels may have six opened files.
71	DIR (ectory) ERROR	The BAM does not match the internal count. There is a problem in the BAM allocation or the BAM has been overwritten in DOS memory. To correct this problem, reinitialize the diskette to restore the BAM in memory. Some active files may be terminated by the corrective action.
72	DISK FULL	Either the blocks on the diskette are used or the directory is at its limit (152 entries).
73	DOS MISMATCH	Data written to a diskette using any one version of DOS may be read using any other version of DOS. However, you must write to a diskette using the same DOS version with which the diskette was initialized. Error 73 is reported if you attempt to write to a diskette using a different version of DOS from the one which created and initialized the diskette.
74	DRIVE NOT READY	An attempt has been made to access the 8050 diskette unit with the selected drive.

Appendix C

BASIC Bibliography

Advanced BASIC. James S. Coan, Hayden Book Co., Rochelle Park, New Jersey.

BASIC. Albrecht, Finkle, and Brown, Peoples Computer Company, Menlo Park, California, 1967.

BASIC: A Computer Programming Language. C. Pegels, Holden-Day, Inc., 1973.

Basic BASIC. James S. Coan, Hayden Book Company, Rochelle Park, New Jersey.

BASIC Programming. J. Kemeny and T. Kurtz, Peoples Computer Company, Menlo Park, California, 1967.

Entering BASIC. J. Sack and J. Meadows, Science Research Associates, 1973.

A Guided Tour of Computer Programming in BASIC. T. Dwyer, Houghton Mifflin Company, 1973.

Hands-On BASIC with a PET. Herbert D. Peckham, McGraw-Hill Book Company, New York, 1979.

Programming Time Shared Computers in BASIC. Eugene H. Barnett, Wiley-Interscience, Library of Congress #72-175789.

What to Do After You Hit Return. Peoples Computer Company, Menlo Park, California 94025.

CBM Newsletters and References

This appendix contains a listing of CBM-related publications for CBM users who want to seek out continuing sources of information on the CBM computer. Many of these sources contain notices of PET/CBM user groups and activities. No endorsement of these publications is implied.

Periodicals

Calculators/Computers Magazine, Box 310, Menlo Park, California 94025. Bimonthly. $10.00 year. A magazine that has several PET articles in each issue.

Commodore PET Users Club Newsletter, Commodore Business Machines, Inc., 3330 Scott Blvd., Santa Clara, California 95051. Monthly. $15.00 year U.S., $25.00 year foreign. Official Commodore newsletter in U.S.

Commodore PET Users Club Newsletter, Commodore Systems, 360 Eusten Rd., London, England NW1 3BL. Bimonthly. £10. Official Commodore newsletter in Europe.

COMPUTE!, P.O. Box 5406, Greensboro, North Carolina, 27403. Monthly. $16.00 year U.S., $18.00 year Canada, $20.00 year elsewhere. Each issue has a regular section on PET/CBM products.

CURSOR, P.O. Box 550, Goleta, California 93017. Monthly. $33.00 year. A cassette magazine — you receive a tape cassette of programs that can be loaded into the CBM. Each cassette comes with a 2-page newsletter/program description.

MICRO, The 6502 Journal, 8 Fourth Lane, South Chelmsford, Massachusetts 01824. Bimonthly. Single copies $1.50, $6.00 year. A magazine that has several CBM articles in each issue. For the experienced CBM user.

People's Computers, 1263 El Camino Real, Box E, Menlo Park, California 94025. Bimonthly. Single copies $1.50, $8.00 year. A magazine that has several CBM articles in each issue.

PET Users Group Newsletter, Lawrence Hall of Science, University of California, Berkeley, California 94720. Monthly. $4.50 for 6 integral issues, checks payable to Regents of the University of California. Highly recommended.

Purser's Reference List of Computer Cassettes. Quarterly. Single copy $4.00 domestic, $5.00 foreign. $12.00 year domestic, $16.00 year foreign. Extensive list of CBM programs available on cassette.

Reference Manuals

CBM Floppy Disk User Manual Model 2040, Commodore Business Machines, Inc., 3330 Scott Blvd., Santa Clara, California 95051, 1979. By the manufacturers of the CBM computer.

CBM Printer User Manual Models 2022 & 2023, Commodore Business Machines, Inc., 3330 Scott Blvd., Santa Clara, California 95051, 1979. By the manufacturers of the CBM computer.

Commodore Business Computer User's Guide Series 8000, Commodore Business Machines, Inc., 3330 Scott Blvd., Santa Clara, California 95051, 1980. By the manufacturers of the CBM computer.

MCS6500 Microcomputer Family Programming Manual, MOS Technology, Inc., 950 Rittenhouse Road, Norristown, Pennsylvania 19401. $10.00 (price may vary with location). By the manufacturers of the 6502 microprocessor.

MCS6500 Microcomputer Family Hardware Manual, MOS Technology, Inc., 950 Rittenhouse Road, Norristown, Pennsylvania 19401. $10.00 (price may vary with location). By the manufacturers of the 6502 microprocessor.

PET and the IEEE 488 Bus (GPIB), E. Fisher and C. W. Jensen, Osborne/McGraw-Hill, 630 Bancroft Way, Berkeley, California 94710, 1980. $15.99.

PET 2001-8 Personal Computer User Manual, Commodore Business Machines, Inc., 3330 Scott Blvd., Santa Clara, California 95051. (8K system). $9.95. By the manufacturers of the PET computer.

PET 2001-16, 16N, 32, 32N Personal Computer User Manual, Commodore Business Machines, Inc., 3330 Scott Blvd., Santa Clara, California 95051. (16K and 32K systems.) $9.95. By the manufacturers of the PET computer.

6502 Assembly Language Programming, Lance Leventhal, Osborne/McGraw-Hill, 630 Bancroft Way, Berkeley, California 94710, 1979. $16.99.

Conversion Tables

This appendix contains the following reference tables:

- Hexadecimal-Decimal Integer Conversion
- Powers of Two
- Mathematical Constants
- Powers of Sixteen
- Powers of Ten

HEXADECIMAL-DECIMAL INTEGER CONVERSION

The table below provides for direct conversions between hexa-decimal integers in the range 0 – FFF and decimal integers in the range 0 – 4095. For conversion of larger integers, the table values may be added to the following figures:

Hexadecimal	Decimal	Hexadecimal	Decimal
01 000	4 096	20 000	131 072
02 000	8 192	30 000	196 608
03 000	12 288	40 000	262 144
04 000	16 384	50 000	327 680
05 000	20 480	60 000	393 216
06 000	24 576	70 000	458 752
07 000	28 672	80 000	524 288
08 000	32 768	90 000	589 824
09 000	36 864	A0 000	655 360
0A 000	40 960	B0 000	720 896
0B 000	45 056	C0 000	786 432
0C 000	49 152	D0 000	851 968
0D 000	53 248	E0 000	917 504
0E 000	57 344	F0 000	983 040
0F 000	61 440	100 000	1 048 576
10 000	65 536	200 000	2 097 152
11 000	69 632	300 000	3 145 728
12 000	73 728	400 000	4 194 304
13 000	77 824	500 000	5 242 880
14 000	81 920	600 000	6 291 456
15 000	86 016	700 000	7 340 032
16 000	90 112	800 000	8 388 608
17 000	94 208	900 000	9 437 184
18 000	98 304	A00 000	10 485 760
19 000	102 400	B00 000	11 534 336
1A 000	106 496	C00 000	12 582 912
1B 000	110 592	D00 000	13 631 488
1C 000	114 688	E00 000	14 680 064
1D 000	118 784	F00 000	15 728 640
1E 000	122 880	1 000 000	16 777 216
1F 000	126 976	2 000 000	33 554 432

Hexadecimal fractions may be converted to decimal fractions as follows:

1. Express the hexadecimal fraction as an integer times 16^{-n}, where n is the number of significant hexadecimal places to the right of the hexadecimal point.

$$0. CA9BF3_{16} = CA9 BF3_{16} \times 16^{-6}$$

2. Find the decimal equivalent of the hexadecimal integer

$$CA9 BF3_{16} = 13 278 195_{10}$$

3. Multiply the decimal equivalent by 16^{-n}

$$\begin{array}{r} 13\ 278\ 195 \\ \times\ 596\ 046\ 448 \times 10^{-16} \\ \hline 0.791\ 442\ 096_{10} \end{array}$$

Decimal fractions may be converted to hexadecimal fractions by successively multiplying the decimal fraction by 16_{10}. After each multiplication, the integer portion is removed to form a hexadecimal fraction by building to the right of the hexadecimal point. However, since decimal arithmetic is used in this conversion, the integer portion of each product must be converted to hexadecimal numbers.

Example: Convert 0.895_{10} to its hexadecimal equivalent

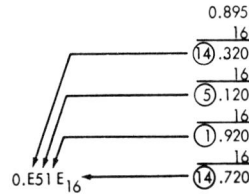

	0	1	2	3	4	5	6	7	8	9	A	B	C	D	E	F
00	0000	0001	0002	0003	0004	0005	0006	0007	0008	0009	0010	0011	0012	0013	0014	0015
01	0016	0017	0018	0019	0020	0021	0022	0023	0024	0025	0026	0027	0028	0029	0030	0031
02	0032	0033	0034	0035	0036	0037	0038	0039	0040	0041	0042	0043	0044	0045	0046	0047
03	0048	0049	0050	0051	0052	0053	0054	0055	0056	0057	0058	0059	0060	0061	0062	0063
04	0064	0065	0066	0067	0068	0069	0070	0071	0072	0073	0074	0075	0076	0077	0078	0079
05	0080	0081	0082	0083	0084	0085	0086	0087	0088	0089	0090	0091	0092	0093	0094	0095
06	0096	0097	0098	0099	0100	0101	0102	0103	0104	0105	0106	0107	0108	0109	0110	0111
07	0112	0113	0114	0115	0116	0117	0118	0119	0120	0121	0122	0123	0124	0125	0126	0127
08	0128	0129	0130	0131	0132	0133	0134	0135	0136	0137	0138	0139	0140	0141	0142	0143
09	0144	0145	0146	0147	0148	0149	0150	0151	0152	0153	0154	0155	0156	0157	0158	0159
0A	0160	0161	0162	0163	0164	0165	0166	0167	0168	0169	0170	0171	0172	0173	0174	0175
0B	0176	0177	0178	0179	0180	0181	0182	0183	0184	0185	0186	0187	0188	0189	0190	0191
0C	0192	0193	0194	0195	0196	0197	0198	0199	0200	0201	0202	0203	0204	0205	0206	0207
0D	0208	0209	0210	0211	0212	0213	0214	0215	0216	0217	0218	0219	0220	0221	0222	0223
0E	0224	0225	0226	0227	0228	0229	0230	0231	0232	0233	0234	0235	0236	0237	0238	0239
0F	0240	0241	0242	0243	0244	0245	0246	0247	0248	0249	0250	0251	0252	0253	0254	0255

HEXADECIMAL-DECIMAL INTEGER CONVERSION (Continued)

	0	1	2	3	4	5	6	7	8	9	A	B	C	D	E	F
10	0256	0257	0258	0259	0260	0261	0262	0263	0264	0265	0266	0267	0268	0269	0270	0271
11	0272	0273	0274	0275	0276	0277	0278	0279	0280	0281	0282	0283	0284	0285	0286	0287
12	0288	0289	0290	0291	0292	0293	0294	0295	0296	0297	0298	0299	0300	0301	0302	0303
13	0304	0305	0306	0307	0308	0309	0310	0311	0312	0313	0314	0315	0316	0317	0318	0319
14	0320	0321	0322	0323	0324	0325	0326	0327	0328	0329	0330	0331	0332	0333	0334	0335
15	0336	0337	0338	0339	0340	0341	0342	0343	0344	0345	0346	0347	0348	0349	0350	0351
16	0352	0353	0354	0355	0356	0357	0358	0359	0360	0361	0362	0363	0364	0365	0366	0367
17	0368	0369	0370	0371	0372	0373	0374	0375	0376	0377	0378	0379	0380	0381	0382	0383
18	0384	0385	0386	0387	0388	0389	0390	0391	0392	0393	0394	0395	0396	0397	0398	0399
19	0400	0401	0402	0403	0404	0405	0406	0407	0408	0409	0410	0411	0412	0413	0414	0415
1A	0416	0417	0418	0419	0420	0421	0422	0423	0424	0425	0426	0427	0428	0429	0430	0431
1B	0432	0433	0434	0435	0436	0437	0438	0439	0440	0441	0442	0443	0444	0445	0446	0447
1C	0448	0449	0450	0451	0452	0453	0454	0455	0456	0457	0458	0459	0460	0461	0462	0463
1D	0464	0465	0466	0467	0468	0469	0470	0471	0472	0473	0474	0475	0476	0477	0478	0479
1E	0480	0481	0482	0483	0484	0485	0486	0487	0488	0489	0490	0491	0492	0493	0494	0495
1F	0496	0497	0498	0499	0500	0501	0502	0503	0504	0505	0506	0507	0508	0509	0510	0511
20	0512	0513	0514	0515	0516	0517	0518	0519	0520	0521	0522	0523	0524	0525	0526	0527
21	0528	0529	0530	0531	0532	0533	0534	0535	0536	0537	0538	0539	0540	0541	0542	0543
22	0544	0545	0546	0547	0548	0549	0550	0551	0552	0553	0554	0555	0556	0557	0558	0559
23	0560	0561	0562	0563	0564	0565	0566	0567	0568	0569	0570	0571	0572	0573	0574	0575
24	0576	0577	0578	0579	0580	0581	0582	0583	0584	0585	0586	0587	0588	0589	0590	0591
25	0592	0593	0594	0595	0596	0597	0598	0599	0600	0601	0602	0603	0604	0605	0606	0607
26	0608	0609	0610	0611	0612	0613	0614	0615	0616	0617	0618	0619	0620	0621	0622	0623
27	0624	0625	0626	0627	0628	0629	0630	0631	0632	0633	0634	0635	0636	0637	0638	0639
28	0640	0641	0642	0643	0644	0645	0646	0647	0648	0649	0650	0651	0652	0653	0654	0655
29	0656	0657	0658	0659	0660	0661	0662	0663	0664	0665	0666	0667	0668	0669	0670	0671
2A	0672	0673	0674	0675	0676	0677	0678	0679	0680	0681	0682	0683	0684	0685	0686	0687
2B	0688	0689	0690	0691	0692	0693	0694	0695	0696	0697	0698	0699	0700	0701	0702	0703
2C	0704	0705	0706	0707	0708	0709	0710	0711	0712	0713	0714	0715	0716	0717	0718	0719
2D	0720	0721	0722	0723	0724	0725	0726	0727	0728	0729	0730	0731	0732	0733	0734	0735
2E	0736	0737	0738	0739	0740	0741	0742	0743	0744	0745	0746	0747	0748	0749	0750	0751
2F	0752	0753	0754	0755	0756	0757	0758	0759	0760	0761	0762	0763	0764	0765	0766	0767
30	0768	0769	0770	0771	0772	0773	0774	0775	0776	0777	0778	0779	0780	0781	0782	0783
31	0784	0785	0786	0787	0788	0789	0790	0791	0792	0793	0794	0795	0796	0797	0798	0799
32	0800	0801	0802	0803	0804	0805	0806	0807	0808	0809	0810	0811	0812	0813	0814	0815
33	0816	0817	0818	0819	0820	0821	0822	0823	0824	0825	0826	0827	0828	0829	0830	0831
34	0832	0833	0834	0835	0836	0837	0838	0839	0840	0841	0842	0843	0844	0845	0846	0847
35	0848	0849	0850	0851	0852	0853	0854	0855	0856	0857	0858	0859	0860	0861	0862	0863
36	0864	0865	0866	0867	0868	0869	0870	0871	0872	0873	0874	0875	0876	0877	0878	0879
37	0880	0881	0882	0883	0884	0885	0886	0887	0888	0889	0890	0891	0892	0893	0894	0895
38	0896	0897	0898	0899	0900	0901	0902	0903	0904	0905	0906	0907	0908	0909	0910	0911
39	0912	0913	0914	0915	0916	0917	0918	0919	0920	0921	0922	0923	0924	0925	0926	0927
3A	0928	0929	0930	0931	0932	0933	0934	0935	0936	0937	0938	0939	0940	0941	0942	0943
3B	0944	0945	0946	0947	0948	0949	0950	0951	0952	0953	0954	0955	0956	0957	0958	0959
3C	0960	0961	0962	0963	0964	0965	0966	0967	0968	0969	0970	0971	0972	0973	0974	0975
3D	0976	0977	0978	0979	0980	0981	0982	0983	0984	0985	0986	0987	0988	0989	0990	0991
3E	0992	0993	0994	0995	0996	0997	0998	0999	1000	1001	1002	1003	1004	1005	1006	1007
3F	1008	1009	1010	1011	1012	1013	1014	1015	1016	1017	1018	1019	1020	1021	1022	1023

HEXADECIMAL-DECIMAL INTEGER CONVERSION (Continued)

	0	1	2	3	4	5	6	7	8	9	A	B	C	D	E	F
40	1024	1025	1026	1027	1028	1029	1030	1031	1032	1033	1034	1035	1036	1037	1038	1039
41	1040	1041	1042	1043	1044	1045	1046	1047	1048	1049	1050	1051	1052	1053	1054	1055
42	1056	1057	1058	1059	1060	1061	1062	1063	1064	1065	1066	1067	1068	1069	1070	1071
43	1072	1073	1074	1075	1076	1077	1078	1079	1080	1081	1082	1083	1084	1085	1086	1087
44	1088	1089	1090	1091	1092	1093	1094	1095	1096	1097	1098	1099	1100	1101	1102	1103
45	1104	1105	1106	1107	1108	1109	1110	1111	1112	1113	1114	1115	1116	1117	1118	1119
46	1120	1121	1122	1123	1124	1125	1126	1127	1128	1129	1130	1131	1132	1133	1134	1135
47	1136	1137	1138	1139	1140	1141	1142	1143	1144	1145	1146	1147	1148	1149	1150	1151
48	1152	1153	1154	1155	1156	1157	1158	1159	1160	1161	1162	1163	1164	1165	1166	1167
49	1168	1169	1170	1171	1172	1173	1174	1175	1176	1177	1178	1179	1180	1181	1182	1183
4A	1184	1185	1186	1187	1188	1189	1190	1191	1192	1193	1194	1195	1196	1197	1198	1199
4B	1200	1201	1202	1203	1204	1205	1206	1207	1208	1209	1210	1211	1212	1213	1214	1215
4C	1216	1217	1218	1219	1220	1221	1222	1223	1224	1225	1226	1227	1228	1229	1230	1231
4D	1232	1233	1234	1235	1236	1237	1238	1239	1240	1241	1242	1243	1244	1245	1246	1247
4E	1248	1249	1250	1251	1252	1253	1254	1255	1256	1257	1258	1259	1260	1261	1262	1263
4F	1264	1265	1266	1267	1268	1269	1270	1271	1272	1273	1274	1275	1276	1277	1278	1279
50	1280	1281	1282	1283	1284	1285	1286	1287	1288	1289	1290	1291	1292	1293	1294	1295
51	1296	1297	1298	1299	1300	1301	1302	1303	1304	1305	1306	1307	1308	1309	1310	1311
52	1312	1313	1314	1315	1316	1317	1318	1319	1320	1321	1322	1323	1324	1325	1326	1327
53	1328	1329	1330	1331	1332	1333	1334	1335	1336	1337	1338	1339	1340	1341	1342	1343
54	1344	1345	1346	1347	1348	1349	1350	1351	1352	1353	1354	1355	1356	1357	1358	1359
55	1360	1361	1362	1363	1364	1365	1366	1367	1368	1369	1370	1371	1372	1373	1374	1375
56	1376	1377	1378	1379	1380	1381	1382	1383	1384	1385	1386	1387	1388	1389	1390	1391
57	1392	1393	1394	1395	1396	1397	1398	1399	1400	1401	1402	1403	1404	1405	1406	1407
58	1408	1409	1410	1411	1412	1413	1414	1415	1416	1417	1418	1419	1420	1421	1422	1423
59	1424	1425	1426	1427	1428	1429	1430	1431	1432	1433	1434	1435	1436	1437	1438	1439
5A	1440	1441	1442	1443	1444	1445	1446	1447	1448	1449	1450	1451	1452	1453	1454	1455
5B	1456	1457	1458	1459	1460	1461	1462	1463	1464	1465	1466	1467	1468	1469	1470	1471
5C	1472	1473	1474	1475	1476	1477	1478	1479	1480	1481	1482	1483	1484	1485	1486	1487
5D	1488	1489	1490	1491	1492	1493	1494	1495	1496	1497	1498	1499	1500	1501	1502	1503
5E	1504	1505	1506	1507	1508	1509	1510	1511	1512	1513	1514	1515	1516	1517	1518	1519
5F	1520	1521	1522	1523	1524	1525	1526	1527	1528	1529	1530	1531	1532	1533	1534	1535
60	1536	1537	1538	1539	1540	1541	1542	1543	1544	1545	1546	1547	1548	1549	1550	1551
61	1552	1553	1554	1555	1556	1557	1558	1559	1560	1561	1562	1563	1564	1565	1566	1567
62	1568	1569	1570	1571	1572	1573	1574	1575	1576	1577	1578	1579	1580	1581	1582	1583
63	1584	1585	1586	1587	1588	1589	1590	1591	1592	1593	1594	1595	1596	1597	1598	1599
64	1600	1601	1602	1603	1604	1605	1606	1607	1608	1609	1610	1611	1612	1613	1614	1615
65	1616	1617	1618	1619	1620	1621	1622	1623	1624	1625	1626	1627	1628	1629	1630	1631
66	1632	1633	1634	1635	1636	1637	1638	1639	1640	1641	1642	1643	1644	1645	1646	1647
67	1648	1649	1650	1651	1652	1653	1654	1655	1656	1657	1658	1659	1660	1661	1562	1663
68	1664	1665	1666	1667	1668	1669	1670	1671	1672	1673	1674	1675	1676	1677	1678	1679
69	1680	1681	1682	1683	1684	1685	1686	1687	1688	1689	1690	1691	1692	1693	1694	1695
6A	1696	1697	1698	1699	1700	1701	1702	1703	1704	1705	1706	1707	1708	1709	1710	1711
6B	1712	1713	1714	1715	1716	1717	1718	1719	1720	1721	1722	1723	1724	1725	1726	1727
6C	1728	1729	1730	1731	1732	1733	1734	1735	1736	1737	1738	1739	1740	1741	1742	1743
6D	1744	1745	1746	1747	1748	1749	1750	1751	1752	1753	1754	1755	1756	1757	1758	1759
6E	1760	1761	1762	1763	1764	1765	1766	1767	1768	1769	1770	1771	1772	1773	1774	1775
6F	1776	1777	1778	1779	1780	1781	1782	1783	1784	1785	1786	1787	1788	1789	1790	1791

HEXADECIMAL-DECIMAL INTEGER CONVERSION (Continued)

	0	1	2	3	4	5	6	7	8	9	A	B	C	D	E	F
70	1792	1793	1794	1795	1796	1797	1798	1799	1800	1801	1802	1803	1804	1805	1806	1807
71	1808	1809	1810	1811	1812	1813	1814	1815	1816	1817	1818	1819	1820	1821	1822	1823
72	1824	1825	1826	1827	1828	1829	1830	1831	1832	1833	1834	1835	1836	1837	1838	1839
73	1840	1841	1842	1843	1844	1845	1846	1847	1848	1849	1850	1851	1852	1853	1854	1855
74	1856	1857	1858	1859	1860	1861	1862	1863	1864	1865	1866	1867	1868	1869	1870	1871
75	1872	1873	1874	1875	1876	1877	1878	1879	1880	1881	1882	1883	1884	1885	1886	1887
76	1888	1889	1890	1891	1892	1893	1894	1895	1896	1897	1898	1899	1900	1901	1902	1903
77	1904	1905	1906	1907	1908	1909	1910	1911	1912	1913	1914	1915	1916	1917	1918	1919
78	1920	1921	1922	1923	1924	1925	1926	1927	1928	1929	1930	1931	1932	1933	1934	1935
79	1936	1937	1938	1939	1940	1941	1942	1943	1944	1945	1946	1947	1948	1949	1950	1951
7A	1952	1953	1954	1955	1956	1957	1958	1959	1960	1961	1962	1963	1964	1965	1966	1967
7B	1968	1969	1970	1971	1972	1973	1974	1975	1976	1977	1978	1979	1980	1981	1982	1983
7C	1984	1985	1986	1987	1988	1989	1990	1991	1992	1993	1994	1995	1996	1997	1998	1999
7D	2000	2001	2002	2003	2004	2005	2006	2007	2008	2009	2010	2011	2012	2013	2014	2015
7E	2016	2017	2018	2019	2020	2021	2022	2023	2024	2025	2026	2027	2028	2029	2030	2031
7F	2032	2033	2034	2035	2036	2037	2038	2039	2040	2041	2042	2043	2044	2045	2046	2047
80	2048	2049	2050	2051	2052	2053	2054	2055	2056	2057	2058	2059	2060	2061	2062	2063
81	2064	2065	2066	2067	2068	2069	2070	2071	2072	2073	2074	2075	2076	2077	2078	2079
82	2080	2081	2082	2083	2084	2085	2086	2087	2088	2089	2090	2091	2092	2093	2094	2095
83	2096	2097	2098	2099	2100	2101	2102	2103	2104	2105	2106	2107	2108	2109	2110	2111
84	2112	2113	2114	2115	2116	2117	2118	2119	2120	2121	2122	2123	2124	2125	2126	2127
85	2128	2129	2130	2131	2132	2133	2134	2135	2136	2137	2138	2139	2140	2141	2142	2143
86	2144	2145	2146	2147	2148	2149	2150	2151	2152	2153	2154	2155	2156	2157	2158	2159
87	2160	2161	2162	2163	2164	2165	2166	2167	2168	2169	2170	2171	2172	2173	2174	2175
88	2176	2177	2178	2179	2180	2181	2182	2183	2184	2185	2186	2187	2188	2189	2190	2191
89	2192	2193	2194	2195	2196	2197	2198	2199	2200	2201	2202	2203	2204	2205	2206	2207
8A	2208	2209	2210	2211	2212	2213	2214	2215	2216	2217	2218	2219	2220	2221	2222	2223
8B	2224	2225	2226	2227	2228	2229	2230	2231	2232	2233	2234	2235	2236	2237	2238	2239
8C	2240	2241	2242	2243	2244	2245	2246	2247	2248	2249	2250	2251	2252	2253	2254	2255
8D	2256	2257	2258	2259	2260	2261	2262	2263	2264	2265	2266	2267	2268	2269	2270	2271
8E	2272	2273	2274	2275	2276	2277	2278	2279	2280	2281	2282	2283	2284	2285	2286	2287
8F	2288	2289	2290	2291	2292	2293	2294	2295	2296	2297	2298	2299	2300	2301	2302	2303
90	2304	2305	2306	2307	2308	2309	2310	2311	2312	2313	2314	2315	2316	2317	2318	2319
91	2320	2321	2322	2323	2324	2325	2326	2327	2328	2329	2330	2331	2332	2333	2334	2335
92	2336	2337	2338	2339	2340	2341	2342	2343	2344	2345	2346	2347	2348	2349	2350	2351
93	2352	2353	2354	2355	2356	2357	2358	2359	2360	2361	2362	2363	2364	2365	2366	2367
94	2368	2369	2370	2371	2372	2373	2374	2375	2376	2377	2378	2379	2380	2381	2382	2383
95	2384	2385	2386	2387	2388	2389	2390	2391	2392	2393	2394	2395	2396	2397	2398	2399
96	2400	2401	2402	2403	2404	2405	2406	2407	2408	2409	2410	2411	2412	2413	2414	2415
97	2416	2417	2418	2419	2420	2421	2422	2423	2424	2425	2426	2427	2428	2429	2430	2431
98	2432	2433	2434	2435	2436	2437	2438	2439	2440	2441	2442	2443	2444	2445	2446	2447
99	2448	2449	2450	2451	2452	2453	2454	2455	2456	2457	2458	2459	2460	2461	2462	2463
9A	2464	2465	2466	2467	2468	2469	2470	2471	2472	2473	2474	2475	2476	2477	2478	2479
9B	2480	2481	2482	2483	2484	2485	2486	2487	2488	2489	2490	2491	2492	2493	2494	2495
9C	2496	2497	2498	2499	2500	2501	2502	2503	2504	2505	2506	2507	2508	2509	2510	2511
9D	2512	2513	2514	2515	2516	2517	2518	2519	2520	2521	2522	2523	2524	2525	2526	2527
9E	2528	2529	2530	2531	2532	2533	2534	2535	2536	2537	2538	2539	2540	2541	2542	2543
9F	2544	2545	2546	2547	2548	2549	2550	2551	2552	2553	2554	2555	2556	2557	2558	2559

HEXADECIMAL-DECIMAL INTEGER CONVERSION (Continued)

	0	1	2	3	4	5	6	7	8	9	A	B	C	D	E	F
A0	2560	2561	2562	2563	2564	2565	2566	2567	2568	2569	2570	2571	2572	2573	2574	2575
A1	2576	2577	2578	2579	2580	2581	2582	2583	2584	2585	2586	2587	2588	2589	2590	2591
A2	2592	2593	2594	2595	2596	2597	2598	2599	2600	2601	2602	2603	2604	2605	2606	2607
A3	2608	2609	2610	2611	2612	2613	2614	2615	2616	2617	2618	2619	2620	2621	2622	2623
A4	2624	2625	2626	2627	2628	2629	2630	2631	2632	2633	2634	2635	2636	2637	2638	2639
A5	2640	2641	2642	2643	2644	2645	2646	2647	2648	2649	2650	2651	2652	2653	2654	2655
A6	2656	2657	2658	2659	2660	2661	2662	2663	2664	2665	2666	2667	2668	2669	2670	2671
A7	2672	2673	2674	2675	2676	2677	2678	2679	2680	2681	2682	2683	2684	2685	2686	2687
A8	2688	2689	2690	2691	2692	2693	2694	2695	2696	2697	2698	2699	2700	2701	2702	2703
A9	2704	2705	2706	2707	2708	2709	2710	2711	2712	2713	2714	2715	2716	2717	2718	2719
AA	2720	2721	2722	2723	2724	2725	2726	2727	2728	2729	2730	2731	2732	2733	2734	2735
AB	2736	2737	2738	2739	2740	2741	2742	2743	2744	2745	2746	2747	2748	2749	2750	2751
AC	2752	2753	2754	2755	2756	2757	2758	2759	2760	2761	2762	2763	2764	2765	2766	2767
AD	2768	2769	2770	2771	2772	2773	2774	2775	2776	2777	2778	2779	2780	2781	2782	2783
AE	2784	2785	2786	2787	2788	2789	2790	2791	2792	2793	2794	2795	2796	2797	2798	2799
AF	2800	2801	2802	2803	2804	2805	2806	2807	2808	2809	2810	2811	2812	2813	2814	2815
B0	2816	2817	2818	2819	2820	2821	2822	2823	2824	2825	2826	2827	2828	2829	2830	2831
B1	2832	2833	2834	2835	2836	2837	2838	2839	2840	2841	2842	2843	2844	2845	2846	2847
B2	2848	2849	2850	2851	2852	2853	2854	2855	2856	2857	2858	2859	2860	2861	2862	2863
B3	2864	2865	2866	2867	2868	2869	2870	2871	2872	2873	2874	2875	2876	2877	2878	2879
B4	2880	2881	2882	2883	2884	2885	2886	2887	2888	2889	2890	2891	2892	2893	2894	2895
B5	2896	2897	2898	2899	2900	2901	2902	2903	2904	2905	2906	2907	2908	2909	2910	2911
B6	2912	2913	2914	2915	2916	2917	2918	2919	2920	2921	2922	2923	2924	2925	2926	2927
B7	2928	2929	2930	2931	2932	2933	2934	2935	2936	2937	2938	2939	2940	2941	2942	2943
B8	2944	2945	2946	2947	2948	2949	2950	2951	2952	2953	2954	2955	2956	2957	2958	2959
B9	2960	2961	2962	2963	2964	2965	2966	2967	2968	2969	2970	2971	2972	2973	2974	2975
BA	2976	2977	2978	2979	2980	2981	2982	2983	2984	2985	2986	2987	2988	2989	2990	2991
BB	2992	2993	2994	2995	2996	2997	2998	2999	3000	3001	3002	3003	3004	3005	3006	3007
BC	3008	3009	3010	3011	3012	3013	3014	3015	3016	3017	3018	3019	3020	3021	3022	3023
BD	3024	3025	3026	3027	3028	3029	3030	3031	3032	3033	3034	3035	3036	3037	3038	3039
BE	3040	3041	3042	3043	3044	3045	3046	3047	3048	3049	3050	3051	3052	3053	3054	3055
BF	3056	3057	3058	3059	3060	3061	3062	3063	3064	3065	3066	3067	3068	3069	3070	3071
C0	3072	3073	3074	3075	3076	3077	3078	3079	3080	3081	3082	3083	3084	3085	3086	3087
C1	3088	3089	3090	3091	3092	3093	3094	3095	3096	3097	3098	3099	3100	3101	3102	3103
C2	3104	3105	3106	3107	3108	3109	3110	3111	3112	3113	3114	3115	3116	3117	3118	3119
C3	3120	3121	3122	3123	3124	3125	3126	3127	3128	3129	3130	3131	3132	3133	3134	3135
C4	3136	3137	3138	3139	3140	3141	3142	3143	3144	3145	3146	3147	3148	3149	3150	3151
C5	3152	3153	3154	3155	3156	3157	3158	3159	3160	3161	3162	3163	3164	3165	3166	3167
C6	3168	3169	3170	3171	3172	3173	3174	3175	3176	3177	3178	3179	3180	3181	3182	3183
C7	3184	3185	3186	3187	3188	3189	3190	3191	3192	3193	3194	3195	3196	3197	3198	3199
C8	3200	3201	3202	3203	3204	3205	3206	3207	3208	3209	3210	3211	3212	3213	3214	3215
C9	3216	3217	3218	3219	3220	3221	3222	3223	3224	3225	3226	3227	3228	3229	3230	3231
CA	3232	3233	3234	3235	3236	3237	3238	3239	3240	3241	3242	3243	3244	3245	3246	3247
CB	3248	3249	3250	3251	3252	3253	3254	3255	3256	3257	3258	3259	3260	3261	3262	3263
CC	3264	3265	3266	3267	3268	3269	3270	3271	3272	3273	3274	3275	3276	3277	3278	3279
CD	3280	3281	3282	3283	3284	3285	3286	3287	3288	3289	3290	3291	3292	3293	3294	3295
CE	3296	3297	3298	3299	3300	3301	3302	3303	3304	3305	3306	3307	3308	3309	3310	3311
CF	3312	3313	3314	3315	3316	3317	3318	3319	3320	3321	3322	3323	3324	3325	3326	3327

HEXADECIMAL-DECIMAL INTEGER CONVERSION (Continued)

	0	1	2	3	4	5	6	7	8	9	A	B	C	D	E	F
D0	3328	3329	3330	3331	3332	3333	3334	3335	3336	3337	3338	3339	3340	3341	3342	3343
D1	3344	3345	3346	3347	3348	3349	3350	3351	3352	3353	3354	3355	3356	3357	3358	3359
D2	3360	3361	3362	3363	3364	3365	3366	3367	3368	3369	3370	3371	3372	3373	3374	3375
D3	3376	3377	3378	3379	3380	3381	3382	3383	3384	3385	3386	3387	3388	3389	3390	3391
D4	3392	3393	3394	3395	3396	3397	3398	3399	3400	3401	3402	3403	3404	3405	3406	3407
D5	3408	3409	3410	3411	3412	3413	3414	3415	3416	3417	3418	3419	3420	3421	3422	3423
D6	3424	3425	3426	3427	3428	3429	3430	3431	3432	3433	3434	3435	3436	3437	3438	3439
D7	3440	3441	3442	3443	3444	3445	3446	3447	3448	3449	3450	3451	3452	3453	3454	3455
D8	3456	3457	3458	3459	3460	3461	3462	3463	3464	3465	3466	3467	3468	3469	3470	3471
D9	3472	3473	3474	3475	3476	3477	3478	3479	3480	3481	3482	3483	3484	3485	3486	3487
DA	3488	3489	3490	3491	3492	3493	3494	3495	3496	3497	3498	3499	3500	3501	3502	3503
DB	3504	3505	3506	3507	3508	3509	3510	3511	3512	3513	3514	3515	3516	3517	3518	3519
DC	3520	3521	3522	3523	3524	3525	3526	3527	3528	3529	3530	3531	3532	3533	3534	3535
DD	3536	3537	3538	3539	3540	3541	3542	3543	3544	3545	3546	3547	3548	3549	3550	3551
DE	3552	3553	3554	3555	3556	3557	3558	3559	3560	3561	3562	3563	3564	3565	3566	3567
DF	3568	3569	3570	3571	3572	3573	3574	3575	3576	3577	3578	3579	3580	3581	3582	3583
E0	3584	3585	3586	3587	3588	3589	3590	3591	3592	3593	3594	3595	3596	3597	3598	3599
E1	3600	3601	3602	3603	3604	3605	3606	3607	3608	3609	3610	3611	3612	3613	3614	3615
E2	3616	3617	3618	3619	3620	3621	3622	3623	3624	3625	3626	3627	3628	3629	3630	3631
E3	3632	3633	3634	3635	3636	3637	3638	3639	3640	3641	3642	3643	3644	3645	3646	3647
E4	3648	3649	3650	3651	3652	3653	3654	3655	3656	3657	3658	3659	3660	3661	3662	3663
E5	3664	3665	3666	3667	3668	3669	3670	3671	3672	3673	3674	3675	3676	3677	3678	3679
E6	3680	3681	3682	3683	3684	3685	3686	3687	3688	3689	3690	3691	3692	3693	3694	3695
E7	3696	3697	3698	3699	3700	3701	3702	3703	3704	3705	3706	3707	3708	3709	3710	3711
E8	3712	3713	3714	3715	3716	3717	3718	3719	3720	3721	3722	3723	3724	3725	3726	3727
E9	3728	3729	3730	3731	3732	3733	3734	3735	3736	3737	3738	3739	3740	3741	3742	3743
EA	3744	3745	3746	3747	3748	3749	3750	3751	3752	3753	3754	3755	3756	3757	3758	3759
EB	3760	3761	3762	3763	3764	3765	3766	3767	3768	3769	3770	3771	3772	3773	3774	3775
EC	3776	3777	3778	3779	3780	3781	3782	3783	3784	3785	3786	3787	3788	3789	3790	3791
ED	3792	3793	3794	3795	3796	3797	3798	3799	3800	3801	3802	3803	3804	3805	3806	3807
EE	3808	3809	3810	3811	3812	3813	3814	3815	3816	3817	3818	3819	3820	3821	3822	3823
EF	3824	3825	3826	3827	3828	3829	3830	3831	3832	3833	3834	3835	3836	3837	3838	3839
F0	3840	3841	3842	3843	3844	3845	3846	3847	3848	3849	3850	3851	3852	3853	3854	3855
F1	3856	3857	3858	3859	3860	3861	3862	3863	3864	3865	3866	3867	3868	3869	3870	3871
F2	3872	3873	3874	3875	3876	3877	3878	3879	3880	3881	3882	3883	3884	3885	3886	3887
F3	3888	3889	3890	3891	3892	3893	3894	3895	3896	3897	3898	3899	3900	3901	3902	3903
F4	3904	3905	3906	3907	3908	3909	3910	3911	3912	3913	3914	3915	3916	3917	3918	3919
F5	3920	3921	3922	3923	3924	3925	3926	3927	3928	3929	3930	3931	3932	3933	3934	3935
F6	3936	3937	3938	3939	3940	3941	3942	3943	3944	3945	3946	3947	3948	3949	3950	3951
F7	3952	3953	3954	3955	3956	3957	3958	3959	3960	3961	3962	3963	3964	3965	3966	3967
F8	3968	3969	3970	3971	3972	3973	3974	3975	3976	3977	3978	3979	3980	3981	3982	3983
F9	3984	3985	3986	3987	3988	3989	3990	3991	3992	3993	3994	3995	3996	3997	3998	3999
FA	4000	4001	4002	4003	4004	4005	4006	4007	4008	4009	4010	4011	4012	4013	4014	4015
FB	4016	4017	4018	4019	4020	4021	4022	4023	4024	4025	4026	4027	4028	4029	4030	4031
FC	4032	4033	4034	4035	4036	4037	4038	4039	4040	4041	4042	4043	4044	4045	4046	4047
FD	4048	4049	4050	4051	4052	4053	4054	4055	4056	4057	4058	4059	4060	4061	4062	4063
FE	4064	4065	4066	4067	4068	4069	4070	4071	4072	4073	4074	4075	4076	4077	4078	4079
FF	4080	4081	4082	4083	4084	4085	4086	4087	4088	4089	4090	4091	4092	4093	4094	4095

POWERS OF TWO

2^n	n	2^{-n}
1	0	1.0
2	1	0.5
4	2	0.25
8	3	0.125
16	4	0.062 5
32	5	0.031 25
64	6	0.015 625
128	7	0.007 812 5
256	8	0.003 906 25
512	9	0.001 953 125
1 024	10	0.000 976 562 5
2 048	11	0.000 488 281 25
4 096	12	0.000 244 140 625
8 192	13	0.000 122 070 312 5
16 384	14	0.000 061 035 156 25
32 768	15	0.000 030 517 578 125
65 536	16	0.000 015 258 789 062 5
131 072	17	0.000 007 629 394 531 25
262 144	18	0.000 003 814 697 265 625
524 288	19	0.000 001 907 348 632 812 5
1 048 576	20	0.000 000 953 674 316 406 25
2 097 152	21	0.000 000 476 837 158 203 125
4 194 304	22	0.000 000 238 418 579 101 562 5
8 388 608	23	0.000 000 119 209 289 550 781 25
16 777 216	24	0.000 000 059 604 644 775 390 625
33 554 432	25	0.000 000 029 802 322 387 695 312 5
67 108 864	26	0.000 000 014 901 161 193 847 656 25
134 217 728	27	0.000 000 007 450 580 596 923 828 125
268 435 456	28	0.000 000 003 725 290 298 461 914 062 5
536 870 912	29	0.000 000 001 862 645 149 230 957 031 25
1 073 741 824	30	0.000 000 000 931 322 574 615 478 515 625
2 147 483 648	31	0.000 000 000 465 661 287 307 739 257 81. 5
4 294 967 296	32	0.000 000 000 232 830 643 653 869 628 906 25
8 589 934 592	33	0.000 000 000 116 415 321 826 934 814 453 125
17 179 869 184	34	0.000 000 000 058 207 66‑˙ 913 467 407 226 562 5
34 359 738 368	35	0.000 000 000 029 103 83ᴗ 456 733 703 613 281 25
68 719 476 736	36	0.000 000 000 014 551 915 228 366 851 806 640 625
137 438 953 472	37	0.000 000 000 007 275 957 614 183 425 903 320 312 5
274 877 906 944	38	0.000 000 000 003 637 978 807 091 712 951 660 156 25
549 755 813 888	39	0.000 000 000 001 818 989 403 545 856 475 830 078 125
1 099 511 627 776	40	0.000 000 000 000 909 494 701 772 928 237 915 039 062 5
2 199 023 255 552	41	0.000 000 000 000 454 747 350 886 464 118 957 519 531 25
4 398 046 511 104	42	0.000 000 000 000 227 373 675 443 232 059 478 759 765 625
8 796 093 022 208	43	0.000 000 000 000 113 686 837 721 616 029 739 379 882 812 5
17 592 186 044 416	44	0.000 000 000 000 056 843 418 860 808 014 869 689 941 406 25
35 184 372 088 832	45	0.000 000 000 000 028 421 709 430 404 007 434 844 970 703 125
70 368 744 177 664	46	0.000 000 000 000 014 210 854 715 202 003 717 422 485 351 562 5
140 737 488 355 328	47	0.000 000 000 000 007 105 427 357 601 001 858 711 242 675 781 25
281 474 976 710 656	48	0.000 000 000 000 003 552 713 678 800 500 929 355 621 337 890 625
562 949 953 421 312	49	0.000 000 000 000 001 776 356 839 400 250 464 677 810 668 945 312 5
1 125 899 906 842 624	50	0.000 000 000 000 000 888 178 419 700 125 232 338 905 334 472 656 25
2 251 799 813 685 248	51	0.000 000 000 000 000 444 089 209 850 062 616 169 452 667 236 328 125
4 503 599 627 370 496	52	0.000 000 000 000 000 222 044 604 925 031 308 084 726 333 618 164 062 5
9 007 199 254 740 992	53	0.000 000 000 000 000 111 022 302 462 515 654 042 363 166 809 082 031 25
18 014 398 509 481 984	54	0.000 000 000 000 000 055 511 151 231 257 827 021 181 583 404 541 015 625
36 028 797 018 963 968	55	0.000 000 000 000 000 027 755 575 615 628 913 510 590 791 702 270 507 812 5
72 057 594 037 927 936	56	0.000 000 000 000 000 013 877 787 807 814 456 755 295 395 851 135 253 906 25
144 115 188 075 855 872	57	0.000 000 000 000 000 006 938 893 903 907 228 377 647 697 925 567 626 953 125
288 230 376 151 711 744	58	0.000 000 000 000 000 003 469 446 951 953 614 188 823 848 962 783 813 476 562 5
576 460 752 303 423 488	59	0.000 000 000 000 000 001 734 723 475 976 807 094 411 924 481 391 906 738 281 25
1 152 921 504 606 846 976	60	0.000 000 000 000 000 000 867 361 737 988 403 547 205 962 240 695 953 369 140 625
2 305 843 009 213 693 952	61	0.000 000 000 000 000 000 433 680 868 994 201 773 602 981 120 347 976 684 570 312 5
4 611 686 018 427 387 904	62	0.000 000 000 000 000 000 216 840 434 497 100 886 801 490 560 173 988 342 285 156 25
9 223 372 036 854 775 808	63	0.000 000 000 000 000 000 108 420 217 248 550 443 400 745 280 086 994 171 142 578 125

MATHEMATICAL CONSTANTS

Constant	Decimal Value		Hexadecimal Value	
π	3.14159 26535 89793		3.243F	6A89
π^{-1}	0.31830 98861 83790		0.517C	C1B7
$\sqrt{\pi}$	1.77245 38509 05516		1.C5BF	891C
$\ln \pi$	1.14472 98858 49400		1.250D	04BF
e	2.71828 18284 59045		2.B7E1	5163
e^{-1}	0.36787 94411 71442		0.5E2D	58D9
$\sqrt{e}$	1.64872 12707 00128		1.A612	98E2
$\log_{10} e$	0.43429 44819 03252		0.6F2D	EC55
$\log_{2} e$	1.44269 50408 88963		1.7154	7653
γ	0.57721 56649 01533		0.93C4	67E4
$\ln \gamma$	-0.54953 93129 81645		-0.8CAE	9BC1
$\sqrt{2}$	1.41421 35623 73095		1.6A09	E668
$\ln 2$	0.69314 71805 59945		0.B172	17F8
$\log_{10} 2$	0.30102 99956 63981		0.4D10	4D42
$\sqrt{10}$	3.16227 76601 68379		3.298B	075C
$\ln 10$	2.30258 40929 94046		2.4D75	3777

POWERS OF SIXTEEN

16^n	n	16^{-n}	
1	0	0.10000 00000 00000 00000	$\times\ 10$
16	1	0.62500 00000 00000 00000	$\times\ 10^{-1}$
256	2	0.39062 50000 00000 00000	$\times\ 10^{-2}$
4 096	3	0.24414 06250 00000 00000	$\times\ 10^{-3}$
65 536	4	0.15258 78906 25000 00000	$\times\ 10^{-4}$
1 048 576	5	0.95367 43164 06250 00000	$\times\ 10^{-6}$
16 777 216	6	0.59604 64477 53906 25000	$\times\ 10^{-7}$
268 435 456	7	0.37252 90298 46191 40625	$\times\ 10^{-8}$
4 294 967 296	8	0.23283 06436 53869 62891	$\times\ 10^{-9}$
68 719 476 736	9	0.14551 91522 83668 51807	$\times\ 10^{-10}$
1 099 511 627 776	10	0.90949 47017 72928 23792	$\times\ 10^{-12}$
17 592 186 044 416	11	0.56843 41886 08080 14870	$\times\ 10^{-13}$
281 474 976 710 656	12	0.35527 13678 80050 09294	$\times\ 10^{-14}$
4 503 599 627 370 496	13	0.22204 46049 25031 30808	$\times\ 10^{-15}$
72 057 594 037 927 936	14	0.13877 78780 78144 56755	$\times\ 10^{-16}$
1 152 921 504 606 846 976	15	0.86736 17379 88403 54721	$\times\ 10^{-18}$

POWERS OF TEN
(Converted to Hexadecimal Values)

10^n	n	10^{-n}	
1	0	1.0000 0000 0000 0000	
A	1	0.1999 9999 9999 999A	
64	2	0.28F5 C28F 5C28 F5C3	$\times\ 16^{-1}$
3E8	3	0.4189 374B C6A7 EF9E	$\times\ 16^{-2}$
2710	4	0.68DB 8BAC 710C B296	$\times\ 16^{-3}$
1 86A0	5	0.A7C5 AC47 1B47 8423	$\times\ 16^{-4}$
F 4240	6	0.10C6 F7A0 B5ED 8D37	$\times\ 16^{-4}$
98 9680	7	0.1AD7 F29A BCAF 4858	$\times\ 16^{-5}$
5F5 E100	8	0.2AF3 1DC4 6118 73BF	$\times\ 16^{-6}$
3B9A CA00	9	0.44B8 2FA0 9B5A 52CC	$\times\ 16^{-7}$
2 540B E400	10	0.6DF3 7F67 5EF6 EADF	$\times\ 16^{-8}$
17 4876 E800	11	0.AFEB FF0B CB24 AAFF	$\times\ 16^{-9}$
E8 D4A5 1000	12	0.1197 9981 2DEA 1119	$\times\ 16^{-9}$
916 4E72 A000	13	0.1C25 C268 4976 81C2	$\times\ 16^{-10}$
5AF3 107A 4000	14	0.2D09 370D 4257 3604	$\times\ 16^{-11}$
3 8D7E A4C6 8000	15	0.480E BE7B 9D58 566D	$\times\ 16^{-12}$
23 8652 6FC1 0000	16	0.734A CA5F 6226 F0AE	$\times\ 16^{-13}$
163 4578 5D8A 0000	17	0.B877 AA32 36A4 B449	$\times\ 16^{-14}$
DE0 B6B3 A764 0000	18	0.1272 5DD1 D243 ABA1	$\times\ 16^{-14}$
8AC7 2304 89E8 0000	19	0.1D83 C94F B6D2 AC35	$\times\ 16^{-15}$

Variations for
Revision Level 2 ROMs

This appendix describes the differences between the Revision Level 3 ROMs, as presented in the chapter material, and the Revision Level 2 ROMs.

Chapter 1: STARTUP

Asterisks (∗) appear in place of the pound signs (#) in the initial display line of the Revision Level 2 ROMs:

∗∗∗ COMMODORE BASIC ∗∗∗

You can use this as an indicator of which ROMs your CBM computer has.

Chapter 4: ARRAYS

On the Revision Level 2 ROMs, the total number of array elements in any one array is limited to 256. For example, for a one-dimensional array, elements may go from 0 to 255. For a two-dimensional array with dimension 2 in the second subscript, elements may go from (0,0), (1,0) to (127,0) or (0,1), (1,1) to (127,1), etc.

An example of programming within this restriction is given below under "Chapter 5: Generating Random Numbers."

Chapter 5: DEVELOPING A PROGRAM, Interactive Programming

In the Revision Level 2 ROMs, the system location that enables the cursor to blink is location 548. To enable the cursor, you would use the statement:

80 POKE 548,0   Enable cursor (Revision Level 2 ROMs)

instead of:

80 POKE 167,0   Enable cursor (Revision Level 3 ROMs)

Chapter 5: RND

RND(0) is non-functional. An argument of zero returns a value that is constant, or nearly constant, and that may vary from CBM to CBM computer.

You will have to use −TI to generate random seeds. This is the method used in all of the examples in Chapter 5 under "Generating Random Numbers."

Chapter 5: GENERATING RANDOM NUMBERS

Do not try to use RND(−RND(0)) to generate random seeds; it will not work. Instead, use −TI as shown in all of the examples.

The RANDOM VERSION 2 sample program in Chapter 5 will not work on the Revision Level 2 ROMs because of the 256-element array limitation. A second version of the program is shown below. It shows the lengths you have to go to in order to program with the 256-element array limitation. In this program the 1000-element table is divided into four quarters of 250 elements each.

```
5 REM RANDOM VERSION 2A
10 REM ******* B L A N K E T *******
20 REM RANDOM DISPLAY OF ONE
30 REM   CHARACTER ENTERED FROM THE
40 REM   KEYBOARD
50 REM ********************************
70 DIM T1(249),T2(249),T3(249),T4(249)
75 T=4    :REM NUMBER OF TABLES
76 N=250 :REM NO OF ELEMENTS
80 GOSUB 200    :REM INITIALIZE TABLES
90 PRINT"HIT A KEY OR <R> TO END";
95 N1=N:N2=N:N3=N:N4=N
100 GET C$: IF C$="" GOTO 100

105 IF C$=CHR$(13) GOTO 170
110 PRINT"⬛";        :REM CLEAR SCREEN
120 X=RND(-TI)       :REM START NEW SEED
125 C=(ASC(C$)AND128)/2 OR (ASC(C$)AND63)
126 FOR L=1TO1000 :REM 1 FOR EACH SPOT
127 T%=T*RND(1)+1  :REM PICK A TABLE
128 ON T% GOSUB 300,400,500,600 :REM GO PICK AN ELEMENT
130 POKE A,C       :REM DISPLAY CHAR
140 NEXT L
160 GOTO 95
170 END
199 REM **SUBR TO INITIALIZE TABLES**
200 FOR I=0 TO N-1:T1(I)=I:NEXT
210 FOR I=0 TO N-1:T2(I)=I+250:NEXT
220 FOR I=0 TO N-1:T3(I)=I+500:NEXT
230 FOR I=0 TO N-1:T4(I)=I+750:NEXT
240 RETURN
299 REM **SUBROUTINE FOR TABLE T1**
```

```
300 N1=N1-1
305 REM IF EMPTY, GO TO ANOTHER TABLE
310 IF N1<0 THEN ON INT(3*RND(1)+1) GOTO 400,500,600
320 A%=(N1+1)*RND(1) :REM PICK AN ELEM
330 A=T1(A%)+32768 :REM FORM POKE ADDR
340 TP=T1(A%):T1(A%)=T1(N1):T1(N1)=TP :REM SWAP ELEMENTS
350 RETURN
399 REM **SUBROUTINE FOR TABLE T2**
400 N2=N2-1
410 IF N2<0 THEN ON INT(3*RND(1)+1) GOTO 300,500,600
420 A%=(N2+1)*RND(1)
430 A=T2(A%)+32768
440 TP=T2(A%):T2(A%)=T2(N2):T2(N2)=TP
450 RETURN
499 REM **SUBROUTINE FOR TABLE T3**
500 N3=N3-1
510 IF N3<0 THEN ON INT(3*RND(1)+1) GOTO 300,400,600
520 A%=(N3+1)*RND(1)
530 A=T3(A%)+32768
540 TP=T3(A%):T3(A%)=T3(N3):T3(N3)=TP
550 RETURN
599 REM **SUBROUTINE FOR TABLE T4**
600 N4=N4-1
610 IF N4<0 THEN ON INT(3*RND(1)+1) GOTO 300,400,500
620 A%=(N4+1)*RND(1)
630 A=T4(A%)+32768
640 TP=T4(A%):T4(A%)=T4(N4):T4(N4)=TP
650 RETURN
```

Chapter 6: FILES

This section is for CBM users who are having problems reading cassette data files using the old ROMs. If your CBM has the Revision Level 2 ROMs and you intend to use data files frequently, you should seriously consider replacing the Revision Level 2 ROMs with the Revision Level 3 ROMs, as the Revision Level 3 ROMs ensure greater reliability when reading and writing data files.

If you do plan to use the Revision Level 2 ROMs, you must do a little extra programming to get around these problems. When writing data to the data tape, the Revision Level 2 ROMs neglect to initialize the pointer to the start address of the cassette tape buffer, and also fail to leave enough blank space on the tape between physical records.[1] Consequently, when the CBM attempts to read the data back from the data tape, the problems may result in lost or garbled data. Here are a few precautions you can take to overcome these obstacles.

1. Initialize the pointer of the cassette buffer start address. Because the Revision Level 2 ROMs fail to initialize the start address to the cassette tape buffer before a file is OPENed, you must be sure to do so before opening a file with a series of POKEs:

```
Cassette #1: POKE 243,122:POKE 244,2:OPEN 1,1,1
Cassette #2: POKE 243,58 :POKE 244,3:OPEN 2,2,1
```

Memory address locations 243 and 244 point to the start address of the current tape buffer. By POKEing in the above values the pointer will be initialized properly.

2. Force interrecord gaps. The Revision Level 2 ROMs do not leave enough blank space on the tape between physical records. When the CBM attempts to read back the data with an INPUT# or GET#, if the physical records are too close together the data cannot be read, resulting in read errors and lost data. To prevent this, you can force larger gaps to be written between records by calling a routine to advance the tape each time the cassette buffer is emptied.

Before forcing an interrecord gap you must detect when the cassette buffer has written out a "physical record" or "block" of data to the tape. The buffer holds 191 characters (or 191 bytes). A full buffer is a signal that a block of data was just written to the tape, since the contents of the buffer are dumped only after it has reached its capacity. By detecting a full buffer, you can infer that a block of data was just written to the tape and an interrecord gap is needed.

How to Detect a Full Buffer

When writing data out to a tape, following each PRINT# statement the length of each data item is calculated and kept in an accumulator, which is then compared to the buffer limit (191 characters). When the accumulator equals 191 the writing to the tape is stopped until an interrecord gap is written on the tape. Below is a sample program:

```
10 POKE 243,122:POKE 244,2:OPEN1,1,1
20 FOR X=1 TO 100
30 PRINT#1,X
40 A=LEN(STR$(X))+1
50 IF (QT+A)>=191 GOSUB 1000      :REM *IF BUFFER FULL CALL SUB. TO ADVANCE TAPE*
60 QT=QT+A
70 NEXT X
80 CLOSE1
90 END
```

Line 20 prints a variable. If the variable printed (in this case, X) is numeric it must be converted to string form so the LEN function may be used to determine X's length, as shown in line 40:

```
40  A=LEN(STR$(X))+1
```

One is added to the lengths of the strings to include the carriage returns that are written on the tape following each data item. Line 50 accumulates the number of characters in the previous strings, (QT), plus A, and compares the total to 191 (the buffer limit). If the number of characters written to the tape (QT + A) is greater than or equal to 191 the entire buffer is written to the tape, and it is time to force an interrecord gap by calling the subroutine at 1000. However, if QT+A is less than 191 (QT+A<191), the buffer is not yet full. Line 60 increments QT by A, and the process keeps repeating until the buffer is full, and all the data is written from the buffer to the tape, interspersed with the interrecord gaps.

Advancing the Cassette Tape

There are three necessary steps in the routine to advance the tape:

1. Turn on the cassette tape motor (POKE 59411,53).
2. Use a wait loop to the stall program while the tape is advancing.
3. Turn off the cassette tape motor (POKE 59411,61).

POKE 59411,53 pokes "53" into memory address location 59411, which controls the cassette motor. Value 53 turns on the motor to advance the tape. Once the motor is on, a wait loop lets the tape advance for a few jiffies. The wait loop will be discussed shortly. To stop the tape, a POKE 59411,61 turns off the cassette motor. The length of the wait loop may be varied or altered, but these two POKEs are absolutely necessary to turn the cassette motor on and off.

Following is a sample wait loop inserted between the two POKE statements:

```
1000 POKE 59411,53        :REM *START TAPE MOTOR*
1010 T=TI
1020 IF (TI-T)<10 GOTO 1020   :REM *WAIT 10 JIFFIES*
1030 POKE 59411,61        :REM *STOP TAPE MOTOR*
1040 QT=0
1050 RETURN
```

Lines 1010 to 1020 make up the wait loop. Line 1010 sets variable T to the current value of TI. TI is the number of jiffies since the PET was powered up or the clock was zeroed. (A jiffy is 1/60 of a second.) TI is incremented once every jiffy, or 60 times a second. By subtracting T from TI, the elapsed time is calculated. The program must wait until ten jiffies (1/6 of a second) has elapsed before the program can continue. While TI increments, until the difference between TI and T equals ten jiffies the program is stalled, letting the cassette tape advance. This blank space on the tape is the interrecord gap. Once (TI−T) equals ten, the next statement turns off the cassette motor with a POKE 59411,61.

The routine calculates the space between each record. The tape is advanced exactly the same amount between each physical record because the time between POKEing on and off the cassette motor will always be ten jiffies. The length of the wait loop may be adjusted by changing the constant of the condition expression:

$$TI-T < X$$

The larger the value of X, the larger the interrecord gap will be. If you're unsure how long the interrecord gap should be, keep the wait loop between 5 and 30 jiffies. It is always better to have the interrecord gap too long than too short.

There is one potential problem with this routine, though it is doubtful you will ever encounter the problem. If the CBM computer has been powered up for close to twenty-four hours, or you have set the internal clock close to the twenty-fourth hour, the routine might hang up during the wait loop. At 24:00:00 the jiffy clock is reset from 5184000 jiffies to zero. If T is assigned within a few jiffies of 5184000 both TI and the jiffy clock will be reset to zero. The result is that the condition TI−T<10 will always be true (0000008−5183998 < 10) and the wait loop will hang up infinitely because TI−T will never be greater than nine. It is very improbable that this will ever happen to you, but you should use caution if the jiffy clock is nearing the twenty-fourth hour.

Here is another way to advance the tape:

```
POKE 59411,53       :REM *START TAPE MOTOR*
POKE 514,0          :REM *ZERO JIFFY CLOCK*
WAIT 514,16         :REM *WAITS 16 JIFFIES*
POKE 59411,61       :REM *STOP TAPE MOTOR*
```

POKE 514,0 pokes a zero into the low-order byte of the internal clock at memory address 514, wiping out the current jiffy time and resetting the clock to zero. The WAIT 514,16 inhibits further program action until the clock has incremented 16 jiffies. Meanwhile, the tape advances until memory address location 514 contains 16 and the following POKE turns the cassette motor off.

There is one drawback with this wait loop. Every time the jiffy clock is reset to zero the CBM loses track of time. Therefore, this routine should *not* be used if it is important within the program that real time be kept or used in any way.

Here is yet another way to implement a wait loop during the data tape advance:

```
POKE 59411,53
FOR I=1 TO 60:NEXT I
POKE 59411,61
```

This method is simple but less accurate than the previous two. Using a FOR-NEXT loop, the program is stalled as the loop increments to the maximum value of I before turning off the motor. However, the time it takes to increment through a FOR-NEXT loop cannot be measured as accurately as time measured in jiffies, and thus the interrecord gaps cannot be precise. One advantage with this method is that it does not alter or inhibit the use of the jiffy clock in any way.

Let's go back to the original wait loop and combine it with the routine that detects a full buffer. Below is a sample program which writes 100 numbers to a data tape with a FOR-NEXT loop. Within the loop is a check for a full buffer. If the buffer is full the data is written to the tape, and the subroutine at 1000 is called to create an interrecord gap:

```
10 POKE 243,122:POKE 244,2:OPEN1,1,1
20 FOR X=1 TO 100
30 PRINT#1,X
40 A=LEN(STR$(X))+1
50 IF (QT+A)>=191 GOSUB 1000          :REM *IF BUFFER FULL CALL SUB. TO ADVANCE TAPE
60 QT=QT+A
70 NEXT X
80 CLOSE1
90 END
1000 POKE 59411,53                     :REM *START TAPE MOTOR*
1010 T=TI
1020 IF (TI-T)<10 GOTO 1020            :REM *WAIT 10 JIFFIES*
1030 POKE 59411,61                     :REM *STOP TAPE MOTOR
1040 QT=0                              :REM *RESET ACCUMULATOR
1050 RETURN
```

where:

A	is the length of the printed string plus 1 for carriage return
QT	is the accumulator to add lengths of printed strings.

If you follow these suggestions and routines you should have little or no trouble writing and reading data files. But, if you find that you cannot get the files to work even with these routines, you should install the Revision Level 3 ROMs in your CBM computer.

Chapter 7: MEMORY MAP

All of the changes in Chapter 7 are based on the fact that the memory map for the Revision Level 2 ROMs was reorganized for the Revision Level 3 ROMs.

The detailed memory maps used by the different versions of CBM BASIC are shown in the back of this appendix.

Table F-1 describes the Revision Level 2 ROMs used in the original PET computers. Table F-2 shows the Revision Level 3 ROMs used in BASIC 3.0 CBM computers. Table F-3 shows the most recent memory map for the BASIC 4.0 CBM computers.

Tables F-1 and F-2 have a similar format; the Table F-3 format differs. Tables F-1 and F-2 show the memory address in decimal and hexadecimal, and also show sample decimal and hexadecimal equivalent values in memory locations. Table F-3 compares the BASIC 4.0 memory map with the BASIC 3.0 revision shown in Table F-2. The DESCRIPTION column provides the location description as currently used by Commodore; the LABEL column shows the assembly language label currently assigned to the location by Commodore. The BASIC 4.0 column gives the hexadecimal address of each location, while the BASIC 3.0 column gives the equivalent BASIC 3.0 hexadecimal

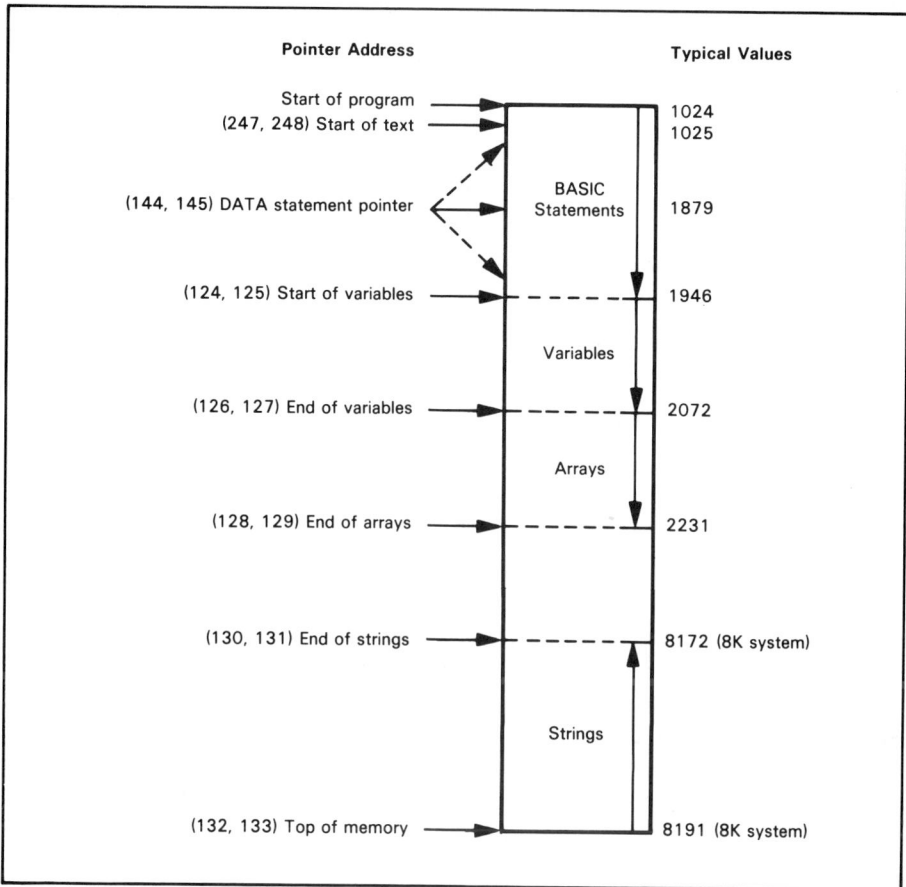

Figure F-1. Principal Pointers in User Program Area

address. To find any BASIC 4.0 location, first find the hexadecimal address given in Table F-2. Find this hexadecimal address in the BASIC 3.0 column of Table F-3 and the comparable BASIC 4.0 hexadecimal address is in the adjacent column.

With the exception of the first two entries in Table F-3, which actually represent memory address 0000, all subsequent 0000 addresses identify entries which do not exist in one version of BASIC or the other. For example, if you see an address in the BASIC 3.0 column with 0000 in the BASIC 4.0 column, then BASIC 4.0 has no equivalent location in its memory map. Conversely, a 0000 address in the BASIC 3.0 column identifies a new entry in the BASIC 4.0 memory map for which there is no BASIC 3.0 equivalent.

Chapter 7: CBM BASIC INTERPRETER

The system locations holding principal pointers in the user program area are different for the Revision Level 2 ROMs. Your pointers, in place of Figure 7-2, are as shown in Figure F-1. Figure F-2, replacing Figure 7-4, also reflects these changes.

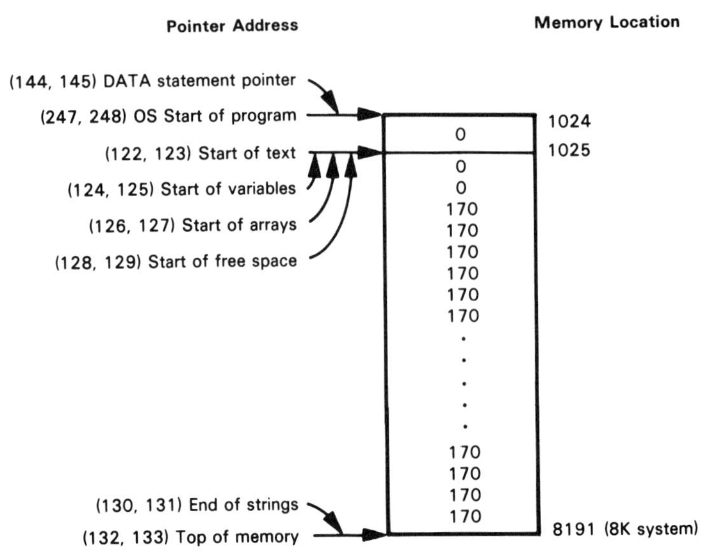

Figure F-2. User Program Area on Power-up

Chapter 7: **VARIABLES, Floating Point Variable Format**

Use the following program to examine floating point representations:

```
10 INPUT A
20 X=PEEK(125)*256+PEEK(124)+2
30 PRINT A;"=";PEEK(X);PEEK(X+1);PEK(X+2);PEEK(X+3);PEEK(X+4)
40 GOTO 10
```

This is the same one given in Chapter 7 except for the system locations at line 20 being PEEKed.

Chapter 7: **CONSTANTS**

Instead of pointer (42,43), the pointer in the diagrams is (124,125).

Chapter 7: **ARRAY STORAGE FORMAT**

Use the following program for viewing sample Array Area entries:

```
10 DIM A(5),B%(2,2),C$(10)        :REM SAMPLE ARRAYS
20 FOR I=0 TO 5:A(I)=I:NEXT
30 FOR I=0 TO 2:FOR J=0 TO 2:B%(J,I)=100+3*I+J:NEXT J,I
40 FOR I=0 TO 10:C$(I)=CHR$(ASC("A")+I):NEXT
50 X=PEEK(127)*256+PEEK(126)       :REM POINT TO ARRAY AREA
60 Y=PEEK(129)*256+PEEK(128)       :REM END OF ARRAYS
70 FOR I=X TO Y
80 PRINT I,PEEK(I)
90 GET D$:IF D$="" THEN GOTO 90:REM HIT KEY FOR NEXT ELEMENT
100 NEXT
```

This is the same as the program in Chapter 7 except for the system locations accessed in lines 50 and 60.

Chapter 7: ASSEMBLY LANGUAGE PROGRAMMING

For the Revision Level 2 ROMs, item 2, Top of Core discussion should read as follows:

2. Top of MEMORY. Memory locations 134 and 135 contain the pointer to the top of memory. On 8K CBMs this value is 8192. You can temporarily set the top of memory pointer to a lower address, thereby reserving a number of bytes from the new pointer value to the actual top of memory for storage of an assembly language program. To set the pointer, say, down 1000 bytes, you will need to store the value 7192 (8192-1000) converted into low, high address order, e.g.:

$$\text{High} \qquad \text{Low}$$
$$7192_{10} = 1C18_{16} \rightarrow 1C_{16} = 28_{10} \text{ and } 18_{16} = 24_{10}$$

So 24 is to be stored at location 134 (low byte), and 28 is to be stored at location 135 (high byte). The following instructions can be used:

```
10 AL=PEEK(134):AH=PEEK(135):    REM SAVE CURRENT POINTER
20 POKE 132,24:POKE 135,28:      REM TOP OF CORE NOW = 7192
      :
      :
      :
100 POKE 134,AL:POKE 135,AH:     REM RESTORE POINTER
110 END
```

Chapter 7: USR

Since the accumulator is maintained in different system locations on the Revision Level 2 ROMs, the accumulator description will read as described below.

The parameter value is passed to the USR subroutine in system locations that function as a floating point accumulator (FAC) for all functions. The FAC resides in six bytes from memory locations 176 to 181 ($B0_{16}-B5_{16}$). The FAC has the following format:

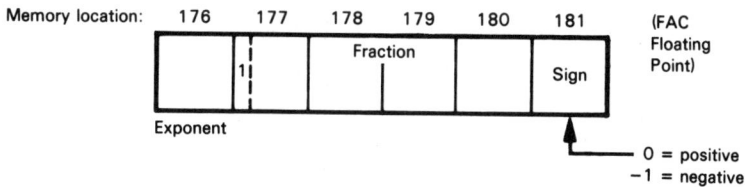

Like floating point variables, the exponent is stored in excess 128 format, and the fraction is normalized with the high-order bit of byte 177 (the high-order byte of the fraction) set to 1. The difference between this format and the variable format is that the high-order 1 bit is present in byte 177 of the FAC. An extra byte (181) is used to hold the sign of the fraction. (This is done for ease of manipulation by the functions that use the FAC.)

1. *PET User Notes*, Volume 1, Issue 6, Sept.-Oct. 1978, p. 14, "Cassette File Usage Summary" by Jim Butterfield.

2. *Best of the PET Gazette*, p. 38, "On Data Files" by Michael Richter.

Table F-1. CBM Memory Map (Rev. 2 ROMs)

Memory Address		Sample Value		Description
Decimal	Hexadecimal	Decimal	Hexadecimal	
				Page 0 (0-255)
				USR Function Locations
0	0000	76	4C	Constant 6502 JMP instruction
1-2	0001-0002	826	033A	User address jump vector
				Terminal I/O Maintenance
3	0003	0	00	Active input device number (0=keyboard)
4	0004	0	00	No. of nulls to print after CR/LF (0=normal)
5	0005	0	00	Cursor position for POS function (0-255)
6	0006	127	7F	Terminal width (unused)
7	0007	127	7F	Limit for scanning source columns (unused)
8	0008	60	3C	Line number storage preceding buffer
9	0009	3	03	Constant
10-89	000A-0059	48	30	BASIC input line buffer (80 bytes)
90	005A	0	00	General counter for BASIC
91	005B	0	00	Delimiter flag for quote mode scan
92	005C	255	FF	Input buffer pointer, general counter
				Evaluation of Variables
93	005D	0	00	Flag for dimensioned variables
94	005E	0	00	Flag for variable type: 00=numeric FF=string
95	005F	0	00	Flag for numeric variable type: 00=floating point 80=integer
96	0060	0	00	Flag to allow reserved words in strings and remarks
97	0061	0	00	Flag to allow subscripted variable
98	0062	0	00	Flag for input type: 0=INPUT 64=GET 152=READ
99	0063	0	00	Flag sign of TAN function
100	0064	0	00	Flag to suppress output: + normal -- suppressed
101	0065	104	68	Index to next available descriptor
102-103	0066-0067	101	0065	Pointer to last string temporary
104-111	0068-006F	2	0002	Table of double-byte descriptors that point to variables (8 bytes)
112-113	0070-0071	14525	38BD	Indirect index #1
114-115	0072-0073	62983	F607	Indirect index #2
116	0074	1	01	Pseudo-register for function operands (6 bytes)
117	0075	234	EA	
118	0076	0	00	
119	0077	0	00	
120	0078	0	00	
121	0079	0	00	

Table F-1. CBM Memory Map (Rev. 2 ROMs) (Continued)

Memory Address		Sample Value		Description
Decimal	Hexadecimal	Decimal	Hexadecimal	
				Data BASIC Storage Maintenance
122-123	007A-007B	1025	0401	Pointer to start of text
124-125	007C-007D	1946	079A	Pointer to start of variables
126-127	007E-007F	2072	0818	Pointer to end of variables
128-129	0080-0081	2231	08B7	Pointer to end of arrays
130-131	0082-0083	8192	2000	Pointer to start of strings (moving down)
132-133	0084-0085	8191	1FFF	Pointer to end of strings (top of available RAM)
134-135	0086-0087	8192	2000	Pointer to limit of BASIC memory
136-137	0088-0089	2000	07D0	Line number of current line being executed −1 in 137=direct mode statement
138-139	008A-008B	110	006E	Line number for last line executed before CONT
140-141	008C-008D	1922	0782	Pointer to next line to be executed after CONT
142-143	008E-008F	1150	047E	Line number of current DATA line
144-145	0090-0091	1879	0757	Pointer to current DATA line
146-147	0092-0093	13	000D	Next DATA item within line
148-149	0094-0095	89	0059	Current variable name
150-151	0096-0097	2032	07F0	Pointer to current variable
152-153	0098-0099	2032	07F0	Pointer to next FOR. . . NEXT variable
154-155	009A-009B	31999	7CFF	Pointer to current operator in ROM table
156	009C	0	00	Mask for current logical operator
157-158	009D-009E	898	0382	Pointer to user function FN definition
159-160	009F-00A0	104	0068	Pointer to a string description
161	00A1	221	DD	Length of string
162	00A2	3	03	Constant used by garbage collection routine
163	00A3	76	4C	Constant 6502 JMP instruction
164-165	00A4-00A5	0	0000	Jump vector for user function FN
166-171	00A6-00AB	129	81	Floating point accumulator #3 (6 bytes)
172-173	00AC-00AD	0	00	Block transfer pointer #1
174-175	00AE-00AF	0	00	Block transfer pointer #2
176-181	00B0-00B5			Floating point accumulator (FAC) #1 (6 bytes)
		0	00	176 00B0 Exponent +128
		0	00	177 00B1 Fraction MSB Floating Point
		0	00	178 00B2 Fraction
		0	00	179 00B3 Fraction MSB Integer
		0	00	180 00B4 Fraction LSB
		0	00	181 00B5 Sign of fraction (0 if zero or positive. −1 if negative)
182	00B6	0	00	Copy of FAC #1 sign of fraction
183	00B7	0	00	Counter for number of bits to shift to normalize FAC #1
184-189	00B8-00BD	0	00	Floating point accumulator #2 (6 bytes)
190	00BE	0	00	Overflow byte for floating argument
191	00BF	0	00	Copy of FAC #2 sign of fraction
192-193	00C0-00C1	258	0102	Conversion pointer

Table F-1. CBM Memory Map (Rev. 2 ROMs) (Continued)

Memory Address		Sample Value		Description
Decimal	Hexadecimal	Decimal	Hexadecimal	
				RAM Subroutines
194-199	00C2-00C7	230	E6	Routine to fetch next BASIC character
200	00C8	173	AD	Entry to refetch current character
201-202	00C9-00CA	1929	0789	Pointer to source text
203-223	00CB-00DF	201	C9	Work area for RND function
				OS Page Zero Storage
224-225	00E0-00E1	33728	83C0	Pointer to start of line where cursor is flashing
226	00E2	0	00	Column position where cursor is flashing (0-79)
227-228	00E3-00E4	33792	8400	Utility pointer
229-230	00E5-00E6	1929	0789	End of current program
231-233	00E7-00E9	254	FE	Utility
234	00EA	0	00	Flag for quote mode. 0=not quote mode
235-237	00EB-00ED	192	C0	Utility
238	00EE	0	00	No. of characters in current file name
239	00EF	5	05	Current logical file number
240	00F0	255	FF	GPIB primary address
241	00F1	63	3F	GPIB device number
242	00F2	39	27	Max. no. of characters on current line (39,79)
243-244	00F3-00F4	634	027A	Pointer to start of current tape buffer (634 or 826)
245	00F5	23	17	Line number where cursor is flashing (0-24)
246	00F6	10	0A	I/O storage
247-248	00F7-00F8	1024	0400	OS pointer to program
249-250	00F9-00FA	3100	0C1C	Pointer to current file name
251	00FB	0	00	Number of Insert keys pushed to go
252	00FC	9	09	Serial bit shift word
253	00FD	0	00	Number of blocks remaining to read/write
254	00FE	0	09	Serial word buffer
255	00FF	243	F3	Overflow byte for binary to ASCII conversions
				Page 1 (256-511)
256-up	0100-up	32	20	Tape read working storage (up to 511) and conversion stg. 256-318 For error correction in tape reads (62 bytes) 256-266 Binary to ASCII conversion (11 bytes)
511-down	01FF-down	0	00	Stack (down to 256)
				Page 2-3 (512-1023)
				OS Working Storage
512-514	0200-0202	3801352	3A0108	24-hour clock incremented every 1/60 second (jiffy). Resets every 5,184,000 jiffies (24 hours). Stored in low to high order.

Table F-1. CBM Memory Map (Rev. 2 ROMs) (Continued)

Memory Address		Sample Value		Description
Decimal	Hexadecimal	Decimal	Hexadecimal	
515	0203	255	FF	Matrix coordinate of key depressed at current jiffy. 1-80=key 255=no key
516	0204	0	00	Status of SHIFT key: 0=unshifted (up) 1=shifted (down)
517-518	0205-0206	37916	941C	Secondary jiffy clock
519	0207	52	34	Interrupt driver flag for cassette #1 ON switch
520	0208	0	00	Interrupt driver flag for cassette #2 ON switch
521	0209	255	FF	Keyswitch PIA
522	020A	0	00	Utility
523	020B	0	00	I/O flag: 0=LOAD 1=VERIFY
524	020C	0	00	I/O status byte
525	020D	0	00	Number of characters in keyboard buffer (0 to 9)
526	020E	0	00	Flag to indicate reverse field on (0=normal)
527-536	020F-0218	85	55	Keyboard buffer (10 bytes)
537-538	0219-021A	34048	8500	Hardware interrupt vector
539-540	021B-021C	0	0000	6502 BRK instruction interrupt vector
541-546	021D-0222			Input routine storage (6 bytes)
		13	0D	542 021E No. of characters on screen line
547	0223	255	FF	Key image
548	0224	1	01	Flag for cursor enable: 0=Enable 1=Disable
549	0225	11	0B	Counter to flip cursor (20 to 1)
550	0226	32	20	Copy of character at current cursor position
551	0227	0	00	Flag for cursor on/off: 0=cursor moved 1=blink started
552	0228	0	00	Flag for tape write
553-577	0229-0241			High byte of screen line addresses 553-559=128 (lines 1-7) 560-565=129 (lines 8-13) 566-572=130 (lines 14-20) 573-577=131 (lines 21-25)
578-587	0242-024B	5	05	Table of logical numbers of open files
588-597	024C-0255	5	05	Table of device numbers of open files
598-607	0256-025F	255	FF	Table of secondary address modes of open files
608	0260	0	00	Flag for input source: 0=keyboard buffer 1=screen memory
609	0261	0	00	I/O utility
610	0262	1	01	Number of open files (index into tables)

Table F-1. CBM Memory Map (Rev. 2 ROMs) (Continued)

Memory Address		Sample Value		Description
Decimal	Hexadecimal	Decimal	Hexadecimal	
611	0263	0	00	Default input device number (0=keyboard)
612	0264	3	03	Default output device number (3=screen)
613	0265	0	00	Tape parity byte
614	0266	0	00	I/O utility
615	0267	0	00	I/O utility
616	0268	0	00	Byte pointer in filename transfer
617	0269	0	00	I/O utility
618	026A	255	FF	I/O utility
619	026B	0	00	I/O utility
620	026C	8	08	Serial bit count
621	026D	0	00	Count of redundant tape blocks
622	026E	0	00	Tape utility
623	026F	0	00	Cycle counter flip for each bit read from tape
624	0270	0	00	Countdown synchronization on tape write
625	0271	0	00	Tape buffer 1 index to next character
626	0272	0	00	Tape buffer 2 index to next character
627	0273	0	00	Countdown synchronization on tape read
628	0274	0	00	Flag to indicate bit/byte tape error
629	0275	0	00	Flag to indicate tape error 0=first half-byte marker not written
630	0276	0	00	Flag to indicate tape error 0=2nd half-byte marker not written /Tape dropout counter
631	0277	0	00	Tape dropout counter
632	0278	128	80	Flag for tape read current function
633	0279	9	09	Checksum utility
634-825	027A-0339	1	01	Tape buffer for cassette #1 (192 bytes)
826-1017	033A-03F9	173	AD	Tape buffer for cassette #2 (192 bytes)
1018-1023	03FA-03FF	28	1C	Utility space/unused.
				Page 4-32 (1024-8191)
1024-8191	0400-1FFF	0	00	User program area
				Page 33-128 (8192-32767)
8192-32767	2000-7FFF	0	00	Expansion RAM
				Page 129-144 (32768-36863)
32768-36863	8000-8FFF	12	0C	TV RAM 32768-33767 Display memory (1000 bytes)
				Page 145-192 (36864-49151)
36864-49151	9000-BFFF	0	00	Expansion ROM
				Page 193-232 BASIC (49152-59391)
				Pointers to BASIC Routines
49152-49153	C000-C001	50973	C71D	Pointer −1 to END*
49154-49155	C002-C003	50760	C648	Pointer −1 to FOR
49156-49157	C004-C005	52277	CC35	Pointer −1 to NEXT

* These memory locations contain the address of the byte preceding the specified BASIC routines.

Table F-1. CBM Memory Map (Rev. 2 ROMs) (Continued)

Memory Address		Sample Value		Description
Decimal	**Hexadecimal**	**Decimal**	**Hexadecimal**	
49158-49159	C006-C007	51183	C73F	Pointer −1 to DATA
49160-49161	C008-C009	51909	CAC5	Pointer −1 to INPUT#
49162-49163	C00A-C00B	51935	CADF	Pointer −1 to INPUT
49164-49165	C00C-C00D	53104	CF70	Pointer −1 to DIM
49166-49167	C00E-C00F	52003	CB23	Pointer −1 to READ
49168-49169	C010-C011	51356	C89C	Pointer −1 to LET
49170-49171	C012-C013	51100	C79C	Pointer −1 to GOTO
49172-49173	C014-C015	51060	C774	Pointer −1 to RUN
49174-49175	C016-C017	51231	C81F	Pointer −1 to IF
49176-49177	C018-C019	50956	C70C	Pointer −1 to RESTORE
49178-49179	C01A-C01B	51071	C77F	Pointer −1 to GOSUB
49180-49181	C01C-C01D	51145	C7C9	Pointer −1 to RETURN
49182-49183	C01E-C01F	51250	C832	Pointer −1 to REM
49184-49185	C020-C021	50971	C71B	Pointer −1 to STOP
49186-49187	C022-C023	51266	C842	Pointer −1 to ON
49188-49189	C024-C025	55041	D701	Pointer −1 to WAIT
49190-49191	C026-C027	65492	FFD4	Pointer −1 to LOAD
49192-49193	C028-C029	65495	FFD7	Pointer −1 to SAVE
49194-49195	C02A-C02B	65498	FFDA	Pointer −1 to VERIFY
49196-49197	C02C-C02D	53908	D294	Pointer −1 to DEF
49198-49199	C02E-C02F	55032	D6F8	Pointer −1 to POKE
49200-49201	C030-C031	51582	C97E	Pointer −1 to PRINT#
49202-49203	C032-C033	51614	C99E	Pointer −1 to PRINT
49204-49205	C034-C035	51012	C744	Pointer −1 to CONT
49206-49207	C036-C037	50599	C5A7	Pointer −1 to LIST
49208-49209	C038-C039	51055	C76F	Pointer −1 to CLR
49210-49211	C03A-C03B	51588	C984	Pointer −1 to CMD
49212-49213	C03C-C03D	65501	FFDD	Pointer −1 to SYS
49214-49215	C03E-C03F	65471	FFBF	Pointer −1 to OPEN
49216-49217	C040-C041	65474	FFC2	Pointer −1 to CLOSE
49218-49219	C042-C043	51870	CA9E	Pointer −1 to GET
49220-49221	C044-C045	50512	C550	Pointer −1 to NEW
49222-49223	C046-C047	56075	DB0B	Pointer to SGN**
49224-49225	C048-C049	56222	DB9E	Pointer to INT
49226-49227	C04A-C04B	56106	DB2A	Pointer to ABS
49228-49229	C04C-C04D	0	0000	Pointer to USR pointer
49230-49231	C04E-C04F	53860	D264	Pointer to FRE
49232-49233	C050-C051	53893	D285	Pointer to POS
49234-49235	C052-C053	56868	DE24	Pointer to SQR
40236-49237	C054-C055	57157	DF45	Pointer to RND
49238-49239	C056-C057	55487	D8BF	Pointer to LOG
49240-49241	C058-C059	56992	DEA0	Pointer to EXP
49242-49243	C05A-C05B	57246	DF9E	Pointer to COS
49244-49245	C05C-C05D	57253	DFA5	Pointer to SIN
49246-49247	C05E-C05F	57326	DFEE	Pointer to TAN
49248-49249	C060-C061	57416	E048	Pointer to ATN
49250-49251	C062-C063	55014	D6E6	Pointer to PEEK
49252-49253	C064-C065	54868	D654	Pointer to LEN
49254-49255	C066-C067	54089	D349	Pointer to STR$
49256-49257	C068-C069	54917	D685	Pointer to VAL
49258-49259	C06A-C06B	54883	D663	Pointer to ASC
49260-49261	C06C-C06D	54724	D5C4	Pointer to CHR$
49262-49263	C06E-C06F	54744	D5D8	Pointer to LEFT$

** These memory locations contain the address of the first byte of the specified BASIC routines.

Table F-1. CBM Memory Map (Rev. 2 ROMs) (Continued)

Memory Address		Sample Value		Description
Decimal	Hexadecimal	Decimal	Hexadecimal	
49264-49265	C070-C071	54788	D604	Pointer to RIGHT$
49266-49267	C072-C073	54799	D60F	Pointer to MID$
49268-57343	C074-DFFF			**BASIC Routines**

Starting Address	Function
49836 C2AC	FOR. . . NEXT stack check
49882 C2DA	Insert line space marker
49949 C31D	Stack overflow check
50007 C357	Error message abort
50057 C389	READY
50068 C394	Execute line
50092 C3AC	Handle new line
50224 C430	Rechain lines after insert/delete
50274 C462	Input line
50297 C479	Get character from input line
50317 C48D	Keyword encoder
50466 C522	Line number search
50513 C551	NEW
50586 C59A	Set pointer to start of program
50600 C5A8	LIST
50761 C649	FOR. . .NEXT
50869 C6B5	Statement processor
50930 C6F2	Statement execute
50957 C70D	RESTORE
50972 C71C	STOP
50974 C71E	END
51013 C745	CONT
51056 C770	CLR
51061 C775	RUN
51072 C780	GOSUB
51101 C79D	GOTO
51146 C7CA	RETURN
51184 C7F0	DATA
51198 C7FE	Next line scan
51232 C820	IF
51251 C833	REM
51267 C843	ON. . . GOTO/GOSUB
51299 C863	Number fetch
51357 C89D	LET=
51484 C91C	Digit check
51583 C97F	PRINT#
51589 C985	CMD
51615 C99F	PRINT
51751 CA27	Print string
51780 CA44	Print character
51831 CA77	Input data error
51871 CA9F	GET

Table F-1. CBM Memory Map (Rev. 2 ROMs) (Continued)

Memory Address		Sample Value		Description
Decimal	Hexadecimal	Decimal	Hexadecimal	
				51910 CAC6 INPUT#
				51936 CAED INPUT
				51991 CB17 Input prompt
				52004 CB24 READ
				52242 CC12 Error messages
				52278 CC36 NEXT
				52370 CC92 Format checker
				52408 CCB8 Expression evaluator
				52538 CD3A Stack argument
				52637 CD9D Symbol evaluator
				52668 CDBC Pi
				53105 CF71 DIM
				53207 CFD7 Variable table look-up
				53415 D0A7 Floating-to-integer
				53860 D264 FRE
				53880 D278 Integer-to-floating
				53893 D285 POS
				53909 D295 DEF
				54089 D349 STR$
				54724 D5C4 CHR$
				54744 D5D8 LEFT$
				54788 D604 RIGHT$
				54799 D60F MID$
				54868 D654 LEN
				54883 D663 ASC
				54917 D685 VAL
				55014 D6E6 PEEK
				55033 D6F9 POKE
				55042 D702 WAIT
				55080 D728 Subtraction
				55103 D73F Addition
				55487 D8BF LOG
				55552 D900 Multiplication
				55646 D95E Load number to AFAC
				55650 D962 Load variable to AFAC
				55780 D9E4 Division
				55924 DA74 Load Accumulator (FAC)
				55928 DA78 Load variable to FAC
				55979 DAAB Store variable from FAC
				56075 DB0B SGN
				56106 DB2A ABS
				56222 DB9E INT
				56868 DE24 SQR
				56878 DE2E Raise AFAC to power FAC
				56992 DEA0 EXP
				57157 DF45 RND
				57246 DF9E COS
				57253 DFA5 SIN
				57326 DFEE TAN

Table F-1. CBM Memory Map (Rev. 2 ROMs) (Continued)

Memory Address		Sample Value		Description
Decimal	Hexadecimal	Decimal	Hexadecimal	
57344-59391	E000-E7FF			**Screen Editor**
				Starting Address Function
				57416 E048 ATN
				57525 E0B5 Initialize BASIC system
				57910 E236 Clear screen
				57981 E27D Character fetch
58004-58986	E294-E66A			Video driver
				58282 E3AA Scroll processor
				58346 E3EA Video display routine
				58185 E349 Quote mode ($EA) switcher
				58346 E3EA Print character
				58713 E559 Scroll 1 line
				58758 E586 Interrupt Request (IRQ)
58987-59012	E66B-E684			Interrupt handler
59013-59198	E685-E73E			Clock update
59199-59227	E73F-E75B			Keyboard scan
59228-59348	E75C-E7D4			Keyboard encoding table
		Page 233-240 I/O Ports and Expansion I/O (PIA's and VIA) (59392-61439)		
				Keyboard PIA (59408-59411)
59408	E810	233	E9	I/O Port A and Data Direction register
59409	E811	60	3C	Control Register A — screen blanking
				52=Screen off (blanked)
				60=Screen on
59410	E812	255	FF	I/O Port B and Data Direction register
				255=all keys except:
				254=RVS key
				253=key
				251=SPACE key
				247= < key
59411	E813	61	3D	Control Register B — #1 cassette motor
				53=motor on
				61=motor off
				IEEE Port PIA (59424-59427)
59424	E820	255	FF	I/O Port A and Data Direction register
				PEEK (59424) reads input data.
59425	E821	188	BC	Control Register A — set output line CA2
				POKE 59425,52=low
				POKE 59425,60=high
59426	E822	255	FF	I/O Port B and Data Direction register
				POKE 59426,data writes output data
				POKE 59426,255 before a read to Port A
59427	E823	60	3C	Control Register B — set output line CB2
				POKE 59427,52=low
				POKE 59427,60=high

Table F-1. CBM Memory Map (Rev. 2 ROMs) (Continued)

Memory Address		Sample Value		Description
Decimal	Hexadecimal	Decimal	Hexadecimal	
				Parallel User Port VIA
				(59456-59471)
59456	E840	254	FE	I/O Port B
				207=#2 cassette motor on
				223=#2 cassette motor off
				WAIT 59456,23,23 waits for vertical retrace of display
				Bit 1=PB1 (NFRD on IEEE connector) output line
				Bit 3=PB3 (ATN on IEEE connector) output line
59457	E841	255	FF	I/O Port A with handshaking
59458	E842	30	1E	Data Direction register for I/O Port B
59459	E843	0	00	Data Direction register for I/O Port A
				For each bit 1=output, 0=input
				=0 all input
				=255 all output
59460-59461	E844-E845	25248	62A0	(Low, high order) Read Timer 1 Counter; write to Timer 1 Latch and (high byte) initiate count
59462-59463	E846-E847	65381	FF65	(Low, high order) Read Timer 1 Latch
59464	E848	113	71	Read Timer 2 Counter low byte and reset interrupt; write to Timer 2 low byte
				PEEK (59464) Clock decrements every microsecond
				POKE 59464,n sets SR rate of shift from high (n=0) to low (n=255) for music from User Port.
59465	E849	200	C8	Read Timer 2 Counter high byte; write to Timer 2 high byte and reset interrupt.
				PEEK (59465) Clock decrements every 256 microseconds
59466	E84A	1	01	Serial I/O Shift register (SR)
				POKE 59466,15 or 51 or 85 to generate square wave output at CB2 for playing music from User Port.
59467	E84B	0	00	Auxiliary Control register.
				=16 Sets SR to free-running mode for music from User Port.
				=0 for proper operation of tape drive
59468	E84C	14	0E	Peripheral Control register
				=12 for graphics on shifted characters
				=14 for lower-case letters on shifted characters
59469	E84D	0	00	Interrupt Flag register
59470	E84E	128	80	Interrupt Enable register
59471	E84F	255	FF	I/O Port A without handshaking
		Page 241-256 Operating System (61440-65535)		
61622-61904	F0B6-F1D0			**File Control**
				Starting Address **Function**
61905-63532	F1D1-F82C			61905 F1D1 Get a character (without cursor)
				61921 F1E1 Input a character (with cursor)

Table F-1. CBM Memory Map (Rev. 2 ROMs) (Continued)

Memory Address		Sample Value		Description
Decimal	Hexadecimal	Decimal	Hexadecimal	
				62002 F232 Display a character
				62026 F24A Close all files
				62121 F2A9 CLOSE
				62250 F32A STOP search
				62278 F346 Tape playback
				62402 F3C2 LOAD
				62481 F411 Display filename
				62515 F433 Fetch file number
				62556 F45C Number fetch
				62647 F4B7 VERIFY
				62724 F504 Fetch filename
				62741 F515 Fetch tape character
				62753 F521 OPEN
				62824 F568 Record SAVE routine
				62894 F5AE Tape header search
				62947 F5E3 Clear current tape buffer
				62957 F5ED Write tape end block
				63101 F67D Set up tape end pointer
				63108 F684 SYS
				63134 F69E SAVE
				63153 F6B1 SAVE memory block on cassette
				63273 F729 Update secondary jiffy clock
				Tape Control
63533-64789	F82D-FD15			
				63582 F85E Check for cassette on
				63615 F87F Tape read to buffer
				63684 F8C4 Write block to tape
				63765 F915 Interrupt wait
64824-65458	FD38-FFB2			**Power-On Diagnostics**
				64824 FD38 System reset
				SYS (64824) simulates power-on reset
				64909 FD8D Reset BASIC (does not affect User Program)
				64912 FD90 EOT-buffer compare
65472-65516	FFC0-FFEC			**Jump Vectors**
65472-65474	FFC0-FFC2	76 62753	4C F521	JMP OPEN
65475-65477	FFC3-FFC5	76 62121	4C F2A9	JMP CLOSE
65487-65489	FFCF-FFD1	76 61921	4C F1E1	JMP RDT
65490-65492	FFD2-FFD4	76 62002	4C F232	JMP WRT
65493-65495	FFD5-FFD7	76 62402	4C F3C2	JMP LOAD
65496-65498	FFD8-FFDA	76 63134	4C F69E	JMP SAVE
65499-65501	FFDB-FFDD	76 62647	4C F4B7	JMP VERIFY
65502-65504	FFDE-FFED	76 63108	4C F684	JMP SYS
65508-65510	FFE4-FFE6	76 61905	4C F1D1	JMP GETC
65514-65516	FFEA-FFEC	76 63273	4C F729	JMP Clock Update
65530-65535	FFFA-FFFF			**6502 Interrupt Vectors**
65530-65531	FFFA-FFFB	51808	CA60	Non-maskable interrupt (NMI)
65532-65533	FFFC-FFFD	64824	FD38	System reset (RESET)
65534-65535	FFFE-FFFF	58987	E66B	Interrupt request, break (IRQ+BRK)

Table F-2. CBM Memory Map (Rev. 3 ROMs)

Memory Address		Sample Value		Description
Decimal	Hexadecimal	Decimal	Hexadecimal	
			Page 0 (0-255)	
				USR Function Locations
0	0000	76	4C	Constant 6502 JMP instruction
1-2	0001-0002	826	033A	User address jump vector
				Evaluation of Variables and Terminal I/O Maintenance
3	0003	0	00	Search character
4	0004	0	00	Delimiter flag for quote mode scan
5	0005	255	FF	Input buffer pointer, general counter
6	0006	0	00	Flag for dimensioned variables
7	0007	0	00	Flag for variable type: 00=numeric FF=string
8	0008	0	00	Flag for numeric variable type: 00=floating point 80=integer
9	0009	0	00	Flag for DATA scan; LIST quote; memory
10	000A	0	00	Flag to allow subscripted variable; FNx flag
11	000B	0	00	Flag for input type: 0=INPUT 64=GET 152=READ
12	000C	0	00	Flag for ATN sign; comparison evaluation
13	000D	0	00	Flag to suppress output: + normal -- suppressed
14	000E	0	00	Current I/O device for prompt-suppress
15	000F	40	28	Terminal width (unused)
16	0010	30	1E	Limit for scanning source columns (unused)
17-18	0011-0012	828	033C	Basic integer address (for SYS, GOTO, etc.)
19	0013	22	16	Index to next available descriptor
20-21	0014-0015	19	13	Pointer to last string temporary
22-29	0016-001D	2	0002	Table of double-byte descriptions that point to variables (8 bytes)
30-31	001E-001F	16451	4043	Indirect index #1
32-33	0020-0021	26119	6607	Indirect index #2
34	0022	1	01	Pseudo-register for function operands (6 bytes)
35	0023	140	8C	
36	0024	0	00	
37	0025	0	00	
38	0026	0	00	
39	0027	0	00	

Table F-2. CBM Memory Map (Rev. 3 ROMs) (Continued)

Memory Address		Sample Value		Description
Decimal	Hexadecimal	Decimal	Hexadecimal	
				Data Storage Maintenance
40-41	0028-0029	1025	0401	Pointer to start of BASIC text
42-43	002A-002B	1920	0780	Pointer to start of variables
44-45	002C-002D	2032	07F0	Pointer to end of variables
46-47	002E-002F	2191	088F	Pointer to end of arrays
48-49	0030-0031	8192	2000	Pointer to start of strings (moving down)
50-51	0032-0033	8191	1FFF	Pointer to end of strings (top of available RAM)
52-53	0034-0035	8192	2000	Pointer to limit of BASIC memory
54-55	0036-0037	2000	07D0	Current line number. Loc. 55=2 if no program yet executed
56-57	0038-0039	110	006E	Previous line number
58-59	003A-003B	1897	0769	Pointer to next line to be executed (for CONT)
60-61	003C-003D	200	00C8	Line number of current DATA line
62-63	003E-003F	1855	073F	Pointer to current DATA item
				Expression Evaluation
64-65	0040-0041	514	0202	INPUT vector
66-67	0042-0043	89	0059	Current variable name.
68-69	0044-0045	2006	07D6	Pointer to current variable
70-71	0046-0047	2006	07D6	Pointer to current FOR. . . NEXT variable
72-73	0048-0049	1279	04FF	Pointer to current operator in ROM table
74	004A	0	00	Mask for current logical operator
75-76	004B-004C	62268	F33C	Pointer to user function FN definition
77-78	0040-004E	26531	67A3	Pointer to a string description
79	004F	243	F3	Length of string
80	0050	3	03	Constant used by garbage collection routine
81	0051	76	4C	Constant 6502 JMP instruction
82-83	0052-0053	0	00	Jump vector for functions
84-89	0054-0059	211	D3	Floating point accumulator #3 (6 bytes)
90-91	005A-005B	0	0000	Block transfer pointer #1
92-93	005C-005D	0	0000	Block transfer pointer #2
94-99	005E-0063			Floating point accumulator (FAC) #1 (6 bytes)
		0	00	94 005E Exponent +128
		0	00	95 005F Fraction MSB Floating Point
		0	00	96 0060 Fraction
		0	00	97 0061 Fraction MSB Integer
		0	00	98 0062 Fraction LSB
		0	00	99 0063 Sign of fraction (0 if zero or positive, --1 if negative)
100	0064	0	00	Copy of FAC #1 sign of fraction
101	0065	0	00	Counter for number of bits to shift to normalize FAC #1
102-107	0066-006B	0	00	Floating point accumulator #2 (6 bytes)
108	006C	0	00	Overflow byte for floating argument
109	006D	0	00	Copy of FAC #2 sign of fraction
110-111	006E-006F	258	0102	Conversion pointer

Table F-2. CBM Memory Map (Rev. 3 ROMs) (Continued)

Memory Address		Sample Value		Description
Decimal	Hexadecimal	Decimal	Hexadecimal	
				RAM Subroutines
112-135	0070-0087	230	E6	Routine to fetch next BASIC character
		173	AD	118 76 Entry to refetch current character
		1904	0770	119-120 77-78 Pointer into source text
136-140	0088-008C	128	80	Next random no. in storage and RND work area
				OS Page Zero Storage
141-143	008D-008F	398710	061576	24-hour clock incremented every 1/60 second (jiffy). Resets every 5,184,000 jiffies (24 hours). Stored in high to low order
144-145	0090-0091	58926	E62E	Hardware interrupt vector
146-147	0092-0093	64791	FD17	6502 BRK instruction interrupt vector
148-149	0094-0095	50057	C389	NMI interrupt vector
150	0096	0	00	Status word ST (1 byte)
151	0097	255	FF	Matrix coordinate of key depressed at current jiffy. 1-80=key, 255=no key
152	0098	0	00	Status of SHIFT key: 0=unshifted (up) 1=shifted (down)
153-154	0099-009A	65282	FF02	Correction factor for clock
155	009B	255	FF	Keyswitch PIA: STOP and RVS flags
156	009C	0	00	Timing constant buffer
157	009D	0	00	I/O flag: 0=LOAD 1=VERIFY
158	009E	0	00	Number of characters in keyboard buffer (0 to 9)
159	009F	0	00	Flag to indicate reverse field on (0=normal)
160	00A0	0	00	IEEE 488 output flag FF=character waiting
161	00A1	13	0D	Byte pointer to end of line for input
162	00A2	0	00	Utility
163-164	00A3-00A4	11, 13	0B, 0D	Cursor log (row, column)
165	00A5	63	3F	IEEE 488 output character buffer
166	00A6	255	FF	Key image
167	00A7	1	01	Flag for cursor enable: 0=Enable 1=Disable
168	00A8	17	11	Counter to flip cursor (20 to 1)
169	00A9	32	20	Copy of character at current cursor position
170	00AA	0	00	Flag for cursor on/off: 0=cursor moved 1=blink started
171	00AB	0	00	Flag for tape write
172	00AC	0	00	Flag for input source: 0=keyboard buffer 1=screen memory

Table F-2. CBM Memory Map (Rev. 3 ROMs) (Continued)

Memory Address		Sample Value		Description
Decimal	Hexadecimal	Decimal	Hexadecimal	
				OS Page Zero Storage (Continued)
173	00AD	0	00	I/O utility; X save flag
174	00AE	1	01	Number of open files (index into tables)
175	00AF	0	00	Default input device number (0=keyboard)
176	00B0	3	03	Default output device number (3=screen)
177	00B1	0	00	Tape parity byte
178	00B2	0	00	Flag for byte received
179	00B3	0	00	I/O utility
180	00B4	0	00	Tape buffer character
181	00B5	0	00	Byte pointer in filename transfer
182	00B6	0	00	I/O utility
183	00B7	0	00	Serial bit count
184	00B8	0	00	Tape utility
185	00B9	0	00	Cycle counter — flip for each bit read from tape
186	00BA	0	00	Countdown synchronization on tape write
187	00BB	0	00	Tape buffer 1 index to next character
188	00BC	0	00	Tape buffer 2 index to next character
189	00BD	0	00	Countdown synchronization on tape read
190	00BE	0	00	Flag to indicate bit/byte tape error
191	00BF	0	00	Flag to indicate tape error 0=first half-byte marker not written
192	00C0	0	00	Flag to indicate tape error 0=2nd half-byte marker not written
193	00C1	0	00	Tape dropout counter
194	00C2	0	00	Flag for cassette read current function 0=scan, 1-15=count, 40_{16}=load, 80_{16}=end
195	00C3	0	00	Checksum utility
196-197	00C4-00C5	33728	83CD	Pointer to start of line where cursor is flashing
198	00C6	0	00	Column position where cursor is flashing (0- 79)
199-200	00C7-00C8	33792	8400	Load start address; utility pointer
201-202	00C9-00CA	0	0000	Load end address
203-204	00CB-00CC	0	00	Tape timing constants
205	00CD	0	00	Flag for quote mode 0=not quote mode
206	00CE	0	00	Flag for tape read timer enable 0=disabled
207	00CF	0	00	Flag for EOT received from tape
208	00D0	0	00	Read character error
209	00D1	0	00	No. of characters in current file name
210	00D2	4	04	Current logical file number
211	00D3	255	FF	Current secondary address
212	00D4	4	04	Current device number
213	00D5	39	27	Current screen line length (39, 79)
214-215	00D6-00D7	0	0000	Pointer to start of current tape buffer (634 or 826)

Table F-2. CBM Memory Map (Rev. 3 ROMs) (Continued)

Memory Address		Sample Value		Description
Decimal	Hexadecimal	Decimal	Hexadecimal	
216	00D8	24	18	Line number where cursor is flashing (0-24)
217	00D9	10	0A	I/O storage: last key input, buffer checksum, bit buffer
218-219	00DA-00DB	0	0000	Pointer to current file name
220	00DC	0	00	Number of Insert keys pushed to go
221	00DD	0	00	Serial bit shift word
222	00DE	0	00	Number of blocks remaining to read/write
223	00DF	0	00	Serial word buffer
224-248	00E0-00F8			High byte of screen line addresses
		128	80	224-230=128 (lines 1-7)
		129	81	231-236=129 (lines 8-13)
		130	82	237-243=130 (lines 14-20)
		131	83	244-248=131 (lines 21-25)
249	00F9	0	00	Cassette #1 status switch
250	00FA	0	00	Cassette #2 status switch
251-252	00FB-00FC	54144	D380	Tape start address
253-255	00FD-00FF	243	F3	Utility
		Page 1 (256-511)		
256-up	0100-up	32	20	Tape read working storage (up to 511) and conversion storage
				256-318 For error correction in tape reads (62 bytes)
				256-266 Binary to ASCII conversion (11 bytes)
511-down	01FF-down	44	2C	Stack (down to 256)
		Page 2-3 (512-1023)		
512-592	0200-0250			BASIC input line buffer (80 bytes)
		12597	3135	512-513 0200-0201 Program Counter
		50	32	514 0202 Processor status
		0	00	515 0203 Accumulator
		171	AB	516 0204 X index
		0	00	517 0205 Y index
		0	00	518 0206 Stack pointer
		15104	3B00	519-520 0207-0208 User modifiable IRQ
593-602	0251-025A	4	04	Table of logical numbers of open files
603-612	025B-0264	4	04	Table of device numbers of open files
613-622	0265-026E	255	FF	Table of secondary address modes of open files
623-632	026F-0278	3	03	Keyboard buffer (10 bytes)
633	0279	28	1C	Keyboard utility
634-825	027A-0339	28	1C	Tape buffer for cassette #1 (192 bytes)
826-1017	033A-03F9	173	AD	Tape buffer for cassette #2 (192 bytes)
1018-1019	03FA-03FB	59383	E7F7	Vector for Machine Language Monitor
1020-1023	03FC-03FF	195	C3	Utility space/unused

Table F-2. CBM Memory Map (Rev. 3 ROMs) (Continued)

Memory Address		Sample Value		Description
Decimal	Hexadecimal	Decimal	Hexadecimal	
				OS Page Zero Storage (Continued)
				Page 4-128 (1024-32767)
1024-32767	0400-7FFF	0	00	User program area and Expansion RAM
				4K PET: 1024-4095 0400-0FFF
				User program area
				4096-32767 1000-7FFF
				Expansion RAM
				8K PET: 1024-8191 0400-1FFF
				User program area
				8192-32767 2000-7FFF
				Expansion RAM
				16K PET: 1024-16383 0400-3FFF
				User program area
				16384-32767 4000-7FFF
				Expansion RAM
				32K PET: 1024-32767 0400-7FFF
				User program area
				Page 129-144 (32768-36863)
32768-36863	8000-8FFF	32	20	TV RAM
				32768-33767 Display memory (1000 bytes)
				Page 145-192 (36864-49151)
36864-49151	9000-BFFF	144	90	Expansion ROM
				Page 193-232 BASIC (49152-59391)
				Pointers to BASIC Routines
49152-49153	C000-C001	51008	C740	Pointer ‒1 to END*
49154-49155	C002-C003	50775	C657	Pointer ‒1 to FOR
49156-49157	C004-C005	52255	CC1F	Pointer ‒1 to NEXT
49158-49159	C006-C007	51199	C7FF	Pointer ‒1 to DATA
49160-49161	C008-C009	51878	CAA6	Pointer ‒1 to INPUT#
49162-49163	C00A-C00B	51904	CAC0	Pointer ‒1 to INPUT
49164-49165	C00C-C00D	53090	CF62	Pointer ‒1 to DIM
49166-49167	C00E-C00F	51974	CB06	Pointer ‒1 to READ
49168-49169	C010-C011	51372	C8AC	Pointer ‒1 to LET
49170-49171	C012-C013	51116	C7AC	Pointer ‒1 to GOTO
49172-49173	C014-C015	51076	C784	Pointer ‒1 to RUN
49174-49175	C016-C017	51247	C82F	Pointer ‒1 to IF
49176-49177	C018-C019	50991	C72F	Pointer ‒1 to RESTORE
49178-49179	C01A-C01B	51087	C78F	Pointer ‒1 to GOSUB
49180-49181	C01C-C01D	51161	C7D9	Pointer ‒1 to RETURN
49182-49183	C01E-C01F	51266	C842	Pointer ‒1 to REM
49184-49185	C020-C021	51006	C73E	Pointer ‒1 to STOP
49186-49187	C022-C023	51282	C852	Pointer ‒1 to ON
49188-49189	C024-C025	55055	D70F	Pointer ‒1 to WAIT
49190-49191	C026-C027	65492	FFD4	Pointer ‒1 to LOAD
49192-49193	C028-C029	65495	FFD7	Pointer ‒1 to SAVE
49194-49195	C02A-C02B	65498	FFDA	Pointer ‒1 to VERIFY
49196-49197	C02C-C02D	53900	D28C	Pointer ‒1 to DEF
49198-49199	C02E-C02F	55046	D706	Pointer ‒1 to POKE
49200-49201	C030-C031	51594	C98A	Pointer ‒1 to PRINT#

* These memory locations contain the address of the byte preceding the specified BASIC routines

Table F-2. CBM Memory Map (Rev. 3 ROMs) (Continued)

Memory Address		Sample Value		Description
Decimal	**Hexadecimal**	**Decimal**	**Hexadecimal**	
				Pointers to BASIC Routines (Continued)
49202-49203	C032-C033	51626	C9AA	Pointer --1 to PRINT
49204-49205	C034-C035	51050	C76A	Pointer --1 to CONT
49206-49207	C036-C037	50612	C5B4	Pointer --1 to LIST
49208-49209	C038-C039	50550	C576	Pointer --1 to CLR
49210-49211	C03A-C03B	51600	C990	Pointer --1 to CMD
49212-49213	C03C-C03D	65501	FFDD	Pointer --1 to SYS
49214-49215	C03E-C03F	65471	FFBF	Pointer --1 to OPEN
49216-49217	C040-C041	65474	FFC2	Pointer --1 to CLOSE
49218-49219	C042-C043	51836	CA7C	Pointer --1 to GET
49220-49221	C044-C045	50522	C55A	Pointer --1 to NEW
49222-49223	C046-C047	56133	DB45	Pointer to SGN **
49224-49225	C048-C049	56280	DBD8	Pointer to INT
49226-49227	C04A-C04B	56164	DB64	Pointer to ABS
49228-49229	C04C-C04D	0	0000	Pointer to USR pointer
49230-49231	C04E-C04F	53849	D259	Pointer to FRE
49232-49233	C050-C051	53882	D27A	Pointer to POS
49234-49235	C052-C053	56926	DE5E	Pointer to SQR
49236-49237	C054-C055	57215	DF7F	Pointer to RND
49238-49239	C056-C057	55542	D8F6	Pointer to LOG
49240-49241	C058-C059	57050	DEDA	Pointer to EXP
49242-49243	C05A-C05B	57304	DFD8	Pointer to COS
49244-49245	C05C-C05D	57311	DFDF	Pointer to SIN
49246-49247	C05E-C05F	57384	E028	Pointer to TAN
49248-49249	C060-C061	57484	E08C	Pointer to ATN
49250-49251	C062-C063	55016	D6E8	Pointer to PEEK
49252-49253	C064-C065	54870	D656	Pointer to LEN
49254-49255	C066-C067	54079	D33F	Pointer to STR$
49256-49257	C068-C069	54919	D687	Pointer to VAL
49258-49259	C06A-C06B	54885	D664	Pointer to ASC
49260-49261	C06C-C06D	54726	D5C6	Pointer to CHR$
49262-49263	C06E-C06F	54746	D5DA	Pointer to LEFT$
49264-49265	C070-C071	54790	D606	Pointer to RIGHT$
49266-49267	C072-C073	54801	D611	Pointer to MID$
49268-49297	C074-C091			Hierarchy and action addresses for operators
49298-49553	C092-C191			Table of BASIC keywords
49554-49833	C192-C2A9			BASIC error messages
				BASIC Routines
				Starting Address **Function**
49834-59343	C2AA-DFFF			49834 C2AA FOR...NEXT stack check
				49880 C2D8 Insert line space marker
				49947 C31B Stack overflow check
				49960 C328 Error message abort
				50057 C389 READY
				50091 C3AB Handle new line

** These memory locations contain the address of the first byte of the specified BASIC routines.

Table F-2. CBM Memory Map (Rev. 3 ROMs) (Continued)

Memory Address		Sample Value		Description
Decimal	Hexadecimal	Decimal	Hexadecimal	
				BASIC Routines (Continued)
				Starting Address Function
				50242 C442 Rechain lines after insert/delete
				50287 C46F Input line
				50325 C495 Keyword encoder
				50476 C52C Line number search
				50523 C55B NEW
				50551 C577 CLR
				50599 C5A7 Set pointer to start of program
				50613 C5B5 LIST
				50776 C658 FOR
				50944 C700 Statement execute
				50992 C730 RESTORE
				51007 C73F STOP
				51009 C741 END
				51051 C76B CONT
				51077 C785 RUN
				51088 C790 GOSUB
				51117 C7AD GOTO
				51162 C7DA RETURN
				51200 C800 DATA
				51214 C80E Scan for next BASIC statement
				51217 C811 Scan for next BASIC line
				51248 C830 IF
				51267 C843 REM
				51283 C853 ON
				51315 C873 Number fetch
				51373 C8AD LET =
				51496 C928 Add ASCII digit to Accumulator #1
				51595 C98B PRINT#
				51601 C991 CMD
				51627 C9AB PRINT
				51740 CA1C Print string
				51769 CA39 Print character
				51791 CA4F Input data error
				51837 CA7D GET
				51879 CAA7 INPUT#
				51962 CAFA Input prompt
				51975 CB07 READ
				52220 CBFC Error messages
				52256 CC20 NEXT
				52345 CC79 Format checker
				52383 CC9F Expression evaluator
				53091 CF63 DIM
				53101 CF6D Variable table lookup
				53249 D001 Create new variable
				53420 D0AC Array table search/ create array

Table F-2. CBM Memory Map (Rev. 3 ROMs) (Continued)

Memory Address		Sample Value		Description
Decimal	Hexadecimal	Decimal	Hexadecimal	
				BASIC Routines (Continued)
				Starting Address Function
				53849 D259 FRE
				53869 D26D Integer-to-floating
				53882 D27A POS
				53888 D280 Valid direct check
				53901 D28D DEF
				54079 D33F STR$
				54726 D5C6 CHR$
				54746 D5DA LEFT$
				54790 D606 RIGHT$
				54801 D611 MID$
				54870 D656 LEN
				54885 D665 ASC
				54919 D687 VAL
				54994 D6D2 Floating-to-integer
				55016 D6E8 PEEK
				55047 D707 POKE
				55056 D710 WAIT
				55091 D733 Subtraction
				55150 D76E Addition
				55542 D8F6 LOG
				55607 D937 Multiplication
				55704 D998 Load number to AFAC
				55818 DA0A Division
				55982 DAAE Load Accumulator (FAC)
				56030 DADE Store FAC
				56072 DB08 Copy AFAC to FAC
				56088 DB18 Copy FAC to AFAC
				56133 DB45 SGN
				56164 DB64 ABS
				56280 DBD8 INT
				56526 DCCE IN line message
				56553 DCE9 Numeric-to-ASCII
				56319 DBFF String-to-floating
				56926 DE5E SQR
				56936 DE68 Power function
				57050 DEDA EXP
				57215 DF7F RND
				57304 DFD8 COS
				57311 DFDF SIN

Table F-2. CBM Memory Map (Rev. 3 ROMs) (Continued)

Memory Address		Sample Value		Description
Decimal	**Hexadecimal**	**Decimal**	**Hexadecimal**	
				Screen Editor
				Starting Address **Function**
57344-5391	E000-E7FF			57384 E028 TAN
				57484 E08C ATN
				57593 E0F9 Subroutine to be moved to
				page 0 ($70-$87)
				57617 E111 Initial RND seed (5 bytes)
				57622 E116 Initialize BASIC system
				57897 E229 Clear screen
				57943 E257 Home cursor
				57989 E285 Character fetch
58100-58906	E2F4-E61A			Video driver
				58100 E2F4 Input from screen
				58175 E33F Quote mode ($CD) switcher
				58188 E34C Print character
				58687 E53F Scroll 1 line
58907-59113	E61B-E6E9			Interrupt Handler
59114-59127	E6EA-E6F7			Keyboard Scan
59128-59241	E6F8-E769			Keyboard Encoding Table
59242-59391	E76A-E7FF			Subroutines for Machine Language Monitor
		Page 233-240 I/O Ports and Expansion I/O (PIA's and VIA) (59392-61439)		
				Keyboard PIA (59408-59411)
59408	E810	249	F9	I/O Port A and Data Direction register
59409	E811	60	3C	Control Register A — screen blanking
				52=Screen off (blanked)
				60=Screen on
59410	E812	255	FF	I/O Port B and Data Direction register
				255=all keys except:
				254=RVS key
				253=[key
				251=SPACE key
				247=< key
59411	E813	61	3D	Control Registers B — #1 cassette motor
				53=motor on
				61=motor off
				IEEE Port PIA (59424-59427)
59424	E820	255	FF	I/O Port A and Data Direction register
				PEEK (59424) reads input data
59425	E821	188	BC	Control Register A — set output line CA2
				POKE 59425,52=low
				POKE 59425,60=high
59426	E822	255	FF	I/O Port B and Data Direction registers
				POKE 59426, data writes output data
				POKE 59426,255 before a read to Port A
59427	E823	60	3C	Control Register B — set output line CB2
				POKE 59427,52=low
				POKE 59427,60=high

Table F-2. CBM Memory Map (Rev. 3 ROMs) (Continued)

Memory Address		Sample Value		Description
Decimal	Hexadecimal	Decimal	Hexadecimal	
				Parallel User Port VIA
				(59456-59471)
59456	E840	223	DF	I/O Port B
				207=#2 cassette motor on
				223=#2 cassette motor off
				WAIT 59456,23,23 waits for vertical retrace of display
				Bit 1=PB1 (NFRD on IEEE connector) output line
				Bit 3=PB3 (ATN on IEEE connector) output line
59457	E841	255	FF	I/O Port A with handshaking
59458	E842	30	1E	Data Direction register for I/O Port B
59459	E843	0	00	Data Direction register for I/O Port A
				For each bit 1=output, 0=input
				=0 all input
				=255 all output
59460-59461	E844-E845	29241	7239	(Low, high order) Read Timer 1, Counter; write to Timer 1 Latch and (high byte) initiate count
59462-59463	E846-E847	65535	FFFF	(Low, high order) Read Timer 1 Latch
59464	E848	147	93	Read Timer 2 Counter low byte and reset interrupt; write to Timer 2 low byte
				PEEK (59464) Clock decrements every microsecond
				POKE 59454,n sets SR rate of shift from high (n=0) to low (n=255) for music from User Port
59465	E849	217	D9	Read Timer 2 Counter high byte; write to Timer 2 high byte and reset interrupt
				PEEK (59465) Clock decrements every millisecond
59466	E84A	0	00	Serial I/O Shift register (SR)
				POKE 59466, 15 or 85 to generate Square wave output at CB2 for playing music from User Port.
59467	E84B	0	00	Auxiliary Control register
				=16 Sets SR to free-running mode for music from User Port
				=0 for proper operation of tape drive
59468	E84C	14	0E	Peripheral Control register
				=12 for graphics on shifted characters
				=14 for lower-case letters on shifted characters
59469	E84D	0	00	Interrupt Flag register
59470	E84E	128	80	Interrupt enable register
59471	E84F	255	FF	I/O Port A without handshaking
		Page 241-256 Operating System (61440-65535)		
61440-61621	F000-F0B5			Monitor messages

Table F-2. CBM Memory Map (Rev. 3 ROMs) (Continued)

Memory Address		Sample Value		Description
Decimal	Hexadecimal	Decimal	Hexadecimal	
				GPIB Handler (IEEE 488 Bus)
				Starting Address Function
61622-61904	F0B6-F1D0			61622 F0B6 Setup for Listen. Talk, etc.
				61678 F0EE Send character
				61736 F128 Output character
				immediate mode
				61750 F136 Error messages
				61796 F164 Send immediate
				Listen command,
				then secondary
				address
				61807 F16F Output characters
				61823 F17F Send Unlisten/
				Untalk
				61836 F18C Input character
				File Control
61905-63493	F1D1-F805			61905 F1D1 Get a character
				(without cursor)
				61921 F1E1 Input a character
				(with cursor)
				62002 F232 Output a character
				to any device
				62062 F26E Close all files
				62066 F272 Restore default I/O devices
				62121 F2A9 CLOSE
				62209 F301 STOP search
				62223 F30F STOP key
				62229 F315 Direct mode test
				62402 F3C2 LOAD
				62474 F40A Display filename/
				fetch file number
				62526 F43E Fetch LOAD/SAVE
				parameters
				62560 F460 Fetch byte paramter
				62566 F466 Send program name
				to GPIB
				62612 F494 Tape header search
				62647 F4B7 VERIFY
				62670 F4CE Fetch OPEN/CLOSE
				parameters
				62753 F521 OPEN
				62886 F5A6 Find any tape
				header
				62938 F5DA Write tape header
				63036 F63C Process tape header
				63108 F684 SYS
				63134 F69E SAVE
				63273 F729 Clock update
				63344 F770 Set input device
				63420 F7BC Set output device

Table F-2. CBM Memory Map (Rev. 3 ROMs) (Continued)

Memory Address		Sample Value		Description
Decimal	Hexadecimal	Decimal	Hexadecimal	
				Tape Control
63494-64720	F806-FCD0			63494 F806 Advance tape buffer pointer
				63541 F835 Gheck for cassette on
				63573 F855 Tape read to buffer
				63622 F886 Write block to tape
				63716 F8E6 Interrupt wait
				Power-on Diagnostics
64721-64784	FCD1-FD10			64721 FCD1 System reset SYS(64721) simulates power-on reset.
				64766 FCFE NMI interrupt entry point
64785-65471	FD11-FFBF			64769 FD01 Table of interrupt vectors
				Machine Language Monitor
				Jump Vectors
65472-65474	FFC0-FFC2	76 62753	4C F521	JMP OPEN
65475-65477	FFC3-FFC5	76 62121	4C F2A9	JMP CLOSE
65478-65480	FFC6-FFC8	76 63344	4C F770	JMP Set Input Device
65481-65483	FFC9-FFCB	76 63420	4C F7BC	JMP Set Output Device
65484-65486	FFCC-FFCE	76 62066	4C F272	JMP Restore Default I/O Devices
65487-65489	FFCF-FFD1	76 61921	4C F1E1	JMP Input Character — RDT
65490-65492	FFD2-FFD4	76 62002	4C F232	JMP Output Character — WRT
65493-65495	FFD5-FFD7	76 62402	4C F3C2	JMP LOAD
65496-65498	FFD8-FFDA	76 63134	4C F69E	JMP SAVE
65499-65501	FFDB-FFDD	76 62647	4C F4B7	JMP VERIFY
65502-65504	FFDE-FFED	76 63108	4C F684	JMP SYS
65505-65507	FFE1-FFE3	76 62223	4C F30F	JMP Test STOP Key
65508-65510	FFE4-FFE6	76 61905	4C F1D1	JMP Get Character
65511-65513	FFE7-FFE9	76 62062	4C F26E	JMP Close all files
65514-65516	FFEA-FFEC	76 63273	4C F729	JMP Clock Update
				6502 Interrupt Vectors
65530-65531	FFFA-FFFB	65766	FCFE	Non-maskable interrupt (NMI)
65532-65533	FFFC-FFFD	64721	FCDI	System reset (RESET)
65534-65535	FFFE-FFFF	58907	E61B	Interrupt request break (IRQ+BRK)

Table F-3. Hex Addresses and Label References: CBM BASICs

BASIC 3.0	BASIC 4.0	Labels	Description
0000	0000	USRPOK	$4C CONSTANT AND ADDRESS TO DISPATCH USR
0000	0000	ERRNF	ERROR CALL VALUE - ECV - NEXT WITHOUT FOR
0001	0001	ADDPRC	X
0002	0002	BUFPAG	INPUT BUFFER AT $0200
0002	0002	ADDPR2	X
0003	0003	STRSIZ	NUMBER OF LOCS PER STRING DESCRIPTOR
0003	0003	INTEGR	ONE-BYTE INTEGER FROM "QINT"
0003	0003	CHARAC	STARTING DELIMITER
0004	0004	ENDCHR	ENDING DELIMITER
0004	0004	ADDPR4	X
0005	0005	COUNT	GENERAL COUNTER FOR BASIC
0006	0006	DIMFLG	FLAG TO REMEMBER DIMENSIONED VARIABLES
0007	0007	VALTYP	FLAG FOR VARIABLE TYPE 0-NUMERIC $FF-STRING
0008	0008	INTFLG	FLAG FOR INTEGER TYPE
0008	0008	ADDPR8	X
0009	0009	GARBFL	X
0009	0009	DORES	FLAG WHETHER CAN OR CAN'T CRUNCH RESERVED WORDS
000A	000A	CLMWID	SIZE OF PRINT WINDOW
000A	000A	SUBFLG	FLAG WHICH ALLOWS SUBSCRIPTS IN SYNTAX
000B	000B	INPFLG	FLAGS INPUT OR READ
000C	000C	DOMASK	MASK USED BY RELATION OPERATIONS
000C	000C	TANSGN	FLAG SIGN OF TANGENT
000D	000D	DSDESC	DS$ LENGTH AND POINTER TO DS$
000E	0010	CHANNL	ACTIVE I/O CHANNEL #
0010	0010	ERRSN	ERROR CALL VALUE - ECV - SYNTAX
0011	0011	POKER	HOLDS ADDRESS FORE POKE COMMAND
0011	0011	LINNUM	LINE NUMBER STORAGE
0012	0012	FORSIZ	AMOUNT OF BYTES USED ON STACK FOR-NEXT
0013	0013	TEMPPT	INDEX TO NEXT AVAILABLE DESCRIPTOR
0014	0014	LASTPT	POINTER TO LAST STRING TEMP LO;HI
0016	0016	TEMPST	STORAGE FOR NUMTMP TEMP DESCRIPTORS
0016	0016	ERRRG	ECV - RETURN WITHOUT GOSUB
0017	0017	NUMLEV	NUMBER OF GOSUB LEVELS ALLOWED
001E	001E	NCMPOS	X
001F	001F	INDEX	INDRIECT INDEX #1
001F	001F	INDEX1	SAME
0021	0021	INDEX2	INDIRECT INDEX #2
0023	0023	RESHO	RES -REGISTER
0024	0024	RESMOH	[
0025	0025	ADDEND	TEMP USED BY "UMULT"
0025	0025	RESMO	[
0026	0026	RESLO	[
0028	0028	LINLEN	LENGTH OF SCREEN LINE 40-COL EDITORS
0028	0028	TXTTAB	POINTER TO START OF BASIC TEXT AREA
002A	002A	VARTAB	POINTER TO START OF VARIABLES
002A	002A	ERROD	ECV - OUT OF DATA
002C	002C	ARYTAB	POINTER TO START OF ARRAY TABLE
002E	002E	STREND	POINTER TO END OF VARIABLES
0030	0030	FRETOP	POINTER TO START OF REAL STRINGS
0032	0032	FRESPC	POINTER TO TOP OF FREE STRING SPACE
0034	0034	MEMSIZ	HIGHEST RAM ADDR AVAILIBLE FOR BASIC
0035	0035	ERRFC	ECV - ILLEGAL QUANTITY
0036	0036	CURLIN	CURRENT LINE BEING EXECUTED
0038	0038	OLDLIN	LAST LINE EXECUTED (FOR CONT COMMAND)
003A	003A	OLDTXT	OLD TXTPTR (FOR CONT COMMAND) AND TEMP STORAGE
003C	003C	DATLIN	DATA LINE # FOR ERRORS

Table F-3. Hex Addresses and Label References: CBM BASICs (Continued)

BASIC 3.0	BASIC 4.0	Labels	Description
003E	003E	DATPTR	DATA STATEMENT POINTER
0040	0040	INPPTR	SOURCE OF INPUT ADDRESS
0042	0042	VARNAM	CURRENT VARIABLE NAME
0044	0044	FDECPT	POINTER INTO POWERS OF TEN FOR FOUT
0044	0044	VARPNT	POINTER TO VARIABLE IN MEMORY
0045	0045	ERROV	ECV - OVERFLOW
0046	0046	LSTPNT	PNTR TO LIST STRING
0046	0046	ANDMSK	THEN MASK USED BY WAIT FOR ANDING
0046	0046	FORPNT	POINTER TO CURRENT FOR-NEXT VARIABLE REFERENCE
0047	0047	EORMSK	THE MASK FOR EORING IN WAIT
0048	0048	VARTXT	POINTER INTO LIST OF VARIABLES
0048	0048	OPPTR	POINTER TO CURRENT OPERATOR IN TABLE
004A	004A	OPMASK	MASK CREATED BY CURRENT OPERATOR
004B	004B	GRBPNT	POINTER USED IN GARBAGE COLLECTION
004B	004B	TEMPF3	A THIRD FAC TEMPORARY 4-BYTES
004B	004B	DEFPNT	POINTER USED IN FUNCTION DEFINITION
004D	004D	DSCPNT	POINTER TO A STRING DESCRIPTION
004D	004D	ERROM	ECV - OUT OF MEMORY
0050	0050	FOUR6	VARIABLE CONSTANT USED BY GARB COLLECT
0051	0051	BUFLEN	INPUT BUFFER MAX SIZE+1
0051	0051	JMPER	$4C CONSTANT AND ADDRESS USED TO DISPATCH FUNCS
0052	0052	SIZE	X
0053	0053	OLDOV	THE OLD OVERFLOW
0054	0054	TEMPF1	A FAC TEMP 4-BYTES
0055	0055	ARYPNT	A POINTER USED IN ARRAY BUILDING
0055	0055	HIGHDS	DESTINATION OF HIGHEST ELMENT IN BLT.
0057	0057	HIGHTR	SOURCE OF HIGHEST ELEMENT TO MOVE
0059	0059	TEMPF2	A FAC TEMP 4-BYTES
005A	005A	DECCNT	NUMBER OF PLACES BEFORE DECIMAL POINT
005A	005A	LOWDS	LOCATION OF LAST BYTE TRANSFERRED INTO
005A	005A	ERRUS	ECV - UNDEF'D STATEMENT
005B	005B	TENEXP	BASE TEN EXPONENT FOR FIN AND FOUT
005C	005C	GRBTOP	A POINTER USED IN GARBAGE COLLECTION
005C	005C	DPTFLG	FLAG IF A DECIMAL POINT HAS BEEN INPUT
005C	005C	LOWTR	LAST THING TO MOVE IN BLT.
005D	005D	EXPSGN	SIGN OF BASE TEN EXPONENT
005D	005D	EPSGN	X
005E	005E	DSCTMP	THIS IS WHERE TEMP DESCS ARE BUILT
005E	005E	FAC	THE MAIN FLOATING POINT ACCUMULATOR
005E	005E	FACEXP	THE EXPONENT BYTE
005F	005F	FACHO	[MOST SIGNIFICANT BYTE OF MANTISSA
0060	0060	FACMOH	[ONE MORE
0061	0061	INDICE	INDICE IS SET UP HERE BY "QINT"
0061	0061	FACMO	[MIDDLE ORDER OF MANTISSA
0062	0062	FACLO	[LEAST SIG BYTE OF MANTISSA
0063	0063	FACSGN	SIGN OF FAC (0 OR -1) WHEN UNPACKED
0064	0064	DEGREE	A CONT USED BY POLYNOMIALS
0064	0064	SGNFLG	SIGN OF FAC IS PRESERVED HERE BY FIN
0065	0065	BITS	COUNTER FOR # OF BIT SHIFTS TO NORMALIZE FAC
0066	0066	ARGEXP	THE ARG REGISTER EXPONENT
0067	0067	ARGHO	[
0068	0068	ARGMOH	[
0069	0069	ARGMO	[
006A	006A	ARGLO	[
006B	006B	ARGSGN	THE SIGN (SAME AS FAC)
006B	006B	ERRBS	ECV - BAD SUBSCRIPT

Table F-3. Hex Addresses and Label References: CBM BASICs (Continued)

BASIC 3.0	BASIC 4.0	Labels	Description
006C	006C	STRNG1	POINTER TO A STRING OR DESCRIPTOR
006C	006C	ARISGN	A SIGN REFLECTING THE RESULT
006D	006D	FACOV	OVERFLOW BYTE OF THE FAC
006E	006E	BUFPTR	POINTER TO BUF USED BY "CRUNCH ROUTINE"
006E	006E	STRNG2	POINTER TO STRING OR DESC.
006E	006E	POLYPT	POINTER INTO POLYNOMIAL COEFFICIENTS.
006E	006E	CURTOL	ABSOLUTE LINEAR INDEX IS FORMED HERE
006E	006E	FBUFPT	POINTER INTO FBUFFER USED IN FOUT.
0070	0070	CHRGET	ROUTINE — GETS NEXT CHARACTER FROM BASIC TEXT
0076	0076	CHRGOT	ROUTINE —REGETS CURRENT CHARACTER FROM BASIC TEXT
0077	0077	TXTPTR	POINTER TO CURRENT SOURCE TEXT
0078	0078	ERRDD	ECV — REDIM'D ARRAY
007D	007D	GNUM	LABEL IN CHRGET
0080	0080	ENDTK	TOKEN — END
0081	0081	FORTK	TOKEN — FOR
0083	0083	DATATK	TOKEN — DATA
0085	0085	ERRDVO	ECV — DIVISION BY ZERO
0087	0087	CHRRTS	LABEL IN CHRGET
0088	0088	RNDX	NEXT RANDOM NUMBER — INITIAL LOAD FROM ROM
0089	0089	GOTOTK	TOKEN — GOTO
008B	008B	ZZ7	X
008D	008D	CTIMR	24 HR CLOCK 1/60 OF SEC
008D	008D	GOSUTK	TOKEN — GOSUB
008F	008F	REMTK	TOKEN — REM
0095	0095	ERRID	ECV — ILLEGAL DIRECT
0096	0096	CSTAT	I/O OPERATION STATUS BYTE (VARIABLE ST)
0099	0099	PRINTK	TOKEN — PRINT
00A2	00A2	SCRATK	TOKEN — NEW
00A3	00A3	TABTK	TOKEN — TAB
00A3	00A3	ERRTM	ECV — TYPE MISMATCH
00A4	00A4	TOTK	TOKEN — TO
00A5	00A5	FNTK	TOKEN — FN
00A6	00A6	SPCTK	TOKEN — SPC
00A7	00A7	THENTK	TOKEN — THEN
00A8	00A8	NOTTK	TOKEN — NOT
00A9	00A9	STEPTK	TOKEN — STEP
00AA	00AA	PLUSTK	TOKEN — +
00AB	00AB	MINUTK	TOKEN — −
00B0	00B0	ERRLS	ECV — STRING TO LONG
00B1	00B1	GREATK	TOKEN — >
00B2	00B2	EQULTK	TOKEN — =
00B3	00B3	LESSTK	TOKEN — <
00B4	00B4	ONEFUN	TOKEN — SGN START OF SINGLE PARM FUNCTIONS
00BF	00BF	ERRBD	ECV — FILE DATA
00C6	00C6	TRMPOS	X
00C7	00C7	LASNUM	TOKEN — CHR$ LAST FUNC WITH ARITHMETIC PARMS
00C8	00C8	ERRST	ECV — FORMULA TOO COMPLEX
00CB	00CB	GOTK	TOKEN — GO (GO TO)
00DB	00DB	ERRCN	ECV — CAN'T CONTINUE
00E9	00E9	ERRUF	ECV — UNDEF'D FUNCTION
00FF	00FF	PI	VALUE OF PI SYMBOL
00FF	00FF	LOFBUF	START OF FOUT STRING FOR STRD AND TI$
0100	0100	FBUFFR	FOUT BUFFER HOLDS ASCII STRING FOR OUTPUT
01FB	01FB	STKEND	TOP OF STACK FOR BASIC
01FF	01FF	ZZ1	X
01FF	01FF	ZZ5	X

Table F-3. Hex Addresses and Label References: CBM BASICs (Continued)

BASIC 3.0	BASIC 4.0	Labels	Description
01FF	01FF	ZZ4	X
0200	0200	BUF	BASIC INPUT BUFFER (80 CHARACTERS-BYTES LONG)
0200	0200	BUFOFS	SAME AS ABOVE
0201	0201	ZZ2	X
0202	0202	ZZ3	X
0400	0400	RAMLOC	BEGINNING OF RAM AVALIABLE FOR BASIC TEXT
0000	8000	OFFSET	*VALUE USED IN ASSEMBLY – ROM VERSION
0000	8BB8	ZZ8	X
C000	B000	ROMLOC	BEGINNING OF BASIC ROMS –V2=$C000 V4=$B000
C000	B000	STMDSP	START OF COMMAND DISPATCH TABLE
C046	B066	FUNDSP	START OF FUNCTION DISPATCH TABLE
C04C	B06C	USRLOC	X
C074	B094	OPTAB	START OF MATH OPERATORS DISPATCH TABLE
C089	B0A9	NEGTAB	UNITARY NEGATE DISPATCH (.BYTE 125,DISPATCH)
C08C	B0AC	NOTTAB	NOT OPERATOR DISPATCH (.BYTE 90,DISPATCH)
C08F	B0AF	PTDORL	COMPARISON DISPATCH (.BYTE 100,DISPATCH)
C092	B0B2	RESLST	START OF RESERVED WORD LIST (ASCII,END(OR $80))
C192	B20D	ERRTAB	START OF BASIC ERROR MESSAGE STORAGE
C28B	B306	ERR	MESSAGE – "ERROR"
C292	B30D	INTXT	MESSAGE – "IN"
C297	B312	REDDY	MESSAGE – "READY"
C2A2	B31B	BRKTXT	MESSAGE – "BREAK"
C2AA	B322	FNDFOR	PEEKS AT THE STACK FOR AN ACRTIVE "FOR" LOOP
C2AF	B327	FFLOOP	X
C2C4	B33C	CMPFOR	X
C2D0	B348	ADDFRS	X
C2D7	B34F	FFRTS	X
C2D8	B350	BLTU	"OPENS UP" A SPACE IN BASIC FOR A NEW LINE
C2DF	B357	BLTUC	X
C2FC	B374	BLT1	X
C308	B380	BLTLP	X
C30C	B384	MOREN1	X
C313	B38B	DECBLT	X
C31B	B393	GETSTK	TEST FOR STACK-TOO-DEEP ERROR
C328	B3A0	REASON	CHECKS FOR AVALIABLE MEMORY SPACE
C332	B3AA	TRYMOR	X
C336	B3AE	REASAV	X
C341	B3B9	REASTO	X
C354	B3CC	REARTS	X
C355	B3CD	OMERR	OUT OF MEMORY ERROR VECTOR
C357	B3CF	ERROR	ERROR HANDLER (ERROR TYPE IN .X)
C364	B3DA	ERRCRD	X
C36A	B3E0	GETERR	X
0000	B3ED	TYPERR	PRINTS OUT THE ERROR MESSAGE
C37E	B3F4	ERRFIN	X
C389	B3FF	READY	PRINTS "READY." GOES INTO MAIN BASIC LOOP (← NMI)
C392	B406	MAIN	MAIN BASIC LOOP, ANALYZES INPUT LINES
C3AB	B41F	MAIN1	LINES THAT START WITH A NUMBER HANDLED HERE
C3E6	B45A	QDECT1	X
C3EE	B462	MLOOP	X
C3FC	B470	NODEL	X
C417	B48B	NODELC	X
C431	B4A5	STOLOP	X
C439	B4AD	FINI	CLEANS BASIC SYSTEM UP; CLR
C442	B4B6	LNKPRG	RELINKS BASIC STATEMENTS IN TEXT AREA
C44B	B4BF	CHEAD	X

Table F-3. Hex Addresses and Label References: CBM BASICs (Continued)

BASIC 3.0	BASIC 4.0	Labels	Description
C453	B4C7	CZLOOP	X
C46E	B4E1	LNKRTS	X
C46F	B4E2	INLIN	INPUT A LINE OF INFORMATION INTO BUF (MAX 80 CHARS)
C471	B4E4	INLINC	X
C47E	B4F8	FININ1	X
C495	B4FB	CRUNCH	LOOKS UP KEYWORDS IN AN INPUT LINE
C49B	B501	KLOOP	X
C4A7	B50D	CMPSPC	X
C4BD	B523	KLOOP1	X
C4C5	B52B	MUSTCR	X
C4CF	B53D	RESER	X
C4D1	B544	RESCON	X
C4E0	B552	GETBPT	X
C4E2	B554	STUFFH	X
C4F5	B567	COLIS	X
C4F7	B569	NODATT	X
C4FE	B570	STR1	X
C507	B579	STRNG	X
C50E	B580	NTHIS	X
C512	B584	NTHIS1	X
0000	B58D	NTHIS2	X
C522	B599	CRDONE	X
C52C	B5A3	FNDLIN	SEARCHES FOR A LINE NUMBER (NUMBER IN LINNUM)
C530	B5A7	FNDLNC	X
C547	B5BE	FNDLO1	X
C550	B5C7	AFFRTS	X
C559	B5D0	FLINRT	X
C55A	B5D1	FLNRTS	X
C55B	B5D2	SCRATH	IMPLEMENTS "NEW" COMMAND – CLEARS EVERY THING
C55D	B5D4	SCRTCH	X
C572	B5E9	RUNC	X
C577	B5EE	CLEAR	CLR – ROUTINE
C579	B5F0	CLEARC	X
0000	B60B	FLOAD	X
C593	B60E	STKINI	X
C5A6	B621	STKRTS	X
C5A7	B622	STXTPT	TXTPTR=TXTTAB–1
C5B5	B630	LIST	ROUTINE – LIST
C5BD	B638	GOLST	X
C5D4	B64F	LSTEND	X
C5E2	B65D	LIST4	X
C5FF	B67A	TSTDUN	X
C601	B67C	TYPLIN	X
C608	B683	PRIT4	X
C60C	B687	PLOOP	X
C619	B694	PLOOP1	X
C62D	B6A8	GRODY	X
C630	B6AB	QPLOP	X
C642	B6C5	RESRCH	X
C645	B6C8	RESCR1	X
0000	B6CE	RESCR2	X
C64D	B6D4	PRIT3	X
0000	B6D5	,PRIT3B	X
C658	B6DE	FOR	ROUTINE – FOR
C669	B6EF	NOTOL	X
C6A1	B727	LDFONE	X

Table F-3. Hex Addresses and Label References: CBM BASICs (Continued)

BASIC 3.0	BASIC 4.0	Labels	Description
C6B5	B73B	ONEON	X
C6C4	B74A	NEWSTT	MAIN STATEMENT DISPATCH LOOP (DO NEXT STATEMENT)
C6D4	B759	DIRCON	X
C6E4	B769	DIRCN1	X
C6F7	B77C	GONE	DISPATCHES NEXT BYTE CHRGET RETURNS
C700	B785	GONE3	DISPATCHES .A IF NONZERO ELSE LOOP TO NEWSTT
C702	B787	GONE2	X
0000	B795	GONE4	X
C717	B7A2	GLET	X
C71A	B7A5	MORSTS	X
C71E	B7A9	SNERR1	SYNTAX ERROR VECTOR
0000	B7AC	GO	HANDLE GO TOKEN CASE (FIND A TO)
C730	B7B7	RESTOR	ROUTINE - RESTORE
C73A	B7C1	RESFIN	X
C73E	B7C5	ISCRTS	X
C73F	B7C6	STOP	STOP - SEC END - CLC
C741	B7C8	END	ROUTINE - END
C742	B7C9	STOPC	ROUTINE - STOP
C751	B7D8	STPEND	X
C759	B7E0	DIRIS	X
C75B	B7E2	ENDCON	X
C768	B7EB	GORDY	JMP READY
C76B	B7EE	CONT	ROUTINE - CONT
C784	B807	CONTRT	X
C785	B808	RUN	ROUTINE - RUN
C790	B813	GOSUB	ROUTINE - GOSUB
C7A4	B827	RUNC2	X
C7AD	B830	GOTO	ROUTINE - GOTO
C7C4	B847	LUK4IT	X
C7C8	B84B	LUKALL	X
C7D9	B85C	GORTS	X
C7DA	B85D	RETURN	ROUTINE - RETURN
C7EB	B86E	USERR	BAD SUBSCRIPT ERROR VECTOR
C7F0	B873	SNERR2	SYNTAX ERROR VECTORY
C7F3	B876	RETU1	X
C800	B883	DATA	X
C803	B886	ADDON	X
C80D	B890	REMRTS	X
C80E	B891	DATAN	SEARCH FOR NEXT '
C811	B894	REMN	LOOK FOR EOL($00) (TXTPTR OFFSET IN .Y)
C819	B89C	EXCHQT	X
C821	B8A4	REMER	X
C830	B8B3	IF	ROUTINE - IF
C83F	B8C2	OKGOTO	X
C843	B8C6	REM	ROUTINE - REM
C848	B8CB	DOCOND	X
C850	B8D3	DOCO	X
C853	B8D6	ONGOTO	ROUTINE - ON (GOTO OR GOSUB)
C85B	B8DE	SNERR3	SYNTAX ERROR VECTOR
C85F	B8E2	ONGLOP	X
C867	B8EA	ONGLP1	X
C872	B8F5	ONGRTS	X
C873	B8F6	LINGET	INPUT A BASIC LINE NUMBER (0-63999)(VALUE IN LINNUM)
C879	B8FC	MORLIN	X
C8A7	B92A	NXTLGC	X
C8AD	B930	LET	ROUTINE - LET

Table F-3. Hex Addresses and Label References: CBM BASICs (Continued)

BASIC 3.0	BASIC 4.0	Labels	Description
C8CA	B94D	QINTGR	X
C8DE	B961	COPFLT	X
C8E1	B964	COPSTR	X
C8E2	B965	INPCOM	X
C8F5	B978	TIMELP	X
C90F	B992	NOML6	X
C91F	B9A2	TIMEST	X
C928	B9AB	TIMNUM	X
C92F	B9B2	FCERR2	ILLEGAL QUANITY ERROR VECTOR
C932	B9B5	GOTNUM	X
C937	B9BA	GETSPT	COPY STRINGS IF NEEDED
0000	B9BE	DSKX0	X
0000	B9D2	DSKX1	X
0000	B9D4	DSKX2	X
C948	B9E1	QVARIA	X
C956	B9EF	DNTCPY	X
C95D	B9F6	COPY	X
C973	BA13	COPYC	X
0000	BA2E	COPY00	X
0000	BA44	COPY01	X
0000	BA46	COPY02	X
0000	BA4E	STRADJ	POINT TO STRING FOR A COPY
0000	BA6C	ADJ	X
0000	BA70	ADJXX	X
0000	BA74	ADJ02	X
0000	BA83	ADJ00	X
0000	BA85	ADJ01	X
C98B	BA88	PRINTN	ROUTINE - PRINT#
C991	BA8E	CMD	ROUTINE - CMD
C99B	BA98	SAVEIT	X
C9A5	BAA2	STRDON	X
C9A8	BAA5	NEWCHR	X
C9AB	BAA8	PRINT	ROUTINE - PRINT
C9AD	BAAA	PRINTC	X
C9D5	BAD2	FININL	X
C9E2	BADF	CRDO	OUTPUT A CARRIAGE RETURN
C9EC	BAED	CRFIN	X
C9EE	BAEF	PRTRTS	X
C9EF	BAF0	COMPRT	X
C9F2	BAF3	MORCO1	X
C9FC	BAFD	TABER	TAB AND SPC HANDLER
CA0C	BB0D	ASPAC	X
CA0D	BB0E	XSPAC	X
CA0E	BB0F	XSPAC2	X
CA11	BB12	NOTABR	X
CA17	BB18	XSPAC1	X
CA1C	BB1D	STROUT	PRINT STRING FROM ADDRESS IN .Y AND .A
CA1F	BB20	STRPRT	PRINT STRING POINTED TO BY INDEX
CA26	BB27	STRPR2	X
CA39	BB3A	OUTSPC	OUTPUT A SPACE
CA40	BB41	CRTSKP	OUTPUT A $1D
CA43	BB44	OUTQST	OUTPUT A ?
CA45	BB46	OUTDO	OUTPUT THE CHAR IN .A
CA4C	BB49	OUTRTS	X
CA4F	BB4C	TRMNOK	HANDLES BAD INPUT DATA
CA59	BB56	GETDTL	X

Table F-3. Hex Addresses and Label References: CBM BASICs (Continued)

BASIC 3.0	BASIC 4.0	Labels	Description
CA5D	BB5A	STCURL	X
CA61	BB5E	SNERR4	SYNTAX ERROR VECTOR
CA64	BB61	TRMNO1	X
CA6D	BB6A	DOAGIN	X
CA7D	BB7A	GET	ROUTINE - GET OR GET#
CA94	BB91	GETTTY	X
CAA7	BBA4	INPUTN	ROUTINE - INPUT#
CAB7	BBB4	IODONE	RESTORE INPUT TO KEYBOARD
CAB9	BBB6	IORELE	X
CAC1	BBBE	INPUT	ROUTINE - INPUT
CAD2	BBCD	NOTQTI	X
CADA	BBD5	GETAGN	X
CAED	BBE8	BUFFUL	X
0000	BBF1	PTHRTI	X
CAFA	BBF5	QINLIN	PROMPTS AND RECEIVES THE INPUT
CB04	BBFF	GINLIN	X
CB07	BC02	READ	ROUTINE - READ
CB0E	BC09	INPCON	X
CB10	BC0B	INPCO1	X
CB16	BC11	INLOOP	X
CB42	BC3D	QDATA	X
CB4B	BC46	GETNTH	X
CB4E	BC49	DATBK	X
CB52	BC4D	DATBK1	X
CB66	BC61	SETQUT	X
CB72	BC6D	RESETC	X
CB73	BC6E	NOWGET	X
CB7E	BC79	NOWGE1	X
CB8A	BC85	NUMINS	X
CB92	BC8D	STRDN2	X
CB9E	BC99	TRMOK	X
CBB9	BCB4	DATLOP	X
CBD2	BCCD	NOWLIN.	X
CBDF	BCDA	VAREND	X
CBEA	BCE5	VARY0	PRINT "EXTRA IGNORED " IF KEYBOARD AND A SEPERATOR
CBFB	BCF6	INPRTS	X
CBFC	BCF7	EXIGNT	MESSAGE - EXTRA IGNORED
CC0D	BD07	TRYAGN	MESSAGE - ?REDO FROM START
CC20	BD19	NEXT	ROUTINE - NEXT
CC26	BD1F	GETFOR	X
CC29	BD22	STXFOR	X
CC34	BD2D	ERRGO5	X
CC36	BD2F	HAVFOR	X
CC76	BD6F	NEWSGO	X
CC79	BD72	LOOPDN	CHECKS DATA FORMAT
CC8B	BD84	FRMNUM	JMP FRMEVL
CC8E	BD87	CHKNUM	CHECK THAT CURRENT TYPE IS NUMERIC
CC90	BD89	CHKSTR	CHECK THAT CURRENT TYPE IS STRING (CHKS VALTYP)
CC91	BD8A	CHKVAL	X
CC97	BD90	CHKOK	X
CC98	BD91	DOCSTR	X
CC9A	BD93	CHKERR	TYPE MISMATCH ERROR VECTOR
CC9C	BD95	ERRGO4	X
CC9F	BD98	FRMEVL	FORMULA EVALUATOR - EVALUATES ALL FORMULAS
CCA5	BD9E	FRMEV1	X
CCAA	BDA3	LPOPER	X

Table F-3. Hex Addresses and Label References: CBM BASICs (Continued)

BASIC 3.0	BASIC 4.0	Labels	Description
CCB9	BDB2	TSTOP	X
CCBC	BDB5	LOPREL	X
CCD8	BDD1	ENDREL	X
CCF1	BDEA	QPREC	X
CCFA	BDF3	DOPREC	X
CCFB	BDF4	NEGPRC	X
CD08	BE01	FINREL	X
CD12	BE0B	FINRE2	X
CD1A	BE13	QPREC1	X
CD21	BE1A	DOPRE1	PUSHES A PARTIAL EVALUATION ON THE STACK
CD31	BE2A	SNERRS	SYNTAX ERROR VECTOR
CD34	BE2D	PUSHF1	X
CD39	BE32	PUSHF	X
CD44	BE41	FORPSH	X
CD59	BE56	QOP	X
CD5C	BE59	QOPGO	X
CD5E	BE5B	QCHNUM	X
CD65	BE62	UNPSTK	X
CD67	BE64	PULSTK	RESTORE ARG FROM STACK (PUSHED EVALUATION)
CD81	BE7E	QOPRTS	X
CD83	BE80	UNPRTS	X
CD84	BE81	EVAL	EVALUATES NUMERIC FORMULAS
CD88	BE85	EVAL0	X
CD8D	BE8A	EVAL1	X
CD90	BE8D	EVAL2	X
CDA3	BEA0	PIVAL	STORAGE — THE BINARY.VALUE OF PI
CDA8	BEA5	QDOT	X
CDB8	BEB5	STRTXT	IMMEDIATE STRINGS HANDLER
CDC1	BEBE	STRTX2	X
CDC7	BEC4	EVAL3	X
CDCF	BECC	NOTOP	EVAL — NOT
CDDE	BEDB	EVAL4	X
CDEC	BEE9	PARCHK	EVALUATE A FUNCTION WITHIN ()'S (FRMEVL)
CDF2	BEEF	CHKCLS	CHECK FOR RIGHT PARENTHESIS)
CDF5	BEF2	CHKOPN	CHECK FOR LEFT PARENTHESIS (
CDF8	BEF5	CHKCOM	CHECK FOR A COMMA
CDFA	BEF7	SYNCHR	COMPARE TXTPTR AGAINST .A IF <> THEN...
CE03	BF00	SNERR	...SYNTAX ERROR VECTOR
CE08	BF05	DOMIN	SET UP FUNCTION FOR FUTURE EVALUATION
CE0A	BF07	GONPRC	X
0000	BF0C	CKSMB0	THE CHECKSUM BYTE FOR THE $B000 ROM
0000	BF0D	ISVJMP	JMP ISVAR
0000	BF10	PABB0	PATCHES
0000	BF10	PATCHG	P
0000	BF1D	PCTH0	P
0000	BF1E	PCTH1	P
0000	BF21	PATCHH	P
0000	BF2E	PATCHI	P
CE0F	BF8C	ISVAR	SET UP A VARIABLE NAME SEARCH
CE11	BF8E	ZZ6	X
CE12	BF8F	ISVRET	X
0000	BFC1	ISVDS	DS$ TEST AND HANDLER
CE42	BFD3	STRRTS	X
CE43	BFD4	G000	X
CE54	BFE5	G00000	X
0000	BFFC	CHKDS	CHECK FOR A DS VARIABLE

Table F-3. Hex Addresses and Label References: CBM BASICs (Continued)

BASIC 3.0	BASIC 4.0	Labels	Description
CE69	C003	GETTIM	ASSIGN TIME TO TI
CE75	C00F	QSTATV	X
0000	C01C	QDSAV	X
CE82	C040	GOMOVF	X
CE89	C047	ISFUN	DISPATCH AND EVAL IF IT'S A FUNCTION
CEB3	C071	OKNORM	X
CEB8	C076	FINGO	PLACE FUNCTIONS DISPATCH ADDRESS IN JUMPER AND GO
CEC8	C086	OROP	EVAL - OR
CECB	C089	ANDOP	EVAL - AND
CEF8	C0B6	DOREL	DO COMPARISONS
CF10	C0CE	STRCMP	X
CF38	C0F6	STASGN	X
CF3D	C0FB	NXTCMP	X
CF43	C101	QCOMP	X
CF48	C106	GETCMP	X
CF54	C112	DOCMP	X
CF5D	C11B	GOFLOT	X
CF60	C11E	DIM3	MULTIPLE DIM RE-ENTRY (CHKS FOR A COMMA)
CF63	C121	DIM	ROUTINE - DIM
CF6D	C12B	PTRGET	SEARCHES FOR A BASIC VARIABLE
CF72	C130	PTRGT1	X
CF74	C132	PTRGT2	X
CF7E	C13C	INTERR	SYNTAX ERROR VECTOR
CF81	C13F	PTRGT3	X
CF91	C14F	ISSEC	X
CF92	C150	EATEM	X
CF9C	C15A	NOSEC	X
CFA6	C164	NOTSTR	X
CFB6	C174	TURNON	X
CFBD	C17B	STRNAM	X
CFD3	C18F	STXFND	X
CFD5	C191	LOPFND	X
CFDF	C19B	LOPFN	X
0000	C1AB	NXTPTR	MOVE SEARCH TO NEXT TABLE ENTRY
CFED	C1AC	NOTIT	X
CFF7	C1B6	ISLETC	X
D000	C1BF	ISLRTS	X
D001	C1C0	NOTFNS	DID NOT FIND VARIABLE - CREATE A NEW ONE
D007	C1C6	LDZR	X
D00C	C1CB	NOTEVL	X
D01C	C1DB	GOBADV	X
D01F	C1DE	QSTAVR	CHECK FOR ST CASE
0000	C1E6	QDSVAR	CHECK FOR DS CASE
D027	C1F2	VAROK	GOOD USABLE VARIABLE
D03D	C208	NOTEVE	X
D448	C21C	ARYVA2	X
D44C	C220	ARYVA3	X
D457	C228	ARYVGO	SEARCH THE ARRAYS
D488	C259	ARYGET	MOVE THRU THE ARRAY TABLES
D492	C263	GOGO	X
0000	C281	GOGO1	X
D4D0	C290	DVARTS	X
0000	C29D	ARYDON	X
D069	C2B9	FINPTR	LOGS BASIC VARIABLE LOCATION
D073	C2C3	FINNOW	X
D078	C2C8	FMAPTR	ARRAY POINTER SUBROUTINE

Table F-3. Hex Addresses and Label References: CBM BASICs (Continued)

BASIC 3.0	BASIC 4.0	Labels	Description
D084	C2D4	JSRGM	X
D089	C2D9	N32768	STORAGE — THEN BINARY VALUE -32768
D08D	C2DD	INTIDX	EVALUATE FORMULA RESULT IS POSITIVE INTEGER VALUE
D093	C2E3	POSINT	CONVERT FLOATING BINARY TO POSITVE INTEGER
D09A	C2EA	AYINT	CONVERT FLOATING BINARY TO INTEGER
D0A7	C2F7	NONONO	ILLEGAL QUANITY ERROR VECTOR
D0A9	C2F9	QINTGO	JMP QINT
D0AC	C2FC	ISARY	LOCATES AND/OR CREATES ARRAYS
D0B6	C306	INDLOP	X
D0F7	C347	LOPFDA	X
D103	C353	LOPFDV	X
D112	C362	NMARY1	X
D120	C370	BSERR	BAD SUBSCRIPT ERROR VECTOR
D123	C373	FCERR	ILLEGAL QUANITY ERROR VECTOR
D125	C375	ERRGO3	X
D128	C378	GOTARY	X
D13C	C38C	NOTFDD	X
D150	C39F	NOTFLT	X
D159	C3A8	STOMLT	X
D162	C3B1	LOPPTA	X
D172	C3C1	NOTDIM	X
D195	C3E4	GREASE	X
D1A4	C3F3	ZERITA	X
D1A9	C3F8	DECCUR	X
D1C6	C415	GETDEF	X
D1CE	C41D	INLPNM	X
D1E4	C433	BSERR7	SYNTAX ERROR VECTOR
D1E7	C436	OMERR1	OUT OF MEMORY ERROR VECTOR
D1EA	C439	INLPN2	X
D1EB	C43A	INLPN1	X
D1FC	C44B	ADDIND	X
D20D	C45C	NOTFL1	X
D213	C462	STOML1	X
D227	C476	DIMRTS	X
D228	C477	UMULT	INTEGER ARITHMETIC ROUTINES FOR MULTI-DIM ARRAYS
D231	C480	UMULTD	X
D23B	C48A	UMULTC	X
D254	C4A3	UMLCNT	X
D258	C4A7	UMLRTS	X
D259	C4A8	FRE	ROUTINE — FRE(X)
D260	C4AF	NOFREF	X
D26D	C4BC	GIVAYF	CONVERTS INTEGER TO FLOATING BINARY
D27A	C4C9	POS	ROUTINE — POS(X)
D27C	C4CB	SNGFLT	X
D280	C4CF	ERRDIR	IF COMMAND TYPE IS INDIRECT ONLY — ILLEGAL DIRECT
D288	C4D7	ERRGUF	UNDEFINED FUNCTION ERROR VECTOR
D28D	C4DC	DEF	ROUTINE — DEF FN()=
D2BB	C50A	GETFNM	X
D2CE	C51D	FNDOER	EVALUATES FN() IN FORMULAS
D2F2	C541	DEFSTF	X
D329	C578	DEFFIN	X
D33F	C58E	STRD	ROUTINE — STR$
D349	C598	TIMSTR	MAKE A STRING OUT OF INFO AT $01FF
D34F	C59E	STRINI	MAKE A STRING OUT OF (FACMO POINTER)
D357	C5A6	STRSPA	X
D361	C5B0	STRLIT	SCANS AND SETS UP STRING ELEMENTS

Table F-3. Hex Addresses and Label References: CBM BASICs (Continued)

BASIC 3.0	BASIC 4.0	Labels	Description
D367	C5B6	STRLT2	X
D371	C5C0	STRGET	X
D37E	C5CD	STRFIN	X
D382	C5D1	STRFI1	X
D383	C5D2	STRFI2	X
D38F	C5DE	STRST2	X
D399	C5E8	STRCP	X
D3A4	C5F3	PUTNEW	CHECK STRING TEMPS PLACE DATA IN TEMPS
D3AC	C5FB	ERRGO2	X
D3AF	C5FE	PUTNW1	X
D3CE	C61D	GETSPA	BUILDS STRING VECTORS
D3D0	C61F	TRYAG2	X
D3DB	C62D	TRYAG3	X
0000	C63A	TRYAG4	X
D3E5	C644	STRFRE	X
0000	C65A	GETRTS	X
D3F0	C65B	GARBAG	X
D400	C66A	GARBA2	DOES 'GARBAGE COLLECTION' – PACKS STRINGS
0000	C67E	GLOOP	X
0000	C68A	COL00	X
0000	C693	COL00B	X
0000	C69E	COL00A	X
0000	C6A9	COL01	X
0000	C6B2	COL02	X
0000	C6CE	GLOP1	X
0000	C6D8	COL02B	X
0000	C6F0	COL02A	X
0000	C700	GRBEND	JMP ENDGRB
0000	C703	COL03	MOVES FRESPC TO FRETOP
0000	C716	ENDGRB	MOVES FRESPC TO FRETOP
0000	C71F	SKIP2	X
0000	C724	SKIP2A	X
0000	C726	MOVPNT	X
0000	C730	MOV00	X
0000	C735	MOVTOP	X
0000	C73F	MOV01	X
0000	C744	SETINX	X
0000	C746	SET00	X
D517	C74F	CAT	CONCATENATE TWO STRINGS (FAC) AND (+←(TXTPTR))
D537	C76F	SIZEOK	X
D554	C78C	MOVINS	X
D562	C79A	MOVSTR	X
D566	C79E	MOVDO	X
D56A	C7A2	MOVLP	X
D573	C7AB	MVDONE	X
D57C	C7B4	MVSTRT	X
D57D	C7B5	FRESTR	X
D580	C7B8	FREFAC	X
D584	C7BC	FRETMP	FREES UP TEMPORARY STRING POINTERS
0000	C7DE	RES00	X
0000	C7F6	FRE01	X
D5AF	C7FC	FREPLA	X
0000	C7FE	FRE02	X
D5B5	C811	FRETMS	X
D5C5	C821	FRERTS	X
D5C6	C822	CHRD	ROUTINE – CHR$(VALUE) (VALUE 0–255)

Table F-3. Hex Addresses and Label References: CBM BASICs (Continued)

BASIC 3.0	BASIC 4.0	Labels	Description
D5DA	C836	LEFTD	ROUTINE – LEFT$()
D5E0	C83C	RLEFT	X
D5E6	C842	RLEFT1	X
D5E7	C843	RLEFT2	X
D5E8	C844	RLEFT3	X
D5FF	C85B	PULMOR	X
D606	C862	RIGHTD	ROUTINE – RIGHT$()
D611	C86D	MIDD	ROUTINE – MID$()
D622	C87E	MID2	X
D63B	C897	PREAM	USED BY RIGHT
D656	C8B2	LEN	ROUTINE – LEN(STRING)
D65C	C8B8	LEN1	X
D665	C8C1	ASC	ROUTINE – ASC(STRING)
D672	C8CE	GOFUC	X
D675	C8D1	GTBYTC	DOES A CHRGET AND GETBYT
D678	C8D4	GETBYT	EVALUATE THE FORMULA AND RETURN A BYTE VALUE (IN .X)
D67B	C8D7	CONINT	X
D687	C8E3	VAL	ROUTINE – VAL(STRING)
D6A7	C903	VAL2	X
D6BD	C918	ST2TXT	X
D6C5	C920	VALRTS	X
D6C6	C921	GETNUM	EVALUATE FORMULA AND RETURN INTEGER VALUE (0-65535)
D6CC	C927	COMBYT	X
D6D2	C92D	GETADR	CONVERT FAC TO VALUE(0-65535) PLACE IN POKER
D6E8	C943	PEEK	ROUTINE – PEEK(X)
D6FB	C94E	GETCON	X
D6FE	C951	DOSGFL	X
D707	C95A	POKE	ROUTINE – POKE X
D710	C963	FNWAIT	ROUTINE – WAIT
D71F	C972	STORDO	X
D723	C976	WAITER	X
D72B	C97E	ZERRTS	X
D72C	C97F	FADDH	ADD 1/2 TO FPB VALUE IN FAC
D733	C986	FSUB	UNPACKS ARGUMENT AND SUBTRACT FPB
D736	C989	FSUBT	FPB SUBTRACTION ARG-FAC
D76E	C998	FADD5	X
D773	C99D	FADD	UNPACK ARGUMENT INTO ARG DO A FPB ADD
D776	C9A0	FADDT	FPB ADDITION FAC=FAC+ARG
D783	C9AD	FADDC	X
D79F	C9C9	FADDA	X
D7A3	C9CD	FADD1	X
D7AF	C9D9	FADD4	X
D7BB	C9E5	SUBIT	X
D7DE	CA08	FADFLT	X
D7E3	CA0D	NORMAL	NORMALIZE ADDITION AND SUBTRACTION RESULTS
D7E7	CA11	NORM3	X
D803	CA2D	ZEROFC	FAC=0
D805	CA2F	ZEROF1	X
D807	CA31	ZEROML	MAKE SIGN POSITIVE
D80A	CA34	FADD2	X
D829	CA53	NORM2	X
D835	CA5F	NORM1	X
D842	CA6C	SQUEEZ	X
D844	CA6E	RNDSHF	X
D852	CA7C	RNDRT5	X
D853	CA7D	NEGFAC	COMPLEMENT FAC ENTIRELY

Table F-3. Hex Addresses and Label References: CBM BASICs (Continued)

BASIC 3.0	BASIC 4.0	Labels	Description
D859	CA83	NEGFCH	COMPLEMENT JUST THE NUMBER IN FAC
D87B	CAA5	INCFAC	INCREMENT FAC
D889	CAB3	INCFRT	X
D88A	CAB4	OVERR	OVERFLOW ERROR VECTOR
D88F	CAB9	MULSHF	SHIFER ROUTINES
D891	CABB	SHFTR2	X
D8A5	CACF	SHIFTR	X
D8B2	CADC	SHFTR3	X
D8B8	CAE2	SHFTR4	X
D8BC	CAE6	ROLSHF	X
D8C6	CAF0	SHFTRT	X
D8C8	CAF2	FONE	FLOATING-POINT-BINARY CONSTANTS
D8CD	CAF7	LOGCN2	X
D8E2	CB0C	SQR05	X
D8E7	CB11	SQR20	X
D8EC	CB16	NEGHLF	X
D8F1	CB1B	LOG2	X
D8F6	CB20	LOG	ROUTINE - LOG(X)
D8FD	CB27	LOGERR	ILLEGAL QUANITY ERROR VECTOR
D900	CB2A	LOG1	X
0000	CB5A	MULLN2	X
D934	CB5E	FMULT	FPB MULTIPLY FAC=FAC*ARG
D937	CB61	FMULTT	FPB MULTIPLY WITH ARG AND .AC LOADED
D965	CB8F	MLTPLY	X
D96A	CB94	MLTPL1	X
D96D	CB97	MLTPL2	X
D989	CBB3	MLTPL3	X
D997	CBC1	MULTRT	X
D998	CBC2	CONUPK	UNPACK MEMORY INTO ARG
D9C3	CBED	MULDIV	CHECK AND ADJUST EXPS OF FPB MULT AND DIV
D9C5	CBEF	MLDEXP	X
D9D0	CBFA	TRYOFF	X
D9E0	CC0A	MLDVEX	X
D9E6	CC10	ZEREMV	X
D9EB	CC15	GOOVER	OVERFLOW ERROR VECTOR
D9EE	CC18	MUL10	MULTIPLY FAC BY 10
D9F9	CC23	FINML6	X
DA04	CC2E	MUL10R	X
DA05	CC2F	TENC	FPB VALUE 10
D30A	CC34	DIV10	DIVIDE FAC BY 10
DA13	CC3D	FDIVF	X
DA1B	CC45	FDIV	UNPACK MEMORY AND DIVIDE
DA1E	CC48	FDIVT	FAC = ARG/FAC
DA35	CC5F	DIVIDE	X
DA4B	CC75	SAVQUO	X
DA58	CC82	QSHFT	X
DA5B	CC85	SHFARG	X
DA69	CC93	DIVSUB	X
DA86	CCB0	LD100	X
DA8A	CCB4	DIVNRM	X
DA96	CCC0	DV0ERR	OVERFLOW ERROR VECTOR
DA9B	CCC5	MOVFR	MOVE RES TO FAC
DAAE	CCD8	MOVFM	MOVE MEMORY TO FAC
DAD3	CCFD	MOV2F	X
DAD6	CD00	MOV1F	X
DADC	CD06	MOVVF	X

Table F-3. Hex Addresses and Label References: CBM BASICs (Continued)

BASIC 3.0	BASIC 4.0	Labels	Description
DAE0	CD0A	MOVMF	MOVE FAC TO MEMORY
DB08	CD32	MOVFA	MOVE ARG TO FAC
DB0A	CD34	MOVFA1	X
DB0E	CD38	MOVFAL	X
DB18	CD42	MOVAF	MOVE FAC TO ARG
DB1B	CD45	MOVEF	X
DB1D	CD47	MOVAFL	X
DB26	CD50	MOVRTS	X
DB27	CD51	ROUND	ROUND FAC
DB2F	CD59	INCRND	X
DB37	CD61	SIGN	EXTRACT SIGN FROM FAC IN .A
DB3B	CD65	FCSIGN	X
DB3D	CD67	FCOMPS	X
DB44	CD6E	SIGNRT	X
DB45	CD6F	SGN	ROUTINE - SGN(X)
DB48	CD72	FLOAT	FLOAT THE SIGNED INTEGER IN FAC
DB50	CD7A	FLOATS	FLOAT THE SIGNED NUMBER IN FAC
DB55	CD7F	FLOATC	X
DB5B	CD85	FLOATB	X
DB64	CD8E	ABS	ROUTINE - ABS(X)
DB67	CD91	FCOMP	COMPARE ARG AND FAC .A=1←A<F
DB69	CD93	FCOMPN	X
DB9E	CDC8	FCOMPC	X
DBA4	CDCE	FCOMPD	X
DBA7	CDD1	QINT	FAC=INT(FAC) SIGNED ROUTINE - INT(X)
DBBB	CDE5	QISHFT	X
DBC6	CDF0	QINTRT	X
DBC7	CDF1	QINT1	X
DBD8	CE02	INT	ROUTINE - INT(X)
DBF5	CE1F	CLRFAC	.A TO ALL POSITIONS OF FAC
DBFE	CE28	INTRTS	X
DBFF	CE29	FIN	FBP INPUT, TXTPTR POINTS TO ASCII, RETURNS IN FAC
DC03	CE2D	FINZLP	X
DC12	CE3C	QPLUS	X
DC16	CE40	FINC	X
DC19	CE43	FINDG0	X
DC1B	CE45	FIN1	X
DC3A	CE64	FINEC1	X
DC3C	CE66	FINEC	X
DC3F	CE69	FNEDG1	X
DC41	CE6B	FINEC2	X
DC4D	CE77	FINDP	X
DC53	CE7D	FINE	X
DC55	CE7F	FINE1	X
DC5E	CE88	FINDIV	X
DC67	CE91	FINMUL	X
DC6E	CE98	FINQNG	X
DC73	CE9D	NEGXQS	X
DC76	CEA0	FINDIG	X
DC7D	CEA7	FINDG1	X
DC8A	CEB4	FINLOG	X
DC9D	CEC7	FINEDG	X
DCAC	CED6	MLEX10	X
DCBA	CEE4	MLEXMI	X
DCBF	CEE9	N0999	FPB VALUE 99999999.90625
DCC4	CEEE	N9999	FPB VALUE 999999999.5

Table F-3. Hex Addresses and Label References: CBM BASICs (Continued)

BASIC 3.0	BASIC 4.0	Labels	Description
DCC9	CEF3	NMIL	FPB VALUE 10-9
0000	CEF8	CKSMC0	CHECKSUM BYTE $C000 ROM
DCCE	CF78	INPRT	PRINT CURRENT LINE NUMBER
DCD9	CF83	LINPRT	PRINT NUMBER IN (.A←HIGH .Y←LOW)
DCE6	CF90	STROU2	JMP STROUT
DCE9	CF93	FOUT	FPB OUTPUT
DCEB	CF95	FOUTC	X
DCF3	CF9D	FOUT1	X
DD0C	CFB6	FOUT37	X
DD15	CFBF	FOUT7	X
DD17	CFC1	FOUT4	X
DD22	CFCC	FOUT3	X
DD2D	CFD7	FOUT38	X
DD34	CFDE	FOUT9	X
DD3B	CFE5	FOUT5	X
DD3E	CFE8	BIGGES	X
DD53	CFFD	FOUTPI	X
DD54	CFFE	FOUT6	X
DD5F	D009	FOUT39	X
DD70	D01A	FOUT16	X
DD72	D01C	FOUT8	X
DD74	D01E	FOUTIM	CLOCK ENTRY INTO FOUT
DD76	D020	FOUT2	X
DD9A	D044	FOUT41	X
DD9C	D046	FOUT40	X
DDA3	D04D	FOUTYP	X
DDBE	D068	STXBUF	X
DDD0	D07A	FOULDY	X
DDD2	D07C	FOUT11	X
DDDF	D089	FOUT12	X
DDEF	D099	FOUT14	X
DDFB	D0A5	FOUT15	X
DE10	D0BA	FOUT19	X
DE13	D0BD	FOUT17	X
DE18	D0C2	FOUT20	X
DE1D	D0C7	FHALF	FPB VALUE 1/2
DE1F	D0C9	ZERO	X
DE22	D0CC	FOUTBL	TABLES OF POWERS OF -10↑X
DE46	D0F0	FDCEND	END OF POWERS TABLE
DE5E	D108	TIMEND	FPB TIME CONVERSION TABLES
DE5E	D108	SQR	ROUTINE - SQR(X)
DE68	D112	FPWRT	ROUTINE (ARG↑FAC)
DE71	D11B	FPWRT1	X
DE8B	D135	FPWR1	X
DEA1	D14B	NEGOP	NEGATE THE NUMBER IN FAC
DEAB	D155	NEGRTS	X
DEAC	D156	LOGEB2	FPB VALUE LOG(E) BASE 2
DEB1	D15B	EXPCON	LOG AND EXPONENT FPB TABLES
DEDA	D184	EXP	ROUTINE - EXP(FAC)
DEEA	D194	STOLD	X
DEF5	D19F	GOMLDV	X
DEF8	D1A2	EXP1	X
DF08	D1B2	SWAPLP	X
DF2D	D1D7	POLYX	POLYNOMIAL EVALUATOR
DF43	D1ED	POLY	POLYNOMIAL EVALUATOR
DF47	D1F1	POLY1	X

Table F-3. Hex Addresses and Label References: CBM BASICs (Continued)

BASIC 3.0	BASIC 4.0	Labels	Description
DF56	D200	POLY3	X
DF5A	D204	POLY2	X
DF67	D211	POLY4	X
DF77	D221	RMULC	X
DF7B	D225	RADDC	X
DF7F	D229	RND	ROUTINE — RND(X)
DF9D	D247	QSETNR	X
DFB2	D25C	RND1	X
DFC2	D26C	STRNEX	X
DFD5	D27F	GMOVMF	X
DFD8	D282	COS	ROTINE — COS(X)
DFDF	D289	SIN	ROUTINE — SIN(FAC)
E011	D2BB	SIN1	X
E014	D2BE	SIN2	X
E021	D2CB	SIN3	X
E028	D2D2	TAN	ROUTINE — TAN(FAC)
E050	D2FA	COSC	X
E054	D2FE	PI2	FPB VALUE PI/2
E059	D303	TWOPI	FBP VALUE 2*PI
E05E	D308	FR4	FPB VALUE 1/4
E063	D30D	SINCON	SIN TABLES FPB VALUES
E08C	D320	ATN	ROUTINE — ATN(FAC)
E094	D334	ATN1	X
E0A2	D342	ATN2	X
E0B5	D355	ATN3	X
E0BB	D35B	ATN4	X
E0BC	D35C	ATNCON	X
E0F9	D399	INITAT	BASIC SYSTEM INITIALIZATION CODE
E0FF	D39F	CHDGOT	X
E110	D3B0	CHDRTS	X
0000	D3B6	INIT	BASIC SYSTEM INITIALIZATION ROUTINE
E131	D3C9	MOVCHG	X
E15D	D400	LOOPMM	X
E165	D408	LOOPM1	X
E174	D417	USEDEC	X
E178	D41B	USEDEF	X
E1B7	D44B	WORDS	MESSAGE — 'BYTES FREE'
E1C4	D458	FREMES	MESSAGE — '### COMMODORE BASIC ###'
E1DE	D472	LASTWR	LAST BYTE OF BASIC SYSTEM CODE+1
0000	DEA4	PATCH2	PATCHES
E844	E844	CHTIM	X
0000	FF93	CONCAT	VECTOR — CONCAT
0000	FF96	DOPEN	VECTOR — DOPEN
0000	FF99	DCLOSE	VECTOR — DCLOSE
0000	FF9C	RECORD	VECTOR — RECORD
0000	FF9F	FORMAT	VECTOR — FORMAT
0000	FFA2	COLECT	VECTOR — COLLECT
0000	FFA5	BACKUP	VECTOR — BACKUP
0000	FFA8	DCOPY	VECTOR — COPY
0000	FFAB	APPEND	VECTOR — APPEND
0000	FFAE	DSAVE	VECTOR — DSAVE
0000	FFB1	DLOAD	VECTOR — DLOAD
0000	FFB4	DIRCAT	VECTOR — DIRECTORY
0000	FFB4	DCAT	VECTOR — CATALOG
0000	FFB7	RENAME	VECTOR — RENAME
0000	FFBA	SCRATC	VECTOR — SCRATCH

Table F-3. Hex Addresses and Label References: CBM BASICs (Continued)

BASIC 3.0	BASIC 4.0	Labels	Description
0000	FFBD	READDS	VECTOR — DS AND DS$
FFC0	FFC0	COPEN	VECTOR — OPEN
FFC3	FFC3	CCLOS	VECTOR — CLOSE
FFC6	FFC6	COIN	VECTOR — SET INPUT DEVICE
FFC9	FFC9	COOUT	VECTOR — SET OUTPUT DEVICE
FFCC	FFCC	CLSCHN	VECTOR — RESTORE NORMAL I/O DEVICES
FFCC	FFCC	CCCHN	SAME AS ABOVE
C481	FFCF	INCHR	VECTOR — INPUT A CHARACTER (FROM SCREEN)
FFCF	FFCF	CINCH	SAME AS ABOVE
FFD2	FFD2	OUTCH	VECTOR — OUTPUT A CHARACTER
FFD5	FFD5	CLOAD	VECTOR — LOAD
FFD8	FFD8	CSAVE	VECTOR — SAVE
FFDB	FFDB	CVERF	VECTOR — VERIFY
FFDE	FFDE	CSYS	VECTOR — SYS
FFE1	FFE1	ISCNTC	VECTOR — TEST STOP KEY
FFE4	FFE4	CGETL	VECTOR — GET CHARACTER FROM KEYBOARD BUFFER
FFE7	FFE7	CCALL	VECTOR — ABORT ALL I/O CHANNELS
000F	0000	CONTW	Z
000D	0000	CNTWFL	Z
000F	0000	LINWID	Z
0010	0000	NCMWID	Z
006C	0000	STRNGI	Z
007F	0000	Q	Z
C494	0000	INCRTS	Z
C721	0000	SNERRX	Z
D404	0000	FNDVAR	Z
D41E	0000	TVAR	Z
D427	0000	SVARS	Z
D433	0000	SVAR	Z
D43B	0000	SVARGO	Z
D440	0000	ARYVAR	Z
D48A	0000	ARYSTR	Z
D497	0000	DVARS	Z
D4A1	0000	DVAR	Z
D4B6	0000	DVAR2	Z
D4C0	0000	DVAR3	Z
D4DB	0000	GRBRTS	Z
D4E0	0000	GRBPAS	Z
D5B0	0000	FRETRT	Z
D745	0000	STORD1	Z
D745	0000	STORD1	Z
D745	0000	STORD1	Z
D745	0000	STORD1	Z

Index

Other OSBORNE/McGraw-Hill Publications